C0-AVW-457

Contents

The Quadrilog:
Tradition and the Future of Ecumenism

Essays in Honor of George H. Tavard

Kenneth Hagen, Editor

Contributors

Marc R. Alexander	Jeffery Hopper
Robert W. Bertram	Frederick M. Jelly, O.P.
Joseph A. Burgess	Mary Charles Murray
David Butler	Walter H. Principe, C.S.B.
Patrick W. Carey	Herbert J. Ryan, S.J.
Simon J. De Vries	J.-M.R. Tillard, O.P.
John Patrick Donnelly, S.J.	Arthur A. Vogel
Avery Dulles, S.J.	Geoffrey Wainwright
Robert B. Eno, S.S.	J. Robert Wright
R. William Franklin	Edward Yarnold, S.J.
Eric W. Gritsch	Norman Young

A Michael Glazier Book
THE LITURGICAL PRESS
Collegeville, Minnesota

BT
90
.Q33
A93

A Michael Glazier Book published by The Liturgical Press.

Cover design by Greg Becker.

Assistant to the editor: Aldemar Hagen

© 1994 by The Order of St. Benedict, Inc., Collegeville, Minnesota. All rights reserved. No part of this book may be reproduced in any form or by any means, electronic or mechanical, including photocopying, recording, taping, or any retrieval system, without the written permission of The Liturgical Press, Collegeville, Minnesota 56321. Printed in the United States of America.

1	2	3	4	5	6	7	8

Library of Congress Cataloging-in-Publication Data

The Quadrilog : tradition and the future of ecumenism : essays in
    honor of George H. Tavard / edited by Kenneth Hagen.
        p.   cm.
    Includes bibliographical references and index.
    ISBN 0-8146-5838-5
    1. Tradition (Theology) 2. Tradition (Theology) and Christian
union. I. Tavard, George H. (George Henry), 1922– . II. Hagen,
Kenneth.
BT90.Q33 1994
231'.042—dc20   93-24302
                                                                          CIP

Preface

Thanks for this project goes first to the president of Marquette University, Rev. Albert J. DiUlio, S.J., for inaugurating the Presidential Chair in Theology and appointing Rev George H. Tavard, A.A., as the first occupant. Secondly, I thank my assistant, Aldemar Hagen, for doing the hard work with the computer equipment, for proofreading, and for help with the editing. Rev. Michael Zamzow, the prodigious indexer, is once again to be acknowledged for the index. The Liturgical Press has been extremely forthcoming, and the international ecumenical community is in their debt. The pleasure of editing this *Festschrift* has been enhanced by the cooperation and diligence of the essayists.

Personally, the presence of George Tavard—the theologian, the Frenchman, the poet—has energized me in many ways and broadened my horizons; I hope I can continue to show him my gratitude beyond this *Festschrift*.

Kenneth Hagen
Advent 1992

Introduction

Kenneth Hagen

In 1960 George Tavard wrote, "As seen in the light of the long life of the Church, it is of no crucial importance whether she recovers from century-old schisms tomorrow afternoon or tomorrow evening."[1] As the afternoons came and went, George Tavard dedicated his life to ecumenical dialogue even before Vatican II gave its blessing to ecumenical endeavors. Much of his career has been spent teaching at protestant colleges and traveling the *oikoumenē* in witness to his convictions about unity. "Rarely a weekend has gone by this fall [1992]" recounts a student of his at Marquette University, "when he hasn't flown off to still another interfaith meeting on our continent or abroad. 'The traveling is boring. All airports are alike,' he insists, but he comes back exhilarated or disappointed at the ecumenical process and its pace."

I. George Tavard to Marquette University

The plan for a *Festschrift* for George Tavard began when he was appointed as the first occupant of the Presidential Chair in Theology at Marquette University to begin the year of his seventieth birthday. After hearing of his appointment (Fall 1991), I called to welcome him to Marquette University and to find out what if any plans were underway for a *Festschrift*, wondering how—in the world he travels—it could be, if my suspicions were true, that no one had been planning a *Festschrift* for one whom many regard to be one of the most influential international and ecumenical theologians in the second half of this century. When I called, erroneously assuming his birthday was in November 1992 (from information in *Who's Who in Relig-*

ion 1985), I was shocked to hear it was in February and too embarrassed, being a historian, to admit to him that my dates were off. I wrote him and explained my embarrassment; he wrote back, "I was born on the day of Pope Pius XI's election!!!"

The rush to put out a *Festschrift* for his seventieth was not necessary nor has it proved necessary to present one during his first year at Marquette University. The tenure of this Distinguished Professor at Marquette University has gone so well from the faculty and student points of view that his life at Marquette University is only beginning during the filling out of his seventieth year. The development of the *Festschrift* during 1992–1993 has been governed by the desire to insure the timely and scholarly quality of the essays and to publish a first-class volume.

II. *Topic of Tradition*

The topic of Tradition has been chosen as the theme of this volume and focus of the essays, since it has been most prominent in George Tavard's writings spanning over forty years. A theme-*Festschrift* also gives prominence to the honoree's writings.

Tavard's forty-five books (and counting) provide a barometer for international theological currents of debate and dialogue that have taken place during the second half of the twentieth century. As it turns out, one key issue still under much discussion going into the mid-1990s is the theme of t/Tradition. It is hard to imagine any theologian interested in t/Tradition over the last thirty years who has not read *Holy Writ or Holy Church*.[2] Typical of divinity students, I poured over the footnotes in *Holy Writ* in the early 60s. While *Holy Writ or Holy Church* has served as a focus and source for the modern discussion on the relationship of Scripture and Tradition, the theme of t/Tradition for this volume was designed to focus on deeper and broader issues that George Tavard's corpus raises in relation to t/Tradition. The authors of this volume reflect the preoccupation of world ecumenism with the subject of tradition, whether tradition with a small "t," large "T," or TRADITION in all caps, whether t/Tradition in the singular or traditions in the plural, whether the *actus tradendi* or the *tradenda/ tradendum*. Many facets of the complicated issue and important nuances have come onto the international scene since Vatican II, where George Tavard served as a *peritus*. Very few people, I am told, see the whole picture. George Tavard is one who does.

Authors in this volume add to the nuances of the international discussion (note that individual author preference for lower case/upper case "T" has been retained to reflect both style and point of view). Usually it is understood that Tradition with upper case "T" for Roman Catholics refers to the life of Catholic faith guarded by the Roman *magisterium* (Catholic substance) and Tradition with upper case "T" for Protestants refers to the life of Catholic and Apostolic faith guarded by the Gospel (Protestant principle). This volume renders such a distinction outdated.

III. To the Reader

Tradition refers to what is believed always, everywhere, and by everyone (the rule of Vincent of Lerins, known as the Vincentian canon) and not ever explicitly and fully written down and codified. Such an understanding of Tradition is similar to the character of sacred Scripture itself in the sense that the writing of Scripture could never encapsulate or codify the living Word of God. No document can ever contain the life of the Trinity.

Tradition understood as the biblical *paradosis* begins with God—God's handing over of Jesus Christ to sinful humanity (the *paradosis* of the *kerygma*). A "virtual consensus" at Montreal put it: "The Tradition is the self-givenness of God in the self-giving of Jesus Christ, 'for us men and for our salvation.' "[3] Tradition is the transitive process by means of which the Christian past is renewed in the living present and made available to the open future. The biblical tradition is the history of God, the history of the Word made flesh in the Man of God's own choosing; THE TRADITION biblically grounded is the life of the Triune God; the Tradition is the faith of Christ handed down in the life of the Church (*ab Abel*). As Christians we live and have our being in the Tradition of the Gospel testified in Scripture, transmitted in and by the Church through the power of the Holy Spirit. The content of Tradition is God's revelation.

When we look at Scripture, we need to realize that the sacred writings are themselves the unfolding of God's revelation, containing, reflecting, and conveying the Tradition or the life of the faith of God's people handed down over many centuries. Tradition is both the container and the conveyer of the sacred. Scripture is the sacred page that bears the imprint of God himself. The sacred page carries and conveys the witness of God's creating, redeeming, and sanctifying work. Such action of God ad extra is the Tradition of God. Every tradition with small "t" seeks to embody the Tradition of God's self-giving life, love, and holiness.

Such simple three paragraphs are my warm-up to the reader to press on through the volume.

IV. Essays

The scope, variety, and international makeup of the contributors have been made possible by the fact that so many came forward to offer original essays. The outpouring of creative and critical scholarship by the authors is a testimony to how the international community of ecumenical scholars regards George Tavard.

The order of the essays is first to present the prominent historical figures in the history of the Western Church to address the topic of Tradition up through the early part of the twentieth century. Three essays on Anglican/ Roman Catholic ecumenism and one on Montreal follow. Next a student of George Tavard's theology (Licentiate at Louvain, S.T.D. in Rome) presents a historical-literary overview. The volume continues with two systematic essays, one essay on the philosophical tradition, one on the tradition of artistic image, and one on Scripture and canonization. The offering to Tavard concludes with a complete bibliography of his works to date.

The focus of the volume is "Tradition and the Future of Ecumenism in the Quadrilog. Essays in Honor of George H. Tavard." The quadrilog refers to the four ecumenical partners of George Tavard involved in this project: Roman Catholic, Anglican, Methodist, and Lutheran. The work of "Mr. Ecumenism" is the center of the four-way conversation.

The configuration of contributors has been designed to reflect some of the traditions, faculties, Dialogues, and colleagues with whom George Tavard has been/is in conversation. Colleagues in the volume from the Methodist Theological School in Ohio are De Vries and Hopper; at Marquette University two of his colleagues are Carey and Donnelly. The essayists with whom George Tavard has been in official dialogue are listed as follows:

Anglican/Roman Catholic Consultation, United States, 1965–
     Franklin, Jelly, Wright
United States Lutheran/Roman Catholic Theological Dialogue, 1965–1992
     Bertram, Burgess, Dulles, Eno, Gritsch, Hagen, Principe
ARCIC I, 1970–1981
     Ryan, Tillard, Vogel, Yarnold
RC/World Methodist Council, 1982–
     Butler, Charles Murray, Wainwright, Young

V. *Curriculum vitae: Georges Henri Tavard*

Born: February 6, 1922, Nancy, France; son of Henri Ernest and Marguerite (Wasser)

United States citizen: came to the United States December 1952, naturalized 1960

Ordained: March 2, 1947

Community: Augustinians of the Assumption (Assumptionists, A.A.); professed 1943

STD: 1949, Facultés catholiques de Lyon

D.D. (hon.): 1965, Bexley Hall, Kenyon College

1948–1951: lecturer in theology, Capenor House, Nutfield, Surrey, England

July 1951–December 1952: "Rédacteur", *La Documentation Catholique*, Paris, France

1953–1957: Theologian in residence, Our Lady of Guadalupe Church, New York City

September 1957–July 1958: Lecturer, Assumption College, Worcester, Massachusetts

July 1958–August 1960: Theologian in residence, Our Lady of Esperanza Church, New York City

1960–1966: Professor of Theology, chairman, Mount Mercy College, Pittsburgh, Pennsylvania

1962–1965: peritus at Vatican II

September 1966–January 1967: Fellow, Center for Advanced Studies, Wesleyan University, Middletown, Connecticut

January 1967–1969: Professor of Religious Studies, Pennsylvania State University, State College, Pennsylvania

1969–1970: Visiting Professor, Princeton Theological Seminary, Princeton, New Jersey

1970–1989: Professor of Theology, Methodist Theological School in Ohio, Delaware, Ohio[4]

1989– : Professor Emeritus, Methodist Theological School in Ohio

1992– : Distinguished Professor (Presidential Chair), Marquette University, Milwaukee, Wisconsin

Roman Catholic/World Methodist Council, 1982–

Anglican/Roman Catholic Consultation, United States, 1965–

United States Lutheran/Roman Catholic Theological Dialogue, 1965–1992

Anglican-Roman Catholic Joint Preparatory Commission, 1967–1968

ARCIC I, 1970–1981

VI. *Profile of the Man*

In 1960 he began his teaching career in the United States as professor and chairman of theology at Mount Mercy College, Pittsburgh, Pennsylvania. Most know his American academic connection as the Methodist Theological School in Ohio. Students at Marquette University now are linked with an international cadre of scholars studying under George Tavard.

It is difficult to gain a profile of the man George(s) Tavard—tidbits and tales about his family background, schooling, religious order, linguistic and cultural milieux, international travels, attachment to water or mountains—except, for this editor, through his poetry. Since his poetry is written under the penname of his mother's maiden name and the inspiration of her father,[5] his attachment to the sea helps explain his international moorings:

LA MER

Quand s'estompe le plan de la douce demeure
nul ne sait si l'eau verte est un lac peu profond.
Quand s'affronte l'esquif à la mer intérieure
sommes-nous embarqués sur l'océan sans fond?

Allons-nous voyager sur des barques chêtives,
chercheurs de paradis, insensés prometteurs
d'infinis au-delà de nos villes votives,
nouveaux explorateurs, lointains navigateurs?

Sera-ce le chemin des pèlerins bouddhistes
vers l'Inde, reposoir du message éternel?
ou la quête du Graal? ou suivons-nous la piste
de saint Brendan parmi les brouillards et les gels?

Par les piliers d'Hercule au bord de l'Atlantique
—porte ouverte—sortons du monde illusionné
sans escale, sans port ou île épisodique,
sans autre repos que le charisme donné,
par les sept océans faisant le tour des mondes
retraçant rudement la route des voiliers
ou perdus dans l'Arctique et ses brumes profondes.
Quel jeu d'enfant cherche le ciel dans les halliers?

La fenêtre intérieure s'ouvre, visionnaire,
sur l'horizon des champs sans espaces, point mort

au centre de l'orage où nous perdons la terre
où l'interne océan se mire sans effort.

Dans la révolution du tréfonds c'est la hune
inversée, et trop tard c'est l'épouvante au quart:
le soleil à minuit et à midi la lune?
Nous écoutons l'écho des chansons du départ.

Il annonce le calme éternel de la vie.
Point de retour. Le vent n'a qu'une direction.
Est-ce vers l'occident ou vers l'anatolie
ou vers le ciel par la cinquième dimension?

Peut-être approchons-nous du port de l'Ogdoade
plus loin que l'infini, au centre du milieu,
parallèle à soi-même en double colonnade,
triple concentration sur eux-mêmes des cieux.

O mer au fond de l'âme, ô Méditerranée,
plus belle encore, plus profonde encore, ô mer,
qui es aussi notre grande sœur étoilée,
ne nous refuse pas nos houles bleu-amer.[6]

When asked to describe George H. Tavard, A.A., one of his students at Marquette University wrote:

"The words that come to mind are 'charming,' 'erudite,' 'droll,' but most of all, 'unpretentious.' That last quality has not failed to surprise us in a scholar of Fr. Tavard's calibre, nor to endear. I recall his pleasure at having lunched with Archbishop Weakland a few weeks ago, or sharing with us a poem written by a friend. Or passing around a photo of his shaking hands with the Austrian president. Reminiscing about an early Lutheran/Roman Catholic dialogue . . . John Courtney Murray, Arthur Carl Piepkorn, Cardinal Sheehan, all dead now. Translating Calvin's French and Augustine's Latin so easily that it seemed he was reading English. Blushing at a compliment. Speaking charitably of separatists, or with gentlemanly bristling at institutional flubbery. A sense of wonder matched to thorough and precise scholarship.

"Father Tavard's mastery of tradition history and its doctrines has enabled a clarity of vision which takes into account the humanity of the church, theology from below fortified by a bottomless cache of anecdotes. At the same time, his compelling high ecclesiology discerns the creative trinitarian

God who empowers word and sacraments—never exclusively either through gender or denomination, but imaging the doxological sense of humanity at prayer in diverse ways.

"While not blinding him to its faults, Fr. Tavard's experience of church in its rich heritage and spiritual beauty resists useless cynicism. Perhaps that hopefulness is the best part of him. He doesn't come to us as an embattled or embittered old warrior. On the contrary, he brings a fresh and perceptive outlook, honest wisdom, and a graceful spirit which makes age inconsequential. It's been an uncommon privilege to study with Fr. Tavard. He gives us hope in the future, an invaluable gift" (Joan).

Another student of his wrote recently: "On one occasion class discussion turned briefly to the issue of blessing animals. Father Tavard mentioned his own aversion to blessing animals in general and rodents in particular. 'I just cannot bring myself to bless a rat or a mouse,' he confessed. He referred to an incident in New York City where a woman approached him at a cathedral. She asked if he was a priest, and when he responded in the affirmative she asked if he would please bless her cat, which was soon to have an operation. Thinking quickly, Father Tavard got himself out of the situation by assuring the woman that her cat's condition was definitely a problem that could best be handled by the pastor.

"Another day the question of the existence of angels received Father Tavard's attention. He asserted their existence by explaining, 'They have to exist, you know, because I once wrote a book about them.' Father mentioned one saint who was thought to have been so convinced of the immediate presence of angels that he always stepped back and allowed any angels who might have been present to pass through a doorway ahead of him. 'I don't hold a door open for angels,' Tavard commented quietly. 'I think that if angels are all they're cracked up to be, they can go through doorways whether or not I hold the door open for them.'

"Father Tavard's assessment of Pope John Paul II's propensity to beatify and canonize saints: 'There must be an inflation in holiness' " (Sr. Pam).

George Tavard is a scholar and writer in many languages; his ecumenical work in Europe and America and voluminous writings have had a pioneering and salutary influence. He writes with the surety of one who is intimately familiar with the sources of the Christian tradition and with the problems and nuances of contemporary theology.

The brilliance and breadth of George Tavard are reflected in my two favorite genre of his literary output: The book on philosophical and theological method *La théologie parmi les sciences humaines: de la méthode en thé-*

ologie, Le point théologique, 15 (Paris: Éditions Beauchesne, 1975), which contains what Marc Alexander calls a simplified formula describing «énergie théologique»:

$$x^n \rangle Sv \Rightarrow Sv' \rightarrow x'^n$$

(The formula is clarified in note 28 of Alexander's chapter [17]).

The one who can probe the depths of interdisciplinary questions of method and linguistics can also create on a different canvas an equally beautiful and joyous picture of

LA LETTRE

La lettre enluminée de rires gothiques
    embellie de rouge et d'or et du mystère du bleu de
                Chartres
    percée de gargouilles gonflées de pluie
    peu à peu dans l'écritoire monastique
    élève entrelacée d'arcs-boutants
    la cathédrale des chants psalmodiés
    Deus in adjutorium meum intende

La lettre
    qui commence l'Au commencement
    qui inaugure l'*incipit* de la création
    et relance la nouvelle créature
    élance des flèches d'église dans le ciel d'été
    départs sans retour des missionnaires autrefois vers
                la Chine
    passages des grands oiseaux triangulaires dans l'or
                des soirs tardifs
    sillage ancré sur l'océan infini des eaux claires

d'où descendent
    quand luit dans les ténèbres le *fiat* la Mère
    les prémices de tout don parfait
    et quand de la lumière
    procède en nous la lumière

La lettre aux traits qui s'estompent
    noue dans les balbutiements surpris de la parole
    image d'art éternel creuset

de l'essentielle beauté
les nœuds de la fantaisie théologale

et la tristesse joyeuse des enfants qui cherchent les mots
— a b c d —
agite en claquant le squelette du langage
du cliquetis des dentales
au b-a ba des labiales
triste joie de la lettre douloureusement docile
sauf chez les barbares qui baragouinent
quand je déambule étranger chez les peuples que
je n'entends pas

La lettre enjolivée
rappelle les rêves de l'ancienne journée
au gré des contours pénombrés où l'on touche
au détour des lacs fluant l'un dans l'autre
le fond de la pensée innombrable

Marche le fantôme du langage
dans le noir de l'espace
sur les brumes de la Manche
et traîne la parole balbutiante
et naît de la matrice archétypale
le verbe qui s'articule au foyer de la phrase

Lorsque nous serons prêts
pour l'engrangement final des attentes lentes
des blés mûrs des orges pleines des seigles
des avoines blanches aux grains détachés comme les
clochettes de Pâques
pour la moisson des pensées
et que l'on aura glané çà et là
quelques mots laissés pour compte
ah   donne-nous de prononcer comme il faut
la parole qui vale pour l'éternité
la parole de l'ultime amour qui vainc la mort
la parole qui est ta Parole

Et Verbum caro factum est
et s'est incarné dans nos cœurs[7]

Notes

[1] *Two Centuries of Ecumenism* (Notre Dame, Ind.: Fides Publishers Association, 1960) 237.

[2] George H. Tavard, *Holy Writ or Holy Church: The Crisis of the Protestant Reformation* (New York: Harper and Brothers, 1959).

[3] See the Burgess essay in this volume.

[4]   OHIO

Terres moutonnantes
á l'inverse des nuages
sous le ciel venteux.

Henri Wasser, *La septiéme vague* (Paris: Éditions Saint-Germain-des-Prés, 1976) 26.

[5]   LE LIVRE DU GRAND-PERE

Je veux relire ce soir le livre du grand-père.
Pendant que l'avenir descend du ciel avec la neige
sur le présent concentré dans la chambre pénombrée,
le passé remonte des pages délicates à papier quadrillé,
de la vie en dix-huit-cent-quatre-vingt-douze
et d'un voyage à Paris avec des fleurs artificielles au
    Rond-Point-des-Champs-Elysées.
Ils revivent hors de ces lignes manuscrites
d'une écriture fine et allongée avec de l'encre noire qui
    se fane:
poèmes sur St-Dié et sur Nancy et sur les grands sapins
    des Vosges,
récits sur la chute de Strasbourg pendant la guerre qu'on
    croyait la plus terrible
—mais on ne connaissait pas la prochaine encore plus
    horrible;—
livre de raison qui est aussi sans le dire un livre
    d'oraison,
priére d'hier et de toujours de l'homme qui regarde sa
    vie
et qui en marque les étapes avec des cailloux blancs sur
    le papier jauni.
Je tourne les pages et je regarde les desseins illustratifs
d'un ouvrier typographe qui est aussi écrivain et artiste,
car de la praxis naissent les grandes visions de la beauté.
J'entends l'écho des temps passés qui appartiennent à ma
    pré-histoire
dans l'eau qui coule, dans le trait de plume et dans le
    chuintement du feu.
J'écoute la voix déjà ancienne de l'avant-hier
    anticipateur
que je reconnais dans mon âme sans l'avoir jamais
    connue.
C'est la voix du grand-pére mort en dix-huit-cent-quatre-
    vingt-seize

d'une maladie que je devais attrapper aussi et dont je ne
  suis pas mort.
Et la grand-mère est restée veuve avec ses trois enfants
et avec ce livre manuscrit à parcourir de temps en temps
pour se rappeler . . . pour se rappeler . . . pour se rappeler. . . .
Et je me rappelle en lisant les souvenirs de mes
  grands-parents.

Henri Wasser, *Le silence d'une demi-heure* (Paris: Éditions Saint-Germain-des-Prés, 1980) 14–15.
  [6]Henri Wasser, *La septiéme vague,* 56–58.
  [7]Henri Wasser, *Le silence d'une demi-heure,* 83–85.

1

Scripture and Tradition in Tertullian

Robert B. Eno, S.S.

Throughout a lifetime of laboring for Christian unity as a theologian and historian, George Tavard has confronted a wide variety of issues, both recent and long-standing. Among these is the question of the relationship of Scripture and the much-disputed category of Tradition. In his significant work *Holy Writ or Holy Church,*[1] he made a noteworthy contribution to the study of this topic, a subject that underwent rapid change in the years leading up to Vatican II. His studies and those of other scholars such as Yves Congar and Josef Rupert Geiselmann transformed the question. The results of their efforts can be seen in the documents of that council.

The question of the relationship between Scripture and Tradition, as we usually phrase it, while it has been heatedly debated since the Reformation, is bound up with the very beginnings of Christianity. In the eyes of the more radical critics, since it is nearly impossible to separate the teachings of Jesus himself from the many alleged traditions about him, the primitive Church of the first two centuries must be seen as a jumble of contradictory teachings and conflicting communities. Each sect claimed to have the teachings of Jesus but, in the opinion of these same critics, they were all equally in error. The triumphant sect(s) proclaimed themselves the orthodox and rewrote the stories that condemned their unsuccessful rivals forever to the scrap heap of history's losers. These particular losers were labeled heretics.[2]

The ancient and classic theory opposed to this modern scepticism was formulated to a large extent by the subject of this article, Tertullian of Carthage (+ after 221). He believed that the truth came before its falsification. Thus it was relatively simple to detect the heresies and to dismiss them while recognizing and preserving the true teachings of Jesus. Over the centuries variations of this view have been held by most Christians who considered themselves orthodox. Bossuet was its most notable Catholic champion in post-Reformation times. Scholars today consider it, at the very least, an over-simplification. But that does not mean that the more radical view mentioned above has carried the day.

For Tertullian, the teaching of Jesus was unified, consistent, and clear.[3] It was passed on in its fullness to the apostles who in turn transmitted it to their successors in the local churches they had founded. As foreseen and foretold, false teachers arose. For their own unworthy reasons, they distorted this teaching which had been clear for all to see. Hence the proliferation of sects. This simple schema was satisfactory for Tertullian, but others raised further questions, especially the basic one: Amid this cacophony of conflicting claims, how discern the truth? This essay is a study of Tertullian's replies to this question. His work *De praescriptione haereticorum* constitutes his major response to the challenge.

I. Heresy Overthrown: Tertullian's Argument

The teaching of Christ is known to us because it comes to us from the apostles. True Christianity is above all apostolic. As Tertullian put it, in phraseology reminiscent of Clement's letter to the Corinthians (42:1-2): "[I]t, without a doubt, holds what the churches received from the apostles, the apostles from Christ and Christ from God."[4] Christ is the fountainhead, of course; that is not an issue among Christians. But, after Christ? For true Christians, fabricating one's own teachings is not an option. Our authorities are the apostles. But even they did not invent. Rather, they faithfully passed on what they had received from Christ.[5] The apostles were the channels of all teaching and the authors of the Gospels, the *evangelicum instrumentum*. In two cases, the Gospels of Mark and Luke, the authors were apostolic men (*apostolici*), coworkers with the twelve and Paul. But their authority is not diminished or brought into question. Any alteration or rather adulteration arose in the postapostolic period.[6]

It is, in Tertullian's view, a common sense axiom, often repeated in his writings, that the original comes before its imitations. Thus the teaching of Christ in history, the apostolic teaching in short, originated and was in possession before its falsifications, the heresies, arose or even could have arisen.

Tertullian's basic assumption and the conclusions based on it are made explicit in his treatise, the *Prescription Against the Heretics* (ca. 203). While he also authored other works against particular heresies, he viewed this work as his general answer to all dissidents. He began by arguing that the existence of heresies should not be seen as alarming. They are one means, along with persecution, by which God tests the fidelity and steadfastness of his followers. In the case of those who fail the test, the Church is purged of hangers-on and the insufficiently fervent.

"Heresy" derives from the Greek word for choice. But Christians by definition are not allowed a further choice once they have found the truth. Their only choice is to adhere to the truth and thereafter to reject other teachings. Briefly attacking philosophy as a source of heresy, already a rather traditional tack for apologists, he noted that the Gnostics' favorite scriptural words were "Seek and you shall find" (Matt 7:7). While we shall look at Tertullian's principles of exegesis later, we note that he here objects that the words of Scripture are not to be removed from their context.[7] Christ's teaching is clear and definite. There is no warrant to go on seeking indefinitely, once his teaching has been found.

For those constitutionally incapable of restraining their curiosity, they may think and ask questions but never against the rule of faith. Provided its *forma* is maintained, one may do some seeking but only within narrow limits and preferably among fellow orthodox believers. It may be better in the long run to suppress such intellectual striving. Too many, even of the well-intentioned, have quickly passed beyond the limits.

Tertullian then states the principle from which the title of the work is derived, the prescription, a legal principle which helped to determine the ownership of property. In this context, the Scriptures are the property of the Church; dissidents have no right to cite or use them or to claim to derive their doctrine from them.[8] It is not only a tactical error to consent to discuss Scripture with heretics, it is also a waste of time. Such debates do not clarify issues, let alone decide them. Spectators leave even more confused than when they entered. Zealous debaters thus exhibit only their well-intentioned naiveté.[9] The true Scriptures are found only where the true faith and teaching are proclaimed. Heretics mutilate Scripture, Marcion above all; or, at least, they put forward faulty interpretations, something that is more difficult to demonstrate.[10]

Here we return once more to the foundations of Tertullian's case, the apostles. Against the assertions of the Gnostics, the apostles received the entire teaching of Jesus. There was no esoteric doctrine for a select group of *illuminati;* no secret teaching for the apostles only or solely for a special group of apostles with a partial doctrine for the multitudes. The chain began with them. The apostles founded churches in each city they visited. Nor at this later stage of development was there any question of a partial transmission of Jesus' words.[11] There were no misunderstandings.

The argument, of course, goes directly against the Gnostic contention that they alone passed on the real teachings of Jesus, an esoteric doctrine hidden from the masses. They derived these doctrines from one of the apostles, usually one of the more obscure of the twelve, through a succession of equally obscure masters. Tertullian developed the counterarguments found in Irenaeus, although he seems to place more emphasis on the churches and less on bishops. No list of bishops is found in his works.

The churches historically founded by apostles were very significant for Tertullian's case. The apostles received all of Jesus' teaching and passed it on in all its integrity, especially to those whom they had put in charge of the local churches they founded. These foundations are recounted in the Acts and the letters of Paul. But the seed of apostolic doctrine was also passed on to other local churches founded later in history after the deaths of the apostles. If these churches teach the same doctrine, they too are apostolic in the most important sense. The "transfusion" of doctrine did not just take place at some given moment in the past. All these local communities were united at their origins and remain linked so that they collectively are simply "the first one that came from the apostles."[12] These ongoing exchanges continue every day and the circulation of Christians in the empire offers concrete proof of the unity of these apostolic churches. They are in peace and communion. Christians call each other brothers and sisters and the churches offer hospitality to all Christians in communion with them.[13] Returning to the blood metaphor, he later said that these communities are linked by a "consanguinity of doctrine."[14]

His argument from prescription demands that only those sent by the apostles should be received as teachers of the doctrine taught by Jesus and guarded and transmitted by the apostles. As a form of historical verification, the churches founded by apostles can be appealed to. They are the ones who received this teaching directly from the apostles. They are the wombs and origins of the faith.[15] Does the teaching of other local churches agree with them? At the heart of their unity is the "handing on of the one faith."[16]

He then returned to the doubts and cavils of the Gnostics. Perhaps the apostles were not told the whole truth or perhaps they misunderstood. Could error have crept in after the apostles? If so, the Holy Spirit, "the vicar of Christ," given to the Church to lead it into all truth, would have failed in his mission. Furthermore, if error had entered in, how is it that today all the apostolically founded churches still have the same doctrine? Error means variation. Thus if there is question of error, these churches could not now have the same teaching.[17] He then reiterated one of his basic arguments. The truth comes first; error, falsely claiming to restore ancient truth, comes later. Hence variations can be expected among the many Gnostic groups. And that is, in fact, what one finds.

The apostolic churches, on the contrary, manifest no such variations and have in effect a historical pedigree to appeal to, a means of tracing their current teaching back to their founding apostle. For example, Smyrna traces its teaching back through Polycarp to John, Rome through Clement back to Peter. They have a list of bishops to show enquirers, a "series of bishops . . . succeeding each other from the beginning." Thus the apostolic seed was planted once but continues to grow and spread even now.[18]

Since the Gnostics claimed the dubious trait of *curiositas* as a virtue, then why should they not exercise this trait to some more fruitful end? They should investigate the claims made here. He then mentioned various apostolic churches in different regions where enquirers could travel to see and hear the teaching of these ancient Christian communities. Philippi, Thessalonika, and Ephesus were some of the historic communities scattered throughout the east. In the west there was only one, Rome, whence he seemed to say, Carthage had received the gospel. He continued with a brief encomium of the Roman Christians whose community was founded by Peter and Paul. He was also aware of the tradition that John visited Rome. Unlike his colleagues, he did not suffer a martyr's death though it was not for lack of trying.[19]

What is this apostolic doctrine? It is at least summarized in a rule (*regula*) usually called the rule of faith, a short list of core beliefs. Tertullian gave this summary on several occasions. While the wording is never precisely the same, the basic doctrines are there.[20] Likewise, while there are variations among the four Gospels, these are not significant because these gospels agree on the essentials.[21]

Tertullian closed this foundational treatment with two final subsidiary arguments. Variation in doctrine leads to adulteration of the Scriptures.[22] This is true in the literal sense in the case of Marcion who simply jettisoned the Jewish Scriptures and bowdlerized the New Testament. But in a more controversial sense, the other heretics adulterate the Bible even when they leave the received texts intact. They accomplish this by their false interpretation. Finally, he attacks the dissenters with another category basic to his world view, they lack *disciplina*.[23] They are not serious and do not deserve to be taken seriously. They lack order. Today's leader is cast aside tomorrow. For Tertullian, discipline is a telltale indicator of the corruption of doctrine.[24] If you lack one, neither do you have the other.

This summarizes the content and the argument of Tertullian's seminal work on how one should deal with heresy and his exposition of his views on the unity of the Church's doctrine derived from the apostles. In a sense, one might truly say that Tertullian wrote the book on the subject. Hence all the greater the consternation among Catholics when he himself became a Montanist. One can imagine the charges of absurd inconsistency against which he was obliged to react. It has been said with justice that much of Tertullian's argument has been taken from Irenaeus.[25] Even if this is so, I believe that it can also be said with justice that Tertullian's formulations and presentation of the argument are more concise and sharp and therefore more effective than those of Irenaeus.

II. The Rule of Faith

Tertullian uses the word *regula* some eighty times. Upon occasion, he uses the word to speak of other matters, but most of the time, he is dealing with questions of Christian teaching. Ellen Flesseman-van Leer speaks of its most common use as a "condensation and formulation of apostolic tradition with special emphasis on its normative function."[26] While Tertullian uses the expression *regula veritatis* occasionally, he much more regularly uses *regula fidei*.[27]

Like the teachings of Christ in general, the rule also comes from the apostles, Christ's companions.[28] Indeed, it comes from Christ himself.[29] Even Paul, the thirteenth apostle, went to Jerusalem to consult with the twelve concerning the content (*Regula*) of his own gospel.[30] Faith itself has been placed within the boundaries of the rule; it has its law, and salvation is found in the observance of this law.[31]

But there are dangers for the rule of faith or, at least, to our fidelity to it. Erudition combined with curiosity pose a threat to remaining faithful to this rule but some thinking and searching are permitted provided one stay within its parameters.[32] Other dangers originate in philosophy.[33] Problems have arisen when individuals like Valentinus, out of frustrated ambition, rebelled against the "Church of the authentic rule."[34] Many others, for a variety of reasons, "fall away from the rule."[35]

There is simply only one rule of faith that comes from the apostles. All others are inventions and frauds. Marcion claimed to have rescued or revived the true rule but, in reality, he simply invented his own.[36] Once more, Tertullian repeated his basic assumption: the truth always comes first.[37] In his letter to the Philippians, Paul had noted the diversity of human temperaments, but nowhere did he admit a diversity in the "rules of Christ's mysteries."[38]

Apart from the places where Tertullian recited versions of the rule of faith with its short creed-like series of tenets, he in addition sometimes noted that this or that assertion of heretics was contrary to the rule, e.g., the rule teaches that there is one God and that God is invisible.[39] In the treatise against Praxeas, he noted that formal heretics were not the only ones who had trouble with the rule. He observed that simple Christians, knowing that the rule had brought them from polytheism to monotheism, at times had difficulties not only in understanding but even in accepting the economy, i.e., the Incarnation with its Trinitarian implications.

In short, anything that diverged from the rule of faith was automatically suspect.[40] Christ himself was portrayed as saying (ironically in the original anti-Marcion context): "At one and the same time, I delegated to my apostles the gospel and the teaching of the same rule."[41] Here, gospel and rule seem to be the same materially with gospel understood not as books of the New Testament but as the essentials of Christ's teachings.

III. Discipline

Key studies of Tertullian's use of the word *disciplina* were published by Valentin Morel just before and during World War II.[42] Discipline is a word used much more frequently than rule by Tertullian. It has a greater range of meanings than *regula* or than even its obvious literal meaning of discipline. In Morel's view, the rule of faith is fixed for Tertullian, but Christian discipline can always be expanded and improved. This, of course, is the reasoning Tertullian will put forward in his Montanist period to argue that he was not violating his own rules of orthodoxy laid down in the *De praescriptione*. His rule of faith, i.e., the theological teaching about God and the economy, the teaching about the incarnation and the work of Christ, had not been abandoned or violated in the least. The Paraclete revealed not a new rule of faith, but he did reveal and require a stricter and more demanding way of life among Christians.

Disciplina, Morel argued, should be seen in Tertullian as encompassing just about everything in Christianity beyond the rule. Thus, ecclesiology and sacramentology which later become strictly theological matters, pertained for Tertullian to *disciplina,* not to the *regula.* Morel speculated that there were so many facets to Tertullian's use of *disciplina,* including what we would consider doctrinal aspects, because of the relative poverty of theological vocabulary at this early point.[43]

Once again, his early use of *disciplina* is seen in the *De praescriptione* where it is a stick with which to beat the heretics. Lack of discipline is itself a sign of heresy. Dissidents try to disguise their nakedness by cloaking their anarchy with the euphemistic title "simplicity" while they call Catholic concerns for good order "artificiality."[44] Such people lack the good old Roman virtue of *gravitas.*[45] If disorder points to heresy, then the presence of discipline proclaims the presence of the truth as well.[46] The Valentinians, for example, were numerous but were without discipline and chaotic in their teaching.[47] Discipline became a more prominent issue later when it emerged as a focus of controversy during his Montanist period.

IV. Tradition

Most commentators[48] agree that while for Tertullian *traditio* can mean both the content transmitted and the act of transmitting, it is the former use that predominates. For Munier, Tertullian's *traditio* is the equivalent of the Greek *paradosis.* In his Catholic period, tradition and apostolic tradition are used interchangeably. Appeal to the apostolic churches is a means of ascertaining the content of this tradition and the succession of their bishops back to the founding apostle, its tangible sign. Antiquity is not the ultimate criterion of the authenticity of tradition but rather apostolicity.[49]

In his earliest antipagan apologetic, Tertullian spoke of the pagan traditions which Christians rejected along with the characteristic pagan veneration for antiquity. Indeed, in a passage of rhetorical power, the whole

Christian enterprise was painted by Tertullian as a violent war against every kind of tradition hitherto received.[50]

But his principal usage of the word was in an intrachristian context. The unity of the Church is ultimately based on "the one tradition of the same mystery."[51] This unified teaching of the churches can come from nothing other than the tradition of the apostles.[52] Such unity and accord in teaching is itself evidence of tradition, not error.[53] Heresy always comes later than the truth but usually claims to correct what is being taught at any given period in favor of a restoration of the past. In fact, it is corruption, not correction.[54] Marcion annulled what had always been believed simply because he did not choose to believe it himself. His problem was that he abolished the truth in favor of falsehood.[55] For the Catholic Tertullian, tradition was essentially the rule of faith and the related aspects of the gospel as taught by Christ, handed down by the apostles and both protected and preached by the apostolically founded churches and those local churches more recent in time but identical in doctrine.

V. How is Scripture to Be Interpreted?

Van den Eynde sees Tertullian following Irenaeus closely in this matter also. Details of Scripture are to be interpreted in harmony with the whole of the Bible. Obscure passages are to be explained by clearer ones and the whole of Scripture is to be interpreted according to the tradition of the Church.[56] Flesseman-van Leer agrees with this but she adds that, while the only legitimate exegesis of Holy Scripture is that which is in accord with the rule of faith, the whole of Scripture expresses the rule. Scripture is to be interpreted according to the meaning of the totality of Scripture.[57] Waszink objects to this.[58] He professes not to know what interpreting the whole of Scripture according to the rule would mean in practice. In a sense, he probably has a point. There are no doubt great sections of the Bible that have little or nothing to do with the rule directly. Perhaps interpretation according to the rule of faith should be understood as a series of subrules of interpretation for relevant sections of Scripture. For example, Scripture is never to be interpreted as denying the unity of God or the reality of the incarnation. It must never be understood as denying the divinity of Christ, etc. Karpp likewise is more restrictive in his view of the relationship between the Bible and its interpretation by the rule.[59]

Protestant authors in particular seek to avoid any appearance of subordinating Scripture to the rule of faith. Waszink cites Kuss: "Though the rule of faith is the last and highest instance of the correct knowledge of divine realities and consequently of the legitimate meaning of Holy Scripture, the Scripture itself remains the source of Revelation."[60] In practice, surely, but Tertullian just as often simply refers to Christ as the source.

As we have seen, Tertullian found Marcion a relatively easy target. Disagreements over the meaning of texts are one thing but Marcion was guilty of butchering the text. He solved the problem of the interpretation of texts by eliminating most of them.[61] Beyond Marcion's wholesale rejection lay the question we refer to as canonicity. Tertullian had little to say directly but where it did emerge, his reaction betrayed his penchant for using all means available to attain his purpose in debate. And in this he seems ironically to resemble Marcion. So, in the *De cultu feminarum,* he argued that Christians should accept the book of Henoch because of the role it assigned to angels.[62] On the other hand, in his later more rigoristic phase, he clearly rejected the *Shepherd* of Hermas, calling it the Shepherd of Adulterers.[63] In a more neutral question, he asserted that what Marcion insisted was Paul's letter to the Laodiceans was really the letter to the Ephesians.[64]

It is more difficult to agree on the exegesis of texts accepted by both sides. But, as Tertullian put it, "An unfaithful interpretation is just as damaging to the truth as a corrupting pen."[65] Heretics single out obscure or ambiguous texts to support their views.[66] It is not enough simply to cite words; meaning in context (*ratio verborum*) must be considered.[67] Heretics seize upon any opportunity offered by the Scriptures. They take simple concepts and twist them to their own purposes.[68] On one occasion, Tertullian speaks of his opponent's *tortuositas.*[69]

Scriptural meaning can be ascertained by observing what has actually happened and looking back to see how these events were described in ancient prophecy.[70] Simplicity is to be preferred; the clearer meaning accepted. Some people strive too hard, looking for obscure meanings. This is one of the bad results of *curiositas* and its accompanying striving (*exercitatio*).[71] One must not go on searching indefinitely.[72] These common sense rules are violated by heretics but as a foretaste of Tertullian's growing arbitrariness of his later period, one should note his comment in the *De spectaculis,* "Divine Scripture may always be extended further, whenever in accordance with its basic meaning, discipline is strengthened."[73]

A much-debated question in Tertullian concerns the importance of Scripture for his theology. It often seems that Scripture is secondary to tradition in the sense that Scripture is to be interpreted in accordance with the faith of the contemporary Church as found primarily, but not exclusively, in the rule of faith. Indeed, some of his remarks are worthy of Counter-Reformation polemics.

A basic premise of the *De praescriptione* is that Christians do not agree on the meaning of very many passages of Scripture. But he goes further and states, "[T]he Scriptures themselves have by God's will been so arranged as to furnish the heretics with their subject matter. . . . There could be no heresy without Scripture."[74] Sacred Scripture offers many opportunities for the heretics and they are not slow to take them up.[75] This is as the apostle warned us, "There must be heresies among you" (1 Cor 11:19). They understand the Scriptures perversely.[76]

Tertullian's argument from prescription claims that the heretics have no right to the Scriptures. "Let them believe without Scripture in order that they may believe against the Scriptures."[77] Faith will save you but this is *fides quae* for Tertullian. The faith is governed by the rule, its law; and salvation will be found in the observance of this law.[78] Where diversity of doctrine is found, two versions cannot both be right. One, at least, has been corrupted.

This problem returns us to the apostolic tradition argument summarized above. Doctrine is not first tested by Scripture. It is the other way around. "One must not appeal to the Scriptures; the fight should not be carried on where victory is either nonexistent, uncertain or barely certain. . . . There where you see the true Christian discipline and faith, there you will find the true Scriptures and their true interpretation and all Christian tradition."[79] "What we are, the Scriptures have been since their beginning."[80]

Here is an example of how false doctrine undermines Scripture. True doctrine, on the other hand, interprets the meaning correctly. Docetists argued that Matthew 12:48, "Who is my mother and who are my brothers?" was a proof text for their contention that Jesus was not truly human, that he had no human mother. The statement was a temptation for Jesus. Tertullian noted that elsewhere in the New Testament, when Jesus is being tempted, it is so noted. Why should one find such a temptation in this passage? Tertullian rejected the interpretation and commented, "I do not accept something which is a conclusion from your own doctrine and which is not in Scripture. . . ."[81] In one of his last works, he claimed that the heretics fashioned their teaching from some kind of wooden conformity to the details of Scripture, whereas the orthodox (or the Montanists in this case) interpreted Scripture in accordance with their doctrine.[82]

Even if pride of place in interpreting Scripture is given to the rule of faith and, more generally, the doctrine of the Church, there are many other things which Christians do which are to be found neither in Scripture nor in the rule as such. The best source for his earlier thoughts on the question of Christian customs is his treatise on the Lord's Prayer (*De oratione*).

After discussing that prayer, Tertullian added comments on a variety of customs practiced by some Christians in his community. He characterized such customs as vain and matters of empty observance because they had emerged without the authority of a precept of the Lord or of the apostles.[83] Some of these foolish things are noted by Tertullian: praying sitting down, supposedly based on the *Shepherd* of Hermas (Vis. 5); refusing to give the kiss of peace while fasting.[84] In this latter instance, whatever command some supposed they were honoring in so acting, it could not have been more important than the Lord's clear command in Scripture to conceal our fasting.[85] No specific rules have been set down concerning times for prayer. When bad customs such as insufficient veiling for women, customs which should be changed, were in question, Tertullian had no hesitation about complaining that certain leaders (bishops?) were being excessively cautious when they refused to overturn the rulings of their predecessors.[86]

VI. How Tertullian Changed in His Montanist Period

In his later works, Tertullian undid himself and his arguments from the Catholic period. Previously he had argued that the apostles had been completely aware of and faithful to the teachings of Jesus. Now he drew a greater divide between the teachings of Jesus in his own lifetime, the lives and teachings of the apostles in their time, and the situations of postapostolic Christians. Jesus, for example, told his disciples to flee to other towns in time of persecution (Matt 10:23). But Tertullian continued, we do not find this command repeated by the apostles. Their disciples therefore are not free to run away. In general, for Tertullian the Montanist, the powers entrusted to the apostles, such as the power to forgive *all* sins, were not passed on to future generations, or at least, certainly not to the bishops![87]

The apostles acted at the instigation of the Spirit who gave them their authority. Since Catholics have not accepted the prophets sent by the same Spirit, they no longer possess the authority of the apostles.[88] What the apostles taught was consistent not only on matters of faith but also on matters of discipline as well.[89] Tertullian's persistent claim was that his Montanist stance was no contradiction to his earlier position outlined in the *De praescriptione*. Catholics were uncertain about the Paraclete, and for this reason the new prophecies were rejected. "Not that Montanus and Priscilla and Maximilla preach another God, nor that they reduce Jesus Christ to nothing, nor that they overturn any particular rule of faith or hope, but that they plainly teach more frequent fasting than marriage."[90]

In reality, Catholics raised objections, Tertullian argued, because they rejected a stricter way of life. Doctrinal scruples were a smoke screen for moral weakness. Are innovations always wrong? Are these new requirements the demands of the Holy Spirit or of evil spirits who seek to confuse Christians and divide the Church? Tertullian's general answer was always that movements toward greater asceticism and self-denial were right by definition. If this movement were the work of the Devil, he would first move to destroy the faith, to attack the *regula fidei* as his first priority. This rule always precedes the *ordo disciplinae*.[91]

But is this stricter discipline really such a novelty?[92] Christ was an example of perfect and complete discipline. The Spirit had earlier revealed that this perfection would eventually be required of all.[93] The discipline of the apostles themselves is or should be the principal element determining the lifestyle of Christians.[94] If stricter discipline was always in our future, at the beginning, for pedagogical reasons, things were a bit more relaxed. But now that Christians had reached maturity, the full rigor of discipline was being demanded of them.[95] It is interesting to note that much later Augustine made use of a similar argument.[96] In general, for Tertullian, when it comes down to more strict vs. less strict, more is not only better, it is the only choice.[97]

While many of his basic principles of interpretation remained unchanged, his Montanist faith now began to affect his reading of the Scriptures. Paul, for example, was to be interpreted as consistent with himself, i.e., rigorist rather than lenient.[98] Any concessions to weakness must be clear and explicit for what Scripture does not mention, it denies.[99] Or, even if Paul is seen as indulgent in certain instances, why could such leniency not be later overruled by the Paraclete? Revelation must be understood in a way that is "worthy" of God and Christ.[100] In questions concerning the Trinity, the Old Testament must be interpreted in the light of the New.[101]

Catholics were now added to the list of those who distorted the meaning of Scripture by emphasizing rare words or phrases to support their idiosyncratic views contrary to the real and manifest intention of God's revelation.[102] But, in fact, that Tertullian himself went to great lengths to interpret scriptural passages to his own doctrinal advantage can be seen in the *De monogamia* and the *De pudicitia*. Bad exegesis, he insisted, was no less serious than bad behavior.[103] But apparently bad exegesis was permitted for the promotion of good behavior. In order to narrow still further the possibilities of postbaptismal penance for serious sins, Tertullian insisted that the gospel parables of mercy were addressed to pagans, not sinful Christians. By interpreting the parable of the prodigal son of sinful Christians, Catholics were destroying the whole *status salutis*. It simply was not expedient to interpret this parable of Christians.[104] For the Montanists, doctrine was the norm for interpreting the parables, not vice versa.[105]

The Montanists, of course, claimed that the Spirit, referred to especially as the Paraclete, had revealed no new doctrines but a new order of greater moral and ascetical rigor. Was it possible for the Paraclete to reveal anything that contradicted the Catholic tradition? It may well be that still more is to be revealed. If and when this happens, the new demands will be authenticated by the "integrity of his proclamation."[106] The task of the Paraclete is to direct discipline, to reveal the Scriptures, to renew the mind, and to make progress toward better things.[107]

VII. The Montanist View of Customs

The question of custom becomes more significant than it was in Tertullian's Catholic period. His broadest term for custom was *observatio* with the term *consuetudo* adding a note of authority to tradition.[108] Montanist customs come from the Paraclete, of course, but a reasonable Catholic should be able to judge the validity of a custom by asking whether (1) it is worthy of God, (2) it conforms to ecclesiastical discipline, and (3) it is useful for eternal salvation. Curiously, the earlier Tertullian of the *De oratione* might be compared to a Protestant, very circumspect about Church practices, seeking a written basis for them. The Montanist Tertullian, on the other hand, is more like the Catholic who scoffs at Protestant scrupulosity in such matters, especially the demand for scriptural proof or precedent.

In the *De virginibus velandis*, Tertullian was faced with the following situation. The local north African practice concerning the veiling of women was more relaxed than that of other regions of the Church, notably in Greece.[109] He appealed for the adoption of the stricter custom. He argued from the unity of the Church. There should be no objection to adopting the stricter practice from another part of the one Church. The local custom of Carthage, though an ancient one, must be deemed to have originated in "ignorance and simplicity.''[110] Since it is a false custom, no argument from prescription can be urged in its favor. Jesus said, ''I am the truth, not, I am the custom.''[111] Even an ancient custom can be heretical.

Even if it were not a bad custom, there is always room for improvement in discipline, especially when the Paraclete shows the way. The rule of faith, of course, remains untouched.[112] He claimed to be unashamed about altering his earlier views as a Catholic because it was no shame to change from worse to better.[113] A bit like a patristic Joachim of Flora, Tertullian saw sacred history progressing from Adam through Moses, not to Christ but through Christ to the Paraclete.[114] With a rhetorical flourish, he wrote ''Rise up, O Truth!'' to trample on the unworthy custom of his own church.[115] When it came to fasting, Catholics objected to the obligatory character of the Montanist practices. Tertullian answered their question by asking his own: On what basis were the differing Catholic customs founded? If you are doubtful about your position, pray for the enlightenment of the Paraclete. Catholics try too hard to constrain God according to their own desires.[116]

What was probably Tertullian's most radical treatment of the question of customs came in his *De corona militis*. Here he praised a Christian soldier who refused to wear the laurel crown on the occasion of receiving an imperial *donativum* or special gift of money. Ultimately the soldier was martyred but his act was not applauded by other Christian soldiers who found fault with what they considered his scrupulosity. Was he better than they? In Tertullian's eyes he certainly was. The critics asked further, ''Where in Scripture are we forbidden to wear a crown?'' Tertullian countered with the much more restrictive, ''Where does it say in Scripture that we are permitted to wear a crown?'' ''Whatever is not specifically permitted is forbidden.''[117] The motives of those who question the validity of a custom which demands more of a Christian are suspect.

This was the last word of Tertullian the Montanist on custom. His earlier position in the *De oratione* now seems to have been superseded. He no longer accepted the view that a custom should be authorized by a written, presumably scriptural, source. He listed several liturgical observances which the Church practiced but for which there was no scriptural authority. No, tradition was their source, custom confirmed them, and faith urged their observance with *ratio* behind all three.[118] ''Simply because it is observed, a nonwritten tradition can be defended, if it is confirmed by custom, which is itself a valid witness to an approved tradition from the mere fact that it has gone on for a long time.''[119] Furthermore, any Christian might originate a custom so long as it was pleasing to God, promoted discipline, and was an aid to salvation.[120]

VIII. Conclusion

Tertullian's initial writings as a Catholic, culminating in the *De praescriptione,* constituted a notable and well-ordered argument about the strength and weakness of Scripture as the bearer of revelation and the necessity of tradition as its interpreter. The rule of faith, the brief summary of Christian teachings, derived from Christ through the apostles, was the unassailable core of doctrine against which the words of Scripture could not be urged. Words were subordinated to meaning; verses taken out of context must not be construed in opposition to the general thrust of Scripture. The Church's tradition from the apostles as preserved in the apostolically founded churches was the guide to the meaning and message of God's word to us.

Unfortunately, this surprisingly early and impressive synthesis was undermined by Tertullian himself in his Montanist period. Despite his assurances to the contrary, his insistence on the ongoing revelations of the Paraclete and his new polemic against his Catholic brothers and sisters did not impact solely on questions of practice, discipline, and custom. His whole admirable structure was threatened with collapse.

The flaws in his character overcame his intellectual brilliance. The remarks of the fifth-century historian of Constantinople, Socrates, à propos of the struggle between Novatian and Cornelius in Rome in the mid-third century can be applied to Tertullian: "Thus as these two persons wrote contrary to one another and each confirmed his own procedure by the testimony of the divine Word, as usually happens, every one identified himself with that view which favored his previous habits and inclinations."[121]

Notes

[1]George Tavard, *Holy Writ or Holy Church: The Crisis of the Protestant Reformation* (London: Burns & Oates, 1959).

[2]Walter Bauer, *Orthodoxy and Heresy in Earliest Christianity,* ed. Robert Kraft and Gerhard Krodel, trans. members of the Philadelphia Seminar on Christian Origins from 2nd German edition (Philadelphia: Fortress Press, 1971) (German original 1934).

[3]Tertullian, *De praescriptione haereticorum* 9 (hereinafter cited as Praescr.). All patristic citations are from the works of Tertullian unless otherwise specified. All citations are taken from the two volumes of Tertullian's works in the *Corpus Christianorum. Series Latina I–II* (hereinafter cited as CCSL) (Turnhout: Brepols, 1954) 1:195.

⁴Praescr. 21.4, CCSL 1:202–03.

⁵Praescr. 6.4 ("auctores"), CCSL 1:191. See Thomas Ring, *Auctoritas bei Tertullian, Cyprian und Ambrosius,* Cassiciacum, 29 (Würzburg: Augustinus-Verlag, 1975) and Charles Munier, "L'autorité de l'église et l'autorité de l'esprit d'après Tertullien," *Autorité épiscopale et sollicitude pastorale IIe–VIe siècles* (Aldershot: Variorum, 1991) 77–80 (originally pub. 1984).

⁶*Adversus Marcionem* (Marc.) IV.2, CCSL 1:547.

⁷Praescr. 9.2, CCSL 1:195.

⁸Praescr. 15, CCSL 1:199.

⁹Praescr. 16, 18, CCSL 1:199–201.

¹⁰Praescr. 17, 19, CCSL 1:200–01.

¹¹Praescr. 22, CCSL 1:203–04.

¹²Praescr. 20.7, CCSL 1:202.

¹³Praescr. 20.8, CCSL 1:202: "communicatio pacis; appellatio fraternitatis; contesseratio hospitalitatis."

¹⁴Praescr. 32.6, CCSL 1:213.

¹⁵Praescr. 21.4, CCSL 1:202.

¹⁶Praescr. 20.9, CCSL 1:202: "[e]iusdem sacramenti una traditio."

¹⁷Praescr. 28, CCSL 1:209.

¹⁸Praescr. 32.1, 3, CCSL 1:212–13.

¹⁹Praescr. 36, CCSL 1:216–17.

²⁰Praescr. 13, CCSL 1:197. *De virginibus velandis* (Virg.) 1.3 CCSL 2:1209

²¹Marc. IV.2.2, CCSL 1:547.

²²Praescr. 38.1–3, CCSL 1:218.

²³Praescr. 41, CCSL 1:221.

²⁴Praescr. 43.2, CCSL 1:223.

²⁵Damien van den Eynde, *Les normes de l'enseignement chrétien dans la littérature des trois premiers siècles* (Gembloux: Duculot, 1933) 202.

²⁶Ellen Flesseman-van Leer, *Tradition and Scripture in the Early Church* (Assen: van Gorcum, 1954) 170.

²⁷Ibid. See also Heinrich Karpp, *Schrift und Geist bei Tertullian* (Gütersloh: C. Bertelsmann Verlag, 1955) 33.

²⁸*Apologeticus* (Apol.) 47.10, CCSL 1:164.

²⁹Praescr. 13.6, CCSL 1:198.

³⁰Marc. V.3.1, CCSL 1:668.

³¹Praescr. 14.4, CCSL 1:198.

³²Praescr., CCSL 1:198.

³³*De anima* (An.) II.5, CCSL 2:784.

³⁴*Adversus Valentinianos* (Val.) 4.1, CCSL 2:755.

³⁵Praescr. 3.5, CCSL 1:188.

³⁶Marc. I.20.1, CCSL 1:460–61.

³⁷Marc. III.1.2, CCSL 1:509. Marc. V.19.1, CCSL 1:720.

³⁸Marc. V.20.1, CCSL 1:723.

³⁸*Adversus Praxean* (Prax.) 14.1, CCSL 2:1176.

⁴⁰Prax. 3.1, CCSL 2:1161. Marc. III.3.2, CCSL 1:511.

⁴¹Praescr. 44.9, CCSL 1:224.

⁴²Valentin Morel, "Le développement de la *'Disciplina'* sous l'action du Saint-Esprit chez Tertullien," *Revue d'histoire ecclésiastique* 35 (1939) 243–65; *"Disciplina.* Le mot et l'idée représentée par lui dans les oeuvres de Tertullien," *Revue d'histoire ecclésiastique* 40 (1944–1945) 5–46.

⁴³V. Morel, *"Disciplina.* Le mot et l'idée," 43–45.

⁴⁴Praescr. 41.3, CCSL 1:221.

⁴⁵Praescr. 43.5, CCSL 1:223.

⁴⁶Praescr. 44.1, CCSL 1:223.

⁴⁷Val. I.l, CCSL 2:753.

⁴⁸Jacob Speigl, "Herkommen und Fortschritt im Christentum nach Tertullian," *Pietas.* Festschrift für Bernhard Kötting. Ernst Dassmann and K. Suso Frank, eds. Jahrbuch für Antike und Christentum. Ergänzungsband 8 (Münster: Aschendorff, 1980) 167; Charles Munier, "La tradition apostolique chez Tertullien," *Autorité épiscopale et sollicitude pastorale IIe–VIe siècles* (Aldershot: Variorum, 1991) 176 (originally pub. 1979).

⁴⁹C. Munier, "La tradition apostolique," 180–81.

⁵⁰*Ad nationes* (Nat.) I.10; II.1, CCSL 1:24–29, 41.

⁵¹Praescr. 20.9, CCSL 1:202.

⁵²Praescr. 21.6, CCSL 1:203.

⁵³Praescr. 28.3, CCSL 1:209.

⁵⁴Marc. IV.4.5, CCSL 1:550.

⁵⁵*De carne Christi* (Carn. Chr.) II.5–6, CCSL 2:875.

⁵⁶D. van den Eynde, *Les normes de l'enseignement chrétien,* 267–68.

⁵⁷E. Flesseman-van Leer, *Tradition and Scripture,* 177–79.

⁵⁸J. H. Waszink, "Tertullian's Principles and Methods of Exegesis," *Early Christian Literature and the Classical Intellectual Tradition in honorem Robert M. Grant,* ed. William R. Schoedel and Robert L. Wilken, Théologie historique, 53 (Paris: Beauchesne, 1979) 24–25.

⁵⁹H. Karpp, *Schrift und Geist* 43.

⁶⁰J. H. Waszink, "Tertullian's Principles and Methods," 22, n. 7.

⁶¹Praescr. 17.1, CCSL 1:200.

⁶²*De cultu feminarum* (Cult. Fem.) I.3.1 CCSL 1:346. In the context of his argument against female coquetry and cosmetics, Tertullian brought up the story of the angels seduced by the daughters of men. Hence the usefulness of the book of Henoch for him.

⁶³*De pudicitia* (Pud.) 10.12, CCSL 2:1301.

⁶⁴Marc. V.17.1, CCSL 1:712.

⁶⁵Praescr. 17.2, CCSL 1:200.

⁶⁶Praescr. 17.3, CCSL 1:200.

⁶⁷Praescr. 9.2, CCSL 1:195.

⁶⁸*Adversus Hermogenem* (Herm.) 19.1, CCSL 1:412.

⁶⁹Carn. Chr. 20.1, CCSL 2:908.

⁷⁰*Scorpiace* (Scorp.) 11.5, CCSL 2:1091.

⁷¹Praescr. 17.2–4, CCSL 1:200.

⁷²Praescr. 9.3, 6, CCSL 1:195.

⁷³*De spectaculis* (Spect.) 3.4, CCSL 1:230.

⁷⁴Praescr. 39.7, CCSL 1:220.

⁷⁵Val. I.3, CCSL 2:753.

⁷⁶*De resurrectione carnis* (Res.) 40.1; 63.7, CCSL 2:973, 1012.

⁷⁷Praescr. 23.5, CCSL 1:205.

⁷⁸Praescr. 14.4, CCSL 1:198.

⁷⁹Praescr. 19.1, 3, CCSL 1:201.

⁸⁰Praescr. 38.5, CCSL 1:218.

⁸¹Carn. Chr. 7.3, CCSL 2:887.

⁸²Pud. 8.12–9.1, CCSL 2:1296.

⁸³*De oratione* (Or.) 15.1, CCSL 1:265.

⁸⁴Or. 16.1; 18.1, CCSL 1:266–67.

⁸⁵Or. 18.6, CCSL 1:267.

⁸⁶Or. 24; 22.10, CCSL 1:272, 271.

[87]Pud. 21.5, CCSL 2:1326.

[88]Pud. 12.1, CCSL 2:1302.

[89]Pud. 19.3, CCSL 2:1320.

[90]*De ieiunio* (Ieiun.) 1.3, CCSL 2:1257.

[91]*De monogamia* (Mon.) 2.3, CCSL 2:1230.

[92]Ieiun. 1.5, CCSL 2:1257–58.

[93]Mon. 3.9–10, CCSL 2:1232.

[94]Pud. 20.1, CCSL 2: 1323–24.

[95]*Exhortatio castitatis* (Cast.) 6.3, CCSL 2:1023–24.

[96]Augustine *Ep.* 29.9, *Corpus scriptorum ecclesiasticorum latinorum*, 34/1:120, ed. A. Goldbacher (Vienna: Tempsky, 1895).

[97]Virg. 2.3, CCSL 2:1210–11.

[98]Mon. 11.13, CCSL 2:1246.

[99]Mon. 4.4, CCSL 2:1233.

[100]Mon. 14.3, CCSL 2:1249.

[101]Prax. 15. 1, CCSL 2:1178.

[102]Pud. 16.24, CCSL 2:1314–15. Prax. 20.1, CCSL 2:1186.

[103]Pud. 9.22, CCSL 2:1299.

[104]Pud. 9.11, CCSL 2:1298.

[105]Pud. 9.1, CCSL 2:1296.

[106]Mon. 2.4, CCSL 2:1230.

[107]Virg. 1.5, CCSL 2:1209 10.

[108]Frans de Pauw, "La justification des traditions non-écrites chez Tertullien," *Ephemerides Theologicae Lovanienses* 19 (1942) 9, 30; C. Munier, "La tradition apostolique," 190.

[109]Virg. 2.1, CCSL 2:1210.

[110]Virg. 1.1, CCSL 2:1209.

[111]Virg., CCSL 2:1209.

[112]Virg. 1.3–4, CCSL 2:1209.

[113]Pud. 1.10–13, CCSL 2:1282.

[114]Virg. 1.7, CCSL 2:1210.

[115]Virg. 3.5, CCSL 2:1212.

[116]Ieiun. 10.1; 11.6, CCSL 2:1267, 1270.

[117]*De corona militis* (Cor.) 2.4, CCSL 2:1042.

[118]Cor. 4.1, CCSL 2:1043.

[119]Cor. 4.4, CCSL 2:1044.

[120]Cor. 4.5, CCSL 2:1044.

[121]Socrates, *Historia ecclesiastica* IV.28; Migne, *Patrologia graeca*, 67:537.

2

The Existential Context of Tradition in the Early Works of St. Augustine

Herbert J. Ryan, S.J.

Almost fifty years ago Germán Mártil published his seminal study, *La tradición en San Agustín a través de la controversia pelagiana*.[1] Mártil's work exemplifies the neo-scholastic treatment of the patristic heritage. Mártil marshals texts from the later works of Augustine and interprets them in a way which would make Augustine's theological understanding of tradition anticipate the distinctions of post-Tridentine apologetic and controversial theology.

In 1958 Henri-Irénée Marrou's *Saint augustin et la fin de la culture antique* appeared at Paris.[2] Marrou's method of interpreting Augustine's writings differed markedly from the neo-scholastic method of analysis which Mártil had used with such startling results fifteen years before. Marrou took great pains to place Augustine in the literary culture of late antiquity. That culture shared a common method for interpreting a written text regarded as integral to the culture itself. One could grasp the meaning of works by Homer, Vergil, Cicero, or even Plotinus by interpreting the written text according to established norms of grammar and rhetoric. Marrou amply illustrated that Christian writers interpreted the texts revered in the Christian community according to these same norms. Marrou calls this phenomenon the inadvertent influence of the traditional literary culture on emerging Christian culture. In Marrou's opinion contemporary theology would hold that this style of interpreting texts would resemble the Alexandrian school of patristic theology with its penchant for the allegorical interpretation of Scripture modeled on Origen's exegesis.

One could easily contrast the neo-scholastic method of Mártil with the literary-historical method of Marrou and imagine that Marrou has unintentionally undermined Mártil's work on Augustine so thoroughly that nothing in Mártil's study merits scholarly consideration. A false assumption underlies the line of thought that would suggest so cavalier a dismissal of Mártil's earlier scholarship once Marrou's work appeared with a different approach to the writings of St. Augustine. If Marrou were maintaining and had established that Augustine's understanding of theological tradition is no more than the literary hermeneutic of late antiquity, then indeed Mártil's work would have little of value to offer the contemporary researcher. But such an interpretation of Marrou's work would be a fanciful distortion of a careful scholar's attempt to illumine the many influences which shaped the subtle and complex mind of Augustine.

Marrou's work attempts to place Augustine in his proper existential setting. Marrou shares with Mártil the conviction that Augustine's own religious experience is the vital center from which Augustine's comprehension of the Christian tradition proceeds.[3] Marrou studies how Augustine uses the literary tools of his era to describe both his religious experience and his deepening understanding of the content and significance of the Christian message. Mártil concentrates on Augustine's later polemical works and attempts to clarify how Augustine vigorously expounds his lived experience of the Christian faith as springing from and being normative for the religious life of Christians. Though Mártil may at times be accused of forcing a text into preconceived categories of thought expressive of theological distinctions alien to the patristic age, Mártil's work still retains value for the researcher seeking to grasp Augustine's understanding of tradition in Christian theology.

That a researcher may accept the insights which both Mártil and Marrou gleaned from the work of Augustine despite the different methods of analysis they used to scrutinize the text is a development in the contemporary reassessment of theological tradition. This new approach to understanding tradition owes much to George Tavard's theological reflection. Almost twenty years ago at John Carroll University, Tavard, in collaboration with Robert M. Grant and Robert E. McNally, gave the Tuohy Lectures on Scripture and Tradition. In a scintillating lecture on "Tradition in Theology: A Problematic Approach," Tavard laid the groundwork for the simultaneous acceptance of the results of diverse methods of analysis of a theological text.

"Yet a catalyst is at work," Tavard writes, "in the gathering together of historical evidence and in the study of the doctrinal and theological docu-

ments of the past. No theological conclusion would emerge from a historical investigation without a mediation. It is precisely the personal reflection
of the enquirer which provides the necessary and sufficient element through
which a return to the past becomes a *ressourcement,* enabling him to understand the thrust of faith and the teachings of the church in the present day.
The past comes to life as tradition through the action of a contemporary
living reflection which cannot avoid being contextual and conditioned by
its time. Tradition exists only as a contemporary interpretation of the past
in the light of the expected future."[4]

When Marrou is at pains to place Augustine within the literary culture
of late antiquity, he shows how carefully and respectfully Augustine becomes engaged with the theological tradition of Christianity. When Mártil
analyses Augustine's anti-Pelagian writings, he reveals Augustine's passionate
experience of the divine initiative in his coming to a mature Christian commitment to God. Both Marrou and Mártil, each in his own way, cast light
on the context in which Augustine meets the tradition of Christianity contemporary with him and each highlights an aspect of the conditions in which
Augustine articulated his understanding of that tradition.[5]

The studies by Marrou and Mártil exemplify complementary aspects of
Augustine's personalizing and restating the Christian message. In their
studies both Marrou and Mártil uncover aspects of the way Augustine develops his theological reflection. Post-Tridentine theology finds an affinity
between Augustine's reflective method of doing theology and the sixteenth-
century's comprehension of the notion of theological tradition. But Augustine's reflective theological method is more subtle than the polemical
theologians of the sixteenth and seventeenth centuries imagined. Actually
what they and Mártil identify as tradition in Augustine's theological reflection bears a closer resemblance to Tavard's conception of tradition than
to their own.

Marrou portrays Augustine, the professional rhetor, analyzing and commenting on the written sources of Christianity. In his own writing Augustine
dazzlingly displays his skill in employing the sophisticated literary tools so
attractive to the educated classes in the era of late antiquity. However, Augustine's application of the rhetorical tradition of that culture to the tradition of Christian faith was not just an exercise in creating Christian literature
acceptable to the elite of the late Roman Empire. As Marrou implies and
Mártil rightly insists, Augustine uses the traditional literary analysis not only
to illumine the Christian tradition but simultaneously also to plumb his
own religious experience.

Mártil realizes that Augustine considered his restatement of Christianity in the light of his own religious experience to be consonant with the Christian tradition. Moreover, Augustine was passionately certain that his personalized restatement of the Christian tradition about salvation encapsulated the teaching of the Church. When he forcefully expressed himself on this topic in his anti-Pelagian writings, Augustine believed his restatement of the tradition merely repeated what the Catholic Church had long taught. As Robert Evans writes, "Of one thing Augustine was certain—that on the important doctrines of sin, grace, and freedom he spoke with no other voice than that of the Catholic Church."[6]

Is there any evidence in Augustine's writing prior to his polemical works against the Pelagians which would indicate that Augustine would be a suitable example to illustrate what Tavard means by "the past coming to life as tradition through the action of a contemporary living reflection" of a theologian's own investigation of the written sources of Christianity in the light of his own religious experience?[7] If Augustine's theological reflection in fact exemplifies what Tavard means by tradition, does this imply that Augustine's restatement of Christian belief was a new paradigm for understanding the Christian tradition?[8]

Book VIII of Augustine's *Confessions* limns the existential context of Augustine's encounter with theological tradition.[9] The Book opens with Simplicianus' recounting to Augustine the story of the conversion at Rome of the famous rhetor Victorinus. Augustine narrates that "[f]inally the hour came for him (Victorinus) to make the profession of faith which is expressed in set form. At Rome these words are memorized and then by custom recited from an elevated place before the baptized believers by those who want to come to your grace. Simplicianus used to say that the presbyters offered him (Victorinus) the opportunity of affirming the creed in private, as was their custom to offer to people who felt embarrassed and afraid. But he preferred to make profession of his salvation before the holy congregation. For there was no salvation in the rhetoric which he had taught: yet his profession of that had been public. How much less should he be afraid in proclaiming your word, when he used to feel no fear in using his own words before crowds of frenzied pagans."[10] There is a clear parallel between the story of Victorinus' conversion and his profession of the faith and the conversion of another well-known rhetor, Augustine.[11] Victorinus proclaims his faith with all the skill of a professional orator. With all the polish of a master rhetor, Augustine proclaims his faith through the *Confessions*.[12]

When Augustine begins his theological reflection on the story of Victorinus' conversion, another element of the professional rhetor's encounter with Christian tradition surfaces. "God of goodness, what causes man to be more delighted by the salvation of a soul who is despaired of but is then liberated from great danger than if there has always been hope or if the danger has only been minor? You also, merciful Father, rejoice 'more over one penitent than over ninety-nine just persons who need no penitence' (Luke 15:4). We too experience great pleasure when we hear how the shepherd's shoulders exult when they carry the lost sheep, and as we listen to the story of the drachma restored to your treasuries while the neighbors rejoice with the woman who found it. Tears flow at the joy of the solemnities of your house (Ps 25:8) when in your house the story is read of your younger son 'who was dead and is alive again, was lost and has been found' (Luke 15:32). You rejoice indeed in us and in your angels who are holy in holy love. You are always the same, and you always know unchangeably the things which are not always the same."[13]

Augustine's initial reflection on the story of Victorinus' conversion unearths deeper levels of the existential context of Augustine's encounter with the Christian theological tradition. Augustine identifies with much in Victorinus' story, especially the hesitancy to yield to grace and to turn away from the values which long had ensnared his will. What Victorinus experienced Augustine depicts as salvation in bold and vivid images selected exclusively from Scripture. But Augustine does not choose the images randomly. Augustine selects biblical passages which suggest images that meld in his highly trained mind with thought patterns he appropriated from Plotinus. It is significant, for instance, that Augustine evokes Luke's parable of the prodigal son to climax the set of biblical images he employs to describe Victorinus' religious experience of salvation. The country far from his father where the prodigal's self-indulgence brought him to near ruin, the *regio egestatis* (land of want), in the Latin version of Luke's parable, is quite akin to the *regio dissimilitudinis* (region of dissimilarity) which Augustine mentions in Book VII of the *Confessions*.[14] These images are commonplaces in the writings of both Plotinus and Porphyry.[15]

Augustine's Neo-Platonic cast of mind certainly constitutes one level of the existential context of tradition in Augustine's early writings. But these few lines of Book VIII of the *Confessions* also help to reveal a deeper level of that existential context, Augustine's own religious experience—the experience of salvation, the paradoxical surrender of self-will to achieve through loving surrender inner freedom and peace which God bestows only in and through Jesus on human beings. Augustine does not starkly give a thumbnail sketch of this central component of the existential context of his treatment of Christian tradition. Rather he indirectly reveals aspects of this most personal and profound area of his inner life. One can discern a pattern in the structure of the last part of Book VII of the *Confessions* and the initial section of Book IX which provides a glimpse at what is occurring deep within Augustine's conscious being. The two sections seem like panels in a diptych each of which depicts Jesus. The latter sections of Book VII discuss Augustine's coming to grasp through Neo-Platonic reasoning about a unique mediator between human beings and God the reasonability of the orthodox doctrine concerning Jesus as the Incarnate Word, while Alypius unwittingly was stumbling into a Photinian Christology.[16] But once Augustine has experienced the liberation of salvation in Jesus, the impersonal intellectual analysis about Jesus with which Augustine concludes Book VII changes under the influence of Augustine's love-filled will into fervent prayer to Jesus in the first section of Book IX. At the heart of Augustine's religious experience was a vibrant faith centered on a dynamic and living personal relationship with the Risen Jesus. Augustine believed in the Christian tradition about Jesus' being the unique mediator between God and the human family. In the light of his lively personal relationship with the Risen Jesus Augustine gratefully received the tradition from the Church and offered to the Christian community a fresh, contemporary expression of the Christian faith. Augustine's profound religious experience of the Risen Jesus constitutes the deepest level of the existential context of tradition in Augustine's writings.

The prayer which Augustine addresses to the Risen Jesus at the opening of Book IX of the *Confessions* indicates the deeply personal character of Augustine's appropriation of the Christian tradition. The passage comes after Augustine's profoundly moving account of his loving submission to God in the garden of his home at Milan.[17] The prayer is the second panel of the diptych in which Augustine paints a literary portrait of Christ by using language evocative especially of love, freedom, and inner peace. Augustine's creative genius gives voice to his personal relationship with the Risen Jesus in describing the Incarnate Word with doctrinal exactness drawn from the Christian tradition which Augustine deepens while he articulates it anew.

"Who am I and what am I? What was not evil in my deeds or, if not deeds, in my words or, if not words, in my intention? But you Lord, 'are good and merciful' (Ps 102:8). Your right hand had regard for the depth of my dead condition, and from the bottom of my heart had drawn out a trough of corruption. The nub of the problem was to reject my own will and to desire yours. But where through so many years was my freedom of will? From what deep and hidden recess was it called out in a moment? Thereby I submitted my neck to your easy yoke and my shoulders to your light burden (Matt 11:30), O Christ Jesus 'my helper and redeemer' (Ps 18:15). Suddenly it had become sweet to me to be without the sweets of folly. What I once feared to lose was now a delight to dismiss. You turned them out and entered to take their place, pleasanter than any pleasure but not to flesh and blood, brighter than all light yet more inward than any secret recess, higher than any honour but not to those who think themselves sublime. Already my mind was free of 'the biting cares' (Horace, *Odes* I. 18. 4) of place-seeking, of desire for gain, of wallowing in self-indulgence, of scratching the itch of lust. And I was now talking with you, Lord my God, my radiance, my wealth, and my salvation."[18]

There seems to be ample evidence to assert that Augustine, even in his early writings, exemplifies Tavard's model of the understanding of Christian tradition. Does this mean, however, that only those theologians who shaped the tradition as markedly as did Augustine could serve as examples of Tavard's understanding of Christian tradition? If this is the case, then an immediate problem arises concerning Tavard's position. The problem can be phrased in the form of a question. Does Tavard's understanding of Christian tradition so closely resemble Thomas Kuhn's theory of scientific change through the articulation of a new paradigm that, in effect, Tavard is applying to theology the insights gained through Kuhn's reflections on the history of science?[19] Briefly put, is Tavard maintaining that the revitalization of tradition takes place in the same way that scientific revolutions occur?

The question epitomizes at least one contemporary approach in grappling with the notion of the development and adaptation of the Christian tradition. Thomas H. Groome appears to assess Augustine's impact on the Christian tradition in terms which seem to blend the insights of Tavard regarding tradition and the advances Kuhn has made in the understanding of scientific revolutions. "With Constantine and the Edict of Milan (313)," Groome writes, "Christianity began to emerge as the established religion of the Roman Empire; its perspective shaped the social, cultural, and intellectual life of the West thereafter. No one person was more influential in forming the thought patterns of 'Christendom' than Augustine of Hippo (354–430). Augustine saw his task as weaving together revelation and reason in a coherent theology to promote the 'spiritual wisdom' of Christian faith."[20]

Tavard's understanding of tradition does not require that the theologian who is recasting the tradition be of the same stature as Augustine. For Tavard, competent theologians who keep the Christian tradition abreast of contemporary religious experience need not bring about the equivalent in theological understanding of what Kuhn portrays as a scientific revolution.[21] In Tavard's view, vital theological reflection passes on the tradition to the community while enriching the tradition with the community's own religious experience. Tavard's understanding of tradition is independent of Kuhn's theory of scientific revolutions. One can show that Augustine does exemplify Tavard's understanding of theological tradition. It is unlikely, however, that one could show that Augustine's enrichment of the Christian tradition constituted a new paradigm and brought about a theological revolution analogous to the scientific revolutions which Kuhn analyzed.

Notes

[1] Germán Mártil, *La tradición en San Agustín a través de la controversia pelagiana* (Madrid: Espasa-Calpe, 1943) 223–25. These pages contain the summary of the work which would have Augustine seemingly anticipate in his understanding of tradition theological distinctions which more properly belong to post-Tridentine apologetic and controversial theology. Henri de Lubac, S.J., *Augustinianism and Modern Theology* (New York: Herder and Herder, 1969) 1–92, illustrates how Baius and Jansenius reinterpreted Augustine, while 118–63 investigates how the polemical and conservative Thomism of the sixteenth century had reinterpreted Augustine a generation earlier.

[2] Henri-Irénée Marrou, *Saint augustin et lafin de la culture antique* (Paris: De Boccard, 1958) 478–98. It is interesting to note that Marrou points out the Donatist exegete Tyconius' rules for the interpretation of Scripture tend towards an allegorical or Alexandrian way of interpreting Scripture.

[3] Robert P. Imbelli and Thomas H. Groome, "Signposts towards a Pastoral Theology," *Theological Studies* 53:2 (March 1992) 127–37, contains an excellent and well-documented discussion of the nature of religious experience as the vital center from which theological reflection flows.

[4] Robert M. Grant, Robert E. McNally, and George H. Tavard, *Perspectives on Scripture and Tradition*, ed. Joseph F. Kelly (Notre Dame, Ind.: Fides Publishers, Inc., 1976) 91–92.

[5] James Mohler would agree with this assessment. In his view Augustine's theology of faith reflects three aspects of his engagement with the Christian tradition of faith: Augustine's search for the truth, his conversion, and his continuing religious experience. James A. Mohler, S.J., *Late Have I Loved You: An Interpretation of Saint Augustine on Human and Divine Relationships* (New York: New City Press, 1991) 27–37.

[6] Robert F. Evans, *Pelagius: Inquiries and Reappraisals* (New York: The Seabury Press, 1968) 85. That Augustine saw his restatement of the Christian tradition's understanding of salvation as normative for the Christian faith is a point frequently made in B. R. Rees, *Pelagius: A Reluctant Heretic* (Woodbridge, Suffolk: Boydell and Brewer, 1988). Rees' latest work is a comprehensive treatment of the surviving sources from the Pelagian side of the controversy.

Cf. B. R. Rees, *Letters of Pelagius and His Followers* (Woodbridge, Suffolk: Boydell and Brewer, 1992). Rees' treatment of the Pelagian controversy is clearer and more detailed than Gerald Bonner's fundamental introduction to the points at issue in the controversy, yet Bonner's work is still very worthwhile. Cf. Gerald Bonner, *St. Augustine of Hippo: Life and Controversies* (Philadelphia: The Westminster Press, 1963). Peter Brown maintains that Augustine's victory over Pelagius meant the suppression of Pelagius' views of the *populus Christianus* with the result that clericalism took hold in the Western Church. Cf. Peter Brown, *Religion and Society in the Age of Saint Augustine* (London: Faber and Faber, 1972) 183–207.

⁷There would appear to be solid ground to support this surmise. John J. O'Meara, *The Young Augustine: The Growth of St. Augustine's Mind up to His Conversion* (New York: Alba House, 1965) 143–55, treats Augustine's formation in the intellectual heritage of late antiquity and 186–90 explores Augustine's initial examination of the human will in reference to the literary and philosophical strands of the intellectual tradition of the later Roman Empire. Emilie Zum Brunn summarizes the fruit of Augustine's quest pithily. "But although these philosophers know what this participation of wisdom consists of, their knowledge paradoxically becomes folly because they are unaware of, or refuse, the temporal condition that alone makes this participation accessible to man: the mediation of Christ. That is why the gold of truth is mixed in them with the matrix of pride, which turns it into idolatry." Emilie Zum Brunn, *St. Augustine: Being and Nothingness in the Dialogs and Confessions* (New York: Paragon House Publishers, 1986) 71.

⁸I am using the term "paradigm" in the sense that Thomas S. Kuhn gave it in his later writings on the history of science. "A paradigm is what the members of a scientific community, and they alone, share. Conversely, it is their possession of a common paradigm that constitutes a scientific community of a group of otherwise disparate men. . . . During what is called in *Structure of Scientific Revolutions* the 'paradigm period,' the practitioners of a science are split into a number of competing schools, each claiming competence for the same subject matter but approaching it in quite different ways. This developmental stage is followed by a relatively rapid transition, usually in the aftermath of some notable scientific achievement, to a so-called postparadigm period characterized by the disappearance of all or most schools, a change which permits far more powerful professional behavior to the members of the remaining community. I still think that pattern typical and important, but it can be discussed without reference to the first achievement of a paradigm. Whatever paradigms may be, they are possessed by any scientific community, including the schools of the so-called preparadigm period. My failure to see that point clearly has helped make a paradigm seem a quasi-mystical entity or property which, like charisma, transforms those infected by it. There is a transformation, but it is not induced by the acquisition of a paradigm." Thomas S. Kuhn, *The Essential Tension: Selected Studies in Scientific Tradition and Change* (Chicago and London: The University of Chicago Press, 1977) 294–95. Initially then it would appear unlikely that Augustine articulated a new paradigm for understanding Christianity in his restatement of the Christian tradition in the light of his personal religious experience.

⁹Henry Chadwick, *Augustine* (Oxford and New York: Oxford University Press, 1986) 66–74, puts the *Confessions* in the context of Augustine's life. The work is a short but excellent scholarly biography of Augustine. A more ample and still valuable biography of Augustine is Peter Brown, *Augustine of Hippo: A Biography* (Berkeley and Los Angeles: University of California Press, 1969). The chronological charts which place Augustine's writings in the sequence of the events of his life are particularly helpful; no. 16 for the years 354–385, nos. 74–76 for the years 386–395, nos. 184–86 for the years 395–410, nos. 282–84 for the years 410–420, no. 378 for the years 420–430.

¹⁰Augustine, *Confessions,* trans. Henry Chadwick (Oxford and New York: Oxford University Press, 1991) 136–37, VIII:ii(5) (hereinafter cited as *Confessions*).

[11]Robert J. O'Connell, *St. Augustine's Confessions: The Odyssey of a Soul* (Cambridge, Mass.: Harvard University Press, 1969) 95. This book is an excellent commentary on the whole of the *Confessions.* Colin Starnes, *Augustine's Conversion: A Guide to the Argument of Confessions I–IX* (Waterloo, Ont.: Wilfrid Laurier University Press, 1990) 213–45, disagrees with O'Connell's assessment that in Book VIII Augustine is discerning whether to be a married or celibate Christian. *Confessions* 151–52, VIII:xi(26–28) seems to support O'Connell's position.

[12]Henry Chadwick gives a masterful summary of Augustine's grasp of the Christian faith as he expresses it in his early writings. "Finally, one must ask what specific ideas about God and man were accepted by Augustine in consequence of his baptism and confession of faith. Reduced to its most basic and skeletal elements, the Christian faith invited him to make the following affirmations. First, the ordered world stems from the supreme Good who is also the supreme Power, not merely the best that happens to exist, but a perfection such that our minds cannot even frame the idea of any superior being. Therefore 'he' is the proper object of awe and worship. We should not think of God as involved in a process of struggling from lower to higher as human beings do (and as the Manichee Light power), but rather as having a consistent creative and redemptive purpose in relation to the universe in general and the rational creation in particular. The supreme level in the ladder of value is the love which is the very nature of God.

"Secondly, human nature as now experienced fails to correspond to the Creator's intentions. Human misery is perpetuated by social and individual egotisms, so that man is haunted by ignorance, mortality and the brevity of life, weakness of will, above all by the arrogant and wilful rejection of his true good. In short, humanity needs the remedy of eternal life and the forgiveness of sins, or restoration under the love of God.

"Thirdly, the supreme God has acted within the time and history in which we live, and which 'he' transcends, bringing to us knowledge, life, strength, and (greatest gift of all) humility without which no one learns anything. This act has its culminating focus in Jesus, model to humanity by his life and wise teaching and by the unique filial relation to the supreme 'Father'. Jesus embodied the gift of God's love by the humility of his incarnation and death. Access to this movement of God to rescue fallen man is found through the assent of faith and through adhesion to the community of Jesus' followers, a structured community entrusted by him with the gospel and with sacramental covenant signs of water, bread, and wine. Thereby the Spirit of holiness unites man to God, to give hope for the life to come, of which Jesus' resurrection is the ultimate pledge, and to transform the individual's personal and moral life to be fit for the society of saints in the presence of God.

"In these themes Christian preaching spoke to Augustine in strongly other-worldly terms which linked arms with Platonic morality and metaphysics. It was momentous that he brought together Plotinus' negative, impersonal language about the One or Absolute and the biblical concept of God as love, power, justice, and forgiveness. It is cardinal to theism that the mystery of God is known not only in the grandeur and glory of nature but also by a self-disclosure— on the analogy of a person making known to others what they could not find out for themselves. From 387 onwards Augustine took these ideas as first principles." Chadwick, *Augustine* 28–29. Another summary may be found in James J. O'Donnell, *Augustine* (Boston: G. K. Bell and Company, 1985) 79.

[13]*Confessions,* 137, VIII:iii(6).

[14]*Confessions,* 123, VII:x(16).

[15]C. Starnes, *Guide,* 51. Starnes gives an extensive bibliography on this point. Unlike some of the authors cited, he prudently refrains from trying to discover the exact measure of influence exerted by either Neo-Platonism or the Christian understanding of the Bible in Augustine's selecting and using the biblical images.

[16]*Confessions,* 128–32, VII:xviii(24) to xxi(27).

[17]See Georges Tavard, *Les jardins de Saint Augustin: Lecture des "Confessions"* (Montreal: Les Éditions Bellarmin, 1988).

[18]*Confessions*, 155, IX:i(1).

[19]Thomas S. Kuhn, *The Structure of Scientific Revolutions* (Chicago: University of Chicago Press, 1971).

[20]Thomas H. Groome, *Sharing Faith: A Comprehensive Approach to Religious Education and Pastoral Ministry* (San Francisco: Harper, 1991) 52. Pages 52–55 contain Groome's pointed critical assessment of Augustine's bequest to Western theology. Groome's assessment looks like the outline of a new paradigm Augustine could have created which swept away previous paradigms and in time held almost exclusive sway among theologians in Western Christendom. In *The Structure*, 4–5, Kuhn explains how this phenomenon takes place and well describes the role education plays in the passing on of a paradigm to a literate elite. A similar blend of insights on the nature of theological tradition quite close to Tavard's position and Kuhn's use of paradigms to understand scientific revolutions can be found in Martin Thornton, *Prayer: A New Encounter* (New York: Morehouse-Barlow, 1948) 68. Thornton views the dominance of Augustine in the Western theological tradition as a beneficent influence. Pages 93–97 give a description of the Augustinian paradigm which Thornton calls the "old map" which even now is influential in Western theology.

[21]This same point is made by Frances Young in her excellent treatment of Theodoret of Cyrrhus' personal reworking of the Christian tradition in his *Graecorum affectionum curatio (Cure for Pagan Maladies)*, a work which is contemporary with Augustine's *City of God*. Cf. Frances M. Young, *From Nicaea to Chalcedon: A Guide to the Literature and the Background* (Philadelphia: Fortress Press, 1983) 35–36.

3

"Tradition" in Thomas Aquinas' Scriptural Commentaries

Walter H. Principe, C.S.B.

Thomas Aquinas' notion of tradition has been examined by authors such as G. Geenen, Yves Congar, and Étienne Ménard. Geenen investigates the way Aquinas views tradition in relation to revelation and as a source of theology.[1] Congar's study of tradition and *sacra doctrina* in Aquinas situates his teaching within the broader context of his theology of sacred teaching and divine government.[2] As the subtitle of Ménard's monograph suggests, his extensive analysis of tradition according to Aquinas establishes its links with the Angelic Doctor's theology of Revelation, Scripture, and the Church.[3] Although Congar and Ménard give a few references to Aquinas' scriptural commentaries, their studies rely mainly on works such as the *Scriptum super Sententiis* and the *Summa theologiae*. These authors were chiefly interested in the positive aspects of tradition within the teaching function of the Church and of theologians, often keeping in mind contemporary ecumenical discussions with Protestants. We shall see that Thomas' scriptural commentaries, while frequently paralleling and corroborating the conclusions of these studies, add significantly to them because the scriptural texts often lead Aquinas to criticize certain kinds of traditions and also to affirm from Scripture itself a key criterion for judging traditions.[4]

This study must limit itself almost exclusively to texts in which *traditio* and its verbal source, *tradere*, are used. As Congar and Ménard have pointed out, a complete study of tradition in Thomas Aquinas would require a much broader examination of all the realities involved than can be had from such a limited study of texts speaking of tradition.[5]

I. Tradere, *the Active Root of* Traditio

The active, dynamic force of Thomas Aquinas' use of the noun *traditio* can be grasped only by examining it in conjunction with the verb *tradere* from which it derives. We shall therefore first examine the variety of meanings he gives to this verb and then see how he expresses these various meanings in the noun *traditio*.

For Thomas Aquinas, the most general sense of *tradere* is that of "handing over" something or someone.[6] What is handed over can be a material thing, such as "armaments to oblivion [in a time of peace after war]," "a drink of water," "vessels of the sanctuary," or an object given over in a sale, or money handed over to investment.[7] In relation to Christ it could be "all things handed over to him by the Father" or his giving over his body in the Eucharist or his handing over the kingdom to the Father.[8]

One can also hand or give over a person, either oneself or another. In one case Thomas speaks of "handing over a friend to forgetfulness [after the friend has died],"[9] but usually such a personal handing over is either a person's handing or giving oneself over to suffering or being handed over by another person to suffering. Thus Thomas, often following the letter of the text, speaks positively of Jesus as handing himself over to suffering and death or of the Father giving Jesus over to the passion and death. Negatively, others such as Judas or even the devil are said to hand over Jesus to death: in the case of Judas, the verb also has the notion of betrayal.[10] God is said to have handed over the ten tribes of Israel to captivity because of their malice.[11]

One of the most frequent uses of *tradere* is its association with *doctrina*. Although, as Congar and others have pointed out, *doctrina* can have a dynamic sense of active teaching, yet when it is combined with *tradere* it has the meaning of a doctrine or truth—that which is communicated in the act of handing over doctrine (*tradere doctrinam*) or in the act of teaching (*docere doctrinam*). In the commentary on Matthew, for example, Aquinas says of Jesus' response to the rich young man: "After he handed over the doctrine of common salvation, here he hands over the doctrine of perfection. And he hands over the doctrine first, then the need for this doctrine, and, third, the reward for observing this doctrine."[12]

The most frequent occurrences of this usage occur in Thomas' commentary on the Gospel according to John. In the prologue Thomas says that John's contemplation was lofty, among other things, "because of the incomprehensibility of the Word, which John transmitted to us in his

Gospel."[13] Explaining why only John's Gospel uses the expression *Amen, Amen,* he says that the other evangelists transmitted matters especially related to Christ's humanity, whereas John treats matters chiefly related to Christ's divinity, whose hidden character requires a stronger affirmation (a double *Amen*) than teachings about his humanity.[14]

Speaking of the Babylonian exile of the ten tribes of Israel, Aquinas states that God gave them over to captivity because of their evil, but sent a certain Jewish priest to them in captivity "to hand over to them the Law of God."[15] Moses' and Jesus' ways of handing over their precepts differed, Moses giving them in writing lest they be easily handed over to forgetfulness, whereas Christ handed over his precepts by words.[16] Again, Thomas says, Christ fulfils in truth what Moses handed over only in figure.[17] When Jesus speaks of sowers and reapers, Aquinas gives, among others, Origen's twofold interpretation. The first of these Thomas relates to the "faculty" (that is, the discipline) of theology. Sowers are those who in any faculty transmit the principles of that faculty; reapers are those who proceed on the basis of these principles—this, he adds, is especially true in this faculty (theology), "which is the science of all sciences." According to Origen's second interpretation, sowers are the prophets who handed over many things about God, whereas reapers are the apostles, who revealed what was obscure in the prophets.[18]

Two texts in Thomas' commentary on Hebrews reveal his ambivalent view about the Old Testament tradition. In one he says that its very *traditio* or handing over shows its weakness because it was handed over (*traditum est*) to slaves and weak people.[19] The other says that the author of Hebrews commends the Old Testament because it was handed over to the fathers and so, being familiar or family-like to us, is received by us.[20]

A number of Aquinas' texts speak of Jesus as handing over doctrine,[21] and one speaks of the Father as handing over knowledge by begetting Christ, who is the knower.[22] "Paul" [i.e., the author of Hebrews] is said in one place to have handed over the mysteries of the Trinity and incarnation,[23] and Paul's several statements that he has handed over doctrines give rise to commentary by Thomas Aquinas.[24] The most extensive discussion of Paul's transmitting doctrines occurs in Thomas' commentary on 1 Corinthians 15. Here Thomas lists and expounds each of the mysteries that Paul says he has handed over and still hands over.[25] These are the mysteries of the incarnation, the death, burial, and resurrection of Jesus, and his appearances to Cephas, to the eleven apostles, to more than five hundred people, to James, and finally to Paul himself.[26] Thomas discusses each of these "handings over" and makes the remark that Paul does not mention all the appearances given in the Gospels; he also states concerning Jesus' appearance to more than five hundred people that "we read nothing about this in sacred scripture except what is said here."[27]

The final distinctive use of *tradere* is important for Aquinas' notion of *traditio* because it refers to the handing over not of doctrines but of practices, ceremonies, or ways of acting. Sometimes persons transmit these by describing the practice or ceremony or way of acting in words, but sometimes the handing over is done by actions rather than by words. The distinction between transmitting doctrines by words and by actions is stated explicitly when Thomas comments on Jesus' baptizing. In the Gospel according to John, he says, Jesus had already handed over the doctrine or teaching about spiritual regeneration through words (to Nicodemus), but here he completes that teaching in action, by baptizing.[28]

Practices that were handed over by description included the precepts and practices of the Old Law which, Thomas says, were handed over in writing for the sake of foreigners and for those who could not hear them verbally.[29] Also, Jesus handed over the Lord's Prayer.[30] And when Paul speaks of the precepts he had transmitted in words, Thomas adds that Paul means that they are to be observed in the same fashion as he handed them over.[31]

Several other passages refer in one way or another to Christ's handing over the Eucharist or his body in this sacrament. He gave it over after sunset, Thomas says, in order to signify his death, since the setting of the sun signifies his death.[32] He handed over the sacrament under a twofold species in order to indicate its perfection, its signification, and its salutary effect.[33] He gave it over at the time of his final departure from the apostles in order to impress this sacrament more firmly in their hearts.[34] Because Christ gave it to the apostles after supper, Thomas comments, the Corinthians first ate their supper together and then celebrated the Eucharist.[35] Later on in the same commentary, however, Thomas specifies that Christ handed over his body during the meal but gave his blood "expressly after the meal." He relates these differing moments to the time of the Law's validity: Christ's body was given over during the meal with reference to the incarnation, which took place while the Law was still to be observed, whereas Christ's blood was given after the meal with reference to the Passion, which brought an end to all legal prescriptions.[36] Finally, Thomas says that one of the several ways that someone can partake of the Eucharist unworthily (Paul's *indigne*) is to celebrate the sacrament of the Eucharist in a manner other than the way in which it was handed over by Christ, for example, by using bread not made from wheat or a liquid not made from wine from the vine.[37]

II. Traditio

We have already seen texts in which *traditio* is explicitly linked with *tradere*.[38] *Traditio* is quite frequently used by Thomas with respect to doctrines or practices. The situations described in the Scriptures frequently elicit from Aquinas a negative view of certain traditions. This applies first of all to human traditions that are opposed to a tradition coming from God.[39] Thomas has an interesting discussion about the text of Colossians 2:8, which warns these Christians against being deceived by philosophy and vain fallacies "according to human traditions." Thomas says that the words *secundum traditionem hominum* are intended to show how deception can arise. Secular or worldly wisdom can deceive either through "real principles of philosophy" or through "sophistic reasons." These latter can be seductive because of something that is not real but only apparent. One source of such apparent truth is the authority of philosophers: this is what is referred to as being "according to human tradition, that is, according to those things that some have handed over on the basis of their own reasoning."[40] Thomas then raises the question whether human traditions and reasonings are always to be rejected. He denies this: only those are to be rejected that rely on "physical reasoning according to these (human traditions) rather than according to Christ."[41]

As might be expected when certain scriptural texts speak about Jewish traditions, Aquinas has comments regarding these traditions. In some cases he speaks favorably about them. He says, for instance, that their fasting practices arose either from their traditions or from the Law;[42] again, they had it from their traditions that Christ would die voluntarily.[43] And when Paul refers to "the traditions of his fathers," Thomas speaks of Jewish traditions that are licit and that Paul calls his own because he thought of them as his own.[44]

Very often, however, Thomas Aquinas speaks quite harshly about these traditions insofar as they are unwarranted or stand in opposition to Jesus and the New Covenant. His views, of course, reflect those of Jesus himself, but his own comments on these texts are interesting. Applying a passage from the psalms to the Jews, he says that "they halted from their paths" because they followed only the traditions of the Pharisees.[45] Jesus refers to the yeast of the Pharisees, Thomas says, because yeast signifies corrupt doctrine, in this case the traditions of the Pharisees, which corrupt the whole of life.[46]

The Jews feared that Christ would destroy their traditions and so, rejecting the yoke of Christ, they suffered the yoke of the Romans.[47] The Pharisees opposed John the Baptist because he had taken on the office of baptizing outside the order of their Law and tradition.[48] The Pharisees, who established ceremonial traditions, did not enter the sheepfold through Christ; they are not shepherds of the sheep.[49] When Paul advises the Corinthians not to bear the yoke with unbelievers, Thomas says that among these unbelievers were those who shared the traditions of the elders with the Jews and that Paul urges them not to share with Jews the traditions of the Law nor with pagans the worship of idols, for, Thomas adds very strongly, "Each are infidels."[50] Speaking of Paul's criticism of the Galatians for turning to "another gospel," that is, to legal prescriptions of the Law, Thomas says that the Old Law was a gospel to the extent that it proclaimed good things but, because these good things—being temporal and carnal—were "small and minimal," it was not a perfect Gospel, as is the New Law with its proclamation of "heavenly, spiritual and eternal goods." For Paul, Thomas says, the "other gospel" of the Old Law is a "gospel according to a pseudo-tradition" but is not a Gospel such as he preaches.[51]

The principle invoked by Christ and therefore followed by Thomas Aquinas when criticizing the traditions of the Pharisees is that some of their traditions are human and are opposed to the laws of God. Examining the text in the Gospel according to Matthew in which the Pharisees accuse Jesus' disciples of transgressing the traditions of the elders (for example, by not washing their hands before meals), Aquinas quotes a passage from Deuteronomy in which Moses forbids adding anything to the words he has spoken. By adding traditions, Aquinas says, they acted against the Law. He continues with a remark that is important for his view of traditions: it was not illicit to establish something, he says, but their fault was that they ordered these traditions to be observed as if they were the Law of God.[52] Thomas adds further that it is more serious to transgress the Law of God than human traditions, the Law of God being greater than these traditions.[53] He uses the same principle about legitimate and illegitimate additions when discussing Paul's references to the traditions of his fathers.[54]

When, facing the Pharisees' reproaches against his disciples, Jesus retorts by accusing them of transgressing God's command through their tradition (Matt 15:3), the text gives Thomas an occasion for a long commentary that continues the principle he has just laid down. A good part of this discus-

sion concerns the honor due to parents and the way the Pharisees dishon-
ored parents by their traditions. Thomas concludes this long discussion by
saying that their traditions are unfitting both to one's neighbor (in this case,
the parents) and to God, because, as Jesus says in the text, they have nullified God's command for the sake of their tradition.[55] When the question
is raised whether the fictitious hypocrisy of the Pharisees has any value for
them, Thomas answers negatively, citing the words that Jesus quotes: "They
worship me without cause."[56] But, it is objected, to fast is a human doctrine and the canons (of the Church) are human traditions: do those who
teach these doctrines worship God without cause? Thomas replies that this
text does indeed apply when these doctrines are prejudicial to God's commands. After adding two scriptural texts to support this view, he concludes:
"From this we have it that a person ought to be more conscientious about
transgressing a command (of God) than about transgressing a constitution
of the Church."[57] The last remark is a rather rare example of Thomas' applying his thought on tradition to the Church of his own day.

This last text, with its ecclesial reference, leads to the final group of texts,
in which Thomas Aquinas speaks about the traditions of the apostles and/or
ecclesiastical traditions. When he comments on Peter's confession of faith
in Christ, he says that the words, "Flesh and blood have not revealed this
to you," mean that Peter did not get this knowledge from the tradition
of the Jews but rather from God's revealing it.[58] This leads Thomas to comment on Christ's promise that "the gates of hell will not prevail against"
the Church. Although Thomas does not use the word *traditio*, the idea seems
to be implied in his remarks. Thus, after some severely negative statements
about other Churches, including that of Constantinople (which, he says,
has had heretics and has lost the pastoral efforts of the apostles), he adds
that the Roman Church, the Church of Peter, was not harmed by heretics
because it was founded on a rock. The Lord's prayer that Peter's faith should
not fail (Luke 22:32) refers, he says, not only to the Church of Peter but
also to Peter's faith and to the whole western Church. "Hence," he concludes, "I believe that western [Christians] owe greater reverence to Peter
than to the other apostles."[59]

Commenting on a discussion about tithing in which Jesus excoriates
the Jews for their added traditions,[60] Thomas asks whether the precept about
tithing is still valid in his day. After an interesting discussion about moral
and ceremonial precepts, he concludes that natural law would hold it to
be fitting that those who serve the community—including preachers!—should
live from the community. But, he continues, to determine how much the

tithes should actually be belongs legitimately to the power of the Church. Therefore, the obligation to pay this or that amount is not of natural law but of the constitution of the Church.[61] Here again, although he does not mention tradition explicitly, Thomas Aquinas sees a role for the Church to determine, in different historical circumstances, detailed applications of the natural law that are not themselves binding by natural law. This seems to indicate on his part a view that there is a living tradition within the Church but that, at the same time, there are differences of degrees in the authority of this tradition.

In his commentary on Paul's account of the Eucharist, which he examines in relation to the words and practices of the liturgy in his day, Thomas notes that Paul's description placing the breaking of the bread before the consecration "seems to be contrary to the usage of the Church," which does the breaking after the consecration.[62] The variations about the words of consecration that are found in Paul and in Matthew and Luke also raise a problem. Although some say that any of these forms of words suffices for consecration, Thomas holds it to be more probable that "the consecration is perfected only by those words which the Church uses as established from the tradition of the apostles." An interesting insight into his view of Scripture and its applicability to later questions is given by his view that the evangelists meant to give a *historical* account of Jesus' words rather than an account of his words as ordered to the consecration of the sacraments. Here, as elsewhere, he explains such unwritten traditions by the need of the early Church to protect the sacred mysteries from unbelievers.[63] Thomas defends the addition of the words "mysterium fidei" to the consecratory words because "mystery" points to the hidden aspect of faith, in this case "faith in the passion of Christ, which was hidden in all the sacrifices of the Old Testament as truth [hidden] in [its] sign." Although the expression is not found in the canon of Scripture, he says, the Church has it from the tradition of the apostles.[64]

Thomas Aquinas' most significant statements about ecclesial tradition occur when he comments on Paul's exhortations to the Thessalonians: "Stand firm and hold fast to the traditions you have learned either by our word or our letter" (2 Thess 2:14), and: "We urge you . . . to avoid any brother who leads a disorderly life that is not in keeping with the tradition you received from us" (2 Thess 3:6). The first passage, which in Thomas' own version reads: "Stand *in the truth* and hold fast etc.," yields the following interpretation: to "stand in the truth," he says, represents Paul's urging them to persevere; to "hold fast to the traditions" indicates Paul's manner of showing them "the *way* to stand" in the truth. These traditions, he says, are the teachings (*documenta*) handed over or transmitted by those who are "greater" (*maiores*). Teachings handed over by those who are "lesser" (*minores*) should not always be followed, i.e., when they are contrary to the teachings of faith. But if they are ordered to the commandments of God, they should be observed.[65] Here again Thomas sees a distinction to be made in the force or authority of different traditions, in this instance because of the greater or lesser authority of those teaching the traditions. The apostles, he adds, gave some of these traditions in word and others in writing. "Hence it is clear," he concludes, "that many things that are not written in the Church are taught by the apostles and therefore are to be observed." It was better, he explains, that many things be hidden; [the Pseudo-]Dionysius speaks of this, and Paul gives evidence of the same elsewhere when he tells the Corinthians that he will settle other matters (than those treated in his writings) when he comes to them.[66]

Commenting on the same epistle further on, Aquinas says that excommunication should be used only for those who, as Paul says, lead disorderly lives because of certain sins that are evil in themselves and against the order of natural law, or that are prohibited and are against the teaching of the Church.[67] According to Aquinas, at this point Paul specifies the tradition, showing what this tradition is and how they have received it from him. This tradition, Thomas comments, is that they should not be idle or curious.[68] He adds that when Paul appeals to the tradition they have received and refers to his own example, this shows that "prelates are not to be imitated in everything but only in those things that are according to the rule of Christ."[69] Here again Thomas glances at contemporary situations.

III. Conclusion

In his references to the act of handing over (*tradere*) or to the resulting traditions (*traditiones*), Thomas Aquinas nowhere presents a formal analysis of the theme of tradition. As was remarked at the beginning, one would have to examine these explicit references to tradition in conjunction with many other comments and themes in his scriptural commentaries (e.g., God's governance and revelation, the sufficiency of Scripture, the continuing presence of Christ and the Holy Spirit, the Church, ecclesial ministry—a theme well developed in his commentary on 2 Corinthians—the sacraments, etc.) in order to have some idea of his full view of tradition. What we have seen, however, shows both a broader and a more concrete perspective than is found in his other writings.

As in his other works, but very concretely in these commentaries, he holds that in some areas of Church life such as sacramental practice, apostolic traditions guarantee the validity of practices not found in Scripture. He also maintains that some apostolic traditions were given in writing but others only by words, and that these apostolic nonwritten teachings are to be observed.

More clearly than in his systematic works, the scriptural commentaries bring out Thomas Aquinas' criteria for judging traditions that are not apostolic. The most basic criterion is that any tradition opposed to God's commands or the Gospel is to be rejected. Even licit traditions added to the law of God must not be imposed as if they are the law of God. It is more serious to transgress God's law than human traditions; one must be more conscientious about transgressing God's command than about transgressing a constitution or canon of the Church. Prelates should be imitated only if they live according to the rule of Christ. Teachings handed over by persons of lesser authority should not always be followed: this seems to indicate that for Aquinas there are different degrees of authority for various traditions.

Anyone who reads extensively in Thomas Aquinas' scriptural commentaries will easily recognize that he frequently has in mind practical applications for his student audience, more so than in his speculative disputed questions, commentaries, or *summae*.[70] For them he emphasized the validity of sound traditions coming from the apostles, traditions that are in accord with the Gospel and God's will. On the other hand, his criteria for rejecting some traditions, especially those that oppose the Gospel and God's will, may have been a warning to his students about such "pseudo-traditions."[71] His statement that we should be more conscientious about transgressing God's command than about transgressing a constitution or canon of the Church, his assertion that traditions handed over by *minores* should not always be followed, his view that even licit additions to the Gospel must not be put on the same level as the Gospel, and his remark that prelates are to be imitated only in matters that are according to the rule of Christ must have evoked reflection in his students' minds. That both the positive and critical views of Thomas Aquinas concerning traditions can still be worth considering in our contemporary ecumenical search for unity must be a source of pleasure to our colleague whose work in this and other areas we honor here.

Notes

[1]"The Place of Tradition in the Theology of St. Thomas," *The Thomist* 15 (1952) 110–35. Some materials on this subject are also to be found in his "Saint Thomas et les Pères," sec. VII, cols. 738–61 of "Thomas d'Aquin," *Dictionnaire de théologie catholique* 15 (1950) cols. 619–761. Geenen indicates the limitations of his essay and promises a further essay, which does not seem to have appeared.

[2]"Tradition et «sacra doctrina» chez saint Thomas d'Aquin," *Église et tradition,* ed. Johannes Betz and Heinrich Fries (Le Puy-Lyon: Xavier Mappus, 1963) 157–94; this first appeared in German as "«Traditio» und «sacra doctrina» bei Thomas von Aquin," *Kirche und Überlieferung (Festgabe J. R. Gieselmann)* [same editors] (Freiburg: Herder, 1960) 170–210. See also Congar's massive study, *La Tradition et les traditions,* 2 vols. (Paris: Fayard, 1960, 1963), trans. Michael Naseby and Thomas Rainborough, *Tradition and Traditions: An Historical and a Theological Essay* (New York: Macmillan, 1967).

[3]*La Tradition: Révélation-Écriture-Église selon saint Thomas d'Aquin,* Studia, 18 (Bruges-Paris: Desclée de Brouwer, 1964). Each of the three themes in the subtitle is examined in separate large chapters.

[4]Busa's new concordance now makes it possible to locate more easily the scattered places in the scriptural commentaries in which Aquinas speaks explicitly about tradition.

Abbreviations of titles of Aquinas' scriptural commentaries and the editions used are those found in the *Index thomisticus: Sancti Thomas Aquinatis operum omnium indices et concordantiae: Concordantia prima,* ed. Roberto Busa (Stuttgart-Bad Cannstatt: Fromann-Holzburg, 1974–1975).

In references, the last item (e.g., 118/2 in RPS below) indicates where the text is found in *S. Thomae Aquinatis opera omnia,* vol. 6: *Reportationes* [= *STO*], ed. Roberto Busa (Stuttgart-Bad Cannstatt: Fromann-Holzburg, 1980).

The abbreviations and references are as follows:

RPS 45:7; p. 329; 118/2 = *In psalmos Davidis expositio,* ps. 45, v. 7; *Sancti Thomae Aquinatis . . . opera omnia,* vol. 14 (Parma, 1863) p. 329; *STO,* p. 118, col. 2.

REM 10:30, lect. 2; #876, p. 137; 162/1 = *Super evangelium S. Matthaei lectura,* ch. 10, v. 30, lectio 2; ed. Raphael Cai, 5th ed. (Rome: Marietti, 1951) #876, p. 137; *STO,* p. 162, col. 1.

REI 3:35, lect. 6; #545, p. 104; 256/3 = *Super evangelium S. Ioannis lectura,* ch. 3, v. 35, lectio 6; ed. Raphael Cai (Rome: Marietti, 1952; 6th ed., 1972) #545, p. 104; *STO,* p. 256, col. 3.

RIC 11:2, lect. 1; #584, 1.344; 375/3 = *Super primam epistolam ad Corinthios,* ch. 11, v. 2, lectio 1; in Raphael Cai, ed., *Super epistolas S. Pauli lectura,* 8th rev. ed., 2 vols. (Rome: Marietti, 1953) #584, vol. 1, p. 344; in *STO,* 375, col. 3.

The same method and the same edition by Cai are used for

R2C   (*Super II ad Corinthios*)
RGL   (*Super ad Galatas*)
RCL   (*Super ad Colossenses*) (This and the following commentaries are found in vol. 2 of Cai's edition and are referred to here as "2." plus the page number).
R2T   (*Super ad Thessalonicenses II*)
RT1, RT2   (*Super ad Timotheum I, II*)
RTT   (*Super ad Titum*)
RHE   (*Super ad Hebraeos*)

[5]Congar stresses this especially in another work, *La Tradition et les traditions*, vol. 1: *Essai historique*, p. 13 (p. 1 in the English translation). See ibid., 17–38 (5–22 in English) for his outline of what he calls "the fact" of "tradition" in the New Testament. While many of the scriptural texts he quotes are those that will call forth an explicit mention of "tradition" in Thomas' commentaries (texts that we shall examine), Congar's study, like Ménard's, reveals the far greater range of themes and texts that would have to be examined in order to get a full view of Thomas' notion of tradition in his scriptural commentaries as well as in his other works.

[6]Our usual translation of *tradere* will be "hand over," but at times, for the sake of variety, other translations such as "give over" or "transmit" will be used.

[7]" . . . et ideo dicit: *Arcum conteret, et confringet arma,* quasi dicat, 'Tamdiu durabit pax, quod omnes tradent oblivioni arma,' quia illa pax diu durabit" (RPS 45:7; p. 239; 118/2); " . . . Dominus sciebat eam non sibi traditurum potum" (REI 4:9, lect. 1; #574, p. 109; 258/2); "sacerdotes tradebant Levitis vasas sanctuarii" (R2C 12:1, lect. 1; #442, 1.539–40; 420/1); " . . . quod per pretium tradis" (REM 10:8, lect. 1; #819, p. 130; 159/3); " . . . qui pecuniam tradunt ad multiplicationem" (REM 25:27, lect. 2; #2070, p. 320; 211/2). Cf. REM 10:30, lect. 2; #876, p. 137; 162/1.

[8]"*Omnia mihi tradita sunt a Patre* . . . ut dicatur Pater omnia in manu Filii tradidisse . . . , et huius traditionis ratio est, quia diligit eum" (REI 3:35, lect. 6; #545, p. 104; 256/3: the link of *traditio* with *tradere* is evident here); " . . . quia tunc tradidit corpus suum in cibum" (REM 14:15, lect. 2; #1240, p. 192; 176/3); " . . . quando tradetur regnum Deo et Patri" (R1C 15:24, lect. 3; #938, 1.413; 393/1: "tradiderit regnum" is in the text itself of 1 Cor 15:24). On this last see also RHE 1:8, lect. 4; #60, 2.349; 518/2.

[9]Tertium [opprobrium] est oblivio. Et hoc est quod ait, *Oblivioni datus sum.* Sed quia homo, quantumcumque diligat aliquem, post mortem tradit eum oblivioni, ideo dicit, *Tamquam mortuus*" (RPS 30:9; p. 252; 89/2).

[10]All these meanings come together in REM 17:22, lect. 2; #1474, p. 224; 185/3–186/1: "Prius tetigit de occisione, sed non de traditione; hic vero tangit de traditione, dicens *Filius hominis tradetur. Et recte dicit Filius hominis,* quia etsi ille qui traditur sit Dominus gloriae, tamen secundum quod filius hominis traditur. . . . Sed non dicitur a quibus traditus est. Quia tradidit se, ad Gal. 2, 20: *Qui tradidit semetipsum pro me.* Traditus est a Patre, *qui proprio Filio non pepercit, sed pro nobis omnibus tradidit illum,* Rom. 8, 32. Item, traditus est a Iuda, supra 10, 4: *Qui et tradidit eum.* Item, a daemonibus, Io. 13, habetur quod diabolus posuit in cor ut traderet eum Iudas. Et Sap. 2, 12: *Venite, occidamus iustum.*"

Other texts: Jesus handed himself over to suffering and death: REM 26:50, lect. 6; #2255, p. 347; 219/1; REI 8:21, lect. 3; #1173, p. 220; 289/1; R1C 11:24, lect. 5; #671, 1.359; 379/3; RGL 2:20, lect. 6; #110, 1.589; 431/1 (the Father and Judas also handed Jesus over); Jesus hands himself over to be touched after his resurrection: REM 28:17, lectio unica; #2455, p. 376; 227/1. The Father handed Jesus over: REM 17:22, lect. 2; #1374, p. 224; 185/3; REM 26:31, lect. 5; #2209, p. 341; 217/2; Peter handed over (betrayed) Jesus: REI 13:24, lect. 4; #1805, p. 338; 321/1. Again, the Son of Man is to be handed over by Judas and by the chief priests and scribes: REM 20:18-19 (*tradere* is in the scriptural text itself), lect. 2; #1652, p. 254; 193/3; REM 26:59, lect. 7; #2273, p. 349; 220/1.

[11]REI 4:9, lect. 1; #574, p. 109; 258/2. Other uses in this sense: despite Paul's many sufferings, God did not hand him over to death: R2C 6:9, lect. 2; #225, 1.491; 410/1; Jesus predicts that his disciples will be handed over in the councils: REM 10:17, lect. 2; ##843–46, p. 133; 160/3; John the Baptist is handed over (or betrayed): REI 2:12, lect. 2; #367, p. 73; 248/1; an excommunicated person is handed over to Satan: R2C 2:6, lect. 2; #59, 1.451; 401/1; those who despair may hand themselves over to every kind of sin: ibid., #62. 1.451; 401/1–2.

[12]"Postquam Dominus tradidit doctrinam communis salutis, hic tradit doctrinam perfec-

tionis. Et primo tradit doctrinam; secundo necessitatem huius doctrinae; tertio praemium observationis" (REM 19:20, lect. unica; #1586, p. 243; 19/3).

[13]"Sic ergo contemplatio Ioannis alta fuit . . . quantum ad Verbi incomprehensibilitatem, quam nobis in suo Evangelio tradidit Ioannes" (REI prologue; #6, p. 2; 224/1).

[14]" . . . Alii Evangelistae ea principaliter tradunt quae ad humanitatem Christi pertinent: ad quae, cum facilius credibilia sint, minor assertio necessaria erat; Ioannes vero ea quae ad divinitatem Christi pertinent, principaliter tractat, quae, cum occulta sint, et a cognitione hominum remota, maiori assertione indigebant" (REI 3:3, lect. 1; #430, p. 84; 251/1). See also REI 12:14, lect. 3; #1626, p. 304; 311/3, in which Thomas says that John "compendio tradidit" that which "per alios diffuse dicta sunt."

[15]"Dominus . . . propter Iudaeorum malitiam tradidit eos [in captivitatem]. . . . Misit ad eos sacerdotem quemdam ex Iudaeis, traditurum eis Dei legem secundum legem Moysi" (REI 4:9, lect. 1; #573, p. 109; 258/2).

[16]"Secundo, per comparationem ad modum tradendi: quia Moyses praecepta dedit in scriptis, quae possunt diutius meditari, nec tradi oblivioni de facili, et ideo magis obligant ad credendum. Christus vero tradidit verbis; et quantum ad hoc dicit *Si non creditis litteris illius,* quarum libros apud vos habetis, *quomodo credetis verbis meis?*" (REI 5:47, lect. 7; #837, p. 158; 272/2).

[17]" . . . velamen *evacuatur,* id est tollitur per Christum, scilicet implendo in veritate quod Moyses tradidit in figura" (R2C 3:12, lect. 3; #105, 1.462; 403/2).

[18]"Secundum Originem vero, seminantes in qualibet facultate dicuntur illi qui quaelibet illius facultatis principia tradunt; metentes vero qui ex illis procedunt ulterius: et hoc multo magis in ista, quae est omnium scientiarum scientia Prophetae seminantes sunt, quia multa de divinis tradiderunt; messores vero sunt Apostoli, qui ea quae non manifestaverunt Prophetae hominibus, praedicando et docendo revelaverunt" (REI 4:36, lect. 4; #651, pp. 123–24; 262/1).

[19]"Deinde cum dicit *In die qua apprehendi,* etc., ostendit defectum Veteris Testamenti et primo, ex eius traditione; secundo ex eventu, ibi *Quoniam ipsi.* Vetus enim Testamentum *traditum* est servis et infirmis. Servis quidem, quia quandoque exierunt de servitute Aegypti . . . Item, infirmis, quia per se non poterant se iuvare" (RHE 8:9, lect. 2; ##400–01, 2.423; 536/3).

[20]"[8] Circa autem Vetus Testamentum quinque ponit. Primo modum tradendi, quia *multifarie multisque modis,* etc. . . . ; secundo, tempus [traditionis], cum dicit *Olim* . . . ; quarto, quibus sit traditum, quia *patribus* nostris. . . . [10] Secundo, tangit tempus traditionis huius doctrinae, quod est tempus praeteritum. . . . [12] Quarto ostendit quibus traditum sit, quia *patribus.* Et ideo est nobis familiare, et acceptum" (RHE 1:1, lect. 1; ##8, 10, 12: 2.337–38; 515/1). The second point again links *traditio* with *tradere.*

Aquinas uses *familiare* and cognate terms quite often; see the references and discussion in Ménard (cited above, n. 3) 24–25. He and Congar think it points to revelation given to a restricted and intimate group rather than to a large public.

[21]REI 3:22, lect. 4; #497, p. 139; 266/3; REI 5:18, lect. 3; #744, p. 139; 266/3; REI 14:20, lect. 6; #1958, p. 367; 329/3; REI 18:20, lect. 3; #2315, pp. 433–34; 347/1.

[22]"*Sed sicut docuit me Pater;* idest, tradidit scientiam generando me scientem" (REI 8:28, lect. 3; #1192, p. 222; 289/3).

[23]The text occurs in an argument against a statement of Aquinas that "children (*pueri*) cannot share in perfect understanding of the words of justice" (RHE 5:15, lect. 2; #269, 2.394; 530/1). "Sed contra: quia Apostolus superius multa valde difficilia tradidit eis, scilicet de mysterio Trinitatis et de sacramento Incarnationis, et multa alia ardua: ergo vel non erant parvuli, vel talia tradenda sunt parvulis" (ibid.; #270).

Against the dilemma proposed, that is, that (contrary to the text of Hebrews) the recipients were *not* "little ones" or, if they were, such difficult mysteries *should* indeed be handed over to them (this, again, seems to be contrary to the text of Hebrews), Aquinas first insists that those receiving the "handing over" of the mysteries were "little ones." As to whether they should have difficult mysteries handed over to them, he makes a distinction: everyone should receive the entire doctrine of faith, he says, but for "little ones" these mysteries should only be presented and not expounded or discussed in detail because their minds could not take this in: "Respondeo. Dicendum est secundum Augustinum quod non est intelligendum quod in doctrina fidei alia sunt tradenda maioribus et perfectis, et alia imperfectis. Non enim est inter eos ista differentia. Eadem enim utrisque sunt tradenda, sed parvulis proponenda sunt, sed non exponenda, nec pertractanda: quia intellectus eorum magis deficeret quam elevaretur" (ibid.).

[24]When Paul says that Timothy *has the sound form of words which you have heard from me,* Aquinas notes that the last words are added "quasi dicat: Non est deceptus, quia hoc tradidi quod a Christo audivi" (RT2 1:13, lect. 4; #30, 2.272; 502/2). And when Paul says he handed over the doctrine about the Eucharist (1 Cor 11:23), Thomas comments that Paul "extols the dignity of this sacrament by handing over [the account of] its institution (*tradens institutionem ipsius*)" (R1C 11:23, lect. 5; #645, 1.355; 378/3).

[25]"*Tradidi enim:* Hoc ostendit propositum. . . . Dicit ergo primo: Istud debetis tenere, id est memoria habere, quod *tradidi* vobis in primis et adhuc *trado*" (R1C 15:3, lect. 1; #894, 1.406; 391/1).

[26]Ibid.; ##894-98, 1.406-08; 391/1-2.

[27]"Notandum autem est quia apparitiones Christi non ponuntur hic omnes, nec illae quae factae sunt mulieribus. Ponuntur autem hic quaedam quae non leguntur in Evangeliis" (ibid.; #899, 1.407; 391/2). Concerning the apparition to more than five hundred, he adds: "Sed de hoc nihil legimus in sacra scriptura, nisi hoc quod hic dicitur" (ibid.; #901, 1.407; 391/2).

[28]"Supra Dominus tradidit doctrinam de spirituali regeneratione per verba; hic vero doctrinam illam implet per opera, baptizando" (REI 3:23, lect. 4; #497, p. 95; 254/2).

The same distinction is also clear in Paul's second letter to Timothy: "Supra ostendit Apostolus quid eis suo exemplo tradidit, ut scilicet non essent inquieti, sed ut operarentur, hic ostendit quomodo hoc praesens verbis et factis tradidit" (R2T 3:10, lect. 2; #76, 2.207; 489/1).

[29]"Lex enim statuta in scriptis aliquid tradit propter extraneos, et eos qui ab eo verbotenus audire non possunt" (RGL 2:10, lect. 6; #105, 1.588; 430/3).

[30]"Unde haec oratio habet tria: est enim brevis, perfecta et efficax. . . . Perfecta est: ipse enim Dominus tradidit hanc, et Dei perfecta sunt opera" (REM 6:9, lect. 3; #583, p. 90; 149/3).

[31]" . . . Quantum vero ad dicta, subdit: *Et sicut tradidi vobis, praecepta mea observatis,* quasi dicat: eodem tenore observatis quo ego tradidi" (R1C 11:2, lect. 1; #584, 1.344; 375/3).

[32]"Dicit ergo *Vespere autem facto,* scilicet solis occubitu, per quod significatur mors Christi, quia tunc tradidit corpus suum in cibum . . . " (REM 14:23, lect. 2; #1240, p. 192; 176/3).

[33]"*Traditur* autem hoc sacramentum sub duplici specie propter tria. Primo quidem propter eius perfectionem. . . . Secundo propter eius significationem. . . . Tertio propter huius sacramenti effectum salutarem" (R1C 11:23, lect. 5; #653, 1.356; 379/1).

[34]" . . . ut arctius imprimeretur hoc sacramentum cordibus discipulorum, quibus ipsum tradidit in ultimo suo recessu" (R1C 11:20, lect. 4; #631, 1.353; 378/1).

[35]"Quia enim Dominus discipulis suis post coenam hoc sacramentum tradidit, volebant etiam Corinthi post communem coenam sumere corpus Christi" (ibid.).

[36]" . . . Christus corpus suum tradidit inter coenam. . . . Sed sanguinem dedit expresse post coenam. . . . Cuius ratio est, quia corpus Christi repraesentat mysterium incarnationis, quae facta est adhuc legalibus observantiis statum habentibus, inter quas praecipua erat coena agni paschalis. Sed sanguis Christi in sacramento directe repraesentat passionem, per quam est effusus et per quam sunt terminata omnia legalia" (R1C 11:25, lect. 6; #675, 1.360-61; 380/1).

[37]" . . . Considerandum est qualiter aliquis indigne manducat et bibat. . . . Primo quidem quantum ad celebrationem huius sacramenti, quia scilicet aliquis aliter celebrat sacramentum

Eucharistiae quam a Christo traditum est: puta si offerat in hoc sacramento alium panem quam triticeum, vel alium liquorem, quam vinum de vite" (RIC 11:27, lect. 7; #688, 1.363; 380/3).

[38]See the texts in nn. 8, 10, 19, 20. See also REM 10:17, lect. 2; #843, p. 133; 160/3; REM 20:18, lect. 2; #1652, p. 254; 193/3; REI 2:12, lect. 2; #367, p. 73; 248/1.

[39]"Sed quare respondet sic [*Unus est bonus, Deus*]? Dicit Hieronymus quod respondet ad mentem ipsius, qui illam bonitatem commendebat, quae solet esse in homine; quia magis adhaerebant traditionibus hominum quam Dei, sicut supra xv, 6 dicitur: *Irritum fecistis mandatum Dei propter traditiones vestras.* Ideo reprehendit eum, quia petebat ab eo tamquam ab homine bono, non autem tamquam a Deo" (REM 19:17, lect. 1; #1582, p. 242; 190/2). Cf. REM 15:1, lect. 1; #1307, p. 201; 179/1· "Unde potest ista plantatio intelligi de traditione hominum, quae est eradicanda si sit contra Deum; sed traditio quae est a Deo numquam est eradicanda. Unde *omnis plantatio,* id est, traditio quae non est a Deo Patre meo, eradicabitur."

[40]"Sed quod aliquis decipiatur per sapientiam saecularem, dupliciter contingit, scilicet quandoque per principia realia philosophiae, quandoque per sophisticas rationes. . . . Eph. V. 6: *Nemo vos seducat inanibus verbis.* Quomodo seducens? Qui seducit, oportet habere aliquid apparens, et aliquid non existens. Ideo primo ponit principium apparentiae; secundo defectum existentiae. Principium apparentiae est duplex, id est, auctoritas philosophorum, et quantum ad hoc dicit *secundum traditionem hominum,* id est, secundum ea quae aliqui tradiderunt propria ratione" (RCL 2:8, lect. 2; ##91–92. 2.144; 476/3).

[41]"Sed numquid sunt semper respuendae traditiones hominum et rationes? Respondeo: Non, sed tunc quando procedit physica ratio secundum illas, et non secundum Christum" (ibid., #93). In the phrase *physica ratio,* "physical" likely means "natural" or "depending on natural reasoning alone."

[42]"Sed unde hoc quod ieiunebant? Respondetur hic ex traditionibus suis, vel ex lege, sicut habetur quod in die propitiationis tenebant ieiunare" (REM 9:14, lect. 3; #767, p. 121; 157/2). See also the text in ii. 54.

[43]"Secundum Originem autem, forte non sine causa Iudaei hoc dicunt [*Numquid interficiet semetipsum?*]. Habebant enim ex traditionibus quod Christus voluntarie esset moriturus . . ." (REI 8:22, lect. 3; #1173, p. 220; 289/1).

A favorable view of Jewish tradition is given, Thomas indicates, by the author of Hebrews when he speaks about "the time of the tradition of this doctrine," that is, the teachings of the prophets before Christ, through whom God spoke (RHE 1:1, lect. 1; #10, 2.338; 515/1).

[44]"Et ideo dicit *abundantius prae aliis aemulator existens,* non solum legis, sed *paternarum mearum traditionum,* scilicet quas habent Iudaei licitas, 'quas boni patres addiderunt,' ut dicitur in Glossa, quas quidem traditiones vocat suas quia ita reputabat eas ac si suae fuissent" (RGL 1:14, lect. 3; #37, p. 571; 427/1).

[45]"Item, *claudicaverunt a semitis suis,* id est, praeceptis legis: quia uno pede incedunt, scilicet sensu litterali, non spirituali. Item literaliter etiam *claudicaverunt* quia sequebantur solum traditiones pharisaeorum . . ." (RPS 17[18]:46; #26, p. 206; 71/3).

[46]"Per fermentum intelligit doctrinam corruptam; unde non intelligit doctrinam legis, sed traditiones pharisaeorum, quae vocantur fermentum, quia sicut ex modico fermento totum corrumpitur, sic ex modico errore tota vita corrumpitur . . ." (REM 16:6, lect. 1; #1364, p. 209; 181/2).

[47]"Et quod est propositum? *Habemus haereditatem eius.* Sciebant enim ex lege quod debebat dominari super iudaicum populum. Unde timebant ne imponeret super eos iugum legis, et traditiones eorum destrueret. Ideo noluerunt pati iugum Christi, unde passi sunt iugum Romanorum" (REM 21:38, lect. 2; #1744, p. 268; 197/2).

[48]". . . Pharisaei movebantur contra Ioannem, quod sibi baptizandi officium praeter ordinem legis et traditionem eorum assumpsisset" (REI 1:22, lect. 12, p. 47; 241/1).

[49]Those who did not enter the sheepfold, according to Thomas, include not only the

Pharisees but also "philosophers who examined the chief virtues": "Si ergo velis intrare . . . sicut pastor, ut oves conserves, oportet te per Christum intrare in ovile, non aliunde quam per Christum; sicut philosophi, qui tractaverunt de principalibus virtutibus, et Pharisaei, qui caeremoniales traditiones statuerunt. Sed isti non sunt pastores neque oves . . ." (REI 10:1, lect. l; #1368, p. 256; 299/1).

⁵⁰"Alii autem erant qui communicabant cum Iudaeis in traditionibus seniorum. Unde Apostolus hortatur eos, cum dicit *nolite,* etc., ut non communicent cum Iudaeis in traditionibus legis, neque cum gentibus in cultu idolorum. Utrique enim infideles sunt" (R2C 6:14, lect. 3; #234, 1.493; 410/2).

⁵¹"Unde dicit *in aliud evangelium,* id est, veteris legis, quae [annuntiatio] . . . non est perfecte et simpliciter evangelium;* quia non annuntiat perfecta et maxima bona, sed parva et minima. Sed lex nova est perfecte et simpliciter evangelium, id est, bona annuntiatio, quia annuntiat maxima bona, scilicet caelestia, spiritualia et aeterna. Et licet sit aliud evangelium secundum traditionem pseudo, tamen secundum meam praedicationem non" (RGL 1:6, lect. 2; #19, 1.568; 426/1).

> *quae . . . evangelium] quae [annuntiatio] . . . non est perfecta et simpliciter,
> sicut evangelium *ed.*

⁵²"Deinde ponitur id in quo accusabant eos: *Quare discipuli tui transgrediuntur traditiones seniorum?* Praeceptum erat, ut habetur Deut. IV, 2: *Non addetis ad verbum, quod vobis loquor, nec auferetis ex eo.* Unde addentes traditiones, contra legem faciebant; non quod non liceret constituere aliquid, sed quod ita praecipiebant observari sicut legem Domini" (REM 15:2, lect. 1; #1284, p. 198; 178/1–2).

⁵³"Constant quod transgredi mandatum Dei est gravius quam traditiones hominum: et ideo qui transgrediebantur mandata Dei in maioribus delinquebant" (ibid., #1286, p. 198; 178/2).

⁵⁴"Dicendum est quod verbum illud Domini [Deut 4:2, quoted in n. 52; really the words of Moses, but confirmed by Christ in the context of Matt 15:1-9] intelligendum est sic: Non addetis aliquid contrarium, seu extraneum verbis quae ego loquor, etc. Addere autem aliqua quae non sunt contraria, licuit eis, scilicet aliquos dies solemnes et alia similia . . . in memoriam beneficiorum quae a Deo recipiebant.—Contra, Matth. XV, 6, Dominus reprehendit eos, dicens: *Irritum fecistis mandatum Domini propter traditiones hominum.* Non ergo sunt licitae traditiones.—Respondeo. Dicendum est quod non arguuntur quod tenent traditiones hominum, sed quia propter traditiones hominum dimittunt mandata Dei" (RGL 1:14, lect. 3; #38, pp. 571–72; 427/1).

⁵⁵"Sed ex ista doctrina sequuntur duo inconvenientia. Unum contra proximum, aliud contra Dominum. . . . Item, contra Deum; unde dicit *Et irritum fecistis mandatum Dei,* quasi dicat: Non solum fecistis contra proximum, immo etiam *irritum fecistis mandatum Dei propter traditionem vestram*" (REM 15:5–6, lect. 1; #1293, p. 199; 178/2–3).

⁵⁶"Sed numquid ista fictio valet eis? Non, quia non placet Domino; unde sequitur *Sine causa autem colunt me*" (ibid.; #1296, p. 199; 178/3).

⁵⁷"Sed quid est hoc dictum? Ieiunare est doctrina hominum, et canones sunt traditiones hominum; numquid qui haec docent, sine causa colunt Deum?—Intelligendum est in praeiudicium mandatorum Dei. Iob XXXII, 21: *Deum homini non aequabo.* Act. v. 9: *Obedire oportet magis Deo quam hominibus.* Quare? Quia Deus decipi non potest. Is. I. v. 13: *Ne offeratis sacrificium frustra.* Ex hoc habemus quod homo magis debeat sibi conscientiam facere de transgressione mandati quam de transgressione ecclesiasticae constitutionis" (ibid.).

⁵⁸" . . . *Caro et sanguis non revelavit tibi,* id est, non habuisti ex traditione Iudaeorum sed ex revelatione Dei" (REM 16:17, lect. 2; #1380, p. 211; 182/1).

⁵⁹"*Et portae inferi non praevalebunt adversus eam.* Ier. 1,19: *Bellabunt adversum te, et non praevalebunt.*—Et qui sunt portae inferi? Haeretici: quia sicut per portam intratur in domum,

sic per istos intratur in infernum. Item tyranni, daemones, peccata. Et quamvis aliae Ecclesiae vituperari possint per haereticos, Ecclesia tamen Romana non fuit ab haereticis depravata quia supra petram erat fundata. Unde in Constantinopoli fuerunt haeretici, et labor Apostolorum amissus erat; sola Petri Ecclesia inviolata permansit. Unde Lc. XXII, 32: *Ego rogavi pro te, Petre, ut non deficiat fides tua.* Et hoc non solum refertur ad Ecclesiam Petri, sed ad fidem Petri, et ad totam occidentalem Ecclesiam. Unde credo quod occidentales maiorem reverentiam debent Petro quam aliis Apostolis" (REM 16:18, lect. 2; #1385, pp. 211–12; 182/1–2).

[60]Thomas comments on Matthew 23:17 (the Pharisees swear by the gold of the temple rather than the temple, which sanctifies the gold), 23:18 (they swear by the gift on the altar rather than on the altar itself), and on 23:23 (the Pharisees tithe mint, etc., while neglecting weightier things of the Law). He lists them as different "traditions," which he sees as designed to obtain more money from people. See REM 23:17–18, 23, lect. 2; ##1863–66, pp. 288–89; 202/1–2).

[61]". . . Dicunt quod praeceptum de decimis partim caerimoniale est, partim morale. Sunt enim ad sustentationem pauperum et eorum qui vacant servitio Dei, vel praedicationi: qui enim servit communitati, convenit ei de communitate vivere, et hoc est de iure naturali; sed quod decimam partem, hoc est caeremoniale.

"Sed numquid tenentur modo? Dico quod determinatio ad quemlibet principem qui habet potestatem legem constituendi pertinet; unde in potestate Ecclesiae est constituere vel decimam vel nonam vel huiusmodi. Unde tenentur, non quia sit de iure naturali sed ex constitutione Ecclesiae" (REM 23:23, lectio 2; #1872, p. 290; 202/3).

The reference to a natural law foundation for support of preachers is another interesting glance by Thomas at his own situation; one recalls his vigorous defense of Mendicant poverty and the right to live from preaching rather than by manual labor.

[62]"Tertium tangit, cum dicit *fregit.* Is. LVIII, v. 7: *Frange esurienti panem tuum.* Sed videtur hoc esse contrarium usui Ecclesiae, secundum quam prius consecratur corpus Christi, et postea frangitur: hic autem dicitur quod prius fregit, postea protulit verba consecrationis" (RIC 11:24, lect. 5; ##656–67, 1.357; 379/1).

Another ecclesiastical usage established by the Church is the Eucharistic fast: "Sed in reverentiam tanti sacramenti postmodum Ecclesia instituit quod nonnisi a ieiunis sumatur, a quo excipiuntur infirmi, qui in necessitate, quae legem non habet, possunt non ieiuni sumere corpus Christi" (RIC 11:20, lect. 4; #631, 1.353; 378/1).

[63]"Dicunt ergo quidam quod quaecumque formae horum verborum proferantur quae sunt scripta in canone sufficere ad consecrationem.

"Probabilius autem dici videtur quod illis solis verbis perficitur consecratio quibus Ecclesia utitur ex traditione Apostolorum structa. Evangelistae enim verba Domini recitare intenderunt quantum pertinet ad rationem historiae, non autem secundum quod ordinabat ad consecrationem sacramentorum, quas in occulto habebant in primitiva Ecclesia propter infideles" (RIC 11:25, lect. 6; #680, 1.361; 380/2).

[64]"Secundo, virtus eius [i.e., Eucharistiae] consideratur per comparationem ad vitam iustitiae, quam facit per fidem secundum illud Rom. III, 24: *Iustificati gratis per gratiam ipsius, per redemptionem quae est in Christo Iesu, quem proposuit propitiationem per fidem in sanguine ipsius.* Et quantum ad hoc dicit: *Mysterium,* id est, occultum fidei, quia scilicet fides passionis Christi erat occulta in omnibus sacrificiis Veteris Testamenti sicut veritas in signo. Hoc autem Ecclesia habet ex traditione Apostolorum, cum in canone scripturae non inveniatur" (RIC 11:25, lect. 6; #682, 1.362; 380/2).

[65]"Et primo monet ad standum cum dicit *State in veritate.* Gal. v. 1: *State, et nolite iterum iugo servitutis contineri.* Secundo docet modum standi, ibi *et tenete traditiones,* id est, documenta quae a maioribus traduntur. Nam documenta quae traduntur a minoribus quandoque non sunt servanda, quando scilicet contrariantur documentis fidei. Matth. XV, 6: *Irritum fecistis*

mandatum Dei propter traditionem vestram. Sed servanda sunt quae ordinantur ad mandata Dei. *Quas didicistis.* Act. XVI, 4: *Paulus docebat ut tenerent traditiones et documenta quae erant decreta ab Apostolis et senioribus qui erant Ierosolymis,* etc.'' (R2T 2:14, lect. 3; #60, 2.203; 488/1–2).

⁶⁶''Et has traditiones dupliciter ediderunt, quasdam verbis, unde dicit *per sermonem,* quasdam in scripturis; ideo addit *sive per epistolam.* Unde patet quod multa in ecclesia non scripta, sunt ab apostolis docta et ideo servanda. Nam multa, secundum iudicium apostolorum, melius erat ut occultarentur, ut dicit Dionysius. Unde Apostolus I Cor. X [XI, 34] dicit: *Caetera cum venero disponam''* (ibid.; 488/2).

⁶⁷''Nec debet fieri excommunicatio nisi pro aliquo peccato, quia hic dicitur *inordinate* etc. Et hoc est quando aliquid est secundum se malum et contra ordinem iuris naturalis, ut Glossa exponit. 1 Cor. XIV, 40: *Ut omnia honeste et secundum ordinem fiant in vobis.* Rom. XIII, 1: *Omnia quae sunt a Deo ordinata sunt.* Vel quia est prohibitum et contra doctrinam ecclesiae. Unde dicit *et non secundum traditionem* etc. Supra secundo huius: *Tenete traditiones quas didicistis sive per sermonem sive per epistolam nostram''* (R2T 3:7, lect. 1; #71, 2.206; 488/3).

⁶⁸''Deinde cum dicit *Ipsi enim* etc., exponit quantum ad ultimum quod dixerat, scilicet *secundum traditiones,* ostendens quae sit traditio haec, et quomodo acceperunt ab ipso. Est autem haec traditio ut non essent otiosi vel curiosi'' (ibid.; #71, 2.206; 488/3).

⁶⁹''Dicit ergo *traditionem quam acceperunt, scitis,* etc., quia praelati sunt imitandi non in omnibus, sed in his quae sunt secundum regulam Christi. 1 Cor. IV, 16 et c. XI, 1: *Imitatores mei estote, sicut et ego Christi.* Et in quo? *Quoniam non inquieti fuimus inter vos''* (R2T ibid.; #72).

⁷⁰This is not to say that these other works are purely speculative. Thomas himself says that if the scientific mode of *sacra doctrina* is primarily speculative, it is secondarily—and therefore really—practical (*Summa theologiae* 1.1.4), and much of the *Summa theologiae* deals with the theology of practical activity, albeit from a speculative point of view. See my Gilson lecture entitled ''Thomas Aquinas' Spirituality'' (Toronto: Pontifical Institute of Mediaeval Studies, 1984). In the scriptural commentaries, on the other hand, his comments are often rhetorical and hortatory in style.

⁷¹See the text quoted in n. 51.

4

Martin Luther's View of Tradition

Eric W. Gritsch

More than three decades ago George H. Tavard offered a brief history of what he called the "disintegration" of the ancient unity of Scripture and ecclesiastical authority.[1] He concluded that "in the person of Martin Luther the cleavage between Scripture and tradition became irreconcilable."[2] That is a sound judgment, given the tragic events labeled "Luther's reformation." But Luther's view of tradition—the process of the historical transmission of what Luther considered "the gospel"—discloses fundamental insights that point to a reconciling relationship between Scripture and tradition. These insights should make Luther scholars and Lutherans converge with Tavard's judgment in the 1950s "that the time may soon be ripe for a reassessment of the basic issue of 'Scripture alone.'"[3]

I. The Use of the Past

John M. Headley and Hans-Ulrich Delius have shown how immersed Luther was in history.[4] He was able to quote from memory a host of pre-Christian writers, ranging from historians to poets. To Luther, history is the playground of God who, as the creator of space and time, hides "under the contrariness" (*sub contrario*) of events. On the one hand, God appears to use his power arbitrarily; on the other hand, God is Christ who seems to succumb to the powers of the world. "Histories are nothing else than a demonstration, recollection, and sign of divine action and judgement. . . . The historians, therefore, are the most useful people and the best teachers, so that one can never honor, praise, and thank them enough."[5] But historiography must communicate the work of God; otherwise, history is meaningless. "For what is history without the Word of God . . . ?"[6] Luther devised his own chronological computations, following a traditional medieval scheme of viewing world history as a succession of millennia analogous to the seven days of creation.[7] He coordinated biblical chronology with the available chronologies of classical antiquity in order to criticize legendary accounts of the origins of the Church. Comparing, for example, biblical statements about Peter and Paul with the length of the Roman emperors' reigns, Luther concluded with a historian's pride "that the first Roman saints who went to heaven had never seen either St. Peter or St. Paul."[8] Following Augustine and his disciples, Luther viewed history as the struggle between good and evil. In this struggle, God selects certain people who embody the divine will, like Hannibal, the great military strategist. He and others were God's "miracle men" (*Wundermänner*) who were called to foil the ambitious "big Johns" (*grosse Hansen*) of this world. One can be a Goliath and still lose in the struggle with David.[9] Scripture, then, was Luther's source for ascertaining the meaning of the past. Accordingly, he saw in Mary's "magnificat" (Luke 1:48-55) a basic clue for discerning the meaning of political power in history. God puts down the mighty and exalts the humble, like the Virgin Mary. The histories of Assyria, Babylon, Persia, Greece, and Rome disclose the powerful hand of God who destroys pride and lifts up reason, wisdom, and right.[10]

Luther also viewed history as the record of the conflict between the true and the false church, between the gathering of those who are faithful to Christ and the gospel and those who, like the sixteenth-century Roman Catholic Church, succumb to the enduring temptation to play God (Gen 3:5). According to Luther, the history of the true Church begins with Adam and Eve who already embodied both belief and unbelief, thus foreshadowing the history of humankind. But there is always the promise that true faith in God will triumph. There will be a Messiah who will crush the serpent's head (Gen 3:15). Luther, therefore, assumes a tradition of God's Word in Scripture, a handing on of the basic meaning of time as God's time, culminating in the first and second advent of Christ. The Church must guard that tradition in the interim between Christ's resurrection and the end of time. Luther believed that the core of the tradition, the transmission of the Word of God, would always be preserved by the power of God, no matter how deformed the Church could become. Even Rome could not completely betray that tradition. "Much Christian good is to be found in the papacy and from there it descended to us."[11] Luther always felt that the "reformation" was not his doing, but the work of God.[12] He was not joking when he declared in 1535: "All we aim for is that the glory of God be preserved and that the righteousness of faith remain pure and sound. Once this has been established, namely that God alone justified us solely by His grace through Christ, we are willing not only to bear the pope aloft on our hands but also to kiss his feet."[13] Thus Luther saw in the Judeo-Christian past a tradition of the Word of God which is guaranteed in Scripture and preserved by those who are faithful to Scripture. The center of this tradition is Christ crucified; after his resurrection and ascension he is the head of the Church, his "body" on earth.

Whenever Luther spoke of the reformation of the Roman Catholic Church, he focused on Scripture as the earthen vessel of Christ, the living Word of God. The principle of "Scripture alone" (*sola scriptura*) is but another way of saying "Christ alone" (*solus Christus*). Here Luther found himself in the company of Paul, Augustine, and Jerome who agreed with the injunction "test everything" and "hold fast to what is good" (1 Thess 5.21). "Holy Scripture must necessarily be clearer, simpler and more reliable than any other writings, especially since all teachers verify their own statements through the Scriptures as clearer and more reliable writings, and desire their own writings to be confirmed and explained by them."[14]

Whenever Luther distanced himself from the "left wing" in his camp, the "enthusiasts" (*Schwärmer*), he focused on Scripture *and* tradition. Two examples clearly show his stance: his defense of infant baptism against those who hold to "believers' baptism" of adults only; and his view of the authority of Church councils, assemblies of bishops who develop rules for faith and morals.

II. The Case of Infant Baptism

When Swiss reformers in Ulrich Zwingli's movement called for the rebaptism of infants and instituted the practice, Luther defended infant baptism in a treatise entitled *Concerning Rebaptism*. Two pastors had asked Luther for advice regarding the heresy of anabaptism in 1527, and Luther responded one year later when the anabaptist leader Balthasar Hubmaier was executed in Vienna; he had claimed Luther as one of his supporters.

Luther criticized rebaptizers as innovators who think they can do without tradition just because the papal tradition is abusive. But just as Christ did not do away with everything Jewish, so Christians should not throw out the baby with the water. Even if the pope is the Antichrist, Luther contends, he still sits in the temple. "And since he is to sit and reign there it is necessary that there be Christians under him. . . . The Christendom that is now under the papacy is truly the body of Christ and a member of it."[15] One could rant and rave against the veritable Antichrist in Rome, as do the *Schwärmer* and anabaptists. But one should not reject everything that is papal. "Dear friend, this is not the way to blast the papacy while Christian saints are in his keeping. One needs a more cautious, discreet spirit, which attacks the accretion which threatens the temple without destroying the temple of God itself."[16] The rebaptizers argue that they are truly baptized when they had voluntarily consented to be baptized. They rely on personal experience rather than on the word of others. But it is safer to rely on others than on oneself. Believers' baptism is based on personal testimony rather than on the testimony of others. "The one who believes and is baptized will be saved" (Mark 16:16). But if personal faith is the reason for baptism, Luther argues, then baptism is based on a great presumption.

> For if they follow this principle they cannot venture to baptize before they are certain that the one to be baptized believes. How and when can they ever know that for certain? Have they now become gods so that they can discern the hearts of people and know whether or not they believe? If they are not certain if they believe, why then do they baptize, since they contend so strenuously that faith must precede baptism? Are they not contradicting themselves when they baptize without being certain if faith is there or not? For whoever bases baptism on faith and baptizes on chance and not on certainty that faith is present does nothing better than he who baptizes him who has no faith.[17]

Luther used the same argument against believers' baptism as did his opponents against him: that subjectivism subverts Scripture and tradition! As a matter of fact, Luther even defends tradition against Scripture by contending that the custom of infant baptism is orthodox because of its longevity. "If we are going to change or do away with customs that are traditional, it is necessary to prove convincingly that these are contrary to the Word of God."[18] What is not contrary to Scripture may become a solid tradition of the Word of God, Luther contends. "Now it is up to you to bring forth a single Scripture verse which proves that children cannot believe in baptism."[19] As long as baptism is administered correctly, it is valid, whether faith was present or not. "For the words were spoken and everything that pertains to baptism was done as fully as when faith is present."[20] Luther advocates the efficacy of Word and sacrament. They are more reliable than faith. Baptism based on faith is not true baptism. "Were we to follow their reasoning we would have to baptize all the time."[21] Moreover, reliance on personal faith alone creates a works-righteousness, a *Werkteufel,* who feigns faith, whereas he really has a work in mind.[22] Baptism is based on a divine command. That is why one should say: "I thank God and am happy that I was baptized as a child, for thus I have done what God commanded. Whether I have believed or not, I have followed the command of God and been baptized and my baptism was correct and certain."[23]

Luther sums up his defense of infant baptism in six theses:

1. Infant baptism is derived from the apostles and has endured. "God is wonderful in his works. What he does not will, he clearly witnesses to in Scripture. What is not so witnessed to there, we can accept as his work."[24]

2. If infant baptism were a heresy, it would have disappeared. But the custom endured, just like the Bible, the Lord's Prayer, and faith. There is, to be sure, no clear proof from Scripture. "But you can well conclude that in our day no one may reject or neglect the practice of child baptism which has so long a tradition, since God actually not only permitted it, but from the beginning so ordered, that it has not yet disappeared."[25]

3. Infants who have been baptized received "great and holy gifts" from God and accomplished great things. Luther singles out John Huss among others who faithfully lived out his baptism. "Since he [God] thus gives such gifts as we must admit to be holy gifts of God, he confirms, of course, thereby the first baptism and considers us rightly baptized."[26]

4. If infant baptism "were not right, it would follow that for more than a thousand years there was no baptism or any Christendom, which is impossible."[27] Sounds as if *"sola scriptura"* is complemented by *"sola traditio"*!

5. Infant baptism may have occurred in the temple of God invaded by the Antichrist. But that does not invalidate the custom. Moreover, there is some evidence in Scripture that whole households were baptized (Acts 16:15); infants could have been included. Infant baptism "is nowhere contrary to Scripture, but is rather in accord with Scripture."[28]

6. God has offered his love to the whole world. Why would such love exclude infants? "Since God has made a covenant with all heathen through the gospel and ordained baptism as a sign thereof, who can exclude children?"[29]

Anabaptists should be called "anabelievers," Luther declares, because "according to their peculiar logic they should be urging a rebelieving, not a rebaptizing." The devil always stirs up people to follow their own logic rather than the Word of God. "In the cloud he dazzles us with will o' the wisps to mislead us."[30]

III. The Authority of Councils

Luther honored the tradition of conciliarism. Shortly after his hearing with Cardinal Cajetan in Augsburg, Luther formally appealed to have his case heard before a general council. The appeal was drafted by a lawyer and was read aloud by Luther on Sunday, November 28, 1518, in the Holy Spirit Chapel of the Wittenberg Town Church.[31] Rome was reluctant to call a council but was finally pressured by Emperor Charles V to do so. Pope Paul III called such a council to meet at Trent in 1545. German Lutheran princes, who had formed the Smalcald League, had agreed in 1537 to participate in such a council if its decisions were based on Scripture and if it were held in Germany. Rome, of course, refused to accept such conditions.

Luther had been quite interested in the history and authority of councils since he had declared at the Leipzig debate in 1519 that John Huss had been right and that councils could err. Moreover, humanist scholars had provided numerous sources, including the records of councils and popes.[32] In 1539, Luther published his own account of the authority of councils in a lengthy treatise entitled *On the Councils and the Church (Von den Conciliis und Kirchen).*[33]

In the first part of the treatise, Luther argues that councils have imposed unnecessary burdens on the Church. Augustine had already complained about it, saying that one may ignore some conciliar decisions without sin.[34] He also declared that only the councils of Nicaea and Constantinople had authority. Luther adds that the name "council" was derived from the fact that bishops were summoned by the emperor. "If Emperor Constantine had not convoked the first council in Nicaea, the Roman bishop Sylvester [I] would have been obliged to leave it unconvoked."[35] Concerning the authority of councils, Luther shows that Augustine held only Scripture as inerrant, not also councils. "If we should take the church back to the teaching and ways of the fathers and the councils, there stands St. Augustine to confuse us and thwart our plan. . . ."[36] The first council of the apostles and its decision (Acts 15:28-29) is a case in point: "should we, in obedience to this council, refrain from blood, then we shall let the Jews become our masters in our churches."[37] Thus those who cry "council, council" all the time should be more careful in invoking the authority of councils. One council orders this, another that. "Put them all together, both fathers and councils, and you still will not be able to cull from them all the teachings of the Christian faith, even if you culled forever.''[38] That is why Luther wants to speak more realistically about the authority of councils than Rome since there is now solid historical evidence about the development of conciliar authority.

In the second part, Luther discusses the significance of the first four councils: Nicaea (325), Constantinople (381), Ephesus (431), and Chalcedon (451).

The council of Nicaea was called by Emperor Constantine because of the Arian heresy that threatened Christian unity in the empire. Luther describes in great detail how the council was called by the emperor and how it proceeded, how it got mired in debate over the date of Easter, and how the emperor almost succumbed to the Arians. What makes the council authoritative is its preservation of the article of Christ's divinity. "One can see clearly that this council neither thought up nor established anything new, but only condemned Arius' new error against the old faith on the basis of Scripture.''[39]

The council of Constantinople was convened under the emperors Gratian and Theodosius because the bishop of Constantinople, Macedonius, opposed the Nicene party and sided with heretics. Luther again describes in great detail the proceedings of the council: how bishops were divided, how Rome tried to dominate, and how Rome and Constantinople became estranged. According to Luther, the sole reason for holding this council was the affirmation that the Holy Spirit is true God because Bishop Macedonius had denied that. Other decisions are not articles of faith but "human good intentions," such as creating a patriarch in Constantinople.[40]

The council of Ephesus was summoned by Theodosius II who recognized the equal authority of the bishops of Rome and Constantinople. According to Luther, this council disclosed the increasing weakness of councils when they are quite distanced from the apostolic tradition and the great fathers of the Church—Ambrose, Jerome, Augustine (who died in 430). Nestorius was not their equal at all, and it showed in his view that Mary was the mother of Christ (*"christotokos"*) rather than the "God bearer" (*"theotokos"*). The council reaffirmed what the other two councils had declared, based on Scripture: "that Christ is true God. . . . The other decrees established there apply to bodily matters and are not articles of faith; these we drop.''[41]

The council of Chalcedon is difficult to reconstruct, according to Luther, "for no trustworthy history has been transmitted. . . . ''[42] At issue was the proper understanding of the *communicatio idiomatum,* the relationship of Christ's two natures. Again, the ancient Christology was upheld: "it [the council] furnishes no proof that councils are vested with the authority to foist new doctrines on Christendom."[43] Luther read about much "bickering, confusion, and disorder" in this council, and he quotes Gregory of Nazianzus' judgment "to flee all the councils of bishops; for I saw nothing good resulting from the councils. . . . "[44]

Luther sums up his view of councils in ten theses:

1. "A council has no power to establish new articles of faith, even though the Holy Spirit is present." The chief article must be protected: "that one is to be saved without the laws, solely through the grace of Christ."[45] Here Luther uses his gospel hermeneutic to assess the significance of conciliarism.

2. "A council has the power—and is also duty-bound to exercise it— to suppress and to condemn new articles of faith, in accordance with Scripture and the ancient faith."[46]

3. "A council has no power to command new good works; it cannot do so, for Holy Scripture has already abundantly commanded all good works."[47]

4. "A council has the power—and is also duty-bound to exercise it— to condemn evil works that oppose love, according to all of Scripture and the ancient practice of the church."[48] Luther cites monasticism as an example: the story of a saintly hermit should not make ordinary Christians feel guilty, as if the monastic "good work" was the standard of Christian life. One must not look for something extraordinary to be or do good. When people admired St. Jerome, he told them that they were as good as he since they had the precepts of prophets and apostles preached to them.[49] But to have something new is the way of the world, Luther warns. "So we fall, in throngs and with all our might, away from the Christian faith and into the new holiness, that is, into the devil's trap and lime-rod."[50]

5. "A council has no power to impose new ceremonies on Christians, to be observed on pain of mortal sin or at the peril of conscience—such as fast days, feast days, food, drink, garb."[51]

6. "A council has the power and is bound to condemn such ceremonies in accordance with Scripture."[52] To impose them is idolatrous.

7. "A council has no power to interfere in worldly law and government."[53]

8. "A council has the power and is bound to condemn such arbitrary

ways or new laws, in accordance with Holy Scripture."[54] Luther views papal decisions as such "new laws."

9. A council has no power to create statutes that are tyrannical, such as the power of bishops "to command what they will."[55]

10. A council has the power to institute some "ceremonies" if they are "useful and profitable to the people and show fine, orderly discipline and conduct."[56]

A council, then, according to Luther, "is nothing but a consistory, a royal court, a supreme court, or the like."[57] Its law is Scripture which reveals the Word of God. A council must be the servant of the people of God, not their tyrant. Conciliar authority is valid only when it confesses and defends "the ancient faith," especially when it is in jeopardy.[58] Luther called for such a council because the pope betrayed the ancient faith by instituting "human ordinances" that violate the chief article of faith: that righteousness is granted by faith in Christ alone, not as a reward for good works.[59]

Luther had given up hope for a council that would correct papal abuses. He surmised that even temporal government could not summon such a council, as was once done by Emperor Constantine and his successors. The reform of the Church had to be done by the people of God in their various educational and parochial settings. "We shall promote the small and the young councils, that is, parishes and schools," Luther advises.[60] They represent to him part of the "hierarchy" God created for life in the world: family, government, and Church. "These are the three hierarchies [*Hierarchien*] ordained by God, and we need no more; indeed, we have enough and more than enough to do in living aright and resisting the devil in these three."[61]

IV. Tradition, Scripture, and Church

Luther used the term "tradition" (in Latin and in German) to designate aspects of biblical and Christian history: Old Testament teachings, especially Mosaic law, knowledge of Christ, the gospel, the teachings of Church fathers, doctrine, and human customs in general.[62] According to Luther, there is always a conflict between the divine tradition of the Word of God, preserved in Scripture, and human traditions, infested by sin. Luther dealt often with this conflict, especially when opponents used Augustine to subordinate the authority of the Word of God to the authority of the

Church. "I truly should not believe the gospel," wrote Augustine against the Manicheans, "unless I am moved to do so by the authority of the catholic church" (*ego vero Evangelio non crederem, nisi me catholicae Ecclesiae commoveret auctoritas*).[63] Luther contended that this saying could not be used to defend papal authority. For "Augustine speaks of the whole of Christendom," not just of the Roman Catholic Church which has subverted the authority of Scripture by creating doctrines that cannot be reconciled with Scripture.

> We do not condemn human teachings just because they are human teachings, for we would gladly put up with them. But we condemn them because they are contrary to the gospel and the Scriptures. While the Scriptures liberate consciences and forbid that they be taken captive by human teachings, they [the consciences] are taken captive. . . . Therefore we request that the papists first reconcile their doctrine with the Scriptures. If they accomplish that, we will observe their doctrines. But that they will not do until the Holy Spirit first becomes a liar.[64]

In 1522, Luther no longer expected a reconciliation between reformers and Rome. Accordingly, he began to speak of two opposing traditions in the Church: the papal tradition which claims to be divinely instituted, and an ecumenical tradition which claims the apostolic succession of the gospel, independent of any structure. According to Luther, the papal tradition has secular roots in Roman law and custom;[65] the ecumenical tradition is anchored in Christ's commissioning of the apostles and their successors to make him known in the world as the mediator of God's salvation for all humankind. Christ gave the Church the authority to communicate his gospel of salvation from sin and death, regardless of human merit. But the Church's mission involves a struggle between the Word of God and the devil. Luther saw this struggle intensify in his encounter with the papacy. "Therefore whoever desires to see the Christian Church existing in quiet peace, entirely without crosses, without heresy, and without factions, will never see it thus, or else he must view the false church of the devil as the real church."[66] But the Church will endure despite treason and error. "To err does not harm the church, but to remain in error—this is intolerable."[67]

Although the Church may be organized in a variety of ways, its "marks" (*notae*) are universally the same, Luther contends. There are seven such marks which could be called "sacraments":[68] (1) proclamation, (2) baptism, (3) Lord's Supper, (4) the power of the keys (penance and absolution), (5) ordination, (6) public worship, and (7) suffering (*Anfechtung*). These seven marks are signs of authority and power. They are exhibited in the communication of the gospel in Word and sacrament. Luther distinguished between the seven marks of the Church and "adiaphora" (things neither commanded nor prohibited—*Mitteldinge*), like liturgy, polity, or other functions in the Church for the sake of a more efficient mission. When adiaphora implement the Word of God in Christ, the very center of Scripture, they are truly ecumenical. Luther claimed that his movement was part of the Church catholic because it adhered to Scripture and tradition. "We are the true, ancient church, one body and one communion of saints with the holy, universal, Christian church. Now you too, papists, prove that you are the true church."[69]

Luther clearly saw himself and his reform movement as a faithful extension of the ancient Christian tradition. That tradition affirmed the history of salvation from the fall to the Jesus of Israel, God incarnate. For Luther, the authority of the Church is not so much expressed in doctrine as in the proclamation of the mighty acts of God in history, centered in the Christ crucified. Doctrine was to enable proclamation rather than to explain its content; and theology was not just God-talk, but talk about God saving sinners "The proper subject of theology is man guilty of sin and condemned, and God the Justifier and Savior of man the sinner. Whatever is asked or discussed outside this subject is error and poison."[70] Scripture, tradition, theology, and the Church are to return to and retrieve what Luther called "the true treasure of the church": "the most holy gospel of the glory and the grace of God."[71] Authority, therefore, meant returning to origins (as the term *"auctoritas"* suggests) and ensuring a faithful transmission of what Scripture and the earliest tradition proclaimed. Luther found that proclamation especially in the Gospel of John because it coordinated so well the doctrine of justification and the dogma of the Trinity. As Jaroslav Pelikan put it: "when Christ in that gospel said, 'He who believes has eternal life [John 6:47]' this text was, according to Luther, 'the cornerstone of our justification.' For the issue was not one of terminology, but of the gospel message, whose doctrine of 'justification' was synonymous with the gift of 'eternal life'."[72]

When Luther discovered that his Church refused reform, he concluded that Rome no longer cared for the unity of the Church. He was convinced, however, that he and his reform movement were one with the ancient Church whose legacy had been preserved by the Churches in the East.[73] Luther thought that the recovery of the gospel from Scripture and the Trinitarian creedal tradition would restore the sense of true catholicity in the West. Accordingly, he used the gospel to correct a schismatic tradition; he even expected a reform of the existing structure of ecclesiastical authority, but lost hope in the face of Rome's recalcitrance.[74]

V. Conclusions

1. Luther meant by "tradition" the life of the Word of God in time, beginning at creation and ending at the Last Day. The Word of God reveals God's will for law and order in the face of chaos resulting from the violation of the first commandment ("You shall have no other gods"). But the Word of God also discloses God's love for the world in Christ, the good news that in the man Jesus the sin of disobedience has been forgiven.

2. Scripture is the God-willed vessel of the Word of God. Its center is Christ who is proleptically already present in the Old Testament.[75] The New Testament is the apostolic witness of the final act of God in the history of salvation, the resurrection of Jesus as the foundation of a future without sin and death for all who, like the first disciples, have faith in him alone.

3. The Trinitarian creeds (Apostles', Nicene, Athanasian) summarize Scripture in the face of heresy, focusing on the incarnation of God in Christ. Luther accepts the doctrinal decisions and formulations of the first four ecumenical councils as adequate summaries of the biblical-Christocentric Word of God; he regards these councils as guardians of the truth of God's incarnation in Christ.

4. Luther distinguishes between Scripture and tradition only when the original tradition of the Word of God is threatened by what could be called an "under-development" of dogma and praxis, that is, by a falsification, indeed denial, in thought and action, of Christ as the sole mediator of salvation.

5. Luther, therefore, calls for a proper distinction of the "divine tradition" from "human traditions." He labeled the latter "adiaphora"—things not necessary for salvation, but good for the mission of the Church to communicate salvation in Christ in the interim between his first and second advent.

6. In the light of these findings, the so-called principle of "Scripture alone" (*sola scriptura*) needs to be reassessed. George H. Tavard has pointed the way by calling for "an inclusive concept of Scripture and of the Church." They belong together.[76]

Notes

[1]George Tavard, *Holy Writ or Holy Church: The Crisis of the Protestant Reformation* (New York: Harper and Brothers, 1959) vii.

[2]Ibid., 80.

[3]Ibid., 246.

[4]John M. Headley, *Luther's View of Church History* (New Haven and London: Yale University Press, 1963). Hans-Ulrich Delius, "Zu Luthers historischen Quellen," *Lutherjahrbuch* 42 (1975) 71–125. See also Eric W. Gritsch, *Martin—God's Court Jester. Luther in Retrospect,* 2d ed. (Ramsey, N.J.: Sigler Press, 1990) 92–110 ("Scripture and Tradition").

[5]"Preface to Galeatius Capella's History," 1538. *Luthers Werke*. Kritische Gesamtausgabe (Weimar: Boehlau, 1833–) 50:384.2–4, 15–17 (hereinafter cited as WA). *Luther's Works,* American edition, 55 vols., ed. Jaroslav Pelikan and Helmut T. Lehmann (Philadelphia: Fortress Press; St. Louis: Concordia Publishing House, 1955–1986) 34:275–76 (hereinafter cited as LW).

[6]"Lectures on Genesis," 1542. WA 43:672.17. LW 5:353.

[7]"Supputatio annorum mundi," 1541. WA 53:22–182.

[8]"Against the Roman Papacy," 1545. WA 54:276.13–14. LW 41:348. Luther sided with Paul against Peter in their dispute over Jewish Christianity. See Hayo Gerdes, "Luther und Augustin ueber den Streit zwischen Petrus und Paulus zu Antiochien (Galater 2,11ff.)," *Lutherjahrbuch* 29 (1962) 9–34.

[9]"Commentary on Psalm 101:1," 1534. WA 5.208.20–36.

[10]"The Magnificat," 1521. WA 7:590.9–18. LW 21:344.

[11]"Concerning Rebaptism," 1528. WA 26:147.13–15. LW 40:231.

[12]A collection of Luther sayings on "reformation" is offered by Erwin Muehlhaupt, "Was Luther selber von der Reformation hielt," *Luther* 38 (1967) 97–113. See also Wilhelm Maurer, "Was verstand Luther unter der Reformation der Kirche?" Luther 28 (1957) 49–62.

[13]"Lectures on Galatians," 1535. WA 40/1:181.10–14. LW 26:99.

[14]"Defense and Explanation of All the Articles Which Were Rejected by the Roman Bull," 1521. WA 7:317.1–4. LW 32:11–12.

[15]"Concerning Rebaptism," 1528. WA 26:147.32–33.35–36. LW 40:232.

[16]WA 26:149.5–8. LW 40:233–34.

[17]WA 26:154.6–14. LW 40:239–40.

[18]WA 26:155.32–34. LW 241.

[19]WA 26:157.2–4. LW 40:243.

[20]WA 26:159.32–34. LW 40:246.

[21]WA 26:160.39–40. LW 40:247.

[22]WA 26:161.35–37. LW 40:248.

[23]WA 26:165.34–37. LW 40:253.

[24]WA 26:167.13–15. LW 40:255.

[25]WA 26:168.1–5. LW 40:256.

[26]WA 26:168.20–22. LW 40:256.

[27]WA 26:168.27–29. LW 40:256.

[28]WA 26:169.18–19. LW 40:257.

[29]WA 26:169.20–22. LW 40:257.

[30]WA 26:172.33–35; 174.3–4. LW 261.

[31]"Appelatio F. Martin Lutheri ad concilium," 1518. WA 2:40.9–20. On the origin and meaning of Luther's conciliarism see Christa T. Johns, *Luthers Konzilsidee in ihrer historischen Bedingtheit und ihrem reformatorischen Neuansatz* (Berlin: Toepelmann, 1966).

[32]Evidence cited in LW 41:7.
[33]WA 50:509–653. LW 41:9–178.
[34]WA 50:525.32–36. LW 41:27.
[35]WA 50:522.31–523.2. LW 41:23.
[36]WA 50:525.31–33. LW 41:27.
[37]WA 50:527.5–7. LW 41:28.
[38]WA 50:546.29–547.2. LW 41:52.
[39]WA 50:575.3–5. LW 41:86.
[40]WA 50:580.9–10. LW 41:92.
[41]WA 50:583.20–21.24–25. LW 41:96.
[42]WA 50:592.3. LW 41:106.
[43]WA 50:603.16–18. LW 41:118.
[44]WA 50:604.11–15. LW 41:119–20.
[45]WA 50:607.7–8.10–11. LW 41:123.
[46]WA 50:607.13–15. LW 41:123.
[47]WA 50:607.18–21. LW 41:123.
[48]WA 50:607.27–28. LW 41:124.
[49]WA 50:609.1–4. LW 41:125.
[50]WA 50:611.23–25. LW 41:127.
[51]WA 50:613.19–21. LW 41:130.
[52]WA 50:613.27–28. LW 41:130.
[53]WA 50:613.31–32. LW 41:130.
[54]WA 50:613.34–36. LW 41:131.
[55]WA 50:614.1–4. LW 41:131.
[56]WA 50:614.10–11. LW 41:131.
[57]WA 50:615.28–29. LW 41:133.
[58]WA 50:618.36–37. LW 41:136.
[59]WA 50:621.18–22. LW 41:139–40.
[60]WA 50:623.28–30. LW 41:142.
[61]WA 50:652.18–20. LW 41:177.

[62]The verb *"tradere"* and the noun *"traditio"* as well as their derivations (*"traditionarius,"* *"traditiuncula,"* *"traditor"*) appear about four hundred times in Luther's works. The German *"Tradition"* appears only seven times. This evidence was provided by the Kommission zur Herausgabe der Werke Luthers at the Institut für Spätmittelalter und Reformation, University of Tübingen.

[63]"Avoiding Human Doctrines and Reply to the Texts Cited in Their Defense," 1522. WA 10/2:89.8. LW 35:150. This statement of Augustine was frequently cited in the Middle Ages as a definition of the apostolicity of the Church and its relation to apostolic Scripture. See Jaroslav Pelikan, *The Christian Tradition: A History of the Development of Doctrine,* 5 vols. (Chicago and London: University of Chicago Press, 1971–1989). Vol. V: *Reformation of Church and Dogma (1300–1700)* 125–26.

[64]WA 10/2:91.21–24.92.1–4. LW 35:153. I have changed the LW translation at the end of the first part of the quotation: "they [the consciences] are taken captive (*so fangen sie die menschen lere*)."

[65]"The Smalcald Articles," 1537. *The Book of Concord,* ed. and trans. Theodore G. Tappert (Philadelphia: Fortress Press, 1959) 301:14. See also Eric W. Gritsch, "The Orthodoxy of Conflict: Luther's Ecumenism," *Encounters with Luther.* Lectures, Discussions and Sermons at the Martin Luther Colloquia 1970–1989, 4 vols., ed. Eric W. Gritsch (Gettysburg: Institute for Luther Studies, 1980–1990) 3:115–34.

[66]"The Three Symbols or Creeds of the Christian Church," 1538. WA 50:272.34–273.1. LW 34:215.

[67]"The Private Mass and the Consecration of Priests," 1533. WA 38:215.35–36. LW 38:171.

[68]"On the Councils and the Church," 1539. WA 50:643.2–3. LW 41:166.

[69]WA 50:487.18–21. LW 41:199.

[70]"Commentary on Psalm 51," 1532. WA 40/2:328.17–20. LW 12:311.

[71]Thesis 62 of "The Ninety-Five Theses," 1517. WA 1:236.22–23. LW 31:31.

[72]Pelikan, *Reformation of Church and Dogma,* 148.

[73]George Pósfay, " 'The Whole Christian Church on Earth'—Luther's Conception of the Universality of the Church," *Luther and Global Christianity.* The Martin Luther Colloquium 1991. *Bulletin* (Gettysburg: Institute for Luther Studies, Lutheran Theological Seminary, Winter 1992) 32–34.

[74]Bernhard Lohse, "Die Einheit der Kirche bei Luther," *Luther* 50 (1979) 18: "Das Evangelium ist das Korrektiv gegenüber der Tradition, nicht aber schafft es selbst die Ordnung; vielmehr kann das Evangelium auch angesichts anderer Strukturen als der herkömmlichen wirken."

[75]Heinrich Bornkamm, *Luther and the Old Testament,* trans. Eric W. and Ruth C. Gritsch, ed. Victor I. Gruhn (Philadelphia: Fortress Press, 1969).

[76]Tavard, *Holy Writ or Holy Church,* 246.

5

How Scripture Is "Traditioned" in the Lutheran Confessions

Robert W. Bertram

My first encounter with George Tavard, long before I met him face to face, was as a beneficiary of his early book *Holy Writ or Holy Church: The Crisis of the Protestant Reformation*. Ever since then and especially in my years with him in the United States Lutheran/Roman Catholic Theological Dialogue, I have been unable to think of Holy Writ and Holy Church as separable, seeing that both are one sequential "traditioning" of the same Word of God, first in its scriptural origins and then in Scripture's "echoes," the Church's creeds and confessions. True, it is in my own confessional tradition that I have had to rediscover that Scripture-Church continuity. But even there, within Lutheranism, Father Tavard has often been my mentor and I his debtor.

I. Judge and Witnesses

"We [the subscribers of the Formula of Concord] pledge ourselves to the prophetic and apostolic writings of the Old and New Testaments as the pure and clear fountain of Israel, which is the only true norm according to which all teachers and teachings are to be judged and evaluated." But then how in the same breath can these concordists claim that their own recent symbol, the Augsburg Confession, coming more than a millennium after the close of the biblical canon, likewise constitutes "a single, universally accepted, certain, and common form of doctrine" by which all other

76

churchly writings are to be "judged and regulated?"[1] *Is* Scripture "the only true norm" or does it, after all, share its normativeness with other writings than itself? Answer: yes, to both questions.

1.1. The biblical Word shares its unique normativeness with such post-biblical confessions only because, and if, that is what they are: "con-fession," *Bekenntnus, homologia,* a same-saying, a saying-back of that original scriptural Word. According to the concordists, the Augsburg Confession's claim upon our faith ("a genuinely Christian symbol which all true Christians ought to accept") *is* its scripturalness or, may we say, its "Wordedness"— "drawn from and conformed to the Word of God."[2]

1.2. Actually, the English "conformed *to* the Word of God" may give the misimpression of a second document standing outside Scripture looking in, trying to emulate it. The German original (*aus und nach Gottes Wort . . . zusammengezogen*) stresses a much more internal connection between biblical Word and confession, almost to the point of identity. The "form of doctrine" (*Form der Lehre*) which defines the confessions is not merely like but *is* the selfsame form which defines Scripture and which the confessions have simply "drawn together" and "summarized" from Scripture, professedly intact (*Form der Lehre . . . aus Gottes Wort genommen*).[3] Thus Scripture and confessions are literally uni-form, their common identity being the one Word of God.

1.3. In this context where "Scripture and tradition" means Scripture and *confession,* there are not two magisterial authorities—for instance, as in canonical text and normative interpreter—the later, lesser one augmenting the earlier one with some incremental authority of its own. The confessions' doctrinal authority is not original but altogether derivative. On the other hand, that much authority it is, a reassertion of the scriptures' own authority, whose very "form of doctrine" the confessions are claiming to have "drawn" forth and "taken" to themselves.

1.4. Even that metaphor, the extractive image of "drawing out" and "taking" and "summarizing" is not the concordists' boldest metaphor. If that were all, the reader might still be left with the relatively modest picture of confession-making as the human doing of the confessors themselves: latter-day extractors and quarriers who like archaeologists return *ad fontes,* to Scripture as an ancient closed norm, fixed there in its sheer givenness and challenging later reconstructions to fathom it. The Formula of Concord does employ such metaphors, too, portraying Scripture as an independent criterion (*Regel, Richtschnur*) obliging the confessors to adjust to its hard data, its original intentions, its over-and-done-with events.[4] But the Formula's dominant metaphor, as already hinted by the word "confession," moves in the opposite direction, not from the present back to the past but vice versa. And here the doer, the driving, effectual agent is the Word of God itself, the confessors being but its most recent respondents.

1.5. The biblical Word is pictured as the ever-contemporary "judge," "the only judge" (*der einig Richter*) which in each new age calls forth "witnesses" to itself. The "confessions" (another forensic image) are that judge's witnesses. They are the *Zeugen* in which, as in the ancient creeds, "the doctrine of the prophets and apostles" is again brought to speech "in post-apostolic times" (*nach der Apostel Zeit*) and "in our times" (*dieser Zeit*).[5] The confessions are what the *judge* evokes—not merely agrees or disagrees with after hearing them but, typically of the courtrooms of that day, what the judge actively prompts the witnesses to testify. Confessions have been called reverberations, echoes. They are the scriptural Word of God hearing itself coming back, if always in new historical contexts.

1.6. So the biblical Word of God is not first of all a critical "norm." It is that, too, but only secondarily. Primarily the Word is creative and authorial. It is the judge not just judging testimony but, before that, eliciting it and, only insofar as that fails, standing aloof as an external norm. Before the Word is a "norm" (*Richtschnur*) it is "the pure and clear fountain [*Brunnen*] of Israel." Before the Word is a norm it is a "form," and more as an active verb than a noun, formative of and informing its later witnesses with its own unique "form of doctrine," "the pure doctrine of the holy Gospel"—freely translated, "the fresh teaching of the hallowing Good News."[6]

1.7. What is true of the scriptural Word, that it is formative before it is normative, is true also of the confessions as responses to that Word. "The Symbols," as Piepkorn observes, "can serve as a legal club, in order to enforce conformity with their teaching. . . . But this is certainly an *opus alienum*. Their proper office includes serving as . . . a *confession*, that is, a classic formulation of our own grateful response to the divine revelation."[7] A confession, as dogma, "does contain an obligation to teach but," says Elert, "it does not contain an obligation to believe." For that is not how confessions, anymore than their originative Word, evoke faith, namely by obligation.[8]

1.8. The concordists say of the confessions that they came into being *nach Anleitung Gottes Worts,* which again might better be translated not "in conformity with God's Word" but more causally, "under the direction [or the guidance] of God's Word.'"[9] By the same token the confessions themselves are not so much doctrinal "standards," as the English puts it, as they are landmarks of the Word's "leading," which same leading (*nach dieser Anleitung*) by the Word of God other future teachers and teachings will realize through exposure to the confessions.[10]

1.9. Never mind that this Word of God, the effectual subject of action, is from our viewpoint also an object over which we dispose as subjects. Granted, considered objectively, the prevenient Word of God does come as quite human "writings" (*Schriften*) produced by quite human (*prophetischen und apostolischen*) authors, publicly datable in historical time (*Altes und Neues Testaments*), to which we the confessors, acting as subjects, now in turn "pledge ourselves" (*uns bekennen*) in the form of confessions of our own, which again are objects of human making. In fact, for the confessors this objecthood of the divine subject—the Word's "externality," as they would describe it—is not at all an embarrassment but, as we shall see, a mark of the Word's very efficacy.[11]

1.10. It must be admitted that confessions do introduce something new which was not previously in the scriptures they echo, if only that be the new heresies which confessions have to combat. And combative a confession surely is, by definition, even though it is spoken not by the court's plaintiffs but by the defendants. Polemic is inherent in the forensic metaphor. As the Word of God, the judge, calls forth witnesses to itself, it does so only in antithesis to those witnesses' current accusers—in the sixteenth century, "the papacy and other sects." In the course of the trial the confessors, who as we said are the ones on trial, can be vindicated only as their "adversaries" are refuted.[12]

1.11. Because the confessors must take into account the new challenges of their day, their confessions are already by that additional component considerably more than a literal, tautological "summary" of Scripture. Nor are they just any meaningful "correlation" between the original *kerygma* and whatever their contemporary culture might offer, which in some instances might well be benign and opportune. No, here the correlation is decidedly adversarial: "how at various times [*jderzeit*] the Holy Scriptures were understood in the church of God by contemporaries [*von den damals Lebenden*] with reference to controverted articles [*streitigen Artikeln*]."[13]

1.12. Do these creedal and confessional encounters with later heresies yield a new *source* of doctrine, albeit a negative one, over and above that primary source which is Scripture? That is a fair question, especially in any discussion of "Scripture and tradition," where the talk is sometimes about "two sources." The truth is, the concordists do not explicitly say, as later Lutheran Church constitutions sometimes do, that Scripture is the "only source" of doctrine. Only norm? Yes. But the question of sole source is not addressed as such. At the very least, creeds and confessions are re-Sources or Source-lets, if such punning conveys that they are reiterations of one and the same Source, the biblical Word. (More on "sources" later.)

1.13. What the concordists do make quite clear is that the Church's creedal and confessional decisions are compelling for posterity not only in what they affirm but also in what they reject. Historic heresies, postcanonical as they are and of course only as negatives, become definitive of the Church's evolving witness to the Word of God. The implication is that the scriptural Word of God has a history. Far from being confined to its canonical epoch, that Word continues to carve out a career in the subsequent life of the Church. It encounters along the way always new opposition and sometimes (not always) succeeds in subjecting its opponents to Christ, if only by its anathemas. On a few rare occasions it prevails so memorably that these historic victories of the Word of God, verbalized as creeds and confessions, constrain all later teachers and teachings, formatively as well as normatively.

1.14. What is hazardous about the confessional metaphor is not just that it attributes such prestigious pedigree to admittedly human confessions but that, by such attribution, it is God who is made ultimately responsible for them. What such a claim risks, in other words, is not just arrogance but blasphemy. That is a metacognitive consideration which today's hermeneutics are apt to mute or even find incomprehensible.

1.15. Notice, to say that considerations of blasphemy are metacognitive is not to say that the *confessions* themselves are metacognitive, and certainly not that they are metacritical, beyond criticism. The confessions do make truth claims and these are open to criticism. Indeed, to acknowledge the risk of blasphemy is, in a soteriological and not only a methodological sense, critical in the extreme. The concordists never pretend that because their confession came into being *nach Anleitung Gottes Worts* they are thereby absolved from having to document their exegetical and doctrinal claims before the critical forum of Church and world. Quite the opposite. Especially in "a time for confessing," confessors, who see themselves on trial *coram Deo,* are impelled by their Lord's word, "Whoever confesses me *before human beings* I also will confess before my Father in heaven." But confessing *coram hominibus* requires exactly that confessors open their books for public audit to expose their scriptural and creedal bases.[14]

1.16. It is no wonder that the twentieth-century Lutheran confessor,

Bonhoeffer, rediscovered in the Formula of Concord a major resource, though that fact is seldom acknowledged by either his Barthian or his Lutheran reporters.[15] For he, too, acutely aware of the tensions of the Christian *martys*, felt called to speak out with eschatological certitude, often misperceived by his critics as illiberal and intolerant, yet simultaneously felt committed to their polemical give-and-take to heed their criticisms and to adduce the best theological, ethical, and historical arguments he could. He renounced the arbitrariness which he perceived in Barth as "revelational positivism."[16]

1.17. Similarly, the Lutheran theologian Pannenberg faults his fellow Lutheran, Bayer, for invoking "speech-act theory," specifically for construing the proclamation of "gospel and law" as a "performative linguistic act" in such a way as to evade critical accountability. "In this approach the truth of the propositions proclaimed is supposedly not bound to answer the human question of verification or falsification." Inexcusably, that renders "the proclamation immune against critical reflection." The point is well taken, with the additional reminder (perhaps also for Pannenberg) that not only systematic theologies but in their own way also "confessional" theologies are accountable to processes of verification.[17] Especially so.

1.18. Take the Formula of Concord itself. Formally it had no other purpose than to establish consensus among subscribers of the Augsburg Confession as to what that earlier confession actually meant. That limited, in-house aim, one might suppose, could have been met by confining attention to the Augustana's own text and by appeal to only those "Lutherans" who by now still had some stake in that text. Instead, the concordists explicate the Augustana not primarily by reference to itself but almost entirely to Scripture and the catholic tradition, thus rendering their confessional stance vulnerable at its very base. Moreover, the concordists, painfully conscious of their dissent from "so many nations" and of the stigma of being called "schismatics," nevertheless submit their case before "all Christendom among both our contemporaries and our posterity."[18] The concordists and even their most "confessional" descendants did not regard their confession as in principle beyond criticism or irreformable.

1.19. At the same time, in view of how momentous and nonpostponable is a "time for confessing," and such "times" are exceptional, the confession has to be made with eschatological finality—not "insofar as" it agrees with the Word of God (*quatenus*) but "because" it does (*quia*). Its confessors expect to be judged in The Final Analysis on the basis of this here-and-now confession. "Nor shall we speak or write anything, privately or publicly, contrary to this confession," so the concordists pledge, "but we intend through God's grace to abide by it." For this "is our teaching, belief and confession in which by God's grace we shall appear with intrepid hearts before the judgment seat of Jesus Christ and for which we shall give account."[19] Jesus Christ: then is that who *der einig Richter* is who all along, through the Spirit, was believed to be prompting the witnesses?

II. Scripture as Source(s)

"To substantiate our Confession," says Melanchthon's Apology of the Augsburg Confession, "and to refute the objections of our opponents, we shall have to say a few things by way of preface so that the sources [*fontes*] of both kinds of doctrine, the opponents' and our own, might be recognized." Given that preface the reader might expect that the "sources" behind this controversy will be, in the case of the confessors' doctrine, Scripture, and in the case of the opponents' doctrine, Scripture and tradition. Instead, what Melanchthon identifies as the confessors' "sources" (note the plural) are "the law and the promises," both of them squarely within Scripture yet at times, right within Scripture, squarely "opposed." On the other hand, the opponents' "sources" (again plural) are the biblical "law," and that merely in truncated form, plus a second source which is not biblical but also not simply equatable with "tradition."[20]

2.1. The opponents' second, extrabiblical "source" lies rather in the peculiar "conviction" they harbor about tradition (*persuasio de traditionibus*), namely, that the observing of certain traditions "serves to earn grace and make satisfaction for sin."[21] Many a church tradition, by itself quite edifying, thus becomes tyrannical by the "addition" of this salvational expectation.[22] This additive "source" is something alien to Scripture and often alien to churchly "traditions." But being endemic to human interpreters, all interpreters, this soteriological illusion cannot help but vitiate their understanding of the thing they interpret.

2.2. That was why the biblical Word needed first to be formative, actually reformative, not just normative of the Church's traditioners, lest through them their built-in soteriological bias become institutionalized for the Church as a whole. The extrabiblical *fons* which Melanchthon detects in the opponents' doctrine resembles, formally if not substantively, what a later Lutheran, Bultmann, would warn against in the Church's interpreters, their reactionary "pre-understanding" (*Vorverständnis*), that is, a prejudicial assumption.[23] This soteriological prejudice, according to the confessors, was one very real "source" of some traditions, a pernicious source. It is no secret that Luther suspected this source of having crept into even *that* "tradition" which is the biblical canon itself.

2.3. For Melanchthon the reactionary preunderstanding at the root of his controversy was what he, following Luther, referred to as *opinio legis,* which we might roughly translate as "legalistic bias."[24] It is humanity's congenital misconstrual of "the law" imbuing our observances of the law with a redeeming value which Scripture does not accord them but does accord the "promises."

2.4. However, if it is indeed the law, the biblical law, which is being misinterpreted, the problem must not lie with the misinterpreters exclusively. Must there not be something about the law itself which, at least in their hands, is amenable to such misinterpretation? The opponents do after all cite Scripture in support of their doctrine, at first glance often plausibly. Though the *opinio* they import is merely that, an unfounded opinion, still what it distorts *is* founded in Scripture, the biblical *lex*. They have elevated to a saving truth what, though it is not saving, is still truth.

2.5. By "law" Melanchthon means "the commandments of the Decalogue, wherever they appear in the Scriptures." That definition already brackets from consideration large tracts of legal material in Scripture, like "the ceremonial and civil laws of Moses," material which is obviously biblical yet not a doctrinal "source," even as law.[25] The same may be said of similar prescriptions in the New Testament. "So Paul directed . . . that women should cover their heads in the assembly." However, nowadays "no one would say that a woman commits a sin if without offense to others she goes out with head uncovered."[26]

2.6. But in the opponents' misuse of the law their graver error, graver than their retaining too much of its civil and ceremonial legislation, is in what they leave out. They suppress the law's most demanding features, *coram Deo*. They tend to confine attention to the law's "civil works." "But the Decalogue . . . also requires other works far beyond the reach of reason, like true fear of God, true love of God, true prayer to God, true conviction that God hears our prayer, and the expectation of God's help in death and all afflictions."[27]

2.7. These most critical demands of the law, because they expose our inability to meet them, are ignored through a kind of tacit denial—what a current popularizer of Luther, Justo Gonzalez, calls "avoidance," "selective forgetfulness."[28] The radically accusatory law of God in Scripture—"God's wrath or judgment"—is toned down to a mere whisper of itself. And by what? By that second, extrabiblical "source" which lulls the opponents' doctrine, namely, their rationalistic, commonsensical assumption that the law must be do-able since it must be saving. "This view naturally flatters," says the Apology, but only at the price of veiling the law of God.[29] Soft bias drives out hard Scripture.

2.8. Furthermore, that two-source hybrid of minilaw and *opinio legis* drives out what truly *is* saving in Scripture, its "promises." True, the promises are still dutifully quoted and invoked, if nothing else as "the history about Christ."[30] But for all doctrinal and pastoral purposes they now become superfluous, unused, "unnecessary." If all that is being promoted is a sinner's manageable version of biblical law, manageable perhaps through an emergency infusion of grace, then "what need is there of Christ?"[31] This rhetorical question reflects a basic methodological concern of the confessors. It is the old Aristotelian rule that true science "saves the phenomena," in this case the biblical "sources," and saves them by "showing the need of them." Else, "of what use [*quorsum opus*] is Christ?"—the embarrassing question which Abelard had raised, and not just rhetorically.[32]

2.9. It should be admitted that later Lutherans quite as much as the original pontifical *Confutatores*, not to mention later Protestants generally, operated with grossly reductionistic views of biblical law, thanks no doubt to their own brands of the *opinio legis*. These same Lutherans have settled for equally insipid Christologies, under-using, under-necessitating the Christ of the biblical promises. In these theological circles a "legalist," a favorite pejorative, is thought to be someone who has "all law and no gospel." For the confessors, that would have been at best a half-truth. For them legalists had also no *law* to speak of, in any authentically biblical sense, and so had to badger people instead with moralisms and bylaws. Legalism was but the converse of antinomianism.

2.10. If the underemployment of Scripture is as perennial as that, doesn't Melanchthon's type of "source" analysis, starting with Luther's prior distinction between law and gospel, continue to have a role in the one catholic Tradition long after the original adversarial "trial" at Augsburg between papal and reform Catholics? Granted, the distinction between law and gospel with its use in biblical hermeneutics has come to be seen as idiosyncratically Lutheran. Perhaps it is one of those elusive things which has been labeled a Lutheran "mode of thought."[33] But a law and gospel hermeneutical theology, if it is a "mode of thought," is one with broad and deep doctrinal import.

2.11. The confessors at Augsburg could not explain Scripture without explaining their "accusers." They could not get to the one without passing through the other. Was that only because the accusers happened also to be the ones in power? If that were all, we might understand why later Protestants, once out from under the papacy, felt free to ignore the kind of biblical exegesis advanced by large tracts of Roman Catholic tradition. For the Lutheran confessions, however, that Roman Catholic exegesis poses a deeper, abiding challenge. For all of its legalism the opponents' exegesis does present a show of right, biblically. It appears to have a leg to stand on within Scripture itself and so deserves an explanation.

2.12. In the Apology to the Augsburg Confession, Article 4 runs longer than all the rest of the Apology because there especially Melanchthon takes pains to examine one biblical passage after the other which the opponents have cited "to prove that we are justified by love and works." The passages are not easily dismissed. "You see that a person is justified by works and not by faith alone" (Jas 2:24). "If I have all faith, . . . but have not love, I am nothing" (1 Cor 13:2). "Love covers a multitude of sins" (1 Pet 4:8). "The doers of the law will be justified" (Rom 2:13). "Forgive and you will be forgiven" (Luke 6:37). "Redeem your sins by showing mercy" (Dan 4:27). "Blessed are the merciful, for they shall obtain mercy" (Matt 5:7). And on and on.[34]

2.13. The title (added later) to this long fourth article of the Apology reads *De Iustificatione*. It could just as well have read, in Melanchthon's own words, How to "praise works in such a way as not to remove the free promise."[35] For that is what the confessors had found so appealing about Scripture. It does indeed extol good works and rewards them, but why? Because in Scripture these are always the works of those who believe the promise. It is not because of the goodness of the works as such, which are always at best ambiguous, but rather because the believers who do the works are themselves good. Thanks to Christ they are, who is good *for* them who trust his promise. It is not their works which endear believers to God but Christ endears them to God, works and all. And so, believing that, it is no wonder that they work as well as they do and are rewarded as they are.

2.14. The troublesome passages which the opponents invoke to the contrary Luther might have called "dark" passages, though the Apology is more apt to ascribe the darkening to how the passages are misinterpreted. Melanchthon thought that the passages themselves, especially when read in context, "contain two elements"—hardly obviously, one should add. The first element "is the proclamation of the law or of penitence, which condemns wrongdoers and commands that they do right. The other is a promise that is added."[36] Here are the confessors' two "sources," both biblical: *lex* and *promissio*. Both are present in all the key passages, though often only implicitly and in a way which requires augmentation.

2.15. As for the legal element, Melanchthon now adds, two simple biblical *regulae* must always apply: "Apart from [Christ] you can do nothing" (John 15:5) and "Without faith it is impossible to please God" (Heb 11:6).[37] Admittedly, such a "regulative" upping of the legal ante, however scriptural, has the daunting effect of stretching some rather straightforward biblical commands ("forgive," "show mercy," "give alms," "love") into virtual impossibilities. For with the heightened demand to do all this in a way that "pleases God" and to do it in "faith," the commands actually become frustrations. As Paul saw, "the law works wrath." The law saps the joy of one's salvation. By itself it does. But then the law need not be by itself. It is only one of scripture's two *fontes*.

2.16. Enter the second "addition." That is, also the promissory element in the opponents' favorite passages must be "added" to, intensified, in effect rendered more promising. Recall, in Scripture the whole intention is that works should be done in the confidence that the doer delights God, right in the face of God's contrary law which always accuses. How else can that be achieved except we "add the Gospel promise"? In the passages invoked by the opponents there are already promises like "and you will be forgiven," "and the Lord will answer," "for they shall obtain mercy." What remains is to intensify these promises with THE promise, "the *Gospel* promise, that for Christ's sake [*propter Christum*] sins are forgiven and that by faith in Christ [*fide in Christum*] we obtain the forgiveness of sins."[38]

2.17. This "adding" of the "Gospel" promise to Scripture's other, less explicitly evangelical promises is supported by a corresponding *regula*, Romans 5:1, "Since we are justified by faith we have peace with God through our Lord Jesus Christ."[39] Is this regulative "addition," "through Christ by faith," in this case a promissory addition, what has been called a "canon within the canon," what a Lutheran like Käsemann refers to as the scriptures' "key" or "centre"?[40] Perhaps. However, nowhere does the Apology suggest that the choice of this "rule" is at all arbitrary or privileged, unique, say, to "Lutherans" or to those who are privy to some unusual existential discovery of the Gospel. On the contrary, the "rule" of *propter Christum, propter fidem,* whether from Romans or somewhere else in Scripture, is assumed to be publicly testable, all in the confidence that proof from Scripture and Church tradition is at hand. Does that confidence deserve to be put to the test, ecumenically? Or is it now too late for that?

2.18. The Apology leaves no doubt about what is at stake. Without these "additions," without Scripture "added" to Scripture, without its Law "added" to its laws and its Promise "added" to its promises—without, as Lutherans used to say, Scripture interpreting Scripture—good works may still be praised, though then probably only the works of the law's "Second Table." What is worse, through insufficient "need of Christ" the promise will be lost as well. For in the absence of such radicalizing, intrabiblical "additions" what will have intruded instead is an "addition" that is not only extrabiblical but essentially reactionary, that regressive "source," the Scripture-diminishing *opinio legis*.

III. Reception: "Keeping" the Tradition

The purpose of this law-gospel hermeneutical theology is thoroughly practical. One might call it a hermeneutics of praxis were it not for the Marxist anachronism that term evokes. According to the Apology the goal of the Church in interpreting Scripture—"preaching" Scripture, the confessors would have said—is to "keep" Scripture's law and promise. Scripture itself is a transmitting (*tradere*) and in that sense is part of the traditioning process, relaying to us what flows from the "sources," God's law and God's promise.[41] We who stand downstream from this "fountain" (*Brunnen*) are to "receive" or "obtain" or "retain" the original law and promises or, as Melanchthon likes to say, to "keep" them.

3.1. "Keep" in this case is a fortunate pun, one English word translating several words in Melanchthon's original Latin, *facere, retinere, custodire*.[42] First, to "keep" the law or the promise means to "do" them. Secondly, to "keep" them means to keep custody of them, keep from losing them, for instance by "using" them in one's exegesis or doctrine, scientifically to "save" them in the Aristotelian sense—as a "hermeneutics of retrieval" might, to keep them from going to waste.

3.2. In the Apology, however, these two meanings of "keep" are inseparable, defying, shall we say, any subject-object antithesis. There is no "keeping" law and promise in theology and preaching, objectively, without that preaching being "kept" in the hearts and lives of hearers, subjectively. Literally, the truth of the preaching lies in the believing of it. Preaching comes true in its being heard and heeded.

3.3. This is directly the case with the biblical "promise," only indirectly with biblical "law." The law is true, "objectively," whether or not we believe it "subjectively." But that is not the case with the promise. It is true, or at least it comes true, only if and as it is believed. The law, recall, is not only commandment but also indictment, a critique (*accusatio*), and that accusation does not depend on the accused to acknowledge it. In a promise, however, the promisor and the promisees are not that separable. The former promises to love the latter, but if they disbelieve the promisor they are not receiving the promised love. They are not "getting loved." The promise does not come to pass. And it is meaningless to speak of a promise as true if it does not materialize.

3.4. That inseparable is the promise's truth (*theoria*) from its being believed (*praxis*). "That is why [the promise] depends on faith," says Paul, "in order that the promise may . . . be guaranteed" (Rom 4:16). So Paul, says Melanchthon, "correlates . . . promise and faith."[43] This close "correlation," which did not escape the Lutheran Tillich, has often tempted Lutheran pietists and existentialists to fideism, where faith becomes faith in faith itself, and also Lutheran orthodoxy with its opposite retreat into objectivism. Both reactions assume a subject-object antithesis which puts asunder what Melanchthon, following Luther, believed God had joined together. Not only does faith need the promise in order to have something to believe, likewise "the promised mercy correlatively requires faith [*correlative requirere fidem*]."[44]

3.5. How ironic that even Lutherans have at times inferred from this link between God's promise and our faith that that must diminish God's prevenience or sovereignty? The whole point of Melanchthon's linkage, or Luther's "Glaubst du hast du," was to clinch thereby the "need" of Christ, God's sheer graciousness. That is "why [the promise] depends on *faith*," Paul said. And why is that? "In order that the promise may rest on *grace*."[45] How does that follow? By a Pauline analogy, grace is to faith the way a promise is to faith. If a promise of love, in order to come true, depends instead on some deservedness within the promisees, that hedges the promise with conditions, but it also hedges any confidence of theirs in that promise. Only an unconditional promise, gratis, such as Christ is, warrants unconditional trust. By the same token only unconditional trust can do justice to an unconditional promise.

3.6. Maybe the real reason Lutherans have sometimes hesitated to let the promise depend on faith lies not in some subject-object antithesis but rather in the fear that faith must then become a new condition for grace.

But a moral condition, a "legal" one, a condition of eligibility? That could happen only on the presupposition of the *opinio legis*.

3.7. If that is the case with the biblical promise, that it is true only of those who trust it, how about biblical law? The law as *accusatio,* we noted, holds true with or without the acquiescence by the accused. But the law as commandment is another matter. The commandment does come true, or begins to, depending on the faith or unfaith of the human subject. And by saying the commandments "begin" to be kept, the Apology does not mean they are now being kept only "outwardly." That much keeping can be done by unbelievers. With believers, however, the commandments begin to be kept "inwardly" as well. For instance, one of the law's most ambitious demands is that our life and work should delight God, and that we should be confident it does. Yet isn't that exactly what faith in Christ does believe, that "on account of Christ we please God"?[46]

3.8. As believers "we please God" even in our works, ambivalent and sinful as they are, and fraught with regret as well as joy. Though this "incipient keeping of the law is impure and far from perfect," "it is pleasing to God for the sake of Christ" (*propter Christum*) "on account of faith" (*propter fidem*). In Scripture even the commandments of the law have promises attached to them. And those promises too, when "added" to by "the Gospel promise," begin to be actualized in those who trust that promise. That is how the Tradition of the Word is received, or "kept, namely, *sola fide.*"[47]

3.9. Not all hermeneutics deal in truth claims. Some may content themselves simply with "interpretation," "understanding," "meaning" and suspend questions of truth or falsity. The law-gospel hermeneutical theology in the Lutheran confessions definitely means for its biblical interpretations to be true, and not only true to the biblical texts or its writers or its contexts (that, most immediately) but thereby and finally true to God, *coram Deo,* whose own intention or Word the scriptures "transmit" (*tradunt*). The verb, *tradere,* is significant, for that is what the scriptures are said to do. They are themselves a "traditioning," a handing on. And *what* they hand on is what comes from the "sources," law and promise, the way a stream proceeds from its "fountainhead" (*Brunnen, fons*).

3.10. So far, it makes little difference whether we say Scripture is a transmitting *from* the Source or we say Scripture *is* the Source, as long as it is the same "pure and fresh" living water, the same *Form der Lehre* as the original Word of God. Either way, to be true to the Writings is to be true to God or God's Word. If, however, as we have seen, God's Word of "promise" comes true only as its promised Christ is believed, and if only then the Word of "commandment" begins to come true, consider what that entails for a hermeneutics constrained by questions of truth.

3.11. For example, suppose I as an interpreter quoted the biblical text as saying, "I am justified by grace through Christ," yet did not personally believe that. Then my statement, while it may be textually accurate, would be not only insincere but also untrue. "I" am *not* "justified by grace through Christ" if I do not *believe* that I am. Linguistically, I may have caught Scripture's "usage," but the Apology would say I have failed to put Christ to "use." Stated positively, the one way finally to "keep" the scriptural law and promise, to "save" them even in the Aristotelian sense, is for us to be saved by them, "by faith." Only that way is the Tradition finally received.

IV. The Word's Externality

If the traditioned Word is finally received only by faith, if only then does it come true, the temptation is to be preoccupied with the believers' subjective reception and to neglect the objective, "external" process of transmission by which the Word reaches them—and not only to neglect such externality but to derogate it and short-circuit it. This distorting of the *sola fide* into an aversion against all *Äusserlichkeit,* aversion even against the publicly transmitted Word and sacraments by the anti-Tradition "Enthusiasts" and "sects," was for Luther perhaps the most grievous miscarriage of the Reformation. For to bypass the Church's external Word and to retreat instead into the immediacy and inwardness of private revelations is nothing short of forfeiting the Holying Spirit, the very Spirit whom the *Schwärmer* so yearned to possess—free at last from all human, historic intermediaries.

4.1. In that Lutheran confession called The Smalcald Articles, specifically the article on private absolution, Luther turns his polemic against those "Enthusiasts" who "boast that the Spirit came upon them without the testimony [literally, "the preaching"] of the Scriptures." Luther had been arguing that absolution, the speaking out loud of forgiveness to the penitents, must be retained in the Church, because it "was instituted by Christ in the Gospel" but also because it is a powerful "consolation and help against sin and a bad conscience." This saving benefit of the externality of the gospel "should be highly esteemed and valued, like all other functions [*Ämter*] of the Christian church."[48]

4.2 For, as Luther continues, "God gives no one his Spirit or grace except through or with the external Word which comes before." But this prevenient, traditioned "external Word" encounters enormous resistance from that *Enthusiasmus* which "clings to Adam and his descendants from the beginning to the end of the world." Indeed, this perennial Enthusiasm "is a poison implanted and inoculated in man by the old dragon, and it is the source [*Ursprung*], strength, and power of all heresy, including that of the papacy and Mohammedanism."[49]

4.3. Notice, in Luther's diagnosis "Enthusiasm" functions as a "source" (*Ursprung, origo*) of heresy in much the same way as the *opinio legis* had in Melanchthon's diagnosis of the papacy's second, extrascriptural *fons*. Really, both Luther and Melanchthon are here referring to the same "source," and they both find it vitiating the "papacy" quite as much as it does the "sects." "Muenzer did this. . . . The papacy, too, . . . for the pope boasts that 'all laws are in the shrine of his heart,' and he claims that whatever he decides and commands in his churches is spirit and law, even when it is above and contrary to the Scriptures or spoken Word." Luther calls this *Geisterei* or *Schwarmgeisterei,* "spiritualizing."[50] That is really just another version of the legalism which, according to the Apology, credits our own religious performance with saving significance but does so only by diminishing God's real demands upon us and, in the process, by diminishing Christ.

4.4. "Enthusiasm," in the bargain, diminishes also the Holying Spirit, who is indispensable to the traditioning of the Word. For the Word uses as its witnesses, as its emissaries in the Pentecostal relay, those fallible human agents who transmit the external Word onward, yes, but only as they themselves are holied or hallowed by that Word. "St. Peter says that when the prophets spoke, they did not prophesy by the impulse of man but were moved by the Holy Spirit, yet as holy men of God." Now "the Holy Spirit would not have moved them to speak while they were still unholy." But neither could they have been made holy except by "the external Word."[51]

4.5. Thus the same "form of doctrine" or Word which in-"forms" the scriptures must by the Spirit re-"form" its witnesses and confessors along the way, disabusing them also of their congenital "Enthusiasm." But if so, their confessions may then be uniform with the scriptural Source itself (and its Sources) and, because of that, may share in its authority—and its vulnerability to critical scrutiny.

Notes

[1]Formula of Concord, Solid Declaration (hereinafter cited as FC SD), Rule and Norm 3 and 10; *The Book of Concord: The Confessions of the Evangelical Lutheran Church,* trans. and ed. T. Tappert (Philadelphia: Fortress Press, 1959) (hereinafter cited as BC) 503–04, 506; *Die Bekenntnisschriften der lutherischen Kirche,* ed. H. Lietzmann and E. Wolf, 6th ed. (Göttingen: Vandenhoeck & Ruprecht, 1967) (hereinafter cited as BS) 834, 838.

[2]FC SD, Rule and Norm, Preface (4) and 5; BC 502, 504; BS 830, 835.

[3]FC SD, Rule and Norm, 10, 4, 5; BC 506, 504; BS 838, 834–35.

[4]FC SD, Rule and Norm, subtitle and 9; BC 503, 505; BS 833, 837.

[5]Formula of Concord. Epitome (hereinafter cited as FC Ep), Rule and Norm, 7, 2, 5; BC 465; BS 769, 768.

[6]FC SD, Rule and Norm, Preface (3); BC 501; BS 830.

[7]Arthur C. Piepkorn, "Suggested Principles for a Hermeneutics of the Lutheran Symbols," *Concordia Theological Monthly* 29:1 (1958) 1.

[8]Werner Elert, *The Christian Faith: An Outline of Lutheran Dogmatics,* trans. M. H. Bertram and W. R. Bouman (Columbus, Ohio: Trinity Seminary Bookstore, 1974) 17.

[9]FC Ep, Rule and Norm, title; BC 464; BS 767.

[10]FC Ep, Rule and Norm, 6; BC 465; BS 769.

[11]FC Ep, Rule and Norm, 1–3; BC 464–65; BS 767–68.

[12]FC Ep, Rule and Norm, 4; BC 465; BS 768.

[13]FC Ep, Rule and Norm, 8; BC 465; BS 769.

[14]FC SD, Article H, 10, 17; BC 612, 614; BS 1057, 1059.

[15]Eberhard Bethge, *Dietrich Bonhoeffer,* trans. E. Mosbacher and others (New York: Harper and Row, 1977) 368.

[16]Dietrich Bonhoeffer, *Letters and Papers from Prison,* ed. E. Bethge, trans. R. Fuller and others, The Enlarged Edition (New York: Macmillan, 1972) 280, 286, 329.

[17]Wolfhart Pannenberg, *Anthropology in Theological Perspective,* trans. M. O'Connell (Philadelphia: Westminster, 1985) 387. Also Pannenberg, *Theology and the Philosophy of Science,* trans. F. McDonagh (Philadelphia: Westminster, 1976) 271–72, 340–45.

[18]FC SD, Article H, 23; BC 615; BS 1061. Article HII, 40; BC 636; BS 1099.

[19]Ibid.

[20]Apology (hereinafter cited as Ap), Article IV, 4,5,7,9; BC 108; BS 159–60.

[21]Augsburg Confession (hereinafter cited as AC), Article HHVI, 1,3; BC 64; BS 101.

[22]Ap, Article HI, l; BC 180–81; BS 249, 251.

[23]Rudolf Bultmann, "Is Exegesis Without Presuppositions Possible?" *Existence and Faith,* trans. S. Ogden (New York: Meridian, 1960) 289–96.

[24]Ap, Article IV, 265; BC 146; BS 213.

[25]Ap, Article IV, 6; BC 108; BS 160.

[26]AC, Article HHVIII, 54; BC 90; BS 129.

[27]Ap, Article IV, 8; BC 108; BS 160.

[28]Justo Gonzalez, *Mañana: Christian Theology from a Hispanic Perspective* (Nashville: Abingdon, 1990) 79.

[29]Ap, Article IV, 9 and 10; BC 108; BS 160–61.

[30]Ap, Article IV, 17; BC 109; BS 162.

[31]Ap, Article IV, 12; BC 109; BS 161.

[32]Robert Bertram, "How To Be Technological Though Theological," Proceedings of the Institute for Theological Encounter With Science and Technology (St. Louis: ITEST, 1975) 30, n. 40.

[33]H. G. Anderson, T. A. Murphy, J. Burgess, eds., *Justification By Faith: Lutherans and Catholics in Dialogue VII* (Minneapolis: Augsburg, 1985) 49.

[34]Ap, Article IV, 218; BC 137; BS 201.

[35]Ap, Article IV, 188; BC 133; BS 197.

[36]Ap, Article IV, 255; BC 144; BS 210.

[37]Ap, Article IV, 256, 266, 269, 315, 372; BC 144, 146–47, 156, 164; BS 210, 213–14, 220, 230.

[38]Ap, Article IV, 257; BC 144; BS 210–11.

[39]Ap, Article IV, 91, 195, 217, 304; BC 120, 134, 137, 154; BS 179, 198, 201, 219.

[40]Ernst Käsemann, "Justification and Salvation History in the Epistle to the Romans," *Perspectives On Paul,* trans. M. Kohl (Philadelphia: Fortress Press, 1969) 75–76.

[41]Ap, Article IV, 186; BC 132; BS 197.

[42]Ap, Article IV, 256, 270; BC 144, 147; BS 210, 214.

[43]Ap, Article IV, 50; BC 114; BS 170.

[44]Ap, Article IV, 324; BC 157; BS 122.

[45]Ap, Article IV, 84; BC 119; BS 177.

[46]Ap, Article IV, 124–25; BC 124; BS 185.

[47]Ap, Article IV, 270; BC 147; BS 214.

[48]Smalcald Articles (hereinafter cited as SA) III:viii, 1–6; BC 312–13; BS 453–55.

[49]SA III:viii, 3, 9; BC 312–13; BS 453, 455.

[50]SA III:viii, 3–5; BC 312; BS 453–54.

[51]SA III:viii, 13; BC 313; BS 456

6

Jesuit Controversialists and the Defense of Tridentine Tradition

John Patrick Donnelly, S.J.

I first read George Tavard's *Holy Writ or Holy Church: The Crisis of the Protestant Reformation*[1] thirty years ago when I was a seminarian. Rereading it as a gray-haired historian specializing in the Reformation, I am even more impressed, especially by its historical sweep and by its probing the central question of the Reformation: how does Scripture relate to Tradition and to the teaching authority of the Church? Luther often termed his teaching on *sola fide* the doctrine on which the Church stands or falls, but his teaching on *sola scriptura* is even more fundamental, for on it not only the Church but also *sola fide* stands or falls. Tavard's treatment begins with the patristic era and goes down to the end of the sixteenth century. Later Tavard carried his investigation of the theological concept of Tradition through seventeenth-century France and England in two other works.[2] In *Holy Writ* the Jesuits receive only passing attention, mostly regarding a consultation at the Council of Trent attributed to Claude Lejay.[3] Tavard's two books on Tradition in the seventeenth century likewise contain only passing references to Jesuit theologians. The swirling theological controversies of the sixteenth and seventeenth century produced thousands of books, and no historian of doctrine can be expected even to have read most of them, much less to have discussed them. Still the Jesuits played a prominent role in Counter-Reformation polemics, and a review of their writings on Tradition may provide a useful if modest appendix to Tavard's fundamental studies.

This essay surveys the teaching on Tradition in four prominent Jesuit controversialists: Peter Canisius (1521–1597), Antonio Possevino (1533–

1611), Edmund Campion (1540–1581), and Robert Bellarmine (1542–1621). They constitute an eminent and yet representative cross section of Jesuit writers. Campion, Canisius, and Bellarmine are all canonized saints, and the later two are the only Jesuit Doctors of the Church. Campion and Possevino were better known as men of action than as writers, and Campion paid for his faith and writings with his life in his native London. Canisius, although born in the Netherlands, worked most of his life in Germany. Possevino and Bellarmine were Italians. All four were unusually cosmopolitan. In addition to their respective homelands, Campion taught in Prague, Canisius in Messina, and Bellarmine in Louvain. Possevino spent the most important years of his life in France, Scandinavia, and eastern Europe. Of the writings we will review, those of Canisius and Possevino were aimed mainly against German Lutherans, that of Campion attacked Anglicanism, and Bellarmine aimed to refute Protestantism across the board.

I. Peter Canisius

The *Summa doctrinae christianae* of Peter Canisius was the earliest and most widely published of the four Jesuit treatments of Tradition. It was first published at Vienna in 1553 and became the standard Catholic catechism in Germany for three centuries. Among Catholic catechisms, only those of Bellarmine and the Council of Trent were rivals for durability and influence. The Summa was designed for priests, teachers, and educated laypersons. Later Canisius published scaled-down versions, the *Parvus catechismus* for students and the *Catechismus minimus* for children. In 1566, after the Council of Trent, Canisius published an expanded version of the Summa which is nearly twice as long as the original, but the treatment of Tradition underwent only minor revisions, some stylistic.[4] The three most noteworthy additions defend the power of churchmen, mainly the pope.[5] Throughout his catechisms Canisius tried to avoid mentioning his opponents by name and rarely engages in explicit polemics, but his Summa was designed as a Catholic antidote to Protestant teaching; and the polemics of the German Reformation strongly influenced the attention that he gave to controverted questions.

Canisius located his defense of Tradition in a section devoted to the Precepts of the Church, which falls between the more traditional sections on the Ten Commandments and on the Sacraments. In the section on the Precepts, Canisius asked nineteen questions—four more than he asked regarding the Ten Commandments. He began by citing St. Paul's command that the Churches guard the precepts of the apostles and elders (Acts 16:4). He then asked (Question II) what is the nature of these precepts and answered by quoting Denis the Areopagite (whom he accepted as a disciple of Paul) that the precepts are "partim scripta, partim non scripta."[6] The phrase is significant because Canisius was clearly picking up a famous phrase that was proposed and argued over at Trent, but not incorporated into the Tridentine Decree on Scripture and Tradition.[7] The *scripta* are clearly contained in the canonical books. The *non scripta* "are accustomed to be embraced by the one name of traditions and are so designated by the Fathers."[8]

Canisius then argued (Question III) that Christians must observe these precepts and traditions. To the question of how do we know which traditions are apostolic and approved in the Church (Question IV), he quoted St. Augustine: "Those which we guard as handed down, not written down, which are observed in the whole world."[9] What sorts of traditions should be observed (Question V)? Canisius answered with several examples, each buttressed by references to the Church Fathers: infant baptism; prayers for the dead; fasting, especially during Lent; the veneration of images of Christ and the saints. His choice of examples had a clear polemical edge—he said nothing about Mary's perpetual virginity, which is not explicit in Scripture but was acknowledged by most of his Protestant opponents.[10]

Canisius devoted his next two questions (VI and VII) to an attack on those who "today are in error about apostolic and ecclesiastical tradition." As usual, Canisius named no names but scorned those who imagine them to be mere human institutions or regard them as adiaphora. The last word is printed in Greek, and Canisius obviously had in mind Philip Melanchthon, an old opponent whom he had confronted face to face on this point at the Colloquy of Worms in 1557.[11] Such persons, Canisius argued, "are condemned by God's Word, which has determined that traditions be observed when it ordered the Church to hear and keep the precepts of the Apostles and elders."[12] Here Canisius invoked the duty of Christians to obey civil and ecclesiastical authorities. Those who reject such authorities "are not so much as spurning men as God himself" (1 Thess 4:8).[13]

In his treatment of Tradition as in his Summa generally, Canisius was at pains to buttress his teaching with references to and quotations from the Church Fathers. Here he devoted a separate question (VIII) to: "What do the Fathers think about this matter?" He cited Origen: "Only that truth is to be believed that at no point differs from church tradition." He then called on St. Jerome: "ecclesiastical traditions . . . are to be observed just as our ancestors handed them down." Augustine agrees: "On those questions about which divine scripture has determined nothing with certainty, the custom of God's people or the practices (*instituta*) of our ancestors are held as a law." Canisius closed with a quotation from Tertullian who, Canisius noted, wrote his whole *Liber de praescriptione haereticorum*[14] against those who accepted nothing which was not explicit in Scripture.[15]

The next eight questions (IX–XVI) in the Summa deal with the Church, its authority, its guidance by the Holy Spirit, the dignity of its officials, and the need for Church authority. It is largely here that Canisius added new material to the 1566 edition. He took special pains to uphold the Roman See and the chair of St. Peter, arguing that the peace of the Church cannot be long maintained without a supreme bishop. He strengthened his defense of Roman preeminence with quotations from Optatus, Cyprian, Ambrose, and Irenaeus. Irenaeus argued that "the whole Church must agree with this [Roman] church because of its preeminent leadership" because it has always preserved Tradition from the Apostles.[16] Canisius added a comparison between the guilt of the Jews of old who defied the high priest who held the chair of Moses and that of those who oppose general councils or "the supreme pontiffs who have always possessed supreme power to define sacred questions."[17]

After his treatment of the Church, Canisius returned to the question (XVII): "What is the use and fruit of the whole teaching on the precepts and traditions of the Church?" He replied, "First, that we understand that we are by no means bound only by the divine letters or scriptures." He then urged that the devout observance of Church traditions greatly aids the charity of the Spirit. Heretics in contrast depart from the simplicity of faith and the approved teaching of their mother the Church of the Fathers.[18]

Perhaps the greatest strength of Canisius's Summa is its use of the Church Fathers to prove that its teachings are firmly rooted in Tradition. Canisius kept adding references to the Fathers until they counted some twelve hundred; in contrast he rarely cited the medieval scholastics. In 1577 a fellow Jesuit, Peter Buys or Busaeus, printed the Summa together with the complete texts of all its citations as the *Opus catechisticum* in some four volumes and 2500 pages![19]

II. Edmund Campion

Our second Jesuit controversialist is Edmund Campion, who spent his first six years as a priest teaching rhetoric and writing and producing plays at the Jesuit college in Prague before being sent to start the Jesuit mission in his native England. He and his companion Robert Persons entered England in disguise in June 1580. Campion considered it a suicide mission, but he managed to escape arrest for about a year. As a counter to government propaganda in case he was captured, Campion issued a challenge to the Privy Council, known as Campion's Brag, which insisted that his mission was religious, not political. Two Anglican ministers, Meredith Hanmer and William Charke, answered it in print. Campion replied to them in his *Decem rationes,* which was written hurriedly and printed on a secret press in England in June 1581.[20] Within two weeks Campion was arrested, tortured, brought before a board of Anglican theologians for a disputation, and finally executed on December 1, 1581. The printer of the *Decem rationes* and his four assistants were also arrested. Over the years some fifty editions of the *Decem rationes* have appeared in print, and some twenty refutations were published against Campion, his Brag, and the *Decem rationes* by English Protestants. Even the Regius Professors of Theology at both Oxford and Cambridge were recruited for the task.[21]

Of the ten reasons Campion gave to support Catholicism against Protestantism, Reasons 1, 4, 5, 6, and 7 deal with the question of Scripture and Tradition. The thrust of Reason One is that Holy Writ cannot stand without Holy Church. Only Church authority can determine the proper canon of Scripture. Campion charged Luther with dismissing the Epistle of James as "contentious, turgid, arid, a thing of straw" and with excluding the deutero-canonical books from the Bible.[22] Calvinists also cut seven books from the Old Testament, while Sebastian Castellio argued that the Song of Solomon was a mere love song. Campion claimed that Luther, Johann Brenz, and Martin Chemnitz were inclined to throw out the Book of Revelation.[23] Campion contrasts his Protestant opponents with St. Augustine, who took "that Spirit wherewith Christ animates the whole Church" as his guide to canonicity.[24] While Protestants claim that the Spirit guides their decisions both in determining the canon and in interpreting Scripture, they are in fact falling into mere subjectivism: "In short, in believing all things every man in the faith of his own spirit, they horribly belie and blaspheme the name of the Holy Ghost."[25]

Reasons 4 to 7 all deal more directly with Tradition, although Campion did not employ the term. The thread that runs through his Reasons is simple: "I say that your exposition of the word of God is perverse and mistaken: I have fifteen centuries to bear me witness: Stand by an opinion, not mine, nor yours, but that of all the ages."[26] Reason 4 urges that since the English Church reverences the first four ecumenical councils, it should also accept "the Synods of other ages, and notably the Synod of Trent," which "have been of the same authority and credence as the first."[27]

Campion's Reasons 5 and 6 take up the Church Fathers. "Men who measure faith by their own quips and quirks, must they not be angry with Augustine" . . . who "professes himself to assent to Antiquity, to Consent, to Perpetuity of Succession, and to the Church which, alone among so many heresies, claims by prescriptive right the name of Catholic?"[28] Here it is worth noting that it was the study of the Church Fathers when Campion was preparing for Anglican ordination that led him to convert to Catholicism. He recalled a conversation during his student days at Oxford with Toby Matthews, later Archbishop of York; he asked Matthews if one who read the Church Fathers closely could belong to the Anglican Party. Matthews replied, according to Campion, he could not if he believed the Fathers as well as read them.[29] Campion compiled a considerable catalogue of Protestants who had mocked the Fathers or dismissed them as worthless. Thus Cyprian was stupid and God-forsaken, Hippolytus was an owl, Gregory Nazianzus a chatterbox, whereas they claim that "Calvin alone is worth more than a hundred Augustines."[30]

Campion's Reason 7 is an appeal to the history of the Church. The great church historians from Eusebius onward bear witness to a continuity of faith and religious practice and to the preeminence of the Roman See in preserving them. "It is clear, I say, that the historians are mine, and that the adversary's raids upon history are utterly without point" unless one assumed that "all Christians of all ages had lapsed into gross infidelity" until Luther.[31]

Campion closed his little book with a double appeal. The first was to Queen Elizabeth: time "will show thee clearly which have loved thee, the Society of Jesus or the offspring of Luther."[32] The second was to the gentlemen of Oxford and Cambridge: "what a piece of stupidity it would be to prefer" his attackers such as Hanmer and Charke "to Christian antiquity."[33]

In contrast to the sober and straightforward catechism of Canisius, Campion's *Decem rationes* swarms with rhetorical flourishes and bitter jibes; Campion mentions by name a host of Protestant writers: Luther, Zwingli, Calvin, Melanchthon, Vermigli, Bucer, Brenz, Chemnitz, Beza, Jewel, and the Magdeburg Centuriators to mention the most famous. In his zeal to attack the enemy, Campion merely claimed Tradition for the Catholic cause, but made little effort to present examples of that Tradition or to develop a theology of Tradition. Perhaps we are expecting too much from a booklet of fifty-seven small pages written by a man working under desperate conditions who was not a theologian but a professor of rhetoric.

III. Antonio Possevino

Our third controversialist is Antonio Possevino, who was a warm admirer of both Canisius and Campion and valued their writings.[34] Possevino's work as papal nuncio and legate in Scandinavia and eastern Europe between 1577 and 1587 brought him into contact and controversy with many Protestant and Orthodox leaders. Possevino was easily the most pugnacious of the four Jesuits under consideration here; one of his many controversies was with the distinguished Lutheran theologian David Chytraeus. In 1582 Chytraeus published *Tractatus de statu ecclesiarum hoc tempore in Graecia, Asia et Hungaria* (Wittenberg, 1582) which Possevino attacked in his *Adversus Davidis Chytraei imposturas* (Ingolstadt, 1583). Chytraeus answered with his *Responsio ad Antonii Possevini et Mylonii cuiusdam criminationes* (Wittenberg, 1584). Possevino's final response to Chytraeus, which dealt with the inevitable questions of Scripture, Church, and Tradition, was his *Notae divini verbi et apostolicae ecclesiae fides ac facies ex quatuor primis oecumenicis synodis* (Posnam, 1586).[35]

The prefatory letter of the Notae, addressed to King John III of Sweden, together with its first section (Sectio Prima, capita I–IV) discusses the background of Possevino's controversy with Chytraeus. The second section devotes five chapters to Scripture and Tradition. Possevino's tone is more personal than that of the other Jesuit controversialists, both in addressing Chytraeus directly and in recalling incidents from his own life to confirm his argument. Possevino began by dismissing with contempt Chytraeus's claim that Protestant teaching is based on the Word of God, for all heretics down through history have made the same claim. Possevino stated that he first got hold of a copy of Chytraeus's Responsio at Posnam—a city in which there were Lutherans, Calvinists, Anabaptists, and two sorts of Antitrinitarians. He traced this multiplication of sects to the principle of *sola scriptura* and recounted examples from his own experience in dealing with Antitrinitarians who began their doctrinal slide with Lutheranism but were led on to a denial of the Trinity and even to atheism.[36] Possevino concluded his first chapter, "Because he [Chytraeus] utterly rejects the Word of God inserted and handed down [in the Church], he does not accept the integral written word and far less does he possess the meaning of the written Word."[37]

Possevino devoted his next chapter to showing that Lutheran teachers want the Word of God only insofar as they can limit its power to printed letters, but they spurn as human traditions what the Apostles, guided by

the Holy Spirit, left as a heritage. This is precisely what all the heretical
sects in the early Church did. Despite their claims, Protestants do believe
many things which are not explicit in Scripture, for instance, the Apostles'
Creed, infant baptism, Mary's perpetual virginity, that heretics are not to
be rebaptized, that the Holy Spirit is to be adored, that the Son is consub-
stantial with the Father, the canon of the Scriptures, and many other things.
The only way that Lutherans can effectively refute the appeal to Scripture
by Anabaptists and Antitrinitarians is by having recourse to apostolic Tradition, as Sts. Cyprian and Augustine pointed out long ago. Here Possevino
employed the same argument and the same passage from St. Irenaeus[38] that
Canisius had used, that even before the Scriptures there was a Tradition
handed down which should be followed. The Protestant failure to accept
Tradition is the reason why they reject most of the sacraments and why
"six hundred" other problems have arisen from their putting Bibles in the
hands of the uneducated.[39]

"Both the Apostles and later the Fathers taught us that the written Word
of God is other [*aliter*] than the non-written Word, but . . . we should
have the same faith in them both. If one is rejected, the other is over-
turned."[40] Possevino reinforced his point with many quotations from the
Fathers, the longest of which is from St. Vincent of Lerins and urges that,
as regards Tradition, the Christian should be "a guardian not an author,
a disciple not an innovator, a follower not a leader. You have received gold,
hand on gold."[41] Perhaps it is significant that Possevino did not quote the
famous passage in which Vincent discussed how to distinguish legitimate
doctrinal development from distortions of the original heritage.[42]

Possevino did devote a chapter (III) to discerning true Tradition. The
Catholic Church does not accept as apostolic Tradition what was taught
by just one Church Father but what has continued with unanimous consent down through the ages, lest human errors creep in. Traditions must
be double-checked both on their being handed down through the ages and
on their agreement with the written Word. After several long passages from
St. Augustine, Possevino again cited Vincent of Lerins: "That is truly
handed down from our Lord and the Apostles which is believed everywhere,
always, and by everybody."[43] Following Augustine, Possevino added another way of discerning true Tradition: whatever has been determined by
the ecumenical councils is divinely handed down. Likewise practices which
are approved in the Church by universal consent are necessarily derived from
apostolic Tradition, for otherwise the Church, which is the column of truth
and is guided by the Holy Spirit, would have gone astray.[44] Chytraeus and

other Protestants say they accept the first four ecumenical councils, but for Possevino their acceptance was a sham and only partial.[45] Possevino also developed the argument which Campion had used earlier: that the Protestants refused to accept the deutero-canonical books of the Old Testament and had cast aspersions on several of the New Testament epistles, but Possevino like Campion did not enter into a serious discussion of the thorny problem of the biblical canon.[46] For both of them Trent had settled that problem.[47]

IV. Robert Bellarmine

Easily the most lucid, learned, and well organized of the Jesuit defenses of Tradition is that found in Robert Bellarmine's De Controversiis, first published in 1586.[48] Bellarmine devoted four books to De Verbo Dei; the last deals with De Verbo Dei non scripto or Tradition. Bellarmine began with two short bibliographies, one of Catholic authors who had defended Tradition and the other of Protestant authors who had attacked it. His first list includes Canisius but omits Campion and Possevino. His second list includes works by Calvin, Brenz, Chemnitz, and Hermann Hamelmann, but it is the first volume of Chemnitz's *Examination of the Council of Trent* that draws the most fire. While Bellarmine's stance toward his adversaries is hostile, it is far less personal and rhetorical than the attitudes of Campion and Possevino.

Bellarmine then moved on to define Tradition as any teaching, written or unwritten, that one person commits to another, but it usually means unwritten teachings, that is, things not written by the person who began the teaching. Tradition can be divine (begun by Christ himself), apostolic (begun by the Apostles under the guidance of the Holy Spirit), or merely ecclesiastical (early customs which have by tacit approval acquired the force of law). The Word of God gets its authority because it comes from God, either directly or indirectly—it has no special authority just because it is written on a page. Ecclesiastical traditions have the same force as written Church decrees and can deal with either faith or morals. Some traditions are universal in the Church, others are only local; some are obligatory, others optional.[49]

According to Bellarmine, Catholics insist against Protestants that the written Word has to be supplemented regarding both doctrine and morals by unwritten divine and apostolic traditions. For Protestants apostolic traditions either are no longer extant outside Scripture or cannot be proven.[50] Bellarmine devoted a chapter to showing that the Scriptures are not sufficient without Tradition, that Tradition relates to both faith and morals and to showing how we can be certain what are true traditions. The Church in some sense reaches from Adam to the end of the world; much of that time antedated the Old Testament, and even after Christ there was a period before the Scriptures were completed, and there were nations belonging to the early Church which did not possess the Scriptures.[51] The Gospel was originally spread by word of mouth. Faith in the existence of inspired Scriptures had to come from outside the biblical text, to say nothing of what was the proper content of the canon. Why, for example, is the gospel of Mark canonical and not that of Thomas? According to Bellarmine, Calvin [Institutes, I, 7, 12] thinks that this is as easy to discern as sweet from bitter, but had not Luther dismissed James as an epistle of straw? Augustine in contrast said that he would not believe in the Gospel unless the Church taught it. Brenz and Chemnitz are more honest when they admit one exception to the rule of *sola scriptura:* the content of the canon. Scripture touches on many points, such as original sin and the Trinity, whose meaning becomes clear only from Tradition. There are other doctrines such as Mary's perpetual virginity and infant baptism which cannot be proved *sola scriptura*. Clearly Bellarmine like the other Jesuits believed in a *partim/partim* division of beliefs.[52]

Bellarmine devoted another chapter to proving that Scripture itself teaches belief in traditions not in Scripture, citing passages such as John 21:25, 1 Corinthians 11:23, 2 Thessalonians 2:15, and 3 John 1:13.[53] He also added a short chapter on passages from the early popes and councils dealing with Tradition,[54] then a very long chapter of eleven folio columns printing and discussing passages from the Church Fathers that assert the role of Tradition.[55] Here there is space for only two of these quotations. The first is from St. Irenaeus: "Even if the Apostles had not left us the Scriptures, should we not follow the ordination of Tradition which they handed down to those to whom they had committed the churches?"[56] The second is from St. Basil the Great: "The dogmas which are preserved and preached in the Church we have partly [*partim*] from written teaching, partly [*partim*] from the Tradition of the Apostles carried down to us in secret [in mysterio]. They both make the same contribution toward religion."[57]

In addition to his arguments for Tradition drawn from Scripture and the Fathers, Bellarmine put forward several additional arguments. Thus he noted that in the early Church it was the heretics such as the Arians and Donatists who rejected arguments drawn from Tradition and appealed to *sola scriptura*. Many ancient legal systems such as that of Lycurgus at Sparta functioned effectively without being written down. Several ancient philosophers such as Pythagoras and Socrates taught orally without leaving a written corpus.[58]

A serious problem faced Bellarmine: How are we to discern true traditions? He offered five rules for this. (1) Whatever the universal Church embraces is a dogma of faith, for instance Mary's perpetual virginity. (2) Things preserved in the universal Church which no mere individual could have established must come from Christ or the Apostles, for instance infant baptism. (3) What is preserved in the universal Church at all times should be attributed to the Apostles, for instance fasting during Lent. (4) What all the Doctors of the Church teach with consensus comes from the Apostles, for instance the veneration of images. (5) What is handed down in unbroken succession in the Churches founded by the Apostles such as Rome, Ephesus, Corinth, Antioch, Alexandria, and Jerusalem should be accepted as coming from the Apostles if there is no contrary evidence of innovation. Of these early Churches, only that of Rome has enjoyed unbroken succession.[59]

Bellarmine devoted a chapter to answering objections drawn from Scripture against his teaching,[60] and another chapter to objections drawn from the Fathers.[61] The final chapter of his book De Verbo Dei non scripto answers objections against Tradition drawn from reason. Thus traditions cannot be preserved down the centuries in the face of human forgetfulness, negligence, and perversity. Thus the laws of Lycurgus mentioned earlier have all disappeared. Bellarmine answered with what his adversaries would have deemed a Deus ex machina: God directs the Church and protects her from her enemies. He can also preserve her traditions despite human weakness. Moreover, traditions need not be preserved unwritten for fifteen centuries—in fact they have been written down over those centuries by later ecclesiastical writers. Continual usage and monuments and buildings have all contributed to preserve Tradition. Paradoxically, the heretics too have helped to preserve Tradition by their attacks, because down the ages they have forced orthodox scholars to study and defend authentic traditions.[62]

V.   Conclusion

The four Jesuits investigated here shared several characteristics, but they did not constitute a school or specifically Jesuit approach to Tradition. Despite many parallels, they seemed not to have borrowed much from one another.[63] Neither do they seem to have been particularly innovative in their teaching on Tradition, but Canisius, Possevino, and Bellarmine were exceptionally learned in the history and theology of the early Church, and they were able to bring that learning to bear on the question of Scripture and Tradition.[64] None of the four Jesuits were mere scholars, all were heros of the Counter Reformation, second class, and this gave what they wrote an added influence. Most importantly, the writings of Campion and Bellarmine went through dozens of editions, and the Canisius Summa was reprinted hundreds of times. Their teaching became the common coin of the Counter Reformation.

All four Jesuits accepted a two-source theory of revelation: God's revelation comes to the human race in written form in the Scriptures and in unwritten form, at least initially, in Tradition. The Jesuits do not in fact often use the formula *partim/partim*—when it does appear in their treatises, it is usually in quotations from the Church Fathers—but they clearly see Tradition as containing some revealed truths not found in Scripture.

The four Jesuits agreed entirely with Trent's statement that Scripture and Tradition should be accepted and venerated with the same loyalty and reverence.[65] Still, it is obvious that quantitatively, even if not qualitatively, Scripture is overwhelmingly the main source of revelation for them. Significantly, Bellarmine devoted only one of his four books on the Word of God to the unwritten Word of God. The four offered only a short and repetitious list of examples of doctrines found in Tradition alone. The doctrinal importance of these examples, such as infant baptism (an example also used by Luther to show the weight of tradition[66]), is minor compared to the central teachings which could be derived from Scripture. When both sources taught the same doctrine, there was little need to appeal to Tradition. It was always easier to cite chapter and verse than to sift through the Fathers to determine that a consensus existed on a point of doctrine.

For the four Jesuits, Tradition tended to be static. There was no continuous revelation that augmented the deposit of faith left by the Apostles. Here the Jesuits broke with several Catholic theologians writing on the eve of Trent who had argued that God continued to give fresh revelation to his Church in addition to the guardianship and guidance of the Holy Spirit in protecting and interpreting the deposit of faith.[67] Trent's statement about all saving truths and moral teaching being preserved by a continuous succession in the Catholic Church seemed to cut against any permanent or postapostolic revelations adding to the deposit of faith.[68] But the theology of Tradition of the four Jesuits is static in another and more important sense: they leave little room for any dynamic development of doctrine by a progressively deeper understanding of the original revelation. This sort of dynamic understanding of Tradition is now commonplace among Catholic theologians after the writings of John Henry Newman, Maurice Blondel, and Yves Congar;[69] Vincent of Lerins, as noted earlier, had partially anticipated this development, but the Jesuits ignore him on this point. For them it was enough that the original gold was passed down the centuries unsullied and unalloyed; there was no need to refine and polish it. At the end of his treatise Bellarmine opened the door to a more modern and dynamic understanding of Tradition when he noted that heretics down the centuries had stimulated scholars to "investigate diligently the doctrine of the Church and ancient traditions."[70] But Bellarmine does not walk through the open door and suggest how their investigations could lead to a deeper understanding and clearer formulation of doctrine. In this respect Albert Pigge (1490–1542) was more modern in his attention to doctrinal development than the later Jesuit controversialists.[71]

Given the Jesuit tradition of loyalty to the papacy, one might expect an exaltation of the papal teaching office in determining authentic traditions; the four Jesuits studied here were strongly devoted to the papacy, but their treatment of Tradition dwells less on the role of the pope than did several of the theologians writing before Trent whom Tavard has studied.[72]

The polemical context in which the Jesuits wrote often skewed their treatment. They all seemed to believe that the best defense is a good offense, hence they devoted more effort to scoring debating points by attacking *sola scriptura* and highlighting the problem of determining the canon than to developing a balanced theology of Tradition. In this their writings were no better or worse than most polemics of the Reformation era.

Notes

[1]London: Burns & Oates, 1959.

[2]*La tradition au XVIIe siécle en France et en Angleterre* (Paris: Éditions du Cerf, 1969); *The Seventeenth Century Tradition: A Study in Recusant Thought* (Leiden: E. J. Brill, 1978).

[3]George Tavard, *Holy Writ or Holy Church: The Crisis of the Protestant Reformation* (London: Burns & Oates, 1959) 197–98, 201. Robert Parsons's *Defence of the Censure,* 1582, is noted on pages 229–30.

[4]*Sancti Petri Canisii doctoris ecclesiae Catechismi latini et germanici,* ed. Friedreich Streicher, T. I, 1 (Rome/Munich: Pontificia Universitas Gregoriana, 1933); this edition provides a critical text of both the 1555 Summa (3–75) and the 1566 Summa (79–204).

[5]Ibid., 108–11. The fact that Trent formulated its decree on Scripture and Tradition during its fourth session, well before the first edition of Canisius's Summa, may largely account for

the relatively few additions to Canisius's discussion of Tradition found in his later edition.

[6] Ibid., 106.

[7] Henricus Denzinger and Adolfus Schönmetzer, eds., *Enchiridion symbolorum* (Barcelona: Herder, 1963) ¶1501. Hereinafter cited as D.S. Tavard's *Holy Writ* discusses the debate over the *partim/partim* formula (196–208).

[8] Streicher, 106: "praecepta et instituta . . . quae uno traditionum nomine comprehendi et sic a patribus nuncupari solent."

[9] Ibid., 106. Augustine, Letter 118 to Januarius (PL 33, 200).

[10] Ibid., 107.

[11] Canisius had helped torpedo the Colloquy at its outset by pointing out that Scripture alone was not a sufficient criterion of religious truth because it did not prevent Protestants from doctrinal differences. James Brodrick, *St. Peter Canisius, S.J., 1521–1597* (New York: Sheed and Ward, 1935) I:398–409.

[12] Streicher, 107.

[13] Ibid.

[14] PL 2:10–74.

[15] Streicher, 108.

[16] Ibid., 109.

[17] Ibid., 110.

[18] Ibid., 113–14.

[19] Brodrick, 248.

[20] Evelyn Waugh, *Edmund Campion* (Garden City, N.J.: Image Books, 1956) 116–18. Edmund Campion, *Ten Reasons* (St. Louis: Herder, 1914) 17. References are to this edition, which contains an Introduction by John H. Pollen (1–29), the Latin text of the *Decem rationes* (30–87), and an English translation (89–145). I have also examined a photo reprint of the 1581 first edition (London: Scolar Press, 1971); the first edition has one notable advantage over many editions: it has Campion's copious marginal references to his biblical, patristic, and contemporary sources.

[21] Campion, 17, 29; Waugh, 128–29, 137.

[22] Campion, 95–96.

[23] Ibid., 93–96.

[24] Ibid., 94.

[25] Ibid., 96.

[26] Ibid., 132.

[27] Ibid., 105.

[28] Ibid., 112.

[29] Ibid., 115–16.

[30] Ibid., 110–11. Campion followed the tactic of most Reformation-era controversialists—he combed the writings of his opponents in search of compromising statements, in this case concerning the Church Fathers. Campion did not try to assess the real use of patristic argument among Protestant theologians. For an excellent treatment of that complex question, see Pierre Fraenkel, *Testimonia Patrum: The Function of the Patristic Argument in the Theology of Philip Melanchthon* (Geneva: Droz, 1961).

[31] Campion, 121.

[32] Ibid., 142.

[33] Ibid., 145.

[34] Brodrick, 249; John P. Donnelly, "Antonio Possevino's Tribute to Edmund Campion," *Archivum Historicum Societatis Iesu* 57 (1988) 163–69.

[35] The controversy is briefly treated by Walter Delius, *Antonio Possevino und Ivan Groznyj* (Stuttgart: Evangelisches Verlagswerk, 1962) 92–94. Here I use the edition of the Notae pub-

lished in Possevino's *Moscovia et alia opera* ([Cologne]: Birckmann, 1587; photo reprint by Gregg International Publishers, 1970). The same volume also prints (278–300) Possevino's first book against Chytraeus under the title *Retectio imposturarum cuiusdam Davidis Chytraei.*

[36]Notae, 124–26.

[37]Ibid., 126.

[38]*Adversus haereses,* 3:4 (PG 7:855).

[39]Notae, 127.

[40]Ibid., 128.

[41]Ibid., 128.

[42]PL 50:667.

[43]Notae, 130–31.

[44]Ibid., 131.

[45]Ibid., 144–46. Possevino's Notae goes on for six more sections (143–278), but these add little to his discussion of Tradition.

[46]Ibid., 132. Somewhat later (140) Possevino makes explicit reference to Campion's *Decem rationes.* Possevino reprinted the *Decem rationes* in his own *Bibliotheca selecta* (Rome, 1593).

[47]The Council of Trent (see D.S. 1502 and 1503) listed the canon of Scripture accepted by Catholics. In doing so, Trent was following a decree issued in the aftermath of the Council of Florence (see D.S. 1334–1336).

[48]*De Controversiis christianae fidei adversus huius temporis haereticos* I; citations here are to the *Opera omnia* edition (Naples: G. Giuliano, 1856). Bellarmine's treatment of Tradition, unlike that of the other Jesuits considered here, has been the subject of previous study: Johannes Beumer, "Die Frage nach Schrift und Tradition bei Robert Bellarmin," *Scholastik* 34 (1959) 1–19.

[49]Bellarmine, 115–16.

[50]Ibid., 117.

[51]Bellarmine's argument that the Church goes back to Adam was earlier developed by Johannes Driedo (d. 1535) in his pioneering treatise on Tradition. Tavard's *Holy Writ* discusses it on the point (138). Bellarmine listed Driedo (as Johannes a Lovanio) among earlier Catholic authors treating Tradition (115).

[52]Ibid., 119–21.

[53]Ibid., 122–24.

[54]Ibid., 124.

[55]Ibid., 124–30.

[56]Ibid., 123.

[57]Ibid., 126. The *partim/partim* formula also appears in a passage from Irenaeus that Bellarmine quoted (p. 124): " . . . primi . . . duces summa illa et supersubstantialia partim scriptis, partim non scriptis institutionibus suis, nobis tradiderunt." Bellarmine himself used the formula later in his tract (133): "Cum enim Paulus loquatur in genere de praedicatione apostolica, et illa partim sit scripta, partim non scripta; possumus inde recte probare, non licere aliquid asserere contra scriptam praedicationem Apostolorum." Beumer discusses the *partim/partim* question in Bellarmine, 4–6.

[58]Bellarmine, 130. Augustine (*De Consensu evangelistarum,* I, vii, 12; CSEL 43, 12) and Aquinas (S.T., III, Q. 42, a. 4c.) both make the same point about Pythagoras and Socrates.

[59]Bellarmine, 131–32. Here Bellarmine doubtless has in mind the decree of the Council of Trent (D.S. 1501): " . . . traditiones . . . continua successione in Ecclesia catholica conservatas. . . " But significantly Bellarmine has narrowed the "continua successione" phrase used by Trent by restricting it in practice to the Roman church.

[60]Bellarmine, 132–35.

[61]Ibid., 135–39.

[62]Ibid., 139–41.

[63]Such borrowings and parallels would show up most obviously in quotations from the Church Fathers, but it is surprising how seldom they used the same quotations. For example, Canisius (113) used a quotation from Irenaeus (PG 7, 855): " . . . si neque apostoli quidem scripturas reliquissent nobis, nonne oportebat ordinem sequi traditionis, quam tradiderunt iis, quibus committebant ecclesias?" Possevino certainly knew Canisius's catechism and used the same quotation (127) but his phrasing differs on minor points.

[64]The four Jesuit treatises very rarely refer to the Scholastics.

[65]D.S. 1501: " . . . pari pietatis affectu ac reverentia suscipit et veneratur. . . ."

[66]See Knut Alfsvåg, "Language and Reality: Luther's relation to classical rhetoric in *Rationis Latomianae confutatio* (1521)," *Studia Theologica* 41 (1987) 85–126. For a treatment of Luther's work *Von der Wiedertaufe* (1528), see the chapter by Eric Gritsch in this volume [ed. note].

[67]Tavard's *Holy Writ* devotes ch. 10 (The Permanent Revelation, 151–71) to this school which included John Fisher, Alberto Pio, Johannes Faber, Nikolaus Ellenbog, and Nicholas Herborn.

[68]D.S. 1501.

[69]Yves Congar, *The Meaning of Tradition*, trans. A. N. Woodrow (New York: Hawthorn Books, 1964) 30–31, 105–19.

[70]Bellarmine, 140.

[71]Tavard, *Holy Writ or Holy Church*, 148–49.

[72]Notably Cardinal Cajetan, Johann Eck, and Albert Pigge: Tavard, ibid., 114–15, 118–19, 148.

7

Wesley and Newman on Conscience and Tradition: A Contribution to Ecumenical Dialogue

Norman Young

The word "Tradition" signifies the living transmission of the gospel of Christ, by manifold means, for the constant renewal of every generation.[1] That way of understanding tradition, set out in the report by the fifth Roman Catholic-Methodist International Commission, was significantly influenced by Father Tavard, author of a seminal paper[2] which gave initial impetus to the four years of discussion that led up to this report entitled *The Apostolic Tradition*. As a Methodist member for many years of that dialogue and as a friend, colleague, and admirer of George Tavard, I offer this article as a tribute to him and as a small contribution to the strengthening of ecumenical bonds. It is my intention here to reflect on ways in which John Wesley and John Henry Newman participated in this "living transmission," inheriting, themselves being renewed, and contributing to the renewal of their generation and those that have come after.

I. Wesley and Newman

To begin on a personal note, one of the "manifold means" by which the Gospel was transmitted to me and which renewed my appropriation of the faith has been my reflection on the life and work of these two highly influential scholars. By the time I began postgraduate study I had worked my way through more of Newman's writings than of Wesley's, unusual

to say the least for a Methodist candidate for ordination.[3] Over the years
I have redressed the balance somewhat, if not tipped it the other way, but
my appropriation of the Church's tradition continues to be greatly influenced by both men. To mention the two in the same breath as contributing to the Church's tradition may seem to testify to just how broad the
spectrum of tradition is. Does it not take a pretty deep breath to name them
together? Can the movements they founded be any closer together than
Tertullian's Athens and Jerusalem? In fact, of course, they have a great deal
in common, and clearly Nicholas Lash's description of the one could apply
equally to the other:

> It was more a movement of the heart than of the head. . . . It always saw
> dogma in relation to worship, to the numinous, to the movement of the heart,
> to the conscience and the moral need, to the immediate experience of the
> hidden hand of God.[4]

And the more one thinks of the men themselves, the more the parallels
multiply.

Ordained to the ministry within the Church of England, they both became in their own ways profoundly concerned by what they saw as her failure to hold fast to the faith and be true to her tradition, which failure they
saw as both a symptom and a contributing factor to the malaise of the nation itself. In particular they deplored the easy acceptance of a religious attitude that allowed one to believe almost anything one liked. "Speculative
latitudinarianism" Wesley called it; Newman, "liberalism in religion" which
maintained, as he put it, that the first principles and elements of religion
are mere matter of opinion.[5]

Oxford loomed large for both of them. Both set out while dons there
(Wesley at Christ Church and Lincoln, Newman at Trinity and Oriel) on
programmes of reform. The term "Methodist" was first coined there by
the detractors of the Wesley brothers and a few close friends who met daily
for prayer and bible study, weekly for communion (quarterly was the norm
in parishes, yearly in some) and engaged in good works such as prison visitation. And Newman became a leader of that other Oxford Movement,
the Movement of 1833. As Dean Church put it, "it was Keble who inspired, Froude who gave the impetus and Newman took up the work."[6]
And the first indications of how both men would set their lives off in a
new direction was given in sermons they preached at St. Mary's.

Only a month after Wesley's "heartwarming experience" at Aldersgate
Street when as he was later to write, "I felt I did trust in Christ, Christ

alone, for salvation,''[7] he preached the University Sermon on "By grace
are ye saved through faith." That exposition was the charter for a new
Methodism, and for Wesley himself it marked the beginning of fifty years
of travelling the length and breadth of England, tirelessly proclaiming the
grace of God, "free in all and for all." Here then was Tradition in action,
"the living transmission of the Gospel of Christ . . . for the constant renewal of every generation."

The same parish Church about a hundred years later was to witness the
beginning of another and different phase of this "living transmission."
There, in a side chapel, Newman gave his lectures promoting the role of
the *via media* for the Church of England. There also he preached his Parochial Sermons which, published along with his volumes of University Sermons, Owen Chadwick holds to be

> the most important publication not only of his Protestant days but of his
> life. . . . He never wrote better, never more powerfully, never more per-
> suasively. These books of sermons made the heart of that body of thought
> which came in history to be known as the Mind of the Oxford Movement.[8]

Yet both were to find Oxford finally inhospitable. Hardly surprising in Wesley's case, given his University sermon of 1744:

> Ye venerable men who are more especially called to form the tender minds
> of youth . . . do you inculcate upon them, day by day, that without love
> all learning is but splendid ignorance, pompous folly, vexation of spirit?[9]

Answering his own question, as preachers are inclined to do, he accused
the senior members of the University of "pride, haughtiness of spirit, im-
patience and peevishness, sloth and indolence, gluttony and sensuality, even
proverbial uselessness."[10] Not surprisingly, he was never again invited to
preach at St. Mary's Oxford. Newman mounted no such attack on the city
or its University, but after Tract 90[11] his popularity in Oxford declined significantly. He spent more and more time at the secluded community at
Littlemore, then left the Oxford area altogether in 1846. Thirty-one years
later his first College, Trinity, offered him an Honorary Fellowship, which
he was delighted to accept, but his dream of returning to Oxford as superior of a proposed branch of the Oratory there was shattered by another
Tractarian-become-Cardinal, Henry Manning.

The Wesley-Newman parallels multiply and need no more than a mention here. In their appeal to tradition in the narrower sense of postbiblical
teaching of the Church, both went back to the early fathers, particularly

the Greek, in order to find new direction in their own time. They laid great emphasis on holiness, and Newman's sermon "Holiness without which none may see the Lord" shows remarkable resemblance to Wesley's "Circumcision of the heart" preached from the same pulpit a century earlier. As well, both spread their influential views through polemical tracts and longer published works. As Anglicans they were, or in Newman's case, became, High Church, and their attitude toward the Roman Catholic Church was remarkably open for Englishmen of the time, given that the prevailing stance was what one historian of the period has called "untroubled anti-Romanism."[12]Wesley could, on occasion, inveigh against the Pope with the rest of his countrymen, as Newman did in his younger days, but Wesley's concern to be reconciled with Roman Catholics and his resolve to work together in love is well documented and makes moving reading even today.[13] And well before he recanted his criticism of Rome, Newman took a more positive view of that Church than did most Anglicans of the day.

Most people with any acquaintance with Newman are familiar with what he wrote in his Introduction to the Tracts. After citing the defects of the Church of England which effectively deprived the people of what they needed and had the right to expect, he affirmed "Popery is the refuge of those whom the [Anglican] Church stints of the gifts of grace." But few recall the whole sentence:

> Methodism and Popery are in different ways the refuge of those whom the Church stints of the gifts of grace; they are the foster-mothers of abandoned children.[14]

II. Wesley on Conscience

So far I have been comparing the ways in which Wesley from the Protestant side and Newman from the Catholic participated in the Tradition of the Church, i.e., engaged in the "living transmission of the Gospel of Christ" that issues in the renewal of a generation. I want now to illustrate that somewhat discursive comparison by focusing on the place of conscience in the theological reflection of each scholar. Both saw conscience as more than a faculty to assist ethical decision-making. It was for them a primary source of God's self-revelation and gracious provision for human need. Both used this understanding as an aspect of their reinterpretation (living transmission) of the Gospel for their own generation. Yet both affirmed the limitations of individual conscience and the need to supplement and modify in order to come to genuine knowledge of God and faithful response to God's grace.

A. CONSCIENCE IN WESLEY'S THEOLOGY

In his sermon "On Conscience" Wesley defines it as

> That faculty whereby we are at once conscious of our own thoughts, words and actions; and of their merit and demerit, of their being good or bad, and, consequently, deserving either praise or censure.[15]

He goes on to maintain that there is clear evidence of the presence of conscience in everyone born into the world, "as soon as the understanding opens, as soon as reason begins to dawn."[16] Not that this universal faculty gives unchallengeable and detailed direction about how one should act in all circumstances; what it does is to enable everyone to know *that* there is a difference between good and evil, and it provides insight into the broad moral principles such as the need to honor parents and to do to others as we would have them do to us.

Wesley's next paragraph is highly significant, for it both locates him in the stream of tradition in which he participates and foreshadows the direction in which he will channel that stream, for the refreshing of his own generation and, I believe, for the nourishing of a doctrine that continues to bear ecumenical fruit:

> This faculty seems to be what is usually meant by those who speak of "natural conscience"; an expression frequently found in some of our best authors, but not yet strictly just. For though in one sense it may be termed natural, because it is found in all . . . yet properly speaking it is not natural, but a supernatural gift of God, above all his natural endowments. No; it is not nature, but the Son of God, that is the "true light that enlighteneth every man that cometh into the world." So that we may say to every human creature "He" not nature "hath shown thee, O man, what is good." And it is his Spirit who giveth thee an inward check, who causeth thee to feel uneasy, when thou walketh in any instance contrary to the light which he hath given thee.[17]

With this view of conscience as supernatural rather than natural gift of God, Wesley puts himself within the stream of Tradition, albeit toward one edge. More important for our purpose is to recognize a view of conscience consistent with, and indeed constituent of, his understanding of "prevenient (or preventing) grace"; for his exposition of that doctrine has significant and ongoing ecumenical implications, overcoming as it does what has frequently been seen as a great Protestant-Catholic divide in the area of moral theology.

This impasse has traditionally been described in terms of "Natural Law theory" versus "Ethics of Revelation." Whatever variations there are in the natural law approach, common to all is the fundamental contention that God has, in creation, ordered the world according to the Creator's own rational will. What accords with that will is good, and what is not is evil. Human beings, since in the image of God, are rational and consequently have valid insight into the rational will of God for the world. They share in a finite way, Aquinas would have put it, in God's own judgment of good and evil; "the light of natural reason whereby we distinguish good and evil, which is the function of natural law, is nothing but the impress upon us of the divine light itself."[18]

The Reformers, however, could have none of this. This divine light in human beings has been extinguished, they insisted, by the Fall, or so refracted by our sinfulness that it highlights only our distorted desires and proud self-justification. The image of God has been destroyed, or so marred that the creature no longer possesses the capacity to discern the will of the Creator.

What then is the Protestant alternative? Not knowledge of God through our own natural capacity to recognize the Creator's will but God's self-revelation in Jesus Christ, breaking into our human situation with both saving grace and renewed power of discernment. All true knowledge of God, therefore, and all understanding of what it is to live faithfully in the world stems from this unprecedented and unparalleled action in Jesus Christ; thus it is our grace-healed rather than natural capacities that discern the work and will of God, and this is found not by looking at the world of nature but at the uniquely revelatory Christ event.

Is there any way of overcoming this long-standing impasse? I believe there is and that Wesley has shown the way with his view of conscience and its relation to prevenient grace.

> Allowing that all the souls of men are dead in sin *by nature,* this excuses none, seeing there is no man, unless he has quenched the Spirit, that is wholly void of the grace of God. No man is entirely destitute of what is vulgarly called *natural conscience.* But this is not natural; it is more properly termed *preventing grace.* . . . Everyone, unless he be one of the small number whose conscience is seared with a hot iron, feels more or less uneasy when he acts contrary to the light of his own conscience.[19]

Wesley then, by reiterating his view of conscience as belonging to supernature rather than nature, is able to stand with the Reformers' view of what the Fall has done to human beings and yet with Catholics who maintain the universal sense of right and wrong. "Prevenient grace" for Wesley is that grace which stems from God's act in Jesus Christ which is free in all and for all. One of its effects is to restore lost freedom to respond in faith to God,[20] the other is to restore in all the in-built sense of right and wrong—and that prior to or even without prior appropriation of that grace. Not that this prevenient grace, the strongest evidence for which is the existence of conscience, gives us full knowledge of God's will. To go beyond the sense of unease when we have gone wrong to the joy of conforming to what we know to be right comes only when we faithfully take to ourselves God's saving grace. Then, through the intercession of the Son, the Holy Spirit is given to "renew us both in knowledge in his natural image . . . and also in his moral image, viz., righteousness and true holiness."[21]

In Wesley's theology, as we can see, conscience played a key role, pointing as it did to prevenient grace—the renewing effect on all human beings of the Christ-event, whereby we are no longer "dead in our sins" because of the Fall, but granted once again freedom to accept God's saving love and insight into the Creator's will and purpose. Here, I believe, is an example of what Fr. Jared Wicks, in his response to the Dialogue report *The Apostolic Tradition*, refers to as "the fecundity of the Tradition for positive development and growth"[22]—positive because it provides a way of overcoming one of the major issues that has been seen to divide Reformed from Catholic approaches to Natural Law.

B. The Limits of Conscience

Nevertheless, Wesley was ready to acknowledge the limitations of conscience—its limitations both as a human faculty and as a theological concept. More than once he indicated that its effects could be nullified, "blinded by the prejudices of education," for example, or deadened by "every act of disobedience . . . that it may not feel self-condemnation when we act in opposition to it."[23] Gift of God though it is, and supernatural gift at that, it needs the human nurturing of awareness and response:

> If you desire to have your conscience always quick to discern and faithful to accuse or excuse you, if you would preserve it always sensible and tender, be sure to obey it at all events; continually listen to its admonitions, and steadily follow them. Whatever it directs you to do, according to the word of God,

do; however grievous to flesh and blood. Whatever it forbids, if the prohibition be grounded on the word of God, see you do it not; however pleasing it may be to flesh and blood.[24]

It is important to note here Wesley's repeated "according to the word of God," emphasizing as it does that conscience must not be understood as a faculty that enables the individual to tap a private line to the Almighty and claim a special revelation not open to query or challenge. Conscience does not convey a private word that adds to what God has already revealed but enables us to get the point and feel the force of the written word. By the gracious action of God, conscience brings us under that rule which is to direct us in every particular, "none other than the written word of God."[25]

To relate conscience and Scripture in this way, however, appears to identify another Protestant-Catholic divide. Avoid the natural law/supernatural revelation dichotomy it may, but does it not warrant the Catholic suspicion of overemphasis on individual experience and *sola scriptura?* Those who have dismissed Wesley because in their view he identifies religion with "a real or supposed experience"[26] are hardly likely to be won over by adding an appeal to Scripture if this Scripture is in its turn to be interpreted only by individual experience. It is therefore important to recognize that Wesley does not restrict the authority under which every Christian stands to the experience of conscience and the written words of Scripture. As Albert Outler in particular has made clear in coining the phrase "Wesleyan Quadrilateral," Scripture, reason, tradition, and experience were all expected to play their part.

> Thus we can see in Wesley a distinctive theological *method,* with Scripture as its pre-eminent norm, but interfaced with tradition, reason and Christian experience as dynamic and interactive aids in the interpretation of the Word of God in Scripture. Such a method takes it for granted that faith is human *re*-action to an antecedent action of the Holy Spirit's prevenience, aimed at convicting our consciences and opening our eyes and ears to God's address to us in Scriptures. . . . This complex method, within its fourfold reference, could be more fruitful for contemporary theologizing than has yet been realized. It preserves the primacy of Scripture, it profits from the wisdom of tradition, it accepts the discipline of critical reason, and its stress on the Christian experience of grace gives it existential force.[27]

That way of describing Wesley's theological method, and indeed any use of that fourfold designation, has its limitations, for it retains a restricted understanding of tradition as something different from Scripture rather than seeing Scripture as already part of tradition in the wider sense of "living transmission of the Gospel." Nevertheless it has proved to be remarkably fecund, to use Father Wicks's term again, not least in contributing to the major advances represented in the latest Catholic-Methodist Report, for it is not a giant step, albeit a critical one, to move from Outler's view of the *inter-relation* between Scripture, reason, tradition, and experience to seeing that all four are essential aspects of that wider understanding of Tradition. So the report, by insisting that Scripture and experience on the one hand and Church and postbiblical teaching (tradition in the narrower sense) on the other are all brought into being by God's Creative Word, enables Catholics and Protestants to affirm together:

> The Tradition received by the apostles itself continues an unbroken process of communication between God and human beings. Every possible human resource is employed to sustain and deepen this process: linguistic, ritual, artistic, social and constitutional. The written word of Scripture is its permanent norm. Through the sacraments of baptism and the eucharist the memory of events whereby the Church came into being is preserved. The living Word has made a living community in which men and women converse with God and speak their faith to one another. Guided by its pastors and teachers, the Church continues to communicate with all generations, preserves its own identity and message, and is daily renewed in its obedience.[28]

III. Newman on Conscience

A. CONSCIENCE IN NEWMAN'S THEOLOGY

Newman held, as Wesley did before him, that the importance of the phenomenon of conscience is not restricted to its capacity to help us make moral decisions. It plays a key role in his theological account of how we come to knowledge of God. In recognizing its limitations, however, he goes further than Wesley, for whereas Wesley was prepared to allow for its limitations by setting it within a larger framework of "authorities," Newman finally left this appeal to conscience behind, turning to other authorities as alternatives rather than cooperating sources for the knowledge of God.

It was in his first sustained attempt to combat "liberalism in religion," referred to earlier, that Newman made a systematic appeal to conscience—to the fact that it exists and to what it does. He undertook to refute the notion on which liberalism fed, viz., that religion is one of those subjects on which truth cannot be discerned, and on which one conclusion is pretty much on a level with another.[29]

He believed that existing theological approaches, both Protestant and Catholic, were failing to meet the challenge and were bound to fail because the liberal approach undermined the very basis from which current theologies operated. They maintained that knowledge of God began with faithful appropriation of revealed truth; liberals insisted that real knowledge came only by way of the scientific method based on experience and experiment. So there was no common ground on which the battle could be joined.

Newman therefore chose to have the issue settled by meeting the liberals on their own ground. Following the scientific method of inductive reasoning from observed phenomena, he sought to demonstrate that the same kind of certainty could be achieved in the field of religion as in that of science. In his *A Grammar of Assent,* Newman analyzed the way in which we come to knowledge of the world around us. Beginning with sensory perceptions of people, things, and events, we put these together into a unified impression and form hypotheses about their nature and their relationship to others. But they remain hypotheses to which we can give what he called only "notional assent" until we test these hypotheses in various particular situations and discover by experience whether they hold up. If and when such experience confirms the hypothesis, notion and reality are identified as one; assent to them is said to be real rather than notional and certitude follows.

Does this method also apply in the field of religion?

> Can I attain to any more vivid assent to the Being of God than that which is given merely to the notions of the intellect? . . . Can I believe as if I saw?[30]

Yes, he maintains, there is a direct parallel between the process of physical perception outlined above and that of spiritual.

> When it is said that we cannot see God, this is undeniable; but still in what sense have we discernment of his creatures, of the individuals which surround us? The evidence which we have of their presence lies in the phenomena which address our senses, and our warrant for taking these for evidence is our instinctive certitude that they are evidence.[31]

But what, in the process of knowing God, plays the role that the phenomena which address our senses play in the discerning of God's creation? Newman answers, conscience.

> We may, by means of induction from particular experiences of conscience, have as good warrant for concluding the Ubiquitous presence of one Supreme Master as we have, from parallel experience of sense, for assenting to the fact of a multiform and vast world, material and mental.[32]

It is significant that Newman found the phenomena from which to build an idea of God not in the world outside himself but from the experience of conscience. The empirical argument that begins from nature or history and moves on to the notion of Creator of nature or Lord of history he rejected, claiming that the suffering in the world made him feel as though "some malignant nature has got hold of us, and is making us his sport."[33] A study of world history, for much the same reason, warrants the conclusion either that there is no creator or that he has disowned the creation.[34]

In thus appealing to conscience as the first element in the knowledge of God, Newman believed himself to be on firm ground, since convinced that the existence of conscience was universally acknowledged. But he also recognized the need to find agreement not only on the existence of conscience but also on what gave rise to that common experience. If one acknowledged the existence of conscience but denied its origin in the voice of God, then the attempt to use conscience as the means of coming to belief "as if one saw" would fail. So Newman set out to refute the most persistent attempts to explain the existence of conscience without recourse to God in much the same way as Wesley had before him.[35] In opposition to all such explanations, Newman insisted that the emotions that are aroused as sanctions of right conduct can be adequately explained only by assuming the existence of a Superior Being:

> If, as is the case, we feel responsibility, are ashamed, are frightened at transgressing the voice of conscience, this implies that there is One to whom we are responsible, before whom we are ashamed, whose claim upon us we fear . . . these feelings in us are such as to require for their exciting cause an intelligent being.[36]

However, this idea of a Supreme Being that comes from the experience of conscience is, according to Newman's own terminology, only notional. Certainty that there is a God follows only when the notional idea is put to the test and confirmed in experience. So he goes on to maintain, when we live our lives believing that there is such a God, the events of life will confirm such belief.

> When men begin all their works with the thought of God . . . they will find that everything that happens tends to confirm them in the truths about Him

which live in their imagination. They are brought into His presence as that of a living Person.[37]

Thus obedience to the voice within us leads us to recognize the author of that voice.

B. The Limits of Conscience

Newman remained consistently within the framework of his experimental epistemology in this demonstration of how we can give real assent to the proposition that "God exists." But however consistent he may have been, it is clear that he became dissatisfied with this inductive approach. The reason for this dissatisfaction is already evident in his novel *Callista*. Callista, speaking to Palermo (a Greek philosopher representing the view of the liberals in Newman's time), says of God:

> I feel myself in his presence. He says to me "Do this; don't do that." You may tell me that this dictate is a law of my own nature, as to joy or grieve. I cannot understand this. No, it is the echo of a person speaking to me. . . . You will say "Who is He, has He ever told you anything about Himself?" Alas, No! the more's the pity.[38]

Newman thus would have agreed with Wesley that conscience, while universal, is not strictly speaking "natural"—not part of the natural order of things but a supernatural gift from God. He also recognizes the same limitation, that conscience is not so much a source for adequate knowledge of God as a faculty to keep us loyal to what we know of God from other sources, Scripture in particular. The knowledge of God that comes from the experience of conscience is confined, as Newman put it, to the recognition of a divine speaker who is to be loved and feared, but no more than this.

But whereas Wesley's theological approach retained a positive role for conscience and the reasoned appeal to experience, appropriating the knowledge of God provided by Scripture and tradition, Newman found no such accommodation. He turned away from the inductive or experimental path to knowledge of God because he concluded that what conscience provided was not merely limited but most unreliable:

> The sense of right and wrong is so delicate, so fitful, so easily puzzled, obscured, perverted, so subtle in its argumentative methods, so impressible by education, so biassed by pride and passion, so unsteady in its course, that, in the struggle for existence amid the various exercises and triumphs of the human intellect, this sense is at once the highest of all teachers, yet the least

luminous; and the Church, the Pope, the Hierarchy are, in the Divine purpose, the supply of an urgent demand.[39]

IV. Conscience and Authority[40]

We have already noted that in his sermon *On Conscience* Wesley too acknowledged an "urgent demand" to inform and strengthen the conscience. Not, it is true, with Church, Pope, and Hierarchy (although with two of these he had no quarrel in principle!) but with the written Word of God. We have also seen that for Wesley this "written word" in Scripture does not stand alone in informing conscience. Reason, tradition, and experience play a vital and interdependent role.

In the reading and hearing of Scripture, reason is to be used, employing all the scholarly methods of biblical interpretation available. Wherever possible the plain meaning of the text is to be preferred, with due reference to the original languages; and texts are to be compared with, and understood in the light of, others. The meaning of the text, however, is not thereby exhausted. The tradition of the Church draws out the meaning and clarifies the doctrine implied therein, but all of this comes alive only when appropriated by faith and lived out in experience. Then and only then can we know that the word of salvation set forth in Scripture, interpreted by tradition, and expounded by reason is a word spoken to us with power to heal and save. In the same way for Wesley, tradition, reason, and experience can all be shown to enhance, depend upon, and stand under the judgement of the others.

Nevertheless, for Wesley the prior authority of Scripture is never in doubt—read with reason, interpreted through tradition, and appropriated through experience, yes; but Scripture so read, interpreted, and appropriated remained the touchstone of faith and practice.

It would be tempting at this point to claim ecumenical convergence by citing the Catholic-Methodist *The Apostolic Tradition* document which, in line with Vatican II, maintains of tradition that "the written word of Scripture is its permanent norm."[41] But that would be too easy, and would in fact set back the ecumenical cause by refusing to acknowledge an issue that has yet to be resolved. Father Wicks's response to the Report alludes to this issue. He makes the point that Scriptures which play a normative role are never "bare uninterpreted texts that are just out there as a normative instance in the Church or over against the Church. The Bible expresses itself normatively only when it is interpreted."[42] But of course not every interpretation is acceptable; not every "living transmission" witnesses authentically to the Gospel; "not all developments are positive and not all innovation is enrichment."[43] Consequently, "the Apostolic Faith is beset by myriad threats to its authentic meaning and full ideals of life."[44] How then to meet these threats, to distinguish between positive and negative developments, to guard against those that are destructive?

> A Catholic reflection . . . quite naturally leads to the perception of the spiritual empowerment given to the corporate body that succeeds the apostolic college, an empowerment to resolve controversies in a binding way through teaching that in its solemn forms is maintained in the truth by God's Spirit.[45]

And for a Roman Catholic, of course, that corporate body affirms the authority of the Pope as its head.

That sharpens the issue, for in the very document in which he insists that the distinguishing marks of a Methodist are not opinion, words, actions, or emphases, but "having the love of God shed abroad in his heart by the Holy Spirit," Wesley affirmed, "We believe the written word of God to be the only and sufficient rule of both faith and practice." Superficial ecumenical politeness might then drop the rest of the sentence, "and herein we are fundamentally distinguished from the Romish Church."[46] But a deeper commitment to ecumenism demands that we acknowledge it and face the question of whether that really was such a fundamental distinction.

It was if we hold Wesley to the more restrictive way of applying this "rule of faith and practice," viz., that nothing is acceptable unless specifically enjoined in Scripture. This method he did on occasion follow, especially when engaged in polemical writing.[47] Nevertheless it is clear that he was also prepared to adopt a more expansive method of interpretation, to allow (although not insisting upon as essential) what is not expressly forbidden in Scripture. Wesley remained a priest of the Church of England, for example, believing her doctrines and loving her liturgy; yet he acknowledged that there were no grounds in the New Testament for a national Church.[48] Nor did he claim that her liturgy was prescribed in Scripture. And while he asserted of the threefold order of ministry that it was described in the New Testament and generally obtained in the apostolic era, he did not deny the validity of other orders:

> If this plan [the threefold order of ministry] were essential to a Christian Church, what must become of all the foreign Reformed Churches? It would

follow that they were no part of the Church of Christ—a consequence full of shocking absurdity.[49]

Had Wesley been prepared to test the development of doctrine and Church order within the "Romish Church" in the same expansive way as he applied it to the Church of England, then he may not have seen the distinction at this point between himself and those of the "Romish persuasion" to have been so fundamental.

Nor is it so fundamental now. Those who follow Wesley at his best as it were, with the more expansive application of the rule of faith, can certainly recognize the authority of the hierarchy and the primacy of Peter as a legitimate development within the Catholic Church, without necessarily acknowledging the authority of the pope and hierarchy for themselves and without accepting those formulations of infallibility which they cannot see as consistent with Scripture. But more than that, those Methodists who find their views upheld in the *Apostolic Tradition* report will affirm that some such authoritative process for interpreting Scripture and some such means of discerning legitimate development among a riot of strident claimants is a matter of urgent necessity for them as well. What form that may take and the extent of future ecumenical convergence on this issue is, as Father Wicks remarks, "material for another phase of dialogue."[50]

V. A Whimsical Coda

In drawing this to a close, I cannot resist the temptation of wondering what Wesley and Newman would have thought of each other had they been contemporaries instead of failing to overlap by just a decade. Idle speculation perhaps; nevertheless at least some historical data can be brought to bear on the question.

Of Wesley, Newman once wrote, "personally I do not like him, if it were merely for his deep self-reliance and self-conceit . . . ,"[51] and while of course Wesley made no reference to Newman, we do know what some of his followers thought of the Oxford Movement. In 1868 Edward Pusey, hopes of union with Rome waning and disappointed that Anglicans had not responded more warmly to his *Eirenicons,* wrote a letter to the President of the Wesleyan Conference proposing a rapprochement between Anglo-Catholics and Methodists. The President addressed a polite but discouraging response, maintaining that the proper role for Wesleyans was, as he put it with gentle irony, "the *via media* between Anglicanism and Dissent," and went on,

While we hold this midway position we are still prepared to regard . . . with respect and affection, the State Church, so long as she remains faithful to her calling.[52]

Some lively members of Conference were less polite and composed a piece of doggerel to a popular tune of the time:

> You offer one hand to the papal band
> And the other to us extend.
> Can you really hope that we and the Pope
> Can acknowledge a mutual friend?
> You tell us our barque is not an ark
> We don't believe that's true.
> We'd trust a raft before your craft,
> Just paddle your own canoe.[53]

So much for rapprochement! It would, however, be a mistake to conclude from these quotations that Newman left the Church of England to head off in one direction and Wesleyans took off in the other, so that the gulf between Newman and Wesley is as wide as the whole breadth of the Anglican Church, than which there is none broader. For these quotations tell only half the story. The context for Newman's comment about Wesley was that of a wider appreciation of him and the Methodists. He maintained that if what secured for Anglicans a place in the Holy Catholic Church was visible evidence of supernatural grace, then they could hardly deny that place also to Wesley and his followers who in that regard were clearly superior:[54]

> Have they not more remarkable phenomena in their history, symptomatic of the presence of grace among them, than you can show in yours? If you wish to find the shadow and suggestion of the supernatural qualities which make up the notion of a Catholic saint, to Wesley you must go, and to such as him. Personally I do not like him, if it were merely for his deep self-reliance and self-conceit; still I am bound, in justice to him, to ask, and you in consistency to answer, what historical personage in the Establishment, during its whole three centuries, has approximated in force and splendour of conduct and achievements to one who began by innovating on your rules and ending by contemning your authorities? He and his companions, starting amid ridicule at Oxford, with fasting and praying in the cold night air, then going about preaching, reviled by the rich and educated, and pelted and dragged to prison by the populace, and converting their thousands from sin to God's service—were it not for their pride and eccentricity, their fanatical doctrine and untranquil devotion, they would startle us, as if the times of St. Vincent Ferrer or St. Francis Xavier were come again in a Protestant land.[55]

So Newman on the Wesleyans. But what of Wesley and the Tractarians? Would Wesley have turned away, as his followers did, from those who "offered their hand to the papal band"? In Dublin in 1749 Wesley wrote and later published his *Letter to a Roman Catholic*. After setting out what he along with other "true Protestants" believe, maintaining its consistency with the "old religion," Wesley concludes:

> In the name then, and in the strength of God, let us resolve first not to hurt one another. . . . Rather let us endeavour after every instance of a kind, friendly and Christian behaviour towards each other. . . . Let us resolve secondly, God being our helper, to speak nothing harsh or unkind of each other . . . to use only the language of love. . . . Let us thirdly, resolve to harbour no unkind thought, no unfriendly temper towards each other. Let us lay the axe to the root of that tree. . . . Let us fourthly, endeavour to help each other on in whatever we are agreed leads to the Kingdom. So far as we can let us always rejoice to strengthen each other's hands in God. Above all, let us each take heed to himself that he not fall short of the religion of love.[56]

I think, therefore, a *Punch* cartoonist in 1868 interpreted Wesley better than did the Wesleyan Conference that year in its response to Pusey. The cartoon depicted Edward Pusey, dressed in clerical attire, inviting a Wesleyan lady to accompany him to Church. She politely declines. Yet above her is a portrait of Wesley—a mirror image of Pusey, down to the last detail of cassock, gown, and bands![57]

"Rejoice to strengthen each others' hands in God." That is why this heir of Wesley is more than happy to teach in a United Faculty of Theology with Anglican and Catholic colleagues and to be a long-standing member of Catholic-Methodist dialogue, in joyful hope that what we are able to say and do together anticipates what God will bring about in the wider Church which we serve in God's name.

Notes

[1] *The Apostolic Tradition*. Report by the fifth Roman Catholic-World Methodist International Commission, *Catholic International* (February 1992) 3:3, 107ff.

[2] George Tavard, "Tradition as Koinonia in Historical Perspective," *One in Christ* 24 (1988) 97–111.

[3] For some months during 1954, I was involved as co-author with Rev. Dr. Hugh Mitchell of Melbourne, preparing for publication an article based on his doctoral dissertation. Unfortunately he became too ill for the work to be completed. I am glad that some of his insights into Newman's view of conscience can now be more widely known.

⁴Nicholas Lash was referring to the Tractarians, but I have been unable to trace whether in a lecture or written work.

⁵John Henry Newman, *A Grammar of Assent* (New York: Longmans Green, 1891) 237.

⁶"Newman," *Encyclopedia Britannica,* 16.

⁷John Wesley, *Works* 1:97; journal entry for May 1738.

⁸Owen Chadwick, *Newman* (Oxford: Oxford University Press, 1983) 18–19.

⁹John Wesley, *Journal* (August 28, 1744); cited in S. Ayling, *John Wesley* (London: Collins, 1979) 151–52.

¹⁰Ibid.

¹¹In which he advocated interpreting *The Thirty-Nine Articles* in line with the Council of Trent.

¹²Paul Misner, *Papacy and Development: Newman and the Primacy of the Pope* (Leiden: E. J. Brill, 1976) 7.

¹³See esp. Wesley's "Letter to a Roman Catholic," *Works* 10:77–83.

¹⁴John Newman, *Tracts for the Times* (London: Rivington, 1839) 1:12.

¹⁵Wesley, *Works* 6:485.

¹⁶Ibid.

¹⁷Ibid., 178–79.

¹⁸Thomas Aquinas, *Summa Theologiae I–II,* q. 91 a. 2; cited in J. V. Dolan, *Conscience: Its Freedom and Limitations* (New York: Fordham, 1971) 11.

¹⁹Wesley, *Works* 6:485.

²⁰Thus avoiding the contention on which the doctrine of predestination is built, viz., that since not all are saved and human beings no longer have the freedom to choose God's saving grace, they are saved by God's election before the foundation of the world.

²¹Wesley, *Works* 6:209.

²²Jared Wicks, "An Advance in Ecumenical Understanding," commentary on and assessment of *The Apostolic Tradition,* 124.

²³Wesley, *Works* 7:183.

²⁴Ibid., 180.

²⁵Ibid., 181.

²⁶Ronald Knox, *Enthusiasm* (Oxford: Oxford University Press, 1950) 547.

²⁷Albert Outler, *The Wesleyan Theological Heritage,* ed. Oden and Longden (Grand Rapids, Mich.: Zondervan, 1991) 25–26.

²⁸*The Apostolic Tradition,* 109.

²⁹Newman, *A Grammar of Assent,* 237.

³⁰Ibid., 102–03.

³¹Ibid.

³²Ibid., 63.

³³John Henry Newman, *Apologia Pro Vita Sua* (London: Longmans, 1903) 241.

³⁴Ibid., 10.

³⁵Newman in his Parochial Sermons, for example, and Wesley in his sermon "On Conscience" in which he joined issue with one Professor Hutcheson, "late of Glasgow."

³⁶Newman, *A Grammar of Assent,* 110.

³⁷Ibid., 117.

³⁸John Henry Newman, *Callista: A Sketch of the Third Century* (London: Burns & Oates, 1876) 244.

³⁹John Henry Newman, *Difficulties of Anglicans* (New York: Logmans Green, 1891) 237.

⁴⁰I incorporate here some material presented to an earlier Catholic-Methodist dialogue, and which appeared in amended form in an essay "Conscience and Authority," *The Answer Lies Below,* ed. Henry Thompson (New York: University of America, 1984).

[41]*The Apostolic Tradition,* 108.

[42]Wicks, "An Advance in Ecumenical Understanding," 123.

[43]Ibid., 124.

[44]Ibid.

[45]Ibid.

[46]John Wesley, "The Character of a Methodist," *Works* 8:326.

[47]When, for example, he criticizes the Bull of Pius IV for "adding to the book of life," *Works* 1:209.

[48]Minutes of Conference, 1749; cited by Colin Williams, *John Wesley's Theology Today* (London: Epworth, 1960) 222.

[49]Ibid.

[50]Wicks, "An Advance in Ecumenical Understanding," 124.

[51]Newman, *Difficulties of Anglicans,* 90.

[52]Cited in J. M. Turner, *Conflict and Reconciliation* (Epworth: London, 1985) 146.

[53]Ibid.

[54]Although by this time Newman held that no such grounds alone could validate claims to belong to the Church, Catholic and Apostolic.

[55]Newman, *Difficulties of Anglicans,* 109.

[56]Wesley, "Letter to a Roman Catholic," *Works* 10:82–83.

[57]Cited in Turner, *Conflict,* 146.

8

Tradition as a Liturgical Act

Geoffrey Wainwright

"Le principal instrument de la Tradition de l'Église," wrote George Tavard's fellow-countryman, Bishop J. B. Bossuet of Meaux (1627–1704), "est renfermé dans ses prières."[1] While there is obvious truth to Bossuet's thesis that the liturgy is the principal instrument of the Church's Tradition, I wish to suggest that the obvious truth rests on a deeper truth that is discovered only when the thesis is turned around. Bossuet's formulation makes it appear that there has always already existed a substantive Tradition which the continuing liturgy subserviently hands on to the future; liturgy is thereby adjectival to Tradition, or even a mere *locus theologicus* from which doctrines may be proven. Thus Bossuet went on: "The solemn conclusion of all the Church's prayers 'through Jesus Christ,' and 'in the unity of the Holy Spirit,' shows the necessity of express faith in the Trinity, in the incarnation, and in the mediation of the Son of God."

In turning around Bossuet's thesis, my hypothesis is rather that the traditionary process takes its origin from, and finds its goal in, worship, and that this thorough subservience of tradition is meanwhile demonstrated by its ongoing character as a liturgical act. Liturgy *constitutes* the Tradition. Or even more boldly: Liturgy *is* the Tradition, and (more boldly yet) the Tradition *is* liturgy. My method and purpose here are systematic, offering a theological interpretation of Scripture and Christian history for the sake of a constructive understanding and practice of liturgy and tradition in the ecumenical present.[2]

I. The Lord's Supper

We may begin with 1 Corinthians 11:23-26, where the Apostle Paul employs the technical rabbinical terms for traditioning, *mâsar* and *qibbêl*, or *paradounai* and *paralambanein:* "For I *received* (*parelabon*) of the Lord *what* (*ho*) I also *delivered* (*paredôka*) to you, *that* (*hoti*) the Lord Jesus on the night when he was betrayed took bread, and when he had given thanks, he broke it, and said, 'This is my body, which is for you. Do this in remembrance of me.' In the same way also the cup, after supper, saying, 'This cup is the new covenant in my blood. Do this, as often as you drink it, in remembrance of me.' For as often as you eat this bread and drink this cup, you proclaim the Lord's death until he comes."

That is usually called, even by liturgists, "the institution narrative." It is in fact much less a narrative than a "rubric," culminating in the two-fold "command to repeat": "Do this in remembrance of me." Now the proper thing to do with a rubric is not to read it but to perform it, as Pierre Benoit said in accounting for the absence of "the command to repeat" from Matthew and Mark and (we might extend the argument) of the entire "institution narrative" from some early eucharistic prayers: "On ne récite pas une rubrique, on l'exécute."[3] Without endorsing Hans Lietzmann's exegesis that Paul is in 1 Corinthians 11:23-26 claiming to be the *first* to receive from the Lord (a new form of) the Lord's Supper (a Hellenistic memorial meal rather than the Jerusalemite festive meal),[4] we may therefore suggest that *what* St. Paul received "from the Lord," doubtless by a traditionary process, was in fact the beginning of Christian worship, "the first Mass" (as they used to say). At the Last Supper Jesus provided his Church with the means of perpetuating the redemptive event of his own impending death and resurrection, the offering which inaugurated the new covenant. The ecclesial celebration of the sacrament carries forward the history of salvation and of the Church. It will be celebrated "until he comes" or—taking up Joachim Jeremias' observation that *achri ou* with aorist subjunctive often carries a final sense—"with a view to His coming" (*bis [es so weit ist, dass] er kommt*).[5] At the last, the sacrament will give way to what it anticipates, namely the Marriage Feast of the Lamb (Rev 19:7-9).

II. Preaching

Moving on to 1 Corinthians 15:1-7, we find the same terminology for the traditionary process and the same substantive content, only the form is now that of preaching rather than the eucharistic meal: "Now I would remind you in what terms I preached to you the gospel (*to euangelion ho euêngelisamên humin*), which you *received* (*ho kai parelabete*), in which you stand, by which you are saved, if you hold it fast (*katechein*)—unless you believed in vain. For I *delivered* (*paredôka*) to you as of first importance *what* I also *received* (*ho kai parelabon*), *that* (*hoti*) Christ died for our sins in accordance with the scriptures, that he was buried, that he was raised on the third day in accordance with the scriptures, and that he appeared to Cephas, then to the twelve. . . . " What Paul hands on is "the gospel," or the Paschal Mystery itself: "Christ, our paschal lamb, has been sacrificed" (1 Cor 5:7). The core of the *kerygma* is "Christ crucified" (1 Cor 1:23), whom God has raised from the dead (1 Cor 15:12-20).

During his earthly ministry, Jesus had said to those whom he sent out in his name, "Whoever hears you hears me" (Luke 10:16). After his death and resurrection, his promised accompaniment of his apostles to the close of the age, as in Matthew 28:16-20, grounds a perhaps even stronger identification between his messengers and the One who has become the Proclaimed: Lutheran exegetes in particular are fond of arguing that, according to Paul's use of the noun *euangelion* and the verb *euangelizesthai*, "gospel" is both content and action, with Christ both its author and its object.[6] Or in the words, on the Reformed side, of the marginal addition to the Second Helvetic Confession: "The preaching of the Word of God is itself the word of God (*praedicatio verbi divini est verbum divinum*)."

According to Romans 10, the purpose and result of preaching is that people may "confess with [their] lips that 'Jesus is Lord' and believe in [their] hearts that God raised him from the dead," so that they may "call on the name of the Lord" and "be saved." Thus they join in the anticipation of that final worship when "at the name of Jesus every knee shall bow, . . . and every tongue confess that 'Jesus Christ is Lord,' to the glory of God the Father" (Phil 2:10-11). Or, to put the apostolic testimony in another way: as believers speak out, so the grace of God abounds to more and more, and the eucharistic chorus is swelled: "We too believe, and so we speak, knowing that he who raised the Lord Jesus will raise us also with Jesus and bring us with you into his presence. For it is all for your sake, so that as grace extends to more and more people it may increase thanksgiving, to the glory of God" (2 Cor 4:13-15).

Having begun with the Eucharist and with preaching, which are the preeminent instances of "word and sacrament," we turn now to other forms of worship which in their very substance and action constitute the Tradition. First we examine a trio that employs above all the spoken word: the recitation of creeds, the saying of prayers, and the singing of hymns. The point is neatly made in a verse by the nineteenth-century Anglican hymn-writer Samuel John Stone:

> Ancient Prayer and Song liturgic,
> Creeds that change not to the end,
> As His gift we have received them,
> As His charge we will defend.[7]

We note at the outset that each appears as "gift" and "charge," "Gabe" and "Aufgabe," as is characteristic of the traditionary process.

III. Creeds

From the fourth century we know of a ceremony that took place some weeks or days before baptism, the *traditio symboli,* whereby the creed was "passed on" to the candidates who then, after learning it, "returned" it—the *redditio*—to the bishop.[8]

The *traditio et redditio symboli* is best viewed as a rehearsal for the act of confessing the faith that was integral to baptism itself.[9] The first form that we know of the words spoken at baptism consists in the threefold creedal questions put by the minister to the candidate and the latter's responses of "I believe," upon which the candidate was each time immersed. Thus, in the so-called *Apostolic Tradition of Hippolytus* which dates from the early third century:

> The minister of baptism shall lay hand on the candidate, saying:
> "Do you believe in God the Father almighty?"
> And the one who is being baptized shall say: "I believe."
> And forthwith the giver, having his hand placed upon the baptizand's head, shall baptize him once.
> And then he shall say: "Do you believe in Christ Jesus, the Son of God, who was born of the Holy Spirit from the Virgin Mary, and was crucified under Pontius Pilate, and died, and rose again on the third day alive from the dead, and ascended into heaven, and sits at the right hand of the Father, and will come to judge the living and the dead?"
> And when he has said, "I believe," he shall be baptized again.
> And the minister shall say again: "Do you believe in the Holy Spirit and the Holy Church and the resurrection of the flesh?"
> Then the one being baptized shall say: "I believe," and thus he shall be baptized a third time.[10]

The Trinitarian creedal structure clearly matches the "command to baptize" recorded of the risen Lord in Matthew 28:19: "Go therefore and make disciples of all nations, baptizing them in the name of the Father and of the Son and of the Holy Spirit, teaching them to observe all that I have commanded you; and lo, I am with you always, to the close of the age." That justifies the fact that, even after he had ceased to hold that the Apostles' Creed was dictated by Christ himself, the great nineteenth-century Danish preacher and theologian N.F.S. Grundtvig could still consider the Western baptismal creed as "a word from the Lord's own mouth."

The significance of that baptism "in the name of the Father, the Son, and the Holy Spirit" has been well brought out by Markus Barth in terms of Matthean exegesis: it is baptism into the crucified and risen Christ, the Father's chosen and anointed Son, who himself baptizes with the holy Spirit that is now being poured out on all flesh.[11] According to the Church's canonical reading of the broader apostolic witness contained in the entire New Testament, baptism in the water of God's creation signifies and effects: inclusion, by grace and faith, into the redeeming death and resurrection of Christ; the gift of the Holy Spirit whereby the children of God *in Filio* cry "Abba, Father"; incorporation into the Church; and inheritance in the promised final kingdom. Thus each later confession of the baptismal creed, as the anamnesis of baptism, summarizes and takes up the history of salvation and locates the believer within it. And thus does the *traditio symboli* contribute to the formation and renewal of the worshipping community.

IV. The Lord's Prayer

Emerging perhaps at a slightly later date in the patristic period than the *traditio et redditio symboli* was another double ceremony of "handing over" and "rendition," the *traditio et redditio orationis dominicae*. The Lord's Prayer was taught to the baptismal candidates after they had "returned" the creed, and, still before baptism, they had to "repeat" the prayer in preparation for their first "sacramental" use of it, which would occur at the eucharistic communion that followed immediately on their baptism.[12]

Jesus had promised his disciples that whenever they gathered in his name for prayer, he would be in the midst of them. That would ensure the Father's hearing them (Matt 18:19-20). The presupposition was that their prayer would follow the model and spirit of Jesus' instruction:

> Pray then like this:
> Our Father who art in heaven,

Hallowed be thy name.
Thy kingdom come,
Thy will be done,
    On earth as it is in heaven.
Give us this day our bread for the morrow;
And forgive us our debts,
    As we also have forgiven our debtors;
And lead us not into temptation,
    But deliver us from evil (Matt 6:9-13).

When the Church Fathers discuss prayer, this is *the* prayer they write about. Tertullian calls it a "summary of the entire Gospel" (*brevarium totius evangelii*), and Cyprian a "compend of our heavenly teaching" (*nostris coelestis doctrinae compendium*).[13] In our own time, the exegete Heinz Schürmann says the Lord's Prayer is "the key to the preaching of Jesus";[14] and the theological historian Yves Congar writes that "When I say the 'Our Father,' I have already included everything which will be given me to know only in the Revelation of glory."[15]

Three instances may be given of the ways in which the Church continued to pray after the fashion of the Lord's Prayer and thereby allowed the prayer to constitute its Tradition in the interval between Christ's announcement of the kingdom and the kingdom's final arrival. First we know from Justin Martyr, in the middle of the second century, that petitionary and intercessory prayers formed part of the regular Sunday gathering for worship: common prayers were made "for ourselves . . . and for all others everywhere, that, having learned the truth, we may be deemed worthy to be found good citizens also in our actions and guardians of the commandments, so that we may be saved with eternal salvation."[16] The classical "prayers of the people" continued to seek the spread of the gospel, the conversion of the world, and the perseverance of the faithful, all with a view to the coming of God's kingdom.[17]

Second, we may notice a prayer from the ancient *Didachè* which has found favor as an offertory prayer in modern liturgical revival:

As this broken bread was scattered over the mountains, and when brought together became one, so let your Church be brought together from the ends of the earth into your kingdom; for yours are the glory and the power through Jesus Christ for evermore.[18]

Finally may be mentioned the Sanctus, which is found already in Revelation 4:8 and came to be a fixture in the eucharistic anaphora or great prayer of thanksgiving. With the "Holy, holy, holy" the Church on earth joins in the hallowing of God's name which is the accomplishment of "angels and archangels and all the company of heaven."[19]

V. Song Liturgic

Twentieth-century biblical scholarship has recalled attention to the primitive Christian hymns embedded in the texts of the New Testament. Christocentrically, but always with reference to God the Father, they celebrate the divine origin of Christ, his role in creation, redemption and consummation, and his sovereign status. Characteristic are Colossians 1:15-20 and, most famously, Philippians 2:5-11.

An early postapostolic example is the *Phôs hilaron:*

> Hail, gladdening light, of His pure glory poured,
> Who is the immortal Father, heavenly, blest,
> Holiest of Holies, Jesus Christ, our Lord!
> Now we come to the sun's hour of rest.
> The lights of evening round us shine.
> We hymn the Father, Son, and Holy Spirit divine.
> Worthiest art Thou at all times to be sung
> With undefilèd tongue,
> Son of God, giver of life, alone;
> Therefore in all the world Thy glories, Lord, they own.[20]

In the fourth century this was joined by the Western *Te Deum*. Both have remained in constant use in the Churches. Addressed in the present to the divine Persons, they enact the praise that is due God's being, nature, and works and thereby locate the worshippers in the salvation which God graciously bestows and will bestow in the final kingdom. The same is achieved by the Church's constant use of the Psalms of David, often interpreted Christologically (whether as *vox Christi* or as *vox ad Christum*) and concluding with a Trinitarian doxology.

Later hymn writers frequently take up the practice of patristic preachers in focusing the past and future of salvation history upon a liturgical "today," whereby that history is resumed, advanced, and anticipated. I select two examples from my own Methodist tradition. First, some verses from Charles Wesley's "Hymn for Ascension Day":

> Hail the day that sees Him rise,
> Ravished from our wistful eyes!

Christ, awhile to mortals given,
Reascends His native heaven.

Him though highest heaven receives,
Still He loves the earth He leaves;
Though returning to His throne,
Still he calls mankind His own.

See! He lifts His hands above;
See! He shows the prints of love;
Hark! His gracious lips bestow
Blessings on his Church below.

Master, parted from our sight,
High above yon azure height,
Grant our hearts may thither rise,
Following Thee beyond the skies.[21]

And then from another Wesley hymn, in anticipation of the final Advent:

Lo! He comes with clouds descending,
Once for favoured sinners slain;
Thousand thousand saints attending,
Swell the triumph of His train:
Hallelujah!
God appears on earth to reign.[22]

After the oral forms of "ancient prayer and song liturgic, creeds that change not to the end," we turn to two sacraments that in our context are also to be considered in their constitutive function for Tradition. Medieval Western theology appropriately viewed baptism and ordination as *deputationes ad cultum*. Baptism and ordination are themselves liturgical acts that induct persons into membership of, and particular roles in, the worshipping community. Thereby the baptized and the ordained become, "incidentally," carriers of the Tradition.

VI. Baptism

According to the *Apostolic Tradition of Hippolytus,* it is baptism which first allows a person to "pray with the faithful," to exchange the kiss of peace, to offer gifts at the Eucharist, and to receive the communion. Henceforth one becomes no longer merely a receiver of the gospel through listening to teaching, the reading of the Scriptures and the oral word of the sermon, but now one who, as a member of the celebrating community, actively embodies the faith. A secondary sign of this is the putting on of the white "garment of righteousness," having been "washed in the blood of the Lamb" (cf. Rev 7:14).[23]

Here the existential and ethical implications of baptism come into play. The *results* of participation in Christ's death and resurrection and incorporation into his body are presented by the New Testament in liturgical or cultic terms In 1 Corinthians 6:19-20, St. Paul asks the rhetorical question: "Do you not know that your body is a temple of the Holy Spirit within you, which you have from God? You are not your own; you were bought with a price. So glorify God in your body." And similarly in 2 Corinthians 6:16–7:1: "What agreement has the temple of God with idols? For we are the temple of the living God; as God has said, 'I will live in them, and I will be their God, and they shall be my people.' . . . Since we have these promises, beloved, let us cleanse ourselves from every defilement of body and spirit, and make holiness perfect in the fear of God." Or again in Romans 12:1-2: "I appeal to you therefore, brothers and sisters, by the mercies of God, to present your bodies as a living sacrifice, holy and acceptable to God, which is your spiritual worship. Do not be conformed to this world but be transformed by the renewal of your mind, that you may prove what is the will of God, what is good, and acceptable, and perfect."

The existential and ethical comportment of Christians may, by the witness it makes, have the incidental effect of bringing others to glorify God. So, according to Matthew 5:16: "Let your light so shine before others, that they may see your good works and give glory to your Father who is in heaven." Or, as echoed by 1 Peter 2:12: "Maintain good conduct among the Gentiles, so that in case they speak against you as wrongdoers, they may see your good works and glorify God on the day of visitation."

VII. Ordination

The prayer for the ordination of a bishop in the *Apostolic Tradition of Hippolytus* exercised great influence, directly or indirectly, in many parts of the East, and in our time it has reemerged as a source for the revision of the rite in several Western Churches. While "princely"' and "pastoral" themes echo the Old Testament notion of a "royal shepherd," they are integrated into a priestly framework which makes the principal ministry of a bishop liturgical. The prayer of Hippolytus reads in large part:

God and Father of our Lord Jesus Christ, you foreordained from the beginning a race of righteous men from Abraham; you appointed princes and priests, and did not leave your sanctuary without a ministry. From the beginning of the age it was your good pleasure to be glorified in those whom you have chosen: now pour forth that power which is from you, of the princely Spirit which you granted through your beloved Son Jesus Christ to your holy apostles who established the Church in every place as your sanctuary, to the unceasing glory and praise of your name.

You who know the hearts of all, bestow upon this your servant, whom you have chosen for the episcopate, to feed your holy flock and to exercise the high-priesthood before you blamelessly, serving night and day; to propitiate your countenance unceasingly, and to offer you the gifts of your holy Church; and by the Spirit of high-priesthood to have the power to forgive sins according to your command, to confer orders according to your bidding, to loose every bond according to the power which you gave to the apostles, to please you in gentleness and a pure heart, offering to you a sweet-smelling savor, through your child Jesus Christ our Lord, with whom be glory and power and honor to you, with the holy Spirit, both now and to the ages of ages. Amen.[24]

Correspondingly, Vatican II's Constitution on the Sacred Liturgy calls the worship assembly "the preeminent manifestation of the Church," marked by the "full, active participation of all God's holy people, especially in the same eucharist, in a single prayer, at one altar at which the bishop presides, surrounded by his college of priests and by his ministers."[25]

The building up of this worshipping community is the purpose of the traditionary process. In the patristic and medieval periods, the bishop's duties were recognized to include evangelizing, preaching, and teaching.[26] At the ordination of a bishop, the eighth-century Byzantine rite prays for "him who has been elected to undertake the gospel."[27] The ninth- or tenth-century Armenian rite of ordination to the priesthood contains the petition for the ordinand "that he may stand firm and without blemish in the priesthood before you in the catholic Church, built and established on the rock of faith; without shame, to epitomize rightly the word of the preaching, to sow abroad the quickening and orthodox faith of the apostolic Church in all places to them that listen."[28]

Ancient prayers of ordination do not forget that the gospel is to be spread outward. In closely similar phraseology, a Georgian prayer for the ordination of a bishop refers to "teachers, by whom has been spread over the whole earth the knowledge of your truth, vouchsafed to those born of men by the Prince your only-begotten Son, whom from generation to generation you manifested to your chosen ones"; the East Syrian rite to "apostles and prophets, teachers and priests, by whose work might be multiplied the knowledge of the truth which your only-begotten Son gave to the human race"; and a West Syrian prayer to the gift of "leaders, so that we might please you by making the knowledge of the name of your Christ multiplied and glorified throughout the world."[29] In the medieval West, a Gallican prayer in the Roman rite for bishops asks that "their feet, by your aid, may be beautiful for bringing good tidings of peace, for bringing your good tidings of good [Isa 52:7; Rom 10:15]. Give them, Lord, a ministry of reconciliation [2 Cor 5:18] in word and deeds and in power of signs and of wonders [Rom 15:18-19]. May their speech and preaching be not with enticing words of human wisdom, but in demonstration of the Spirit and of power [1 Cor 2:4; 1 Thess 1:5]."[30]

The strongly Pauline character of those prayers recalls the ministry of the apostle, who saw his evangelizing work in liturgical terms. Paul uses the verb *latreuô* in Romans 1:9, the sense of which C. K. Barrett nearly captures as "I render God spiritual service in proclaiming the Gospel of his Son."[31] In Romans 15:15-16, the apostle writes: "On some points I have written to you very boldly, by way of reminder, because of the grace given me by God to be a minister (*leitourgos*) of Christ Jesus to the Gentiles in the priestly service (*hierourgón*) of the Gospel of God, so that the offering (*prosphora*) of the Gentiles may be acceptable, sanctified by the Holy Spirit." His expected apostolic martyrdom, which was but the culmination of a ministry of mortal hardship (2 Cor 4:7-12; 6:4-5; Gal 6:17), St. Paul interpreted in terms of sacrifice (2 Tim 4:6), "poured out as a libation upon the sacrificial offering of your faith" (Phil 2:17). The successors in the apostolic tradition may expect no less: it is their service to the worshipping community's service of God.

After the spoken word and the sacramental act we may now turn to two objects whose liturgical use also constitutes the Tradition. I refer to the book of the Scriptures and to icons.

VIII. *The Scriptures*

Some weeks before the *traditio symboli* and the *traditio orationis dominicae,* candidates for baptism in the patristic Church in parts of the West also received the *traditio evangelii* to which was transferred the name of *apertio aurium.* The candidates had their "ears opened" by the "tradition of the

Gospel," as the beginnings of the four Gospels were read and expounded to them, and they could thenceforth "hear the Gospel" in the eucharistic assembly.[32] They thus became part of a community that was so deeply constituted by the gospel that it was considered an act of apostasy to "surrender" its Scriptures into the wrong hands in times of persecution: in a kind of negative example of tradition, the *traditores* were betrayers or traitors.

When the Churches confess the divine inspiration of the Scriptures, room is left for various modalities of the Spirit's action in the composing, sorting, and understanding of the texts, and among these must certainly be included the creative, selective, and interpretative force of the liturgy. As to the origin of the Scriptures, much of their material—and by no means only the hymns we mentioned earlier—has been judged by contemporary scholarship to have had its *Sitz im Leben* in the worship of the believing community.[33] As to the choice of the writings that would eventually be recognized as canonical, George Tavard has rightly stressed the part played in the "reception" of a book by the "experience of the Word" as he "imposed himself with power" in the reading of the book "in the continued Pentecost of liturgical worship."[34] Finally, therefore, as to the hermeneutic of Scripture, the liturgical assembly and rite provide a connatural context and purpose.

The canonical Scriptures serve as the internal norm of the Tradition and thereby also as an instrument of its transmission. The fact that, at the sheer level of producing manuscripts, the Scriptures were copied principally for liturgical use is an indication of the purpose of the Tradition in worship. The normativity for the Tradition of the liturgically preserved Scriptures is illustrated by the way their reading has, ordinarily, provided guidance for the ongoing life of the Church and of the individual faithful—and, extraordinarily, sparked reformation or renewal where need or opportunity arose.

IX. Icons

Liturgical icons are characteristic of the Eastern Churches rather than the Western, but help toward understanding and appreciating their action upon the Tradition can be found in some observations of George Tavard concerning the communion of saints. When the international dialogue between the Roman Catholic Church and the World Methodist Council began to tackle the theme of the apostolic Tradition, Tavard proposed to the Joint Commission the serendipitous and fruitful motto of "koinonia in time."[35] Viewing the proclamation of the Gospel in the administration of the sacraments, he noted that "receiving and transmitting the Gospel manifests and promotes the communion of saints, both holy things and holy persons": "Tradition is the tradition of holy things; their reception makes the faithful holy (*Ta agia tois agiois,* 'holy things for the holy,' in the liturgy of St. John Chrysostom)." At each moment, "this Tradition lives from the riches of the Gospel as received from the previous generation[s]," and while "Tradition looks forward, beyond history, to the full epiphany of the divine glory in the kingdom of God," there are "anticipations and previews of the kingdom, when the Church is truly experienced as the communion of saints."

Tavard's stimulation allowed the Singapore 1991 report of the Catholics and the Methodists at several places to view the communion of the saints as both an agent in and a purpose of the apostolic Tradition:[36]

> To be sure that we are hearing the Word, we maintain communion with those who have heard and obeyed the Word before us (18)

> The Holy Spirit has enabled the faithful to confess Christ in every generation, and the Church continues in this communion of saints (33).

> When Christians recite the Creed within a liturgical setting, they do more than list a set of beliefs; they identify themselves with that great company "whose lives are hid with Christ in God" (37).

> In places that are hostile to Christianity, missionary endeavour has been difficult, and fidelity to the Gospel has proved very costly. The picture in Hebrews of the saints who watch from heaven and encourage us is pertinent here (47).

> While all the baptized make up the communion of saints, they also recognize the conspicuous presence of divine grace in specific persons—the Saints—whose lives and example testify, even to the shedding of their blood for Jesus, to the transforming action of the Spirit of God in every generation. The "cloud of witnesses" transcends denominational barriers (66).

> The saints in heaven are held as instances of Christ's "closest love" and as present tokens of the ultimate fulfillment of all God's purposes (75).

Against that background, Western Christians also should be able to recognize that liturgical icons—on the ceilings, walls, screens of the churches—are signs of the cumulative transgenerational presence of the saints amid the earthly worshipping community; or we may say that the contemporary generation of worshippers is lifted to join the heavenly company from all times and places. Once more, the Tradition is displayed as a liturgical event which gathers up past, present, and future.

Everything that has so far been said about varieties of word and sacrament, of persons, functions and liturgical objects, presupposes the presence and action of the Holy Spirit to constitute Christian worship and *ipso facto* the Tradition. As a final, but fundamental, feature of the liturgy we must therefore treat the explicit invocation of the Holy Spirit.

X. The Invocation of the Spirit

In the Eastern Churches again, the Tradition is customarily understood in strongly pneumatological terms. Vladimir Lossky called Tradition "the life of the Holy Spirit in the Church, communicating to each member of the Body of Christ the faculty of hearing, of receiving, of knowing the truth in the Light that belongs to it, and not according to the natural light of human reason."[37] Paul Evdokimov called the Holy Spirit "l'Esprit de la Transmission": "The time of the Spirit is the time of Tradition, essentially marked by its apostolic origins and its openness to the Parousia. . . . The *Acts of the Apostles,* Acts of the Church until the end of the world, constitute the *Gospel of the Holy Spirit.* . . . Even outside the gathering of councils, the epiclesis of conciliarity is permanently operative; it is the epiclesis of Tradition, of the uninterrupted life of the Church."[38]

The term "epiclesis" gives the clue to the constitutively liturgical character of the Tradition. In its technical sense among liturgiologists, the *epiclesis* is the specific prayer to God, appropriately for the Holy Spirit, to consecrate the materials, the assembly, and the action for the realization of the sacramental event. Typical is the *epiclesis* in the Byzantine Liturgy of St. John Chrysostom: "We pray and beseech and entreat you, send down your Holy Spirit on us and on these gifts set forth; and make this bread the precious body of your Christ, changing it by your Holy Spirit, Amen; and that which is in this cup the precious blood of your Christ, changing it by your Holy Spirit, Amen; so that they may become to those who partake for vigilance of soul, for fellowship with the Holy Spirit, for the fullness of the kingdom of heaven, for boldness toward you, not for judgement or condemnation."[39] Suitable variations are made in the case of the elements, actions and purposes of baptism and chrismation,[40] while ordination prayers often have the appearance of a single expanded *epiclesis.*

Despite lingering controversies between East and West over a "moment of consecration" at the Eucharist (reflecting different views on the respective roles of the Trinitarian persons and even perhaps the *filioque* debate), and despite continuing Protestant hesitations over the propriety of invoking the Spirit on "inanimate" elements, the twentieth-century liturgical movement has rediscovered for the West the pneumatological, and even the specifically epicletic, dimension of Christian worship.[41] An ecumenical indication of this is provided by the quite widespread welcome given, even from unexpected quarters, by the responding Churches to the theme of "invocation of the Spirit" in Faith and Order's Lima text, *Baptism, Eucharist and Ministry*.[42] The Anglican Church of Canada, for example, notes that "the emphasis on epiklesis not only restores the importance of the role of the Holy Spirit in the operation of the sacraments, but also it makes clear that the sacraments are prayer actions and not mechanical means of grace," and the Evangelical Lutheran Church of Bavaria "sees expressed [in the efficacy of the Holy Ghost] that the church does not control the gift of the sacrament, but entreats the presence of God. This wards off at the same time a magical understanding of the *verba testamenti*."[43]

What applies focally to specific moments in sacramental rites applies generally to Christian worship in its entirety and thereby to the Tradition: the Holy Spirit is integral to its substantive content and to the traditionary process. Without the Spirit who is invoked in Worship, there is no Tradition or tradition.

XI. *Conclusion*

Two points remain to be briefly made. Defensively, it may be necessary to ward off any charge of "liturgical fundamentalism" that may be raised against the foregoing argument. Positively, I need to redeem my obliquely made promise at the start that my thesis has hopeful implications for ecumenism.

Against any charge of mindless, passive invariability it should be sufficient to affirm that the active and intelligent receptivity called forth by divine Revelation in its originating moments continues to mark Christian worship and the ongoing traditionary process it constitutes. What is received has in fact to be actively and intelligently appropriated, assimilated, and applied in the ever-new here and now. The present and local horizon is intergral to the hermeneutical procedure and to the ritual performance. George Tavard has put the matter well in terms of culture: "At first sight there would seem to be no diversities in regard to the reception of the gospel: all must listen to it (*fides ex auditu*, Rom 10:17), accept it, and live a life of obedience to it (the 'new obedience' of the Reformers). But in fact there is diversity in reception that is due to the inculturation of the gospel in the many cultures of the world. . . . What one receives is the gospel as previously received in a certain culture, expressed in a given language, embodied in certain customs and institutions. This gospel is always in tension with its social context. For the context has been shaped by human traditions that preceded the preaching of the gospel, or that have grown outside of it, or that are more or less in conflict with it, or even that have been inspired by it."[44]

As Tavard recognizes, complex and subtle discernment is therefore required: "The present in which we live affects our reception of the gospel. It colours the way we assimilate it and pass it on. In other words, Tradition, both as reception and as handing on, requires discernment. One should assess the meaning and value of past documents, and one can do this only in the light of contemporary culture and of present needs. Yet there must also be a critical discernment of one's discernment. In the cumulative effect of the Tradition, many things—customs, practices of piety, pious opinions, methods of meditation and self-discipline, ethical conclusions, practical applications—have accrued to the core of Tradition. The community and its members must be capable of sorting out the essential from the permissible, the permanent from the provisional."[45]

That is where the liturgical nature of Tradition comes in and the ecumenical promise of such an understanding and practice. For communities that gather faithfully and expectantly in the name of "Jesus Christ, the same yesterday, today, and forever" open themselves to reformation and renewal by the Triune God who is the origin, sustenance, and goal of the Tradition. It is no accident that the twentieth-century liturgical and ecumenical movements have gone hand in hand, allowing the Churches to converge in their understanding and practice of the gospel as, with the help of the biblical and patristic movements, they have sought to penetrate again to the core of the Tradition and allow it to reconfigure them.[46]

There is still a way to go. But the recovery of unity *coram Deo* is vital, for only as they live together in harmony with one another and in accord with Christ Jesus can Christians fulfill the purpose and reach the goal of Tradition: "with one heart and one voice to glorify the God and Father of our Lord Jesus Christ" (Rom 15:5-6).

Notes

[1] J. B. Bossuet, *Instruction sur les états d'oraison* (1697) Book VI.

[2] It is useful, though sometimes difficult, to make a distinction between Tradition (initial capital) and tradition (lower case). I have tried to follow the usage of the World Conference on Faith and Order at Montreal in 1963 by using a capital T where the stress is on the substantive "*paradosis* of the *kerygma*" and a small t for the transmission process or for particular traditions.

[3] Pierre Benoit, "Le récit de la cène dans Lc. xxii, 15–20," *Revue Biblique* 48 (1939) 386.

[4] Hans Lietzmann, *Messe und Herrenmahl,* 3rd ed. (Berlin: de Gruyter, 1955).

[5] Joachim Jeremias, *Die Abendmahlsworte Jesu,* 3rd ed. (Göttingen: Vandenhoeck & Ruprecht, 1960) 244.

[6] See, for instance, G. Friedrich, *euangelizomai, euangelion,* in G. Kittel, *Theologisches Wörterbuch zum Neuen Testament,* 2:715–33.

[7] Samuel John Stone, *Poems and Hymns* (London: Methuen, 1903) 245.

[8] We know of the practice in Jerusalem from Etheria's *Pilgrimage,* in Rome from Rufinus's *Commentary on the Apostles' Creed,* and in North Africa from Augustine's *Sermons* (56–59 or 212–15). The two-part rite was spread throughout the West. There was geographical variety in the days appointed for its performance. The history may be traced in Alois Stenzel, *Die Taufe: Eine genetische Erklärung der Taufliturgie* (Innsbruck: Rauch, 1958) or in J.D.C. Fisher, *Christian Initiation: Baptism in the Medieval West* (London: SPCK, 1965).

[9] Stenzel distinguishes between a stress at the *redditio symboli* on the accuracy of the candidate's learning of the *content* of the faith (the *fides quae creditur*), on the one hand, and on the other hand, the profession of faith at the baptism itself as the commitment of belief (the *fides qua creditur*). But such a distinction seems a trifle artificial in this context.

[10] Translation largely borrowed from G. J. Cuming, *Hippolytus: A Text for Students* (Bramcote, Notts.: Grove Books, 1976) 19. In a recovery of the Tradition, modern liturgical revision has reclaimed the interrogative form of the profession of faith immediately *before* the baptism, while retaining also the pronouncement by the minister, "I baptize you . . . ," which appears to have been unnecessary as long as the baptismal questions and responses occurred in the water.

[11] Markus Barth, *Die Taufe—ein Sakrament?* (Zollikon-Zürich: Evangelischer Verlag, 1951) 525–54.

[12] For the history, see again Stenzel or Fisher.

[13] Tertullian, *De Oratione,* 1; Cyprian, *De Oratione dominica,* 9.

[14] H. Schürmann, *Das Gebet des Herrn,* 4th ed. (Freiburg: Herder, 1981) 14.

[15] Y. M.-J. Congar, *La Tradition et les traditions* (Paris: Arthème Fayard, 1963) 2:185. In that section (181–91), Congar is treating the liturgy as the first among "les principaux monuments de la Tradition."

[16] Justin, First Apology 67 (for regular Sunday worship) and 65 (for the content of the prayers). Translation from R.C.D. Jasper and G. J. Cuming, *Prayers of the Eucharist: Early and Reformed,* 3rd ed. (New York: Pueblo, 1987) 28–29.

[17] See Paul de Clerck, *La "Prière universelle" dans les liturgies latines anciennes: témoignages patristiques et textes liturgiques* (Münster: Aschendorff, 1977).

[18] Translation from Jasper and Cuming, *Prayers of the Eucharist,* 23.

[19] The dating of the Sanctus in the Eucharistic Prayer and its place in the structure of the various anaphoras is historically debated. See, most recently, B. D. Spinks, *The Sanctus in the Eucharistic Prayer* (Cambridge: Cambridge University Press, 1991).

[20] Translation by John Keble.

[21]First published in 1739, the hymn is found in *The Poetical Works of John and Charles Wesley,* ed. George Osborn (London: Wesleyan-Methodist Conference Office, 1868) 1:187–88, and in many Methodist and other hymnals.

[22]First published in 1758 under the title "Thy Kingdom Come," the hymn is found in *The Poetical Works,* ed. Osborn (1870) 6:143–44, and in many Methodist and other hymnals.

[23]It is, of course, the martyrs who by their "baptism of blood" most powerfully embody the Tradition of the gospel and the faith.

[24]Translation from Paul F. Bradshaw, *Ordination Rites of the Ancient Churches of East and West* (New York: Pueblo, 1990) 107.

[25]*Sacrosanctum Concilium,* 41. Translation from the International Commission on English in the Liturgy, *Documents on the Liturgy 1963–1969* (Collegeville: The Liturgical Press, 1982) 12–13.

[26]See Bernard Cooke, *Ministry to Word and Sacraments* (Philadelphia: Fortress Press, 1976) 78, 85, 255–56, 430.

[27]Bradshaw, *Ordination Rites, 133.*

[28]Ibid., 130.

[29]Ibid., 171–72, 164, 184 respectively.

[30]Ibid., 229.

[31]C. K. Barrett, *The Epistle to the Romans* (London: Black, 1957) 24.

[32]See Stenzel, *Die Taufe,* esp. 64–67, 151–52 (n. 251), 189–93.

[33]For a summary including both the Old Testament and the New Testament material, see G. Wainwright, *Doxology* (New York: Oxford University Press, 1980) 151–63.

[34]George Tavard, *Holy Writ or Holy Church: The Crisis of the Protestant Reformation* (London: Burns & Oates, 1959) 6–8.

[35]George Tavard, "Tradition as Koinonia in Historical Perspective," *One in Christ* 24 (1988) 97–111.

[36]*The Apostolic Tradition: Report of the Joint Commission between the Roman Catholic Church and the World Methodist Council, Fifth Series, 1986–1991,* reprinted in several places, such as *Origins* 21 (September 19, 1991) 237–47, *Catholic International* 3 (February 1–14, 1992) 106–20, and *One in Christ* 28 (1992) 49–73.

[37]Vladimir Lossky, *In the Image and Likeness of God* (Crestwood, N.Y.: St. Vladimir's Seminary Press, 1974) 141–68 ("Tradition and traditions") here 152.

[38]Paul Evdokimov, *L'Orthodoxie* (Neuchâtel: Delachaux et Niestlé, 1959)196–97.

[39]Translation from Jasper and Cuming, *Prayers of the Eucharist,* 133.

[40]See E.G.C.F. Atchley, *On the Epiclesis of the Eucharistic Liturgy and in the Consecration of the Font* (London: Oxford University Press, 1935).

[41]See John H. McKenna, *Eucharist and Holy Spirit: The Eucharistic Epiclesis in Twentieth-Century Theology* (Great Wakering, Essex: Mayhew-McCrimmon, 1975).

[42]See *Baptism, Eucharist and Ministry 1982–1990: Report on the Process and Responses,* Faith and Order Paper No. 149 (Geneva: World Council of Churches, 1990) 67–68, 114–16.

[43]Ibid., 68.

[44]Tavard, "Tradition as Koinonia in Historical Perspective," 101–02.

[45]Ibid., 107.

[46]See G. Wainwright, "Renewing Worship: The Recovery of Classical Patterns," *Theology Today* 48 (April 1991) 45–55.

9

Tradition as a Point of Contact between Anglicans and Roman Catholics in the Nineteenth Century: The Case of Johann Adam Möhler and Edward Bouverie Pusey

R. William Franklin

I.

Johann Adam Möhler (1796–1838) was one of the circle of young Roman Catholic theologians at the University of Tübingen in the south-western German kingdom of Württemberg who provided a Christian response to modernization during the middle years of the age of revolution, 1825 to 1838. Möhler was born into the patchwork of tiny German states stitched together between Bavaria in the east, Baden in the west, and the Rhineland in the north. He grew up amid the ruination of Roman Catholic institutions in Germany which was the result of Napoleon's *Reichsdeputationshauptschluss* of 1803, at a time when such aspects of Tradition as celibacy for the ordained and allegiance to the papacy were being questioned by German Catholics.

At one point Möhler was educated in Berlin under the shadow of a militaristic Prussia rising among the German states. In 1835 he was forced out of the University of Tübingen by the Protestant king of Württemberg. Napoleon, Prussia, and the plight of Catholics in his native Württemberg set the political stage from which Möhler issued two of the most influential works of nineteenth-century ecclesiology: *Die Einheit*, or *The Unity in the Church*, of 1825, and *Der Symbolik*, or *The Symbolism*, of 1832.[1]

To Möhler the essence of the Church of 1825 was the entire people of God, not the hierarchy alone. The fundamental shift in his ecclesiology matched the radical change in Europe from monarchy to an era when "We the People" had become the motto of an age. In an age of revolution that witnessed not only the liberation of the people but also the threat of a new absolutism as represented by Napoleon, Prussia, or Württemberg, Möhler beheld Christianity not as the rules and dogma of hierarchy, but as a higher way of life made available to all people.

From this perspective it is possible to place Möhler in the nineteenth-century pantheon alongside Daniel O'Connell or Abraham Lincoln, as a theological emancipator of the laity, and yet it is also possible to define the Möhlerian project as a significant restatement of Catholic teaching on Tradition for the new conditions of the nineteenth century. Möhler manufactured an ecclesiology that was an alloy, a dynamic evolving along a creative "middle-way" that was at once conservative, in that it looked to the Tradition of the past defined as the institutional structures of the Christian faith that had grown up during the first centuries, as a standard for the contemporary church, and progressive, in that it sought to create a revived community life for the laity appropriate to modern conditions.

On the progressive side, because he believed that the celebration of the Eucharist pointed to the essential communal nature of the Church, Möhler issued a revolutionary call for a return to the earliest structures of Christian worship in which the assembly of the laity united in the closest possible manner with everything that was said and done at the altar by the presider. At a time when Roman Catholic prelates were not disturbed that the laity had little idea of what was happening at a Mass, did not receive communion within the Mass, and did not join their voices to the priest during the Mass propers, Möhler campaigned against private Masses, he called for a return of the communion cup to the laity at Mass after a millennium of denial, and in the Tübingen Catholic journal *Theologische Quartalschrift* he mocked the current arguments that the language of the liturgy should be Latin because of its antiquity and its ability to build up a worldwide human unity. "Such a unity!" he wrote in 1825, "a unity based on ignorance and as for antiquity, why not use Hebrew in the liturgy? . . . Let the people understand their prayers."[2]

On the conservative side, Möhler defended Catholic Tradition as the institutional arch upon which each Christian community must be constructed so that the *koinonia* of worship, participation and fellowship, might be translated into the concrete realities of *diakonia*, Christian service that humanizes an increasingly fragmented modern society. "Tradition," in Möhler's definition, "is the expression through the centuries—at every moment living, and at the same time taking body—of the Holy Spirit who animates the totality of the faithful."[3]

Such a definition of the Church as corporate totality with mystical Spirit, rather than as a legal entity in the manner of the seventeenth-century theologian Robert Bellarmine who perceived the Church as a militant *perfect society* of ordered ranks "like the Kingdom of France or the Republic of Venice," is based by Möhler on the incarnation.[4] From the perspective of the Vatican II era, the significant advance of Möhler's incarnational ecclesiology was that it bridged the post-Tridentine chasm between people and Tradition, fusing the two with his popularization of the term *sensus fidelium* and narrowing the distinctions for the future by reviving the Pauline and patristic metaphor of the Church as "the body of Christ." In the fifteenth century a book that had sought to revive Augustine's formulation of the Church as "body of Christ" had been condemned by the Council of Basel as "offensive to pious ears."[5] Now in Möhler the Church, with its structured tradition of primate, episcopate, presbyterate, and *sensus fidelium*, is a visible divinely constituted body which is the manifestation of Christ's saving mercy. The celebration of the Eucharist is the supreme action by which each Christian comes into her or his own as a member of Christ's body. This linking of Eucharistic fellowship to the concrete institutions of the Church, Möhler's revival of the phrases "the Church as the mystical body of Christ" and *sensus fidelium*, and as well as the merging of Tradition into "the flow from the same divine well spring" as Scripture, each of these advances in ecclesiology came to stand behind the thinking of the German and French Roman Catholic theologians, including George Tavard, who fashioned a revised understanding of Tradition at Vatican II.[6]

Those theologians who prepared the way for a change of thinking on Tradition, from Cardinal Ratzinger and Hans Küng to Yves Congar, would all admit of some debt to Möhler. Congar wrote: "Thanks to Pierre Chenu, I was given the first idea, global in its implication, of Möhler. . . . I felt that I had not only found a breach in the bastion of the post-Tridentine Church, but an inspiration, a source, a new synthesis."[7] And George Tavard has defined Möhler's significance this way: "Modern Catholic ecclesiology . . . began to mushroom in the second half of the nineteenth century. The movement started in Germany where the school of Tübingen, notably with Johann Adam Möhler . . . saw the Church primarily as a living organism led by the Spirit."[8] The strength of Möhler's synthesis of people and Tradition was that it was grounded upon a return to the Church of the first seven centuries, to the patristic era, as the model of a new Catholicism for the age of revolution.

II.

Edward Bouverie Pusey (1800–1882) was, with John Keble and John Henry Newman, one of the leaders of the Oxford Movement (1833–1845), the beginning of a revival of Catholic Tradition within the Church of England. Pusey and his allies maintained that the established Church was not the *Protestant* Church *of* England but the *Catholic* Church *in* England, and they fashioned their *Tracts for Times* into instruments for a second, and Catholic, reformation in England. In its own day the Oxford Movement was viewed by some as a suspect, Continental challenge to Protestant hegemony, though it was launched by a group of Anglicans at the heart of the British academic establishment. Yet in reviving Catholic Tradition within Anglicanism, Pusey, like Möhler, rejected the Continental, Roman concepts of his day, such as "perfect society" that identified the Church with hierarchy. He came to see, with Möhler, that the times required communities of faith showing how to keep the fast as well as the festival.

It was Pusey who turned the Oxford Movement away from the better-funded parishes controlled by some of the most reactionary elements in British society and urged that the Anglican Catholic revival should focus on the modern cities and outcasts of urban society, rather than on the gentry and on areas of former population concentration where the comfortable parishes were located. The established church had based its power and its privileges upon an alliance with the country gentry. Pusey had grown up among the landed aristocracy, and he had been appointed Regius Professor of Hebrew at Oxford in 1828 by the Tory Duke of Wellington when the previous incumbent in the chair, Dr. Nicoll, had died prematurely, some said, from breathing too much dust in in Oxford's Bodleian Library.[9]

But to the new Regius Professor at Oxford the old Anglican establishment, with episcopal palace, country parsonage with fire and sherry, the bare worship, these were not to be the ideal for modern Anglicanism. It is for this reason that in September 1833 Pusey launched a campaign to build "Eucharistic" parish churches in the new industrial cities of Britain.

Pusey linked the network of new parishes as liturgical, architectural and pastoral advisor and guest preacher until his death in 1882.[10]

A central theme in Pusey's preaching and in the practical machinery of these parishes was the patristic focus on the incarnation of Jesus and on Christian Tradition, handed down in both the institutions and liturgies of the Church, as a reflection of the incarnation and therefore central, not peripheral, to the life of the Christian community. Christ-Church-Eucharist: for Pusey, as for the Fathers and Möhler, these three are essentially one mystery; the liberating power of God is unleashed through the coming of Christ, through the Church, and the Eucharist to restore the dignity of man and woman amid dehumanizing circumstances through the liturgical and institutional Tradition of the Church.

The Fathers thus provided the theological vocabulary for Pusey as he turned the Anglican Catholic revival into a movement that focused primarily on the restoration of the centrality of Eucharistic worship in the life of a parish. In the atmosphere of the mechanized world of Victorian Britain, Pusey found that in order to make worship the act of all present who are members of Christ's body, the people's work—the patristic word for Eucharist until the fifth century is *leitourgia* (the people's work)—the Eucharist, rather than morning prayer, should be celebrated weekly. Pusey's revival of the patristic tradition that held the Eucharist to be the action of a communal body is expressed in two lines from a hymn of his ally, the prime minister of England, W. E. Gladstone:

> We who with one blest Food are fed
> Into one body may we grow.[11]

The Church as a community under the figure of the body of Christ, worship as the act of a community that receives this body of Christ under the form of bread: these key themes of Puseyite Anglican Catholicism are all a part of a nineteenth-century revival of patristic Tradition within the Church of England. Pusey himself defined "Puseyism" as "in a word, reference to the Ancient Church, instead of the Reformers, as the ultimate expounder of our Church."[12]

From this perspective it is possible to view Puseyism as a distinctive stream within the Anglican Catholic revival, one that was patristic rather than Roman in its definition of Catholicism, one that was urban rather than rural in defining the new focus of Christian action in the era of modernization. In 1943, in his classic *The Shape of the Liturgy,* Dom Gregory Dix, the most influential figure in the enterprise of twentieth-century Anglican liturgical revision, captured the significance of the urban, parochial expressions of Puseyism in one sentence: "The Oxford Movement turned to the parishes and taught the parish priests and the laity in great numbers to think of the eucharistic action as the patristic authors had thought of it."[13] It is this pointing to a local community centered about the Eucharist that distinguished Pusey's revival of patristic Tradition from that of the seventeenth-century Anglicans Pearson and Bull or that of the nineteenth-century American High Church Episcopalian John Henry Hobart.[14] In time Pusey's revival of patristic Tradition that focused on the Eucharistic liturgy transformed the worship of the Church of England in such a way as to lead to the parish communion, to the replacement of morning prayer as the normal way of Anglican Sunday worship. As a result of this process initiated within Anglicanism by E. B. Pusey and from the perspective of the change to a vernacular Roman Catholic liturgy at Vatican II, at last the English liturgy derived from Thomas Cranmer and the Catholic liturgy derived from the Council of Trent were hardly to be distinguished.

III.

In a commentary on the parallel evolution of Anglican and Roman Catholic understanding of Tradition and liturgy which achieved this remarkable convergence in the 1960s, the Archbishop of Canterbury Michael Ramsey, wrote: "It is of little importance here to know whether this point of convergence is eschatological or belongs to history. . . . It is a process in which the Catholic Church will continue to reform and purify herself, to develop in herself, and if need be to rediscover any values which are hers but which, in her present state in time, she does not integrally honor."[15] The coincidence of the appearance, of the survival, and of the eventual triumph of these two figures in England and Germany, quite similar in their expressions of Christianity, demands a proper explanation today. The Oxford Tractarians and Pusey, Möhler and the Tübingen school were each movements launched to restore the Catholic conception of Christianity for the first generation of Europeans forced to confront a democratic, industrial, and predominantly secular civilization. Their similarities suggest that a root of the modern ecumenical movement can be found in the parallel attempts, a century and a half ago, in a variety of nations and denominations, to adapt Christianity to the forces of modernization, political, and industrial revolution.

The hunt for a connection between the Tübingen School and the Oxford Movement has in fact engaged scholars since the nineteenth century. Lord Acton was convinced that Möhler had directly influenced the Tractarian view of apostolic Tradition as an authoritative tradition, derived from the Lord, and transmitted through the Christian community to the present. Gladstone reviewed Möhler's *Symbolism* in 1845 and noted with appreciation the German's reconciliation of Tradition with history understood as movement and change. Frederick Oakely and W. G. Ward cited Möhler frequently in their articles in the *British Critic,* one of the main organs of the Oxford Movement. William Palmer went as far as to say that Möhler and de Maistre were the two favorite authors of the *British Critic.* In *The Development of Christian Doctrine* Newman himself cites Möhler as one who had already said much the same thing on the living Tradition of the Church embodied in the liturgy and in the episcopate, as well as in the *sensus fidelium,* as Newman had, in the preface to his *Die Einheit* and in *Der Symbolik.*[16]

On the German side, the Tübingen theologian maintained a great interest in the Church of England, but his only direct contact with Anglicanism was the Anglican congregation at Baden-Baden, to which Möhler would travel for leisurely summer cures. He wrote four articles in 1827, 1828, and 1830 on the Church of England. Two are on Anselm and the Church of his time, and two deal with England in the era of Bishop Milner.[17] There were two important discussions of Puseyism in the *Theologische Quartalschrift* written by Möhler's teacher J. S. Drey, emphasizing the parallel concerns of the Tübingen School and the Oxford Movement: "Das Wesen der Puseyitischen Doctrin" and "Die rückläufige Bewegung im Protestantismus und ihre Bedeutung."[18] Möhler was also convinced that a new theology of the Church, written in the spirit of the times, would be a point of contact for the future. He predicted in the *Symbolik* "that this is the point at which Catholics and Protestants will, in great multitudes, one day meet, and stretch a friendly hand one to the other. Both, conscious of guilt, must exclaim, 'We all have erred—it is the Church only which cannot err; we all have sinned—the Church only is spotless on earth.' "[19]

IV.

Yet beyond all these connections there is one overriding fact that explains a convergence in Möhler and Pusey on Tradition. Northern German Protestantism, decisively shaped by Romanticism, nurtured Möhler's concept of Tradition when the Tübingen Catholic faculty made the extraordinary gesture of sending the young priest north to the University of Berlin for further study from the fall of 1822 to the spring of 1823. Möhler travelled to Berlin not without a certain anxiety, and he found himself harassed there by the extremely high cost of food and lodging and by the excessive police-like ambience of Prussia. But such discomfort was dislodged by the learning and piety he found in the city, and he wrote back to the Tübingen faculty: "This place where Schleiermacher, Neander, Marheinecke, Strauss . . . teach deserves alone a half-year visit. The spirituality, the deep earnestness, with which scientific investigation is carried on, the true religiosity which penetrates all the teachers, the unusual recognition of the contributions of other churches . . . the love of the students and the lively interest in their education as well as for their spiritual advancement distinguishes this theological faculty above all others."[20]

In a parallel gesture, knowing of Pusey's troubles with the interpretation of Scripture, Dr. Lloyd, the Bishop of Oxford and Pusey's patron, suggested to him in 1825 that a young English theologian might best acquire the tools of biblical scholarship at the German universities. Pusey remembered years later: "One day Dr. Lloyd said to me, 'I wish you would learn something about those German critics . . . .' My life turned on that hint of Lloyds's."[21] Pusey left London for Göttingen and Berlin in 1825, and he returned again in 1826. Remaining in Germany through late 1827, he mastered enough Syriac, Chaldee, and Rabbinic to read the Jewish and Arabic commentators on the Hebrew Bible; but what was to be most important for the future development of Anglicanism was that through Schleiermacher Pusey also became acquainted with the Berlin church historian Augustus Neander, whose lecture series "Introduction to the Fathers" Pusey audited in 1825 and whose entire course on ecclesiastical history he attended in 1826. That same year Pusey formed a lasting friendship with Augustus Tholuck, the director of the German Bible Society, who had popularized in Germany the patristic method of interpretation of biblical texts.

Thus both Möhler and Pusey arrived in Berlin at almost the same time amid a great flowering in north German Protestantism, characterized by Lord Acton as having "no parallel in modern history except the revival of the fifteenth century, to which it bears a real resemblance."[22] A revival of patristic Tradition formed a central part of this Protestant renaissance, for Möhler and Pusey were in Berlin while Augustus Neander was lecturing from the notes of the first volume of his *Allgemeine Geschichte der Christlichen Religion und Kirche,* which covered the first seven centuries of the Church. Neander had been converted to Christianity by Schleiermacher's

Halle lectures in 1806, and he began teaching history at the University of Berlin in 1813. He began his career with studies of the fourth century, *Über den Kaiser Julianus und sein Zeitalter* (1812), and then he wrote on the Gnostics, *Genetische Entwicklung der Vornehmsten Gnostischen Systeme* (1818), and the eras of Chrysostom, *Der heilige Chrysostomus und die Kirche in dessen Zeitalter* (1820) and *Tertullian* (1825). In these books and in his lectures Neander presented this patristic material in the context of a contemporary dilemma: Europeans were now living "in a time of great crisis" and God was working in this generation of revolution to set right the imbalances of Christianity. For the Enlightenment had turned faith into a rational exercise divorced from liturgy, and the Evangelical movement of the German Pietists had dangerously weakened the institutional expressions of Christianity.[23] By contrast, Neander maintained that Jesus Christ had left institutional and liturgical means, Tradition, to his Church for the purposes of stability and growth. In this passage Neander provided a definition of a living and growing Tradition, rooted in the Fathers, that would prove useful to others later on: "With the inner fellowship, Christianity produced among its professors from the first a living outward union, whereby the distantly separated were brought near to each other. This union must be realized in a determinant form, which later was conditioned by the existing forms of social life."[24] Neander the German Protestant thus set before the Roman Catholic and the Anglican the forgotten world of the patristic Church: the intense consciousness of human solidarity in the institutions of the Church expressed in the writings of the Fathers and Mothers; the fellowship, sharing, and corporate celebration the Church experienced in its liturgical worship; the essential vision of the patristic Church as an institution propagating itself in opposition to the dominant pagan power.

These ideas were immediately attractive to Möhler. He wrote back to Tübingen in 1824: "Neander's lectures will be unforgettable to me. . . . He knows no one among his colleagues as thoroughly as he knows Origen, Tertullian, Augustine, Chrysostom, and St. Bernard. I went often to see him when he was alone as well as when he was in society. I spoke with him about the great historical subjects and works which I have had in view."[25] To Möhler's friend Heinrich Kihn, the contact with Neander in Berlin was the central turning point of Möhler's life, for it was the Protestant historian who directed him to the study of the Fathers, the inspiration that shaped all of his later work. In turn, through the *Theologische Quartalschrift* Möhler introduced Neander to the Roman Catholic priests of Württemberg. From 1824 at the University of Tübingen he conducted a lecture series on the patristic era, and the notes for his discussion of Jerome, Augustine, Leo, Gregory the Great, Athanasius, Chrysostom, Gregory of Nazianzus, and Basil the Great are all taken from Neander. Möhler remarked that this literature was "the tableau of my being";[26] he confided to his friend Lipp in 1825: "Earlier I had only the word, only the naked concept of Christianity. . . . The earnest study of the Fathers excited me. In them I have discovered for the first time a . . . Christianity as Christ himself wanted it . . . ."[27] We witness Möhler in these lectures translating the Romantic concept of community into an ecclesiology which associates the people once again with Tradition through the concept of *sensus fidelium*. It was Neander who opened the door to this synthesis which would be so vital for the future of Roman Catholicism.

V.

For his part, in a letter to Bishop Lloyd in August 1826, Pusey noted also his acceptance of the habit of "the orthodox [school in Berlin's characteristic of] going back almost exclusively to the Fathers."[28] Pusey also returned from Berlin with twelve volumes of Chrysostom and with the works of Clement of Alexandria, Tertullian, Gregory of Nazianzus, Cyril of Jerusalem, Cyprian, Jerome, Irenaeus, and Augustine, as well as Neander's own monographs devoted to the study of Chrysostom, Bernard, Tertullian, the Gnostics, and the era of Julian. In 1832 he was still using these volumes when he wrote to Newman, "I should be also much obliged to you to send me the three first volumes of Neander's *Kirchengeschichte* in my study . . . ;"[29] and A. P. Stanley has provided this description of Pusey's Oxford classroom in 1838:

> The whole atmosphere of the Professor breathed the spirit of Germany to a degree which I am convinced could have been found in no other lecture room in Oxford. . . . The table was piled with German commentaries . . . to these lectures I certainly look back as to the most instructive which I attended in Oxford. . . . And it is certainly not from agreement with the peculiar views which the Professor extracted from the Fathers. . . .[30]

We see three results in Anglicanism of these "peculiar views which the Professor extracted from the Fathers" after his period of study in Berlin. Pusey's Oxford lectures in the Hebrew Chair, which reached a final form in 1836 under the title "Lectures on Prophecies and Types of Our Lord in the Old Testament," provided a national platform for Pusey's revival of patristic Tradition within nineteenth-century Anglicanism. The lectures present salvation history as a story of God's choice of men and women as members of a given community, "a people"; and the relationship of the Jewish people to God is presented as typical of the understanding of the Christian Church as a community under the figure of the body of Christ. One continues in this living, organic relationship with others in the Church through an aspect of Tradition, by taking nourishment, Christ's body and blood, at the Eucharist.[31]

The Library of the Fathers of the Holy Catholic Church, whose publication was begun in 1838 and continued until 1885 when forty-eight volumes had been issued, was a second attempt by Pusey to propagate the tradition of the Fathers in order to reform the English Church. In 1845, the year of Newman's conversion to Rome, Pusey wrote to W. J. Copeland that these editions of the Fathers had provided a foundation of Catholic Tradition that was not threatened by the spectre of the Roman See:

> Then as to authorities: when not employed in Hebrew, I used to live "in the Fathers." . . . They have been these many years the same comfort to me as modern Roman writers have been a discomfort to you. . . . I read them, learn of them, live among them, as a child; adopt their words, say what they say, do not say what they do not. . . . Theirs is my native language.[32]

Baron Bunsen, the most distinguished representative of German Protestantism in Britain, went to Christ Church in the 1830s to visit the Professor of Hebrew, in order to discuss the patristic authors Ignatius of Antioch and Hippolytus of Rome, and he wrote later in his journal: "Breakfasted with Pusey upon ham and speculative philosophy. . . . He is a most unique union of a practical Englishman and an intellectual German."[33] What is interesting here is not only the German reference but the mention of Pusey's practicality, for Bunsen knew that in the 1830s Pusey advocated the founding of a series of parish churches as the practical laboratories of his revived interest in patristic Tradition in the nineteenth century. For example, at Christ Church, Hoxton, in 1851 Pusey wished the priest to face the congregation across the altar at the celebration of the Eucharist, as had been the custom in the first centuries. "One most grievous offense seems to be turning your back to the people," he wrote the Vicar. "It certainly seemed against the Rubric, that the consecration should take place so that they cannot see. . . . It was, as you know, in some old Roman churches the custom to consecrate behind the altar [facing the people]. This too might have its meaning; and the eyes of the people might be more directed to the oblation."[34]

Though this instruction must have seemed odd at the time, it has now become almost the universal practice of Anglican Christendom. By such liturgical, architectural, and pastoral means, nineteenth-century parish churches in England were a third venue which was crucial to the survival of Pusey-ism as a distinctive movement outside the lecture room and into the twentieth century.

VI.

The role of Berlin in these Catholic revivals of the nineteenth century was later denied by both Anglicans and Roman Catholics, and two world wars did not help matters any. Yet to be understood in its fullness, the Catholic revival must be seen as part of such an international cultural dynamic in which Christianity, confronted by modernization, turned back to themes of people and Tradition which marked the pre-Constantinian era, a dynamic that owed much to the realization that, with the spread of mechanical power and the displacement of monarchy, the social order that had been in existence for over a thousand years in western civilization had come to an end. In 1842 the great Catholic church historian J.J.I. von Döllinger recognized the same spirit of this dynamic growing in Pusey that he saw dawning in his Munich colleague Johann Adam Möhler. Döllinger wrote to Pusey in 1842 and again in 1866 that "everything with us in Germany also points more and more distinctly towards a drawing together of kindred elements . . . . Inwardly we are united in our religious conviction, although externally we belong to two separated churches."[35]

From the perspective of the ecumenical movement, this point of contact between Anglicans and Roman Catholics in the nineteenth century is an important phenomenon because it demonstrates the existence of a much more venerable dynamic toward Christian unity between Anglican and Roman Catholics than many may have imagined, one that has taken many forms and has many sources and lines of descent far transcending the fortunes of twentieth-century ecumenism. The forces of history, the chance encounter, the accidental friendship all play a role in this dynamic, alongside the official texts and congresses that constitute the history of the ecumenical movement. But amid all of this the constant factor has been the Christian individual, more often than not the quiet academic, who has seized the opportunity and marshalled the potential of each ecumenical moment that has marked the stages of this dynamic. George Tavard can best be understood against this background, which is far larger than Vatican II and his generation, a background before which he, with resources of faith and hope like Möhler and Pusey, beckons us forward to see a Christian *consummatio* as part of the fulfillment of humanity destined for the future.

Notes

[1] *Die Einheit in der Kirche oder das Prinzip des Katholizismus, dargestellt im Geiste der Kirchenvater der drei ersten Jahrhunderte,* ed. and commentary Josef Rupert Geiselmann (Cologne. Jakob Hegner, 1957); other editions of this in 1825, 1843, and 1925. *Symbolik oder Darstellung der dogmatischen Gegensätze der Katholiker und Protestanten nach ihren öffentlichen Bekenntnisschriften* (Cologne: Jakob Hegner, 1958). Thirteen editions of *Symbolik* have been published in Germany. For a complete bibliography of the works of Möhler, and list of all translations, see Jochen Köhler, Carola Zimmermann, and Rudolf Reinhardt, *Verzeichnis der gedruckten Arbeiten Johann Adam Möhlers (1796–1838)* (Göttingen: Vandenhoeck & Ruprecht, 1975).

[2] J. A. Möhler, "Rezension: F. Walter, *Lehrbuch des Kirchenrechts mit Berucksichtigung der neuesten Verhaltnisse,*" *Theologische Quartalschrift* (hereinafter cited as ThQ) 5 (1823) 263–99; "Rezension: C.F.L. Schaaf, *Die Kirchen-Agendensache in dem preussischen Staate,*" ThQ 7 (1825) 285–92.

[3] *Einheit,* 121. The most important work on Möhler and tradition is Josef Rupert Geiselmann, *Lebendiger Glaube aus geheiligter Überlieferung; Der Grundgedanke der Theologie Johann Adam Möhlers und der katholischen Tübingen Schule* (Freiburg: Herder, 1966).

[4] Bellarmine in Peter Nichols, *The Pope's Divisions* (London: Penguin Books, 1981) 107. On the contrasting ideal of the Church as "perfect society" see Patrick Granfield, "The Church as *Societas Perfecta* in the Schemata of Vatican I," *Church History* 48 (1979) 431–46; and Knut Walf, "Die katholische kirche—eine 'Societas Perfecta'?" ThQ 157 (1977) 107–18.

[5] The Council of Basel (1439) in Godfrey Diekmann, *Come, Let Us Worship* (Baltimore: Jelicon Press, 1961) 15.

[6] *Dei verbum* (1965) ¶9. For an overview of the evolution see K. McNamara, "From Möhler to Vatican II: The Modern Movement in Ecclesiology," ed. K. McNamara, *Vatican II, the Constitution on the Church: A Theological and Pastoral Commentary* (Chicago: Franciscan Herald Press, 1968).

[7] Yves Congar, "Johann Adam Möhler," ThQ 150 (1970) 47; see also Yves Congar, "Sur l'évolution et l'interpretation de la penseé de Moehler," *Revue des Sciences Philosophiques et Théologiques* 27:2 (1938) 204–12. See also Yves Congar, *Tradition and Traditions: An Historical and a Theological Essay* (New York: Burns & Oates, 1966).

[8] George H. Tavard, *The Church, Community of Salvation: An Ecumenical Ecclesiology* (Collegeville: The Liturgical Press, 1992) 8.

[9] A bibliographical list of the printed works of Pusey appears in H. P. Liddon, *Life of Edward Bouverie Pusey* IV (London: Longmans, Green, and Co., 1898) 396–446. Aside from this monumental biography of Liddon, Pusey is without a full modern life, though there have been recent studies of aspects of him in A. G. Lough, *Dr. Pusey* (1981), *Pusey Rediscovered,* ed. Perry Butler (1985), and David Forrester, *Young Dr. Pusey* (1989).

[10] By the year of his death in 1882 more than five hundred out of fourteen thousand Anglican parishes in England and Wales were celebrating the Eucharist as the principal service of worship on Sunday morning, with the clergy often wearing Eucharistic vestments, the invariable standard of a Puseyite church. For recent surveys of Puseyism in the parish see Geoffrey Rowell, *The Vision Glorious* (Oxford: Oxford University, 1983) 71–97, 116–40; and Stephen Savage and Christopher Tyne, *The Labours of Years* (Cowley: Church Army Press, 1976).

[11]*The English Hymnal*, 1933, no. 322. For the extent to which Gladstone might be described as a Puseyite see Perry Butler, *Gladstone: Church, State, and Tractariansim* (Oxford: Oxford University Press, 1982).

[12]E. B. Pusey, "What is Puseyism?": H. P. Liddon, *Life of Pusey II* (London: Longmans, Green, and Co., 1894) 140–41. To Victorians generally, "Puseyism" was, in the words of John Wolffe, "an unfocused term of abuse," as in Thomas Carlyle's phrase "to procreate a spectral Puseyism."

[13]Gregory Dix, *The Shape of the Liturgy* (London: Dacre Press, 1945) 717. See also Donald Gray, *Earth and Altar: The Evolution of the Parish Communion in the Church of England* (Norwick: Alcuin Club, 1986) which charts the terrain from the nineteenth-century parishes to Dix; and also Kenneth W. Stevenson, *Gregory Dix Twenty-Five Years On* (Bramcote: Grove Books, 1977).

[14]For a comparison of these patristic models see Robert Bruce Mullin, *Episcopal Vision/American Reality: High Church Theology in Evangelical America* (New Haven: Yale University Press, 1986).

[15]Michael Ramsey and Leon-Joseph Cardinal Suenens, *The Future of the Christian Church* (New York: Paulist Press, 1970) 66.

[16]These connections are discussed in Owen Chadwick, *From Bossuet to Newman* (Cambridge: Cambridge University Press, 1957) 112, 114–18; Edmond Vermeil, *Jean-Adam Moehler et l'École Catholique de Tübingen* (Paris: Armand Colin, 1913) 454ff.; Henry Tristram, "J. A. Möhler et J. H. Newman, la penseé allemande et la renaissance Catholique," *Revue des Sciences Philosophiques et Théologiques* 2 (1938) 184–204; and Robert Greenfield, MS., "The Attitude of the Tractarians to the Roman Catholic Church: 1833–1850" (D.Phil. diss.: Oxford University, 1957) 368–73.

[17]J. A. Möhler, "Anselm, Erzbischof von Canterbury," ThQ 9 (1827) 435–97, 585–664; and "Die Scholastik des Anselmus," ThQ 10 (1828) 62–130; "John Milner, Ziel und Ende religiöser Controversen," ThQ 10 (1828) 337–47; and "John Milner, Briefe an einen Pfründer," ThQ 12 (1830) 118–51.

[18]ThQ 26 (1844) 4–56, 417–57. For the connections see Stephan Lösch, "J. A. Möhler und die Theologie Englands im 19. Jahrhundert," *Rottenburger Monatschrift für praktische Theologie* 6 (1922–1923) 198–202, 221–27; and I. A. Willoughby, "On Some German Affinities With the Oxford Movement," *The Modern Language Review* 29:1 (1934) 52–66.

[19]*Symbolik*, 349.

[20]Stefan Lösch, *Johann Adam Möhler: Gesammelte Aktenstücke und Briefe* (Munich: Beck, 1928) 89–90.

[21]H. P. Liddon, *Life of Pusey I* (London: Longmans, Green, and Co., 1893) 72.

[22]J.E.E.D. Acton, *Essays on Church and State* (London: Hollis and Carter, 1952) 66. A recent article that sets the context for the revival of Church history in Germany at the turn of the nineteenth century is Gustav A. Benrath, "Evangelische und Katholische Kirchenhistorie im Zeichen der Aufklarung und der Romantik," *Zeitschrift für Kirchengeschichte* 82 (1971) 211–31.

[23]Augustus Neander, *History of the Planting and Training of the Christian Church* (Edinburgh: T. & T. Clark, 1842) VI.

[24]Ibid., 181, 201–02.

[25]Lösch, *Möhler*, 83–84.

[26]Alois Knöpfler, *Johann Adam Möhler: Ein Gedenkblatt zu dessen hundertstem Geburtstage* (Munich: Reinhardt, 1896) 42. Möhler discusses Neander in "Über Justin Apologie I c. 6 Gegen die Auslegung dieser Stelle von Neander," ThQ 15 (1833) 49–60; and in reviews of Neander's books in the same journal: 6 (1824) 262–80 and 7 (1825) 646–64.

[27]Lösch, *Möhler*, 251.

[28]MS. letter of Pusey to Bishop Lloyd, August 29, 1826, Pusey House, Oxford. Pusey's detailed reports and letters from Germany are documented at Pusey House in the collection of manuscripts "German Correspondence of E. B. Pusey."

[29]MS. letter of Pusey to Newman, July 13, 1832, Pusey House, Oxford.

[30]E.G.W. Bill, *University Reform in Nineteenth Century Oxford 1811–1885* (Oxford: Oxford University Press, 1973) 252–53.

[31]The lectures have never been published and they are found among the manuscript volumes of Pusey House. However, the arguments appear in germ in Pusey's *Tracts 67, 68, 69* (1835) and in a more developed later form in his *Tract 81* (1837). On the role of the lectures see David Jasper, "Pusey's Lectures on Types and Prophecies of the Old Testament": Butler, *Pusey Rediscovered*, 71–118.

[32]MS. letter of Pusey to W. J. Copland, 1845, Pusey House, Oxford. On these points see particularly Pusey's introductions to *Tertullian* (1854) and *The Confessions of Saint Augustine* (1876). The Library initially secured eight hundred subscribers who wished to see "the Fathers of the Catholic Church rather than non-Conformist authors in the hands of the clergy."

[33]*Memoirs of Baron Bunsen* (1838) quoted in *Literary Supplement of Agricultural Gazette* (March 3, 1879) n.p.

[34]Letter of Pusey to W. Scott, January 1, 1851, in Liddon, *Life* 4:210–11.

[35]MS. letters of Johann Joseph Ignaz von Döllinger to E. B. Pusey, February 7, 1842, and May 30, 1866, Pusey House, Oxford.

10

Orestes A. Brownson on Tradition and Traditionalism

Patrick W. Carey

The concept of tradition in the religious culture of the United States has had few defenders. Between the American Revolution and the 1840s in particular, as Ralph E. Morrow has argued, tradition "suffered the perverse fortune of having only the case against it presented fully and explicitly."[1] Separately and in combination, the Protestant principle of *sola scriptura* and the Enlightenment's fascination with reason made the principle of tradition seem like a barrier to human freedom and progress. Religious liberty, separation of Church and state, and the general sense that the United States belonged to a new order of the ages combined to make tradition—generally understood as the confining, static, historical, and authoritarian structures of religion and politics—a part of the dead past which liberated Americans had transcended. Reason alone, private interpretation of the Bible (under the guidance of the Holy Spirit's enlightenment), and/or a natural religious sentiment provided the foundation for a knowledge of divine truth. In addition to this general cultural mind set, deism had revolted against traditional Christianity, Unitarianism and Universalism against the Calvinist tradition, Transcendentalism against Unitarianism, Mormonism against the Christian view of revelation, and various democratic forms of popular Christianity against traditional Christian structures of authority.[2] The case against tradition was also being made here and there by a Kantian critique and an incipient biblical and historical criticism.

By the late 1830s and early 1840s, a few minor theological impulses called into question this general cultural denial of the value and importance of tradition in Christianity. The so-called "Church question" of the early 1840s—advocating a reappraisal of the nature, role, and necessity of the Church itself—arose here and there, particularly within the quasi-Oxford movement of General Theological Seminary in New York and the Mercersburg theology of Philip Schaff and John Williamson Nevin.[3] These movements argued for an organic and incarnational approach to Christianity, emphasizing the continuity and development of the Christian tradition. They had little lasting impact, though, upon American religious culture. American Catholic apologists, moreover, had supported one or another of the post-Tridentine interpretations of the interrelationship of Scripture, tradition, and Church in coming to a knowledge of divine revelation; but they, too, were on the outskirts of American culture.[4]

The concept of tradition was also defended by Orestes A. Brownson (1803–1876) whose evolving views reflected at different stages of his career both the dominant American cultural bias and an incipient critique of that bias. His theology of tradition is important, moreover, not so much because it embodied any seminal ideas but because it illustrated so clearly some vital currents of Protestant and Catholic thought during the mid-nineteenth century. Brownson's own religious pilgrimage carried him from Presbyterianism to Universalism, Unitarianism, Transcendentalism, and ultimately to Catholicism in 1844.[5] He changed his mind so many times on religion (and the idea of tradition) in reaction to what he was currently reading and to how he interpreted the needs of his culture that James Russell Lowell called him a "weather vane." He was in succession influenced by and/or reacted to the writings of the Universalists, the Unitarians, the Transcendentalists, the French St. Simonians, Félicité de Lamennais, Johann Adam Möhler, John Henry Newman, Philip Schaff, John Williamson Nevin, the Louvain and French traditionalists, and the Italian ontologist Vincenzo Gioberti. Yet there was something of a consistent dialectic between revelation and its reception that ran through his changes.

Brownson's various conceptualizations of tradition must be seen as a mirror of the times in which he lived, but they also must be interpreted within the context of his own very personal search for an adequate rule of faith. In *The Convert* (1857), his intellectual and spiritual autobiography, he indicated that from his earliest youth he was plagued by the question "by what authority I was to obey, or on what authority I was to take my belief?"[6] What, in the midst of so much religious and cultural diversity, provided a guide for understanding the Christian faith? In his responses to this question, Brownson passed through different stages of development until he reached during his Catholic period what he considered a sound rule which included a dialectical synthesis between Scripture, tradition, and the Church.

Owen Chadwick once argued that "Nothing looks so ossified in the theology of the nineteenth century as the doctrine of tradition in Newman's critic Orestes Brownson, who was trying to defend an incipient Ultramontanism of the nineteenth century with a theory taken verbally from the seventeenth century, while he disallowed the only historical method which had once sought to justify that theory."[7] Such a judgment cannot be sustained by a historical examination of Brownson's actual thought. Before, after, and during his controversy with Newman on development (1846–1848), Brownson was creating a dynamic view of tradition that tried to incorporate into one dialectical whole tradition's creative as well as conservative dimensions. His view was much more an incarnation of nineteenth-century Christian thought than it was of Chadwick's seventeenth century.

I. *An Enlightenment Approach, 1826–1831*

In his earliest writings, as a Universalist minister in upstate New York, Brownson, like many of the youthful American religious leaders of what Nathan Hatch has called "popular theology,"[8] had eclectically combined the worlds of a supernaturalist evangelical pietism and an anticlerical deistic rationalism into an odd mixture that fits into none of the classical patterns of religious thought. Like a number of young populist theologians who felt themselves freed from all traditions, he asserted the rights of individual conscience in all matters relative to religion and politics, and, yet, he held on to a pious supernaturalism.

As a young Universalist minister, Brownson launched repeated Marxist-like attacks upon all organized religion, seeing the clerical ministry and all ecclesiastical creeds in particular as human institutions constructed to protect the vested interests of powerful elites within a community. The Bible, too, came under his critical suspicion because of its many contradictions, irrational and absurd assertions, errors of historical fact, and anthropomorphic approaches to God. The Churches, moreover, had used the Bible as the sole criterion for religious faith and practice in order to safeguard their sectarian enterprises.

Only an appeal to reason, which was created by God and therefore common to all, could help human beings escape the machinations of the past and reach temporal and spiritual happiness, the goal of all true, nonsectarian religion. Although reason was a divine gift intended to be the authentic interpreter of nature and all communications from God, it was not itself the source of the idea of God—revelation was. The realization of the necessity of revelation came from an awareness of the limits of reason. "From the study of nature, he [a person] cannot ascertain that there is a God, much less that God exists in a three-fold form."[9] The idea of God's existence comes from a primitive revelation and this revelation is transmitted to all human beings through tradition (understood as a universal cultural phenomenon). "We consider revelation a communication made from God to man, and made in the early ages of the world. Being made before the dispersion of mankind, it was easily carried with them as they wandered from each other, and thus became spread over the earth."[10] His idea of a common cultural tradition, which is here undeveloped, provided an explanation for the universal belief in God. Throughout his life Brownson struggled to find a way to reconcile the relationship between revelation as source of our ideas of God and reason as the receptacle and interpreter of that revelation.

This primitive revelation came down to us through a common tradition and through the sacred books of all nations which exhibited some traces of the primitive revelation. The Bible, especially the New Testament, however, provided the purest and most authentic account and safeguard of this primitive revelation. In this sense the Bible was inspired and therefore had authority for Christians. The Bible was the inspired Word of God, but inspiration did not belong to every word or judgment that was contained in the text. The Bible contained matters that were traditional, historical, moral, and doctrinal, but only "the doctrinal parts of the Christian Scripture, or of the New Testament" are inspired. The other parts of the Bible require no extraordinary inspiration.[11]

The Bible functioned not only to safeguard the primitive revelation but also to increase the human capacity "to understand and obey the laws of nature."[12] The Bible was also Brownson's "spiritual telescope, with which I survey the world of spirits, and regions after death." The Bible, therefore, was "infallible where the light of nature fails."[13]

Although inspired and authoritative, the Bible provided only the weakest kind of evidence for faith. Much like John Locke, Brownson argued that faith arose from intuitive perception, experience, or from testimony. Intuition provided the strongest evidence for faith, followed by experience and then testimony. The Bible came under testimony, the weakest category of evidence for faith. The Bible, furthermore, could never authorize humans to believe what contradicted their intuitive perceptions or experiences. It may have infallible authority when it conveys things beyond our reason but not when contradictory to it. "What contradicts reason or experience, our intuitive perception, or our own knowledge, we are to reject, bible or no bible: what is beyond our reason or experience, may or may not be true."[14] The doctrine of the Trinity, for example, was a human tradition and being contrary to reason it was not to be believed. On the other hand, the resurrection of Jesus, being beyond reason but not indeed contrary to a future understanding of the laws of nature, may be a doctrine worthy of belief.

Although Brownson recognized the necessity of a primitive revelation and saw the biblical revelation as consistent with it in its doctrinal assertions, he still made reason alone the interpreter and arbiter of that revelation, and, in effect, the only rule of Christian faith and practice. Being a book like any other book, the Bible must be interpreted according to the normal canons of literary interpretation. Reason must prevail in constructing and using these canons and reasonable people must avoid at all costs explaining the text "by the analogy of faith, or by one's creed."[15] Such a procedure would put sectarianism and authority above reason.

II. A Romantic Development, 1831–1841

For a variety of reasons, which are unimportant for this essay, Brownson left the Universalist ministry at the end of 1829 and gradually made his way into the Unitarian ministry. Although he continued to see revelation in much the same way as he had during his Universalist period, he began, under the influence of his reading of William Ellery Channing and Benjamin Constant, to emphasize more and more the limits of reason and the necessity of an internal revelation in the heart as the source of Christian truth and life. There is, as Constant and Channing held, a natural religious sentiment in all human beings which leads them to seek and embrace God as a benevolent and loving parent. By 1832, he asserted: "My own faith rests on this internal revelation from God to the inner man. I have thus a witness within; and, having this witness, I can find its testimony corroborated by the whole of external nature."[16]

Human beings have only to listen to the voice of the Divinity within their souls in order to be able to read the Bible and the book of nature. According to Brownson, it is not necessary to prove this internal witness; it is self-evident; humans see, feel, and know it immediately. The written word alone, therefore, is "not a revelation to us. It is only a record of the views taken of a revelation made to others. It is valuable; it is of immense importance; but it is not alone sufficient."[17]

During this period reason has been replaced to a considerable extent by "that 'true light which enlighteneth every one that cometh into the world.' "[18] This universal light conveyed to the heart the whole message of Christianity and enabled all human beings to interpret the Scriptures. To a certain extent this light itself now became for Brownson the rule of faith and practice. Brownson's move in this direction was in continuity not only with the post-Kantian Romantics but also with the more traditional Calvinist view of the relationship between the Bible and the Christian believer. In fact, by 1839 he was quoting Jonathan Edwards' sermon on the *Divine and Supernatural Light* to reinforce the necessity of appealing to the internal sense in order to obtain a truly committed understanding of revelation in the Bible. For Edwards the divine light within brought with it "a sense of the divine excellency of the things revealed in the word of God, and a *conviction* of the truth and reality of them thence arising."[19]

Like some other Transcendentalists,[20] Brownson had placed so much emphasis upon the inner sense that he believed it possible ultimately "to know Christian truth, the truths of religion, and to believe in them, independently of the 'written word.' "[21] Brownson could easily have agreed with George Ripley who asserted that the Transcendentalists maintained that "the truth of religion does not depend on tradition, nor on historical facts, but has an unerring witness in the soul."[22]

By 1841, however, Brownson was beginning to reexamine this position and for the first time in his career he appealed to the Church's tradition to demonstrate that his own emphasis upon the inner light departed less from the "sense of the Church, than some may suppose."[23] Christianity, he argued, existed before the Scriptures were written and the early Christian fathers believed that the Scriptures had value only when interpreted authentically according to their inspiration. The Catholic Church, too, had always asserted "a means of arriving at spiritual truth, beside [*sic*] the Bible, and even denied the sufficiency of the Bible, without an authoritative expounder, to make us wise unto salvation. Fénelon, the Quakers, and Jonathan Edwards, all assert the reality of the Inner Light, that the soul may hold direct communion with the spiritual world." Even evangelical Protestants looked to "religious experience" as a direct communication from God. Much of the Christian tradition had recourse to a source other than the Bible as the foundation of true religion.[24]

Although this interior light was universal, it was not natural. "It results not from the natural and spontaneous nor the reflective exercise of our faculties, but is the infusion of light from a source foreign to us." Unlike the Transcendentalist Theodore Parker, Brownson was becoming more and more an objective idealist who interpreted the inner light as an objective force, not merely a human or natural religious sentiment. The light came from God as the "inshining of the Divine Logos, or Intelligence, and is impersonal and independent in relation to us, personal and dependent in relation to God." This interior light is discerned, moreover, by criteria analogous to the Vincentian canon: the light is "known by its character of uniformity, fixedness, and universality, making it the same at all times, in all places, and with all individuals."[25] The Bible had inspiration as a particular reflection of this inner light and in this it had an authority that is "ultimate in all matters of doctrine, whether of faith or practice."[26] But, the Bible can never be "sufficient authority for us in relation to any proposition which we do not understand, or which does not commend itself to our own sense of right, to our own reason, judgment, and conscience."[27] Ultimately it was the combination of the inspiration of the Bible and that of the soul that provided certitude. "By the interior inspiration, we detect that of the written word, and by that of the written word, we in part, determine and limit the interior inspiration. In the correspondence of the two, in their united testimony, which is the testimony of two independent witnesses, we have our highest degree of certainty."[28]

III. Life by Communion, 1842–1844

Until 1841, Brownson emphasized almost exclusively the universal and self-progressive dimensions of inspiration and revelation. The Bible had an importance and authority for the individual, but only as a safeguard and reflection of the general inspiration and revelation. He began to change his perspective dramatically during 1842 under the primary influence of the French St. Simonian Pierre Leroux.

From Leroux he discovered a doctrine he called "Life by Communion," and in a series of essays in 1842 and 1843[29] he applied Leroux's philosophical insights to theology, making a case for the objective authority of the Bible and tradition and for the Church's authority to interpret them. From this period onward he began to develop arguments for the organic interrelatedness of the Bible, tradition, and the Church.

According to Leroux and Brownson, all life, as all knowledge, is the result of the mutually interactive communion of a subject and an object.[30] Human life is twofold. It is always the result of two factors of which I, the subject, am one, and they with whom I commune, and who commune with me, are the other. Both the me and the not me are active in the production of life. Thus, all life, as all knowledge, is simultaneously subjective and objective. In life, "the subject and object are not only placed in juxtaposition, mutually acting and reacting one upon the other, but are in fact unified, if we may so speak, *soldered* together."[31] The very act of teaching illustrates the doctrine of life by communion. "In teaching, whether by precept or example, the teacher imparts, communicates, a portion of his own life, and the reception of this is the being taught;—not, indeed, the passive, but the active reception of this; for it requires action to receive, no less than to impart."[32] The student, the subject in this case, is active as well as the teacher, the object.

This doctrine of life by communion helped Brownson to explain not only how all human life was organically related to nature, other humans, and to God (i.e., the objective parts of all human life) but also how human life itself was progressive and developmental. All human growth and development was not the result of some inherent natural human potency but the result of communion with objects that were foreign to the self and that possessed a life superior to that of the self. All human growth, in fact, was by accretion, and by assimilation, not by natural self-development. As a plant only grows as a result of assimilating the benefits of the soil, water, and the sun, so also human beings and the human race grow only by assimilating to their own life a higher form of life that comes to them only through special divinely endowed individuals whom Leroux and Brownson called "Providential Men." These men (e.g., Plato, Aristotle, Confucius, Jesus) come into communion with individuals and the race and raise the level of individual and communal life. Thus, we of today have been enlarged by the past accumulations of the race and progress only through this process. We thus have an organic relation to the past and cannot, even if we wanted to, divest ourselves of tradition. Tradition is indeed an active and objective part of our entire life. Progress through this tradition of "providential men," however, could not be explained "without assuming the supernatural, the miraculous [and constant] intervention of Divine Providence."[33] Supernaturalism is needed to explain growth because there is within the human race no self-germinating principle of growth toward a higher life. A single human being can stand above the human race by no natural or inherent power. Growth is provided for by a supernatural change in the object ("providential men").

Of all the "providential men" who have advanced the life of the human race, Jesus has had the most significant impact because "in him dwelt all the fullness of the Godhead bodily."[34] Those human beings who come after Jesus live according to a life already above that of the race, and it is through communion with those who interacted with Jesus himself that the race is raised to a higher level of moral and social existence. Thus, Jesus lives in his disciples by virtue of the law of life, and by that same law his life is communicated to us through our interaction with the disciples and their successors. Brownson accepts a concept of apostolic succession as a means of communion with Jesus, even though he does not accept it in its episcopal sense in 1842.[35]

Within this context of his doctrine of life by communion and Christian life by communion with Jesus through the tradition of the Christian community, Brownson developed a new understanding of the Bible, tradition, and the Church. Now, Brownson argued against Theodore Parker and his own former position that the Bible is inspired not because of the authors' "greater fidelity to their own moral and religious motives"[36] but because it is as supernaturally inspired as are "providential men." Unlike his earlier position, therefore, Brownson now holds that the Bible belongs to a "different category from that of all other books." Thus, the inspiration, authority, and sufficiency of the Bible is seen in the fact that it is "the life of this very Church of the Disciples."[37] But still its inspiration is limited because it is produced by limited, though providential, men.[38]

Brownson continued to deny the all-sufficiency of the Bible, but for the first time he criticized the so-called right of private interpretation. If once admitted to its full extent, private interpretation would involve the "destruction of all social, moral, and religious order." And, once this principle of private interpretation is admitted, in Parker's sense of inner light, even the need for a biblical revelation vanishes.[39] Private interpretation only reinforced a doctrine of individualism that warred against the communal nature of the Christian community. The Bible is sufficient, but not in itself. It is insufficient "without the authoritative interpretation of the Church."[40] The true interpretation of the Bible belonged to the Church, not to an individual or to a pope. "But its [the Bible's] real significance we obtain only from the commentaries of the Holy Ghost, the Spirit of Truth, the Comforter, which is the living Jesus, who was to be with us unto the end of the world, and of which the true Church, the one Catholic [i.e., universal] Church, is the real, literal, and living God.''[41] Because of Brownson's doctrine of communion, the universal Church now replaced the individual as the true interpreter of the Bible because the Church is itself the living expression and consciousness of Jesus, and it is the Church that puts individuals in communion with the life and meaning of the text and not just with the dead letter.[42] Thus, through the Church, human beings have a continuous inspiration that is derivative and mediatorial yet full and authoritative.[43]

By 1843, Brownson was aware of how Catholic his ideas and even his language had become. But, at this point, he could not accept the Catholic Church as the universal Church that he was speaking about. At this point he considered himself neither a Protestant nor a Catholic. He admitted the need for a universal Church, but he could not acknowledge any one of the claims of the historical Churches to authority and universality.

Throughout 1844 the primary issue for Brownson, as for a number of other Americans, was the question of the necessity of the Church for salvation. Second, he raised the issue of the nature and office of the Church. Third, and finally, he came to the practical question of which of the historically existing Churches was the true catholic and apostolic Church, the one in continuity with the gospel and able to provide an authentic and authoritative interpretation of the gospel and to apply it most effectively to the present.

Because he saw the Church's vital principle or organic force as the *"indwelling Life, or Spirit, of Christ,* not the mere fact that she is the depositary of *past* revelations and inspirations,'' Brownson asserted the unity, catholicity, apostolicity, and what he called the "continuous inspiration" of the Church. At the beginning of 1844, however, he found this theory of the Church nowhere realized or put into practice in any of the existing historical Churches. The Catholic Church had the theory most clearly, but Catholics were unable to square tradition with progress or continuous development. Instead of seeing the Gospel as given to the Church "merely in germ, to be subsequently developed and applied," most Catholics have perceived it "as a perfect code drawn out in all the minuteness of detail, and that her sole mission is, to preserve the original deposite [*sic*] unaltered, unenlarged, undiminished.'' By confining herself to ancient tradition and to primitive usage, the Catholic Church had been too dependent upon antiquity and had not taken seriously her mission of carrying on the progress of the human race. Her error had not been, as most Protestants charge, in making arrogant and pretentious claims, but "in *not* asserting, her independence in regard to tradition, written or unwritten." In this regard, Protestantism was no better off because "Protestantism asserts the supremacy of the Written Word, not as the principle, but as a full and perfect code, needing and admitting, no farther developments, and, therefore, tends to subject the Church to Antiquity."[44]

Although Brownson had asserted his law of life or continuity and respected tradition as a life-giving and living force within history and within personal, communal, and ecclesial development, he could not accept the mistaken notion of tradition

> as already complete, and, therefore, as a law that must bind us, and as an inheritance which must supersede all necessity of any acquisitions of our own. While we accept tradition with all sincerity and reverence, we should carefully avoid this fatal mistake, which would be a bar to all farther progress. In accepting tradition, we must regard it as our duty to carry it on, by supplying its deficiencies, and enriching it by new discoveries. We must guard against the error of believing, that the canon of authentic tradition is closed, and that the human race must henceforth feed solely on its past inspirations.[45]

The present as well as the future is in continuity with past inspirations, but because of the "continuous inspiration" within the Church, the present and the future may indeed enlarge, while never overriding or superseding, past inspirations. Neither Catholics nor Protestants were open to this view of development.

The life of the Church, i.e., the indwelling force of the Holy Spirit, changes not; "but its assimilation to human nature, and practical realization in the life of man and of men, is a progressive work, and involves development and growth."[46] In a remarkable paragraph, Brownson outlines his position on development, a position that he will modify later in reacting to John Henry Newman's theory.

> The philosophy of the Church, that is, its exposition, interpretation, and practical application of the law of life, must needs be subject to development and growth. In this mutable world, and changing life, new questions are perpetually coming up, or old questions in new forms, which are to be decided. The written Word, no doubt, contains the principle, the law applicable to each particular case; but the application itself demands an authoritative interpreter. The law does not change, but men's views of it change, and so do the questions to which it needs to be applied. The outward *form* and *discipline* of the Church, while the principles of each remain unaltered and unalterable, may often need modifying, to adapt them to the altered conditions of society.

The Church, we contend, has the inherent power to make such alterations in them, from time to time, as in her wisdom are necessary; and this power she has always claimed and exercised. No man will venture to say, that the outward form, the usages, and discipline of the Catholic Church, have remained unvaried from the time of the apostles.[47]

Gradually throughout 1844 Brownson came to face the question of which Church was the true catholic apostolic Church. The issue that turned his face toward Rome was eventually the question of who decides in controversies over doctrine and practice the correct interpretation of the Scriptures. By July of 1844 he was taking instructions in the Catholic Church and decided that he must "go to Rome" to find a Church that upheld its own right and authority to interpret authentically the Word of God. Only in this way could he avoid the "absolute individualism" and the "no Churchism" that was so prevalent in American Christianity.[48] By making this decision, he held, he had not abandoned his belief in progress and improvement, but he had definitely changed his mind on the source of progress. He abandoned the idea he once held that progress was the result of some inherent force. Under the influence of Leroux, he maintained that all progress and development of the individual and the race came from above and not from below, from a source outside of the individual and the race—in other words, from God's providential interventions. The Church, as the continuation of the incarnation, was the providential source and condition of all authentic unity, liberty, and progress.

IV. The Catholic Period, 1844–1876

Brownson was received into the Catholic Church in October of 1844; and, under the increasing influence of instructions from Boston's Bishop John Bernard Fitzpatrick, he began to accept a post-Cartesian Catholic apologetic which proceeded from the veracity of God revealing and stressed the authority of the Church as the basis for the motives of the credibility of Christianity. He was also beginning to sound more like Bossuet than the Brownson of January 1844. In a dramatic turnabout he wrote approvingly in October that the Catholic believes that the "Church came into the world *perfectly formed,* and that it received all truth from the beginning, and therefore, can make no progress, save in the application of truth to the life and progress of individuals and society. It effects a growth in individuals and society, but it has no growth of its own. It is immutable, like its Author, and is unchangeable amid all changes, immovable amid all fluctuations, the representative of the eternal and unchangeable God. What it was eighteen hundred years ago, it is now, and will be to the end of time."[49] Such a view pushed Brownson more and more away from his earlier subject-object synthetic dialectic and toward an almost exclusive emphasis upon the object (whether the revealing God or the Church).

The Christian believes the truths revealed as the object of faith and these truths are "fixed and unalterable, universal and permanent." And, indeed, the revealed truth itself must be clearly distinguished from "our notions or apprehensions of them, which are dependent on our mental states or conditions, and change and fluctuate as we ourselves change and fluctuate. These notions are not the matter of faith."[50] The Church is the guarantee that what we believe is revealed truth and not just our notions of the truth. Without the Church's infallible authority, moreover, it was impossible to settle the canon, establish the sufficiency and inspiration of Scriptures, and determine their genuine sense.

Although the Catholic Brownson emphasized the role of the Church, and especially of the magisterium (the *ecclesia docens*), in securing a true sense of the Scriptures, he did not completely abandon the Calvinist and Edwardsean notion of divine illumination as a means to authentic interpretation and a committed understanding of the revealed Word of God. From Edwards and the Calvinists he learned to appreciate the fact that the whole gospel was present in the hearts of the converted through divine illumination, and in the early 1840s he also learned that this conception was not entirely foreign to Johann Adam Möhler's idea of internal tradition.[51] "That there is a Christian sense, so to speak—internal tradition, as it is sometimes called, to distinguish it from the external—which belongs to Christians, and which makes them altogether better judges of what is Christian truth than are those who are not Christians, and that the just, those who belong to the soul of the Church, have a clearer perception, a more vivid appreciation, of the truth, beauty, grandeur, and work of Christian faith than have the unregenerate or the unjust, we of course very distinctly and cheerfully admit."[52] One can accept this view of an internal tradition or internal witness in the heart as long as it does not deny the need for a corresponding external tradition to confirm, verify, and express the public nature of this Christian sense of revelation.

Brownson's polemically anti-Protestant post-Cartesian Catholic apologetic, mixed as it was with some of his former notions, was a significant departure from his earlier synthetic and developmentalist approach to Christianity. It was during this early Catholic period (1844–1855) that he reacted so strongly against the theories of development in John Henry Newman and the Mercersburg theologians Philip Schaff and John Williamson Nevin. Historians have frequently failed to note that Brownson's severe criticism of Newman in his early Catholic period was conditioned by his extreme movement to a post-Cartesian apologetic that was foreign both to his earlier and to his later intellectual developments.[53]

Brownson, always somewhat polemical, was particularly so against Newman's *An Essay on the Development of Christian Doctrine* (1845). It is interesting to compare, though, Brownson's 1846 judgment that the *Essay* was "essentially anti Catholic and Protestant"[54] with his 1862 view that it was "a highly important contribution to modern theology" and contained a great truth or seminal principle "which it is necessary to accept, if we would not leave Catholic theology to stagnate and die, or if we would reconcile authority with reason, the immobility of the Church with the progress of civilization, the immutability of dogma with the development of intelligence, the divine unchangeableness with human variableness, or retain the past without foreclosing the future."[55] These two apparently contradictory judgments are in fact not as contradictory as they appear when one examines precisely what Brownson rejected and what he accepted of the developmentalist theory even in his early Catholic period.[56]

Brownson's primary objection to Newman's theory of development was that it was fatal to any understanding of the permanency of an original revelation. He believed, mistakenly, that Newman's theory undermined the unchangeableness and invariableness of the divine element in Christianity. Unlike Newman, Brownson argued that "Christian doctrine is revelation itself, not the view which men take of that revelation."[57] He identified revelation and Christian doctrine and in this sense Christian doctrine was not changeable and variable. Brownson feared that Newman's view so threatened the permanency of the original divine deposit that there was no telling where development might end. Could the idea of development, for example, end up in something like John Robinson's (1575–1625) conception of a new extrabiblical revelation or in a theory of "continuous inspiration" which Brownson himself had most recently held?

Brownson also objected to Newman's understanding that Christianity came into the world as an idea and not as an institution. For Brownson, there was no parity between Christian doctrine and human ideas. Brownson's quasi-Platonic understanding of idea, furthermore, conflicted with Newman's quasi-empirical understanding of idea. For Newman the idea developed in the human mind and in the mind of the Church. For Brownson, ideas are subsistent and have an objective existence over against us. Here Brownson and Newman are speaking about two very different realities, and Brownson does not take the difference into account when he criticizes Newman. Ultimately Brownson fears that Newman's theory of development gives too much play to the human mind itself, making doctrine itself the product of the mind. He sees in Newman's theory the kind of subjectivism and developmentalism that he saw in American Unitarians and feared that Newman's theory would only give support, for example, to the idea that the Trinitarian developments of the fourth century were mere human additions to the faith and not a part of the original deposit. The idea of development, moreover, could support the Reformation and Protestantism in general—and indeed the Mercersburg theologians, Nevin and Schaff, were using the idea in this way.

Brownson's objective idealist approach to the Church, too, contrasted sharply with Newman's historical approach. Like the quasi-idealist he was, Brownson saw the Church as the ideal body of Christ; and because it belonged to the order of grace and not to that of nature, it had no natural history. For him, the Church sprung into existence "full grown" like Mineva from the brain of Jupiter.[58] Of course, the grace-given reality of the Church needed to be actualized in history, but the grace-given reality itself did not change or grow. He believed, moreover, that Newman gave too much weight to the learning Church and not enough to the teaching Church in his theory of development, threatening the divinely commissioned role of the teaching Church.

In the end, Brownson thought that Newman failed to distinguish Christian doctrine (i.e., revelation), which did not change and develop, from Christian theology and discipline, which did. Even during his early Catholic period, though, Brownson was not opposed to all ideas of development. He had in fact argued for the idea of development prior to becoming a Catholic and continued to do so after becoming one. But, his own view of development was restricted primarily to ecclesiastical government, discipline, worship, and theological science.

In the area of Christian dogma, too, he was willing to admit some development as long as the permanency of the original divine revelation was preserved. But, this development was always the result of the communion of the divine and the human, where the divine was the agency of change and development. Christianity developed or progressed only as a result of the action of the Holy Spirit upon the Church. What Brownson opposed was a concept of doctrinal development that was exclusively the result of ecclesial self-development. "What is to be denied is not the progressiveness of past revelation by divine agency, but the development and growth of doctrine by the mental or moral action of the faithful."[59] Nonetheless, there was a sense in which Christian teaching did develop. There were indeed new definitions (like Chalcedon) of the faith and new explications (not new revelations) of what must be believed. In this sense it is true that everything was not explicit from the beginning of Christianity in the believing Church. Like Bossuet and Vincent of Lerins, Brownson acknowledged some sense of development. New definitions of the faith, for example, raised to the level of formal faith what was only previously in the realm of material faith. In the course of history, the Church's faith gains in evidence, clarity, precision, and distinctness. The new definitions, moreover, gave a clearer understanding not of what the faith is but of what it is not. Brownson can, therefore, accept Giovanni Perrone's view that there are "new modes of expression adopted on the occasion of novel errors" and Möhler's view of development as logical deduction and coherence. What Brownson denied in the theory of development was the *creation* of new doctrines from the mind of the historical Church, a development that occurred, as he understood Newman, as a result of the Church's reflection.

Brownson's reactions against Newman, as those against the Mercersburg theology, reflect his intense period of objective idealism, a period in which he wanted in particular to assert that all reality, Christian reality included, was independent of the minds that conceived of it. This led Brownson to some extreme emphases upon the objective order, the teaching Church, authority, and a view of revelation independent of its reception. Brownson continued to object to Newman's notion of doctrinal development for the remainder of his life, but after 1850 his opposition was modified considerably and his support for Newman's understanding of development in the Church's reception of the original revelation was much warmer and more enthusiastic.

After 1850, Brownson moved more and more away from his early Catholic post-Cartesian apologetic. His reading of Vincenzo Gioberti and some of the Louvain and French Traditionalists helped him to realize that his pre-Catholic theological approach was not entirely inconsistent with Catholic theology as he had been led to believe by Bishop Fitzpatrick.[60] Brownson had always accepted some kind of traditionalism, believing that in fact knowledge of God's existence and revelation came to human beings through the medium of tradition. He had also believed in some form of intuitive awareness of God's existence as a precondition for the reception of revelation through tradition. By the 1850s, these general concerns of his earlier period returned in the form of French traditionalism and Italian ontologism. Gradually after 1850, Brownson retrieved his former doctrine of life by communion and elaborated it along lines of Gioberti's ontologism and modified traditionalism. In this movement he renewed his emphasis upon the dialectic between the subjective and the objective and refined his earlier emphasis upon intuition, reason, and tradition as the complementary means of knowing God and as the conditions for the reception of a supernatural revelation. It was within this new context that he recaptured and developed his understanding of the relationship of the Bible, tradition, the Church, and the Magisterium.

By the mid-1850s and early 1860s, because of the Roman condemnations of traditionalism and ontologism, Brownson began to sort out what he considered the strengths and weaknesses of the two systems of thought, but throughout the remainder of his life he never completely abandoned a modified ontologism and traditionalism. The benefit of traditionalism was that it could explain the universal presence of theism and the origin of human desires and aspirations for God. Theism and the human need for God were the results of a primitive revelation of God to the first human being—a revelation which was communicated to all subsequent ages through the medium of language, which was the medium of tradition. One, therefore, did not have to have recourse to some doctrine of pure nature, a belief in the natural desire for God, or some theory of natural beatitude to explain why human beings seek God and a supernatural beatitude as their ultimate end. Primitive revelation transmitted through tradition created the wants and aspirations for God. All human beings have this as a reminiscence of a primitive revelation. Our own human feelings and experiences of inadequacies, too, are vague reminders of the primitive revelation and are thus unimpeachable witnesses to the fact of this supernatural revelation. All human beings are

> under a supernatural Providence, and have everywhere reminiscences of a supernatural revelation which surpasses the strength of natural reason. Every man bears about with him, whether he knows it or not, the evidence that God has revealed to the world an order of life above our natural life. The revelation has been made, and man is nowhere, not even in the savage state, what he would have been if left to the simple lights of natural reason. The sound of the Gospel has gone out into all the earth, and reverberates in all hearts from first to last, as a prophecy or a tradition. The intimation of a God-man, of the fact of the Incarnation, as a fact that is to take place, or that

has taken place, has in some form reached all the sons and daughters of Adam, and man is nowhere what he else would have been. It, with the universal strivings of grace, excites hopes and fears, and develops wants in all hearts to which neither natural reason nor natural strength suffices. Our Lord has a witness in all hearts, and in all hearts there are cravings, there are hopes which only the great fact of the Incarnation, the elevation of human nature to be the nature of God, can satisfy. Here is the grand fact; man has, universally, glimpses, though brief and dim they may be, of something more than nature, and which render him too large for the natural order.[61]

This primitive revelation was not completely destroyed even by the Fall. The recollections of the revelation received in integral nature and the reminiscences of original endowments were never, except here and there, completely lost to the human race. They were transmitted down the ages to us through a variety of traditional forms, but the reminiscences were kept alive most purely through the patriarchs, the synagogue, and especially the Church.[62]

Although Brownson accepted this traditionalist perspective, he believed that some French traditionalists had pushed this doctrine so far that they denied at least by implication the value of all reason or the ability of reason to know God. Traditionalism's greatest weakness was its attempt to build science on faith, i.e., making all knowledge and reason depend upon revelation received through tradition. Many of the French traditionalists (like the Roman neoscholastic theologians), moreover, did not distinguish clearly reason's order of intuition and its order of reflection. Extreme traditionalism needed to be modified by emphasizing the role of reason in understanding God and revelation. Tradition was indeed necessary to bring reason to reflective awareness of what was ontologically present in intuition (i.e., God, the immortality of the soul, free will, and moral obligation). Here Brownson's traditionalism was modified by his ontologism. For him, it was necessary to assert, as did Gioberti, that "God affirms his own being to reason intuitively in the very act of creating it, so that God is always present to reason as the ideal." Reflection brings to conscious awareness what is present in intuition. "We know intuitively that which is God, but we know and are able to say it is God only by reflection, through the agency of language, the instrument of reflection, or if you please, social instruction and development."[63]

Tradition, too, is the "proper medium" for detecting and establishing the fact of a supernatural providence and revelation.[64] But, the Church is the authentic depository, preserver, witness, and interpreter of that tradition. And, the evidence for the Church's role as interpreter, Brownson argued, came not only from history but also from what he and Möhler called an internal tradition—i.e., the Church's living self-consciousness of her own identity, a living tradition of awareness of the life force of the apostolic preaching and teaching, a Christian sense or Christian instinct.

> The Church is a living body, informed by the Holy Ghost, and is a real person, having her personality in the Word made flesh. Christ lives in her, and teaches at all moments in and through her, infusing his knowledge and grace into her, in some sense, as the Word infused knowledge and grace into the humanity he assumed when he became incarnate. For herself, she has the witness in her ever present, and has no occasion to go beyond her own consciousness, if we may so speak, to know the validity of her claims, or the dogmas or precepts revealed by our Lord. If she consults historical documents, if she appeals to records, to the teaching of the fathers and doctors, it is not because she needs to learn for herself the tradition of faith and morals, but because she operates *more humano,* and because she wishes to enlighten and convince those who need to be set right.[65]

The external tradition of documents and Church teachings is the complement to the internal tradition and is in fact the historical expression or actualization of the Church's internal consciousness which develops throughout history. These two forms of tradition correspond to one another and are related one to another as the reality to the sign, as meaning to its symbolic expression.

> Tradition, we have said, is both external and internal, and, rightly considered, is the continuity in the external and internal life of the Church of the word speaking and of the word spoken. . . . The Church speaking speaks always according to this interior tradition, her present interior life; and as this life is a continuous evolution and explication of the Word [immanent in the Church], it gives always to the external tradition a broader and a deeper significance; it destroys not its truth, renders it not false, but shows that there is more in it than was at first apprehended, that it covers a broader field or has a deeper and richer meaning than was at first supposed. There is in this way, or in this sense, a continuous development and progress of truth in the Church.[66]

How, then, does the Bible fit into this conception of a double tradition? The Bible is a part of the external tradition. "The Catholic, no doubt, holds the Bible to be the written word of God, and he is ready to concede at once, that if the Church were to contradict it, her teaching would be false. But before one can establish the fact of the contradiction, he must know exactly what is the true sense of Scripture, and what it is the Church really teaches."[67] Brownson never separates the Bible from tradition and the Church, but he undoubtedly gives the Church the primacy as a witness and interpreter. He sees the Bible as the fountain or locus of faith, but it is not the sole rule of faith; it is a rule of faith only in its true sense. The "Catholic tradition," including the Bible and its true sense, is the rule of faith.[68] Even Protestants, he asserted, read and interpreted the Scriptures within a tradition of oral preaching and teaching and thus in practice they did not accept the *sola scriptura* principle. Many Calvinist Protestants, moreover, upheld the necessity of divine illumination for a sound interpretation of Scripture and thus departed somewhat from the principle.[69]

After 1864 Brownson's views on the relationship of the Bible, tradition, and the Church changed very little except for his more forceful emphasis upon the role of the papacy in the interpretation of Scripture and tradition. Since the late 1840s, Brownson considered himself an ultra ultramontane and after 1870 he became a follower of Archbishop Henry Edward Manning's interpretation of Vatican I. According to Brownson, Vatican I had introduced into Catholicism an "important innovation" in the mode of presenting doctrine. For the first time the Catholic Church had treated the primacy of the pope before treating the body of the Church. Brownson saw this development as providential for clarifying the Church's constitution, and, of course, forecasted what would happen to the tract *De Ecclesia* after Vatican I.[70]

Brownson still argued that the Scriptures contained, explicitly or implicitly, the whole faith, and that Catholic tradition was the key to unlocking the real sense of the Scriptures. "Read in the light of tradition, what is implicit in the text becomes explicit, what is merely referred to as wholly known becomes expressly and clearly stated, and we are able to understand the written word, because tradition interprets it for us, without any demand for a knowledge or judgment on our part that exceeds our natural powers."[71] To the Church's tradition one has recourse to uncover the faith in its unity and integrity.

Although Brownson never identified the Church's tradition with the papacy, as Pope Pius IX is reported to have done, he made it clear after 1870 that an infallible papacy was responsible for preserving and applying the tradition for the people.[72] To a certain extent the pope became in Brownson's view the public rule of faith in the sense of preserving, bearing witness, authentically interpreting, applying, and defining the Christian faith. The living voice of the Church became for him the present voice of the pope.

Although individuals needed the enlightenment of the Holy Spirit to receive the Christian tradition in faith and reason to understand it, they were incapable as private persons of providing a public interpretation of the faith. The same could be said of scholars. Brownson greatly disapproved what he called the "Döllinger rule," i.e., the view of Johann Joseph Ignatz von Döllinger which assumed, as Brownson interpreted it, that the Church was to be "controlled in her definitions of faith by the investigations and conclusions of the learned professors." What need was there for the scholars' biblical and historical investigations if the magisterium, through the power of the Holy Spirit residing in it, possessed the living tradition and its authentic interpretation? Without taking into consideration the assistance of the Holy Spirit in the Church, Döllinger's position was only a "reproduction of rationalism." The Church's definitions are infallible not by human learning or science but by supernatural assistance.[73]

Brownson never had much knowledge of or sympathy for historical science, which he called the "least certain" of all the sciences. For him, as for Manning, "historical science is so far from controlling the Church in her decisions, that it is the Church that must control the conclusions of the historian. The Church is the controlling fact of the universe, and in her alone is to be found the key to all history and to all science."[74] Brownson here was fighting against a kind of historicism that raised brute historical facts to a level of intelligibility they did not possess. All real facts, according to Brownson, have their intelligibility only in their relation to the central Christian mysteries. "The truth of dogma is the key to the true fact, and controls its sense, and therefore must control the judgment of the historian." Thus, Brownson concluded, "dogma controls history, not history dogma, and dogma is determined by the Church through the supernatural and infallible assistance of the Holy Ghost, who leads her into all truth."[75]

Brownson was led to this position not because of a skepticism regarding reason or science, but because he believed that reason and faith formed one dialectical whole and that the realms of reason and faith, although never completely separated, must be clearly distinguished. In Brownson's perspective, "the rational is for the super-rational and the natural is for the supernatural [human beings, i.e., have always been under a supernatural providence], in which it has its principle, medium and end, reason has not her complement in herself, and is completed only in revelation."[76] Dogma controls history in the sense that the whole of the natural order is oriented to a supernatural end, and all history, therefore, must be understood ultimately in light of the revealed end. Nature as well as grace are equally God's works and form ontologically one whole. Thus, there can never be a real contradiction between the work of reason and that of faith, between papal infallibility and reason. Such a view does not make critical investigation useless; it puts it in service to a higher end and makes it a part of an organic whole. Science is not an isolated or autonomous enterprise. Although Brownson asserts the complementariness of reason and revelation, science and faith, he never demonstrates how science and faith can in practice be complementary.

V. Conclusion

Even a cursory review of the evolution of Brownson's thinking on tradition makes it difficult to agree with Owen Chadwick's judgment that Brownson's doctrine of tradition was "ossified," that it was nothing but a throwback to the rigid traditionalism of Bossuet. Brownson's idea of tradition developed; and from the early 1840s onward, he upheld a view of the mutual coinherence of Scripture, tradition, and the Church. He knew nothing of the so-called two-source theory, that the Word of God was partly in the Scriptures and partly in tradition. For him the whole Word of God was contained in the Scripture and in tradition, both Scripture and tradition were in the Church, and the Church's magisterium was the authentic witness and interpreter of both and the judge of controversies concerning the interpretation of both. And even though the original revelation did not develop, the Church's understanding of it did develop in the course of history. As was clear in his controversy with Newman, though, he did not distinguish between Christian doctrine and revelation.

Brownson's understanding of the Church as the continuation of the incarnation, influenced as it was by an objective idealism, however, made it difficult, if not impossible, for him to distinguish between Christ and the Church. This ecclesiological monophysitism, although it avoided the dangers of historicism and a separation of the human and the divine within the Church, made his understanding of the Church ahistorical. He placed so much emphasis upon the Church and the Church's Magisterium, the papacy in particular, in the transmission of Scripture and tradition that it is difficult to see how Scripture and tradition as content and deposit functioned in his thought. Although he never identified tradition with the teachings of the Magisterium (because for him the Magisterium was always the witness and interpreter) and even though he repeatedly asserted that the

Church could never contradict the Word of God, he did not make clear precisely how the Church was to use Scripture and tradition as objective norms for judging the Church's own life and thought. For him, of course, such a judgment was a theological impossibility, given the presence of the Holy Spirit's guidance within the Church. For him the Church accredits itself and has the norm of its own interior life within itself, and thereby in a sense he set up the Church's own interior life as the norm of that self-same life. But, this did not mean even for him that the Church's external life, government, worship, discipline, and morality were freed from all criticism. In fact, unlike many in the ethnic Catholicism of his day, he distinguished clearly between tradition and the traditions. Superstition and error as well as religion and faith may be transmitted by tradition. "The pastor himself, but poorly instructed in his theology, as is sometimes the case, may fail now and then to distinguish between the true and the false tradition," and mistake the traditions of his own countrymen for Catholic tradition itself.[77]

He acknowledged that although the magisterium had the Holy Spirit's assistance in discernment, it was not itself a source of the Word of God nor did it possess infused knowledge. But, he said nothing about what responsibility, even *more humano,* the magisterium had to consult the learned in coming to an understanding of the Bible and tradition. Because his concept of tradition did not emphasize historical records, but the living tradition, it gave little value to even honest historical and scientific investigation of those records to ascertain before the demands of reason the documentary basis of the Church's faith and doctrinal tradition. And, thus, the relationship between learning and discernment was not clear in his writings. His modified form of traditionalism, furthermore, led to a quasi-fideistic approach to the Catholic tradition—a position he tried to escape by assertion but one that he in fact never completely avoided. His fideism made belief in the Church almost the sole criterion of the sense of the Word of God and Christian doctrine.

Brownson's position on tradition manifested the vitality and problematic of mid-nineteenth-century Catholic theology. In the polemical context in which it arose, it was first of all an attempt to revive a concept of tradition that would counteract the prevailing Protestant rule of faith and to call attention to organic continuity in the Christian tradition. For him, and for other Catholics of the period, it was an apologetical attempt to make intelligible the principles of unity, universality, consent, and development that were essential to Christianity—especially in the face of what he and others perceived to be the breakdown of all respect for tradition and authority, the rapid multiplication of new religious denominations, and the increasing diversity within American Protestantism. In this effort he, like the Mercersburg theologians, was largely unsuccessful.

Brownson's views of tradition had very little effect upon the development of thought in what there was of an American Catholic intellectual community in the nineteenth century. Most of his contemporaries, Catholic as well as Protestant, were more concerned with the important practical issues of religious life than the serious academic issues that had been raised for Christianity by the Kantian critique and the incipient biblical and historical criticism of the eighteenth and early nineteenth centuries. Later generations of American Catholic intellectuals, moreover, found it difficult to discern Brownson's views on tradition simply because his opinions were frequently changing and because they were buried in periodical literature and not readily available in major systematic studies. His own views on tradition, moreover, would be superseded within the Catholic communion by the post-Vatican I neoscholastic handbooks of theology which trained future priests to look upon tradition in a static fashion. The idea of a living tradition open to growth in conceptualization largely escaped American Catholic thinkers until the short-lived American Catholic modernist movement (1895–1910)[78] and until John Courtney Murray, S.J., took up the problem of religious liberty and the growing edge of that tradition within the modern world and modern papal teachings. In the 1950s, too, the first American Catholic systematic historical and theological studies of tradition were published by the French émigré George Tavard.

Notes

[1]"The Great Revival, the West, and the Crisis of the Church," *The Frontier Re-examined*, ed. John F. McDermott (Urbana, Ill.: University of Illinois Press, 1967) 70.

[2]On the popular theological movements, see the excellent study by Nathan O. Hatch, *The Democratization of American Christianity* (New Haven: Yale University Press, 1989).

[3]On these movements, see Sydney E. Ahlstrom, *A Religious History of the American People* (New Haven: Yale University Press, 1972) 615–32, and James Hastings Nichols, *Romanticism in American Theology: Nevin and Schaff at Mercersburg* (Chicago: The University of Chicago Press, 1961).

[4]Gerald Fogarty, *Nova et Vetera: The Theology of Tradition in American Catholicism* (Milwaukee, Wis.: Marquette University Press, 1987). Fogarty shows that some Catholic apologists had adopted a dynamic concept of tradition prior to Vatican I and thereafter followed the neoscholastic interpretation of tradition as one of two sources of Christian doctrine. Fogarty's study does not treat Orestes Brownson.

⁵On Brownson's life and thought, see in particular Thomas R. Ryan, *Orestes A. Brownson: A Definitive Biography* (Huntington, Ind.: Our Sunday Visitor, Inc., 1976); Arthur M. Schlesinger, Jr., *Orestes A. Brownson: A Pilgrim's Progress* (Boston: Little, Brown, and Co., 1939); Richard Leliaert, "Orestes A. Brownson (1803–1876): Theological Perspectives on His Search for the Meaning of God, Christology, and the Development of Doctrine" (Ph.D. diss., Graduate Theological Union, Berkeley, 1974); Arie Griffioen, "Orestes Brownson's Synthetic Theology of Revelation, (1826–1844)" (Ph.D., diss., Marquette University, 1988); and the selected bibliography and the introduction in my *Orestes A. Brownson: Selected Writings* (New York: Paulist Press, 1991).

⁶*The Works of Orestes A. Brownson*, ed. Henry F. Brownson, 20 vols. (Detroit: Thorndike Nourse, Publisher, 1882–1887) 5:16. Hereinafter cited as Works.

⁷*From Bossuet to Newman: The Idea of Doctrinal Development* (Cambridge: Cambridge University Press, 1957) 192.

⁸N. Hatch, *The Democratization of American Christianity,* 34–40.

⁹"An Essay on Christianity," *The Gospel Advocate and Impartial Investigator* 7 (January 24, 1829) 21.

¹⁰"Mr. Reese's Letter," *The Gospel Advocate and Impartial Investigator* 7 (July 25, 1829) 239.

¹¹Ibid., 7 (March 21, 1829) 87.

¹²"New Birth," *The Gospel Advocate and Impartial Investigator* 6 (August 16, 1828) 259.

¹³"Vindication of Universalism," *The Gospel Advocate and Impartial Investigator* 7 (May 2, 1829) 141.

¹⁴"An Essay on Christianity," *The Gospel Advocate and Impartial Investigator* 7 (February 7, 1829) 37.

¹⁵Ibid., 7 (April 18, 1829) 118–19.

¹⁶"Essay on Reform," *The Philanthropist* 2 (February 14, 1832) 115; cf. also ibid. (March 13, 1832) 134–35.

¹⁷"Spirituality of Religion," *The Unitarian* 1 (September 1834) 410.

¹⁸Ibid.

¹⁹"Norton on the Evidences of Christianity," *Boston Quarterly Review* 2 (January 1839) 99–105. Hereinafter cited as *BQR.*

²⁰In 1836, Brownson became an original member of the Transcendentalist Club, and although he had ideological sympathies with the Transcendentalists for a number of years thereafter, he was always moderately critical of what he believed were the subjectivist, idealist, and pantheistic tendencies in the thought of Ralph Waldo Emerson and Theodore Parker—preferring himself the eclecticism and what he considered the objective idealism of Victor Cousin.

²¹"Transient and Permanent in Christianity, etc.," *BQR* 4 (October 1841) 448.

²²George Ripley, *A Letter Addressed to the Congregational Church in Purchase Street* (Boston: Freeman and Bolles, 1840) 15.

²³"Transient and Permanent in Christianity," 448. The appeal to the "sense of the Church" was a recurring theme in Brownson's thought in the late 1830s and early 1840s. He admitted in January of 1840 that as he grew older and reflected more deeply upon Christianity, he had a "natural tendency to return to the simple faith of our childhood, and we become less and less inclined to depart from commonly received opinions." Although he acknowledged his reliance upon his own experience and inner light, he also gave presumption of truth to doctrines long held by the human race. The Church's own symbols and doctrines, however, had to be interpreted anew—i.e., in ways contemporaries could understand. "Introduction," *BQR* 3 (January 1840) 4–7. He warned his readers in his 1841 essay on Parker, however, that they should "mistake not innovation for progress, and to bear in mind, that a departure from old beaten tracks is not necessarily to be on the road to truth," "Transient and Permanent," 474.

²⁴Ibid., 449.

[25]Ibid., 460.

[26]Ibid., 453–54.

[27]Ibid., 455.

[28]Ibid., 460.

[29]"Reform and Conservativism," *BQR* 5 (January 1842) 60–84; "Leroux on Humanity," *BQR* 5 (July 1842) 257–322; "Parker's Discourse," *BQR* 5 (October 1842) 385–512; *The Mediatorial Life of Jesus. A Letter to William Ellery Channing, D.D.* (Boston: Charles C. Little and James Brown, 1842); and "The Mission of Jesus and the Church," *The Christian World* 1 (January 7, 14, 21, 28; February 4, 11, 25; April 15, 1843).

[30]It is not important here to outline the philosophical and epistemological foundations of Leroux's and Brownson's doctrine of life by communion. For such a view see my introduction to *Orestes A. Brownson*, 27–36.

[31]"Leroux on Humanity," *BQR* 5 (July 1842) 296.

[32]"The Mission of Jesus," *The Christian World* 1 (January 21, 1843).

[33]"Parker's Discourse," *BQR* 5 (October 1842) 445.

[34]Ibid., 450.

[35]Works, 4:162.

[36]"Parker's Discourse," *BQR* 5:478.

[37]"The Church and Its Mission," *The Christian World* 1 (February 4, 1843).

[38]"Parker's Discourse," *BQR* 5:486; see also Works, 4:149.

[39]"Parker's Discourse," *BQR* 5:487–88.

[40]"The Church and Its Mission," *The Christian World* 1 (February 25, 1843).

[41]"Parker's Discourse," *BQR* 5:489.

[42]Ibid., 490.

[43]Ibid., 500–01.

[44]"Introduction," *Brownson's Quarterly Review* 1 (January 1844) 16, 11–12. Hereinafter cited as *BrQR*.

[45]Ibid., 17.

[46]"Nature and Office of the Church," *BrQR* 1 (April 1844) 254.

[47]Ibid.

[48]"Bishop Hopkins on Novelties," *BrQR* 1 (July 1844) 367.

[49]"Fourierism Repugnant to Christianity," *BrQR* 1 (October 1844) 477–78.

[50]"The Church Against No-Church" (April 1845), Works, 5:357.

[51]Brownson had been reading Möhler's *Die Einheit* (1825) and *Symbolik* (1832) in the early 1840s, and after 1842 his writing shows some influence from these sources.

[52]Works, 5:362–63.

[53]This was true of Chadwick in particular. But others have also failed to mention the dramatic shift in Brownson's thought on the question of development. I cannot do justice here to the numerous arguments Brownson makes against Newman. For more extensive treatment see R. Leliaert, "Orestes Brownson," 211–51; T. Ryan, *Orestes A. Brownson*, 366–80; Edwin Ryan, "Brownson and Newman," *American Ecclesiastical Review* 52 (1915) 406–13; Theodore Maynard, *Orestes Brownson: Yankee, Radical, Catholic* (New York: The Macmillan Co., 1943) 198–210; and esp. Daniel Barnes, "Brownson and Newman: The Controversy Re-examined," *Emerson Society Quarterly Supplement* 50 (1968) 9–20. I believe much more needs to be done on this debate, with special attention being paid to the philosophical, methodological, and cultural differences. Many Newman scholars are excessively critical of Brownson's rejection of Newman's theory without ever examining Brownson's position in its own intellectual and social context.

[54]"Newman's Development of Christian Doctrine" (July 1846), Works, 14:5.

[55]"The Reunion of All Christians" (January 1862), Works, 12:473–74; cf. also 12:491–92.

⁵⁶For his views during this period see the following: "Newman's Development of Doctrine," *BrQR* 8 (July 1846) 342–68; "Newman's Theory of Christian Doctrine," *BrQR* 9 (January 1847) 39–86; "The Dublin Review on Developments," *BrQR* 9 (October 1847) 485–526; "The Dublin Review and Ourselves," *BrQR* 10 (April 1848) 265–72; "Doctrinal Developments," *BrQR* 10 (October 1848) 525–39; "Reply to the Mercersburg Review," *BrQR* 12 (April 1850) 191–228 and (July 1850) 353–78; "The Mercersburg Hypothesis," *BrQR* 16 (April 1854) 253–65.

⁵⁷Works, 14:15.

⁵⁸Works, 14:25.

⁵⁹"Saint-Bonnet on Social Restoration" (October 1851), Works, 14:207.

⁶⁰Brownson's changes after 1850 and especially after 1855 can also be attributed to other factors. His perceptions of political changes in Europe, moreover, forced him to reexamine his own ideological emphases. Between 1846 and 1850 the real dangers in Europe and in the United States, as he saw them, came from the freedom-seeking and revolutionary forces of socialism, communism, and red republicanism. That situation called for support of authority, law, and order. But, after 1850 the counterrevolutionary powers became organized to crush the rebellion and the revolutionary forces for freedom. This new situation called for a rehabilitation of reason and freedom in politics and in religious thought more generally. In 1855, furthermore, Brownson decided to move his family from Boston to New York, and with this move he left once and for all the theological tutelage of Bishop Fitzpatrick.

⁶¹"The Church an Organism" (January 1858), Works, 12:101.

⁶²On this see, "Maret on Reason and Revelation" (July 1858), Works, 1:480–83.

⁶³"Rationalism and Traditionalism" (October 1860), Works, 1:506.

⁶⁴"Maret on Reason and Revelation," Works, 1:489.

⁶⁵"The Church an Organism" (January 1858), Works, 12:99.

⁶⁶"The Reunion of All Christians" (January 1862), Works, 12:491–92.

⁶⁷"The Bible Against Protestants" (January 1860), Works, 7:585.

⁶⁸"The Protestant Rule of Faith" (January 1872), Works, 8:419–20, 429.

⁶⁹"Reading and Study of the Scriptures" (October 1861), Works, 20:177–78.

⁷⁰"The Constitution of the Church" (July 1875), Works, 8:527.

⁷¹"Authority in Matters of Faith" (November 1871), Works, 8:589.

⁷²"The Protestant Rule of Faith" (January 1872), Works, 8:434–38.

⁷³"The Dollingerites, Nationalists and the Papacy" (January 1873), Works, 13:365.

⁷⁴Ibid.

⁷⁵Ibid., 366–67.

⁷⁶Ibid., 367.

⁷⁷Works, 12:377.

⁷⁸See R. Scott Appleby, *"Church and Age Unite!" The Modernist Impulse in American Catholicism* (Notre Dame, Ind.: University of Notre Dame Press, 1992).

11

Tradition as the Development of Dogma According to Yves Congar

Frederick M. Jelly, O.P.

In the teaching of Vatican II, the notion of Tradition as dogmatic development is found in the context of the Dogmatic Constitution on Divine Revelation, *Dei Verbum* (DV), Chapter II, "The Transmission of Divine Revelation." The second paragraph of DV 8 in the text declares:

> The Tradition that comes from the apostles makes progress in the Church, with the help of the Holy Spirit. There is a growth in insight into the realities and words that are being passed on. This comes about in various ways. It comes through the contemplation and study of believers who ponder these things in their hearts (cf. Luke 2:19 and 51). It comes from the intimate sense of spiritual realities which they experience. And it comes from the preaching of those who have received, along with their right of succession in the episcopate, the sure charism of truth. Thus, as the centuries go by, the Church is always advancing towards the plenitude of divine truth, until eventually the words of God are fulfilled in her.[1]

Commenting upon this section of the conciliar document, Joseph Cardinal Ratzinger asserts: "It is not difficult (as in the additions in which Article 7 goes beyond Trent) to recognize the pen of Yves Congar in the text and to see behind it the influence of the Catholic Tübingen school of the nineteenth century with, in particular, its dynamic and organic idea of tradition, which in turn was strongly impregnated by the spirit of German Romanticism."[2]

The principal purpose of this essay is to examine Father Congar's influence upon the development of the Roman Catholic teaching about tradition, particularly as expressed in the above text from Vatican II. Concerning DV 8 of the Dogmatic Constitution, René Latourelle observes: "This is the first time that any document of the extraordinary Magisterium has proposed such an elaborate text on the nature, object and importance of Tradition."[3] To identify and assess any influence upon this official teaching about tradition is theologically and ecumenically significant, especially as it addresses the difficulties in explaining the different ways in which dogmas develop.

This essay considers (1) Congar's thought about "Tradition as History and Development,"[4] a brief but extremely rich section of Part Two, "A Theological Essay" in his monumental *Tradition and Traditions,* (2) the influence that his thought seems to have had on *Dei Verbum* and generally on theological theories of dogmatic development, and (3) the theological and ecumenical contributions made by Congar, with a few comments about their lasting influence upon the future dialogue on the topic of Tradition.

I. *Tradition as History and Development in Congar's Thought*

The initial point emphasized by Congar in his theological essay is that "What is passed on is received by a living, active subject."[5] The persons who receive the realities and words of redeeming faith are not merely passive in their reception of that which is transmitted to them as though they were just repeating it mechanically. The distinction that has been drawn between active and passive tradition tends to minimize the role of the recipient in the process of appropriating the objects being passed on. While this distinction is indeed valid and useful, it must be interpreted properly. There is really no word or communication from one to another without some response on the part of the hearer to the speaker who not only impresses information upon the mind as a seal upon wax but summons the other to enter into an interpersonal relationship.[6] What is true about human language generally is analogously verified in the revealing Word of God which calls us to a religious relationship with the Trinity through faith in Jesus Christ our Savior.

Congar points out that the Bible has this structure of a dialogue between God and ourselves. Such expressions in the New Testament as "obedience to the faith" (Rom 1:5; Acts 5:32), or to "obey the gospel" (2 Thess 1:8; Rom 10:16), or "obedience in acknowledging the gospel" (2 Cor 9:13) indicate clearly that the Word must be actively "received" (1 Thess 4:1), "heard" (Rom 10:17), and "welcomed" (1 Thess 1:6) by a living, active subject. He states: "The New Testament presents Mary as the perfect example of responsive faith. She welcomes the Word in her heart (Luke 2:19, 51)."[7] These are the two biblical references found in Vatican II's text cited above: " . . . a growth in insight into the realities and words that are being passed on . . . comes through the contemplation and study of believers who ponder these things in their hearts" (DV 8). "But Mary kept all these things, pondering them in her heart" (Luke 2:19). " . . . and his mother kept all these things in her heart" (Luke 2:51). The Greek words for "to keep" (συντηρεῖν, διατηρεῖν) and "to ponder" (συμβάλλειν) imply much more than a mere recalling. As Congar puts it: "This is the living fidelity of a mind reflecting upon the meaning of what it has heard, drawing conclusions, trying to determine the boundaries between what is true and what is not."[8] In this context he quotes quite at length from the last of the *University Sermons*, preached by John Henry Cardinal Newman on February 2, 1843, commenting on St. Luke's words about Mary whom he proposes to be

> our pattern of Faith, both in the reception and in the study of Divine Truth. She does not think it enough to accept, she dwells upon it; not enough to possess, she uses it; not enough to assent, she develops it; not enough to submit the Reason, she reasons upon it; not indeed reasoning first, and believing afterwards with Zacharias, yet first believing without reasoning, next from love and reverence, reasoning after believing. And thus she symbolizes to us, not only the faith of the unlearned, but of the Doctors of the Church also, who have to investigate, and weigh, and define, as well as to profess the Gospel; to draw the line between truth and heresy; to anticipate or remedy the various aberrations of wrong reason; to combat pride and recklessness with their own arms; and thus to triumph over the sophist and innovator.[9]

And so the Mother of the Lord, the God-Bearer, did indeed conceive Christ in her heart through faith before doing so physically in her womb—*"in corde priusquam in carne"* or *"in mente priusquam in ventre"* as the Latin Fathers of the Western Church were wont to say. Through the saving grace of her Son, she is the exemplar *par excellence* of receptive righteousness. Her *"fiat"* to the Word of God at the annunciation was an active response flowing from her graced freedom. It was not a consent of faithful and loving obedience resting upon reason alone but a complete self-giving to the infinite self-giving of God.

Like Mary each one of us is called to respond wholeheartedly to the Word of God which addresses not only our intellects but our hearts, not only as individuals but as members of the Church, the body of Christ. No one of us is ever saved in isolation within the Judaeo-Christian tradition. And we are saved to share the good news with others that Christ suffered, died, and rose for the sake of us all. Congar explains: "This presupposes on our part something quite different from a purely passive receptivity; rather does it call for an exchange of gifts. Yes, God gives all, and yet we must nourish with our living substance his action in us. One cannot nourish one's own life on the Word, without a self-giving. We have here a mutual giving, a spiritual banquet wherein Christ is incorporated into us, we into Christ. The covenant that makes the people of God becomes a spiritual marriage, and thus a sharing, a reciprocal relation, ultimately 'one flesh', one body of Christ."[10] In a footnote he acknowledges the inspiration of a passage from Martin Luther's works for the image of our mutual incorporation with Christ.[11] The mystery of the Church must always be at the center of the notion of tradition, particularly as history and development. Our faith is always ecclesial, i.e., circumscribed by the historical and concrete reality of the Church which is the bearer of tradition and, at the same time, is ever being conserved by that tradition.

At this juncture in Congar's thought, we are introduced to a consideration of the Church's historicity. She is made up of human members whose consciousness is intrinsically conditioned by time or who live in a present that joins an accomplished past with an anticipated future. This historical continuum enables us to transcend time by continuously reactualizing the past to release its virtualities in an ever new and dynamic present so that we may have a hand in shaping the future. This is development and progress in human history with all of its cultural, social, political, economic, and military dimensions. And so our deeper insights into the achievements of the past preserve it as potentially productive for new ideas and inventive ways of doing things. The past is never quite finished in the march of time that is our history. It is constantly being recreated into fresh forms through which old implications now become explicit expressions of the richness that had been hidden. Continuity and change are at the very heart of all human tradition. The science and technology of our contemporary world would never have produced its marvelous achievements without building upon those of the past. At the same time, such magnificent accomplishments as the exploration of outer space, heart transplants, computers, etc., are truly innovative creations.

As members of the Church, we are called to translate secular history into salvation history which can be done only if the grace of Christ transforms each one of us personally and corporately. Salvation history is not a separate series of events but the activity of the triune God as it penetrates and permeates our experiences in time and space. The axiom of St. Thomas Aquinas that "grace perfects nature and does not vitiate it" applies to us as individuals within our historical relationships.[12] The sanctifying power of the Holy Spirit does not work in us apart from our essential human characteristic of historicity as though it separated us from space and time. It is a constant conviction of the Judaeo-Christian tradition that the "mighty deeds of God"—indeed the very Person of the divine Son—enter into our history. This is consistent with another principle frequently invoked by Aquinas, namely, "Whatever is received, is received in accord with the condition of the recipient."[13] We receive the revealing Word of God through the various media of divine communication in accord with the condition of our human receptivity requiring teaching, dialogue, social life, etc., if our discursive minds and hearts are to respond as living, active subjects. The historicity that is a natural component of our human existence personally and communally is transformed by the supernatural mystery of the Church so that we become instruments of the Spirit in making salvation history. As Congar puts it: "Created once for all, and continually re-created by *God's* gracious initiative, the Church's own proper time is that of sacred history."[14]

Here Congar embarks upon an analysis of "The time of sacred history."[15] His explanation of the "sacramental nature" of time as experienced in the Church is the second major point of this theological treatment of tradition as historical development of our Christian faith. Sacred or salvation history has both a divine and a human aspect as does the Church herself. God has set that history in motion during two successive phases: (1) the gradual setting up of the covenant, and (2) the entrance of human persons into that covenant in their free response to the divine election at the particular period of history when they are alive. The religious relationship between the triune God and the human race was initiated by a series of divine interventions in history which culminated in the Christ-event. The Bible gives testimony to the living tradition beginning with the call of Abraham at the dawn of salvation history and reaching the perfect revelation of the religious relationship in Christ, particularly in his paschal mystery, the new and eternal covenant in his blood. The Word of God incarnate is the definitive disclosure of human historicity breaking through the barriers of cosmic time. In Christ eternity elevates time without destroying its historical nature. The incarnation and the passover of Jesus Christ do not annul the revelations of the old covenant but bring them to final fulfillment. Congar expresses this truth eloquently: "We can justifiably take up St. Gregory of Nyssa's remark about Moses, David and all the other men of God through whose hearts he effected the successive stages in the progress of sacred history: 'He who ascends will not stop to make a halt, but must be ever moving forward in an unending succession of new beginnings.' The crucial initiatives taken by God in establishing the covenant relationship in Jesus Christ remain not only as truths and memories but also as a dynamic influence: John the Baptist comes 'in the power of Elias'; we pray, 'Remember David, O Lord' (Ps 131); and the elect will sing in heaven the song of Moses, freed from the deep waters."[16]

The second phase of the divine activity begins with the completion of Christ's salvific paschal mystery in the sending of the Pentecostal Spirit who brought original or foundational revelation to its final form in the witness of the apostolic Church. Congar says of this very special time in the historical tradition of the Church: "Words, divine interventions, the events of the life and *transitus* of Christ, the institutions he set up, are so many elements inaugurating the covenant relationship, and they will henceforth bring it to its universal consummation 'through an unending succession of new beginnings'."[17] This inauguration of the new and eternal covenant launches the period of the postapostolic Church or that of dependent revelation which interprets the original revelation constituted in Christ adding only what is already implicit or divinely insinuated and suggested in it.[18] And so until the Second Coming of Christ an ever new structure of relationships has been divinely established in the world which God graciously offers to every human person who is called to enter the covenant and is graced to accept the divine invitation freely. Like Mary we are called to respond with our *"fiat"* to the Word of God. Our "yes" is made possible only by the action of the Holy Spirit who enables each one of us to appropriate the saving truth and power of Christ which transforms our moment in world history into salvation history. Always remaining rooted in the archives of the Church's apostolic consciousness, our own personal faith is a new moment in salvation history representing a development in tradition. The growth and progress is not merely a quantitative increment of another individual added to the number of members in the Church, but more profoundly a qualitative increase of the life of Christ in our world born of the uniqueness of each new personality becoming a new creation in the Spirit. As Congar asserts: "And yet, all is new at each instant in which a man's freedom is engaged, with the aid of divine grace, and all is in movement towards a conclusion, which is purely and simply the end of universal history as a whole."[19]

The nature of the time of salvation history, the time of the Church, is sacramental. According to Aquinas, each of the sacraments of the Church has a threefold significance that telescopes the past, the present, and the future of time: (1) every sacrament symbolizes the past as the accomplishment of our redemption in the completion of the paschal mystery of Christ, (2) each one of the sacraments of the Church signifies a special grace of our present Christian life which it efficaciously bestows upon us in accord with our free dispositions of faith, and (3) all of the sacraments refer to our future glory in heaven of which grace is the seed.[20] The Eucharist, the sacrament of the Church *par excellence* to which all the others lead, may be called an "eschatological miracle." In this sacrament we really and truly receive the risen Lord whose past activity in our history has redeemed us, who in the present Holy Communion personally comes to nourish our spiritual lives, and who will come again at the end of time. As Congar puts it: "Thus the sacraments have a peculiar temporal duration, in which past, present and future are not mutually exclusive, as in our chronological time. Sacramental time, the time of the Church, allows the sharing by men who follow each other through the centuries in an event which is historically unique and which took place at a distant time; this sharing is achieved not merely on the intellectual level, as I could commune with Plato's thought, or with the death of Socrates, but in the presence and action of the mystery of salvation."[21] This "presence-in-mystery" of the historical deeds and sufferings of Christ that have redeemed us is much more than a memorial of past events since they are rendered present or re-presented to us in their redemptive efficacy, particularly in the liturgical celebration of the Eucharist.[22] It is by the power of the Holy Spirit working within her that the Church upon earth transcends in some way her temporal limits and is united with the heavenly Church in the communion of saints.

These gifts of God—indeed the gift of God's own self in the indwelling of the Holy Trinity—do not make salvation history any less a human history. Without this human aspect of sacred or salvation history, there would be no context for our free response to the divine initiatives inviting us to believe, to bear witness to our faith, and to hand it on to the next generation intact and interpreted by our living it in love. Every "visitation" or "coming" of God is a gradual growth of our covenant relationship destined to develop throughout the course of history till the Trinity becomes "all in all." According to the theology of the "divine missions" the Son who was made flesh and the Pentecostal Spirit are continuously being sent into our midst by the Father who always comes with them to take up his abode within us.[23] This activity of the self-giving triune God always works through the sacred humanity of Jesus Christ, our Head, as through a "conjoined animated instrument."[24] This means that Christ is consciously involved in every act of the saving God that makes it possible for us to live freely by faith in history. Our affirmative responses to God's will for us personally and communally in the Church flow from the apostolic and prophetic deposit of faith as their objective source, and from ourselves as their active, living subjective principle moved by the Holy Spirit. Congar sums up his second major point about "the time of sacred history" by concluding: "The time of the Church is thus the time of those responses that are stirred up in us, in the order of truth and love, by the 'divine missions' or visitations of the God who is, who was and who is to come, by which he brings this relationship, revealed and definitively established in Christ, to its final fulfilment. Each moment of this time is thus the present reality of the relationship, the active presence of what brought it about once and for all, and at the same time the beginning of its final consummation."[25]

The third and final point in this part of his theological essay discusses "Tradition: the time of the Church and the time of the Holy Spirit."[26] Now Congar turns to a reconsideration of present time in relation to the past and to the future. He believes that it is more precise to speak of "the continuing presence of the past in the present" than merely "the relation of the present to the past."[27] The theological sense of the expression is more than the sociological since it signifies not just the fidelity of the inheritors of the tradition to their origin but also the identity of its ultimate subject from beginning to end, namely, the Holy Spirit. The Christian Tradition is ever new because "(it) is not the simple permanence of a structure, but a continual renewal and fertility *within* this given structure, which is guaranteed by a living and unchanging principle of identity."[28] This divine principle is the same work done by our risen Lord and the Pentecostal Spirit which, however, is appropriated to each in different ways. The Incarnate Word reveals the Father, and by instituting the sacraments, the apostolate, and the Church definitively establishes the new and eternal covenant. The Pentecostal Spirit vitalizes this structure as the "heart" or "soul" of the mystical body and enables us to interiorize the gifts won for us by Christ. Under the influence of the Spirit the tradition of our faith never grows old but is constantly renewed.

The same Holy Spirit who keeps the deposit of our apostolic faith ever fresh at the same time keeps the eyes of our faith upon the future. God's immutable will to save us is radically eschatological, a promise that can find its fulfillment only in the gradual growth of grace toward its full flowering in a future glory beyond space and time. This postterrestrial future can be reached only through the successive stages of a historical future during which the Holy Spirit will teach us all things and bring to our remembrance all that Christ said to the apostles (cf. John 14:26) and will guide us into all the truth (cf. John 16:13). It is in this context that Congar comments: "Thus tradition is development as well as transmission. It is impossible that the religious relationship of men with God should be preserved without its substance bearing fruit. That which was received and professed in baptism becomes, in the context of the Christian life, praise, service, witness, response and decision."[29]

Even a cursory glance at our tradition shows that the Fathers and early councils of the Church, the theologians of the Middle Ages, etc., were deeply conscious of development in the Church under the guidance of the Holy Spirit as the implications of the deposit of faith were gradually drawn out. Congar speaks of Scripture "explaining itself" in tradition so that it may be said there is "more" in the ecclesial explanation and dogmatic definition than in the text of the Bible, " . . . understood at the purely philological and historical level."[30] He is careful to note immediately, however, that the magisterium and the Church as a whole must ever return to the normative source of the transmitted deposit of faith which always contains more than we can possibly receive or express. The Church's tradition "treasures" its inexhaustible source both by preserving it and by actualizing its spiritual richness for each generation of believers. Without this actualization of God's revealing Word for every moment of salvation history, the Church is not really preserving the apostolic faith as the "continuing presence of the past in the present" since that Word would not be addressing us today but presenting us with a historical record of our past.

The continuity and change within the living tradition of the Church maintains us in a dynamic communication with all the saints of salvation history and with the apostles themselves by and through whom we are in communion with the very consciousness of our Lord's risen humanity where the whole of the divine mystery resides eternally. That mystery is continually being made manifest to us as meaningful in our own cultural context which requires explicitations that were not necessary for the apostles themselves. And it is the totality of the mystery of Christ which is made accessible to us, not merely the nucleus of the Christian message in its origins.

We cannot share in the consciousness of Christ without receiving the mystery as a whole, without accepting all its richness as handed on to us in the Church. Although the richness of the treasure of our faith can never be fully expressed at the level of explicit understanding, of historical research and even of dogmatic definition, whatever is necessary for the salvation of any participants in the tradition is continually developed and made available in the ecclesial communion of faith. New revelations are not made in and by the Church since the apostolic era, but she is called to continue the essential structure of the covenant relationship by drawing out its implications for the faith of every age.

While the entire Church is the agent or efficient cause of handing on and developing the monuments of tradition, the magisterium is endowed by the Spirit with the special normative role of judging the authenticity of such developments. Far from being a "source" of revelation, its functional charism for the sake of the whole Church is to discern without error through the assistance of the Spirit what are the authentic dogmatic developments which requires the hard work of "positive theology" beginning with a thorough exegetical study and proceeding through the significant moments of the unfolding of the Scriptures as they yield a fuller meaning in the course of tradition. But the necessary task of positive theology is not the final word since, like all the other parts of theology such as systematics, it must continuously learn as well as teach. In Congar's own words: "The last word belongs to the Holy Spirit, and to his human instrument, set up by God among his people the magisterium of the episcopal college, the heir of the apostolic college in the order of the ministry."[31] At the very end of his three-volume work *I Believe in the Holy Spirit,* he seems to sum up his thought about tradition as a historical development of dogma by speaking of "The Life of the Church as One Long Epiclesis."[32] Basing himself upon the epiclesis or invocation of the Holy Spirit as it appears in the anaphora of the Eucharistic Liturgy, he shows how it is also expressed in the celebration of other sacraments and sacramentals in the Church. He explains the aptness of calling the Church's life "one long epiclesis":

> The Church can be sure that God works in it, but, because it is God and not the Church that is the principle of this holy activity, the Church has to pray earnestly for his intervention as a grace. As an apostle, Paul was convinced that he was proclaiming the Word of God, yet he still prayed and had others pray for it (see Col 4:3; Eph 6:19). Jesus was sure that he was doing God's work, yet he too prayed before he chose his apostles (see Luke 6:12-13). The same way, the Church does not in itself have any assurance that

it is doing work that will "well up to eternal life"; it has to pray for the grace of the one who is uncreated Grace, that is, the absolute Gift, the Breath of the Father and the Word.[33]

II. *Influence of Congar's Thought upon* Dei Verbum *and Theories of Development*

As mentioned in the introduction of this essay, Cardinal Ratzinger acknowledges Congar's influence upon DV 8. And in the context of our exposing the first major aspect of his thought about tradition as history and development, we also indicated that the same conciliar text uses the identical scriptural references (Luke 2:19, 51) as does Congar who interprets the New Testament as thereby presenting Mary to be the perfect example of responsive faith illustrating the first way that tradition develops, namely, "through the contemplation and study of believers" (DV 8). Even a quick comparison between Vatican II's teaching on the topic and the ideas of Congar as we have presented them could cause one to say that his theological essay was a commentary upon DV 8 before it was finally formulated and that the council's text itself is a brief but brilliant summary of his most salient points.

The phrase of the text " . . . with the help of the Holy Spirit" certainly resonates with the constant refrain in Congar's essay which insists in a variety of ways that the Holy Spirit's activity in the tradition of the Church is always its ultimate principle of authentic development. The supernatural character of any progress and growth in the faith demands that its principal cause be above the innate capacities of the human person. Faith itself and all that it encompasses in terms of creed, cult, and a code of ethical behavior is beyond the natural endowments of our cognitive, affective, and conative drives. And so any theories of development that limit its source to our unaided reason, our finite free will, or any other nongraced power of our embodied spirits are *ipso facto* inadequate to explain how the tradition of faith unfolds.[34] There have been "logical" theories of development which have not only failed to account for the supernatural character of progress in faith but do not provide a suitable explanation of the nonrational factors involved in "a growth in insight into the realities and words that are being passed on" (DV 8). Such are the aspirations that inspire the devotion of our worship and the dedication of our witness to Christ. Congar's thought includes these nonrational (not irrational) factors within the matrix of development. Surely the nonverbal realities that are transmitted in our tradition as the ritual acts of liturgical celebrations, the so-called "matter" of the sacraments as water in baptism, bread and wine in the Eucharist, etc., actions of the various ministries in the Church, and the like, are a precious part of its object or content. Ordinarily they are accompanied by words to bring out their rich symbolic meaning which is always the case with the sacraments in which the words are the "form" giving precise significance to the material used and the action administered. This sacramental structure is characteristic of original revelation itself with its intimate unity of historical deeds as the quasi matter and prophetic interpretation of the events as the quasi form determining under divine charism God's intentionality or the salvific meaning of the event.[35] Similarly dependent revelation in the postapostolic tradition under the impact of the Holy Spirit weds words and deeds, especially in the sacraments of the Church, to disclose the divine will for our salvation today. But the Word of God addresses us not only on the intellectual level, as Congar clearly teaches, but on the noncognitive levels as well. And so we cannot abstract the words from the sacramental matter and acts as is done when we do theology. Theology, truly a science and a wisdom which proceeds from revelation and faith as its principles, is not to be confused with faith as such. Although supernatural in its source, it is unable of itself to engender or develop that faith. In the history of the Church, theology along with devotion and witness to contemplative and apostolic holiness and zeal has been an important instrument in development of our faith but *per se* is powerless to produce its supernatural activity. Only the Holy Spirit working within the graces and charisms of the faithful Church as a whole and of the normative Magisterium can constantly make us the new creation in Christ. Theology and any of its ancillary disciplines are truly an intellectual service to the Church and its Magisterium, but it is not designed or equipped to effect of itself more than theological development even when it is reflecting upon and explaining the supernatural and the nonrational aspects of our Christian Tradition. We must, therefore, understand Vatican II's " . . . the contemplation and study of believers . . . " (DV 8) as more than a theological enterprise but as the acts of supernatural faith, enlightened and inspired by the Holy Spirit, gaining deeper insights into our Christian Tradition because theology, though instrumental, cannot be a principle of such growth.

The second way identified by Vatican II as a means of development in our tradition of faith is the " . . . intimate sense of spiritual realities which they (we) experience" (DV 8). This would support the proper understanding of the principal cause of development proposed thus far, whether the first or ultimate principal activity of the Holy Spirit or the secondary principal causality of the acts flowing from our own faith. One cannot have an authentically religious experience of God's activity in his/her life and what is its ultimate meaning and value without a supernatural sharing in the consciousness of our risen Lord working with and through the Holy Spirit. As Congar clearly teaches, the sacraments are the special spiritual realities of the Church which enable us to penetrate more profoundly the paschal mystery so that we are graced to grow in our insights into the redemptive mission of Christ as the past is made continually present to our faith. Unlike a "transformistic" theory of development, particularly at the heart of Modernism according to which there is no real identity between original revelation and dogmatic definitions, there must always be preserved the continuity with the past Christ-event in any authentic progress of our faith.[36] Dogmas cannot be based upon a pragmatic notion of their truth which would consider them as necessary only for the sake of a purely external unity in professing the same creed without any intrinsic meaning shared by the community of faith. Dogmas would then be only functional formulations so that a congregation at worship might use the same words as they recite the articles of the Christian creed together. They would have no value as vehicles of manifesting the truths of God's revealing Word as it directs us in our beliefs and behavior toward the fullness of salvation. To transform the truth that alone can make us free (cf. John 8:32) into merely useful phrases and purely subjective sentiments is indeed diametrically opposed to the teaching of Vatican II about "the intimate sense of spiritual realities" (DV 8) that we are called to experience in our Christian lives as well as to the theological doctrine of an Yves Congar.

The third way in which our tradition of faith develops according to the conciliar text is that " . . . it comes from the preaching of those who have received, along with their right of succession in the episcopate, the sure charism of truth" (DV 8). It is evidently an essential element in Congar's position that our faith as individuals or even as members of the Church does not give us the assurance that we are being faithful to the apostolic witness apart from the Magisterium or the infallible teaching authority of the college of bishops as successors of the apostles. The "sure charism of truth" under the enlightenment and inspiration of the Holy Spirit authorizes them to serve in the ministry of preserving the essential unity of the Church's faith in collaboration with the bishop of Rome. This charism differs from the charisms of biblical inspiration and prophetic revelation since the pope and his brother bishops in the universal Church are called to make judgments about the truth or falsity of developments in dogma based upon the apostolic deposit of faith. They are not exempt in their preaching and teaching from searching the Scriptures and apostolic traditions as they have been preserved and developed in the tradition. This task of "positive theology," whether done directly by the bishops or by others who do not have their "sure charism of truth," must also carefully consider the *sensus fidelium* or the faith-understanding of the Church as a whole which is the total agent of development under the influence of the Spirit. The normative judgment of the episcopate, however, is a necessary condition for the certitude of divine Catholic faith.

A Roman Catholic "theological" theory of development of dogma, informed by the thought of Congar, attempts to resolve the dialectical tensions between the "logical" theories and a "transformist" theory.[37] The logical theories reduce the truths of revelation and dogmas of faith to a number of propositional statements about God, while the transformist theory reduces them to a subjective experience unfounded upon objective truth. The former tends toward an objectivistic rationalism and the latter leads to a subjectivistic immanentism. A theological theory of the development of dogma generally gives each element in the process its proper place: logic, historical research, theological reasoning, implicit knowledge in the context of the whole person and of the Church with the special activity of the Holy Spirit in each of the faithful and in the Magisterium. Such a theory tries to depolarize the dialectical tensions between the extreme positions in the logical and transformist theories by uniting the elements of truth in each type into a higher synthesis that accounts for the respective roles of the supernatural (the influence of the Holy Spirit on the faith of the whole Church and magisterial judgments), of theological reasoning (historical research and theological reflection), and of the influences of noncognitive factors upon human consciousness in tradition (affective and conative dimensions of our Christian faith in worship, witness, etc.) as principles and instruments in the development of dogma.

The second paragraph of DV 8 concludes: "Thus, as the centuries go by, the Church is always advancing toward the plenitude of divine truth, until eventually the words of God are fulfilled in her." This concurs completely with Congar's comments concerning John 16:13, "When the Spirit of truth comes, he will guide you into all the truth." His understanding of the Church's life as "one long epiclesis" puts the development of dogma into eschatological perspective. Although at no particular moment within time, even the sacramental time of salvation history, do we grasp the "plenitude" explicitly; we are advancing toward the vision of the total mystery in the eschaton, the final fulfillment of all our yearnings in the supra-historical Church of heaven. St. Augustine's "Our hearts are made for thee O Lord, and they will not rest till they rest in thee" sums up so eloquently the eschatological finality of our faith with its inner dynamism of development during the spiritual pilgrimage of this life.

III. Congar's Contributions to the Ongoing Theological and Ecumenical Dialogue

Yves Congar, a French Dominican who has been one of the outstanding ecumenists of this century, is essentially a positive theologian and not a speculative or a systematic theologian. He has, however, helped to provide reflections upon tradition, as those summarized in this essay, which have contributed to the theories of dogmatic development constructed by a number of systematicians who continue to be influenced by his thought not only to the benefit of theological speculation but also of the ecumenical movement.[38]

The final paragraph of Chapter II, "The Transmission of Divine Revelation," in Vatican II's DV 10 is both the fruit of the work done by such theologians as Congar, Karl Rahner, and Edward Schillebeeckx, as well as the seed of their further reflections about Tradition as dogmatic development: "It is clear, therefore, that, in the supremely wise arrangement of God, sacred Tradition, sacred Scripture and the Magisterium of the Church are so connected and associated that one of them cannot stand without the others. Working together, each in its own way under the action of the one Holy Spirit, they all contribute effectively to the salvation of souls."[39] This conciliar text avoids the two-source theory as a necessary interpretation of the Council of Trent, namely Scripture and Tradition, and so is much more conducive to the ecumenical dialogue between Protestants and Catholics with regard to the *sola scriptura* principle of the Reformation. The organic interdependence between Scripture and Tradition has contributed to a mutual understanding of the "material" sufficiency of Scripture in the development of dogma while at the same time allowing for the necessity of Tradition to have a "formal" sufficiency. As already indicated, Congar speaks of Scripture "explaining itself" within the Tradition wherein the ecclesial statement or dogmatic definition does express something "more" than the biblical text " . . . understood at the purely philological and historical level." This qualification seems to leave enough room in the ongoing theological and ecumenical dialogue to explore mutually acceptable explanations of *sola scriptura* in our Churches. In fact this has been actually going on during Round IX of the U.S. Lutheran/Roman Catholic Theological Dialogue.[40]

As we Catholic participants in this dialogue have learned from our Lutheran partners, *solus Christus* (Christ alone) "radically entails" *sola gratia* (grace alone), *sola fides* (faith alone), and *sola scriptura* (Scripture alone). This means that only Scripture can clearly proclaim that Christ alone saves sinners by grace through faith. The Lutheran side strongly suspects that the Catholic position on Tradition and the Magisterium tends to undermine this teaching that human persons are justified by the grace of faith alone. In the context of dogmatic development, the Catholic side of this bilateral conversation should strive to show that the proper interpretation of Vatican II's DV 10, far from undermining this Lutheran teaching, really considers that Tradition supports Scripture in its proclamation. That the Magisterium also supports it may be inferred from the second paragraph of the same conciliar text:

> But the task of giving an authentic interpretation of the Word of God, whether in its written form or in the form of Tradition, has been entrusted to the living teaching office of the Church alone. Its authority in this matter is exercised in the name of Jesus Christ. Yet this Magisterium is not superior to the Word of God, but is its servant. It teaches only what has been handed on to it. At the divine command and with the help of the Holy Spirit, it listens to this devotedly, guards it with dedication and expounds it faithfully. All that it proposes for belief as being divinely revealed is drawn from this single deposit of faith.[41]

Given the clear biblical revelation of the "good news" that Christ alone saves us by grace through faith, and indeed not through our good works or those of any other, Vatican II's teaching along with that of a Congar awards to Tradition and the Magisterium a formal authority that can only confirm and develop the material content of this fundamental Christian conviction. It would be too much to assert that the conciliar doctrine explicitly holds for the "material" sufficiency of Scripture in all matters of faith and dogma since the text does not restrict the "Word of God" to its "written form" but includes the "form of Tradition." And so a theological theory of Tradition as development might maintain that its Spirit-inspired process in the Church of Christ gives rise to a material or conceptual content of faith in a dogmatic definition that is not clearly and explicitly proclaimed in the Bible, e.g., the canon of Scripture and the defined dogmas of Mary's

Immaculate Conception and Assumption. Just how such a theory can account for these developments without disparaging the "material" sufficiency of Scripture is still a part of the ongoing ecumenical dialogue. Likewise, although considerable progress has been made about justification by faith alone, further conversation seems necessary, particularly between Lutherans and Catholics, concerning the cooperation with Christ's saving grace on the part of justified human freedom.[42] Congar's theological reflections upon the role of the active, living subject in receiving and responding to the Word of God as a "mutual exchange of gifts" entirely made possible by grace can also contribute to this part of the dialogue.

Just how nature and grace or reason and faith are intimately united without suppressing either aspect of our redeemed human freedom is a special problem in any theory of Tradition as the development of dogma. This essay has tried to show that Congar's thought in the matter has contributed greatly toward a solution and should continue to do so. His influence ought to endure through the teaching of Vatican II which, according to George Tavard "For the first time in a council, connected tradition and progress in doctrine, this being a deepening insight into divine truth."[43] He also seems to have influenced the systematic theology of Schillebeeckx who holds " . . . that there is an inherent logical aspect in the process of development but that the process as a whole is pervaded with and directed by a divine beyond, guiding the Church into conclusions that cannot be adequately controlled by reason."[44] Theological reasoning in the service of the Church is an instrumental part of the process; but authentic dogmatic development, ever faithful to the Word of God, can only have the Holy Spirit as its ultimate principle which makes the living Tradition of the Church "one long epiclesis" to borrow once more Congar's inspiring image.

Notes

[1] Austin Flannery, O.P., gen. ed., *Vatican Council II: The Conciliar and Post Conciliar Documents,* Study Edition (Northport, N.Y.: Costello Publishing Co., 1987) 754.

[2] *Commentary on the Documents of Vatican II,* ed. Herbert Vorgrimler (New York: Crossroad, 1989) 3:184.

[3] René Latourelle, S.J., *Theology of Revelation* (Staten Island: Alba House, 1987) 476.

[4] Yves M.-J. Congar, O.P., *Tradition and Traditions: An Historical and a Theological Essay* (New York: The Macmillan Co., 1966) 253–70.

[5] Ibid., 253.

[6] Cf. Latourelle, *Theology of Revelation,* 315–28.

[7] Congar, *Tradition and Traditions,* 253.

[8]Ibid., 254.

[9]Ibid., who quotes from *University Sermons*, XV, ¶3.

[10]Ibid., 255.

[11]Ibid., quoted in note 3 from *Dictata super Psalterium* (on Psalm 68) WA 3:434.

[12]*Summa Theologiae*, Pt. I, q. 1, a. 8, ad 2.

[13]Ibid., q. 75, a. 5, co.; cf. q. 79, a. 6, co.; q. 84, a. 1, co.; q. 89, a. 4, co.; Pt. III, q. 11, a. 5, co., and q. 54, a. 2, ad 1.

[14]Congar, *Tradition and Traditions*, 257.

[15]Ibid.

[16]Ibid., 258.

[17]Ibid.

[18]Cf. Gerald O'Collins, S.J., "Revelation Past and Present," *Vatican II: Assessment and Perspectives Twenty-Five Years After,* ed. René Latourelle, S.J. (New York/Mahwah: Paulist Press, 1988) 1:125-37.

[19]Congar, *Tradition and Traditions*, 259.

[20]*Summa Theologiae*, Pt. III, q. 60, a. 3, co.

[21]Congar, *Tradition and Traditions*, 260.

[22]Cf. Adrian Nocent, O.S.B., *The Liturgical Year: Volume One—Advent, Christmas, Epiphany,* trans. Matthew J. O'Connell (Collegeville: The Liturgical Press, 1977) 187–89.

[23]Cf. Aquinas, *Summa Theologiae*, Pt. I, q. 43.

[24]Cf. ibid., Pt. III, q. 62, a. 5, co.

[25]Congar, *Tradition and Traditions*, 264.

[26]Ibid.

[27]Ibid.

[28]Ibid., 264–65.

[29]Ibid., 266.

[30]Ibid., 267.

[31]Ibid., 270.

[32]Congar, *I Believe in the Holy Spirit: Volume III—The River of Life Flows in the East and in the West,* trans. David Smith (New York: Seabury Press; London: Geoffrey Chapman, 1983) 267–74.

[33]Ibid., 271.

[34]Cf. Edward Schillebeeckx, O.P., *Revelation and Theology,* trans. N. D. Smith (New York: Sheed and Ward, 1967) 1:64–68; Jan Walgrave, O.P., *Unfolding Revelation: The Nature of Doctrinal Development* (Philadelphia: Westminster; London: Hutchinson, 1972) 164–78.

[35]Cf. Latourelle, *Theology of Revelation*, 462.

[36]Cf. Walgrave, *Unfolding Revelation*, 245–53.

[37]Cf. ibid., 332–47.

[38]Cf. Aidan Nichols, O.P., *From Newman to Congar: The Idea of Doctrinal Development from the Victorians to the Second Vatican Council* (Edinburgh: T. & T. Clark, 1990) 248–78.

[39]Flannery, *Vatican Council II*, 756.

[40]Cf. "Scripture and Tradition" to be published as a "Common Statement" in Lutherans and Catholics in Dialogue IX.

[41]Flannery, *Vatican Council II*, 755–56.

[42]Cf. *Justification by Faith: Lutherans and Catholics in Dialogue VII,* ed. H. George Anderson, T. Austin Murphy, and Joseph A. Burgess (Minneapolis: Augsburg Publishing House, 1985) and what has been regarded as the "first big test case for justification by faith alone" (*The One Mediator, the Saints, and Mary: Lutherans and Catholics in Dialogue VIII,* ed. H. George Anderson, J. Francis Stafford, Joseph A. Burgess [Minneapolis: Augsburg, 1992]) which has surfaced the need for further dialogue about our mutual understanding of *sola fides* and

sola gratia particularly in the context of invocation, intercession, and mediation of Mary and all the saints in heaven.

[43]George H. Tavard, "Tradition," *The New Dictionary of Theology,* ed. Joseph A. Komonchak, Mary Collins, and Dermot A. Lane (Wilmington: Michael Glazier, Inc., 1987) 1041.

[44]Walgrave, *Unfolding Revelation,* 347; cf. Schillebeeckx, *Revelation and Theology,* 68–83.

12

The Methodist Perception of Tradition

David Butler

Merely to mention the word Tradition in connection with the Methodist Church is to invite disbelief and even ridicule. Surely the Methodist movement began with the rediscovery of the gospel of Christ based on the Scriptures and had no reference to anything as vague as Tradition? Up to a point this is true, and yet it has to be said that nobody comes to the faith without the presuppositions of his own period of understanding. John Wesley was of course an Anglican who came to his own experience of justifying faith within the tradition of an Anglicanism in which he had been raised by an imaginative mother and by a father who was a born loser. This Anglican tradition of faith included the formulations of Richard Hooker and later authors such as William Laud and Francis White who regarded the faith as resting on the three legs of Scripture, Tradition, and Reason.[1] Because of his own knowledge and experience Wesley was forced to add a fourth, that of Experience. Thus came about the famous Wesley Quadrilateral. The first side of the Quadrilateral can be found in Wesley's affirmation that he always desired both to be a man of one book, "homo unius libri,"[2] and to read and study the Bible as the one, the only standard of truth, and the only model of pure religion.[3] The third side, that of Reason, may be best illustrated by the almost Lockeian use of reason in many of his sermons and pamphlets,[4] such as his "Appeals to Men of Reason and Religion."[5] Henry Rack used appropriate language when he called Wesley a "reasonable" enthusiast.[6] The fourth side, of Experience, is manifest in one who put the assurance of salvation as one of the main tenets of Methodism (the "inward impression of the soul" that we are children of God).[7]

We turn to the second side, that of Tradition. As an Anglican, Wesley claimed that he stood within the Tradition of the Church of England of the eighteenth century. Within that Tradition he gave a prime position to the Fathers:

> . . . the most authentic Commentators on Scripture, as being both the nearest the fountain and eminently endued with that Spirit by whom "all Scripture was given."[8]

His concern was to canonize those writers who were nearest to the New Testament period, even though some might not have possessed much learning and sometimes made mistakes:

> And yet I exceedingly reverence them as well as their writings, and esteem them very highly in love. I reverence them, because they were Christians, such Christians as are above described. And I reverence their writings, because they describe true, genuine Christianity, and direct us to the strongest evidence of the Christian doctrine.[9]

The basis of the authority of the early Fathers of the Church was for Wesley their agreement with the biblical witness to authentic faith:

> But still they never relinquish this: "What the Scripture promises, I enjoy. Come and see what Christianity has done here, and acknowledge it is of God."[10]

For an even higher estimate of the authority of the early Fathers, we turn to the preface to the Apostolic Fathers in the first volume of the Christian Library first published in 1749:

> The plain inference is, Not only that they were not mistaken in their interpretations of the gospel of Christ; but that in all the necessary parts of it, they were assisted by the Holy Ghost, as to be scarce capable of mistaking. Consequently, we are to look on their writings, tho' not of equal authority with the Holy Scriptures, (because neither were the authors of them called in so extraordinary a way to the writing them, nor endued with so large a portion of the blessed Spirit) yet as worthy of a much greater respect, than any composures which have been made since; however men have afterwards written with more art, and a greater stock of human learning, than is to be found not only in the following pieces, but even in the New Testament itself.[11]

The opening sentence of this passage almost offers the Apostolic Fathers the status of quasi infallibility. His main interest in the Fathers, however, is to use them as sources for the doctrines which were controverted by other less enthusiastic members of the Church of England of his day, in particular the witness of the Spirit, the assurance of faith and justification by faith. In his letter to "John Smith" in 1747 he offers evidence for the doctrine of the witness of the Spirit from Scripture, Reason and from the Fathers Origen and Chrysostom.[12] As far as I have been able to discover, this seems to be the only clear reference in Wesley to the Anglican triple criteria for doctrinal pronouncements, those of Scripture, Tradition, and Reason. When he wants to affirm the doctrine of assurance as part of the doctrines of the primitive Church against Richard Tompson in 1755, he turns to the authority of the early centuries and specifically to Clement of Rome, Ignatius, Polycarp, and Origen.[13] His 1762 list of patristic authorities for the doctrine of justification by faith is even more impressive, and here he moves into the later patristic period with Origen, Cyprian, Chrysostom, Hilary, Basil, Ambrose, and Augustine.[14] Other important references give an important place to Irenaeus,[15] and to both Macarius the Egyptian and to Ephraim Syrus, mainly because they offered something of the earliest authentic Christianity, as Wesley wrote of Ephraim:

. . . The most awakened writer, I think, of all the ancients.[16]

That he could be guilty of undue reverence for antiquity can be seen from an early reference in his Journal. At first the appeal to antiquity was very strong for him, in particular due to the influence of John Clayton.[17] In his Journal he states his initial adherence to the Vincentian canon of quod ubique, quod semper, quod ab omnibus creditum est. Later he claims that his bow was bent too far the other way (1) by making antiquity a coordinate rather than a subordinate rule with Scripture, (2) by admitting several doubtful writings as undoubted evidences of antiquity, and (3) by extending antiquity too far, even to the middle or end of the fourth century.[18]

Wesley seems to have evinced little or no respect for the writers between the Fathers and the Reformation. In one passage for example he complains that "the damnable predestination doctrine" hatched by Augustine was made by Peter Lombard into a complete system which was then explained and confirmed by Thomas Aquinas and Duns Scotus.[19] Since he believed that the doctrine of predestination represented God as worse than the devil, more false, more cruel, more unjust, he could hardly have appreciated the systematization of the doctrine by the scholastics.

Thou can'st not mock the sons of men,
   Invite us to draw nigh,

Offer thy grace to all, and then
    Thy grace to most deny! . . .

Doom them an endless death to die,
    From which they could not flee—
No, Lord! Thine inmost bowels cry
    Against the dire decree![20]

"In order to be clearly and fully satisfied what the doctrine of the Church of England is," Wesley simply listed extracts from the Liturgy, Articles, and Homilies of that Church.[21] He believed the liturgy of the Church of England to be solid and scriptural, as he stated in the preface to the Sunday Service of the Methodists in the United States of America in September 1784:

> I believe there is no Liturgy in the world, either in ancient or modern language, which breathes more of a solid, scriptural piety, than the Common Prayer of the Church of England.[22]

On occasions he was forced to defend himself by an appeal to the Thirty-Nine Articles and the Anglican Homilies against fellow members of the Church of England who suspected his orthodoxy.[23] However, when he came to his revision of the Book of Common Prayer for America, he did not hesitate to prune the thirty-nine down to twenty-four, centering on the mainly theological articles, omitting scripturally suspect articles, and abbreviating the whole to about half of the original size. Rupert Davies has pointed out that he was prepared to disagree with Article 19 with its classical definition of the Church as that place where the pure Word of God was preached and the sacraments duly administered. Although this definition did not apply to the Church of Rome, even so Wesley was not prepared to unchurch the Romans.[24]

A part of the Anglican Tradition that he notoriously failed to uphold was that of the historic episcopate. While he believed that episcopacy was essential to the Church, his reading of Lord Peter King[25] and Bishop Stillingfleet[26] led him to the view that in the early Church bishop and presbyter were equal and that episcopal ordination was not always essential. Although he began to consider these matters as early as 1745, it was not until 1784 that he took the monumental step of ordaining Richard Whatcoat and Thomas Vasey for the work in America. The argument was that the Anglican Tradition could not be followed against the consensus of the early

Church if human salvation were at stake.[27] His doctrine of the episcopate can perhaps be best summarized in one illuminating sentence:

> I firmly believe that I am a scriptural "episcopos" as much as any man in England or in Europe; for the *uninterrupted succession* I know to be a fable, which no man ever did or can prove.[28]

John Wesley's reverence for the early Fathers has been noted, but he was also concerned to illustrate the movement of Christian thought and devotion down the centuries and to compile a sort of "third testament" or "part three" made up of selected authors and put together in his fifty-volume "Christian Library" (1749–1755). If we include the biographers, over ninety authors find their place in the Library, and the catholicity of the choice is really quite amazing. By my estimate, about forty-five percent of the Library has Anglican roots. The Anglican authors include John Foxe, John Preston, Jeremy Taylor, Thomas Ken, Anthony Horneck, Simon Patrick, and John Tillotson. The most surprising figure is that of the Puritans who contribute some thirty-five percent of the Library. From this section of the Church we have works by Robert Bolton, Richard Sibbes, Thomas Goodwin, Isaac Ambrose, John Owen, Joseph and Richard Alleine, John Bunyan, Samuel Annesley (John Wesley's grandfather), and Richard Baxter. In descending order we then have the Reformed tradition with six percent (Samuel Rutherford, the Shorter Catechism of the Church of Scotland, a life of Calvin, Henry Scougal, and other Scottish notables), the Roman Catholic tradition with five percent (Blaise Pascal, Antoinette Bourignon, Archbishop Fénélon, Brother Lawrence, Miguel de Molinos, and Gregory Lopez), the Lutheran tradition with four percent (Johannes Arndt, Melanchthon), and the early Fathers with one percent (Clement of Rome, Ignatius, Polycarp, and Macarius of Egypt). These eclectic volumes were produced by Wesley at a considerable loss but were meant to offer his people a selection of the true Christian spiritual tradition. It has often been pointed out that the percentage of Catholic literature is very high for an eighteenth-century work in England; the equivalent of some two and a half volumes out of fifty.

The orthodoxy of the nineteenth and early twentieth centuries in Methodism was to dismiss Tradition and Reason and to pass from Scripture to Experience.[29] Davies suggests that the two major causes for this were the influence of Schleiermacher's concept of religion as a "feeling of dependence" and a considered reaction against the rise of the Tractarian or Oxford Movement. Since the Oxford Movement emphasised the early

Fathers as a major source of Christian truth and led many such as Ward and Newman to Rome, it was perhaps inevitable that Methodists might in some places be moved to feel that Experience rather than Tradition was the greater help in the elucidation of the truth. This comes out most starkly in the correspondence between the Tractarian Edward Bouverie Pusey and the Wesleyan Thomas Jackson in 1842. Pusey in his "Letter to the Archbishop of Canterbury" accused the Wesleyans of teaching the heresy of justification by feelings, as the extracts below show.

> The root of that heresy consists in the way in which the doctrine of Justification is held, being in fact, and *practically,* a "Justification by feelings". "Believe (not 'in Christ' but) that you will be saved, and you will be saved," was early a Wesleyan doctrine; but its character was long held in check, partly by the Church-system, in which those who adopted it had been educated, partly by the continued use of the Sacraments of the Church.

After an unfortunate accusation against Dr. Thomas Coke for aspiring to be a bishop in the Church and being prepared to abandon his Wesleyanism to this end, Pusey makes the accusation that the Wesleyans have abandoned the central Tradition:

> Wesleyanism, then, was said to be "degenerating into a developed heresy", in that it substitutes for the Catholic teaching, a doctrine of Justification for which there is "no warrant in the Word of God", involving the principle of Antinomianism, and, in many cases, practically leading into it, effacing the doctrine of Repentance, and the real character of good works, and virtually superseding the Sacraments.[30]

Jackson was quick to realize that Pusey had neither read John Wesley nor understood him and countered with the argument that feelings, though important, must extend to altered behavior:

> Those persons are most esteemed who attain to the greatest proficiency in these "feelings", at the same time exhibiting the genuine effects of them in their lives.[31]

He aims a few swipes at the inconsistency of one who could remain within the Church of England while holding a doctrine of justification similar to that of the Council of Trent and holding a Catholic view of the Thirty-Nine Articles, as evinced by Tract XC. Jackson then adopts a stance which is nearer a Scriptura Sola position than that held by John Wesley:

> The Wesleyans have been taught by the revered Founder of their societies,
> to be "men of one book"; and to teach nothing as binding upon the con-
> sciences of mankind, but what is clearly taught in the inspired records. . . .
> For religion, in its scriptural simplicity, power, and life, they will not cease
> to contend, leaving all mere ceremonies of human invention, whether de-
> rived from the Nicene Church, or the Church of the Scribes and Pharisees,
> to those who admire them.[32]

Gordon Rupp has pointed out the obtuseness of Thomas Jackson at
this point in his vision of Rome. The encroachments of Catholicism via the
Tractarians, the threat of a renascent Catholicism after the Emancipation
Act of 1829, the Irish immigrations, and the conversions of the intelligent-
sia are offered as excuses for Jackson's stance.[33] The founder of Methodism
was of course equally obtuse in his later years concerning the Catholics, and
the Wesley of the Letter to a Roman Catholic of 1749 is not the same one
as the writer to the editor of the Public Advertiser in 1780. The later Wesley and the bulk of his nineteenth-century followers seem to have used the
word "tradition" in a pejorative sense as "mere ceremonies of human invention." We take William Burt Pope (1822–1903) as an example and quote
from his three-volume "Compendium of Christian Theology" published
in 1880:

> Methodist theology, which has spread during the last century over a very wide
> area of Christendom, is Catholic in the best sense, holding the Doctrinal Ar-
> ticles of the English Church, including the Three Creeds, and therefore main-
> taining the general doctrine of the Reformation. . . . Its peculiarities are
> many, touching chiefly the nature and extent of personal salvation; and with
> regard to these its standards are certain writings of John Wesley and other
> authoritative documents.[34]

This position would be essentially the same as that of the uniting Methodist Churches in 1932, but Burt goes on later to speak of the abuse of
the Tradition within the Catholic community:

> The co-ordinate Rule is that of Oral Tradition, adding doctrines not contained
> in Scripture; or Development, expanding those revealed in germ. It has never
> been authoritatively settled what is the "Verbum Dei non scriptum", or what
> constitute the APOSTOLIC TRADITIONS; but some of the leading Articles
> of Faith and practice are generally included.[35]

As the negotiations for Methodist union began after World War I, the
main point at issue was the question concerning the doctrinal standards of
the united Church.[36] The Wesleyans were concerned that the doctrinal stan-

dards should be those of the founder and the first draft of the scheme in 1919 contained these words:

> That the evangelical doctrines for which Methodism has stood from the be-
> ginning, as held by the three Conferences, and as generally contained in John
> Wesley's *Notes on the New Testament* and the first four volumes of his *Sermons*,
> shall be the doctrinal basis of the Methodist Church.[37]

A. S. Peake, the lay Primitive Methodist biblical scholar, objected strongly to the canonization of Wesley's *Notes* since Wesley had depended on Bengel for many of his ideas, and clearly by 1920 Bengel was not regarded as having said the last word on biblical scholarship.[38] Peake was happy that the qualifying word "generally" was in the statement and even happier that the Wesleyan Conference of 1919 had stated that the *Notes* and the Sermons "were not intended to impose a system of formal or speculative theology on our preachers." Peake hoped that such a phrase could be a basis for the interpretations of Wesley in the united Church. In these negotiations we note that Wesley is being used as a conveyor of the Tradition, in much the same way as Augustine or Gregory the Great were used in the Middle Ages. But even this was not enough for some of the high Wesleyans. Ernest Rattenbury and Sir Henry Lunn, among others, were concerned that the catholic emphases of Methodism were being forgotten in this emphasis on Scripture, even if Scripture interpreted by John Wesley was at issue. They suggested an appeal to the historical emphases of the faith, particularly the anchorage in the ancient Creeds and in the principles of the continental Reformation. If these were omitted, any reconciliation with the Church of England at some future date would be extremely difficult. This argument was not readily accepted by many in all three branches of Methodism, partly because creeds were hardly recited in many parts of Methodism and partly because reconciliation with the Church of England seemed a hopelessly far-off event in the England of the 1920s. When the doctrinal section was finally drafted, most of the objections of the Rattenbury camp had been taken into account and paragraph 30 of the Deed of the Union read:

> The Methodist Church claims and cherishes its place in the Holy Catholic
> Church which is the Body of Christ. It rejoices in the inheritance of the
> Apostolic Faith and loyally accepts the fundamental principles of the historic
> creeds and of the Protestant Reformation. It ever remembers that in the Provi-
> dence of God Methodism was raised up to spread Scriptural Holiness through-
> out the land by the proclamation of the Evangelical Faith and declares its
> unfaltering resolve to be true to its Divinely appointed mission.

> The Doctrines of the Evangelical Faith which Methodism has held from the beginning and still holds are based upon the Divine revelation recorded in the Holy Scriptures. The Methodist Church acknowledges this revelation as the supreme rule of faith and practice. These Evangelical Doctrines to which the Preachers of The Methodist Church both Ministers and Laymen are pledged are contained in Wesley's Notes on the New Testament and the first four volumes of his sermons.

> The Notes on the New Testament and the 44 Sermons are not intended to impose a system of formal or speculative theology on Methodist Preachers, but to set up standards of preaching and belief which should secure loyalty to the fundamental truths of the Gospel of Redemption and ensure the continued witness of the Church to the realities of the Christian experience of salvation.[39]

Within this doctrinal section there are obvious signs of the theological horse trading involved in Methodist union. The high Wesleyans achieved their desire for the mention of the Catholic Church, the historic Creeds, and the principles of the Reformation, while the Primitive Methodist theologians such as Peake (although Peake did not live to see the union) received the necessary qualification that they requested to the use of Wesley as the touchstone of Methodist orthodoxy. There is of course enormous difficulty in deciding what the "fundamental principles" of the historic Creeds are. The Deed probably meant the three historic Creeds and certainly Wesley as an Anglican using the Book of Common Prayer would have believed that it implied the three from the Book of Common Prayer, namely the Apostles', the Nicene, and the Athanasian. It does not in fact specify which creeds it means and certainly a large number of modern Methodists would not be too happy to include the Athanasian Creed with its damnatory clauses. Since it mentions "the fundamental principles" of the ancient Creeds without specifying what they are, it might be worth asking the question whether historically those "principles" included the veneration of the Blessed Virgin Mary as the Mother of God. Certainly she was defined as such at the Council of Ephesus in 431, and the doctrinal work of all the previous councils, Nicea, Constantinople, and Ephesus, was reaffirmed at the fourth ecumenical council at Chalcedon in 451. Thus the affirmation of the "fundamental principles" of the historic Creeds might be implied to have taken the Methodist Church further than she intended to go in 1932.

When the conversations between the Church of England and the Methodist Church began in 1956, it quickly became clear that a statement of the position regarding Scripture and Tradition would need to be made. In

1963 this was a small section of the booklet called "Conversations." The section states that Scripture is the rule of faith and that it is not lawful for the Church to ordain anything contrary to God's written Word. One or two sentences may be quoted which give the feel of what followed:

> Scripture contains the indispensable essentials of salvation but it does not contain all things expedient or even needful for the proper conduct of the life and ordering of the Church.[40]

> Scripture does not prescribe exactly and in all detail those "traditions, rites and ceremonies" which may form a valuable part of the life of the Church, and these are a sphere of the Church's life in which there may be many things determined by the use of reason or the acceptance of custom. It is further recognised that where Scripture gives no clear guidance, and where there is permitted the exercise of human authority, it is the Church and not the individual who decides what is to be done.[41]

The statement later goes on to make clear that what is handed down by the process of tradition is the apostolic testimony of Scripture. When the sixteenth-century reformers attacked the concept of tradition, they attacked not the testimony to Scripture that tradition unfolded but customs which were against the tenor of Scripture:

> When the reformers attacked tradition, it was to oppose the customs of men which had intruded themselves into the Church and which were repugnant to Scripture. They refused to conceive of tradition as a separate source of divine revelation to be given equal authority with Holy Scripture. But they in no wise despised what they had received from the past and appealed confidently to the great creeds and doctors of the Church.[42]

The statement quoted the Edinburgh Conference in 1937 which defined tradition as "the living stream of the Church's life." After a fairly comprehensive look at the elements in tradition, the Scriptures, the "ordinances made in the prime of the christian religion" (the Creeds and the work of the Fathers in particular), and the continuing theological conversation, the statement ended with a positive affirmation:

> Tradition, therefore, should give the Church momentum rather than acting as an inertia from the past. It must be forward rather than backward looking, for the life of the Church is directed forward along the plane of history to the coming of its Lord in judgment and in grace. As it guards and keeps the apostolic testimony and ponders these sacred things in its heart, its aware-

ness of their meaning must deepen and its understanding of their implication widen.[43]

All twelve of the Anglican members signed the report but only eight of the Methodists. The four Methodists, Rev. Dr. Kingsley Barrett, Dr. Thomas Jessop, Rev. Thomas Meadley, and Rev. Dr. Norman Snaith, wrote a dissentient view of the report. In their view the normative and pre-eminent place of Scripture was not recognized nor was its relation to Tradition set out satisfactorily. They made the point that traditions within the Church are of mixed value and must be continually tested by Scripture:

> In a word, tradition represents the worldliness of the church, scripture points it to its supernatural origin and basis.[44]

Many things could be said concerning this dissentient view but perhaps one might be sufficient here. The authors have a view of tradition with a small "t", in the sense of "differing churches' ways of doing things." Clearly this view of tradition was not being discussed in the report for in the document that view of Tradition (capital "T") is meant which is "the living stream of the Church's life." The sentence which suggests that tradition is worldly and Scripture supernatural shows some disregard for the facts of history. When Scripture alone could not sort out the Arian dispute or the doctrine of the nature(s) of Christ, then Councils had to decide the matters, the living presence of the Holy Spirit in some sense making the leaders of the Church conscious of the true Tradition. It is interesting that the four dissentients were none of them historians or systematic theologians.

The later publications had to clarify the relationship between Scripture and Tradition more thoroughly than had been done in 1963. The 1967 interim statement "Towards Reconciliation" had a much more nuanced statement on Scripture and its relation to Tradition so that the reservations of the Methodist dissentients could be met. The primacy of Scripture according to both Churches was underlined from the Thirty-Nine Articles and the Deed of Union. An important clarification was made, first by means of a quote from 1963:

> Every tradition, whether of teaching, custom, or institution, will enrich the Church from age to age . . . just in so far as it witnesses to Christ as the deed of God in the world and as the source and centre alike of Christian faith and Christian community.[45]

Then followed an explanatory sentence:

That is to say, only items of tradition which express and elucidate the norm—that is, the apostolic witness to Christ, as the New Testament records it—are of value.

Many forms of Tradition should therefore be received thankfully as gifts of God; the writings of the Fathers, the Reformers, the classical Anglican divines and the Wesleys, the historic Creeds, and the liturgies and formularies of the great communions of Christendom. The interim statement was followed in its entirety by The Scheme of 1968 in its description of Scripture and Tradition and only two paragraphs were added, one containing the new canon on the subject from the Church of England's canon law, and the other one making it clear that the agreement on Scripture and Tradition was enough for Stage 1 of the reunion but might need further clarification before Stage 2. Methodist comments at the time included the thought that few would maintain that no teaching could be entertained that was not found in Scripture, though some of course clearly still did. Harold Roberts, the Methodist chairman of the commission, insisted that there were doctrines and practices built into the life, worship, and teaching of the Church which were not found explicitly in Scripture. Since one of these was stated to be the historic episcopate, it gave some Methodists one more reason for regarding tradition as something which should not be entertained happily in an official document. That the Deed of Union contained a paragraph concerning tradition was conveniently forgotten or it was felt that the Deed of Union conserved Methodist tradition (small "t") and gave no real place for Tradition (capital "T").

What place then does the Methodist Church have for Tradition? Clearly the Deed of Union insists that there is a Tradition which is consistent with the gospel. That Tradition of faith is found in the writings and teachings of John Wesley (specifically the *Notes* and the *Sermons*), in the teaching of the Reformers, and in the classical Creeds (probably the Nicene Creed and the Apostles' Creed are meant). Any traditions that are repugnant in some way to Scripture cannot be allowed as they go against the apostolic witness of the New Testament. Whether therefore the Methodist Church could ever accept, with whatever qualifications, the Immaculate Conception, Papal Infallibility, or the Assumption of the Virgin Mary is very doubtful. The argument against these is that they are not demanded either explicitly or implicitly by Scripture and in any case are not crucial for human salvation. As has often been stated, the Catholic case for these dogmas depends less on Scripture than upon a sense of the "living Tradition" in the Church.

Yet could it be that as Methodists grow closer to Catholics and understand Catholic devotion, these doctrines which seem strange might become understood as part of the Tradition of the whole Church, rather than being the preserve of one particular part of the Church? The dogmas are understood better when we get inside the community that holds them and can seem less strange when looked at from within that communion with its perspective of faith rather than from outside with our perspective of criticism.

Another matter to be considered is the work of the Holy Spirit in the Christian community. Is the work of the Holy Spirit confined to one period, namely that which preceded the canon of the New Testament, or is his work continuous through the centuries? The exegesis we give to John 16:13 may here be crucial; "when the Spirit of truth comes he will guide you into all the truth." Some Protestants take the view that this word was given only to the apostles and that after their demise the Church has to make do with the Scriptures alone. Other theologians and biblical scholars, both Catholic and Protestant, take the view that the Holy Spirit is present in the Church down the ages, drawing out the implications of the faith of the apostles. Catholics have often formulated their views by means of the doctrine of development, a doctrine most usefully expounded by Newman in 1845, making explicit what has hitherto been only implicit. If any doctrine of development were to be acceptable to Methodists, it would probably have to be made in terms that make it consistent with Scripture. For example, Methodists might be happy to accept the possibility of development in the Church's understanding of the Trinity or even in the growth of the episcopate. It would probably stretch their credulity too far however to accept dogmas such as the Immaculate Conception or Assumption on the basis of a doctrine of development going in the wrong direction, against what they see to be the consensus of true faith in the Church. Since a part of the Church made definitions from a position where it was divided from other parts of the Church, as happened in 1854, 1870, and 1950, they wonder whether Vatican II would have made these definitions, assuming of course that they had not been made before 1962, or would the new ecumenical climate have forced them into the background of Catholic thinking? Finally, perhaps it would be fair to ask how far Catholics can now believe that the Reformation and the Methodist movement can be seen as legitimate events within the Tradition of the whole Church.

Abbreviations

WJW   *Works of John Wesley*. Abingdon Edition. Nashville 1975ff.
JWL   *The Letters of John Wesley*, ed. Telford. London 1931.
JWJ   *The Journal of John Wesley*, ed. Curnock. London 1938.
Works   *The Works of John Wesley*, ed. Jackson. London 1872.

Notes

[1] Richard Hooker, *Laws of Ecclesiastical Polity*, II.viii.7. William Laud, *Library of Anglo-Catholic Theology*, II:1639. Francis White, *Treatise on the Sabbath Day* (London: 1635) 97ff.

[2] John Wesley, *A Plain Account of Christian Perfection* (London: 1952) 11, ¶10.

[3] Ibid., 6, ¶5.

[4] E.g., *Thoughts upon Liberty*, Works XI. 38ff.

[5] WJW 11:37ff.

[6] Henry Rack, *Reasonable Enthusiast* (London: 1989).

[7] WJW 1:267ff.

[8] WJW 1.105.

[9] JWL II:387.

[10] Ibid.

[11] *A Christian Library*, 1749 ed. 1:ix.

[12] JWL II:100.

[13] JWL III:137.

[14] JWL IV:176.

[15] JWL II.387.

[16] JWJ I:284.

[17] See A. B. Lawson, *John Wesley and the Christian Ministry* (London: 1963) 8–9.

[18] JWJ I:419.

[19] JWL VI:175.

[20] WJW 3:542ff. *Sermon on Free Grace*.

[21] WJW 11, ed. Gerald Cragg, 111. *A Farther Appeal to Men of Reason and Religion*.

[22] Works XIV:304.

[23] JWL III:125; IV:379–81.

[24] *History of the Methodist Church in Great Britain*, ed. Gordon Rupp and Rupert Davies, 1:174. See also Sermon 38 *A Caution Against Bigotry* in WJW 2:61ff., esp. 71.

[25] JWL II:54, VII:238.

[26] JWL III:182.

[27] JWL VII:21, 238–39, 284–85.

[28] JWL VII:284.

[29] See Rupert Davies, *The Truth in Tradition*, ed. Davies (London: 1992) 40.

[30] Thomas Jackson, *A Letter to the Rev Edward Pusey D.D.* (London: 1842) 4, 6.

[31] Ibid., 106.

[32] Ibid., 107.

[33] Gordon Rupp, *Thomas Jackson, Methodist Patriarch* (London: 1954) 38.

[34] William Burt Pope, *A Compendium of Christian Theology* (London: 1880) I:20–21.

[35] Ibid., I:211–12.

[36] See John Kent, *The Age of Disunity* (London: 1966) and Robert Currie, *Methodism Divided* (London: 1968).

[37] *Agenda of the Wesleyan Methodist Conference* (London: 1919) 296.

[38] J. Bengel, *Gnomon* 1742 (Stuttgart: 1970) 2 vols.

[39] *Constitutional Practice and Discipline of the Methodist Church* (Peterborough: 1991) 2:212.

[40] *Conversations between the Church of England and the Methodist Church* (London: 1963) 16.

[41] Ibid., 16.

[42] Ibid., 17.

[43] Ibid., 19.

[44] Ibid., 58.

[45] *Anglican-Methodist Unity. The Scheme* (London: 1968) 2.19.

13

The Problem of Tradition in the Definitive Response of the Vatican to the Final Report of the ARCIC I

J. Robert Wright

The concept of tradition in the "definitive response" of the Vatican to the Final Report of the first Anglican-Roman Catholic International Commission (ARCIC),[1] to which George Tavard devoted so much of his intellectual ability and creative energy over the years from 1970 to 1981, is of concern not only to students of "tradition" but also to all who pursue the current ecumenical dialogue between Anglicans and Roman Catholics. This essay will investigate the problems it poses from the perspective of one Anglican/Episcopalian who has been a member of the second ARCIC (1983–1991) but not of the first commission (that actually produced the report). On some points it will also be my contention that the Vatican response has been unfairly criticized.

From a first but careful reading of this response, one could easily conclude, at least from an Anglican perspective, that the Vatican has replaced the agreed criterion of the original mandate by a standard of "complete agreement" and even "identity" with particular doctrinal formulations unique to the Roman Catholic Church in order to establish its judgment that "it is not yet possible to state that substantial agreement has been reached on all the questions studied by the commission." According to the original mandate of Pope Paul VI and Archbishop Michael Ramsey establishing this commission (1966), its work was to be "founded on the Gospels and on the ancient common traditions,"[2] and from this perspective many Anglicans will be inclined to agree with the present Archbishop

223

of Canterbury that the Vatican has now at the end unilaterally shifted the methodology and asked instead whether the Final Report is "identical with the teachings of the Roman Catholic Church," thus requiring that Anglicans "conform to its own theological formulations" and from this unilateral perspective judging the Final Report to be defective.[3] From this perspective, one might understandably conclude that the work of George Tavard and his colleagues has been rejected, as their own Church has replaced the standard of the ancient common traditions, which they did so much to unfold and explicate in ARCIC, by a standard of conformity to certain doctrinal expressions from more recent Roman Catholic tradition. In one sense, as an Episcopalian/Anglican, I am sympathetic with this view, but at a deeper level I believe the problem of tradition in the Vatican's response is far more complex and must be examined under a number of related questions and concepts. The problem, as I shall show, is not only that the ancient common traditions have been replaced by recent Roman Catholic doctrinal formulations as the Vatican's criterion, but that the Vatican response itself has now become an official formulation of "Catholic doctrine," a new statement of "tradition," to which future conformity is expected.

For the purposes of this essay it should be noted at the outset that the official or authoritative status of the Vatican response as it was issued is not entirely clear. At one point it describes itself as "the fruit of a close collaboration between the Congregation for the Doctrine of the Faith and the Pontifical Council for Promoting Christian Unity," but, uncharacteristically for such documents, it was not released at any public press conference in Rome, and it has appeared in technically anonymous form, signed by neither department within the Vatican nor by Cardinals Ratzinger or Cassidy or by the Pope himself.[4] It does, nonetheless, claim to be both "an official response" and the "definitive response of the Catholic Church" and as such does seem to meet the criteria for magisterial documents demanding at least "firm assent" or "religious acceptance" as recently defined by the American Roman Catholic hierarchy.[5] For this reason it is now difficult for theologians or professional ecumenists of the Roman Catholic Church to distance themselves from this document, no matter how much they may wish to do so. I shall have more to say regarding its authoritative and magisterial status near the end of this essay when the problem of "tradition" that it poses is summarized. At this point, though, it must be noted that ultimate responsibility for the message it conveys, according to the Vatican rules established in 1988, belongs to the Congregation for the Doctrine of the Faith, not to the Pontifical Council for Promoting Christian Unity. Moreover, as Fr. Francis Sullivan, S.J., of the Pontifical Gregorian University has observed, the document gives no reference to any contribution that the responses of Roman Catholic regional episcopal conferences might have made to it, and it bears no resemblance to those responses of episcopal conferences that were published prior to the Vatican's directive that such documents not be released to the press.[6]

Let us now turn to the problem of tradition in the official response itself. The very word "tradition" occurs only five times in the document, once in a quote from Vatican II that is paraphrasing St. Irenaeus and four times in the discussion of Scriptural interpretation, where the response asserts that the historical-critical method of interpretation "cannot be separated from the living tradition of the church" and that there is therefore "need for further study concerning Scripture, tradition, and the magisterium and their interrelationship" (a subject on which Cardinal Ratzinger has independently called for discussion). For the authors of this document, therefore, there is a "living tradition" that has a vital relationship to the Church's "magisterium," as we shall see. The document does not comment upon what the Final Report had said is meant by Christian tradition: "permanence in the revealed truth and continuous exploration of its meaning."[7]

Apart from these five references, which are not instances in which the Final Report is being evaluated either on the basis of the ancient common traditions or on the basis of recent Roman Catholic doctrinal formulations, there is only one other reference in the document that even touches on the concept of tradition as it appeared in the original mandate, and this is an affirmation that comes near the beginning of the Explanatory Note forming the bulk of the response: "The members of the commission are seen as speaking together out of a continuum of faith and practice which has its roots in the New Testament and has developed under the guidance of the Holy Spirit throughout history." Here we can imagine a nod of approval from Pope Paul and Archbishop Ramsey, but even this statement is not an evaluation of some particular point in the Final Report by an explicit reference to the ancient common traditions. It is only an affirmation of the original standard, but that criterion is not the one that the Vatican document adopts.

The standard or criterion of tradition that the Vatican document does follow is not that of the ancient common traditions, but that of recent Roman Catholic tradition, generally asserted without any particular source reference. Five times such sources are cited as criteria: Vatican Council I at one point and Vatican Council II in four places (*Lumen gentium* three and *Dei verbum* one). Apart from these instances, there are no less than twenty-five other places where the Vatican's response makes a negative judgment about the ARCIC Final Report on the basis of what seems to be recent Roman Catholic tradition but which is not identified by reference to anything more specific than "Catholic doctrine" or "Catholic faith"— suspended, as it were, midway in the air, presumably obvious to all and needing no documentation whatsoever. It is important now to chronicle these phrases in their actual wording, and in the order in which they appear in the (unnumbered) paragraphs of the document, for collectively they constitute the method by which tradition, recent Roman Catholic tradition, is used as a criterion in the Vatican response's objections to the work of ARCIC I:

"Important differences regarding essential matters of Catholic doctrine," "do not satisfy fully certain elements of Catholic doctrine," "will assure that these affirmations are understood in a way that conforms to Catholic doctrine," "essential to Catholic doctrine on which complete agreement or even at times convergence has eluded," "For the Catholic Church," "The Catholic Church believes," "does not express the fullness of the Catholic faith," "From a Catholic viewpoint, it is not possible," "The Catholic Church sees rather," "need for greater clarification from the Catholic point of view," "The faith of the Catholic Church would be even more clearly reflected if," "For Catholics, . . . must include," "is part of the Catholic faith," "can certainly be interpreted in conformity with Catholic faith. They are insufficient, however," "The Catholic Church holds that," "creates concern from the Roman Catholic point of view," "is central to the Catholic understanding," "The view of the Catholic Church in this matter," "stand in need of further clarification from the Catholic perspective," "The Catholic Church recognizes," "the Catholic doctrine affirms," "according to Catholic teaching," "required before it can be said that the statements made in the Final Report correspond fully to Catholic doctrine," "consonant with the faith of the Catholic Church," "an official response as to the identity of the various statements with the faith of the Church."

These several assertions about "living tradition," about recent and now official (Roman) Catholic doctrine, constitute the basis upon which the Vatican's "official response as to the identity of the various [ARCIC] statements with the faith of the Church" is made as well as its judgment that "it is not yet possible to state that substantial agreement has been reached on all the questions studied by the commission." Yet these assertions nowhere make specific reference to any particular writers or councils within "the ancient common traditions" shared by both Anglicans and Roman Catholics before the Reformation, the basis upon which Pope Paul VI and Archbishop Michael Ramsey founded the ARCIC dialogue. Of course it might be said in reply that these twenty-five negative assertions in the Vatican's response are permeated through and through with the ancient common tradition, and that this should be obvious at least to any good catholic theologian who reads them. The "living tradition of the church" is supposedly identical with the ancient common tradition. But the problem is that this was not obvious to the Roman Catholic members of ARCIC I. The Roman Catholic members of ARCIC I who agreed to the contents of its Final Report, whose names (including that of George Tavard) are appended to it on page 106 for all to see, obviously did not believe that in any of these twenty-five instances they were deviating from "the Catholic faith" or stating it inadequately, or they would not have assented to the texts of the Final Report. Presumably they thought they were doing what they had been mandated to do, establishing their agreements on the Gospels and the ancient common traditions. But the problem is that what they agreed has now been found deficient by their own Church on the basis of criteria that are either referenced to Vatican Councils I and II at best (five instances), or, for the most part (twenty-five instances), linked vaguely to an undifferentiated Roman Catholic tradition of the last five centuries but referenced to nothing in particular, so that intelligent discussion of them is impossible.

One can understand how the Anglican members of the commission, proceeding only from the ancient common traditions and the post-Reformation Anglican tradition, might not have recognized, or at least not have agreed with, these twenty-five or thirty defects in "Catholic doctrine" as discerned by the Vatican. But is it possible that the nine outstanding Roman Catholic members of ARCIC I, listed on page 106, would have so extensively misunderstood the ancient common traditions, or would have misrepresented their own Church's "living" and present "Catholic" teaching on some thirty or thirty-five specific points that the Vatican has discovered and cited in its official response? This, from the viewpoint of the present Anglican writer who was a member of ARCIC II but not of ARCIC I, is indicative of the problem of tradition in the Vatican's definitive response to the ARCIC Final Report.

And yet, the problem is even more complex and must be examined in relation to certain other problems, of which the first is the concept of tradition in the Final Report itself. Since this topic is the subject of another essay in this volume, under the broader heading of tradition in the agreed statements of ARCIC, it will not be treated in any detail here beyond the mention of two points that are especially pertinent. The first of these needs only brief mention, and it concerns the way in which the commission's mandate, "founded on the Gospels and on the ancient common traditions," is rephrased in the statements that the commission itself produced. In the opening paragraph of its first statement on Eucharistic Doctrine (1971), the commission asserted that its intention had been to seek a deeper understanding "which is consonant with biblical teaching and with the tradition of our common inheritance," but at the beginning of its second statement on Ministry and Ordination (1973), the same clause echoing the mandate was repeated but the word "tradition" was changed to the plural "traditions." Understanding how "the Gospels" could easily be broadened to mean "biblical teaching," our attention for the purpose of this essay must focus upon the shift from "tradition" to "traditions." Whether this was an intentional shift due to the difference in subject matter of the second statement, or whether the commission was rephrasing to reflect more precisely the wording of the mandate it had been given, or whether the difference was merely accidental and unintentional, or whether in the commission's view there was no difference between "the tradition of our common inheritance" and "the traditions of our common inheritance," we are not told. At any rate, the difference is not picked up at all in the Vatican's response (nor, for that matter, in the Anglican one), and the wording of the mandate is not even paraphrased in the commission's elucidations or in its statements on authority.

The second point relating to the concept of tradition in the Final Report is more fundamental. It is the question, to what extent did the commission itself explicitly identify or document the "ancient common traditions" as the basis for its various assertions? A survey of the seven statements comprising the Final Report reveals the following numbers of citations (depending, of course, on how the reader identifies them, and understanding the "ancient common traditions" as being post-Scriptural, pre-Reformation, and primarily patristic):

Eucharistic Doctrine: No direct references to the ancient common traditions (ACT), one direct reference to post-Reformation Roman Catholic tradition (RCT), and one direct reference to post-Reformation Anglican tradition (AT); Eucharist Elucidation: ACT-7, RCT-4, AT-4; Ministry and Ordination: ACT- 6, RCT-0, AT-1; Ministry Elucidation: ACT-10, RCT-2, AT-2; Authority I: ACT-7, RCT-9, AT-4; Authority Elucidation: ACT-3, RCT-l, AT-6; Authority II: ACT-4, RCT-17, AT-5. Thus, all told: ACT-

37, RCT-33, AT-22. That is, in the total contents of the Final Report, there are thirty-seven direct references to the ancient common traditions, thirty-three direct references to post-Reformation Roman Catholic tradition, and twenty-two direct references to post-Reformation Anglican tradition.

Presumably the commission would claim that all of its assertions having no precise reference or citation were based, in one way or another, upon the Gospels and the ancient common traditions, and certainly the thirty-seven ACT references purport to be founded on such a basis by the very fact that they are labeled as such. It is not the place of this essay to ascertain the veracity of these assertions, the degree to which they can in fact be justified from the evidence of the early Church; but it is enough to note from this survey that, in addition to the more recent citations from the understanding or tradition of each separate Church, the commission did make many references to the ancient common traditions.

These, if not also the many more general assertions having no particular source reference, could have been critiqued by the Vatican response (and, for that matter, by the Anglican one) on the basis of their veracity, of their faithfulness, to the ancient sources. In fact, as recently as 1980, very early in the pontificate of John Paul II and well before Cardinal Ratzinger was appointed to his position at the head of the Congregation for the Doctrine of the Faith, it looked like this was what might happen, for the Pope in that year commended the commission's methodology in these words: "Your method has been to go behind the habit of thought and expression born and nourished in enmity and controversy, to scrutinize together the great common treasure, to clothe it in a language at once traditional and expressive of the insights of an age which no longer glories in strife but seeks to come together in listening to the quiet voice of the Spirit."[8] The Pope's words have their parallels in the various declarations he has signed with the Oriental Orthodox that do not insist upon acceptance of the Chalcedonian definition, and in Cardinal Ratzinger's 1976 proposal, recently reaffirmed by him (1991), that the Eastern Orthodox not be compelled to accept any doctrine of primacy formulated in the Western Church since the time of the Great Schism of 1054.[9] The question thus could have been asked (and answered): to what extent is the Final Report faithful to the ancient common traditions that it claims (even without source references) to be its basis?

But by the mid-1980s the "ancient common traditions" approach was apparently not to be the criterion put to either Church in Anglican-Roman Catholic dialogue. By the time that official responses were expected from both Churches it had somehow become assumed or agreed that the recent and even present and "living" faith-tradition of each Church, presumably the way in which Scripture is received and lived in each Church today, rather than the original mandate of the Gospels and the ancient common traditions, would be the basis upon which each Church would evaluate the final document. The Vatican response cannot, therefore, be faulted for its attention to recent and present Roman Catholic teaching.

Before evaluating this development, it is next appropriate to ask, at least for the sake of comparison, what concept of tradition we find in the Anglican response to the Final Report, which was completed and published more than three years earlier than the Vatican response?[10] The answer to this question must be: not much at all, apart from an expressed desire that ARCIC II "continue to explore the basis in Scripture and Tradition of the concept of a universal primacy, in conjunction with collegiality, as an instrument of unity." The Anglican response, like the Roman Catholic one, contains no evaluation based specifically upon the Gospels and the ancient common traditions, as the original mandate had put it, but only an answer, more positive than that of the Vatican, to the question whether the agreed statements of the Final Report are "consonant in substance with the faith of Anglicans." Like the Roman Catholic response, it evaluates the report on the basis of more recent Anglican tradition, summarized in the phrase "the faith of Anglicans," but also without precise source references.[11] Indeed, "tradition" seems less of a problem in the Anglican response only because its discussion of specific points in the report is much less extensive than the Roman Catholic response and because it reads on the whole like a more positive document. Anglicans may object that the Roman Catholic response seems more critical of the report than does the Anglican response, but they cannot fault the Roman Catholic response any more than the Anglican one for neglecting the ancient common traditions and responding only in terms of recent and present faith. Both Churches did the same, and the problem of tradition in the Vatican response, in my view, lies elsewhere.

Before a final evaluation of the problem of tradition in the Vatican's response to the ARCIC Final Report can be given, one other point must be explored. Some note must be taken of the commission's use of the term "substantial agreement" that was developed over the course of time, and of the possible reasons why that term, or rather variations of that term having reference to the present faith of each Church instead of referring to the terms of the original mandate, became the basis for the questions finally posed by the Anglican Consultative Council and the Pontifical Council for Christian Unity to the two Churches for their response. I have already pub-

lished a detailed study of the several stages that constitute that term's evolution in the commission's documents, including my own critique of the
term's ambiguity that agrees with many of the objections against that term
raised in the Observations of the Congregation for the Doctrine of the Faith
(1982), and that study will not be repeated here.[12]

Suffice it to say, though, that early-on the commission's point of reference became "substantial agreement," or "basic agreement," or "substantial
consensus," or "consensus at the level of faith," or "agreement on essential matters where [the commission] considers that doctrine admits no diver-
gence," or "consensus on questions where agreement is indispensable for
unity." These are the most common verbal formulations it used to express
its intention, its goal, and its conclusions. Although reference was still occasionally made to "the ancient common traditions," the thrust of the commission's statements was not toward the Gospels and the past tradition that
was held in common before the Reformation but rather toward the living
reality of faith in both Churches today, with more and more references being made to the separate and recent traditions of each Church with an attempt to show how they could be held together in "substantial agreement."
To repeat, there are thirty-three RCT references in the report and twenty-
two AT references. Presumably this was thought necessary if the report was
to receive the assent of both Churches at the highest level. Although I voiced
some hesitations about the vagueness and ambiguities inherent in the term
"substantial agreement" when I became a member of ARCIC II, I was assured by a significant Roman Catholic member of the commission that this
was the methodology that the Vatican wanted, that such agreed statements,
once they were accepted officially by the Churches, would themselves become contemporary statements of the faith that we hold in common, and
that reference could thereafter be made to these statements as contemporary,
authoritative, and official formulations of both Churches.[13]

This, I believe, explains the similarity of both responses in their relative
neglect of explicit reference to the ancient common traditions. It also explains the differing texture of both responses, for Roman Catholics place
much more emphasis upon a living tradition, a recent and present tradition, even a *magisterium*, than do Anglicans, and so it is understandable
that the Roman Catholic response is much more highly nuanced in terms
of "conformity" and even "identity" to recent and present Roman Catholic
doctrine whereas the Anglican response does little more than assert a broad
and vague compatibility with "Anglican faith" together with a few minor
reservations. If the subject of this essay were "the problem of tradition in

the *Anglican* response to the Final Report," the problem would be to identify upon what particular sources of Anglican tradition the Anglican response
is based and then to attempt to demonstrate how there could really be a
"substantial agreement" or a "consonance in substance" with Anglican
faith given the number and weight of the reservations that are known to
stand behind the Anglican response in the sources from which the Emmaus
Report was compiled in preparation for the 1988 Lambeth Conference.[14]
The problem of tradition in the Roman Catholic response, however, is not
the same, nor is it that negligible reference is made to the "ancient common traditions," nor is it that the Roman Catholic response is made on
the basis of the presently accepted norms for determining the "living tradition" of Roman Catholic doctrine. Rather, the problem is, in my view:

1. that the process, methodology, and agreed statements of faith in the
Final Report endorsed by the Roman Catholic membership of ARCIC I
have now, on these some thirty-five counts, been rejected by the highest
Roman Catholic authority in the Vatican response as being inadequate ex-
pressions of tradition as it lives and is received and taught in the Roman
Catholic Church today;

2. that in some thirty of these instances no documentary references are
made to any particular Roman Catholic formularies, with the result that
the "official" Roman Catholic position cannot be known except in terms
of "complete agreement" or "identity" with the wording of the Vatican
response itself;

3. that the teachings of "Catholic doctrine" precisely as they are worded
in the Vatican response have apparently for the most part become (if one
takes at face value the November 1991 statement of the United States Catholic hierarchy on degrees of magisterial authority) "non-revealed truth definitively taught by the magisterium" or at least "ordinary, non-definitive
teaching," in either case now demanding "firm assent" or at least "religious acceptance" on the part of the Catholic faithful;[15] and

4. that it is all this teaching in the Vatican response, in precisely this
wording, now called "Catholic doctrine," with hardly any citations from
either the ancient common tradition or even from the documents of recent
Roman Catholic tradition, with which Anglicans (and presumably Eastern
Orthodox, Lutherans, Methodists, and others) are henceforth expected to
be in "complete agreement" and "identity" before it is "possible to state
that substantial agreement has been reached."

This is the problem, and it is a major one, but from an Anglican perspective not all the news is bad. The Vatican response also, almost as though another hand were now editing it, does affirm that "points of convergence and even of agreement" have been reached which "many would not have thought possible," that the Final Report does constitute "a significant milestone" in the ecumenical movement, that "substantial agreement" (however defined) is a legitimate expression of the goal of ecumenical dialogue, and that the Roman Catholic Church remains committed "to the restoration of visible unity." And there are even glimpses of actual "agreement" in the Vatican's comments upon the report's treatment of certain areas of the doctrines of the Eucharist and of Ministry and Ordination.

These are always qualified, however, in such a way that on virtually no point is it possible to say that the Vatican regards the agreement as "complete" or even fully "substantial," and it would be misleading to suggest that any single point of agreement is ever clearly described in this way. One leading Roman Catholic theologian has published a list of "points of agreement" that he states the Vatican response "notes with approval," and an Anglican commentator published a remarkably similar list of points about two months later, but the present writer has been unable to trace any of the points in either list to any corresponding unequivocal statement of substantial agreement in the document itself.[16] Whenever substantial agreement is mentioned in the response, it is always modified in such a way as to suggest that it has been, at best, not quite attained.

In defense of the Vatican's position, it does seem a legitimate concern that for the unity of two Churches a common language, even an agreed formulation of the faith that is accepted by both Churches and could be used in catechetical teaching, is necessary. Yet in no case, not on any one point, has the Vatican been willing to let the agreed statements of the Final Report, endorsed by its own delegates to ARCIC, become those formulations. Rather, the text of its own response is the wording upon which it insists,[17] and this wording is not the product of ecumenical dialogue. Such an insistence, it would seem, runs counter to the principle that Pope John XXIII formulated at the opening of Vatican II: "The substance of the ancient doctrine of the deposit of faith is one thing, and the way in which it is presented is another."[18]

On the contrary, to reach a "complete agreement" of the kind the Vatican now says it wants, to "conform to Catholic doctrine" as it demands, Anglicans are now asked to accept the Vatican's own formulations expressed in its official response, and this, as the Anglican Communion of Churches, they could not and would not do. There is no way that some future Lambeth Conference would make such alterations to the response that the 1988 Lambeth has already given. Nor, I dare say, would the Eastern Orthodox, the Lutherans, or the Methodists, or any other Church be willing to revise the agreed statements coming from their own dialogues with the Roman Catholic Church in order to allow them to be "conformed" in this way to what is claimed to be "Catholic doctrine." Ecumenical dialogues can continue to meet, but with this sort of methodology being demanded from one side "substantial agreement" will never be reached, whether it be agreement with an ancient common tradition or an agreement that is consonant with the present faith of each Church.

Let us take one example of the implications of this sort of methodology, of what is now presumably expected in ecumenical dialogue if the Vatican response is "definitive," as it says it is. The Roman Catholic Church is the largest in the world, and its doctrine of the papacy is already widely acknowledged (even by the Pope) to be the most difficult for other Churches in ecumenical dialogue. Based upon the "official" and "definitive" status claimed by the Vatican's response to the ARCIC Final Report, what understanding of the living "Catholic" tradition as regards the papacy will other Churches in dialogue now be expected to meet, and what interpretations will Roman Catholic scholars and theologians chosen for ecumenical dialogues be expected to defend? They must now be expected to seek "complete" and "identical" agreement with the following formulations of tradition (among others) that are defined within the Vatican response to ARCIC I and which, in contrast to the agreements of the Final Report itself, are now official statements of "Catholic doctrine" possessing "magisterial authority," even as it has been recently defined:

1. that the universal primacy of the Pope is "a permanent institution . . . directly founded by Jesus during his life on earth . . . something positively intended by God and deriving from the will and institution of Jesus Christ,"

2. that in the apostolic succession there is "an unbroken line of episcopal ordination from Christ through the apostles down through the centuries to the [Roman Catholic] bishops of today and an uninterrupted continuity in Christian doctrine from Christ to those today who teach in union with the college of bishops and its head, the successor of Peter," and that these "unbroken lines of episcopal succession and apostolic teaching stand in causal relationship to each other,"

3. that any "church outside of communion with the Roman pontiff lacks more than just the visible manifestation of unity with the Church of Christ which subsists in the Roman Catholic Church," and

4. that there is a "guaranteed . . . gift of divine assistance in judgment necessarily attached to the office of the bishop of Rome by virtue of which his formal decisions can be known to be assured before their reception by the faithful."

The Roman Catholic members of ARCIC I, including George Tavard, capably represented their Church and even brought it ecumenical credibility in reaching a considerable measure of agreement on the place of the papacy in past and recent tradition, a measure of agreement that has been widely appreciated. Who will be interested in continuing a dialogue on the papacy with their successors if these are the formulations to which any such agreement must now "conform"?[19] No matter how well intentioned and irenical Roman Catholic ecumenical officers and representatives may continue to be, no matter what they may say (and believe) in the context of the dialogue, their Church now has a greatly expanded list of defined positions that at the highest official level they are expected to meet. And even if the surviving Roman Catholic members of ARCIC I choose to make a public and documented defense of the report they signed, a defense of the thirty or more challenged positions that they endorsed and presumably thought were "catholic," it seems unlikely that the stalemate now created at the highest official level will change for several decades.[20]

The Vatican response, unlike the earlier Observations of the Congregation for the Doctrine of the Faith (1982), says that it has accepted the concept of "substantial agreement" as the basis for its evaluation, but its methodology in defining "the living tradition of the church" has made such an agreement impossible for any other Church to accept without complete submission to the terms of the other side. Even though the Vatican response states at one point that what is sought are merely "certain clarifications which will ensure that these affirmations are understood in a way that conforms to Catholic doctrine," it would have been one thing to tell this to its own representatives while that dialogue was still in process and the statements not yet completed, but it will be quite another thing to demand that the entire process of reception be reopened in order to persuade each Church of the Anglican Communion that it must now "conform" to these various changes in wording and substance. Regretfully but firmly, it must be emphasized that this will never happen. And I think it unlikely that any other Church would ever agree to such a process of unilateral reception.

The dialogue must now turn to a frank and open discussion of methodology, of whether "tradition" is to be understood unilaterally as conformity to current Roman Catholic doctrine, and of the relation of contemporary "tradition" in each Church to "biblical teaching and the tradition of our common inheritance." Such a discussion can only be of benefit to Anglicans as well, lest disillusionment set in, lest winter descend, and lest weariness prevail.[21]

Notes

[1]*Origins* 21:28 (December 19, 1991) 442–47; also printed, among other places, in *The Tablet* (December 7, 1991) 1521–24, and in *Catholic International* 3:3 (February 1–14, 1992) 125–30. The paragraphs are not numbered in the original text and therefore the locations of quotations in the document cannot be given precisely. After the first four paragraphs the remainder of the document is labeled "Explanatory Note," but it is clear from context that the Explanatory Note is an integral part of the response, since it is introduced in the third paragraph as being "a detailed summary of the areas where differences or ambiguities remain which seriously hinder the restoration of full communion in faith and in the sacramental life" and since the final paragraph of the Explanatory Note returns to the term "official response." It has been suggested that the "response" itself consists of only the first four paragraphs, which do not contain the detailed criticisms; but the commentaries of Fr. Edward Yarnold, S.J., Fr. Francis Sullivan, S.J., Professor Henry Chadwick, and Canon Christopher Hill all assume that the Explanatory Note is an integral part of the official, definitive response, and this article will do the same. (*The Tablet* [December 7, 1991] 1524–27, [February 1, 1992] 136–38, [February 8, 1992] 166–67; *Bulletin: Centro Pro Unione* 40–41 [Fall–Spring 1991–1992] 36–41).

[2]Anglican-Roman Catholic International Commission, *The Final Report* (London: SPCK; Cincinnati: Forward Movement Publications, 1982) 118.

[3]"Archbishop of Canterbury on Vatican Response," *Origins* 21:28 (December 19, 1991) 447.

[4]Its text does not appear in the (monthly) *Acta Apostolicae Sedis* for December 1991 or for January, February, or March of 1992. The text that appeared in both the English and Italian editions of the *Osservatore Romano* was unsigned.

[5]"The Teaching Ministry of the Diocesan Bishop: A Pastoral Reflection," *Origins* 21:30 (January 2, 1991) 473, 475–92.

[6]*Bulletin: Centro Pro Unione* 40–41 (Fall–Spring 1991–1992) 36–41, esp. 36.

[7]"Elucidation" to "Authority in the Church I," 70. For the compatibility of this phrase with the Anglican understanding of tradition, see Gillian R. Evans, "Permanence in the Revealed Truth and Continuous Exploration of its Meaning," *Quadrilateral at One Hundred*, ed. J. Robert Wright (Cincinnati, Ohio: Forward Movement Publications, 1988) 111–25.

[8]The Secretariat for Promoting Christian Unity, *Information Service* 44 (1980/III–IV) 90; *One in Christ* 16 (1980) 341.

[9]For references, see *Catholic International* 3:3 (February 1–14, 1992) 140; *Doing the Truth in Charity*, ed. Thomas F. Stransky and John B. Sheerin (Ramsey, N.J.: Paulist Press, 1982) 233–34, 237–38, 246–48; and cf. *The Tablet* (February 8, 1992) 170.

[10]Definitive text printed in *The Truth Shall Make You Free. The Lambeth Conference 1988. The Reports, Resolutions & Pastoral Letters from the Bishops.* (London: Church House Publishing, 1988) 210–12. The Lambeth response gives "a clear 'yes' " to the Final Report's state-

ments on Eucharistic Doctrine and on Ministry and Ordination, though questions are raised about the two statements on Authority in the Church.

[11]As in the case of the responses from regional episcopal conferences that preceded the definitive Roman Catholic response but are not mentioned in its final text, so likewise there are many regional background reports and evaluations that lie behind the official Anglican response but are not mentioned in it. For an undocumented, provisional, and unofficial summary of these from the Anglican side, see *The Emmaus Report* (London: Church House Publishing, 1987) 42–77. Where are these files of regional responses kept for each church now, and are they open to the public? What understandings of "tradition" will they reveal?

[12]"Fundamental Consensus: An Anglican Perspective," *In Search of Christian Unity,* ed. Joseph A. Burgess (Minneapolis: Augsburg Fortress, 1991) 168–84, esp. 179.

[13]This has not, of course, happened.

[14]See n. 11.

[15]See n. 5.

[16]Thus Edward Yarnold, S.J., wrote in *The Tablet* of December 7, 1991 (1524): "The particular points of agreement which the document notes with approval concern eucharistic sacrifice, the real presence, the distinction between the ordained and the common priesthood, the sacramental nature of ordination, the necessity of ordained ministry in the Church, the need for an ordained minister to preside at the Eucharist, the recognition that universal primacy is not contrary to the New Testament and within God's purpose for his Church, the truths underlying the Marian dogmas, and the place of magisterial authority in the Church." And R. William Franklin wrote in *The Living Church* of February 2, 1992 (8): "Rome now, for the first time in 400 years, records official agreement with Anglicans on the following: the real presence, the Eucharist as a sacrifice, the distinction between ordained priesthood and the priesthood of all believers, holy orders as a sacrament, the requirement that an ordained person should preside at the Holy Eucharist, the recognition that a universal primate is not contrary to the New Testament or God's plan." Notwithstanding the remarkable similarity of discernment on the part of both these writers, I cannot believe that the authors of the Vatican response would agree with either of them; if so, the response would be worded with fewer equivocations, qualifications, and reservations. I note that Pope John Paul II at his first meeting with Archbishop George Carey (May 25, 1992) did not cite any of these so-called "points of agreement," but rather stated categorically that "the response was not able to endorse the claim of ARCIC I to have reached 'substantial agreement' between Anglicans and Roman Catholics on the eucharist and the ordained ministry" (*Origins* 22:4 [June 4, 1992] 51).

[17]Almost in confirmation of this observation, Fr. Francis Sullivan (see n. 6) writes: "The conclusion I come to after studying this *Response* to ARCIC I is that what the CDF would require of an agreed dialogue statement is that it fully correspond to Catholic doctrine, and that, to do so, it must use the language in which the Roman Catholic Church has expressed that doctrine."

[18]*The Documents of Vatican II,* ed. Walter M. Abbott, S.J. (New York: The America Press, 1966) 715. On the translation and interpretation of this sentence, see n. 6 and p. 40, n. 7.

[19]Almost as a warning to ecumenists of the Eastern Orthodox, Lutheran, Methodist, and other traditions, Fr. Francis Sullivan remarks (see n. 6): "If the Vatican is going to continue to apply the criteria which it has used in judging the work of ARCIC I, then I fear that the ecumenical dialogues in which the Catholic Church is involved have a rather unpromising future ahead of them."

[20]They are intelligent and committed ecumenists, but they are also loyal Roman Catholics. What will they do? What will George Tavard say? To what extent does the "magisterial authority" of the Vatican response (cf. nn. 5, 15) prevent public or private dissent from it on their part, or on the part of other Roman Catholic scholars?

[21]Pope John Paul II, at his first meeting with Archbishop George Carey of Canterbury (May 25, 1992), "assured" the archbishop that the Vatican's response "should not be interpreted as putting a brake on the dialogue" but rather "should be seen as a stimulus to the resolution of outstanding differences" (*Origins* 22:4 [June 4, 1992] 51). Given the content of the Vatican's definitive response and given the improbability that the Anglican Communion will be likely to agree to any such demand for revision of the ARCIC I statements at some future Lambeth Conference, and thus given the failure of a methodology based upon "agreed statements" that claim "substantial agreement," I believe that some new methodology must be proposed directly by the Vatican's Congregation for the Doctrine of the Faith which, if followed, will be acceptable to them. Realistically speaking, for the dialogue to proceed on any other basis (even if some new and optimistic proposal from the Pontifical Council for Christian Unity) is only to be, in the words of the London *Times,* "engaged in designing cathedrals in the air" (leader, May 25, 1992, 11).

14

Tradition in the Agreed Statements of the Anglican-Roman Catholic International Commission

Edward Yarnold, S.J.

George Tavard's distinguished services to the cause of ecumenism included eleven years as a member of the Anglican-Roman Catholic International Commission from 1970 to 1981. As a member of the Preparatory Commission which met three times in 1967, he had helped to produce the Malta Report (1968) which suggested the subject matter and the procedures not only for ARCIC when it met in 1970, but also for the two Churches' general growth toward unity.[1] It was the Preparatory Commission which first formulated the strategy of "reunion by stages" which governed all the work of ARCIC. That many of the Preparatory Commission's wise suggestions have still not been adopted a quarter of a century later is sad evidence of the slow speed of the grinding of the ecumenical mill. (If x = the number of years it takes to establish a schism, the number of years it takes to heal it seems to be in the order of 100x.) Not having been a member of the Preparatory Commission, I cannot speak for George Tavard's contribution to that commission's work, but I well recall occasions when ARCIC was kept from error by his keen logician's eye or when misunderstandings were dispelled and new visions opened by his ability to discern the essentials of a question and to share his insights with others. And all was done with a smiling good humor which disarmed opposition and made it impossible to take offence. That the Malta and Final Reports give so full an account of tradition must be due in large measure to the perspicacity and the authority of George Tavard.

From the very beginning tradition lay at the heart of the deliberations of both the Preparatory Commission and of ARCIC. At the historic Rome meeting in 1966 when Pope Paul VI and the Archbishop of Canterbury Michael Ramsey inaugurated the dialogue between the two communions in the search for "that unity in truth, for which Christ prayed," they recognized that the discussions must be "founded on the Gospels and on the ancient common traditions" (Common Declaration, March 24, 1966).

The reference to *"common* traditions" is significant. The Declaration which the two primates issued understandably refrained from discussing the status of those traditions held *separately* by each of the two Churches. One might venture to make the missing stages in the argument explicit. The virtue of hope requires us to believe that in the fifteen hundred years which preceded the Reformation the Holy Spirit had "reminded" the Church of all the essentials of the gospel truth (cf. John 14:26). Consequently the traditions which evolved in each of the Churches after their separation must be interpreted in the light of the earlier common traditions. The common traditions therefore not only provide a criterion for discerning between true and false subsequent developments; they also offer a means by which one Church can be led to recognize the gospel truth that lies beneath the other Church's unfamiliar formulations and practices.

The Malta Report took the first steps toward articulating this understanding of the relation between the common and the separate. Before proceeding to make recommendations, it recorded "with great thankfulness our common faith in God our Father, in our Lord Jesus Christ, and in the Holy Spirit; our common baptism in the one Church of God; our sharing of the holy Scriptures, of the Apostles' and Nicene Creeds, the Chalcedonian definition, and the teaching of the Fathers; our common Christian inheritance for many centuries with its living traditions of liturgy, theology, spirituality, Church order, and mission" (Malta Report 3). It then turned to the divergences which have arisen since the sixteenth century. They "have arisen not so much from the substance of this common tradition as from our separate ways of receiving it." These differing ways of "receiving" the common faith are said to derive from different *experiences* of its "value and power," differing *"interpretation* of its meaning and authority," differing *"formulation* of its content," differing *"theological elaboration"* of its implications, and differing *"understanding"* of its pastoral applications (italics mine). It is recognized that "further study is needed to distinguish between those differences which are merely apparent, and those which are real and require serious examination" (MR 4).

Although the Report does not itself attempt to answer the question whether one of the two Churches will have to change its position to resolve these "real" differences, it does indicate some of the issues which are relevant to an answer: the "historically conditioned" character of the thought-forms and language in which dogmatic definitions and even Scripture itself are expressed; the way in which dogmatic truths are apprehended and interpreted; and the value and limits of doctrinal comprehensiveness (MR 5). It is recommended that the dialogue between the two Churches should deal with certain relevant ideas of Vatican II (MR 6): the "hierarchy of truths" (*Unitatis Redintegratio* 11), the difference between revealed truths and the manner in which they are formulated (*Gaudium et spes* 62), and the complementary nature of many diversities in theological tradition (*Unitatis Redintegratio* 17).

ARCIC was to go some way toward meeting these perceptive recommendations made by the Preparatory Commission, though not at the depth which some critics were to demand. Cardinal Ratzinger, for example, regrets the absence of a clear formulation of the distinction between tradition and traditions.[2] George Tavard himself, following Yves Congar, has done much to clarify this distinction: tradition is the Church's action of handing down the good news from generation to generation, not by automatic repetition, but by a living process, under the guidance of the Holy Spirit, of deeper penetration and creative application of revealed truth to new situations.[3] Traditions are the particular verbal or practical forms which the Church has evolved to meet particular historical needs. In fact, though ARCIC regularly speaks of traditions, it rarely [if at all] uses the term "tradition" in the sense of the Church's continuing reassimilation of the truth of revelation. Nevertheless the Final Report does provide the material for a systematic theology of tradition of some depth and comprehensiveness, particularly in the first statement on Authority.

In the second paragraph of that document the Commission sets out its answer to the divisive question of the relation between Scripture and tradition. True to its method of seeking agreed statements rather than the precise formulation of historical points of difference between the two Churches, ARCIC provides no signal for the reader of the ecumenical importance of this paragraph. Consequently its significance has escaped the attention of many readers and commentators, who have seen the Statement as simply a discussion of the ministerial structures of authority which the Church needs, rather than on the nature of authority itself.

The understanding of tradition contained in this paragraph can be analyzed into several stages. First come the words and deeds of Jesus himself, through whom "God has spoken finally to men." Next comes the *recognition* by the "apostolic community" of Jesus' words and deeds as "the saving activity of God" and the source of their own "mission to proclaim to all men the good news of salvation." The third stage consists of *transmission,* when the apostolic community "assisted by the Holy Spirit . . . transmitted what they had heard and seen of the life and words of Jesus and their interpretation of his redemptive work." Thus already at this third stage tradition includes in an inseparable union the reporting of the Lord's deeds and words, and the interpretation of them. Fourthly, this interpretative reporting is put in *writing* under the inspiration of the Holy Spirit. The fifth stage is *the Church's acceptance* of these documents as "a normative record of the authentic foundation of the faith," [NB "a" not "the"] which provides the Church with "inspiration" (in the loose sense) for its life and mission; "through these written words the authority of the Word of God is conveyed." (ARCIC prudently declined to enter the debate whether Scripture itself *is* God's Word or is more accurately described as the medium by which the event of God's Word takes place.) The sixth stage occurs when the Church, through using Scripture as a *criterion* for assessing its teaching and practice, "is . . . given the capacity to assess its faith and life." Finally, in a seventh stage this living tradition is the source of the *authority* with which the Church speaks to the world in the name of Christ.

The document makes it clear that what is operative at the sixth stage is not the words of Scripture, as interpreted by the individual through the interior guidance of the Spirit, but rather the community, which with the help of Scripture is "enabled" by the Holy Spirit to "live out the Gospel and so to be led into all the truth" (cf. John 16:13). The Holy Spirit, whose action had been noted before in the inspiration of Scripture, is now seen to be at work at this stage too. The result is the creation of a "common mind" in the community through "shared commitment and belief." "By reference to this common faith each person tests the truth of his [or her] own belief."

This close analysis of the argument of paragraph 2 reveals the mutual dependence of Scripture and tradition. The Church's continuance in a life and a faith which are true to the Gospel is brought about by the possession of the Scriptures with which the Church is entrusted. But, contrariwise, the Scriptures themselves are dependent upon tradition; the Holy Spirit was at work helping the apostolic community to transmit its memory and interpretation of Jesus' words and deeds before that memory was entrusted to writing (in stage 4). Tradition is prior to Scripture, but once Scripture is inspired, written, and canonized, the two are inseparable. Tradition is the living interpretation of Scripture; the Church is guided by Scripture as interpreted within a living tradition. There is no suggestion here that tradition is a source of revelation distinct from Scripture which may preserve truths on which Scripture is silent. *Sola scriptura,* yes; but Scripture interpreted and applied within the Church *is* tradition.

As the document develops, the role of the Holy Spirit is clarified. His indwelling is not only in each Christian (cf. AI 4),[4] but in the Christian community itself (AI 3), where he "continues to maintain the people of God in obedience to the Father's will" and "safeguards their faithfulness to the revelation of Jesus Christ." In this way the Holy Spirit makes Christ's authority "active in the Church" (AI 3). The Spirit does this in two interrelated ways. On the one hand, he acts among all the Christian community: "by sharing in the life of the Spirit all find within the *koinonia* the means to be faithful to the revelation of their Lord" (AI 4), so that "all who live faithfully within the *koinonia* may become sensitive to the leading of the Spirit and be brought towards a deeper understanding of the Gospel and of its implications in diverse cultures and changing situations" (AI 6). Later in the document there is an allusion to Jesus' promise of the Spirit to "remind" the Church of his teaching. "Through reflection upon the word, through the proclamation of the Gospel, through baptism, through worship, especially the eucharist, the people of God are moved to the *living remembrance* [italics mine] of Jesus Christ and of the experience and witness of the apostolic community" (AI 15). On the other hand the Spirit acts through the ordained ministry, whose members receive from him a special gift for the building up of the Church's *koinonia* (AI 5); their task is to "discern" the insights with which the Holy Spirit has equipped the faithful and to "give expression to them" (AI 6). The statement on Ministry had already hinted at this understanding of the role of the ordained ministry in preserving the Church in the truth of the Gospel. "The Christian message needs . . . to be unfolded to the faithful, in order to deepen their knowledge of God and their response of grateful faith" (M 10); part of the meaning of apostolic succession is that bishops are "representative of their churches in fidelity to the teaching and mission of the apostles" (M 16).

Hence tradition involves a dialogue between the ordained and the whole community, in which the roles of witness and listener are exchanged from side to side. "Through this continuing process of discernment and response, in which the faith is expressed and the Gospel is pastorally applied, the Holy

Spirit declares the authority of the Lord Jesus Christ'' (AI 6). This is another passage the subtlety of which escaped the attention of many critics, who maintained that the share of the faithful in the process of tradition had been overlooked.

As we saw above, the Malta Report indicated that the language and thought-forms of dogmatic formulations and of Scripture itself are "historically conditioned." This point, reaffirmed (at least as far as dogma is concerned) by ARCIC, is sufficient to refute the criticism made by Paul Avis that the Final Report takes a "crude propositional" view of revelation, as simply a series of verbal formulas demanding literal acceptance.[5] ARCIC's fullest treatment of this question comes in the section of the first statement on Authority headed "Authority in Matters of Faith," where it is made clear that the fundamental object of the Church's proclamation is "God's saving work in Christ." To clarify and transmit this object, the Church must use many types of verbal formulation, such as creeds and definitions; but these forms of words are only "instrumental to the truth which they are intended to convey" (AI 14). It follows that they are not themselves the ultimate object of faith. One is reminded of St. Thomas's dictum that the ultimate object of faith is not propositions but "First Truth" (namely God himself),[6] and Newman's insight (already formed in his first book) that verbal formulations are imperfect realizations in a "foreign medium" of the ultimate Object of devotion, which is God himself.[7]

It is at this point that the statement develops its understanding of the "living remembrance of Jesus Christ," which was anticipated above. The Church's proclamation is shaped not only by its historical origins, but also by the series of its subsequent attempts to "make the relevance of the Gospel plain to every generation" (AI 15). The remembrance is "living" for two reasons. First, it consists of a developing history of proclamation, sacrament, and worship. In other words, tradition is not the handing on of tablets of stone for the guidance of every age: in this process the act of applying the word to the situation becomes itself a part of the tradition. What the Church proclaims today becomes in its turn part of the reservoir of memory on which tomorrow's proclamation will draw. "This remembrance supports and guides them [the people of God] in their search for language which will effectively communicate the meaning of the Gospel" (AI 15).

There is a second way in which the remembrance of Jesus Christ is living. It is "not enough for the Church simply to repeat the original apostolic words"; the Church must "prophetically . . . translate" these words according to the needs of "all generations and cultures" (AI 15). It follows that no single formulation of doctrine can claim exclusive rights. As Popes Paul VI and John Paul II frequently observed,[8] pluriformity of doctrine is both tolerable and desirable. In the same vein Cardinal Ratzinger wrote of the incomplete understanding of the truth when one Church is deprived of the insights of another Church from which it is separated, and the consequent need which Christians have for the practice of "hermeneutics of unity."[9]

But this series of historically conditioned "restatements" of the good news has a "ground of consistency." First, they must be "consonant with the apostolic witness recorded in the Scriptures." Secondly, some of the restatements themselves are seen to be of "lasting value." "This is why the Church has endorsed certain formulas as authentic expressions of its witness, whose significance transcends the setting in which they were first formulated." However, the permanent, definitive status conferred on formulas in this way does not imply that they are "the only possible, or even the most exact, way of expressing the faith, or that they can never be improved": they in turn will need subsequent restatement (AI 15). We have reached here one of the most difficult questions which ecumenical dialogue has to answer: By what criteria can we judge whether a restatement is consonant with the apostolic witness and with subsequent definitions?[10]

This question is closely associated with the one which ARCIC I was later to put to the authorities of each Church: Is the Final Report "consonant with" *your* faith? The two Churches in fact gave very different answers. The Anglican answer, expressed in resolutions passed by the Lambeth Conference of 1988, was affirmative, at least so far as the statements on Eucharist and Ministry were concerned. The Roman Catholic answer was contained in the Vatican Response of 1991 and was negative. A number of considerations however suggest that the two Churches' judgments on the Final Report were not so radically opposed as they appear at first sight.[11] First, the two sides understood the question in different senses: Lambeth seemed to take "consonant" to mean "logically compatible" or "noncontradictory," while Rome took it to refer to identity. Secondly, the faith in relation to which the ARCIC Report was to be measured is conceived by the two Churches in different ways. Roman Catholics are committed to a number of permanent and irrevocable dogmatic definitions which any ecumenical agreement will be expected to satisfy. The Anglican Communion on the other hand possesses no such body of defined dogma (apart from the definitions of the early councils, which enjoy a unique status), not even the Thirty-Nine Articles or the Book of Common Prayer; indeed the draft answer to the question drawn up by the Church of England's Faith and Order Advisory Group explicitly excluded conformity to past statements as a necessary criterion of consonance. Consequently the two Churches' apparently conflicting verdicts on the Final Report were answers to different questions.

ARCIC itself does go a short way toward explaining how previous dogmatic definitions control subsequent restatements. "Although the categories of thought and the mode of expression may be superseded, restatement always builds upon, and does not contradict, the truth intended by the original definition" (AI 15). Consonance, in other words, is less a matter of logical coherence than of continuity of "intention."[12] But the questions then arise: How can the "intention" of the original definition be recognized, and how can I be sure that the new definition is "building upon" the truth intended by the old?

The second statement on authority returned to the topic in its treatment of infallibility and gave a similar answer, though in different terms. New definitions must be "consonant with the community's faith as grounded in Scripture and interpreted by the mind of the Church" (AII 23). Although this might seem at first reading to be a return to an unhistorical *scriptura sola* position, in reality this is not so: the criterion is not the letter of Scripture but the scripturally-formed faith and mind of the Church. Scripture and tradition are not divorced. The reference to the community's faith and the mind of the Church comes close to Authority I's appeal to the "intention," except that instead of the intention of the original definition what is now at issue is the intention throughout history of the believing community.

Authority II later gives further indications of the way in which the "intention" of the Church's teaching is clarified. "The purpose of this service [of making decisive judgments in matters of faith] cannot be to add to the content of revelation, but is to recall and emphasize some important truth; to expound the faith more lucidly; to expose error; to draw out implications not sufficiently recognized; and to show how Christian truth applies to contemporary issues. These statements would be *intended* [italics mine] to articulate, elucidate or define matters of faith which the community believes at least implicitly" (AII 27). The presupposition must be that just as (once again) the fundamental object of revelation is not verbal formulas but the whole Christ-event (though this of course includes words), so too the "intention" of the Church is deeper than the words of a dogmatic formula and is revealed in deeds as well as words: the action of the liturgy as well as the prayers which the Church uses in it; the moral teaching which springs from the doctrine; the lives of the saints who live by it. The law of prayer is the law of belief; orthopraxis (right action) is orthodoxy (right believing).

We have already quoted the authority of Cardinal Newman, and he can help us again here. The search after criteria for recognizing teachings which are faithful to the "intention" of the Church is none other than his search after tests of true developments of doctrine. He proposed "seven Notes of varying cogency, independence and applicability, to discriminate healthy developments of an idea from its state of corruption and decay."[13] However, to provide criteria (such as "chronic vigour" and "preservation of type") for recognizing true developments is only to push the problem back one stage in the argument, for there then arises the need for criteria for recognizing the authentic presence of the Notes themselves. Is *this particular case* an example of chronic vigour or preservation of type? In fact even in the first edition (written just before he became a Catholic) he had recourse to the existence in the Church of an infallible authority,[14] who presumably in the last resort will make a decision which is not based totally on logic, but on something akin to Newman's "illative sense" which enables a person to go beyond logical necessity in recognizing when in *practical* cases converging evidence points to a certain conclusion.[15]

This paper is not the place for discussing ARCIC's crablike but determined approach toward the subject of papal infallibility which Newman's words raise. Let us consider instead what the Final Report has to say about the teaching authority of ordained ministers, particularly bishops. This authority is in several places expounded in terms of responsibility for "discerning" the truth, for the first time in the statement on ministry, in the paragraph which explains the relationship between the role of the ordained and that of the common priesthood of the whole Christian community. "The goal of the ordained ministry is to serve this priesthood of all the faithful," to "provide a focus of leadership and unity," and to "discern what is of the Spirit in the diversity of the Church's life and promote its unity" (M 7). The idea is amplified in the first authority statement: the ordained minister must not only "discern" the insights of the faithful, but "give authoritative expression to them" (AI 6). We have already considered that the fundamental object of revelation is not verbal formulas but Jesus Christ himself. It is now implied that insight into this fundamental revelation is the common property of the whole Christian community, but not necessarily in an articulated verbal form. The responsibility of the ordained on the other hand is threefold: to recognize what is true in these insights, to articulate this truth in words, and to attach to these formulations the seal of authority. Here we have the elements of what Catholic ecclesiology calls *magisterium*.

However, the task of the faithful is not completed when the ordained ministry has discerned and authoritatively expressed the truth of their insights. Though "the bishops have a special responsibility for promoting truth and discerning error," the process involves "the interaction of bishop and people," which is "a safeguard of Christian life and fidelity" (AI 18). The whole community participates in a process of *reception*. "The Church in all its members is involved in such a definition which clarifies and enriches their grasp of the truth. Their active reflection upon the definition in its turn clarifies its significance. . . . [The] assent of the faithful is the ultimate indication that the Church's authoritative decision in a matter of faith has been truly preserved from error by the Holy Spirit. The Holy Spirit who maintains the Church in the truth will bring its members to receive the definition as true and to assimilate it if what has been declared genuinely expounds the revelation" (AII 25). This section ascribes to the faithful a share in the process of reception which is both confirmatory and explanatory. On the one hand their acceptance of the definition is the "ultimate indication" of the truth of the definition, though not the source of the definition's authority; on the other, they reflect on the definition and clarify its significance.

ARCIC II, though it did not have the benefit of George Tavard's presence, resumed and developed some of the ideas of the first commission on the subject of tradition in its document on *The Church as Communion*.[16] The idea of tradition as the Church's living memory, which we have already noted in the Final Report, now receives fuller treatment in the section headed "Communion: Apostolicity, Catholicity and Holiness." "The content of faith," which is (not verbal propositions but) "the truth of Jesus Christ as it has been transmitted through the apostles," "cannot be dissociated from the gift of the Holy Spirit," who acts by "the safeguarding and quickening of the memory of the teaching and work of Christ and of his exaltation"; this living memory "is present and active within the Church as a whole." Thus the Gospel is not "transmitted solely as a text. The living word of God, together with the Spirit, communicates God's invitation to communion to the whole of his world in every age." To "safeguard" the memory the Church was led (the context implies, by the Spirit) to acknowledge the canon of Scripture as "both test and norm." Moreover the Holy Spirit "quickens" the memory he creates. This implies more than the "repetition" of the words of Scripture: it implies also the "unfolding" of revealed truth. "In every age and culture authentic faithfulness [to the memory of Christ] is expressed in new ways and by fresh insights through which the understanding of the apostolic preaching is enriched" (CC 26–27). The Holy Spirit makes the apostolic tradition a living memory by sacrament as well as word, "pre-eminently in the eucharistic memorial of the once-for-all sacrifice of Christ, in which the Scriptures have always been read." As the creative link between present and past, "apostolic tradition is fundamental to the church's communion, which spans time and space" (CC 31).

ARCIC II ascribed to the Church's living memory a more radical scope than its predecessor. "Since faith seeks understanding, this includes an examination of the very foundations of the faith. As the social setting of the Christian community changes, so the questions and challenges posed both from within and from without the church are never entirely the same" (CC 28). The result will be pluriformity. "Diversity of cultures may often elicit a diversity in the expression of the one Gospel. . . . All authentic insights and perceptions, therefore, have their place within the life and faith of the whole church, the temple of the Holy Spirit" (CC 29). Such diversity at times leads to "tensions," which will be "healthy" if they are "creative," but in other cases may disrupt communion (CC 30). Hence once more the need for an ordained ministry with responsibility to "discern" the insights of the people (CC 31). Healthy diversity is one aspect of the catholicity which is a mark of the Church: "the church in its catholicity is the place where God brings glory to his name through the communion of those he created in his own image and likeness, so diverse yet profoundly one"—a unity in diversity expressed at every Eucharistic celebration, where "it is the same one and indivisible body of Christ reconciling divided humanity that is offered to believers" (CC 36).

Though much of this is a restatement in different (and sometimes more radical) terms of the ideas already expounded more briefly by ARCIC I, two points seem to be new. The first is the association of this living memory with the "communion" which is God's gift to the Church through the Holy Spirit, and which is the theme of the whole statement. The second is the link between two aspects of the Holy Spirit's action as the memory of the Church: the creation of Scripture and the "unfolding" of revealed truth for the needs of each age and culture. This is an affirmation of capital importance for Catholic dialogue with other Christians who are not so ready to see in tradition the work of the Holy Spirit.

The importance of the Final Report's understanding of tradition seems to have escaped the notice of the official Catholic Response to the document which was formulated by the Congregation for the Doctrine for the

Faith (under Cardinal Ratzinger) "in consultation with" the Council for Christian Unity (now, on Cardinal Willebrands' retirement, under Cardinal Cassidy).[17] The Response devotes little space to the subject, and at one point indeed seems totally to misunderstand the mind of ARCIC. For it clearly intends to be criticizing the Final Report when it states that "the Catholic doctrine affirms that the historico-critical method is not sufficient for the interpretation of Scripture. Such interpretation cannot be separated from the living Tradition of the Church which receives the message of Scripture." In fact this declaration is exactly in accord with ARCIC's understanding of the relationship between Scripture and tradition as we have expounded it above and not in contradiction of it.

However, there is another criticism of the Final Report's understanding of tradition where the Response correctly understands ARCIC's mind, namely concerning the Commission's understanding of reception, which has been set out above. The Response finds fault with the Final Report for holding that the assent of the faithful is "required for the recognition that a doctrinal decision of the Pope or of an Ecumenical Council is immune from error (AII 27 and 31)." The Response then sets out its own position: "For the Catholic Church, the certain knowledge of any defined truth is not guaranteed by the reception of the faithful that such is in conformity with Scripture and Tradition, but by the authoritative definition itself on the part of the authentic teachers."[18]

Presumably ARCIC II will have to reply to this criticism: we may perhaps be allowed to suggest some points which they might make. First, the belief that subsequent reception by the *sensus fidelium* confirms the authenticity of a definition (though it does not *constitute* it: ARCIC was very clear on this point) follows logically from the statement of *Lumen Gentium* (n. 25) that "to the resultant definitions the assent of the Church can never be wanting, on account of the activity of that same Holy Spirit, whereby the whole flock of Christ is preserved and progresses in unity of faith." This conclusion, which was pressed frequently and vigorously by Bishop Christopher Butler during ARCIC's discussions, exerted a vital influence on the relevant part of the second statement on Authority. Secondly, there have been moments in Christian history when the refusal by the Church as a whole to accept some teaching of a council or a pope has been the decisive evidence that the teaching was not in fact an authentic act of the magisterium. Examples can readily be found in history, notably in the Church's subsequent rejection of the Arianizing councils of the fourth century, and of the teaching of Pope Honorius that Jesus Christ had only one will. It was some such point that Newman had in mind when he wrote his essay *On Consulting the Faithful in Matters of Doctrine*.[19] Thirdly, as ARCIC I itself stated (AII 25), the reaction of the Church to a definition can help to clarify (and, one may add, perhaps deepen) the meaning of the definition. It is not always possible to be certain of the meaning of a definition intended at the time by the pope or council which defined it. (We are back with the subject of intention again.) This is particularly true of councils, where it may be impossible to be sure that the bishops all understood the words of the definition in the same sense, especially when, as seems to have happened for example at Nicaea in 325 in connection with the word *homoousios*, a precise explanation of the terms was not put before them. Moreover, even if the mind of the defining person or body is discoverable, it may be only at a later date that the Church can sift the fundamental truth which is of permanent validity from the historically conditioned cultural presuppositions in which that truth is expressed. A good example can be found in the Council of Trent's decree on original sin (Denzinger-Schönmetzer 1510–1516), in which the essential truth of mankind's inherited alienation from God is expressed in terms of a belief that few theologians today would regard as true, let alone as defined doctrine, namely the descent of the whole race from one historical forefather.

It is a pity that George Tavard is not a member of ARCIC II, for he perhaps more than anyone except Congar has penetrated to the center of the question of reception.[20] I have in mind particularly his lecture entitled "Tradition in Theology: a Problematic Approach," in which he distinguishes between two criteria for judging the authenticity of a tradition, the formal and the material.[21] The Catholic Church emphasizes the formal criterion, judging the authenticity of a definition to depend upon the authority of the pope or council which has made the definition. The Churches of the Reformation on the other hand have placed their trust in the material criterion, looking to the content of the doctrine: Is the doctrine in conformity with Scripture, or with Scripture interpreted according to protestant tradition, above all according to the doctrine of justification by faith? It is Tavard's contention that "even for Catholics at the highest levels of authority, the form is not always a sure warrant for orthodoxy." He cites as cases in point the twenty-eighth canon of Chalcedon (on the privileges of Constantinople) and the fifth session of Constance (on the supremacy of general councils), which pass the formal criterion, but were subsequently rejected by the Church because the material criterion was not fulfilled. "The full Catholic criterion for the Catholic tradition would be the concordance of a formal criterion (the source or organ which teaches a doctrine) and a material criterion (the agreement of a doctrine with the sum total of the other Catholic doctrines).'' One must therefore "renounce the hope that we may have at our disposal absolute criteria that may serve as touch-stones of orthodoxy" (p. 102). The only practical criterion is the moral unanimity of the faithful (p. 103). Thus, as Tavard sees, the Catholic insistence on the formal criterion and the Protestant insistence on the material are brought into conjunction with the Orthodox criterion of *sobornost,* or the mind of the faithful.

This lecture of Tavard's contains many ideas which confirm and go beyond ARCIC's thinking on tradition. Delivered in the academic year 1974–1975, it reveals the ideas which he brought to the discussions leading to the completion of the two statements on Authority in 1976 and 1981 respectively. Especially evident is the fundamental conviction that "the key to the tradition is always the living and lived self-consciousness of the thinking members of the church" (p. 90). It follows that in Christian proclamation documents are not to be interpreted according to what the CDF calls the "historico-critical method," but in such a way that "each event is explained by all the others. . . . Illustrations are sought both in the synchrony of each period and, since the time limits of historical periods are little more than views which need to be constantly corrected by attention to the flow of events, in the diachrony of each movement of thought. A sort of collective meaning of documents and events is thus elicited from the facts as they are known. This collective meaning yields the *sensus ecclesiae,* the mind of the church, the growing self-awareness of the Christian community, the guidance of the Spirit toward the full truth of Christ's revelation" (pp. 90–91).[22]

It follows for Tavard that "tradition is built up for us and by us out of the past under the felt influence of the Spirit in today's church" (p. 92). Tradition therefore is the Church's memory of itself and of its Lord, at the heart of which lies the memorial of the Eucharist, which is "at the origin and center of tradition, both in the passive sense of what is transmitted (the eucharist as Christ given for the many) and in the active sense of the act of transmission (the eucharist as the central action of Christian initiation, preaching and teaching). Likewise, all Christian tradition is eucharistic, because to hand on the memory-memorial of the *acta et passa Christi* implies giving thanks to the Father for the philanthropy which bestowed on us the gift of his Son" (p. 94).

Another important contribution to the understanding of tradition which ARCIC bore in mind in producing its own work was the sermon delivered in Cambridge, England, a few days after the Commission's first meeting by Cardinal Jan Willebrands, then President of the Secretariat for Promoting Christian Unity.[23] Willebrands put forward the idea of "a plurality of *typoi* within the communion of the one and only Church of Christ." He explains the meaning of the term *typos* as follows. "Where there is a long coherent tradition, commanding men's love and loyalty, creating and sustaining a harmonious and organic whole of complementary elements, each of which supports and strengthens the other, you have the reality of a *typos.*" Among such "complementary elements" are "a characteristic theological method and approach," "a characteristic liturgical expression," "a spiritual and devotional tradition," and "a characteristic canonical discipline." Willebrands concludes that "the tradition which is shared and enriched in a true typology is a *living* tradition—something which looks to the past only as it has vital meaning for the present and contributes dynamically to the future."[24] "The life of the Church *needs* [italics mine] a variety of *typoi* which would manifest the full catholic and apostolic character of the one and holy Church. . . . If a typology of Churches, a diversity in unity and unity in diversity, multiplies the possibilities of identifying and celebrating the presence of God in the world; if it brings nearer the hope of providing an imaginative framework within which Christian hope can transform human consciousness for today, then it has all the justification it needs."

"A variety of *typoi* which . . . manifest the full catholic and apostolic character of the one and holy Church." That sentence can serve as a summary of ARCIC's theology of tradition.

Notes

[1] The Malta Report is included as an appendix to the edition of the Final Report published by S.P.C.K. (London, 1982).

[2] Josef Ratzinger, "Anglican-Catholic Dialogue: Its prospects and hopes," *Church, Ecumenism and Politics* (New York: Crossroad, 1988) 65–88, esp. 78–80.

[3] I return to Tavard's views on tradition toward the end of this article. Cf. Yves Congar, O.P., *Tradition and Traditions: an historical and a theological essay,* trans. Michael Naseby and Thomas Rainborough (London: Burns & Oates, 1966).

[4] I use the following abbreviations in referring to the sections of the ARCIC Statements: M = Agreed Statement on Ministry and Ordination; AI and AII = respectively the first or second Agreed Statement on Authority in the Church; AIE = the Elucidation to AI; CC = The Church as Communion.

[5] Paul Avis, *Ecumenical Theology and the Elusiveness of Doctrine* (London: S.P.C.K., 1986) 11.

[6] *Summa Theologiae,* IIa IIae qu.1 art. 1 and 2.

[7] "The systematic doctrine of the Trinity may be considered as the shadow, projected for the contemplation of the intellect, of the Object of scripturally-informed piety: a representation, economical; necessarily imperfect, as being exhibited in a foreign medium." J. H. New-

man, *The Arians of the Fourth Century* (London: Lumley, 1871) 149 (the first edition was published in 1833 by Rivington). The epistemological position implied in this passage remained characteristic of Newman's thought throughout his life. He was of course still an Anglican when he wrote these words, but he did not see fit to change them when the book was republished after he became a Catholic.

[8]An example is provided by Pope John Paul II's address at Constantinople in 1979 in the presence of the Ecumenical Patriarch: "For nearly a whole millennium, the two sister-Churches [Rome and Constantinople] grew side by side, as two great vital and complementary traditions of the same Church of Christ" (*One in Christ* 16 [1980] 44–45).

[9]Ratzinger, "Anglican-Catholic Dialogue," 82–83.

[10]George Tavard's answer to this question is discussed toward the end of this article.

[11]I have gone into this point in greater detail in my article "Roman Catholic Responses to ARCIC I and II," *Reconciliation*, ed. Oliver Rafferty (Blackrock, Co. Dublin: Columba Press, 1993) 32–52, a *Festschrift* in honor of my Jesuit confrère and friend Michael Hurley; a section of this is to be printed separately in a dossier of comments on the Vatican Response to the Final Report, which I have edited jointly with Canon Christopher Hill.

[12]Maurice Wiles had earlier identified continuity of intention as the sign of an authentic development of doctrine. See M. Wiles, *The Making of Christian Doctrine: A study in the principles of early doctrinal development* (London: C.U.P., 1967). We shall return to the subject of intention when we come to consider reception.

[13]J. H. Newman, *An Essay on the Development of Christian Doctrine* (Notre Dame, Ind.: University of Notre Dame Press, 1989; reprint of the 1878 edition) 171.

[14]" . . . in proportion to the probability of true developments of doctrine and practice in the Divine Scheme, so is the probability also of the appointment in that scheme of an external authority to decide upon them. . . . This is the doctrine of the infallibility of the Church" (1878 edition, p. 78).

[15]J. H. Newman, *An Essay in Aid of a Grammar of Assent,* ed. I. T. Ker (Oxford: Clarendon Press; New York: O.U.P., 1984).

[16]A convenient source is *Origins* 20 (April 11, 1991) 719–27.

[17]Published in many places; for an English edition, see *Osservatore Romano* (December 16, 1991) 21–22.

[18]See George Tavard's own discussion of material and formal norms summarized below.

[19]New York: Sheed and Ward, 1962. The Original appeared in 1859 in *The Rambler* during Newman's brief editorship of that journal.

[20]Yves Congar, O.P., "La 'réception' comme réalité ecclésiologique," *Revue des Sciences Philosophiques et Théologiques* 56 (1972).

[21]*Perspectives on Scripture and Tradition*, ed. J. E. Kelly (Notre Dame, Ind.: Fides Publishers, 1976) 84–104.

[22]I vividly remember the twinkle in George's eye when he explained to ARCIC members passionately committed to the purity of the English language the meaning of the terms "synchronicity" and "diachronicity." In fact he writes himself in an English which is both lucid and elegant.

[23]*Documents on Anglican/Roman Catholic Affairs* (Washington: United States Catholic Conference, 1972).

[24]"If we are only going to fossilize, common sense would seem to suggest that it is not very important whether we do so together or separately."

15

Tradition: The Contingency Factor

Arthur A. Vogel

All would agree that, in a most basic sense, Christian tradition is no different than, and so no less than, the Christian life in its entirety. The difficulties and problems of the one are the difficulties and problems of the other: we speak of Christian tradition when the Christian life is viewed in the course of history—when we see it extended through time—but the Christian life itself is an activity extended through time. It is able to be itself only in the course of time.

As John Henry Newman knew, life is movement bringing with it constant change and organic transformation. Tradition, as the Church's "living voice," must manifest those same dynamic qualities. It would be hard to deny, however, that the passage of time often seems to bring the loss of Christianity's vitality rather than its conspicuous continuation. Indeed, the loss has sometimes been attributed to what is called "the tradition." "Tradition" is so criticized when it has become no more than the residue of a life once lived rather than being the dynamic continuation of that life through time.

The Christian life often seems to become less than itself—at least less than its former self—as time passes. The flower of its life fading, and few if any new buds appearing, the attempt is frequently made to get back to Christian roots, to the fervor of the past. Frightened by perceived weakness in the present, the temptation grows to equate the fervor of the past with the past, and so the revitalization of faith is sought in a return to the past—or, at the very least, the revitalization of faith is attempted by denying the fullness of life in the present.

The loss of the vitality of past human acts is an in-built hazard of the human condition. Encounter with God, as the encounter of any two persons, is a spontaneous activity involving the free exercise of our will and of our ability to express ourselves. Such activity is the most significant dimension of personal living we know, but such encounters have something about them that is also the most fleeting aspect of the reality we are. The very reality that makes personal encounters themselves is a temporal, changing reality; it leaves no trace or lasting product. If such activity is to endure, it needs constantly to be renewed; it does not last in itself. Personal agreements, vows exchanged, kindness offered, love professed, and goals set pass without visible trace.

Material things, on the other hand, and especially manufactured products in those dimensions of their being added by their human fabrication, remain just what they are when their production is over. The words in a book and the proportions in a painting never change, even though the material pages of the book may turn yellow and the pigment in the paint may fade.

Because of their transitory nature, our inclination is to try to memorialize and remember human events in a tangible manner. For memory's sake and in recognition of past achievement, we "materialize" bygone spontaneous actions. A wedding ring materializes the wedding vow, and a peace treaty materializes the consent that terminated the war. But both the ring and the treaty are different from, and less than, the human acts they memorialize. Such "means" of memory—of maintaining the tradition—point to, but they do not contain, the free act of the spirit from which they arose.

It is not difficult to understand the human attempt to remember past events by their materialization, and it is with the same ease that we can understand the futility of trying to equate a material memorial with a free act of personal encounter. It is obvious that a theological proposition does not substitute for life in the presence of God. The Christian tradition is not a *thing*, not even a *theological* thing; it is always a new and living encounter of persons.

What may be called the problem of Christian tradition is the problem of Christianity's effectiveness through time. Christian conviction claims that Christianity's ineffectiveness in the course of time is due to the religion's being reduced to something less than its full self. We have just given a generic description of such reduction, and, if we are honest, we can all give specific illustrations from our own lives of having reduced our faith to something less than itself. Are there not times at which we could all have been said to have been carrying our religion with us rather than living it? Religion can become a thing we carry—or bear—rather than live.

Instead of looking just at ourselves, however, if we look at our pluralistic society as a whole, we will discover another way, perhaps the prevalent way today, Christianity is rendered ineffective in the passing of time.

Opposition to Christianity is not new. Christianity has been a scandal in the world and to the world from its origin. Paul tells us it was "a stumbling block to Jews and folly to Gentiles" (1 Cor 1:23). Opposition to Christianity has been constant throughout its life, but that fact does not deny that the opposition can be of different kinds at different times. Direct opposition that attacks Christianity within and because of its terminology might appear to be the most devastating criticism leveled at it. Actually, of course, it is not, for in such a direct attack both the attacker and the attacked share a common vocabulary. Such attacks are the easiest to which to respond, for all parties to the disagreement share a vocabulary and horizon of meaning.

A much more difficult and devastating attack is what might be called an indirect attack. It is the most characteristic form of opposition to Christianity in the Western world today. In such an assault, Christianity is simply by-passed; no argument is made against it, for it is held to be irrelevant. In this instance, there is no common ground between the attacker and the attacked that can furnish a battlefield upon which a confrontation can occur.

An exponent of such a method of dismissing Christianity is Richard Rorty, who describes himself as a "liberal ironist." He enthusiastically proclaims the present-day world to be both post-religious and post-philosophical; and, in the freedom afforded human beings in such a world, he describes the human vocation to be that of self-creation through the invention of new word games. Rorty sees the history of language as the history of metaphors. Old metaphors die off and new ones arise. A metaphor dies when it begins to be taken literally, i.e., when its use is governed by what gradually becomes an old theory. Metaphors interrupt the coherent expectations of old language systems and are held by Rorty actually to be events that disrupt the literal expectations of language usage. Following the lead of Donald Davidson, Rorty compares a metaphor to someone suddenly, in the midst of a conversation, pointing to something or slapping the face of the person with whom he or she is talking. A metaphor produces an effect, but it does not convey a message that is of one kind with the terms of the conversation interrupted.

In describing the process of self-creation, Rorty offers, at the same time, a criticism of what he takes to be the religious understanding of the world. There is no doubt that Rorty has caught something of the moving spirit of our times, and there is no doubt that he has accurately pointed to a symptomatic inefficacy of a great deal of religion, including Christianity, in our day. He describes a condition I believe any serious observer of the world today will recognize and acknowledge. Yet, as critical as he is of religion, I believe his criticism, rather than confirming the ineffectiveness of Christianity, offers a catalyst capable of restoring the Christian tradition to its true self. I believe that what Rorty offers as a substitute for Christianity is, in many ways, what Christianity actually is. That, at any rate, is what I maintain and the view I will attempt to justify.

As an "ironist," Rorty is a historicist and nominalist; as a "liberal," he thinks that cruel acts are the worst things people can do. Contingency and process are the key ingredients of Rorty's view of the human quest. The search for meaning is not the attempt to discover ideas which most correspond to the inner nature of external reality. Truth is not the correspondence of thought to reality; truth is "what comes to be believed in the course of free and open encounters."[1] Coherence within vocabulary systems rather than correspondence to reality defines truth. In such a coherence theory, the dialectical engagement of persons using different vocabulary systems replaces the attempt to discover the "real nature of things."

Hegel is held up as an example of one who criticized his predecessors not because what they said was false but because their languages were rendered obsolete. The quest for meaning and truth as Rorty understands them thus depends upon the establishment of a liberal society, a society which allows the free, open dialogue of vocabularies. Only in such a society can people work out their private salvation. Rorty's historicist, nominalist platform presents a model of human life that is exciting, dynamic, and challenging. Meaning in such a life is always personal and experiential. Permanent, ahistorical, transcendent "truths" manifest their meaninglessness by their inability to motivate and change human behavior.

Rorty contrasts the different vocabularies—and so worlds—to which he is referring by contrasting the life of a "strong poet" with that of a philosopher—or priest. A philosopher or religionist typically tries to discover the intrinsic nature of reality and speaks about the necessary, essential, and telic nature of human beings. Beneath the contingent features of reality, the "philosopher" tries to discover universal and necessary truths. The search for the intrinsic nature of reality is possible, Rorty says, only if reality is the product of a personal creator. Only in such a circumstance is it reasonable to hold that reality can speak to us having, as it were, a language of its own.

Poetry more adequately describes the immediate, human world in which we live than does transcendent, necessary truth, however, and so it is that poets are more humane and compelling in their work than Rorty's philosophers are in their work. Priests claim to hold up eternal truths. Poets are more modest; they describe the accidental, idiosyncratic, and contingent dimensions of our experience. Poets deal with the particular contingencies of human life; from the point of view of philosophy such details are unimportant, but it is the immediate "thickness" of the contingencies we experience, described by poets, that most readily moves us to action.

The search for universal natures and absolute certainty leads to platitudes or mathematics, neither of which is "central to anyone's sense of who she is or what she lives for."[2] Appeals to common sense and to a basic human nature in which all persons participate are singularly ineffective in changing human behavior. A precise illustration of Rorty's point is offered by Pope John Paul II's Christmas message of 1991. Referring to the fighting then going on in Yugoslavia and the suffering caused by the warring factions in Croatia, the Pope called for an end to hatred and oppression in which "passions and violence are defying reason and common sense." Even though the conflict does defy reason and common sense, does knowledge of that fact move people to change their behavior, it may be asked. That the creating God gave all the participants in the conflict the same human nature appears to be a meaningless and gratuitous irrelevance judged by the hostile actions of those who share that nature. Christians still fight Christians.

If we "poeticize" the situation in the name of operative contingencies taken from the lives of those who are fighting rather than trying rationally to resolve the situation in the name of God's creation, however, we seem to come nearer the lives people are actually living. Rorty approvingly refers to Michael Oakeshott who, "following Hegel, suggests . . . [that] we can keep the notion of 'morality' just insofar as we can cease to think of morality as the voice of the divine part of ourselves and instead think of it as the voice of ourselves as members of a community of speakers of a common language. . . . Oakeshott's answer coincides with Wilfrid Sellars's thesis that morality is a matter of what he calls 'we-intentions,' that the core of meaning of 'immoral action' is 'the sort of thing *we* don't do.' "[3]

The operative morality that moves a person to action is thus said to be a contingent product of the lived metaphors defining the localized community to which one belongs, rather than being the "voice of a divinized portion of our soul."[4]

It is precisely here that Freud made his great contribution to our self-understanding, for it was he who showed that meaning cannot be separated from our personal lives. Freud, in other words, de-universalized conscience by letting us see how it is historically conditioned by the contingent circumstances of our experience. Recognizing the "tissue of contingencies" that constitutes our lives helps us understand why we feel guilt, anxiety, or rage on certain occasions and with certain people, rather than at other times with other people. Unlike the virtues and vices abstractly defined in Greek and Christian usage, the meaning content of the terms Freud uses—"infantile," "sadistic," "obsessional," "paranoid"—is filled with the concrete experience of people we have known and with the lived engagement constituting our lives in the world. Such meaning is of one piece with the narrative of our lives rather than consisting of abstract concepts that equally apply—or equally do not apply—to anyone's life. The dramatic narrative of one's own life and the life of the community in which one lives are the sole context and content of meaning for Rorty.

Human solidarity, just as human meaning, is something that is created, not discovered. Rorty criticizes theology, along with philosophy and science, for trying to base human communality, and so morality, on a common human nature, a universal essence in which all human beings participate. The "strong poet," the ironist, on the other hand, seeks such identity through the private and idiosyncratic. Solidarity is constructed within and out of human experience rather than being supplied by a universal reality underlying experience.

Rorty speaks to the experience of each one of us when he says that "our sense of solidarity is strongest when those with whom solidarity is expressed is thought of as 'one of us,' where 'us' means something smaller and more local than the human race. That is why 'because she is a human being' is a weak, unconvincing explanation of a generous action."[5] Rorty criticizes the Christian tradition—thus contrasting it to his position—by reducing the Christian tradition to the abstract universalism we have seen him criticize under the label "philosophy." For a Christian to feel closer to some people than to others is a temptation according to Rorty: all human beings are children of God and so, upon pain of sin, an equal obligation must be felt for the well-being of all. "Secular ethical universalism," he says, "has taken over this attitude from Christianity."[6]

Rorty sees the core of Christian moral tradition perpetuated in the categorical imperative of Kant, thus reducing the Christian moral tradition to an abstract conceptualism. Although Rorty opposes a universalism based on an abstract essence common to all human beings, he says that his position is not incompatible with trying to extend the sense of "we" to as many people as possible in the world. It is just that, in making "we" ever more inclusive of people to whom we formerly referred as "they," we must expand the inclusiveness through the medium of detailed descriptions and stories rather than trying to base it on a common nature said already to be present but unrecognized.

Having observed Rorty's description of life in the postreligious age, we will now turn to an examination of the Christian tradition to see whether or not, as we have previously claimed, Rorty's proposed substitute for it does not rather more enable it to be itself. It is not our intention to examine Rorty's position in order to criticize and refute it as such. By his own admission, he allows that there is no noncircular way he can justify his stance. As an "irony," his position is necessarily reactive, always depending upon the prior existence of something else from which it is able to be alienated. It is especially suited for university professors during class hours!

On the other hand, in the course of distinguishing himself from the Christian world he claims has been left behind, he sometimes expresses himself in the very terms a Christian apologist would use. "Nothing," he writes, "can serve as a criticism of a person save another person, or of a culture save an alternative culture—for persons and cultures are, for us, incarnated vocabularies."[7] Only agreement to that remark can be elicited from those who believe in the Word Incarnate, from those who believe that the Word was made flesh. There is no Christian meaning apart from an "incarnated vocabulary." It will now be our purpose to see whether or not the Christian tradition, as we understand it, corresponds to Rorty's positive insights without justifying his reasons for wanting to disregard it.

Rorty, we have seen, treats religion as if it were of one kind with philosophy; both attribute the greatest importance and highest reality to abstract essences that enable individual things and persons to be themselves. Once an "essential nature" is discovered, deductions about individuals who have those natures can be made and laws can be established. Although Rorty occasionally refers to Christians who have been set afire with the love of Christ, on the whole his characterization of Christianity and religion in general equates them with deism. When God created the universe, he gave it and the things within it essential natures, and it is the nature of things that is within things with which science, metaphysics, ethics, and religious morality are concerned. The difficulty is that, although essential structures and universal natures are held to underlie and make the human world possible, their universality gives them no specific location within the human world. The lived world of every human person is a localized world; thus, as we have seen, universal insights make no difference in the way we live our lives.

Rorty reduces Christian tradition to a thing—an ideational understanding of the world based on God's act of creation. A personal God may be said to have started things out, but impersonal deductions based upon his first act become the reading of his will for human living.

Christian understanding of reality is anchored in the creative will of God to be sure, but no believing Christian will consent to the reduction of his or her religion to a mind game that can be played apart from the personal presence of God in Christ. Since God created the universe, he must will something specific both about it and for it; the universe must be of one kind rather than another, and it must have one purpose and goal rather than another. But does that admission staticize and universalize the world as Rorty contends?

History is rife with illustrations of the Christian tradition being reduced to a deductive process applied in the name of God but within which it is hard—if not impossible—to discern the living presence of God. In the course of its history, Western Christianity has shown essentialistic tendencies that subject it to the type of characterization Rorty makes of it. Essentialism never completely captured the Western Church, however, for there were always protests—by Aquinas and the nominalists, for example—made against it. The Eastern Church has better withstood the essentialistic reduction of Christian tradition, although it, too, has not been totally immune from such contamination.

A reassertion of the personal and communal nature of the Christian tradition has been forcefully made recently by John D. Zizioulas. He finds Christianity to be both radically different from and radically critical of the essentialistic universalism Rorty condemns. As commended by Zizioulas, it may be possible that the recovery of ancient insights can lead us to an understanding of Christian tradition that prevents essentialistic residualism and which requires the Christian tradition to become its full self by recognizing its nature as a never-ending personal dynamic oriented toward the future.

Anything impersonal is totally foreign to the Christian tradition. Zizioulas thus commends the Cappadocian Fathers of the fourth century for contradicting the classical, impersonal claim of Greek philosophy that being is the primary reality. Especially in Basil is the primacy of freedom of the person over being-itself stressed. For Basil, God's being is identified with—and in a sense results from—his personal freedom, rather than his freedom resulting from his Being. God as Father manifests his freedom in and by his existence; there is no being of God prior to or apart from the personal freedom of the Father. That is the meaning of God's telling Moses that his name is "I will be what I will be."

God exists because he is a free, willing Person. It is better to say that God wills to exist than that he wills because he exists. Only so can God truly *be* love; he exists *because* he loves. The Son and Holy Spirit exist by being freely begotten and freely spirated by the Father. The Father must be *because* he eternally "begets" the Son and "breaths" the Spirit.

God is God, in this view, because he is a Person, not because he is Being. Human beings are persons only because they are created by and participate in the life of the only true Person, God the Father in his life with the Son and Holy Spirit. To be a person is to be singular and unique; it is to be a historical life with a unique identity, not merely an instance of a universal essence. A person is more than an individual example of some kind of being, e.g., a rational animal. A person as a person is a singular, historical identity whose singularity is indicated by his or her proper name; a person as a person cannot be identified by genus and species alone.

A striking corollary to this totally personalist view of God is that neither human beings nor God are immortal because of their essential natures. There is no such thing as "necessary immortality" because of a substantial nature. Immortality is not a property of a substance. "The survival of a personal identity is possible for God not on account of His substance but on account of His trinitarian existence. . . . The life of God is eternal because it is personal, that is to say, it is realized as an expression of free communion, as love. Life and love are identified in the person . . . outside the communion of love the person loses its uniqueness and becomes a being like other beings, a 'thing' without absolute 'identity' and 'name,' without a face. Death for a person means ceasing to love and to be loved, ceasing to be unique and unrepeatable . . . ."[8]

"Salvation," Zizioulas continues, is the "eternal survival of a person as a unique, unrepeatable and free 'hypostasis,' as loving and being loved."[9] It is "participation not in the nature or substance of God, but in His personal existence."[10]

Christian truth—and so Christian tradition—is not a "passing on" but a "communion in." If we reflect upon it, "passing on" is basically an impersonal process. Persons are present; things pass on. In fact, when we speak of a person's "passing on," we refer to the person's death, when he or she ceases to be a person in the world and when the person's body—instead of being the person—becomes a thing, what the person leaves behind. The enduring nature of truth is the lasting nature of life: immutability becomes immortality. For the Christian, life is truth and truth is life. The Word of God *is* life and truth; the Word does not just *have* life and truth. Life and truth last in each other because they are each other. It is significant to observe that Rorty attributes the decline of religious faith to the inability of people nowadays seriously to expect life to continue after death with any attendant moral significance. Christianity is much more radical than Rorty, for, whereas Rorty advocates a life that is free as long as we live, Christianity understands life as the freedom to live. In Christ, life is freedom from death.

For the Cappadocians, as understood by Zizioulas, life does not flow necessarily from an essence. God's life does not flow from God's essence; if it did, the personal would flow from the impersonal. Life is participation in a communion of Persons; it is the free gift of love, not the property of an essence.

It is intriguing to observe the similarity of Rorty's and Zizioulas' terminology and yet how different their meaning is. As the Christian tradition is presented by Zizioulas, God's Truth is "communion," and creaturely truth is participation in that communion. Thus truth and meaning result from personal presence and interaction, none of them being themselves without the others. Truth and meaning arise from "language" and communication, and the consistency of that participation even leads to a coherence theory of truth. Life and love are an act of coherence out of which truth flows. Truth is not the correspondence of an idea to something outside— or beyond—the "language game," that is, the communion of love from which it arises. Ultimately there is nothing (i.e., no essence or thing) other than or less than loving communion for a true idea to refer to. There is no "thing-in-itself"—even a nonmaterial thing such as an idea or essence— that is prior to loving personal presence and that stands outside of such presence as a constraint upon it and to which personal presence must somehow correspond. There is, for example, no restraint of external essences on the will of God according to Maximus the Confessor because God knows things through his will rather than through their essences. It is the act of God's creating will that constitutes the objectivity of truth, the "primacy of being," which human beings discover when they are born into the world that precedes and receives them.

In summary it may be said that Christian truth is a kind of life; it is an orientation of personal communion, not an abstract, epistemological object. Christian truth is always a communal truth; it is communally acknowledged and communally confessed. It is a way of living that involves the totality of one's life; it is not an idea that can be known and exhausted either by ideation, deduction, or intellectual contemplation.

If the primacy of God as a Person is understood to be *the* Christian revelation in Jesus Christ, the Word made flesh, linear history becomes itself only in a moving presence. Christian tradition, then, is not a "thing" originating in the past and being passed on in the present; Christian tradition—as the Christian life—is participation, through the Spirit of the glorified Christ, in an open-ended presence that is always new. The Christian tradition is thus understood to be a never-ending action, not an unchangeable explication; it is an unending event rather than an abstract nature that remains unchanged—and so lifeless—in time.

For the ironist and for the Christian, the former represented by Rorty and the latter by Zizioulas, there is no "essence out there" that can be discovered apart from personal dialogue and communion. But how different the meaning of life is in the ironist tradition and the Christian tradition!

In the light of our discussion, we may now turn to a description of Christian tradition we think reveals its true nature by, at one time, embracing the concreteness and dynamism of Rorty's historicism without accepting the consequences of his nominalism. As we have indicated, a Christian who believes in a creating God cannot deny that the universe and everything in it has a nature and a goal, but that does not mean that human life—or the universe—is governed by impersonal, abstract essences that can be considered apart from the singularity of personal presence and the specificity of historical concreteness.

The Christian understanding of God is not an intellectual discovery from which necessary deductions can be made. Christianity is a revealed religion claiming that its "understanding" of God is a gift uniquely given in a historical event by the God who wants human beings to know him. That event is an act of love, and, as such, it is a personally free act of self-disclosure. The absolute dependence on God Christians profess in Christ arises from an event believers acknowledge did not have to occur. The Christian paradox is that the necessary arises from the contingent. The contingency of God's personal revelation freely offered in the historical life of Christ qualifies every aspect of Christian reality. It is for that reason that response to God is a life of thanksgiving. Christian living is a grateful response to God for the gift of his love that could not be anticipated; it is not the kind of response a researcher could make about a successful experiment saying, "I knew it would happen."

Because Christian life is an activity, so is Christian tradition. Both have a historical singularity that can never be reduced to or adequately represented by propositional descriptions. Life is a narrative rather than a treatise. Different theological systems bear the mark of historical personal decisions, as their terminology and nuances vary from one to another, but, even though their varying styles are the mark of onetime spontaneous expression, the systems themselves are fabrications that are less than the lived decisions that produced them.

Ironists as well as Christians acknowledge the importance of community for human living. Language and communication require community, as well as helping constitute human community. We have seen that membership in a "we" community is the ultimate basis of morality for Rorty; Christians would agree.

Rorty believes that the sense of "we" should be extended to as many people as possible in the world; it is just that the extension must occur through stories and descriptions that incorporate more and more people into a personal experience rather than trying to base communal life on abstract natures discovered by the intellect. Rorty contends, as we have seen, that human community can be inclusive without being "universalized." Community is personal, and thus can become itself only through the concreteness of the contingent; that is, significant membership in a community for me can occur only through activity that is historically identified with the ongoing history of my life, rather than being based on something that is true *about* me and so separated from the singularity that *is* me as a person.

Rorty states that the growing inclusiveness of a "we" community is not incompatible with his position; the growth of such a "we" community for the Christian tradition is not just a compatible possibility—it is the singular purpose of human life. Christianity may, in a summary sense, be thought of as supplying the *means* by which such community is brought about. Both the means of achieving community and the nature of the community achieved are, for Christianity, of one kind with those advocated by Rorty. But although the kind of activity that produces and constitutes human community may be the same for the ironist and Christian, the historical source from which such activity springs is radically different for the two.

In Jesus, the Word made flesh, Christians find themselves confronted by and called into precisely the type of singular, historical narrative Rorty commends. In the Spirit, the inner disposition of Jesus' historical life becomes the inner disposition of the historical lives of believers; the narrative of Jesus' life becomes the narrative continued in the lives of those who live with him. Nothing short of the fullness of that life is the Christian tradition.

The community of faith that is the Church is a network of personal relations. Christian tradition is the continuation of that network through time; it is the common living of a personal life by people in time. The Christian tradition is a shared activity, which, in the sharing, eliminates defensive fear of and separation from others, thus becoming its full self only by the incorporation of all people within it.

God's Word spoken in Jesus is a historical event in which all people are called actively to participate; the whole process is historical and communal. God calls a people to himself in Christ; and ever since the Spirit, whose presence in Jesus' life made him the Christ, was poured out upon people in the eschatological event of Pentecost, it has become impossible to think of Jesus in *himself* without including in him the Spirit-filled members of his mystical body in the world. Jesus and the community of God's people are forever inseparable; it is the unique presence of Jesus in the lives of those open to him that creates the intimacy that eventually enables all of humankind to constitute a single community. In the Spirit of the glorified Christ, there is no quantifiable threshold that can destroy, through the sheer weight of numbers, the intimacy necessary for community.

Incorporating all people in the world within the common living of a personal life is not impossible, as John Macmurray has pointed out, if every person in the world, and all persons whom that person regards as "other," stands in a relation to a personal Other who has the *same* intimate and mutual relation to every one of them. In such a commonly lived relation of every person to a singular Other, each person experiences his or her relation to all of the members of the worldwide community through his or her immediate relation to the One person. That is what happens when every believer relates to Jesus as his or her Savior and, as a result, finds himself or herself immediately related to every other person in Jesus.

In terms of the Christian revelation, it is not impossible to understand how all humankind can be called to membership in a single community. In God's gift of himself in his Word and Spirit, the dynamics of such a community are neither self-contradictory nor foreign to human experience. The Christian hope for life in a single communion of saints is a reasonable hope. To say that the goal of Christian living in the communion of saints is a reasonable goal, and even to say that participation in that life is possible for believers still living in this world, is not to say that the goal has already been achieved. The reign of God has obviously not been fully established in the world, so the features of the reign are imperfectly seen in the world. Full participation of all persons in a "we" community that includes everyone in the world is far removed from our present experience. Community is broken even among those who call themselves Christians by denominationalism and factionalism; apart from internal divisions, Christians are a minority in the world.

Even though Christians should regard strangers who are in need to be their neighbor, illustrated by the parable of the good Samaritan, in the present state of the world, few people, including Christians, feel communal inclusiveness with the same intensity with people who live continents away that they feel with members of a community in which they live their daily lives. If for no other reason, personal familiarity requires that time be spent together.

Recognition of the general fact to which we are referring is found even in the New Testament. Writing to the disciples in Galatia, Paul exhorts them to do good to all people as opportunity may present itself, but he especially urges them to do so "to those who are of the household of faith" (Gal 6:10). The kingdom grows as God's reign is exercised where its agents are, and that means where each believer lives his or her daily life. Located in the world through our bodies, we will necessarily have "thick" and more intimate relations with those who live in close proximity to us. Still, in Christ, we can experience life in a historical community that exceeds those with whom we are in daily contact. Even though we cannot recognize it fully achieved, we can recognize that the legitimate means for establishing an all-inclusive, historically achieved human community has been offered to us through the revelation of God in Jesus Christ.

In the historical life of Jesus, believers find themselves called in history to make a new history: they are called by a historic action to historic action; they are called by an agent to continue an agency. Such communality is not that of an abstract essence. Christian community needs constantly to be made. In that sense it needs to be constructed, as Rorty commends, but it can be produced only in and by the immediate presence of the Other. The traditional name of that presence is "grace." Although only human beings can make human community, the community does not come from them; they can achieve it only in and by God's presence to them in Christ in the Spirit.

Christian tradition is a communal act. The paradigmatic act of Christian community is Eucharistic celebration, which means that Christian tradition is ultimately the ongoing life of the Eucharistic community. In

Eucharistic celebration, God calls his people together, unites them with himself and in him with each other, in a historical action that will never end. Further elaboration of Christian tradition will be an elaboration of Eucharistic community; such an elaboration is precluded in this essay, but such an elaboration will further develop, we believe, the dynamics we have described.

Notes

[1]Richard Rorty, *Contingency, irony, and solidarity* (Cambridge: Cambridge University Press, 1989) 68.

[2]Ibid., 47.

[3]Ibid., 59.

[4]Ibid., 60.

[5]Ibid., 191.

[6]Ibid.

[7]Ibid., 80.

[8]John D. Zizioulas, *Being as Communion. Studies in Personhood and the Church* (Crestwood, N.Y.: St. Vladimir's Press, 1985) 48f.

[9]Ibid., 49.

[10]Ibid., 50.

16

Montreal (1963): A Case Study

Joseph A. Burgess

Georges Tavard has played a significant role in modern ecumenism, most particularly in ecumenical deliberations about the meaning of "tradition." Already in 1959 he had published a major volume on this theme: *Holy Writ or Holy Church*.[1] At the Fourth World Conference on Faith and Order held in Montreal in 1963, Tavard was one of five official Roman Catholic observers. As a survey of his bibliography indicates, he has continued to write about this issue throughout his entire career.

Montreal (1963), one of the key events in the ecumenical surge of the 1960s, has diminished in importance. The pre-history of the text on tradition from Montreal (1963), the actual drafting of the text, especially as light is thrown on the process by Tavard's personal recollections, and the reception of the text in the past thirty years help us understand why the ecumenical movement ebbs and flows.

I. The Pre-History of Montreal (1963)

In 1952 at the Third World Conference on Faith and Order held in Lund, a resolution suggested by Albert C. Outler was inserted at the end of a paragraph called "The Nature of Continuity": "We propose the establishment of a Theological Commission to explore more deeply the resources for further ecumenical discussion to be found in that common history which we have as Christians."[2] In 1953 at the meeting of Faith and

Order Working Committee in Bossey, Georges Florovsky, in a memorandum based on discussion with Outler, stated: "There are manifold traditions in which the divided Christian bodies actually live and dwell. It is of great importance to define their relation to what should be described as Tradition."[3] The Working Committee then appointed an Interim Committee "to study the problem of Tradition."[4] In 1954 the Working Committee met again, this time in Evanston and Chicago, and appointed a "theological commission on tradition which will normally operate in two sections, one European, the other North American, in close cooperation."[5] For financial reasons collaboration was only possible by mail and through occasional personal contacts. The WCC archives contain some forty papers, largely unpublished, from the eleven years of deliberations.[6] In 1961 the Theological Commission published an interim report, *The Old and the New in the Church*,[7] and in 1963 the two sections printed their reports as *The Report of the Theological Commission on Tradition and Traditions*.[8] These reports are separate reports of their deliberations, not a unified proposal, and are written by the co-chairmen, A. Outler for the North American section and K. Skydsgaard for the European section.

A. North American Section

The North American section emphasized "the traditionary process in its actual operation in specific 'cases' of 'traditions in transit' " (TCTT 11). More importantly, it developed "working definitions" of "tradition," "traditions," and *"the* Tradition" (TCTT 16–18) that became the basis for the definitions accepted at Montreal (1963).[9] By themselves, to be sure, these definitions are inadequate unless "Scripture" and "Church" are also defined.

1. *Scripture.* The members of the North American section found themselves "in substantial agreement as to the validity of the Reformation slogan, *sola scriptura,* insofar as it asserts and identifies *the* Tradition as the prime datum of the New Testament" (TCTT 18:42-44). There is the need for "some sort of reference to the primacy of Scripture, yet every appeal to Scripture bears the cachet of its denominational hermeneutical style" (TCTT 19:11-13). Many Protestants hold "the tradition of *sola Scriptura* despite the historical actuality of *Scriptura numquam sola:* Scripture is nowhere by itself alone" (TCTT 21:2-4). *The* Tradition is "witnessed to in Scripture" (TCTT 24:23-24; cf. "the 'charter' for this *traditio constitutiva* is uniquely and decisively present in the Scripture's witness to . . . ." [27:22-43]; " . . . to which the Holy Scriptures bear witness" [18:8]).

2. *Church*. On the other hand, the historian "sees the Church as the locus of God's revelation but not the proprietor thereof" (TCTT 19:42-43). The Church "bound itself to *the* Tradition in Scripture by closing the canon" (TCTT 19:10), yet the "Church, living as she does by *the* living Tradition, still cannot make the slightest claim to possessing it by right or merit" (TCTT 27:18-19). *"The* Christian Tradition may be discerned but never defined exactly" (TCTT 27:14); "the Church's one foundation is *the* Tradition . . . whenever and wherever the Word is truly preached and the Sacraments rightly administered" (TCTT 27:8-11). This Tradition is "continuing in the history of the Church" (TCTT 18:18), Christ continues "to renew and renovate his Church" (TCTT 18:27), the Holy Spirit is "resident Governor of the Church" (TCTT 20:14-15), the Church sets "the stage for that *actus tradendi* by which the Holy Spirit leads" (TCTT 22:32-33), and the Christian Tradition is "renewed with every renewal of the Church" (TCTT 24:23-24).

3. *Tradition*. Thus *"Scriptura numquam sola!"* (TCTT 21:2-4), and it "witnesses to" *the* Tradition (TCTT 24:23-24). The Church "bound itself to *the* Tradition in Scripture by closing the canon" (TCTT 19:10), yet *the* Tradition may never be "defined exactly" (TCTT 27:14); the Church set "the stage" (TCTT 22:32- 33), but the Holy Spirit is the instrument. What then is *the* Tradition? In "a virtual consensus" the section stated: in sum, *"The Tradition is the self-givenness of God in the self-giving of Jesus Christ,* 'for us men and for our salvation' "* (TCTT 18:31-32; emphasis in the text). Neither Scripture nor Church is part of the definition. The section agreed that "criteria of authenticity" such as Scripture and legitimate development are "normative notions" which "are not formally precise" (TCTT 20:9-16); *"The* Christian Tradition may be discerned, but never defined exactly . . . "* (TCTT 27:14). In Platonic fashion, just as multiple traditions in the Christian community presuppose *"the* people of God" (TCTT 17:45-18:4; emphasis in the text), so "traditions" *(phenomena)* point beyond themselves to *the* Tradition (TCTT 17:43; 19:4-5).

The report, to be sure, was only a report, not a consensus document asking for adoption. It reflects the strong hand of Albert Outler and his writings, particularly *The Christian Tradition and the Unity We Seek*.[10] The two Lutherans, S. Ahlstrom and J. Pelikan, were no doubt content with the obvious use of Augsburg Confession 7 (TCTT 27:10-11). Georges Florovsky, the one Orthodox member of the section, could find ample references to the way the Orthodox emphasize the interrelationship of Scripture, Tradition, and Church. For the rest—D. Hay (Presbyterian), R. Beaver

(United Church of Christ), Y. Clebsch (Episcopalian), D. Mathers (United Church of Canada), G. Routt (Disciples of Christ), and H. Walsh (Episcopalian)—the report was close enough to modern reflection on the subject to create little difficulty.

B. European Section

The European section was "to concentrate upon historical and systematic reconsideration of the term *traditio* in its biblical and historical aspects" (TCTT 11; emphasis in the text). While assuming the basic distinction between Tradition and traditions, the section focused on the criteriological question. The last part of the report (TCTT 56–63), strictly speaking, is a paper written by Jean-Louis Leuba, in which the members of the section "have recognised the main lines of their studies and discussions" (TCTT 56).

1. *Scripture.* Scripture, as the "bearer of the very Word of God which creates the Church and its faith, . . . has, therefore, an absolute priority in relation to the faith of the Church through all ages" (TCTT 53:39-42). "But Scripture as such is ineffective, even a dead letter, unless it is made living and active by the Spirit of God" (TCTT 58:40-41).

2. *Church.* Similarly, "Unity in the Church was not a theological, doctrinal uniformity, but unity in faith" (TCTT 45:25-26). Thus, with respect to the "doctrine" of the Church, "doctrinal thinking is always open, never closed" (TCTT 54:7, 11-12). Nevertheless, the "Church does not constantly 'spring up' out of the void. It is already in existence, and that is why it is able to confirm the work of the Holy Spirit" (TCTT 60:46-48); "the Church has had a continuous existence, which is both the consequence and the instrument of God's work in Christ through the Holy Spirit" (TCTT 61:2-4).

3. *Tradition.* The apostolic tradition is *tradere Christum,* "and in this sense there is only *one* Tradition—although in different forms and wordings" (TCTT 36:26-27; emphasis in the text). "The new tradition contains the break with an old tradition, indeed a break with any human tradition" (TCTT 48:15-16). "Every Christian church must keep on confronting itself with the question whether its own doctrine and preaching is not being mistaken for the living Word of God which is above and before every tradition" (TCTT 54:1-4). What remains is "the fundamental question: What is it in the final analysis, that divides us in the question of what God's Word is, and in the question of the relation between Scripture and Tradition?" (TCTT 54:26-29, cf. 58, #3).

Beginning in 1956 J.-L. Leuba wrote a series of papers for the European section describing the *traditum* as the apostolic witness, not Christ himself. S. L. Greenslade and G. Ebeling rejected this approach, emphasizing the human aspect of the apostolic witness. Leuba's point of view did not carry the day, and in the final report he joined the majority.[11] Y. Congar, in an unpublished paper (1963) on both reports of the Theological Commission, commented: "The impression given is that the Church is not really the *subject* of the Tradition, but the Tradition is effected *by the Holy Spirit* using the actions of the Church";[12] "The criterion of judgment is clear: it is Scripture. The Church is added, timidly (Leuba)."[13] Congar then summarized the situation:

> It could be asked whether, finally, the difference does not come down to the idea of Revelation. Catholic theology insists on Revelation as communication of understanding through a "locutio formalis", a Word properly so called. It has a historical and objective idea of Revelation. The Council of Trent itself, when considering tradition, speaks of "the Gospel", not of "Jesus Christ". Protestant theology has an idea of Revelation as something contemporary and active, less historical and objective (but this last adjective misrepresents our meaning).[14]

As co-chairman and author of the final report for this section, K. Skydsgaard, a Lutheran, included the Lutheran emphasis on the Word of God, with which the other two Lutherans, G. Ebeling and E. Molland, could only concur. J.-L. Leuba, Swiss Protestant and author of the final section, brought in the instrumentality of the Church (TCTT 60:46-48; 61:2-4), and K. Bonis from the Greek Orthodox tradition could subscribe to that. S. L. Greenslade (Anglican), G. Caird (Congregational), and E. Flesseman-van Leer (Dutch Reformed) were also able to support this combination of viewpoints.

II. Montreal (1963) on Tradition

Montreal (1963) brought together nearly five hundred delegates, observers, guests, and staff, with almost a hundred assigned to Section II on "Scripture, Tradition and Traditions." Roman Catholic observers participated freely, and a main paper at one General Session was given by a Sulpician Father, Raymond E. Brown. Although the Orthodox had been involved with Faith and Order since its first planning session in 1920, their full participation "was much assisted by a consultation of Orthodox and non-Orthodox theologians held immediately before the Conference opened."[15]

Sections were to produce a three-thousand word report for later consideration in Plenary Sessions; these reports were to be in "terms which ordinary Christians without theological training could understand."[16] The work of Section II was divided into three Subsections, but because of the lack of time only the report of Subsection 1 "received a full discussion and the complete approval of the Section"; the Section "in general" recommended the remaining two reports for study.[17]

Tavard was assigned to Section II, which met in a classroom at McGill University. Einar Molland was chairman. The discussion was free and open, so open that strangers felt free to walk in and speak to the question! The Orthodox were active participants, especially Archbishop Basile of Belgium. Much of the time was taken up by debate between Molland and Leuba. Molland kept firm control of the final results. He was chairman of the drafting committee, and he determined where there was consensus. Tavard drafted the Roman Catholic sentence in section 53 of Subsection 1. The minutes of the proceedings are sketchy.[18]

A. SCRIPTURE

In the famous definition "By *the Tradition* is meant the Gospel itself, transmitted from generation to generation in and by the Church, Christ himself present in the life of the Church" (M 39; emphasis in the text), Scripture is not mentioned, though the Church is. "The very fact that Tradition precedes the Scriptures points to the significance of tradition, but also to the Bible as the treasure of the Word of God" (M 42). The Tradition is "testified in Scripture" (M 45). For the postapostolic Church appeal to the Tradition received from the apostles became "the" criterion; as this Tradition "was embodied in the apostolic writings," they became "an" authority for determining the "true Tradition" and they have "a special basic value, because of their apostolic character" (M 49). "The Tradition in its written form, as Holy Scripture . . . , has to be interpreted by the Church" (M 50). "The Scriptures as documents can be letter only. It is the Spirit who is the Lord and Giver of life" (M 52).

B. CHURCH

The Tradition is "transmitted from generation to generation in and by the Church" (M 39). Tradition is "transmitted in and by the Church through the power of the Holy Spirit" (M 45) and the Tradition as Scripture "has to be interpreted by the Church in ever new situations" (M 50). The content of Christian Tradition "is God's revelation and self-giving in Christ, present in the life of the Church" (M 46).

C. TRADITION

The Tradition is "the Gospel itself, . . . Christ himself present in the life of the Church" (M 39). The Tradition "precedes the Scriptures" (M 42); "the Tradition of the Gospel (the *paradosis* of the *kerygma*)[19] . . . is actualized in the preaching of the Word, in the administration of the Sacraments and worship, in Christian teaching and theology, and in mission and witness to Christ by the lives of the members of the Church" (M 45). "Where do we find the genuine Tradition, and where impoverished tradition or even distortion of tradition?" (M 48). "These questions imply the search for a criterion" (M 49).

The North American section of the Theological Commission had defined Tradition without using either Scripture or Church: *"The Tradition is the self-givenness of God in the self-giving of Jesus Christ,* 'for us men and for our salvation' " (TCTT 18:31-32). In fact, in the full page devoted to defining the Tradition the North American section only mentions Church three times, "continuing in the history of the church" (TCTT 18:13), "his intercession for the Church" (TCTT 18:25), and "he will continue to renew and renovate his Church" (TCTT 18:27). The Church is "the locus of God's revelation but not the proprietor thereof" (TCTT 19:42-43), according to the discussion on the following page. This North American understanding continues at Montreal (1963) in Section II, 2, which, however, was only recommended for study: "The Tradition of the Church is not an object which we possess, but a reality by which we are possessed" (M 59). But in Section II, 1, which received "complete approval,"[20] the Church is no longer the "locus" (TCTT 19:42-43) or "the stage for that *actus tradendi* by which the Holy Spirit leads" (TCTT 22:32-33); instead, the phrase "by the Church" has been added in three key places (M 39, 45, 50). Nor is such an emphasis on the Church as instrument found in the Report of the European section except in the final part; the Church is "the instrument of God's work in Christ through the Holy Spirit" (TCTT 61:2-4; cf. 60:46-48), but this part, strictly speaking, is a paper written by J.-L. Leuba in which the members of the section "have recognized the main lines of their studies and discussions" (TCTT 56) and can hardly be said to represent their viewpoint in every turn of phrase.

In Section II Erich Dinkler, possibly in an attempt to accommodate J.-L. Leuba and his supporters, proposed adding *sola traditione*,[21] and the following paragraph was presented to the Plenary:

> In our present situation, we wish to consider the problem of Scripture and Tradition, or rather that of Tradition and Scripture. Our starting-point is that we are all living in a tradition which goes back to our Lord and has its roots in the Old Testament, and we are all indebted to that tradition, inasmuch as we have received the revealed truth, the Gospel, through its being transmitted from one generation to another. Thus we can say that we exist as Christians *sola traditione*, by tradition alone. Tradition then in this sense includes the preaching of the Word and worship, Christian teaching and theology, missions, and also witness to Christ in the lives of members of the Church.[22]

Both M. Thurian and E. Käsemann, although obviously for different reasons, agreed to *sola traditione*, but they argued that when *sola traditione* would be used in another context, it would create serious misunderstanding. In the final version of the Report, *sola traditione* was omitted.[23] The fact that persons holding such divergent viewpoints could find *sola traditione* acceptable indicates how imprecisely the phrase was being used.

III. The Impact of Montreal (1963)

Already at Montreal (1963) the Commission on Faith and Order recommended that the Working Committee of Faith and Order arrange for "an ecumenical study of the councils of the early Church."[24] Then at its meeting in 1964 the Faith and Order Commission and Working Committee authorized a study on the hermeneutical problem.[25] What was intended by these two studies was progress in the remaining issues on tradition.

Yet at the Bristol meeting in 1967 the Faith and Order Commission sounded a different note. The report of the section on hermeneutics, admittedly not "final" but "notes from the discussion" as "a starting point for further work,"[26] quotes the famous definition from Montreal (1963) of "the Tradition of the Gospel (the *paradosis* of the *kerygma*), testified in Scripture, transmitted in and by the Church through the power of the Holy Spirit" (M 45), and then candidly states:

> This sentence expresses an agreement which we all can support. It covers, however, different possible positions. In accepting this statement the rela-

tionship between Scripture and the Church can still be understood differently depending on the emphasis laid upon the various elements of the
sentence.[27]

Three positions on Scripture are identified: (1) Scripture as sole norm; (2)
Scripture as the product of tradition; and (3) Scripture as one element along
with other factors.[28] Three similar positions could have been identified for
the Church.

At Louvain in 1971 the Commission, in its report on the authority of
the Bible, again after quoting the famous definition of Tradition from Montreal (1963) (M 45), states: "Important as this agreement undoubtedly is,
it still leaves room for different emphases," that is, Scripture or Tradition.[29]
The Working Committee then recommended a study of the problem of
change and identity.[30]

At the Bangalore meeting of the Commission in 1978, Committee II
on "Authority in the Church" recommended a consultation on the relation "between the authority of the Scriptures and the authority of the ongoing tradition process," especially the creeds, and defended its recom-
mendation by pointing to the same basic problem:

> Ever since the Fourth World Conference on Faith and Order in Montreal
> (1963), (Scripture, Tradition and Traditions, No. 45), uncertainty about this
> relation has caused problems. The exact interpretation of the phrase "the
> apostolic Faith according to the Scriptures handed down to us through the
> centuries" (see the third paragraph of the Preamble of "A Common State-
> ment of our Faith") was an important point of debate in our commission.
> For some of us this implies the affirmation of the binding authority of at least
> some elements in the ongoing transmission process, like the creeds of the An-
> cient Church. For others, according to Montreal, there is no dichotomy or
> duality; the living Tradition is the life of the Gospel and of the Spirit in the
> Church through the centuries, interpreting the Word of God again and again
> in new situations and cultures: this produces an inheritance which is impor-
> tant for us as the faith of our fathers, but the Tradition is also actual as the
> present proclamation of Word of God in the Church.[31]

It is therefore surprising that in 1982 the Commission in the introduction
to *Baptism, Eucharist and Ministry* asks the churches to describe "as precisely as possible—*the extent to which your church can recognize in this text the
faith of the Church through the ages.*"[32]

The Orthodox, in spite of the major investment they have in the subject of Tradition, virtually ignore Montreal (1963), even though the Or-

thodox were active participants at Montreal (1963) and the Orthodox delegates there accepted Section II, 1. On the one hand, the Orthodox have reservations about what Montreal (1963) implies. In fact, Nikos Nissiotis, a well-known Orthodox ecumenist and a member of Section II at Montreal (1963), wrote soon after the Conference that there are Protestants who understand "Tradition as identical with the Gospel event" and "are ready to go so far as to say *sola Traditione*. For the Orthodox this is impossible" because Tradition is "both the act of *traditio* of God Himself . . . and the process of this *traditio*."[33] On the other hand, in a sense Montreal (1963), from the Orthodox point of view, added little. As Meyendorff points out, "the great Byzantine theologians were always conscious of the necessary distinction between 'Tradition' and 'traditions.' "[34] This distinction, furthermore, had already made its presence felt at the beginning of the Faith and Order Movement at Lausanne (1927),[35] then at Edinburgh (1937),[36] and expressly at Evanston (1954).[37] At first glance the Orthodox seem to have a well worked out and definitive case: Truth = Revelation = Scripture = Tradition = Christ = Church.[38] Nissiotis, however, points out that the "Eastern Orthodox, especially, rely too much on such abstractions" and that such an answer to the problem will be ineffective "if one does not specify how this understanding of the teaching authority operates in detail."[39]

Ecumenical bilateral dialogues at the international level do not refer by name to Montreal (1963) on Tradition, even though virtually every dialogue takes up the question of Scripture and Tradition in one way or another. This raises the possibility that Montreal (1963) has carried the day and is simply taken for granted. A word of caution is in order, however. Not every "Tradition" with a capital "T" reflects Montreal (1963). At times such "T"'s are merely typographical errors. More frequently, capital "T" in Tradition is based on standard Orthodox usage. Some non-Orthodox usage of capital "T" for Tradition is no more than occasional emphasis and hypostatizing. Often one may conjecture Montreal (1963) lies in the background, although perhaps in garbled form, because there is an echo of specific words and phrases, and on a few occasions Montreal (1963) has definitely been used.

At the national level, multilateral meetings where Protestants dominate have tended to cite Montreal (1963) but with a definite emphasis on the ultimate authority of Scripture. At the first British Conference on Faith and Order held at Nottingham in 1964, after citing the famous definition of Tradition (M 45) from Montreal (1963), the appendix on Scripture and Tradition describes Scripture as "the criterion,"[40] and in the United States the Consultation on Church Union in *The COCU Consensus: In Quest of a Church of Christ Uniting* clearly uses Montreal (1963) to define tradition but also states that Scripture is "the supreme norm."[41] Bilateral dialogues in the United States, while very occasionally using or referring to Montreal (1963) on tradition,[42] do not use it precisely.

At times Montreal (1963) is not mentioned where it would be expected, where tradition is a major theme, as, for example, in a recent article by Georges Tavard.[43] This is not so surprising, however, when one discovers how critical he has been of the distinction at Montreal (1963) between Tradition, tradition, and traditions:

> Une telle diversification des sens du mot voile le fait fondamental que la Tradition, au sens défini, ne vit et ne se transmet que par un, ou plutôt, par des processus de transmission, lesquels sont eux-mêmes inseparables des diverses formes d'expression choisies pour opérer ce processus et communiquer la Tradition. Autrement dit, on se fait illusion si l'on imagine pouvoir dissocier le contenu du message (la Tradition) des formes multiples (les traditions) par lesquelles s'en fait le transmission (la tradition).[44]

Other reasons why Montreal (1963) has not carried the day are: (1) the distinction between upper-case "T" and lower-case "t" does not work in languages such as German, where all nouns are capitalized; (2) the Orthodox naturally use their conceptuality in their dialogues and writings; and (3) during this period of time there has been strong competition from what Vatican II stated about tradition in *Dei Verbum,* for Roman Catholics naturally use this conceptuality in their dialogues and writings.

The claim has been made, to be sure, that there is "a remarkable convergence" between Montreal (1963) and *Dei Verbum* on the basic question: "What do we mean when we talk about Tradition?"[45] These two documents should, therefore, tend to support each other instead of the one displacing the other. On the positive side is the fact that *Dei Verbum* emphasizes

> that revelation is personal: fundamentally the self-revelation of God in Christ. The "deposit of faith" is then ultimately Jesus Christ himself. As expressed in the documents of Montreal and the Vatican Council the realization of the inevitability of tradition and the evaluation of revelation as personal are probably the outstanding areas of agreement.[46]

"There is, however, a certain tension between these two documents. . . . In principle, no tension exists between Scripture and Tradition"[47] in *Dei Verbum*. Already J. Ratzinger, commenting on a speech by Cardinal Meyer at Vatican II in September 1964, noted that Vatican II "has more or less ignored the whole question of the criticism of tradition. By doing this, it has missed an important opportunity for ecumenical dialogue."[48] Further, there is a "fundamental difference" between Montreal (1963) and *Dei Verbum* on how the Spirit acts; for Montreal (1963) "it is not possible to be certain . . . whether the Spirit's work is bound to any determinable organ within the Church."[49]

IV. Montreal (1963) Thirty Years Later

Was Montreal (1963) on tradition "a remarkable point of convergence,"[50] even a kind of breakthrough? Intervening history has made Montreal (1963) seem less remarkable, but its accomplishments "must not be undervalued." What was accomplished "is more easily seen in the new Spirit of positive toleration and openness on this question, rather than in any sudden and dramatic new agreement."[51] Protestants became aware "of the inevitability of tradition in every human institution, and therefore its legitimacy as a central theological idea."[52] What Montreal (1963) did was to raise this awareness, including the awareness of how the Orthodox distinguish between Tradition and traditions, to a world level.

Responses to *Baptism, Eucharist and Ministry* (1982) throw significant light on what role Montreal (1963) continues to play in the ongoing discussion of Scripture and tradition. Seven of the approximately twenty-five Lutheran churches responding assert that "the faith of the Church through the ages" asked about in BEM's initial question to the churches "is not a clearly definable norm of faith; it presupposes a dubious concept of tradition."[53] Eight Lutheran churches, largely not those just mentioned, said "further study of the problem of Scripture and Tradition in the ecumenical context is necessary and desirable."[54] And *Baptism, Eucharist & Ministry 1982–1990,* reporting on all responses to BEM, notes that "all churches affirm the authority of Scripture," but then that "the degree of 'over-againstness' of Scripture to Tradition and traditions varies."[55] Of the 186 official responses none uses the consensus reached at Montreal (1963) as the basis for analyzing the problem of the relation between Scripture and tradition; Montreal (1963) is mentioned several times, but simply as past history.[56]

In a chapter entitled "Major Issues Demanding Further Study: Provisional Considerations" *in Baptism, Eucharist & Ministry 1982–1990. Report on the Process and Responses,* a report received by the Faith and Order Commission at Budapest in 1989, there is a critical evaluation of Montreal (1963) on tradition. "[T]he hermeneutical problem . . . was not made sufficiently clear . . . . Montreal only listed the various positions within the ecumenical spectrum."[57] Montreal "could not go beyond a mere juxtaposition of three factors in the transmission process"—events and testimonies leading to Scripture, Scripture, and ecclesial preaching and teaching.[58] "No criteria were offered in Montreal, only questions asked."[59] Thus it has become clear there is a need "for further clarification of the differences in regard to the roles which Scripture, Tradition and traditions actually play in the teaching of the churches . . . . Even where the priority of Scripture is affirmed, it can mean different things to different churches."[60]

The report then describes steps taken and to be taken in order to solve these problems.

> The report on "Scripture, Tradition and Traditions" had no intrinsic relation to the other findings of Montreal . . . . It was precisely in drawing from these sections of Montreal and relating them to the idea of a living ecclesial Tradition that Faith and Order developed the convergence process represented in BEM.[61]

In 1978 at Bangalore Faith and Order formulated the common conviction:

> Before the church performs acts of teaching, she exists and lives. Her existence and her life are the work of the Triune God . . . . The authority of the church has its ground in this *datum* of her being. The whole church teaches by what she is, when she is living according to the gospel.[62]

The report draws two conclusions from this common conviction: (1) "The ecclesial character of the transmission process;" and (2) The criterion is the apostolic gospel.[63] Further, "The Tradition means a permanent dialogue of the church with Christ, an unbroken communion with divine life, a permanent presence of the Holy Spirit."[64] Therefore future work, helped by understanding "Tradition as an ecclesial, dynamic event . . . would include two essential criteria," faithfulness to the apostolic Scriptures and conciliarity.[65] Apostolic Tradition "means continuity in the permanent characteristics of the Church of the apostles."[66]

> "Tradition" (*paradosis*) and "communion" (*koinonia*) intend both past and present: there is need to discern a continuity of the apostolic faith and of the believing community in history; there needs to be also a contemporary solidarity of local churches united in faith and reconciled in a universal communion.[67]

Producing definitions of Tradition, tradition, and traditions at Montreal (1963) proved to be a helpful heuristic exercise, even though the results were limited. It now remains to be seen if the current shift in emphasis from Scripture and tradition to tradition and church, particularly conciliarity and *koinonia,* while helpful, will lead to more precise conclusions than Montreal (1963). Just as after Montreal (1963) at Bristol (1967) three positions on Scripture were identified: (1) Scripture as sole norm; (2) Scripture as the product of tradition; and (3) Scripture as one element along with other factors,[68] will there be three parallel positions on *koinonia?*

Thus the problem of tradition remains difficult and dominant. "Das Traditionsverhältnis und -verständnis gehört ohne Zweifel zu den ungeklärtesten und zugleich folgenreichsten Problemen der gegenwärtigen Kirche."[69] Wiedenhofer states further that what is needed is renewed, intensive systematic reflection and historical research, which in his view are "in der gegenwärtigen Theologie noch kaum ernsthaft in Angriff genommen."[70] Even so itself a document as the German study *The Condemnations of the Reformation Era* states that "there is yet no explicit consensus about the critical function of Scripture over against the formation of the church's tradition."[71] Basically the problem of Scripture and tradition is part of every theological dispute even though, because controversy tends to focus on particular questions, the larger question of the process of transmission is usually not in the foreground. Georges Tavard points out that Scripture and tradition "is an all-embracing theme which reaches to the heart of all theology and which touches on all aspects of Church life"[72] and that Scripture and tradition are in a sense "coinherent."[73]

Notes

[1]George Tavard, *Holy Writ or Holy Church: The Crisis of the Protestant Reformation* (London: Burns & Oates, 1959).

[2]Lukas Vischer, ed., *A Documentary History of the Faith and Order Movement 1927–1963* (St. Louis: Bethany, 1963) 96.

[3]*Minutes of the Working Committee of Faith and Order,* Bossey, 1953; Faith and Order Paper 17 (Geneva: WCC, 1953) 32.

[4]*Minutes* 1953, 36.

[5]*Minutes of the Commission and Working Committee of Faith and Order,* Evanston and Chicago, 1954; Faith and Order Paper 21 (Geneva: WCC, 1954) 29.

[6]Míceál Ledwith, "The Theology of Tradition in the World Council of Churches," *Irish Theological Quarterly* 43 (1976) 106.

[7]*The Old and the New in the Church* (Minneapolis: Augsburg, 1961).

⁸*The Report of the Theological Commission on Tradition and Traditions,* Faith and Order Paper 40 (Geneva: WCC, 1963). Hereinafter cited as TCTT.

⁹In 1959 at the meeting of the Central Committee of the WCC in Rhodes, C. Konstantinidis presented a paper suggesting that the period of oral transmission be named "tradition" with a lower-case "t", the period of written transmission be named "Scripture" with an upper-case "S", the period of further written formulation be named "scripture" with a lower-case "s", and finally there is "Tradition" in "the proper sense of the word" with upper-case "T"; see Chysostomos Konstantinidis, "The Significance of the Eastern and Western Traditions within Christendom," *Ecumenical Review* 12 (1960) 146. It is but a short step from this suggestion to the proposal of the North American Section in 1963 for "tradition," "traditions," and "the Tradition" (TCTT 16–17).

¹⁰Albert Outler, *The Christian Tradition and the Unity We Seek* (New York: Oxford University Press, 1957).

¹¹See TCTT 56–63. The process is described in Brian Gaybba, The *Tradition: An Ecumenical Breakthrough? (A study of a Faith and Order study)* (Rome: Herder, 1971) 135–36, 177–81, 184–85; cf. Ledwith, "The Theology," 110, 112, 116–18.

¹²Cited in Gaybba, *Tradition,* 154. Emphasis in the original.

¹³Cited in Gaybba, *Tradition,* 195.

¹⁴Cited in Gaybba, *Tradition,* 98.

¹⁵*The Fourth World Conference on Faith and Order. Montreal 1963,* ed. P. C. Rodger and L. Vischer (New York: Association Press, 1963) 20. Hereinafter citations from Section II at Montreal (1963) are indicated by the abbreviation M and the paragraph number.

¹⁶*Montreal 1963,* 19.

¹⁷*Montreal 1963,* 50.

¹⁸Personal reminiscence by Georges Tavard. Used by permission.

¹⁹The definition "the *paradosis* of the *kerygma*" was created by Molland. Personal reminiscence by Georges Tavard. Used by permission.

²⁰*Montreal 1963,* 50.

²¹Personal reminiscence by Georges Tavard. Used by permission.

²²*Montreal 1963,* 24.

²³*Montreal 1963,* 25.

²⁴*Minutes of the Faith and Order Commission and Working Committee,* Faith and Order Paper 41 (Geneva: WCC, 1963) 21.

²⁵*Minutes of the Meeting of the Faith and Order Commission and Working Committee,* Faith and Order Paper 44 (Geneva: WCC, 1965) 41–42.

²⁶*New Directions in Faith and Order. Bristol 1967,* Faith and Order Paper 50 (Geneva: WCC, 1968) 33.

²⁷*Bristol 1967,* 39.

²⁸*Bristol 1967,* 39–40.

²⁹*Faith and Order. Louvain 1971,* Faith and Order Paper 92 (Geneva: WCC, 1971) 10.

³⁰*Louvain 1971,* 215.

³¹*Bangalore 1978. Sharing in One Hope,* Faith and Order Paper 92 (Geneva: WCC, 1978) 259; internal citation, 245.

³²*Growth in Agreement. Reports and Agreed Statements of Ecumenical Conversations on a World Level,* Ecumenical Documents 2; ed. H. Meyer and L. Vischer (New York/Ramsey: Paulist; Geneva, WCC, 1984) 489; emphasis in the text.

³³Nikos A. Nissiotis, "The Unity of Scripture and Tradition," *Greek Orthodox Theological Review* 11 (1965–1966) 185.

³⁴John Meyendorff, "The Meaning of Tradition," *Scripture and Tradition,* ed. L. Swidler (Pittsburgh: Duquesne, 1965) 54.

[35]Vischer, *A Documentary History,* 34.

[36]Vischer, *A Documentary History,* 44, 53.

[37]Vischer, *A Documentary History,* 141–43.

[38]Cf. Meyendorff, "The Meaning," 44: "veneration of Scripture is to suggest to the faithful that it contains the very Truth of Revelation, which the Church possesses precisely in a given, written form"; 48: "The Church's awareness of possessing a living Truth which cannot be limited by purely biblical wording"; 50: "the absolute Truth of Christ, living in his Church"; 51: "The one Holy Tradition, which constitutes the self-identity of the Church through the ages."

[39]Nikos A. Nissiotis, "Faith and Order 1976. How Does the Church Teach Authoritatively Today?" *One in Christ* 12 (1976) 246.

[40]*Unity Begins at Home. A Report from the First British Conference on Faith and Order. Nottingham 1964* (London: SCM, 1964) 60–61.

[41]*The COCU Consensus: In Quest of a Church of Christ Uniting* (Princeton: COCU, 1985) 30 = V:6–7.

[42]Cf. *Building Unity. Ecumenical Dialogues with Roman Catholic Participation in the United States,* Ecumenical Documents 4; ed. J. A. Burgess and J. Gros (New York/Mahwah, N.J.: Paulist Press, 1989) 166, #11; *Called to Full Unity. Documents on Anglican-Roman Catholic Relations 1966–1983,* ed. J. W. Witmer and J. R. Wright (Washington: United States Catholic Conference, 1986) 149.

[43]Georges Tavard, "Tradition as Koinonia in Historical Perspective," *One in Christ* 24 (1988) 315–24.

[44]Georges Tavard, *La Théologie parmi les sciences humaines. De la methode in théologie,* Le Point théologique 51 (Paris: Beauchesne, 1975) 123: "Such diversity in the meaning of the word obscures the fact that the Tradition, in the sense defined, only lives and is transmitted by a, or rather, by several processes of transmission which are themselves inseparable from the various forms of expression chosen to develop this process and to communicate the Tradition. In other words, one is mistaken if one imagines it is possible to separate the content of the message (the Tradition) from the multiple forms (the traditions) in which the transmission (the tradition) is being carried out."

[45]Francis A. Sullivan, "The Role of Tradition," *Theological Reflections on Charismatic Renewal,* ed. J. C. Haughy (Ann Arbor: Servant Books, 1976) 79; cf. Harding Meyer, "The Ecumenical Reconsideration of Tradition. An Evaluation," *The Gospel as History,* ed. V. Vajta (Philadelphia: Fortress Press, 1975) 181 and the literature cited there.

[46]Ledwith, "The Theology," 121.

[47]K. E. Skydsgaard, "Écriture et Tradition, un problème résolu?" *Irénikon* 42 (1969) 446.

[48]J. Ratzinger, *Das Zweite Vatikanische Konzil, Teil II. Lexikon für Theologie und Kirche,* 2nd ed. (Freiburg, Basel, Vienna: Herder, 1967) 520.

[49]Ledwith, "The Theology," 122–23.

[50]*Baptism, Eucharist & Ministry 1982–1990. Report on the Process and Responses,* Faith and Order Paper 149 (Geneva: WCC, 1990) 136.

[51]Ledwith, "The Theology," 121.

[52]Ibid.

[53]Michael Seils, *Lutheran Convergence? An Analysis of the Lutheran Responses to the Convergence Document "Baptism, Eucharist and Ministry" of the World Council of Churches Faith and Order Commission,* LWF Report 25 (Geneva: LWF, 1988) 21.

[54]Ibid., 142.

[55]*BEM 1982–1990,* 132.

[56]E.g., "Roman Catholic Church," *Churches respond to BEM,* Faith and Order Paper 144; ed. M. Thurian (Geneva: WCC, 1988) 6:7.

[57]*BEM 1982–1990,* 136, referring to M 53.

[58]Ibid., 136.

[59]Ibid., 136, referring to M 48, 54, 55.

[60]Ibid., 132.

[61]Ibid., 140.

[62]Ibid., 137.

[63]Ibid.

[64]Ibid.

[65]Ibid., 141–42.

[66]Ibid., 139.

[67]Ibid., 140.

[68]*Bristol 1967,* 39–40.

[69]Siegfried Wiedenhofer, "Grundprobleme des theologischen Traditionsbegriffs," *Zeitschrift für katholische Theologie* 112 (1990) 18.

[70]Ibid.

[71]*The Condemnations of the Reformation Era. Do They Still Divide?,* ed. K. Lehmann and W. Pannenberg (Minneapolis: Fortress Press, 1989) 27.

[72]Georges Tavard, "Scripture and Tradition," *Journal of Ecumenical Studies* 5 (1968) 325.

[73]Tavard, *Holy Writ,* 224.

17

G. H. Tavard's Concept of Tradition

Marc R. Alexander

In 1969 George Tavard commented autobiographically: "The question of tradition has, more than any other single problem, retained my attention; and what I consider my major writings have dealt with it."[1] Even from the vantage point of a casual reader, quickly surveying Tavard's substantial corpus, his remark is promptly verified. There are not only his classic historical studies[2] but also other more theoretical works, perhaps less well known yet very important for a correct understanding of Tavard's theology of tradition.[3] His numerous articles address such topics as tradition's relationship to Scripture, dogmatic development, and orthodoxy. His principal writings on this topic span some four decades beginning with "Scripture, Tradition and History," *The Downside Review* in 1954. Even a conservative accounting would require that over twenty of his books and over one hundred of his articles be analyzed in order to gain some grasp of Tavard's vision of tradition. It is evident, therefore, that a complete exposition of Tavard's theology of tradition cannot be attempted within these few pages. In order to highlight the key elements of his theology of tradition, while emphasizing his more recent contributions and contemporary concerns, this study is divided into three sections: (1) Tradition as Transmission, (2) Tradition and Development, and (3) Tradition as the Memory of the Church.[4]

I. Tradition as Transmission

Tavard offers several compact definitions of tradition.[5] For example: "Tradition is the pneumatic understanding of Scripture by the Church";[6]

Tradition is "the communication of the Gospel";[7] "Tradition is the Spirit at work, the unchanging, unmoving yet all-encompassing and all-enlightening Spirit";[8] or, more recently,

> [b]y any definition, tradition has to do with the transmission of something. In an objective sense it is what is transmitted. In an operative sense, it is the process of transmission and the means of this process.[9]

In 1991 Tavard notes that transmission is the common denominator in the various explanations of tradition:

> There have been several definitions of the theological tradition. They are all related to the basic fact that, as it has transmitted the gospel and the Scriptures that embody the catechetics of the first Christians, the Church has not only tried to be faithful to the Scriptures. It has also built up a continuum of fidelity. As theologians have reflected about the nature of this fidelity they have seen it as a transmission of data.[10]

If we focus our attention on tradition as a process of transmission, at least three elements immediately come to mind. First, there is a sender or a subject from whom something comes; second, there is a receiver or the one to whom something is given; finally, there is the "something" which is transmitted or for lack of a better word, the "deposit."

The process of transmission might seem a simple matter to comprehend. What is transmitted from one generation to another or from one believer to another is the deposit of faith, the gospel of Jesus Christ, which is held in Scripture, the Church's documents, the creeds, and the works of theologians. However, upon reflection, the complexity of transmission becomes painfully lucid. For, "[t]o transmit anything, one must at the same time retain and impart."[11]

Several questions may be posed about transmission. First, can one argue that in transmitting the text of Scripture and its "commentaries" that we transmit the faith, or do we instead occasion the reception of faith by the receiving subject(s)? Second, since each element is linguistically encased, how does this affect their transmission? In other words, is the faith transmitted in the mere denotation of the words or also in the connotations? If in the connotations (which a kerygma seems to imply), how are these controlled? Finally, just as it is often said that a translation can never replace the original text (due to the inherent untranslatableness of *every* language), how does one deal with the necessity for translation between different generations, languages, and cultures? Tavard offers some assistance toward further understanding these issues.

Tavard identifies three moments in the transmission process: the moment of reception or invention, the moment of possession, and the moment of communication.[12] The moment of reception refers to our having received, invented, or discovered something. The moment of possession is a time of mutual enrichment between the possessor and the thing which is possessed.[13] The moment of communication is the most delicate, for it involves our perception of the future. We never pass on something without some project in mind. And we only retain that which we believe will be able to survive in the future. Hence, there is, in the very process of communication, a kind of purification and simplification. In other words, we remember and pass on to others what is important to us, that which will have an impact on the future, as we prevision it.[14] The subjective influence within the human act of transmission is carefully recognized in this perspective.

The character of this transmission involves three aspects to be considered. First, a tradition is always living. We do not merely repeat the past when we recall a tradition or transmit an experience. We make it come alive. This is very evident in the case of an expression of faith. In repeating the Apostles' Creed, one does not, hopefully, merely mouth words or repeat formulas. One instead *makes* an *act* of faith. The Creed provides the occasion and immediate mechanism for the living expression of faith, but it is lifeless without our praxis.[15] And it is this praxis which also has a direct bearing on the tradition. Tavard writes: "Our conduct bends the sense of what we have learned."[16] For better or for worse, the wisdom which we have received is touched by our way of life, never to be passed on to others in exactly the same way it was received.[17]

Furthermore, one must keep in mind that the communication of a formula does not communicate the totality of the Christian message, for there is a spiritual dimension which must also be communicated.[18] Drawing on some of the insights of contemporary linguistics,[19] Tavard makes the following application: When the Gospel is communicated, two elements must be distinguished (though never separated)—the formula (expression, form, signifier) and the spiritual meaning (content, substance, signified). When we preach the gospel, we only communicate the former; it is the Holy Spirit who communicates the latter, derived from grace. Without grace, the gospel cannot be successfully communicated.[20] But because of the uniqueness of every person and their call from God and God's action upon them, the message preached "is never understood as presented."[21] Thus, there is a sort of loss of energy, which cannot be avoided by the very nature of the communication process.[22]

The third aspect is that the communication of the tradition always involves language, in its spoken and written forms, as well as in liturgy, the sacraments, and art (LaTh, 119). At this point, two further problems emerge. First, language itself, in whatever form, is always changing and evolving. Or, " . . . the tools at our disposal to communicate our traditions, and specifically the Christian tradition, are equally under the statute of tradition."[23] The language system is inherited from the past, transformed by our usage in the present, and passed on to the future. Consequently, "[a]bsolute communication is then a long shot."[24]

A further complication is introduced when one realizes that the Christian tradition, by definition, is attempting to communicate divine realities in human language, the infinite through the finite. Even Sacred Scripture cannot escape the fact that it uses human language, and hence, even if inspired and authored by God, is "subject to the fundamental incertitudes of all language."[25] Needless to say, the same may be said of the other documents of our tradition.

With so many variables involved in the transmission of the tradition, one wonders how we can be sure that the Christian message is being faithfully transmitted. Tavard offers that "moral certitude" may be obtained by looking at the *intention* of the transmitter or acting subjects to transmit the message faithfully (LaTh, 121). The fact that the intention never exists *in se* but is always connected again with a linguistic and semiotic system (which is imperfect to its task) takes us back to uncertainty. The very network of language which renders communications uncertain also provides its life and vitality. In order for the tradition to be true, it must take a chance on being false. Otherwise said, it is impossible to communicate anything without also taking the chance of being misunderstood or never fully understood.

Tavard minces no words in describing the consequences of this analysis:

> Tradition is not then essentially a guarantee, but an intention of fidelity which persists across the succession of dogmatic formulas. It is also a hope that the Lord accompanies this intention and protects from error, in spite of the arbitrariness of semantics, the contingency of syntax, and the radical impotence of every semiotic to express the inexpressible.[26]

Thus it is impossible to speak of passing on something unchanged. That is, the idea of an absolute deposit of faith which is passed on, as such, like a baton, is dismissed. Since the exposition of faith, at all levels, is tied up with language and language changes and is inherently imperfect, the idea of a "baton of dogma" is absurd. Our confidence in the transmission of the authenticity of the Christian message is located not with us or our constructs but with God, in faith and hope, where it alone belongs.

In the transmission process there is what Tavard calls a "loss of energy,"[27] as was mentioned above. The reason for this is not difficult to see. Since theology seeks to communicate a reflection on an original faith experience in an imperfect language, as is every language in consequence of its human component, something is lost in this formulation. A further loss occurs when this discourse is communicated to another person or group, for each receives according to their ability and subjectivity (LaTh, 148–49). Furthermore, the experience created by the reception of the theological discourse differs from the experience of the one who formulated the theological discourse. The law, as Tavard formulates it, is thus: "Every transmission of theological language suffers from a loss of theological energy."[28]

Obviously, if such a transmission took place in this way continually, eventually virtually no theological energy would remain. Compensation must be found. There are in fact multiple sources which help to replenish theological energy. These would include the presence of a Christian family and/or community, active participation within parish life, Catholic action, and lectures. There is also the factor of grace received interiorly. Regardless, as mentioned already, the Church has an obligation to discover and invent new languages, i.e., means of communication, so that theology and faith, the gospel, may be transmitted with as little loss of energy as possible.[29]

Tavard now moves from the individual level of transmission to the communal level, the level of the Church.[30] If there is a loss of energy on the simple level of transmission, e.g., from person A to person B, one must multiply infinitely this loss on the larger scale. Political preferences, cultural developments, secularization, the influence of the various forms of the media, and social pressures are only several factors which contribute to the loss of theological energy. The situation at the present moment is such that Tavard remarks, "The masses already no longer hear the Christian discourse."[31]

Tavard observes that it is pointless to blame this or that group or person for the troubling situation of the present time. Though the present state has been exacerbated by many outside factors, entropy is an inevitable result of the nature of theology as language. "The message is a discourse.

It falls under the laws of theological discourse."[32] There is only one thing which can be done when the "previous compensatory sources"[33] no longer meet the needs of the present age: new ones must be found.[34] It is at this juncture that we enter the field of the development of dogma, to which we now turn.

II. Tradition and Development

In *The Seventeenth-Century Tradition: A Study in Recusant Thought* (1978), Tavard writes in reference to John H. Newman:

> He envisioned the problem of development as the center of the problem of Tradition. Doctrinal development is the test of any theory of Tradition, since it is at the point of its development that the Christian tradition's relation to the norm of Scripture is to be challenged.[35]

Tavard realizes that no discussion of tradition can be complete without some explanation of dogmatic development, with particular reference to its relationship to Scripture.[36] Before turning to his understanding of development, several more introductory remarks should be made.

First, that legitimate development has in fact occurred cannot be denied. One need only look at the history of the Trinitarian and Christological doctrines.[37] Second, tradition involves not only looking to the past and transmitting to the present but also, in the context of development, to formulation in anticipation of the future. The three facets of time must be considered, especially the future.[38]

Third, the structural similarity between mission and development, from the perspective of the communication and translation of the gospel, is highlighted by Tavard. Thus, he writes:

> We may describe the problem of mission as one of translating christian faith and doctrine in another culture, through the medium of another language. Likewise, the problem of the development of doctrine is one of translating christian faith and doctrine in the culture of another time, through the medium of a language that has evolved over a few centuries since the last great age of doctrinal elaboration. Thus mission and development may be seen together. Mission is development in space. Development is, so to say, mission in time. In both cases the chief problem is one of acculturation and translation.[39]

The primary concern of Tavard is how best to communicate to people of every age and culture the message of salvation in Jesus Christ, the gospel. It is the gospel that must always be communicated without compromise, not its formulations which may and must be translated and acculturated.[40]

Tavard provides two principal perspectives for understanding the dynamics of development, one in terms of analogy and the other in linguistic categories. Both are important.

The analogical approach goes back to an article written in 1954, "Scripture, Tradition and History."[41] Tavard quotes extensive portions of this article in the conclusion of his major work of 1969, *La tradition au XVIIe siècle en France et en Angleterre.*[42] Tavard argues that the Catholic notion of tradition is what may be termed analogical, in distinction from both an equivocal and univocal conception. The former sees tradition as being separated from the Scriptural deposit and developing transformationally on its own.[43] A univocal conception suggests that, once the deposit of Scripture was specified, it was and is simply to be passed on as such.[44] Tavard then offers his proposal:

> Catholic tradition is not equivocal, as Brunner affirms. Apostolic tradition is not univocal, as Cullmann thinks. Both form one analogical whole. Apostolic tradition develops itself analogically into Catholic tradition (STH, 237–38).

And how may this analogical development be explained?[45]

One begins by affirming that the New Testament is the written testimony of the apostolic faith to the revelatory act of Christ. This does not reduce the communication of God to a written text, but it does give it a certain primacy.[46] The Canon in some way replaced Apostleship due to the needs of the time to stem pseudo-apostolic literature. The mission of the apostles is in some manner accomplished via the means of the Canon, though the apostolic function terminated with their death. Thus, the apostolic time is singular and closed. Tavard labels this dynamic "Revelation-Apostles." Now one may not reduce the faith experience of the apostolic period to only the faith of the apostles, and by consequence, to only the Canon. Others, noneyewitnesses, also believed, through the testimony of the apostles. Guided by the Holy Spirit moving deep within, they embraced the faith and became members of "God's own people." This dynamic involving noneyewitnesses being moved to faith by the testimony of the apostles is labeled "Scripture-Faith."[47] As God's holy people, they also shared and transmitted the faith.

The two dynamics, Revelation-Apostles and Scripture-Faith, are both intimately related to one another. And both—the Scriptures and the understanding of these Scriptures by the community of faith—are transmitted within the postapostolic Church. This is tradition. In Tavard's own words we read:

> Now, what is transmitted in the post-apostolic Church, what constitutes tradition within the Church, is not simply the New Testament: it is rather the New Testament, the Apostles' testimony, as understood in the declaration of the "wonderful deeds" of God by the "holy nation" of Christians (STH, 239).

At this point, analogy becomes operative. Each element of tradition, while remaining *constant* in its *relationship* to the other elements, *develops* in *continuity* with its own preceding stages. The key elements—revelation, apostles, Scripture, and faith—maintain their same relationship—Revelation-Apostles connected with Scripture-Faith—in every period. However, the Scriptures are never transmitted *in se* but always with the understanding of the previous period.[48] Thus, while it remains true that the apostolic period was unique, it is also correct to say that every period by virtue of its historical context is unique. Just as the faith of the apostles interpreted the revelatory experience of Jesus Christ for those who were not eyewitnesses, the post-Apostolic Church's faith interprets the writings that the apostles left. The chain continues with each generation adding its own link yet always in continuity with the link before.[49] Thus,

> [w]hen a period ends, its faith is, for the following, agglutinated to the original couple "Revelation-Apostles"; it becomes part of the first term in the couple "Scripture-Faith" (STH, 240).

The classical view of mutual coinherence between Scripture and Tradition is affirmed.

Within this process of development, the Church is guided by the Holy Spirit who guarantees the Church's infallibility. Though individual believers may err, the "Church as a whole" cannot. Each period in seeking to understand the Gospel in its own context neither adds nor subtracts from the Gospel.[50]

The primacy of Scripture as the embodiment of Revelation-Apostles is safeguarded within analogical development, because Scripture is the *primum analogum:* "All subsequent formulations of faith" must be tested by Scripture.[51] However, history also has a role to play within the testing process. Since development is analogical, history should reveal the different connections between different elements.[52] Thus the analogical movement assures both continuity and development.

Tavard's second approach to dogmatic development is through linguistic categories. Within this perspective, the problem of development is primarily a problem of translation.[53] The full import of this will now be explained.

We may recall that the linguisticality of theology makes evolution in theology unavoidable. Language does not remain the same. It is at once the result of a long, historical development and at the same time the result of an existential situation, the present moment.[54] Theology, in order to be living and communicable, must operate within similar boundaries and, consequently, must change on that level. Theology will be affected on both the semantic and syntactic levels.[55] Semantically, a given theologeme may have different denotations, connotations, and evocations in one period or another.[56] Syntactically, there may be changes as well, as one era may attach more importance to rational proofs and another to historical proofs.

Then there is the massive problem of the loss of theological energy. In order to curtail the loss of energy, new formulas must be developed.[57] The question at this point is this: How can new formulations be developed which can compensate for this loss of energy? We now turn to Tavard's answer.[58]

The transmission of the gospel from context A to context B, whether that context be a foreign land or a foreign time (for the problems of mission and development are functionally the same), requires acculturation. For,

> [t]o be understood in context B, theological language must be transformed by absorbing the pre-comprehensions, the pre-figurations of itself which B already contains.[59]

Precomprehensions of the Christian faith are present in every culture. By precomprehensions Tavard does not mean ideas which look like Christian doctrines or which can be modified into Christian doctrines. They are, rather, seminal grounds present within a culture which make that culture capable of developing into a Christian culture.[60] These grounds can and must be incorporated into theological language. The ability for theological language to do this is what Newman calls the "power of assimilation" of dogma to which Tavard refers.[61]

The same dynamic must occur when passing from one time to another time. Each time is like a different culture. Hence, as the faith encounters the new time-culture, it must again identify the precomprehensions of the time and incorporate them into the theological language-system. Development takes place

> when the effect of loss from the process of the transmission of theology is compensated for by the qualitative mass of pre-comprehension incorporated into the new theological language.[62]

Through the incorporation of the precomprehensions of a particular language-culture or time-culture, theological energy is gained, a new synthesis emerges, unity is fostered, the gospel is spread, and the kingdom is further unfolded.

Tavard takes his analysis still further. For the development to be adequate, changes will be seen ultimately on both the syntactic and semantic levels.[63] This point is illustrated by Tavard through reference to Aquinas, Bonaventure, and Augustine. While Aquinas and Bonaventure differed significantly on the syntactic level, on the semantic level there was not much difference. They utilized the intellectual fruits and discoveries of their time, being immersed in the same cultural milieu. There were of course differences, but major differences were by far on the syntactic level. Aquinas' differences with Augustine, however, were significant on both the semantic and syntactic levels, for their cultures were very different.[64]

It is, however, correct to say that not every development is acceptable. Tavard points to the Nestorian heresy as an example. The theologemes of the Nestorians were rejected precisely because they were incompatible with other important theologemes.[65] Tavard concludes with the criteria of proper development:

> Negatively, that which does not entail alienation, rupture, to the interior of the language of faith; positively, that which promotes, on the contrary, harmony; that which accentuates the effectiveness of the language of faith and accentuates all those constitutive qualities which one may call beauty.[66]

If it may be accepted that development is required not only on the syntactic level but also on the semantic level, a further point must be emphasized. Semantic development is not just about changing vocabulary. The process of enriching theologemes touches their levels of denotation, connotation, and evocation.[67] In the development of theologemes, their very structure must be altered in order to complete, correct, improve, and perfect[68] that which existed before, not in order to destroy, breakdown, discard, and belittle. Hence, development of doctrine is not exhibited mainly at the level of denotation, i.e., by official definition of doctrine, whether conciliar or papal. When Pius XII defined the doctrine of the Assumption of Mary, the connotative level was untouched. The denotative level was affected, but this alone is insufficient for development to be predicated. Hence, Tavard writes:

> True development is manifested when, before or after a definition (the temporal relation changes nothing within the process), a theologeme incorporates into the whole of Christian consciousness with new connotative and evocative riches. The scope is not infallibility, ecclesial, conciliar or pontifical, but the blossoming of a new theological language in the garden of the Church.[69]

Semantic development necessarily affects syntactic development, as the newly incorporated connotations and evocations will need to be incorporated into a new model.[70] Development may be looked at from the perspective of a series of models, each incorporating the insights of previous models, each only historically comprehensible when seen in relationship to that which came before, but each always imperfect. The ultimate model, able to sustain all verification processes, has yet to be found. Every model before this eschatological model is but an approximation of it. Consequently, in the end, doctrinal development is oriented toward the future, sustained by hope. Or, in the words of Tavard, "[i]t is an eschatological anticipation."[71]

Development, whether viewed primarily from the perspective of analogy or linguistics, holds the key to Tavard's understanding of tradition. One cannot but notice that Tavard has effectively brought together the past, the present, and the future; continuity and growth; stability and dynamism. The mission of the Church is always clear: to take the message of salvation out to the world, whether that be to new lands or new times. Catholicity is ours, Christ's victory is reality, needing only to be unfolded in our temporal and spatial categories.

III. Tradition as the Memory of the Church

Among Tavard's varied approaches to the subject of tradition, one in particular stands out: Tradition as the Memory of the Church. Already in 1976 he remarked:

> Indeed, one could analyze tradition from the standpoint of memory and define it as the church's memory. As such, it includes primarily the remembrance of the great acts of God in Jesus Christ and even, before that, of the interventions of God in the life of his people from Abraham to John the Baptist. It includes also the high moments of the successive existence of the church through ages.[72]

In two more recent articles, "Tradition as Koinonia in Historical Perspective" (1988) and "Vatican II, Understood and Misunderstood" (1991), Tavard has further developed this approach.[73] Although Tavard has not yet fully developed this theme, he has provided the basic components out of which a provisional synthesis may be constructed. A closer look at this approach will advance our appreciation of the riches and utility of Tavard's vision of tradition.

First, the collective nature of the Church's memory is essential. The agent of the memory is the Church, which comprises all of the people of God in some way. Tavard writes:

> Tradition comes into being as the Church's many members remember what they know of the coming of Christ, of his death and resurrection, and of the way his gospel has been taught, understood, and transmitted down the centuries (VUM, 210).

The collective nature does not mean that everyone has the same role to play within the remembrance process and its transmission. Tavard carefully notes:

> In the Church itself, different groups or orders, such as the magisterium and the laity, have different duties in regard to transmitting the gospel: each must transmit it in keeping with the specificity of its divine calling.[74]

If individual praxis is complicated, collective praxis is even more complicated.[75] Thus, we may not expect that looking at tradition as the memory of the Church will simplify our project, though it may explain the phenomenon more accurately.

Second, if we look at how we remember, we would note, as Tavard does, that "our individual memory of events is spontaneously organized according to a hierarchy of relative importance."[76] Some memories are simply more significant to us; others less significant. This hierarchy of memories also applies to the memory of a collectivity. Our hierarchy may be revealed by answering this question: What do we wish to pass on to those who shall come after us?[77] The answer for Christians is the gospel, for "it is the norm that determines what the Church is" (TKHP, 101). What specific memories we pass on reveals our actual understanding or lack of understanding of this core memory or "central tradition" (TKHP, 100). Turning to the vocabulary of tradition, Tavard articulates a general principle: "a central Tradition should act as the norm with which all other traditions must conform in order to be considered binding or authentic" (TKHP, 101).

Third, the passing on of this central memory and its supporting memories is not primarily through our knowledge of doctrines and formulas. The memory at root is a memorial, *anamnesis*.[78] As we have participated in dying and rising with Christ, having been sealed with the Holy Spirit, and shared the Lord's Supper, and experienced "God's grace given to us in Jesus Christ through the Holy Spirit" (TKHP, 106), so we wish others to experience this wonder through their "contemporary participation in the events of the incarnation-redemption" (TKHP, 105). The sacramental dimension is prominent within this perspective, for "[t]he gospel is communicated in the sacraments" (TKHP, 106). As Tavard explicitly notes, there is no conflict here with the Confession of Augsburg, for "[t]he gospel is the substance of the sacraments. The sacraments are means of forwarding the gospel" (TKHP, 106).

Fourth, in respect to the knowledge of documents and doctrines, one must say that though some of this knowledge is necessary, it is never sufficient for the central tradition and its supporting traditions to be passed on effectively. Rather, when we through both the intellect and will experience and recognize in these documents and teachings that the gospel has been faithfully transmitted, that the Holy Spirit has manifested itself, we receive them as gift and we can then pass them on as such.[79] Reception by the Church is essential for the transmission of the gospel. In this sense, we speak meaningfully of receiving the tradition, the transmission of the gospel, under the guidance of the Holy Spirit.

Fifth, whatever is received is received within the present moment. This almost tautological statement condenses two further insights of Tavard. On the one hand,

> [i]f Tradition is memory, it is memory lived in the present. It is today that the gospel is transmitted, that divine grace is received sacramentally, that persons are converted, lives are changed, mentalities are transformed (TKHP, 106).

Or as Tavard says in another place, "[i]f tradition is memory, it is living, not archival, memory" (VUM, 211). The memory of the Church is not about dead things or possibly interesting events of history. It's about the present action of God, made possible by past events, the events of our salvation.

On the other hand, one cannot avoid the fact that,

> one never receives a pure gospel. What one receives is the gospel as previously received in a certain culture, expressed in a given language, embodied in certain customs and institutions (TKHP, 101).

In other words, we, in our own day and age, with its attendant gifts and deficiencies, receive the gospel which was previously received by another age, in its own present moment, with its own set of gifts and deficiencies. In some way, we must learn the language of the previous age from which we receive the gospel in order to understand it and translate it into a form which we can then share and pass on to others here and now and those yet to be. This is the issue of inculturation once again. In addition, our own insights into the past ages which received and passed on the gospel assist us in determining what is truly lasting in what they passed on to us and what is not. Just as they passed on their "constructive remembrance" to us, so shall we pass on ours (see TKHP, 106). Thus, Tavard affirms that,

> the Tradition is always a present event. The present in which we live affects our reception of the gospel. It colours the way we assimilate it and pass it on (TKHP, 107).

Sixth, one may rightly ask how we determine which memories or traditions correctly pass on the gospel and the experience of grace. This requires discernment. Tavard writes:

> One should assess the meaning and value of past documents, and one can do this only in the light of contemporary culture and of present needs. Yet there must also be a critical discernment of one's discernment. . . . The community and its members must be capable of sorting out the essential from the permissible, the permanent from the provisional (TKHP, 107).

The result of the past meeting with the present is a dialogue, which may also include some opposition.[80] For, "[r]eception . . . is in fact a mix of fidelity and confrontation" (TKHP, 107).

Tavard seeks a balance at this point on two levels. On one level, he expresses the need for balance between discernment by the individual Christian believer and the "sense of the community." Thus, he writes:

> Christian believers should try, according to capacities, to discern the "purity of the gospel" in what they read in the Scriptures and in the fathers of the Church and other traditional witnesses. And they should control their reading with the sense of the present Church, as manifested in its contemporary statements and decisions (TKHP, 107).

Now within this dynamic, opposition within the community is not necessarily action against the community or the common good. In this context, Tavard quotes Karol Wojtyla:

> [T]he attitude of solidarity does not contradict the attitude of opposition: opposition is not inconsistent with solidarity. The one who voices his opposition to the general or particular rules or regulations of the community does not thereby reject his membership; he does not withdraw his readiness to act and to work for the common good.[81]

Give and take, agreement and disagreement, are part of the ongoing effort to make the gospel contemporary.

On another level, Tavard acknowledges the need for a balance between material and formal principles of discernment.[82] Each alone is insufficient. What methodological criteria does he offer? In 1976 he is very direct: "such criteria, in my opinion, do not exist" (TTPA, 100). He continues:

> The only concrete criterion which actually functions is the consciousness of the theologian, of the bishop, of the pope, and the corporate consciousness which emerges through the debates of a council. The judgment by which one concludes that the voice of the tradition has spoken and is still valid or, on the contrary, has lost its relevance, is so closely tied to the personal experience of faith that one cannot find universal criteria for it. Such a judgment is composed of variables. The only elements that appear to be constant are the presence of Christ and the guidance of the Spirit, this presence and this guidance being manifested in an experience which is always unique and ultimately incommunicable. In the question of tradition, we therefore deal with a criterion which is also and at the same time a noncriterion. We face an absolute criterion, God in Christ and in the Spirit, whose awareness in us can only be relative (TTPA, 100–01).

It would be a total misunderstanding of Tavard if one were to think that the inability to have absolute criteria would mean that everything goes. Quite to the contrary. Tavard offers the analogy of faith as a viable means for assessing a doctrine's authenticity.[83] The analogy of faith contains three essential elements for Tavard. First, a material principle must be applied. Tavard explains: "What is presented as the gospel should be tested by the faithful in relation to what they already live as the gospel" (TKHP, 108). Second, a more formal principle, which takes into account "[p]ast decisions and formulations of doctrine, and chiefly the biblical witness, . . . properly understood, as norms for further formulations . . . " (TKHP, 108–09). The third element is the communal experience of Christ who is present through the Holy Spirit. What is required in order for these three elements to properly coalesce toward a point of agreement is clearly stated by Tavard:

> [F]reedom of debate and the allowance of a variety of opinions are indispensable for the tradition eventually to emerge from the past. Only from a comparison of divergent opinions can light be obtained on their relative value. Accordingly, freedom of expression in the church is not a luxury, but a requirement of the intelligibility of faith. The time needed for a serene discus-

sion of divergences in matters of faith will allow the Spirit to manifest himself without hindrance and to create step by step the unanimity of believers (TTPA, 103).

Freedom, openness, patience, and time are required for our memory to be sifted for its lasting treasures to be made alive today. Ultimately, we must trust in the Spirit and be open to this Spirit. Tavard sees Vatican II as a testimony of such an experience, which is, in many ways, its lasting contribution to the Church:

> The long-lasting remembrance of Vatican II should be that, in spite of ignorance as to the future, and against all sorts of odds relating to the preparedness of the people and especially the clergy for the updating that was theologically and liturgically desirable, the bishops trusted the Spirit. The Church experienced a moment of grace. At that moment, the magisterium was not dominated, as it commonly is, by habit and custom, by canon law and *praxis curiae,* by concern for self-image or efficacy, or by whatever immediate problems loom large, but by trust in the Holy Spirit (VUM, 214–15).

Seventh, the future-oriented thrust of tradition as the memory of the Church points to the virtue of hope and the eschatological dimension of Christian life.[84] If our discussion thus far has focused on the past and the present, the future dimension has not been forgotten. We remember the past in the present, so that we might pass on what is important to the future. Our view of the future cannot but affect how we choose to act today. Thus, in summary fashion, Tavard observes that "[t]he past becomes tradition insofar as it is shaped by the anticipated future" (TTPA, 95). Turning to the mystical tradition, Tavard links memory and hope when he writes:

> For memory, in the mystical tradition, is the faculty of hope. It is the art of forgetting, of giving up impediments, of placing between us and the world the cloud of unknowing that will enable us to proceed unhampered into the deeper Cloud of Unknowing which is the experience of the living God. We remember insofar as we forget what is not worth remembering. Thus we are able to turn to the future with hope. Likewise, it is in view of the eternal gospel that the Church remembers the gospel in its tradition. The promises are cherished because they tend to a fulfillment.[85]

The eschatological dimension of tradition is revealed when we see that what we formulate in remembering the past in the present for the future is in some sense always transitional, evanescent, and provisional. Thus, Tavard writes:

No historical feature of the Church is permanent and none is absolute. The Church is absolute and permanent only at the point where it is the elected bride of the divine Word and the temple of the Holy Spirit. Everything else should be open for review. . . . Admittedly, the reviewing process, and the outcome, may not be comfortable for everybody. Yet this should itself be welcome if we believe with the epistle to the Hebrews that we have no "abiding city" here on earth, and we seek "the future city" (Heb 13:14).[86]

Once again, this is no invitation to chaos, individualism, and disunity. It represents, instead, a formidable challenge to experience Christ among us, to listen to the Spirit.

What Tavard wrote in 1976 still applies today—perhaps even more so:

We may look for wisdom and strength in the gospel, in the scriptures, in the tradition as the accumulated wisdom of the past. Yet only through purity of heart will wisdom emerge from the documents explaining the gospel, from the scriptures, from the monuments and texts of the past. At the present juncture, both history and theory call us to conversion (TTMA, 124).

Abbreviations

DOT   "The Depths of the Tradition," *Continuum* 7 (1969) 427–37.

LaTh   *La théologie parmi les sciences humaines: de la méthode en théologie.* Le point théologique, 15. Paris: Éditions Beauchesne, 1975.

LaTrad   *La tradition au XVIIe siècle en France et en Angleterre.* Paris: Éditions du Cerf, 1969.

SCT   *The Seventeenth-Century Tradition: A Study in Recusant Thought.* Studies in the History of Christian Thought, 16. Leiden: E. J. Brill, 1978.

STH   "Scripture, Tradition and History," *The Downside Review* 72 (1954) 232–44.

TFM   *A Theology for Ministry.* Theology and Life Series, 6. Wilmington: Michael Glazier, 1983.

TKHP   "Tradition as Koinonia in Historical Perspective," *One in Christ* 24 (1988) 97–111.

TTMA   "Tradition in Theology: A Methodological Approach," *Perspectives on Scripture and Tradition.* Pp. 105–25.

TTPA   "Tradition in Theology: A Problematic Approach," *Perspectives on Scripture and Tradition.* Ed. Joseph F. Kelly. Notre Dame, Ind.: Fides Publishers, 1976. Pp. 84–104.

TVT   *The Vision of the Trinity.* Washington: The Catholic University Press of America, 1981.

VUM   "Vatican II, Understood and Misunderstood," *One in Christ* 27 (1991) 209–21.

Notes

[1] DOT, 432.

[2] See for example, George Tavard, *Holy Writ or Holy Church: The Crisis of the Protestant Reformation* (New York: Harper and Row, 1959) and *The Seventeenth-Century Tradition: A Study in Recusant Thought* (1978).

³See for example, LaTh.

⁴Some readers may be surprised and disappointed that the topic of Scripture and Tradition will not receive distinct treatment. Two reasons may be offered to justify this decision. First, although Tavard has dealt extensively with this subject, his more recent material has moved in a different direction, emphasizing the dimension of transmission. The primary place of Scripture is more readily appreciated within this context. Second, within the less polemical and apologetical climate of theology today, most theologians, Catholic and Protestant, readily embrace the mutual coinherence of Scripture and Tradition. It is a thesis which, one hopes, no longer requires extended argumentation. The real issues are in the arenas of transmission and development.

⁵On the general terminology of tradition see, for example: Yves Congar, *Tradition and Traditions,* trans. Michael Naseby and Thomas Rainborough (London: Burns & Oates, 1966) esp. 296–307; and Gabriel Moran, *Scripture and Tradition* (New York: Herder and Herder, 1963) esp. 17–18 (with a foreword by Tavard). Tavard does not consistently distinguish "Tradition" and "tradition" in his works, although the context usually clarifies his intention. When presenting his thought, we shall follow his usage. In our own remarks we shall use "Tradition" for title headings and for the overall phenomenon. In other instances, "tradition" will be used.

⁶George Tavard, "The Holy Tradition," *Dialogue for Reunion: The Catholic Premises,* ed. Leonard Swidler (New York: Herder and Herder, 1962) 82–83.

⁷George Tavard, "The Meaning of Scripture," *Scripture and Ecumenism: Protestant, Catholic, Orthodox and Jewish,* ed. Leonard J. Swidler, Duquesne Studies Theological Series, 3 (Pittsburgh: Duquesne University Press, 1965) 71–72.

⁸George H. Tavard, "Scripture and Tradition," *Journal of Ecumenical Studies* 5 (1968) 317.

⁹TKHP, 100.

¹⁰VUM, 210.

¹¹LaTh, 115: "Pour transmettre il faut à la fois conserver et communiquer." This translation and all subsequent ones are mine.

¹²LaTh, 115: ". . . l'acte de transmission exige exactement trois moments . . . la réception ou de l'invention . . . la possession . . . la communication."

¹³This mutual influence is clearly noted by Tavard: "le donné reçu dans ma conscience y travaille et me travaille, développant ma vie intérieure, réflexive ou inconsciente, et mon action extérieure. Réciproquement, j'exerce, sans m'en apercevoir peut-être, une action transformatrice sur ce donné, que je ne pourrai jamais transmettre, quoique j'en ai peut-être l'illusion, exactement tel que je l'ai reçu. Désormais, tout en restant sans doute substantiellement le même, il s'est enrichi de mon expérience à moi, et je le transmettrai à mes relayeurs tel que je l'ai moi-même compris et infléchi" (LaTh, 115).

¹⁴LaTh, 115: "[J]e ne peux transmettre quoi que ce soit à d'autres qu'en fonction d'un projet. Je ne retiens comme digne de transmission que ce qui me paraît capable de survivre dans l'avenir. Ma mémoire fait une opération de décantation qui purifie et simplifie ma transmission du donné en fonction de ce que j'en attends pour les temps proches ou lointains que d'autres vivront. Ceci implique qu'il y a, au coeur de l'acte de transmission, une prévision, une pré-compréhension de l'avenir."

¹⁵LaTh, 117–18: "Quand nous récitons le Credo de Nicée-Constantinople, même si nous le faisons en grec, nous ne formulons pas la foi de ces grands Conciles, mais au mieux, nous exprimons la nôtre, au pis nous répétons une formule à laquelle le temps a enlevé son sens et qui ne parle plus à la situation présente." The point which Tavard derives is then expressed as follows: "D'une part, une tradition se vit. Elle n'est pas seulement formule reçue, mémoire des mots, magie des sons, écho des éloquences de nos pères, rayonnement de leur foi et de leur dévotion. On ne répète jamais une tradition; mais on peut la vivre. Le moment actuel de la tradition s'exprime dans une praxis dont il est lui-même fonction."

¹⁶LaTh, 118: "Notre conduite infléchit le sens de ce que nous avons appris."

¹⁷From a slightly different perspective: "What one receives is the gospel as previously received in a certain culture, expressed in a given language, embodied in certain customs and institutions. This gospel is always in tension with its social context" (TKHP, 101).

¹⁸"The spiritual meaning is not really conveyed by the formulations, yet it is not available without these. Without the formulation of doctrine, faith is illuminism, subject to all the vagaries of individual delusions. Without the spiritual meaning, the formulations are magical and ultimately blasphemous" (TFM, 72).

¹⁹Tavard is particularly indebted to Ferdinand de Saussure's *Cours de Linguistique générale,* which he utilized extensively in LaTh.

²⁰TFM, 72.

²¹TFM, 73: "Colored by the spiritual experience of the speaker, it is heard by the listener in the context of another spiritual experience. Thus the content of the message is ultimately incommunicable in its totality."

²²See LaTh, 148–49. This will be discussed in more detail below.

²³LaTh, 120: " . . . les outils à notre disposition pour communiquer nos traditions, et spécifiquement la tradition chrétienne, sont également soumis au statut de la tradition."

²⁴LaTh, 120: "La communication absolue est donc une gageure."

²⁵LaTh, 120–21: "Car, qu'elle soit même «dictée» par l'Esprit, que Dieu en soit l'auteur principal, que l'Église aime à la considérer comme inspirée, inerrante et source de sa foi, l'Écriture ne cesse d'être langage humain. Même si elle était écrite en un langage contemporain, au lieu de l'être en des langues aujourd'hui mortes, elle demeurerait toujours directement, non pas Parole de Dieu, mais paroles d'hommes en langage d'homme, soumises aux incertitudes foncières de tout langage."

²⁶LaTh, 122: "La tradition n'est donc pas essentiellement une garantie, mais une intention de fidélité qui persiste à travers la suite des formules dogmatiques. Elle est aussi une espérance que le Seigneur accompagne cette intention et protège de l'erreur, malgré l'arbitraire de la sémantique, la contingence de la syntaxe, et l'impuissance radicale de toute sémiotique à exprimer l'inexprimable."

²⁷"une déperdition d'énergie" (LaTh, 148).

²⁸LaTh, 149: "Si, par «énergie théologique», nous entendons l'adéquation de l'expression à l'expérience, nous pouvons formuler cette loi comme suit: Toute transmission du langage théologique souffre d'une perte d'énergie théologique."

A simplified formula is given by Tavard in LaTh on p. 148:

$$x^n > Sv \Rightarrow Sv' \rightarrow x'^n$$

This indicates that a given religious experience by person "A" (signified by "x^n") is given particular verbal expression (signified by "Sv"). This is transmitted to person "B" who receives his comprehension of it (signified by "Sv'") which occasions a personal religious experience (signified by "x'^n").

²⁹LaTh, 149–50. It is not difficult to understand why the faith life of so many, especially the young, is at such an inferior level. Many of the elements which one could count on before to bolster theological energy (e.g., Christian values within the community) are now missing. Consequently, the Church must now be even more "energy efficient" than ever before. We should always be energy efficient, but in the midst of much energy, complacency and inefficiency can and do easily set in. Tavard certainly does not intend to reduce faith and theology to the level of gasoline and miles per gallon. However, his point is well explained. We have an obligation to communicate the gospel as efficiently and effectively as possible. And that means, constantly checking our means of communication.

³⁰See LaTh, 150–51.

³¹LaTh, 150: "Les masses désormais n'entendent plus le discours chrétien."

[32]LaTh, 150: "Le message est un discours. Il tombe sous les lois du discours théologique."

[33]Tavard's expression is "les anciennes sources compensatoires" (LaTh, 150).

[34]Some may be tempted to reply that the former sources and language are more than adequate for communication of the Christian message. The problem is not with the language but with the listeners. One might respond to such a critique by observing, in addition to what has already been said, two points. First, it does not take seriously the present moment. If one is dealing with people who do not understand German, it is fruitless, and even stupid, to complain about their ignorance and to continue to speak to them in German. If one desires communication, one must use a language that one's audience is able to understand. Only later may one teach them German, and then communicate with them in German. A similar situation exists in theological transmission. If the language-system that one is using to communicate the faith is unintelligible to one's audience, one must change (translate) one's message into an understandable language system. If the outside distractions and influences are drowning out the whisper of Christ, then perhaps, a different medium must be employed. This is far more difficult than simply continuing to use previous languages, but is likely to be more fruitful.

A second observation is this. Those who want only to grasp onto the past sources and language might conceal a deeper attitude of disgust for our present age. In other, more diplomatic language, they might in fact be guilty af a kind of cultural chauvinism, which sees only superiority in their language-system and inferiority in those systems which cannot comprehend theirs. This attitude is not acceptable, for the receiving party/culture may also have treasures to offer, which have escaped the attention and experience of the transmitting party/culture. This possibility must at least be allowed, even presumed. But this topic will be addressed in our next section on development.

[35]SCT, 264. Tavard has studied the development of doctrine from the historical perspective in several different areas including the doctrines on angels and devils (e.g., *Die Engel* [1968] and *Satan* [1988]) and ecumenical ecclesiology (e.g., *The Quest for Catholicity. A Study in Anglicanism* [New York: Herder and Herder, 1964]). Tavard has expressed a desire to "attempt a theory of development" (DOT, 432). Though he has yet to give a complete theory of development, the principal lines exist in his writings, as we shall see.

[36]For a compact summary of the problem in reference to Vatican II's *Dei Verbum*, see George Tavard, *Dogmatic Constitution on Divine Revelation of Vatican II: Commentary and Translation* (London: Darton, Longman and Todd; Glen Rock, N.J.: Paulist Fathers, 1966) 33–40.

[37]Tavard himself illustrates the point when he writes the following in reference to a portion of the creedal formula of Nicaea ("We believe . . . in one Lord, Jesus Christ, the Son of God, born of the Father, only-begotten, that is, from the *ousia* of the Father, God from God, light from light, true God from true God, born, not made, *homoousion* to the Father . . . "): "Authors have not been wanting to defend the proposition that the adoption of this formula in 325 was the single most important event in the first centuries of the Church, perhaps even in its entire doctrinal history so far. For, consecrating the endorsement of a Greek vocabulary for the formulation of the Christian faith, it accepted the principle of doctrinal development. It made possible future developments and the eventual adoption, in other movements of acculturation, of other formulas in other languages" (TVT, 67). Tavard makes reference to the work of John Courtney Murray, *The Problem of God* (New Haven and London: Yale University Press, 1964) 31–60. Murray: "The prime objection of the Right [re: the Nicene formula] was to the word, but the issue went much deeper, below the level of language, to an issue of most weighty substance. *The real issue concerned development in the understanding of the Christian revelation and faith.* It concerned progress within the tradition. This was the issue that the Eusebians, after the immemorial custom of conservatives, failed to see or, perhaps refused to see. They pretended to be the protagonists of the tradition. In fact, *they were only*

defenders of the status quo, which is quite a different thing. They were fundamentalists, or biblical positivists . . . in their insistence that only in the formulas of Scripture may the Christian faith be proposed" (p. 47; emphases added).

[38]Tavard's clear formulation of his position follows: "Ainsi la tradition ne se situe pas seulement dans la conservation du passé et sa transmission au présent. Il faut encore la voir à l'oeuvre dans l'anticipation de l'avenir. Chaque moment de la communication de la foi se réfère immanquablement à un passé dont l'origine est, dans son ensemble, connue de toujours et dont la compréhension croît à mesure que se déroulent les âges de l'Église, et à un futur encore généralement inconnu, mais dont les traits s'esquissent déjà dans l'effort actuel d'intellection de la foi" (LaTrad, 196 97).

[39]TFM, 64. See also, LaTh, 152-53. Tavard observes that the correlation between two documents from Vatican II *Dei Verbum* 8 and *Ad Gentes* 6–9 is a consequence of "l'analogie profonde entre la structure du développement doctrinal et celle de l'acculturation du message chrétien" (LaTh, 153, n. 4).

[40]The extent of today's challenge of mission and development, broadly understood, cannot be exaggerated. Countries and cultures which have until recently been dominated by Western culture have increasingly asserted their independence, sometimes in the process rejecting the faith which they see as inseparably enmeshed with the "despised" culture of their oppressors. This is not limited to countries, but may also be applied to "sub-cultures." Certain feminist movements ("radical separatist") exhibit clear rejection of Christianity because of what they call its inherent relationship to patriarchy. For a recent article on this latter subject see Mary Grey, "Has Feminist Theology a Vision for Christian Church?" *Louvain Studies* 16 (1991) 27–40, esp. 27–29.

Development, "mission in time," is further complicated because, as Tavard notes, we "can no longer start from a stable base" (TFM, 65). We are now in a time where both great problems are clamoring for attention.

[41]STH, 232-44.

[42]See pp. 507–10.

[43]STH, 236-37. Tavard illustrates this view using Emil Brunner's interpretation of the Catholic notion of tradition in his book, *The Misunderstanding of the Church*, trans. Harold Knight (Philadelphia: Westminster Press, 1953; German, 1951).

[44]STH, 234-36. To illustrate this view, Tavard refers to Oscar Cullmann's conception of tradition, utilizing Cullmann's article "Écriture et tradition," *Dieu vivant* 23 (1953) 47–67. In the following issue there is a response by Jean Daniélou entitled "Réponse à Oscar Cullmann," *Dieu vivant* 24 (1953) 107–16.

[45]The explanation is drawn from STH, 238-43.

[46]Tavard cautions: "God is known through the Canon, but his means of communication with men are not reduced to a written instrument" (STH, 238).

[47]The Scriptures (in this case the New Testament) are the written form of the apostolic testimony. Just as the testimony of the apostles moved people to faith, so the Scriptures also do.

[48]" . . . the faith of the Church represents the Church's understanding of the apostolic deposit of Scripture" (STH, 239).

[49]In order to assure the clarity of Tavard's point, we insert here an extended quotation from one of John Henry Newman's theological papers. Though Tavard has never referred to this particular quotation (he has dealt often with Newman), the passage explains the importance of the contribution of succeeding ages toward deeper understanding of things already given. It is a brilliant passage, not well enough known:

"What do we mean by a man's being *master* of any subject, say science? What is meant by *knowing* the Aristotelic philosophy? Does it mean that he has before his mind always every doctrinal statement, every sentiment, opinion, intellectual and moral tendency of Aristotle?

This is impossible. Not Aristotle himself, no human mind, can have a host of thoughts present to it at once. The philosophy, as a system, is stored in the *memory*, deeply rooted there if you will, but still in the memory, and is brought out according to the occasion. A learned Aristotelian is one who can answer any whatever philosophical questions in the way that Aristotle would have answered them. If they are questions which could not occur in Aristotle's age, he still answers them; and by two means, by the instinct which a thorough Aristotelic intellect, the habit set up in his mind, possesses; next, by never-swerving processes of ratiocination. . . . . In one respect he knows more than Aristotle . . . . There is another point of view in which he seems to have the advantage of Aristotle, though it is no real superiority, viz. that, from the necessities of the interval between Aristotle and himself, there has been the growth of a technology, a scientific vocabulary, which makes the philosophy easier to remember, easier to communicate and to defend . . . . It keeps his learning well about him, and at command at any moment, as being a sort of memoria technica, both as embodying elementary principles, and as condensing the tradition of a thousand questions and answers, of controversies and resolutions of them, which have taken place between Aristotle's time and his'' (paper of February 15, 1868, first published in "An Unpublished Paper by Cardinal Newman on the Development of Doctrine," *Gregorianum* 39 [1958] 595. Ian T. Ker in his work, *John Henry Newman: A Biography* [Oxford: Clarendon Press, 1988] 315, locates the paper also in *The Theological Papers of John Henry Newman on Biblical Inspiration and on Infallibility*, ed. J. Derek Holmes [Oxford: 1979] 156–59).

[50]Tavard's point is unambiguous: "No addition to the original gospel is made. Rather, in the classical expression, 'faith seeks understanding' and if this seeking may be erroneous in an isolated believer, it is infallibly led by the Holy Spirit as far as the Church as a whole is concerned" (STH, 240).

[51]STH, 241, in agreement with Cullmann. The primordial memory of Jesus cannot be removed or displaced by other newer memories. The types of recollective principles developed and utilized by a particular time cannot destroy this primordial memory for it is burned into our collective consciousness, while the Holy Spirit assures its central role.

[52]"Apostleship having passed away forever, the apostolicity of our faith—its analogical connexion with Apostleship—may be checked only by swimming back along the stream of development until we reach its source" (STH, 241).

[53]See above, p. 292.

[54]See above, p. 290.

[55]See LaTh, 154–55. The semantic and syntactic structures of theology are discussed at length by Tavard in LaTh, 55–71, 75–105, respectively. A brief discussion in English of the semantic and syntactic dimensions in regards to the theology of the Trinity may be found in TVT, 123–32. The semantic dimension "refers to the identification and interpretation of the units of meaning of a given language" (TVT, 127). The syntactic dimension deals with the "ways to combine units of meaning in order to express and communicate signification" (TVT, 123).

[56]A theologeme is a basic unit of meaning which has theological sense. Tavard's final definition, after extended discussion, is as follows: "Nous pouvons donc définir le théologème comme une unité de sens exprimant une expérience religieuse, comme un sème se rapportant à une praxis humano-divine (où Dieu et l'homme se rencontrent). C'est en relation à cette praxis que le mot (Dieu, âme, salut, péché . . .), se chargeant de sens, devient théologème: il exprime Dieu-senti, l'âme-en-paix, le salut-désiré, le péché-regretté . . . " (LaTh, 62).

Briefly explained, Tavard's understanding of denotation refers to the bare or conventional meaning to which a particular word directs our attention. Connotation refers to meanings of a term which go beyond the term's raw sense. The semiotic quadrilateral allows rational connotations to be objectified. The connotations of a particular term may vary depending upon the intellectual and emotional context in which it functions and is received. Nonrational connotations, derived from emotional or affective considerations, are called evocations (see LaTh, 63–67).

[57] See above, pp. 291ff.

[58] This discussion follows LaTh, 151–56.

[59] LaTh, 153: "Pour être compris dans le contexte B, le langage théologique doit se transformer en absorbant les pré-compréhensions, les pré-figurations de lui-même que B déjà recèle."

[60] "Car les pré-compréhensions ne sont pas des mimétismes propédeutiques, doublets anticipateurs de la foi qui leur sera proposée. Ce sont, pour adapter une antique théorie biologique, des raisons séminales qui attendent une culture appropriée pour s'épanouir en une vision chrétienne, encore partielle et toujours imparfaite, du monde" (LaTh, 153).

[61] Tavard refers to Newman's work, *Essay on the Development of Christian Doctrine* (1845), part 2, ch. 5, sect. 3, and ch. 8. The power of assimilation designates both the ability to discern the precomprehensions and to utilize them as key points in a new theological language. See LaTh, 153.

[62] "Il y a développement lorsque l'effet de déperdition des processus de transmission de la théologie se trouve compensé par le volume qualitatif de pré-compréhension incorporé au nouveau langage théologique" (LaTh, 153–54).

[63] To keep things clear, one may think of the semantic level as dealing with the meaning of theological concepts/words, while the syntactic level deals with the relationships one develops between/among these concepts/words. Still simpler, the semantic deals with the individual building blocks, while the syntactic deals with their construction into a building.

[64] To continue with the building image: it is not sufficient to just change the design of the theological building, one must at times even change the material out of which the building is constructed.

[65] "Si les Pères réagissent fortement contre les théologèmes des nestoriens, c'est que ceux-ci aliènent d'autres théologèmes importants du langage traditionnel: si le nestorianisme avait raison, il n'y aurait pas un Sauveur, mais deux" (LaTh, 154). Again, using the building image, the new material utilized must be compatible with the previous important material, for without compatibility, unity and continuity are jeopardized. Of course, the point of controversy will be over exactly what is to be considered important, and what is expendable from the tradition inherited.

[66] LaTh, 154: "Négativement, celui-ci n'entraîne pas d'aliénation, de rupture, à l'intérieur du langage de la foi; positivement, il y promeut, au contraire, l'harmonie; il en accentue l'efficacité et toutes ces qualités constitutives de ce que l'on peut en appeler la beauté."

[67] "Le développement doctrinal affecte les connotations et les évocations, non moins que les dénotations théologiques" (LaTh, 155).

[68] See LaTh, 154–55.

[69] "Le développement véritable se manifeste lorsque, avant ou après une définition (la relation temporelle ne change rien au processus), un théologème s'incorpore à l'ensemble de la conscience chrétienne avec de nouvelles richesses connotatives et évocatives. Le ressort n'en est pas l'infaillibilité, ecclésiale, conciliaire ou pontificale, mail la floraison d'un nouveau langage théologique au jardin de l'Église" (LaTh, 155).

[70] LaTh, 155. See LaTh, 43–48, for Tavard's explanation of the role of models within the general structure of theology.

[71] "Il est un anticipation eschatologique" (LaTh, 156). As an addendum, it may be noted that ecumenism should also be seen within the same order as mission and development. Tavard writes: "Le problème oecuménique est donc du même ordre que celui de la mission et celui du développement. Il s'agit d'abord de comprendre la sémantique et la syntaxe des autres; il faut ensuite déterminer les isomorphies et préciser les irréductibilités; il faut finalement, par un processus de développement, découvrir et adopter un nouveau langage" (LaTh, 156).

[72] TTPA, 92, with discussion on the following pages. In a second presentation in the same

book (TTMA), Tavard writes: "It [tradition] is the memory of the community [the Church], identical with the entirety of the Christian past in as far as the past has left visible traces" (p. 119). These two articles appear to be the first time that Tavard speaks of tradition as the memory of the Church in some detail. The idea of memory is certainly addressed by Tavard in some of his earlier works, usually in the context of someone else's thought. For example, in his volume, *Holy Writ or Holy Church* (p. 158), Tavard speaks of "the memory of the Church" in regard to Alonso de Castro (1495–1558). A powerful sense to "remembering" is presented by Tavard in regard to Tillich's idea of symbol in George Tavard, *Paul Tillich and the Christian Message* (New York: Charles Scribner's Sons, 1962) 54–55. Tavard's opus of 1969, LaTrad has several references to memory and remembering in the context of tradition. For example, see p. 322 (in regard to Matthew Wilson, 1582–1656) and p. 411 (in reference to Thomas White, 1593–1673).

[73]These have already been cited above as TKHP and VUM respectively. See esp. TKHP, 105–10, and all of VUM. In TKHP, Tavard identifies three principal elements in "the structure of the Christian Tradition": memory, presence, and hope (p. 105). One section of VUM is simply entitled "Tradition as memory" (pp. 210–11).

[74]TKHP, 102. The magisterium does not only mean here the episcopal hierarchy. "One can discern the existence and the influence of three interlocking magisteria, two of which are not commonly recognized" (TKHP, 102). The three magisteria are the episcopal magisterium, the "magisterium of holiness," and the "magisterium of theologians."

[75]Tavard discusses both the personal and communal acts of transmission with reference to Karol Wojtyla's *The Acting Person*, trans. Andrzej Potocki (Dordrecht, Holland; Boston; and London: Reidel Publishing Company, 1979). See TKHP, 103–05, 107.

[76]VUM, 210–11. Of note, Tavard has written specifically on the hierarchy of truths in " 'Hierarchia veritatum': A Preliminary Investigation," *Theological Studies* 32 (1971) 278–89.

[77]Tavard asks the question in regard to a specific event, Vatican II (VUM, 211). But the principle behind it certainly applies more generally. Tavard speaks of this hierarchy in regard to tradition in general in TKHP as follows: "All societies are nurtured by their traditions, from which they derive their original purpose, their constitution and organization, their basic principles and their ideals, their way of life, their rules and laws. But there is always a hierarchy in what is passed on. The sundry traditions of a given society are relative to a central tradition, that may be in the public domain or may be kept by a few as a precious secret. This central tradition determines the very nature of the society" (p. 100).

[78]TKHP, 105. In the context of tradition, *anamnesis* is discussed by Tavard in TTPA, 93–94.

[79]"The Church's memory is not primarily a knowledge of texts and doctrines that have been learnt by heart. Even when rote memorizing is part of the process of learning the faith, as it used to be in the old-fashioned catechisms by question and answer, the gospel has not truly been transmitted until there has been some understanding and acceptance of what has been learnt. The intellect and the will are at work, no less than memory in the narrow sense of the term. In the Church at large, a council becomes authoritative in its reception, when the people of the Church recognize in it the faithful transmission of the Gospel and its adaptation to the concerns and problems of the time. Or to say it another way, it is not the council [Vatican II] as a human gathering, comparable to a convention or to a parliament, that needs to be remembered. It is the council [Vatican II] as an experience of the Holy Spirit, as a unique *kairos* in the modern history and life of the Church" (VUM, 212–13).

[80]TKHP, 107. Here Tavard is drawing on his interpretation of Karol Wojtyla's discussion of collective action. See TKHP, 104.

[81]See TKHP, 104. The quote is from Wojtyla, *The Acting Person*, 286, in a section entitled "The Attitude of Opposition" (pp. 286–87). In the next section entitled "The Sense of Dialogue" (p. 287), Wojtyla writes the following instructive passage: "Dialogue, in fact,

without evading the strains, the conflicts, or the strife manifest in the life of various human communities takes up what is right and true in these differences, what may become a source of good for men. Consequently, it seems that in a constructive communal life the principle of dialogue has to be adopted regardless of the obstacles and difficulties that it may bring with it along the way" (p. 287).

[82]On this subject, see esp. TKHP, 107–09, and TTPA, 98–104. The material principle refers to the assessment of doctrine on the basis of its content. The formal principle assesses a doctrine on the basis of its sources.

[83]See TTPA, 101, and TKHP, 108–09.

[84]For this section, see esp. LaTrad, 496–97, 502–06; TTPA, 94–96; and TKHP, 109–10.

[85]TTPA, 95. In speaking of the future-oriented thrust of *Dei Verbum* 8 in regard to tradition Tavard observes: "Now, this tallies with the notion that tradition is no other than the Church's memory. The vision it opens is not to the past that it continues but to the future that it prepares. For the purpose of memory, as carefully analyzed, among others, by St. John of the Cross, is so to remember the past that one is freed for the future" (VUM, 219). The key work on John of the Cross for our topic is the *Ascent of Mount Carmel* (to which Tavard refers in both VUM and TTPA), esp. bk. 2, ch.6, and bk. 3, chs. 1–15. Tavard's study of John of the Cross' poetry is helpful in understanding the function of memory. See George Tavard, *Poetry and Contemplation in St. John of the Cross* (Athens, Ohio: Ohio University Press, 1988) esp. 45, 97–98.

[86]VUM, 219. See also LaTrad, 504–05: "Le problème n'est pas d'établir dès aujourd'hui une synthèse totale, mais d'adopter désormais le point de vue de l'avenir, de regarder la tradition dans la perspective de l'espérance, à la lumière de la Parole du Christ, qui n'est pas seulement inscrite ou écrite, une parole passée, mais qui est la Parole aujourd'hui prononcée par le *Christus praesens*. La théologie de la tradition ne doit plus être seulement une analyse de phénomènes passés, mais plutôt une participation aux développements en cours et une anticipation des développements futurs. La tradition, vue sous cet angle, apparaît comme le sein fécond de naissances et de croissances dont l'Esprit se réserve encore la pleine connaissance mais dont la gestation est déjà en cours dans l'Église."

18

Tradition and Creativity: A Theological Approach

Avery Dulles, S.J.

This study is an expression of friendship and respect for Father George Tavard, who combines in himself an outstanding familiarity with the theology of tradition and a creative capacity that manifests itself not only in his theology but also in his poetic works. The *poietes* is par excellence the embodiment of *poiesis* or creativity.

The ideas of "tradition" and "creativity" seem at first glance to be opposed and incompatible. Tradition says continuity; creativity says innovation and hence discontinuity. With the proper distinctions, however, it may be possible to show that the two are not only compatible but mutually supportive.

The question arises on at least two distinct levels. On one level, tradition is considered in the sociological sense, as a factor in the life of society and culture, including the arts. Tradition is the process by which a specific set of ideas or customs is perpetuated, continuing to influence new developments. On a second level, tradition is considered as a specifically theological entity. Christian faith, as generally understood, is built on the conviction that God's saving act in Christ is a definitive reality that is to be proclaimed and believed by all future generations. For its continued existence the Church depends upon the mediation of that saving event. Tradition in the theological sense refers to this process of transmission. Theologically it must be asked whether faithful mediation of the past redemptive act leaves room for, requires, or even perhaps enhances, human creativity, and conversely, whether human creativity contributes to the mediation of the past event.

I. The Concept of Tradition

The concept of tradition has a long history in theology. In the New Testament the noun *paradosis* and the verb *paradidomi* are used in several senses. In the Gospels Jesus sometimes speaks disparagingly of rabbinic or Pharisaic tradition as a device for nullifying the word of God. For example, he reprimands the scribes and Pharisees for attaching too much importance to ablutions before meals, and even more for their practice of dedicating money to God (the *korban*) as a means of evading the obligation to support their aged parents (Matt 15:1-9; Mark 7:1-15). Paul, while he is familiar with the concept of merely human traditions (Gal 1:14; Col 2:8), also uses the term to signify divine or apostolic tradition, to which Christians are bound. He exhorts the Thessalonians to hold fast to the traditions they have learned (2 Thess 2:15). In writing to the Corinthians he reminds them of their obligation to stand by the tradition concerning Christ's institution of the Eucharist (1 Cor 11:23) and the tradition concerning the appearances of the risen Jesus (1 Cor 15:3ff.).

In the early Church, theologians such as Irenaeus and Tertullian insisted against the Gnostics that the authentic doctrine had been passed on in the Church from the apostles to the legitimate pastors, and that it was not to be found through human philosophical constructions. Gregory of Nyssa, a good representative of the fourth century, writes: "We have, as a more than sufficient guarantee of the truth of our teaching, tradition, that is, the truth that has come down to us by succession from the apostles, as an inheritance."[1] Basil and others distinguish between things known from Scripture and things known from tradition. "Among the doctrines and the definitions preserved in the Church," he writes, "we hold some on the basis of written teaching and others we have received, transmitted secretly, from apostolic tradition. All are of equal value for piety."[2]

Until the late Middle Ages the dominant tendency was to treat Scripture as the basic text of revelation and to rely on tradition, especially patristic tradition, for the authoritative interpretation of Scripture. By the fourteenth century, however, some theologians were beginning to look on tradition as an independent source of revealed truths not attested in Scripture.

The problem of the relationship between Scripture and tradition became acute in the sixteenth century, when many Protestants took the position that Scripture alone was the norm by which all doctrines and practices were to be tested. The Council of Trent, relying on authorities such as Basil, responded that Scripture was not a sufficient rule of faith, and that the Church was bound also by traditions concerning faith and morals that had been continuously handed down from Christ and the apostles.

Since the Council of Trent the concept of tradition has been nuanced in several different ways. Many theologians used the term (usually in the plural, *traditions*) in an objective sense to mean revealed truths handed down from apostolic times by channels other than the canonical Scriptures. Others used the term to designate the process of transmitting the apostolic heritage in the Church, regardless of whether the content was also attested by Scripture. Thirdly, tradition came to mean a criterion to which theologians could appeal to establish the authenticity of certain doctrines and practices that were, as the phrase goes, "proved by tradition." The consensus of the Fathers and the testimony of the liturgy were instances of tradition in this normative sense.

More important for our present purposes is the emergence in the nineteenth century of still another usage. Under the influence of romanticism (and, I suspect, also of Kant), the term "tradition" began to be understood more subjectively as a collective sense of the faith supernaturally imparted to the Church by the Holy Spirit. In his *Die Einheit in der Kirche* (1825) the Catholic Tübingen theologian Johann Adam Möhler depicted tradition as a mysterious inner principle or power of spiritual life. "Tradition," he wrote, "is the living influence of the Holy Spirit animating the whole body of the faithful, perpetuating itself through all times, continually living, and yet expressing itself in bodily forms."[3] For Möhler, therefore, tradition or the living Gospel, continuously proclaimed in the Church, extends to the whole spirit of Christianity and to all its doctrines. While recognizing that tradition inevitably embodies itself in language, Möhler spoke particularly of "interior" tradition, by which he meant the "mysterious, invisible side of the spiritual power of life that perpetuates itself and perdures in the Church."[4] Individual Christians, according to Möhler, had access to tradition by their incorporation in the Church, the primary carrier of tradition. The sense of the faith was constant, since the faith did not change, but it was also living and dynamic, since the faith was experienced and articulated in different forms in different times and cultures.

Early in the twentieth century the Catholic concept of tradition was further developed by the lay philosopher Maurice Blondel, who tried to find a via media between the errors he attributed respectively to the Modernists and to the Scholastics. The Modernists, according to Blondel, regarded tradition as a pure process without any stable or determinate content. For them, he said, Christian beginnings were a mere point of departure. Their view of tradition was Protean since the past was always up for reassessment. On the other hand the Scholastics, as perceived by Blondel, fell into a fixist or Procrustean position, which Blondel labeled "Veterist." They inculcated servile conformity to a static given and overlooked the need for personal involvement on the part of the believer.

Blondel attempted to transcend both the Modernist and Veterist positions by proposing a synthesis. Tradition, he said, is not the mere transmission of received teachings, for in that case it would be only a poor substitute for written texts. Unlike written archives, tradition preserves the living reality of the past, including elements that cannot be stated in words. It is the bearer of tacit knowledge and is most effectively transmitted and received through faithful action. The stability of tradition, for Blondel, does not come from verbal or conceptual conformity with prior statements but from fidelity to the reality intended by the statements. That reality points toward the future. "However paradoxical it may sound, one can therefore maintain that Tradition anticipates and illuminates the future and is disposed to do so by the effort which it makes to remain faithful to the past."[5]

On the eve of Vatican II a number of scholarly theologians took up the insights of Möhler and Blondel. The Tübingen theologian Josef Rupert Geiselmann argued that Scripture and tradition should not be seen as two parallel deposits of revelation but as two witnesses to one and the same body of truth. The French Dominican Yves Congar, after a thorough investigation of the history of the question, concluded that "no article of the Church's belief is held on the authority of Scripture independently of Tradition, and none on the authority of Tradition independently of Scripture."[6] The apostolic heritage, initially crystallized in Scripture, continues to be transmitted through living tradition, and only in the light of that tradition discloses its true meaning. Following Blondel, Congar was convinced that tradition in its historical journey "is as much development as memory and conservation."[7] The deposit of faith, as received today, comes with the enrichment that results from its having been "lived, pondered, and expressed by generations of believers inhabited and vivified by the Spirit of Pentecost."[8]

Thanks to the active collaboration of theologians such as Congar, Vatican II espoused a very dynamic concept of tradition. According to the Constitution on Divine Revelation, which devotes its second chapter to the theme, tradition is the way in which the Church "perpetuates and transmits to all generations all that it is and all that it believes."[9] Tradition consists not simply of words ("oral tradition") but also of ways of living and acting. It is, moreover, capable of growth as the Church meditates on the Word of God, undergoes spiritual experiences, and receives instruction from its hierarchical authorities. The tradition is ceaselessly sustained by the Holy Spirit, who makes the voice of the gospel resound in the Church and keeps the Church in uninterrupted conversation with God. "As the centuries advance, the Church constantly tends toward the fullness of divine truth, until the words of God reach their consummation in the Church."[10]

Although there is no contradiction between Trent and Vatican II, the concept of tradition underwent a considerable evolution between the two councils. Trent used the word "tradition" only in the plural, and in an objective sense, to mean particular beliefs and practices that were continuously handed down in the Church, having been entrusted to the apostles by Christ and the Holy Spirit. Although Trent did not explicitly say that there are any truths in tradition alone, it was generally interpreted as teaching that tradition, as a second source, attested to some revealed truths not certified in Scripture.

Vatican II in *Dei Verbum* uses the term "tradition" only in the singular (except in one instance, where it is quoting the New Testament).[11] It speaks of tradition primarily in a subjective or active sense, to mean the process by which the apostolic heritage is transmitted and received in the Church. Whereas Trent had emphasized oral tradition, Vatican II gives equal emphasis to transmission by action. Unlike Trent, which looked upon traditions as invariant, Vatican II understands tradition as a sense of the faith that develops organically under the aegis of the Holy Spirit. Finally, Vatican II seems to suggest that there is no revealed truth that is attested either by Scripture alone or by tradition alone. It declares that Scripture and tradition "form one single deposit of the Word of God" and "are so connected and associated that one does not stand without the other."[12]

The shift in the dominant concept of tradition in twentieth-century Catholicism has facilitated a more positive assessment of the relationship between tradition and creativity. Before looking into this relationship, however, we must examine the meaning of creativity.

II. *The Concept of Creativity*

The term creativity, as currently used, has very little grounding in the classical theological heritage. The ancient and medieval authors held that creative power is proper to God alone. Creation had a generally accepted definition: *productio rei ex nihilo sui et subjecti* (production of something from no preexisting component or material). No creature, even the highest of the angels, could create anything at all. Most theologians have followed St. Thomas in holding that creatures could not even cooperate as instrumental causes in creating.[13] It was commonly taught that each human soul, as an immaterial substance, came into being by a creative act, and hence was immediately produced by God.[14]

Creativity, to be sure, is not God's only property. God conserves and cares for all that he has made. Creation would be pointless unless God preserved creatures in existence and enabled them to achieve their proper goal. God's presence and activity, therefore, may be discerned not only by the occurrence of utter novelty but also, at times, by extraordinary durability and fruitfulness.

The attribution of creativity to human beings seems to have originated in literary and artistic criticism. John Donne in one of his sermons, probably preached in 1632, says: "Poetry is a counterfeit Creation, and makes things that are not, as though they were."[15] Similarly, John Dryden, in a preface to *Troilus and Cressida*, wrote that in the character of Caliban, "Shakespeare seems there to have created a person which was not in Nature, a boldness which, at first sight, would appear intolerable."[16] As Edward Shils remarks with reference to passages such as these, "The artist became a 'creator' and thereby assumed god-like lineaments."[17]

During the hegemony of romanticism it became standard practice to dismiss tradition as a hindrance to spontaneity and creativity. It was widely supposed that artists of genius, having access to immediate inspiration, could do without human instruction. Rousseau and the primitivists urged artists to express their personal emotions without restraint or inhibition. Nietzsche identified enthusiasm not with Apollonian serenity but with Dionysiac intoxication. Modernist critics measured creativeness not by truth but by originality. Thus antitraditionalism, as Irving Babbitt observed, developed a powerful, though misguided, tradition of its own.[18]

The theme of creativity was popularized in philosophy by Henri Bergson among others. Bergson held that the process of evolution is sustained by a vital, creative impulse that continually breaks through to higher levels. Although the *élan vital* eludes the static and abstract categories of discursive reason, it can in some sort be glimpsed by means of intuition. Human beings vaguely intuit their own freedom and are thereby put in contact with the creative activity of the cosmic vital process. Bergson's immanent *élan vital* differs markedly from the Jewish and Christian idea of God as creator, but Bergson in his later work came to recognize the existence of a transcendent creative activity. By means of the creative energy of love, Bergson contended, God brings into being "creators, that He may have, besides Himself, beings worthy of His love."[19]

Among Bergson's disciples we must recognize the Russian Orthodox thinkers Lossky and Berdyaev. Unlike Thomas Aquinas and the theologians of the Catholic tradition, they maintained that human beings, like God, are creative, and that all creation is *ex nihilo*. Human freedom, according to Berdyaev, is self-creation; creation is continuous.

A number of French Catholic intellectuals were influenced by Bergson. Inspired in part by Bergson, the poet Charles Péguy explored the connection between creativity and tradition. He inveighed against the clerical Catholicism of his day for having lapsed into formalism and privatization, and for failing to renew society. Catholicism in the nineteenth century, he commented, had lost its hold on the people and had become "a kind of higher religion for the higher classes of society and of the nation, a miserable sort of distinguished religion for ostensibly distinguished people."[20] Péguy built into the concept of tradition Bergson's idea of *élan vital*. By simply imitating its own past forms, he argued, tradition becomes atrophied and moribund. Tradition must renew itself by constantly returning to its own original inspiration. Tradition is thus, in the most literal sense, a resource. Péguy was apparently the first to use in French the term *ressourcement*, in the sense of the self-renewal of a people from the original sources of its own life. He wrote in 1913: "Nothing is more thrillingly beautiful than the spectacle of a people that is raising itself up by an inner movement, by a deep *ressourcement* of its former pride, by a renewal of the instincts of its race."[21] Against a superficial and imperfect tradition, Péguy maintained, there is no remedy except to reactivate a deeper and more perfect tradition and to sound the depths from which a richer humanity can well up.[22]

The Thomistic philosopher Jacques Maritain, who had been a pupil of Bergson, built bridges between him and Aquinas. In his richly suggestive book *Creative Intuition in Art and Poetry*[23] Maritain sought to incorporate themes from the romantic tradition, comparing its concept of genius with the classical theological doctrine of the infused gifts of the Holy Spirit. Poetic intuition was for Maritain, as for Bergson, something suprarational, resembling in that respect the connatural knowledge of divine things bestowed upon the saints. The sources of creativity, he said, lie at a level beneath the sunlit surface inhabited by explicit concepts and judgments, at a point that is "hidden in the primordial translucid night of the intimate vitality of the soul."[24] Poetry therefore emanates from the spiritual unconscious, which may also be called the preconscious.

Poetic intuition, according to Maritain, has both cognitive and creative components. In its cognitive aspect, it is directed toward concrete realities that speak to the soul in its inmost being. Through intuition poets can perceive the deeper dimensions both of reality and of their own subjectivity.

In its creative aspect poetic intuition is turned toward expressive activity. Picking up certain themes in literary criticism to which I have already referred, Maritain asserted that the poet is like a god. Poetic creativity is free, "for it only tends to engender in beauty, which is a transcendental, and involves an infinity of possible realizations and possible choices."[25] But the poet is only "a poor god" because poetic activity depends on stimulation from an external world and on the mediational function of a language that must be learned.[26] For all that, however, poetry and art express the subjectivity of the author, somewhat as the created world expresses the subjectivity of God.

Before the age of romanticism, Maritain remarked, poets and artists were not interested in reflective self-awareness. The advent of reflexivity could be a gain, but it has unfortunately been accompanied in many cases by an impoverishing shift to the self-centered ego. At its best, Maritain believed, poetic creativity transcends the private concerns of the individual. True creativity engages the deepest recesses of the self but draws them into the service of the transcendent. Thus there is an analogy between the "I" of the poet and that of the saint.[27]

So far as I am aware, Maritain did not apply his reflections on creativity to the theology of tradition. Combining what he says about the gifts of the Holy Spirit with Möhler's mystical ecclesiology, one might say that the person of faith, especially the saint, grasps the profound meaning of past expressions of the faith by dwelling in a community of faith and acquiring a certain connaturality with the things of God. The religious person's awareness of the spiritual realities attested by the tradition is in the first instance prereflexive and suprarational. Tradition therefore expresses itself primarily by life and action and only secondarily by explicit statements. Authentic expressions of the life of faith communicate not simply the insights of individual believers but the faith of the community. The expressions can be creative because the revelation borne by the tradition is transcendent; it is open to an infinite variety of possible linguistic and cultural embodiments.

III. Tradition and Creativity

As I have indicated in my discussion of literary criticism, antitradition-alism has developed a vigorous tradition of its own. Ralph Waldo Emerson is one of the many who railed against tradition as a hindrance to creativity. In his essay on "Nature" (1836), he wrote: "Our age is retrospective. It builds the sepulchres of the fathers. It writes biographies, histories, and criticism. The foregoing generations beheld God and nature face to face; we through their eyes. Why should we not have a poetry and philosophy of insight and not of tradition, and a religion by revelation to us, and not a history of theirs?"[28] The following year, in his famous Phi Beta Kappa address of 1837, Emerson complained that American institutions were overly concerned with the heritage of the past and were failing to arouse the spontaneous powers of students.[29] In his address to the Senior Class in Divinity at Harvard (July 15, 1838) he applied these principles more directly to theology, objecting to the tenets that the Bible was a closed revelation and that inspiration is a thing of the past.[30]

Emerson's complaints contained a grain of truth. Learning about the past should not be a substitute for dealing with the present. But what Emerson assails under the name of tradition is very different from what Péguy, for example, seeks to defend. To clarify the difference one might distinguish, as does Jaroslav Pelikan, between tradition as "the living faith of the dead" and traditionalism, "the dead faith of the living."[31] Traditionalism, he asserts, is what gives tradition its bad name.

Some years earlier T. S. Eliot made a similar observation. In his celebrated essay on "Tradition and the Individual Talent" (1919) he wrote:

> If the only form of tradition, of handing down, consisted in following the ways of the immediate generation before us in a blind or timid adherence to its successes, "tradition" should positively be discouraged. We have seen many such simple currents soon lost in the sand; and novelty is better than repetition. Tradition is a matter of much wider significance. It cannot be inherited, and if you want it you must obtain it by great labour.[32]

Eliot then went on to explain that a writer cannot be traditional without a vivid sense "not only of the pastness of the past, but of its presence." This historical sense, involving a synthetic perception of past and present in relation to each other, "makes a writer most acutely conscious of his own place in time, of his own contemporaneity."[33]

Among theologically alert authors there is a growing consensus that to let the past live, one must grasp its spirit and adapt its forms. Fidelity requires discernment. Building on some texts of Péguy, Congar points out that there are two levels of fidelity. On a superficial level, fidelity may be understood as adherence to the approved forms. But on a deeper level, the faithful adherent is one who penetrates to the meaning, the principle, the intention.[34] Only the latter type of fidelity is open to progress and development.[35] Following in the footsteps of John Henry Newman, Congar asserts that the dynamic idea at the basis of Christianity transcends all the forms in which it can be objectified. Reflection on the idea gives rise to continually new insights and propositions, none of which exhausts what was implicitly known from the beginning. In Newman's perspective, therefore, development is an inner dimension of tradition itself.[36]

Many Christians, as Congar points out, fail to perceive that fidelity to the past calls for creative appropriation. All too often they live their faith on the level of received ideas and customs, which they confuse with tradition.[37] Gabriel Marcel, making essentially the same point, remarked that orthodoxy is commonly confused with mere religious conformism, whereas true orthodoxy "creates those conditions rooted in the supernatural which unfold the most spacious and unbounded horizons for human knowledge and action."[38]

From all of this it follows that to represent the tradition authentically one must be acutely sensitive to the current situation and to present problems. Like the artist and the poet, the theologian must seek to extend the tradition and thereby contribute to it. Mere imitation is never enough. The contemporary work, as Eliot pointed out, takes its place in the succession that comes down from the past.[39] The past is modified by the introduction of each new member in the series and is reinterpreted in relation to what has emerged from it. The extension, I would add, may be creative if the new work actualizes some previously unforeseen possibility.

Those who extend the tradition depend on previous tradition as the matrix of their work. Classical texts are those that retain through the centuries their power to awaken new insights. They give rise to a series of subsequent works that attest to their disclosive power.[40] Especially is this true of canonical texts, which have normative value for an abiding community. Each generation is challenged to interpret and apply the text in ways that are faithful to the original intention and at the same time responsive to the needs and possibilities of the moment. Past interpretations that have been judged successful provide examples and models for the present.

For Christians the Bible is the canonical text par excellence. As an inspired record of a definitive revelation, it generates a long history of interpretation, some instances of which come to be recognized as permanently valid. Confident that Christ abides with the Church in all ages, thoughtful Christians reread the Bible in the light of what it has meant to the believing community down through the centuries.

Confidence in the tradition never excuses the contemporary thinker or writer from going back to the sources. Since subsequent commentary cannot take the place of the foundational records of the faith, the tradition must be continually renewed by reference to its sources. The *nouvelle théologie* of the 1940s was powerful because it went back to earlier and more authentic sources, which had not been sufficiently studied in their own right: the Scriptures, the church fathers, and the medieval *doctores*. The program of *aggiornamento*, articulated by Pope John XXIII at Vatican II, was a direct consequence of the *ressourcement* of the 1940s. The council laid down the principle: "Every ecclesial renewal essentially consists in an increase of fidelity to the Church's own calling."[41] Congar had said almost the same thing more than a decade earlier: "The great law of Catholic reformism will be to begin by a return to the principles of Catholicism."[42]

Even in the secular sphere, tradition has liberative power. It expands our horizons and thereby prevents us from becoming imprisoned in our own personal limitations and in the transitory fashions of our day. It provides us with a platform from which we can look critically at the present and judge it differently than it judges itself. In Christian theology tradition liberates insofar as it binds its adherents to the vital sources of their life— the revealed truth that makes us free (cf. John 8:32). The truth of the Gospel is ever fruitful in new insights. The theologian cannot fail to be stimulated and inspired by gaining familiarity with ideas resulting from what Newman calls "intuitive spiritual perception in scripturally informed and deeply religious minds."[43]

The study of ancient texts and models, even those contained in Holy Scripture, does not automatically yield creative insights. In order to be attuned to the lasting significance of the classics one must have acquired a certain skill or facility in interpretation. As Michael Polanyi explains, this is an art that cannot be learned by prescription. The novice must assimilate a multitude of particulars that cannot be specified in detail. They are normally passed down by example and supervised performance under the guidance of masters.

> By watching the master and emulating his efforts in the presence of his example, the apprentice picks up the rules of the art, including those which

are not explicitly known by the master himself. These hidden rules can be assimilated only by a person who surrenders himself to that extent uncritically to the imitation of another. A society which wants to preserve a fund of personal knowledge must submit to tradition.[44]

By assiduous discipleship one can gain a personal mastery of the art and be liberated from mechanical submission to formal and explicit rules. This aptitude, as Polanyi explains, is especially crucial for making original advances. The more deeply the discoverer is rooted in the tradition, the more resources will he or she be able to bring to unsolved problems. Lively appreciation of the great achievements of the past fires the mind with confidence and zeal and provides hints for the solution of new problems. By drawing analogies from earlier discoveries the creative imagination becomes better qualified to discern intelligible patterns in puzzling or confusing data.

Paradoxically, therefore, the most innovative artists and scientists have often been the most deeply traditional. Each renaissance has been, at root, a *ressourcement*. Literary revolutionaries such as T. S. Eliot were deeply immersed in the classical sources. James Joyce's *Ulysses* must be understood against the background of a long tradition stretching back to Homer. So, likewise, the theologians who have made the greatest contributions by their personal genius have taken pains to labor within the tradition. What would Luther have been without Augustine, Newman without Athanasius, or de Lubac without Origen? One may apply to the theologian what Eliot says of the poet: "We shall often find that not only the best, but the most individual parts of his work may be those in which the dead poets, his ancestors, assert their immortality most vigorously."[45]

A privileged locus of tradition in the life of the Church is the liturgy. Polanyi speaks in this connection of a dialectic of "dwelling in" and "breaking out." The worshiper's tacit powers are trained and activated by participation in the traditional rites. Discovery takes place in a moment of ecstasy produced by dwelling in spirit

> within the fabric of the religious ritual, which is potentially the highest degree of indwelling that is conceivable. For ritual comprises a sequence of things to be said and gestures to be made which involve the whole body and alert our whole existence. Anyone sincerely saying and doing these things in a place of worship could not fail to be completely absorbed by them.[46]

At a later point in his *Personal Knowledge* Polanyi expands on the heuristic character of religious worship:

The words of prayer and confession, the actions of the ritual, the lesson, the sermon, the church itself, are the clues of the worshipper's striving towards God. They guide his feelings of contrition and gratitude and his craving for the divine presence, while keeping him safe from distracting thoughts.[47]

These assertions receive ample confirmation from theology. When the inspired Scriptures are effectively proclaimed and when the community, invoking the Holy Spirit, responds in adoration, the very reality of the *tradendum* makes itself present. By means of the proclaimed word and the sacramental action, the living Christ draws near with his creative power, transforming the mind, heart, and imagination of the worshipers.

In fields such as art, music, and literature, it has been persuasively argued that creativity depends on "a fundamental encounter with transcendence."[48] "In most cultures," says George Steiner, "in the witness borne to poetry and art until the most recent modernity, the source of 'otherness' has been actualized or metaphorized as transcendent. It has been invoked as divine, as magical, or daimonic."[49] In many great works of art, such a referral to the transcendent is explicit.[50] Whatever may be true in other fields, this relation to transcendence is essential in theology. The Christian tradition, stemming as it does from the presence of the God-man within history, perpetuates both the memory and the presence of its founder. Transmitting the ancient heritage in ever new frameworks, the Church continually reactualizes the mystery that is at the heart of its being.

In a certain sense tradition may be regarded as the Christian mystery transmitting itself. It is, in the words of Henri de Lubac, "the very Word of God both perpetuating and renewing itself under the action of the Spirit of God, . . . the living Word entrusted to the Church and to those to whom the Church never ceases to give birth."[51] For this reason, says de Lubac, "Tradition, according to the Fathers of the Church, is in fact just the opposite of a burden of the past: it is a vital energy, a propulsive as much as a protective force."[52]

The Christian mystery transcends past, present, and future; it rejuvenates those who come into contact with it. Pascal put this well in one of his letters to Mademoiselle de Roannez (November 5, 1656):

The truths of Christianity are certainly new things, but they must be renewed continually; for this newness, which cannot be displeasing to God, any more than the old man can please him, is different from earthly newness, in that the things of the world, however new they may be, grow old as they endure; whereas the new spirit continues to renew itself increasingly as it endures.

"The old man perishes," says St. Paul, "and is renewed from day to day," and will only be perfectly new in eternity where the New Canticle, of which David speaks in the Psalm of Lauds, will be forever sung, that is to say, the song that springs from the new spirit of charity.[53]

The novelty in Christianity points beyond all time to the eschatological future. The glorification that has been accomplished in Jesus is still to be accomplished in the Church and the cosmos. Cherishing the memory of its risen Lord, the Church is drawn forward toward its final destiny, which it anticipates in hope. The very process of transmission is affected by the character of that which is transmitted—the Christ who has gone before us into the glory to which we aspire. Jürgen Moltmann shows how this eschatological dimension gives a creative quality to the Christian concept of tradition:

> Christian tradition is then not to be understood as a handing on of something that has to be preserved, but as an event which summons the dead and the godless to life. This is a creative event happening to what is vain, forsaken, lost, godless and dead. It can therefore be designated as a *nova creatio ex nihilo*, whose continuity lies solely in the guaranteed faithfulness of God.[54]

The same conclusion may be reinforced from another point of view. In the perspectives of theology, the primary bearer of tradition is not the individual or even the Church, but the Holy Spirit, who guides the Church into all truth (John 16:12-13). As Möhler pointed out, the Holy Spirit dwells in the hearts of the faithful, giving them a kind of instinct for, and inner affinity with, the truth of revelation. This Holy Spirit is the *Spiritus creator*, the Spirit who makes all things new. What comes from the Spirit is never a stale reproduction of the past.

The interaction between past and present in Christian tradition, though it has certain analogies in other fields, is unique and unparalleled. The apostolic tradition, which remains accessible through the inspired texts of Scripture and through sacramental worship, transmits the living reality of the past and activates the spiritual powers of those who receive it. Rooted in the sources of faith, they can exercise creative fidelity. For the past to be living, it must in some mysterious way transcend the divisions of time; it must become contemporaneous with the present and point the way into the future. Because Christ the Lord is "the same yesterday, today, and tomorrow," Christian tradition can rise to this challenge, ceaselessly bringing forth "new things and old."

Notes

[1]Gregory of Nyssa, *Contra Eunomium,* ch. 4 (PG 45:653); quoted by Yves Congar, *Tradition and Traditions* (New York: Macmillan, 1966) 43.

[2]Basil, *De Spiritu sancto,* 27:66 (PG 32.188A); quoted by Congar, *Tradition and Traditions,* 47.

[3]J. A. Möhler, *Die Einheit in der Kirche,* ed. J. R. Geiselmann (Cologne: Hegner, 1957) §16, 50–51.

[4]Ibid., §3, 11; see additional quotations from *Die Einheit in der Kirche* in Congar, *Tradition and Traditions,* 193–94; also Jan Walgrave, *Unfolding Revelation* (Philadelphia: Westminster, 1972) 286.

[5]Maurice Blondel, "History and Dogma," *Letter on Apologetics and History and Dogma* (New York: Holt, Rinehart and Winston, 1964) 221–87, at 268.

[6]Yves Congar, *The Meaning of Tradition* (New York: Hawthorn Books, 1964) 45.

[7]Ibid., 114.

[8]Ibid.

[9]*Dei Verbum* 8.

[10]Ibid.

[11]The exception is in *Dei Verbum* 8, which quotes 1 Thessalonians 2:15. In other documents, however, Vatican II spoke of traditions in the plural; e.g., *Unitatis redintegratio,* 15 and 17, where the spiritual, liturgical, and doctrinal traditions of the Eastern Churches are praised.

[12]Ibid., 10.

[13]Thomas Aquinas, *Summa theologiae,* 1.45.5.

[14]Ibid., 1.118.2. In 1887 Antonio Rosmini-Serbati was censured by the Holy Office for his opinion that the human soul was capable of being generated by the parents (DS 3220).

[15]John Donne, *Eighty Sermons* (1640), 266; quoted by Logan Pearsall Smith, *Words and Idioms: Studies in the English Language,* 4th ed. (London: Constable, 1933) 92.

[16]Smith, *Words and Idioms,* 90.

[17]Edward Shils, *Tradition* (Chicago: University of Chicago, 1981) 153.

[18]Irving Babbitt, *On Being Creative and Other Essays* (Boston: Houghton Mifflin, 1932) 1–33, esp. 3.

[19]Henri Bergson, *The Two Sources of Morality and Religion* (Garden City, N.Y.: Doubleday Anchor, n.d.) 255.

[20]Charles Péguy, *Notre Jeunesse* in *Oeuvres en prose de Charles Péguy 1904–1914* (Tours: Gallimard, 1968) 596; cf. Yves Congar, *Vraie et fausse Réforme dans l'Église,* 2nd ed. (Paris: Cerf, 1968) 239.

[21]Péguy, *L'Argent (suite)* in his *Oeuvres en prose,* 1303; cf. Congar, *Vraie et fausse Réforme,* 46.

[22]Péguy, "Avertissement," *Cahiers de la Quinzaine* 5:11 (March 1, 1904); in his *Oeuvres complètes,* 12:186-92; quoted in Congar, *Vraie et fausse Réforme,* 543–44.

[23]Jacques Maritain, *Creative Intuition in Art and Poetry* (New York: Pantheon, 1953).

[24]Ibid., 94.

[25]Ibid., 112.

[26]Ibid., 113.

[27]Ibid., 143.

[28]From *Nature; Addresses, and Lectures,* reprinted in *Ralph Waldo Emerson,* ed. Richard Poirier (New York: Oxford, 1990) 1–110, quotation from 3.

[29]Ibid., 40–41.

[30]Ibid., 64.

[31]Jaroslav Pelikan, *The Vindication of Tradition* (New Haven: Yale University Press, 1984) 65–66.

[32]T. S. Eliot, *Selected Essays* (New York: Harcourt, Brace, 1950) 4.

[33]Ibid.

[34]Congar, *Vraie et fausse Réforme,* 166–67.

[35]Ibid., 542.

[36]Congar, *Tradition and Traditions,* 211. He here refers to Newman's *Essay on the Development of Christian Doctrine* and several other works of Newman.

[37]Congar, *Vraise et fausse Réforme,* 164.

[38]Gabriel Marcel, *Creative Fidelity* (New York: Farrar, Straus and Giroux, 1964) 190.

[39]T. S. Eliot, "Tradition and the Individual Talent," 5.

[40]On the power of classical texts to give rise to a history of interpretation see Hans-Georg Gadamer, *Truth and Method* (New York: Seabury/Continuum, 1975) 253–58. David Tracy in his *The Analogical Imagination* (New York: Crossroad, 1981) has popularized the idea of the disclosive power of the classic (e.g., 14, 108, 169).

[41]*Unitatis redintegratio,* 6.

[42]Congar, *Vraie et fausse Réforme,* 303

[43]Newman, *The Arians of the Fourth Century,* 3rd ed. (London, 1871) 179.

[44]Michael Polanyi, *Personal Knowledge* (Chicago: University of Chicago Press, 1964) 53.

[45]Eliot, "Tradition and the Individual Talent," 4.

[46]Polanyi, *Personal Knowledge,* 198.

[47]Ibid., 281.

[48]George Steiner, *Real Presences* (Chicago: University of Chicago, 1989) 228.

[49]Ibid., 211.

[50]Ibid., 216.

[51]Henri de Lubac, *The Motherhood of the Church* (San Francisco: Ignatius, 1982) 91.

[52]Ibid.

[53]Blaise Pascal, *Oeuvres complètes* (Paris: Ollendorff, 1931) 3:451.

[54]Jürgen Moltmann, *Theology of Hope* (London: SCM, 1967) 302.

19

Tradition, Reception

J.-M. R. Tillard, O.P.

In this short study we cannot deal at length with the crucial but difficult theme of the nature of Christian Tradition. We shall only try to give, briefly, a list of affirmations which are the conclusion of a quite long reflection on this issue. They concern the relation between Tradition and *reception*.

The importance of *reception* in the concrete life of the Church has been rediscovered through a study of the conciliar process done by *Faith and Order*[1] at the request of the New Delhi Assembly of the World Council of Churches (1961). This research was pursued in the wake of Vatican II. But further investigations concerning the role of *reception* have normally been limited to the ecumenical context. In this study we shall use this notion in a broader context and show how it belongs to the inner reality of living Tradition.

By Tradition we mean, here, the living Tradition of the Church, that is the constant dynamism by which the work of Christ is actualized and concretely lived out from generation to generation, in every place and human situation. We thus use the word to signify the whole life of the Church, that is the permanent fruit of the work of the Spirit who, according to the johannine Gospel, *"receives* from" Christ (*ek thou emou lepsetai,* John 16:14) and guides the disciples "into all the truth" (*eis pasan tèn aletheian,* 16:13).

I. *Ephapax and Tradition*

A.

Any reflection that seeks to grasp what is specific in Christian Tradition must first consider seriously the place and meaning of the cross and resurrection of Christ at the heart of the Church's experience. They constitute the event on which, radically, everything depends. Without them, faith itself vanishes. Such a supremacy is theologically made clear at different levels, some of which are essential for a right understanding of Tradition. They show that Tradition is a *paradosis* of life.

1. The most striking feature of the New Testament is certainly the strong conviction that the exaltation of Christ, at the right hand of God, coincides with the dawn of the expected eschatological times. This is the way Luke, explicitly in the first speech of Peter, interprets the apocalyptic signs of the Pentecost in Jerusalem (Acts 2:17). The same view appears, with some nuances we cannot explain here, in the designation of Christ as the *eschatos* (Rev 1:17; 2:8; 22:13), in the presentation of the time of Christ as the *pleróma tou chronou* (Gal 4:4), in the description of the time of the Church as the *eschatè óra* (1 John 2:18; cf. 1 Pet 1:20) or the end of the ages (*ta telè tôn aiônôn*, 1 Cor 10:11), in the affirmation that in these days "which are the last ones" (*ep' eschatou tôn emerôn toutôn*, Heb 1:2; cf. 9:26) those who believe already taste "the heavenly gift, . . . the works of power of the coming age" (Heb 6:5), in the assurance that Christians are raised with Christ who is sitting at the right hand of God and consequently that already their life "has been hidden with Christ in God" (Col 3:1-3).

This relation to the *eschata* determines Christian identity. According to pauline theology, the whole of Christian life is already deeply rooted in the eschatological realities. Its leaven is eschatological since it is the possession of the earnest (*arrabóna*) of the Spirit: "We have a building from God, a house not made with hands, eternal in Heaven. . . . He who worked for us this same thing is God, who has given us the earnest of the Spirit" (2 Cor 5:1-5; cf. 1:22; Rom 8:23; Eph 1:14).

In his authentic letters, Paul explains that because of the gift of the Spirit, all Christians are already the temple of God in which the glory of God is now abiding (1 Cor 3:17; 6:19; 2 Cor 6:16). The author of the letter to the Ephesians is more precise: Jews and Gentiles together are "built on the foundations of the apostles and prophets . . . a Holy Temple in the Lord . . . a dwelling-place of God in the Spirit" (Eph 2:19-22); and this is the consequence of the possession of the *arrabón*, of the inheritance (1:13-14). In a very different context, the first epistle of Peter uses expressions like "spiritual house" (*oikos pneumatikos*), "priestly house of the King" (*basileion hierateuma*), "holy priestly community" (*hierateuma hagion*) (1 Pet 2:4-10) to describe the Christian community.

These affirmations show how, in spite of their different theologies, the diverse traditions of the New Testament share the insight that even the relation with God has been changed by the possession of the Holy Spirit. It has an eschatological character.

The johannine Gospel (John 2:13-22; 4:21-24; 7:39) is certainly more radical. The temple itself is no longer to be considered as a reality submitted to the conditions of human history. For the liturgy is now celebrated in an eschatological temple—the body of the Risen Lord (2:21). This is the definitive liturgy, the liturgy of those who worship "in spirit and in truth" (4:21-24). It is also the liturgy of the kingdom of God (18:36-39; 19:14-15, 19-22). In his account of the Last Supper, Luke, who stresses the link between the departure of Christ and the kingdom (22:16, 18, 30; cf. 23:42-43), explicitly links the Twelve to this eschatological kingdom: "I confer a Kingdom on you as my Father conferred one on me: that you may eat and drink at my table in my Kingdom; and you will sit on thrones to judge the twelve tribes of Israel" (22:29-30).

Put together, all these features coming from diverse ecclesiological backgrounds and theological insights are coherent with the description of the heavenly liturgy given in the Book of Revelation. The whole messianic people of God takes part in this liturgy (Rev 7:9-17; 14:1-5; 15:2-4; 17:14; 19:1-9; 20:4-6), in the eschatological Jerusalem whose twelve foundations are called by the names of the twelve Apostles (21:14), and in which there is no temple (21:22). It is impossible to avoid the impression that what happens *here and now* on earth, in the churches dispersed all over the world, is, like faith itself (1 Cor 13:12), the "projection in a mirror" of what has its full evidence only in heaven. But it is this eschatological reality which, nevertheless, is already at work, through the power of the Spirit, in the life of the local churches.

2. The consequences of the eschatological character of the Church are crucial for the nature of living Tradition. Since the city of the Christians "is in heaven" (Phil 3:20) and because Christians are "fellow-citizens of the saints and of the household of God" (Eph 2:19), no one on earth is Christian by birth. The johannine Gospel speaks of the necessity of a rebirth, a birth from above, a birth out of water and Spirit. It affirms that "if one does not receive (this) birth from above, one is not able to see the Kingdom of God" (John 3:1-7). Natural or historical genealogies and ancestries have no specific place in Christianity. They do not matter.

In a very different theological context, Paul—who affirms that Christ is "declared Son of God in power, according to the Spirit of holiness by the resurrection from the dead" (Rom 1:4)—sees this Christian identity as a participation in divine filiation. He writes: "You received a Spirit of adoption by which we cry Abba, Father! The Spirit itself witnesses with our spirit that we are children of God. And if children, also heirs, truly heirs of God, coheirs with Christ; if indeed we suffer together that we may also be glorified with Him" (Rom 8:15-17; cf. Gal 4:7).

This explains why the Church of God is a communion of local churches established in every human race and nation, and why each of these local churches is made of people of every human stock, color, social rank, and gender. To become a Christian, one needs to be *received* into the communion of all those who share this divine origin. It concretely means to be *received* into the communion of the Church and to *receive* there, together with faith, the eschatological gifts of God. Christian identity is acquired only through this *reception*, never by human birth.

Living Tradition may be defined as the process leading to this *reception*, from place to place and age to age, in the power of the Spirit of God. For this reason, its most fundamental feature is *"iam ab Abel iusto,"* as Augustine is bold to say, the *paradosis* of all the elements which make real the presence of the *eschata*, while human history continues according to its own laws. These elements are all unified in the reality of what the letters to the Ephesians and to the Colossians call the *mystery* (*mysterion*, Eph 1:9-10; 3:3-10; Col 1:26-27; see also Rom 16:25-26; 1 Cor 2:7-9), a word from Jewish apocalyptic literature. They are especially the Word of God and sacramental grace, the Word being actualized in the sacraments and the sacraments being formal acts of *reception* through the Spirit. It is interesting to remember that a very important theological school—of which Aquinas is the most brilliant representative[2]—maintains that already in the Old Testament Word and Sacraments were the means by which the living Tradition of the people of God prepared the way for the eschatological gift of salvation in Christ Jesus and for its *reception* by the whole humanity.

In baptism, those who *receive* the invitation of God, with the authentic will to let it transform their lives, are *received* into the Church, the eschatological community of the living God. At the Eucharist they enter into communion with the salvific event and *receive* in the Body and Blood of the Risen Lord the source of the eschatological life. This is the goal of the Word they *received*.

But the Word thus *received* is not the cold and abstract record of what has been done or said by Christ Jesus. It is a Word which through *reception* already became part of the "memory" of the Church; and according to the johannine Gospel (John 14:26) the Holy Spirit himself is the agent of this memory. Similarly, the celebration of the Eucharist is the "memorial" of the salvific event, celebrated in communion with the whole Church of God, that is the eschatological community of the Risen Lord. Thus, the Tradition does not transmit the gift of God by a mere reprinting or repetition of sacred documents and a mechanical distribution of the means of grace. It does it by *receiving* into the communion of the Church those who (through the Holy Spirit) *receive*—that is accept sincerely—the call of God. Thus, the Tradition transmits by giving a share in the experience of the "community of the Lord," through *reception*.

In this process, the Holy Spirit is, indeed, the *didaskalos,* the teacher (cf. John 14:26). But he is a *didaskalos* who teaches through what he does. The Spirit actualizes in the life of the community and engraves into the "memory" of the whole Church a kind of connaturality with the "heavenly realities" which cannot be described and transmitted merely through words and discourses. It is a kind of inner certitude, a spiritual insight or feeling. Its content is deeper than a clear intellectual idea, and sometimes it can only be properly expressed through the use of art and rites.

Usually, the Word of God that the Tradition transmits through the communion in the life of the community is perceived in its fullness thanks precisely to the commitment of the members and especially the common worship. They reveal more of its meaning than the "letter" itself. For "the letter" alone cannot express what may be described as the result of the exegetical power of the "life in the Spirit." It is now a common view that the documents of the New Testament are themselves the fruit of this exegesis by the "life in the Spirit." What they record and transmit is the way the deeds and words of Christ and of the apostolic community were *received* by the local churches.

Such a living Tradition is really the only authentic vehicle of the Word of God, understood and transmitted in the light of the same Spirit that inspired it. The burning issue of the relation between Scripture and Tradition has to be studied in this context: Scriptures are transmitted because what they contain has been *received* and, thus, already tested "in the Spirit." But, more profoundly, since it is the true expression of the life of the eschatological community, the living Tradition is the only way through which "the realities which are not from this world," the seed "of the life which comes from elsewhere," the "generation of those who are born not of blood nor of the will of the flesh," may continue to be kept as a living and actual offer. In this sense, without Tradition there is no Church.

B.

Since cross and resurrection open up the eschatological experience of the "last days," which coincides with the gift of the *arrabóna* of "the life in the Kingdom," they dominate the whole of human history. This history is made up of the sequence of human events. Those events follow each other according to the progress of *chronos,* the word designating the irreversible succession of moments from the past to the future. They correspond to the dynamism that leads cosmic and human destiny from birth to death. Their story is the flow of human generations.

1. Compared with the *chronoi*—that is with the events succeeding each other in the *chronos*—the death and resurrection of Christ are a *kairos;* moreover, they are *the kairos.* A *kairos* is a moment which transcends the succession of the *chronoi* and of everything happening in cosmic and human affairs. Its source is not the result of casual causes, for it is a decisive moment entirely in the power of God. It "recapitulates" the mighty acts God accomplished in the past through the *chronoi,* and it already includes what God will do in the future of humanity—hence its final identification with the event of Christ, culminating in the cross and resurrection, the source of the *eschata* (Matt 26:18; Luke 19:44; Rom 5:6; Col 4:5; Eph 5:16). The author of the first epistle of Peter uses the expression *kairos eschatos* (1 Pet 1:5; cf. 5:6) to designate the great consummation of God's design at the ultimate hour of the whole human history, corresponding to what other documents call Christ's Parousia.[3] But this consummation belongs to the event of Christ and is not added to it. It is its epiphany (1 Tim 6:15) in the universal triumph of God.

Moreover, in the light of this supremacy of the event of Christ Jesus one may understand why the apostolic faith proclaims that salvation has been accomplished *once-for-all* (*ephapax,* cf. Rom 6:10; Heb 7:27; 9:12; 10:10; or *hapax,* Heb 9:26, 28; 1 Pet 3:18; cf. Heb 9:7; 10:2; 12:26-27; Jude 3:5). Cross and resurrection form a single event, complete and sufficient. It does not need to be repeated. It is *the* final act, altogether definitive, decisive and conclusive of God's plan of grace. For apostolic faith, this event is utterly unique. It is the essential content of "the faith *once-for-all* delivered to the saints" (Jude 3).

2. Because it is the *paradosis* of the grace of this supreme and decisive *kairos,* realized *once-for-all,* the living Tradition cannot be confused with the history of Christianity. Its link with the succession of Christian generations has to be qualified. It depends on the way the *kairos* itself embraces and undergirds the sequence of the *chronoi.*

The place of history cannot be denied or diminished. It belongs to the concrete human condition, and this is the material in which salvation has to be realized. It is clear that since God decided to reveal through history the eternal plan of salvation and to choose the specific history of one people to be the instrument of such a revelation, nothing concerning the *kairos* of this salvation can be isolated from the history it dominates and governs. Moreover, in spite of its preeminent position over all the *chronoi*, the *kairos* of the cross-resurrection is accomplished *in* history. The New Testament insists on the historical character not only of the crucifixion but also of the death and even of the ascension. At the heart of Christian Tradition is the testimony of those who were the witnesses of "the things that have happened in Jerusalem in these days" (Luke 24:18). The insistence of the apostolic records on the meals with the Risen Lord, during which he appears visibly, is also to be understood as a will to inscribe the resurrection itself into the reality of human history. Christian Tradition is indeed a kind of epiphany of this insertion of the *kairos,* accomplished *once-for-all,* into the flow of history.

Because of this insertion, the essential character of *paradosis* cannot be identified simply with the way one generation (in its own *chronos*) transmits to the next generation (in its own *chronos*) what the preceding generations (in their own *chronoi*) have transmitted ever since the apostolic generation (in its own *chronos*). In other words, the essential character of Tradition must not be looked for only in the horizontal succession and addition of Christian generations. It has to be sought in the way the *kairos* (*once-for-all* achieved) is *received,* producing its fruits in each Christian generation and in all the places where the Church's mandate to preach the gospel to all nations "unto the end of the world" is carried out.

Tradition (*paradosis*) implies more than succession. Transmission from one generation to another generation—especially through teaching, baptism, and ordination of ministers—has to be done in such a way that it remains within the absolute authority of what has been *once-for-all* "delivered to the saints" (Jude 3). The point of reference is not the sum of what the preceding generations did or said. It is their relation to the *kairos*. This relation is the thread of the *paradosis*.

This point is very important, especially in an ecumenical context. The Tradition cannot be confused with the museum of everything concerning faith. Obviously, the next generation need not necessarily *receive* everything that comes from the preceding generations. What it has to *receive* is essentially the integrity of the *eschata*. This does not exclude indeed what has been an authentic growth in the understanding and living out of revealed truth. But what a generation hands on to subsequent generations is basically the living presence of the *eschata* in a true *koinônia* where the Spirit is at work— essentially in the preaching, contemplation and study of the Word, the Sacraments, the experience of *Agapè*. It is this more than it is a full record of its acts and deeds, an exhaustive list of its doctrinal advances, a catalogue of its cherished devotions. Many of these will have been the fruit of its efforts to cope with its own historical context and its cultural environment and will not be appropriate to the new situations. They would be more of a hindrance or at least an encumbrance than a gift for the next generations in their effort to actualize the Christian faith in their own context.

3. Here again we are facing the problem of *reception*. We said that the main stream, the thread, of the *paradosis* is the encompassing of the sequence of the *chronoi* within the *kairos*. But we also affirmed that, even if many of the peculiar achievements of one generation have not to be *received* by the next one, nevertheless what is an authentic growth in the communion to the *eschata* and in the understanding of God's revelation has to be *received* by the subsequent *chronoi*. Such a *reception* will not be an addition, improving on a sum of existing tenets. This would be contrary to the fullness of the *once-for-all*. It will be the actualization of what the johannine Gospel says concerning the work of the Spirit in the community of the disciples: "the Holy Spirit will guide you into all truth" (*eis pasan tèn aletheian*) (John 16:13). The guidance is realized from within, through the experience of the *eschata*. It is a guidance formally connected to the whole of *koinônia*.

4. But how can a local church *recognize* what it has to *receive*—that is to make its own—from the former generations, and what it has to consider only as the contingent asset of this or that *chronos* and thus as a good it has not necessarily to *receive?* To this question—which is essential for a clear understanding of the living Tradition—the so-called "patristic churches" have a clear answer. They consider this *recognition* to be the fruit of a mutual *reception*: the *reception* of the insights or perceptions of the *sensus fidelium* by the bishops (especially when they act collectively in their capacity of servants of the *koinônia*) and the *reception* of the discernment of the bishops by the whole community.

Through the abiding of the Spirit and the experience of the *eschata* which the Spirit provides, Christians who are faithful to their commitment to Christ possess what the first johannine letter calls "the anointing" (*chrisma*). This teaches them concerning the realities of the kingdom, and they have no need for anyone to teach them at this deepest level of their communion with God (1 John 2:27). The more they are grounded in the *eschata*, through their faithfulness to the requirements of the Church's *koinónia*, the more they will instinctively *recognize* what of the realities coming from the past generation has to be perpetually kept and what has to be changed in order to permit the local church to find new ways appropriate to its own situation. They possess a flair, a kind of spiritual sixth sense, an ecclesiastical instinct, a *sensus fidei*, which is a consequence of their belonging to the body of Christ (Rom 8:9).

But in the body of Christ there exists a ministry, empowered by the same Spirit to be in a very specific manner at the service of the faithfulness of the Church to its own being, grounded in the *eschata*. It is the ministry of *episkopè*, entrusted with the task of *watching over* the way the gift of God is *received* and passed on from one group to the other, one generation to the other. This is why this ministry is mainly the ministry of the "memory" of the Church. Its principal goal is to be the servant of the Spirit in keeping alive and radically unchanged the "memory" of what has been truly revealed and what really the *eschata* are.

Ministers do that, indeed, in communion with the whole Church. *Receiving* the insights, the desiderata of the *sensus fidelium,* the creative impulse of the whole people of God, those who exercise *episkopè* have the responsibility of judging them critically in the light of the whole Tradition. They must discriminate between what is in tune with the normative and permanent values of revelation and what is not consistent with them or needs to be more fully studied before being *recognized* as compatible with them. This *recognition* of the content of the Church's "memory" in the concrete words and deeds of Christian communities is much more than an echo of what has already been said by theologians or done by committed Christians, a kind of subsequent approbation. It is the fruit of a judgment—Aquinas would say a "prudential judgement"—enacted by those who are equipped with a specific gift of the Spirit. This gift is transmitted in the act of ministerial *paradosis* (ordination), right from the origins (cf. 2 Tim 1:6), to those chosen to exercise *episkopè*.

The living Tradition progresses through this interaction of the *sensus fidelium* (with its specific awareness of the *hic et nunc*) and of the "prudential" function of the ministers of *episkopè* (with their specific mission concerning the Church's "memory" of the *once-for-all*).

Vatican II was a perfect illustration of this process. Since Vatican I, the *sensus fidelium* was at the origin of many movements, all dealing with the faithfulness of the Church to the *eschata:* the biblical movement, the liturgical movement, the patristic movement, the missionary movement, the ecumenical movement. At Vatican II, the college of bishops *received* them. But this *reception* was not a mere approbation, based on a kind of democratic principle. It was the result of a long reflection, the norm of which was always the reference to the Church's "memory." Some of the views or desires emerging from within the movements which shaped the life of the Church during the preceding decades (constituting a peculiar *chronos*) were not *received*. Others were rearticulated and modified. It is the result of such a communion of the *sensus fidelium* and of the specific task of *episkopè* which is now officially offered to the local churches to be *received* by them as the form of their communion with the whole Tradition. They have to keep it and to transmit it (*paradosis*) to the next generations.

The Tradition has certainly been enriched by this *reception*. Nevertheless, such a growth is the fruit of a deepening, not of an addition. The *once-for-all* actualized in the *eschata* transcends all the *chronoi* and what is achieved throughout history. They are all encompassed by its power, seized, possessed by it. This is in harmony with the nature of the Church. For the common good of the Church is not the sum of the particular goods. The *sensus fidelium* is not the sum of the opinions of the faithful, the catholicity of the Church is not the sum of the local churches, the fullness of the Eucharist does not come from the sum of the consecrated breads and cups, the *koinônia* is not the sum of the baptized, like the Divinity is not the sum of the three Divine Persons. Everything that reaches out of the *eschata* into our world has a plenitude of an other kind than what in our human experience, marked by its historical and material condition, we call perfection. But this eschatological plenitude is precisely the gift of God, the earnest (*arrabôna*) of which we already enjoy.

II. Tradition and Catholicity

The Church of God is, indeed, a communion of local churches[4] and in each local church where the Eucharist is celebrated according to the apostolic Tradition the Church of God is really present (LG 26). There is no more Church in twenty local churches than in one of them. Nevertheless, because it coincides with the realization of the love of God for the whole of humanity in all ages and all nations, the Church of God has to be *fully* present *everywhere* humanity exists. Consequently, the living Tradition is concerned not only with the transmission of faith from generation to generation but also its transmission from place to place. In other words, Tradition is not only a chronological *paradosis;* it is also a local, cultural *paradosis.* Thus it stands at the heart of the catholicity of the Church. Here again we shall be confronted with the problem of *reception.*

A.

To be really Catholic, the Church has to be what a homily of the sixth century calls "the one Body which speaks all the tongues of the nations" (PL 65:743-744). We may add that, here, tongue means culture, racial stock, sociological context, historical background, national or regional usage, traditional custom, inherited skill. Since all these are a fructification of the gifts associated with creation, they pertain to the personal and collective fulfillment of human vocation. They are then included in salvation. The Church is the communion of all men and women, but concretely rooted in their human milieu, their city, their nation, their region, their cultural surroundings. The *catholica* is the communion of the local churches, that is of the church which is in Corinth, and of the church which is in Antioch, and of the church which is in Rome, in Tokyo, in Kinshasa, in Vancouver . . . . They are all in communion together, precisely because in each local church the *eschata* are utterly present, everywhere the same, and *katholon.* [5] Their power—which is the power of the reconciling God— encompasses diversity without destroying it. This shows the fundamental unity between creation and salvation, in the person of Christ: "all things were created in him . . . and he is the head of the Body, the Church . . . the first-born from the dead" (Col 1:16-18). The Lord of salvation is the Lord of creation: concrete creation indeed in its whole richness.

1. The *paradosis* of the Word of God from Jerusalem to the Gentiles, as recorded in the Acts of the Apostles, was the point of departure of a quite difficult process. It generated a profound crisis, which necessitated the convening of the leaders of the churches—those exercising *episkopè!*—at Jerusalem, around "the apostles and the elders" (Acts 15:2).

The problem at stake was indeed explicitly the transmission of the gospel (and of the sharing in the *eschata*) from its original Jewish form to new forms in harmony with different cultural settings and other sociological origins. The revelation of universal salvation had to be *received* by others than just the Jewish people, since Christ died "for all." But in order to be universally *received,* it had to be *recognized* as really delivered to humanity as such. This was so that the essential requirements of salvation might not depend upon the characteristics of one specific race or culture. They had to be integrally *received* in all the races, all the cultures, all the sociological contexts, even if salvation came through the commitment of "the race of Abraham," if the twelve foundations of the Church bear the names of the twelve Jewish apostles of the Lord and its doors the names of the twelve tribes of Israel (Rev 21:12-14) and if the Risen Lord is "of the seed of David according to the flesh" (Rom 1:3).

2. Christian Tradition started during the first apostolic generation with this process of handing on the integrity of revelation from the Jews to the Gentiles. This is what we call, to clearly distinguish it from the chronological *paradosis* (from generation to generation), the local, cultural *paradosis* (from one cultural area to another). We consider this cultural *paradosis* to be as important as the other. Moreover, we believe that here also there may be a growth (not an addition) in the understanding of what is passed on.

Theological reflection has been quite sober on this issue. One seems to have understood *paradosis* mainly as a historical passing on and to have underestimated the importance of the cultural, local extension of Christian truth from place to place. But the history of the Church shows how schisms originated more in a bad communication of faith to another culture and in a defective *reception* than in its deficient transmission from one generation to another. Usually, the reason why the wholeness of the *eschata* is no longer handed on to the next generations by a community has to be sought in the way faith has been transmitted and *received* in the particular socio-cultural context of this human group. Some elements of Christian doctrine and life are not adequately transmitted to the new *chronos* because they have not been adequately *received* by the generation which is fading away. The history of the first spread of Arianism is typical of this process.

3. In this local, cultural *paradosis,* through which a newly evangelized human setting *receives* fully the earnest of the *eschata,* it is indeed the body of Christ which is involved. The body of Christ also *receives.* Not only the *chronoi* but, together with them, the diverse cultural, native, or racial realities are taken up and encompassed by the power of the *eschata.* They thus become flesh of the eschatological body.

Through this *paradosis* the catholicity of the Church is actualized. For, the result of the process is that the realities of creation and the fruit of people's skill, the variety of situations ordinarily deeply dependent on racial context or on natural and social environment, become the features of a local church. This local church is really the Church of God, alive in this part of the universe and in this very peculiar cultural experience. It does not lack for anything required to be truly the Church of God. Moreover, this local church is in communion with all the other local churches in the world, for they are also really the Church of God in their own part of the universe and in their peculiar cultural experience. Since the Church of God is this communion of all the local churches, hence it follows that the whole concrete humanity is deeply and extensively embraced in the Church of God. In the Church, the power of the *eschata* really encompasses *omnia loca et tempora*. It is the power of the Holy Spirit, the power that makes the Risen Lord already now Lord of creation. Through cultural *paradosis* the living Tradition incarnating faith in the variety of cultures makes the catholicity of the Church of God concrete and actual.

B.

Dealing with the chronological *paradosis* we explained the relationship between the *chronoi* and the *once-for-all,* and we stressed the Christian certitude that the *kairos,* in its plenitude, transcends the sum of the *kairoï.* The same relationship has to be stressed between the plenitude (the *katholon*) of the eschatological Church and the multiplicity of the local churches founded through cultural, local *paradosis.*

1. When at Pentecost, in the apocalyptic manifestation of the Spirit which Luke describes, the Church of God was breaking into the world, it was already catholic. It was not catholic *in via,* expecting to become catholic by the addition of churches subsequently founded at Antioch, Corinth, Rome, Lyons, Canterbury, Kinshasa. It was "the catholic Church of God in Jerusalem entrusted with the mission to expand *its* catholicity to all the nations (*paradosis*)."

This catholicity of the Church of Jerusalem is grounded on two facts. First, the theophany of Pentecost, during the celebration of the feast centered around the promulgation of the Law and the convocation of the *Qahal Yahweh* on Mount Sinai (Exod 19:7-15), manifests that what happens at Jerusalem is the fulfillment (*teleiôsis*) of what God intended in "creating" the Holy Nation in the Desert. The Church of Jerusalem will be called "The Church of the Saints," for this reason.[6] But, secondly, this Church possesses the totality of the *eschata,* the *katholon* of the gifts of God for "the last times." When the church will be founded at Antioch, at Smyrna, at Ephesus, at Pergamos, there will be no growth of the *eschata,* no addition to the *katholon* (how would it be possible?). But there will be a growth in the sharing of the *eschata,* the possession of the *katholon,* the communion in it. This distinction is essential for a right understanding of the local, cultural *paradosis*.

2. The goal of the local, cultural *paradosis* will be, indeed, the expansion of the Church of God from the local church of Jerusalem to the whole universe. This *paradosis* will follow the ways opened up by the cultural consequences of the Roman occupation and reach the whole of the *oikoumenè*, especially its center, Rome.

The result of this process will be crucial. What was first *received* in a Galilean cultural context will be transmitted in Greek. Even the main Christian doctrines will be expressed in Greek, sometimes with the help of a Greek philosophical vocabulary (*homoousios, physis, ousia, hypostasis*). The center of Christianity will no longer be Jerusalem. Such a transition or a passage (local, cultural *paradosis*) will certainly be for the whole living Tradition as essential as the transmission to the next generations. It will, indeed, determine what will be transmitted in the future. As a matter of fact, it is concretely by reference to the result of this first cultural *paradosis*, expressed especially in the dogmatic definitions of the first "ecumenical" councils (the councils of the *oikoumenè*), that faithfulness to apostolic Tradition is actually measured.

Nevertheless, throughout local *paradosis* the intention is always to found or establish new local churches by providing everywhere the possibility of being inserted into the *katholon* of the Church of Jerusalem, that is of the Apostolic Church, given *once-for-all* by the Spirit. Their being has to be a share in its reality, an entry into its catholicity. This is why, in the power of the same Spirit, they enjoy and transmit one and the same gospel, one and the same baptism, one and the same Eucharist, one and the same *episkopè*, one and the same *koinónia*, one and the same hope, one and the same mission. Local, cultural *paradosis* is thus the process through which the huge variety of human contexts and cultures is brought to the inclusive and embracing reality of the *once-for-all*, disclosed at Pentecost in the Apostolic Church.

Newly founded churches, then, do not *receive* specific *eschata* made to their own measure. They actually *receive* what the Apostolic Church *received*. Moreover what they *receive* is not a copy modeled after the gift of the Spirit which made the Apostolic Church. It is this very gift. Because they *recognize* it in each other, they are one Church in the indivisible grace of Pentecost. Since through their variety the *katholon* of the Church of Pentecost is related to the whole diversity of human condition in the *oikoumenè*, their communion makes concrete the catholicity of God's design.

3. What we already explained of the way Tradition and *reception* are linked together is again clearly demonstrated in this process. *Reception* creates newness, since it brings about the realization of the Church of God in new cultures, new human settings. The shape of the church in Antioch, the form of its liturgy, the details of its canonical discipline are different from those of the church in Tokyo, precisely because they are *received* in a different human soil. Through *paradosis* "what has been *once-for-all* delivered to the saints" (Jude 3) becomes perennial, permanent. What it "plants and waters" in every place (cf. 1 Cor 3:6-7) is nothing else than what has been planted "at Jerusalem, in the beginning." If the soils are different, the seed is the very same, fully identical. It is not even a seed produced by the first plant for its multiplication. It is the first seed itself. For it is the same gospel *once-for-all* revealed, the same Eucharist gathering the faithful in the real Body and Blood *once-for-all* offered, the same mission *once-for-all* declared by the Lord after his resurrection, the same communion *once-for-all* constituted around the apostolic ministry after Pentecost. In a word, this seed is constituted of the very same *eschata* as those at work at Pentecost. They are this seed.

The alternating movement of systole and diastole may help to understand how, by *transmission* and *reception*, the body of Christ grows in history while remaining unchangeable. *Ecclesia Dei nunquam eadem, semper ipsa.* The analogy is, indeed, defective. But like a living body, the Church could not be what it is called to be—a reality already eschatological though necessarily realized in the succession of the *chronoi* and the diversity of the cultures or human contexts—without this two-way dynamism. Through *paradosis*, the *eschata* continue to be transmitted as the unchangeable foundation, already grounded in the eternal feast of the kingdom (cf. Rev 7:1-17; 14:1-5; 15:2-4; 17:14; 19:1- 9; 20:4-6). Through *reception*, this salvific gift of God becomes concretely part of human history and the human condition. This defines what the living Tradition of the Church of God really is.

Notes

[1]See especially *Faith and Order Papers, Louvain 1971* (esp. p. 29); also *Councils and the Ecumenical Movement,* coll. *World Council of Churches* 5, Geneva 1968; *Irenikon* 44 (1971) 349–66.

[2]See *Summa Theologiae IIIa,* 61, art.3, c. and ad 1.

[3]See E. G. Selwyn, *The First Epistle of St Peter* (London: 1946) 125; F. Wright Beare, *The First Epistle of Peter* (Oxford: 1970) 85.

[4]See J.-M. R. Tillard, *Church of Churches* (Collegeville: The Liturgical Press, 1992).

[5]*Katholon* = presence of the whole in each part (Aristotle, *Meta* V, 26).

[6]See L. Cerfaux, "Les Saints de Jérusalem," *Ephemerides Theologiae Lovaniensis* 2 (1925) 510–29.

20

Reflections on the Authority of Tradition in the Writings of Heidegger, Jung, and Tillich

Jeffery Hopper

Fr. George Tavard is many things: prolific writer; historical, systematic, and constructive theologian; ecumenist; teacher; priest; and poet. These many talents have enabled Father Tavard to be a bridge between communities and between viewpoints. This has been clear in his role in many interfaith dialogues and in his seventeen-year professorship at the Methodist Theological School in Ohio introducing candidates for Protestant ministry to the disciplines of theology. In addition to being a bridge between Roman Catholicism and Protestantism, this theologian and poet has also been a bridge between apparently incompatible perspectives, as I hope to illustrate in the following.

Early in this century it was common in Protestant circles to hold that one of the basic differences between Protestantism and Roman Catholicism was that the former affirmed the authority (in theology) of Scripture, while the latter followed the authority of its own traditions. It has long since become clear that this was a caricature which grossly misrepresented the actual practices of both branches of western Christianity and seriously oversimplified the issues involved. The Protestant insistence upon *"sola Scriptura"* was itself an appeal to tradition, and the Scriptures were a product of Church tradition. But what tradition *is,* how it is to be interpreted, and what kind of authority it may be judged to have are themselves difficult questions.

I propose here to sketch some aspects of the perspectives opened on these questions by three of the most influential of the twentieth-century's thinkers: one a philosopher, Martin Heidegger; one a psychologist, Carl Gustav Jung; and one a theologian, Paul Tillich. This might well seem like an attempt to compare incompatibles, but Heidegger and Jung both had serious critical and constructive concerns with theology, and the theological outlook of Tillich was influenced by their teachings. I will argue here that there is important and suggestive common ground among the three. I will then raise the question as to what might be judged to be Father Tavard's perspective on this "common ground."

Although a theological audience is likely to find Tillich's work the most familiar and accessible of the three, I shall deal with it last, because it makes some use of the work of Jung and Heidegger.

In order to discern what is suggested for our understanding of the authority of tradition, it will be necessary in all three cases to look at the basic perspective rather than to focus merely on what was said about tradition.

I. *Martin Heidegger*

Martin Heidegger has often been described as an atheistic existentialist. In my judgment, however, he was a profoundly religious thinker. He was puzzled and saddened, as he stated in a conversation which I had with him in 1968, by the charge of atheism. He began his studies in theology, preparing for the priesthood of the Roman Catholic Church. Very early, however, he came to the judgment that Christian theology had long since gone astray, and his lifelong pursuit of the questions of Being and Truth may be seen as an effort to find a way to recover what had been lost. Beda Allemann told me that Heidegger had said to him that perhaps last of all he would write "theology." This would hardly, however, have been theology as it is commonly understood. Indeed, Heidegger argued in some of his earliest lectures that the primordial Christian faith experience described in the letters of St. Paul was hidden by the use of a metaphysical conceptuality employed in Christian theology. This objectifying conceptuality, instead of clarifying that lived experience, obscured it. Although various interpreters such as Augustine, the medieval mystics, the young Luther, and Søren Kierkegaard rediscovered this primordial Christian faith experience, the predominant theological tradition's continued recourse to the metaphysical conceptuality repeatedly hid it again, finally, in effect, "killing God."[1]

In Heidegger's judgment, being had been understood as if it were a being, something at hand to be looked at, and, in like manner, truth came to be understood as the correspondence between a proposition and an objective state of affairs. Heidegger's basic criticism of Kant's work in the *Critique of Pure Reason* was not that Kant had erred in finding all of our experience as subjects to be of phenomena rather than noumena. The limitation was in the starting point. Kant's analysis began with the subject/object structure, subjects experiencing objects.[2] Heidegger argued that there is a more basic human state which he called "Being-in-the-world."[3] Before human being is as subject over against objects, it is immersed in its "world." The subject-object relating is an abstraction from a more primordial state. This abstracting, moving out from that immersion, which has increasingly characterized western thought since the pre-Socratic philosophers, has been immensely useful, making possible science and technology with all of their achievements and effects. In Heidegger's view this has brought with it the forgetting of Being and Truth and "the death of God." If this subject/object structure is taken for granted, Being is thought of as a being, to be looked at and defined. If we ask what is true concerning Being, we ask as subjects seeking to define an object, for that is the presupposition when truth is understood as correspondence. The same is true when we ask about the truth concerning God. Such asking assumes that God is a being which can be an object for us as knowing subjects.

Heidegger sought to re-think the nature of truth to free it from the subject/object structure. Reaching back to pre-Socratic uses of *aletheia,* Heidegger argued for the understanding of truth as "unconcealment." Truth is described here as an event in which Being comes to presence (is unconcealed). But this coming to presence is not as an object for a subject, and this event of Being's coming to presence is also a reconcealing and hiding or withholding.[4]

In one of the figures of speech in which Heidegger sought to suggest the character of this event of Being/Truth revealing and reconcealing, he likened Being to the light *by which* we see objects. In this "seeing" the light which makes possible a subject's experience of objects is not itself such an object. The light itself becomes manifest only in its illuminating of beings, not directly in itself, for it is not a being.[5]

The likening of Being/Truth to light is also suggested in the title of a group of Heidegger's essays which he called *Holzwege.*[6] This word has been translated by such different phrases as "forest trails" and "dead ends." There is some appropriateness in each, for Heidegger's reference was to the foresters' ways which were to be found, for example, near his ski hut above Todtnauberg in the Black Forest. When one hikes along these paths, some frustration is experienced, for they lead to clearings, but (often) they do not continue further; they dead end. The foresters cut the trails to reach a stand of trees to be harvested and to permit the removal of these trees. Then they go to another place and cut a new way to reach another stand of trees. The suggestion in Heidegger's title is that in each of the essays he has sought to make a clearing, to let the light in, but then he has gone on to make another trail and another clearing. He did not settle down and stay in one clearing, for that would have brought to an end the process of letting in the light. Students or interpreters want Heidegger to "settle down," so that they may fix Heidegger's "viewpoint," grasp his teaching clearly, and specify his meaning. But Heidegger's point is that Being/Truth is not thus to be grasped as an object of our knowing.

The event of Being/Truth which is here likened to light is elsewhere spoken of by Heidegger as "Holy."[7] Being is Holy. This is not because there is a God or there are gods within it. The Holy is prior to "the gods." It is that by which they are divine.[8] Being is Holy for it is undefiled and unapproachable.[9] The gods are particular expressions of this more primordial holiness of Being. The coming of Holy Being disrupts all conventional experience. It is "terrible."[10] It is the omnipresence of this Holy Being which gathers everything, letting it be.[11]

In this essay on *Hölderlin and the Essence of Poetry,* Heidegger asserts that it is the poets' role to respond to the approach of the Holy.[12] Holy Being discloses itself; it is not an object. Even in its approach and self-disclosure for the poets' naming, it does not become "available" such that it can be named in itself. This would deny its holiness, treat the Holy as a god, Being as a being.

As one might then expect, Heidegger also spoke of Being in terms of "grace." He did so, however, not with the usual German word *Gnade* but with the Old High German word *Huld.*[13] Presumably, he judged the term *Gnade* to be captive to conventional theological discourse, wherein God is thought about as a being, an object for discussion and description. Therein grace has lost its character as freely self-giving.

Heidegger also spoke of Being/Truth as "mystery."[14] This is implicit in these other ways of characterizing Being and Truth, if it is understood that to speak of Being as "mystery" is not simply to say that it is unknown or forgotten, but to acknowledge that in itself it will ever elude our grasp. Any such "grasping" would belie the holiness and the graciousness. Therefore, Being, in its self-revealing remains concealed. It cannot be made an object or be defined (have its limits set). One of the ways in which Heidegger expressed this was to say that even Being/Truth's self-concealing is concealed.[15]

To emphasize these expressions, that Being/Truth is Holy, gracious, mysterious, self-revealing and self-concealing, is, no doubt, to invite the simple translation that "Being is God, God is Being." The trouble with such a hasty translation is that it would be heard in a way which would assimilate Heidegger's thought to the very metaphysical objectifying mode of thought which in his view has entailed the forgetting of Being by thinking of Being as a being and has resulted in "the death of God." It would contradict the central concern of his work. Instead of facilitating the event of the coming to presence of Being/Truth, it would continue its forgetting. If one might risk theological terms, nevertheless, this would be conducive to idolatry rather than faith.

The foregoing hasty sketches of some of the emphases in Heidegger's thought may themselves constitute an example of this mistake. They seem to present "doctrines" for intellectual affirmation or denial and thereby encourage a settling down in one of the clearings. I can only repeat that this would be an understanding which contradicts all of these "doctrines!"

How then can Heidegger's thought be related meaningfully to the question of the authority of tradition? If our traditions are dominated by a metaphysical thinking which has forgotten the event of Being/Truth and thereby brought about "the death of God," aren't they simply to be rejected? Didn't Heidegger commit himself to "the destruction of the history of ontology."[16] Yet Heidegger also devoted many years of labor to dialogue with the writings of such giants of our tradition as Kant, Nietzsche, Hegel, Plato, Aristotle, and Heraclitus.

This tension of negative and positive appearances in his relation to tradition makes sense in light of the preceding points. In the event of the coming to presence of Being/Truth, the self-revealing is also a self-concealing. The poet or thinker who is a vehicle of this event *cannot* therefore bring Being/Truth to full expression. That limitation is given with the holy, gracious, mysterious character of Being/Truth, as reflected in the nature of the event of Truth as revealing/reconcealing (*Unverborgenheit*). The objectifying conceptuality of traditional metaphysical thinking compounds this limitation. Heidegger's de-struction (one of the sources of the more recent movement of Deconstructionism) was not essentially negative. He sought to work back through the metaphysical interpretations to let the originating event of Being/Truth come to expression again. His aim was not to get back to "what was said." That is the usual aim of historical interpretations. In Heidegger's view, however, even where the poet/thinker responded to Being/Truth's self-giving appropriately, it was inevitable that something remained unsaid (*Das Ungesagte*).[17] Heidegger's project of "destruction of metaphysics" was but an aspect of his effort at "retrieving,"[18] at letting come to utterance that which remained *unsaid*. He was not asking what the poet/thinker *said*. He was entering into dialogue with each one for a very different purpose!

This has some rather obvious implications for the role and authority of tradition. Most obvious is the recognition that from this perspective no traditional teaching can be supposed to be the truth. So to identify any particular teaching would be to lose the character of truth as event by fixing it objectively and to forget that in its self-revealing Being/Truth also reconceals itself. The holiness, graciousness, and mysteriousness of Being/Truth would be obscured even if the teaching in question were that Being/Truth is holy, gracious, and mysterious! By fixing as subject upon that teaching as object, as something present to be grasped intellectually, one would avoid participation in the event. One would have an idea, which, as compared with any number of differing ideas, would be better. But our temptation to see that idea as the truth, rather than as an ambiguous attempt to bring to expression the event of Truth, is all too easily succumbed to; and in a culture which identifies truth with objective correspondence, it is apparently inevitable.

To say that no particular teaching is the truth is not to denigrate all of traditional teaching as lies or as worthless. In Heidegger's view the poets/thinkers of the past have brought to expression events of the self-revealing of Being/Truth. The priority has been with the holy and mysterious source, not with the poet/thinker. We are, therefore, the beneficiaries of the traditions, but we turn these gifts into a prison house when we treat "what they said" as a treasure to be preserved in and for itself. In so doing we forget not only the distinction between the expression and the event, but we also forget that in and with the self-revealing there was also self-concealing. We shut out Being by conceiving it as a being; we substitute an idol for Holy Being.

This is why Heidegger's writings, especially after *Sein und Zeit*, are so strange and frustrating. He meditates upon art or poetry, writes poetry, and carries on dialogues with earlier writers not aimed at pinning down what they said, but at opening a space for the coming to presence of what remained unsaid, pursuing the possibility that Holy Being *may* reveal itself here and now, albeit with a reconcealing. The poet/thinker is called to "shepherd the mystery."[19] This vocation is not limited to a few exceptional persons. It is for all, for, as Heidegger emphasized from Hölderlin, "poetically doth man dwell on earth."[20]

It is interesting to compare this with our common practices in relation to scriptural interpretation. On the one hand, new commentaries appear in every generation, and every week untold numbers of differing expository sermons are preached, all of which bear eloquent witness to the judgment that the meaning is not simply there in the text or to be fully grasped in one interpretation. On the other hand, most of this is done because of the belief that the meaning *is* there in the text, and our only question is "What does the Bible say?" Our only tasks then are to translate and apply, and we can, presumably, build a system of correct doctrines.

Yet, a strong case can be made that "what the Bible says" is that ultimate truth ever remains holy, gracious, and mysterious. One may appeal to Jesus' teaching in parables, not *defining* God and God's will, but telling stories which may enable some hearers to become open to the event of Holy presence.

In such a view, the authority is not in the texts. It remains with the *Source* of revelation.[21] The Scriptures and other texts of tradition have an essential role as mediating witnesses to events of revelation, and revelation does not provide dogma or information, for it is ever the event of self-revealing of that which remains holy, gracious, and mysterious, hence an event which is also self-concealing.

II. Carl Gustav Jung

The most distinctive and the most controversial aspect of Carl Jung's psychology is his affirmation of the collective unconscious, and it is this which has the most important implications pertaining to the authority of tradition. It was, of course, Sigmund Freud whose researches and arguments led to the recognition that the human psyche is not constituted simply by what is conscious and what may readily become conscious. Indeed, his studies of such things as hysteria, dreams, and "slips of the tongue" led to the conclusion that consciousness is but the "tip of the iceberg" of the human psyche, and that human beings are ordinarily much more influenced by instinct, repressions, and the Super Ego than they are by conscious reasoning. As much, however, as Freud's work enlarged our understanding of the human psyche, Carl Jung's teaching of the collective unconscious enlarged it far more.

In Jungian terms, Freud's "unconscious" is called the "personal unconscious," for it is understood to receive its contents during an individual's life and as a result of that individual's particular experiences. By contrast, the collective unconscious is inherited. A person is born with its contents, which Jung called *archetypes*.

An archetype is not something such as a specific symbol which we can perceive in itself. It is rather a potential for a variety of symbolic, mythic, and ritual expression. That there are archetypes of a collective unconscious at work in the psyches of all human beings is a conclusion which Jung reached very gradually over a long period of research, studying the dreams and fantasies of many persons and the myths and rituals of many cultures. It was Jung's conclusion that the same basic mythological/symbolic themes appeared in all of the cultures he studied and reappeared in the dreams of persons today. He was impressed, for example, by some very elaborate symbolic expressions which were reported in persons' (sometimes children's) dreams which were to be found in strikingly similar detail in documents which could not have been known to the dreamer.[22] In his judgment, the reason for such apparently inexplicable appearances of these symbolic patterns in different times, places, languages, and cultures was that they expressed something archetypal, that is, from the collective unconscious present and at work in all persons and cultures. Like the instincts, the archetypes have developed with the evolutionary process. They express aspects of human wholeness and essential processes in the drama of human becoming. When an archetype is constellated for a person or a group, it has a numinous quality and exerts a strong influence.

Ordinarily we do not recognize the archetypes as such. Instead, we are likely to project them, thus endowing particular objects, persons, words, shapes, etc., with holy or magical or malevolent powers. "Projection" is an unconscious process by which that which is within the psyche is seen outside. We "modern persons" suppose ourselves to be past the naiveté of superstition, magic, and idolatry, but the projections which give these things their power are still a lively aspect of our lives, and necessarily so. They often provide the powerful bridge of our important relationships. One example is our having an immediate strong positive or negative reaction to someone when we meet for the first time. We like to assume that this is because of something which we have seen or intuited in them, but, given the immediacy of the reaction and hence the lack of opportunity to gain such knowledge, it is more likely that something about them facilitates our unconscious projecting upon them of contents of our own psyches, either positive or negative.

A common illustration of our projecting may be seen in Jung's teachings concerning the anima and the animus. Jung found that in each human psyche there is a contrasexual factor. In a man there is an archetypal feminine aspect, which he called the anima, and in a woman an archetypal masculine aspect, which he called the animus. Commonly, in each, the early life struggle to become a "man" or a "woman" entails the suppression of this "other side." Though archetypal, these unconscious dynamics differ in particular form from person to person, for they take shape from each person's experiences of primary relationships to persons of the opposite sex. When someone "falls in love at first sight," it is likely that a projection of the anima (or animus) has been evoked by some "fit" of the person and this unconscious aspect of him/herself. Indeed, this is probably at work in most "loves." The power of the attraction is rooted in the fact that the ones who project are thereby dissociated from parts of themselves and are driven to seek would-be wholeness through relating to those projected upon.

Projection, in Jung's view, begins much earlier, however, for the godlike status of the parents is not due simply to their size, power, and authority. It is rooted in the projection of father and mother archetypes.

The collective unconscious manifest in the symbolic and mythic expressions of the archetypes is both "deeper" and greater than the personal unconscious. While Freud's view of the human psyche has been likened to an iceberg whose above-water tenth is representative of consciousness while the underwater nine-tenths represent the unconscious, Jung's view of the collective unconscious has been compared to the ocean in which the icebergs float, for it is shared by all persons, and it is—as far as we can learn—"bottomless." The personal unconscious is "closer" to consciousness and impedes the access of the archetypal to consciousness, distorting its messages. Nevertheless, that deeper unconscious is seen as including a dynamic drive toward wholeness which it ever presses upon the psyche, conscious and unconscious. That "unfathomable" collective unconscious is rooted in the very "ground and power of being," and the wholeness of each individual psyche requires not only insight into the repressions and complexes of the personal unconscious, but an openness to and cooperation with the collective unconscious. More specifically, the ego (basically what one experiences consciously as "I") must, without losing its tenuous hold on "reality," establish a relationship with the "deepest" of the archetypes, the Self, in which the Self rather than the ego becomes the person's center. The Self, said Jung, is indistinguishable from the God representation.[23]

This last statement is considerably more ambiguous than it may sound at first. Note that Jung did not say that the Self is God, only that we cannot distinguish between the Self archetype and the God representation. We do not experience anything more ultimate or more numinous than the archetype of the Self. If God is, our experience of God is most deeply in and through the archetype of the Self, the archetype which expresses our wholeness. A further element of ambiguity lies in the efforts of Jung to speak as a psychologist, a scientist, an empiricist or phenomenologist, describing what he found in his research. He sought to avoid making metaphysical statements (statements about reality itself, which are, accordingly, beyond the reach of scientific observation and verification) and to keep assertions of his own religious beliefs out of his teachings. Hence the affirmation that the archetype of the Self is indistinguishable from "God" is not a statement about the deity, but a statement about human experience. The question as to whether God *is* is not addressed by Jung as psychologist.

Whether Jung affirmed the reality of God depends on how the word "God" is understood. He said that he regarded statements of belief in God as futile, but he also said, "I am well satisfied with the fact that I know experiences which I cannot avoid calling numinous or divine."[24] This "knowledge" is experiential, not theoretical. "Religion," in Jung's view, is essentially a matter of experience. To experience the archetypal is to experience the numinous, the holy, the awe inspiring; it is sometimes terrifying, sometimes an experience of grace. It is this which constitutes human experience of divinity, and it is this experience which, for Jung, constitutes genuine religion.

It was also Jung's judgment that contemporary Christianity is largely out of touch with such original religious experience. Not only Christianity, but other religions are rooted in such experiences of the archetypes. "They contain a revealed knowledge that was originally hidden, and they set forth the secrets of the soul in glorious images."[25] These images and the rituals, sacred writings, and doctrines of the religions bear powerful witness to that revelation. However, in their evolution, the images become more and more removed from the originating experience. The more familiar they become, the more superficial is their meaning.[26] If we are concerned about "orthodoxy" (i.e., "right teaching") and focus attention upon the correctness of doctrinal formulations, we have, from Jung's standpoint, gone seriously astray. To insist upon correct doctrinal formulations is to forget that the truth is in the originating revelatory experience of that which is holy and mysterious and to fix upon a mere object of belief which thereby becomes a barrier to genuine religious experience. Religion is to be distinguished from creed, for religion is a matter of immediate experience.[27]

To illustrate how this perspective affects the issue of the authority of tradition, we may consider Jung's discussion of the Trinity. I do not say here, "the doctrine of the Trinity," for the image is prior to the doctrine. The image is an expression of an archetype, Jung argued, pointing to trinities in ancient Babylonia, Egypt, and Greece. Such a perspective, of course, relativizes Christianity, as Jung was well aware, but it does not make it meaningless. Quite the contrary. That Christianity should have been so grasped by this archetypal image is witness to the validity of the originating revelatory experience upon which it is based. As that statement would imply, the Christian affirmation of the Trinity was not, in Jung's judgment, the result of intellectual cleverness or of political maneuvering, much as these things can be seen at work in and around the Nicean and Chalcedonian decisions. That affirmation was inevitable because the archetype was constellated in that cultural situation.[28] It is an expression of "a higher form of God-concept," for it corresponds to a situation in which humans have become more conscious.[29] The old gods were dying, and a new god was being born in "an occurrence that healed the wound in men's souls."[30]

The trinitarian formulations were required by the Christian affirmation that the God-man had come among us. Here again an archetype was at work. In Jung's view, what made it possible for persons to perceive divinity present in the event of Jesus Christ was a powerful affinity between that life and "certain contents of the unconscious." "The connecting link here is the archetype of the God-man, which on the one hand became historical reality in Christ, and on the other, being eternally present, reigns over the soul in the form of a supraordinate totality, the self."[31]

For Jung, this is a powerful affirmation of the Christian message, but it does not lead to the conclusion that specific doctrinal formulations of the image are to be regarded as having absolute status for all times and cultural settings. It was also his judgment that in our situation we can and must now recognize that the traditional Christian doctrine of the Trinity is a deficient representation of God. It was a patriarchal formulation in a patriarchal cultural setting. The absence of the feminine leaves it inadequate for expressing wholeness.[32] The doctrine of the Trinity and the Christ-image were also deficient because they excluded the "dark side" from both God and Christ.[33] This was not for Jung an insistence that we must make the metaphysical assertion that God includes evil. He is concerned here with the images which seek to express the archetypal. To put the matter far too simply, human life inevitably includes suffering, and the human psyche always has a "dark side," the unconscious. Since the God-image is for us a symbol of wholeness, its exclusion of a "dark side" is a deficiency. This judgment, for Jung, was not primarily a theoretical one, for his work as therapist and his studies persuaded him that another archetypal image, that of the quaternity, is powerfully at work among us today.[34]

These remarks open a host of complex questions which cannot be pursued here, but they may serve to indicate some basic points about the implications of Jung's teachings for the authority of tradition. The general attitude toward tradition required by a recognition of the power of the archetypes of the collective unconscious is dialectical. There is a powerful affirmation of the traditions, for, in Jung's view, they have developed in response to the archetypes and carry images, therefore, which are rooted in genuine revelatory experiences of the holy. But the authority remains with the origin of the experiences and the images, with the living holy being in which the collective unconscious is rooted, not in the doctrinal formulations which developed in response to those archetypal experiences. In addition, the continuing psychic evolution of the human species means that different archetypes are constellated in different times and cultural settings. We are therefore deeply indebted to tradition and even dependent upon it, but we must not be enslaved by it. The images which facilitated genuine religious experience heretofore may not—and in Jung's judgment, generally do not—do so here and now. One implication for the theologians is that doctrinal reformulation is a continuing obligation, and past formulations do not properly constitute fixed boundaries for that work of reformulation. A related implication is that although doctrinal formulations are rooted in revelatory experience, the truth is not in the doctrines themselves, but in the immediate religious experience. The validity of the doctrines must be discerned in the degree to which they facilitate the reccurrence of those numinous events.

The similarities of these conclusions to those which we found implied in Heidegger's work will be considered after we have taken note of some aspects of the teachings of the theologian Paul Tillich, who was in some degree influenced by both the philosopher Heidegger and the psychologist Carl Jung.

III. Paul Tillich

Like both Heidegger and Jung, Paul Tillich had a dialectical view of tradition. On the one hand, we are dependent upon tradition not only as a socio-cultural fact but also and more importantly because the Churches are basically dependent upon the New Being as it appeared in Jesus, received as the Christ; their access to this foundation is by way of tradition.[35] But tradition can be used heteronomously (as an alien law) and lead to "demonic *hubris.*"[36] Tillich pointed out that the Protestant critique of Roman Catholicism was dependent upon elements of the traditions of the latter, including "the Bible, Augustine, the German mystics, the humanistic underground, and so on."[37] Reformation depends upon tradition.

Tradition also depends upon reformation. If the specific formulations of any context are insisted upon in another, the effects will be destructive to the purposes of the Church. This is not only because of the historical and cultural relativity and the linguistic ambiguity which are inevitable aspects of every formulation, but more importantly because the truth to which the traditions have borne witness transcends all such formulations. The essential message is not in the definitions but is mediated by the *symbols* of the traditions.[38]

Both the affirmation and the warning concerning the authority of tradition may be seen in every part and aspect of Tillich's theology. It is present, for example, in his "Method of Correlation" and in his distinction of "Protestant Principle and Catholic Substance." It is required by his major doctrinal emphases, such as his affirmations of God and revelation and his understanding of the theological task itself.

Tillich's approach to systematic theology, the "Method of Correlation," was not—as has sometimes been said—a forcing of traditional doctrines into compatibility with his analyses of the present human situation. He insisted that the "existential questions" and the "theological answers" are mutually interdependent.[39] Neither can be derived from the other, but each is "heard" under the impact of the other. Because Christian theologians function within the theological circle as persons whose lives are lived in relationships and commitments made possible by the witness carried in the traditions, they cannot experience the human predicament with its threats to our very being apart from their faith. As human beings necessarily living in particular historical and cultural circumstances, they cannot help understanding the "theological answers" in light of the "existential questions" of their situation. These "questions" and "answers" are not verbal formulations. We live the questions, which are the ways in which our being is threatened. The "answers" are the symbolic expressions of the experienced reality of what we have spoken of by such expressions as "sovereign grace." The expressions are not the reality, and their ability to evoke openness to that reality is elusive.

Tillich argued that the sacraments, in their character as dramatic symbolisms, are the more powerful vehicle for the "catholic substance," conveyed by the tradition. That substance itself is the Spiritual Presence (in more traditional terms, the Holy Spirit, the living presence of God). A merely intellectual apprehension—as in a conscious response to a doctrine—would not be spiritual, as the "rediscovery of the unconscious" has helped us to recognize.[40]

Tillich's emphasis upon God as Spiritual Presence is less noted than his affirmation that "The being of God is being itself."[41] They are two aspects of the same perspective. Both emphases are rooted in faith's experience. Formally, faith is the state of being grasped by an ultimate concern. The material definition is that "Faith is the state of being grasped by the Spiritual Presence and opened to the transcendent unity of unambiguous life."[42] God cannot, therefore, be appropriately thought of as a being beside other beings, a member of a class, subject to the structures defining that class of beings. No such being could bear the weight of ultimate concern. So the theologian does better to affirm God as being-itself and as the ground and power of being. This transcendence of God is the basis of the immanence of God, the Spiritual Presence. Creaturely existence is an ambiguous participation in being-itself. That such a view is so easily heard as pantheistic is but a measure of the degree to which we are trapped in human thought categories, failing to grasp the meaning of transcendence. The dichotomies required by our language cannot properly apply to God as being-itself. No human statements can be supposed to apply properly to God. To accord absolute status to Scripture, tradition, creed, or dogma is idolatry.

"Revelation" cannot remove this limitation. Even an omnipotent God could not provide creatures with literal information about God, for "literal information" can only apply to the creaturely, being necessarily as limited as the creaturely minds which grasp its meaning. Tillich shared the general view of modern and postmodern theologians that revelation is not an imparting of information. He described revelation in terms of "miracle" and "ecstasy." "Miracle," referring to the giving side, is not intended as a supernatural violation of natural laws, but as in the older meaning of an awe-inspiring event. "Ecstasy" describes the receiving side as a response to such events in which our usual subject-object relating is transcended, "a state of mind in which reason is beyond itself, that is, beyond its subject-object structure."[43] In such ecstatic encounters, "that which concerns us unconditionally manifests itself."[44] In this self-manifestation of being-itself, that which is essentially mysterious, though manifest, remains mysterious. The recipients know of the presence of the mysterious holy being and of their relationship to it, for they have experienced it, but it has not become an object for them as subjects.[45]

These brief sketches should indicate why Tillich's view of tradition is dialectical. The theologian is dependent on tradition which carries the religious symbols which express the originating revelatory encounters. Appropriate "understanding" occurs when those symbols evoke ecstatic encounter with the Spiritual Presence. The "truth" can never be identical with particular forms of witness and interpretation, for they abstract, objectify, and culturally limit when so understood. If we are to be open to that which tradition mediates, we must not be bound by the doctrinal particularities which have assisted this mediation. The theologian reinterprets the symbols given in the tradition, warning against the supposition that their meaning can ever be fully grasped by objectifying statements, seeking to recognize where that which did have symbolic power no longer does, and struggling to discern the emergence of new symbols.[46] The success of these efforts helps to determine whether tradition serves or enslaves.

IV. Converging Implications

It is my hope that the foregoing sketches, in spite of their necessary brevity, show profound agreements among these three scholars. The reader must be wary, of course, of the possibility that my own interests and perspectives have biased the presentation. There are surely differences among the three. Obviously, their subjects and the foci of their researches differed. As psychologist, Jung sought to avoid "metaphysical" judgments, while the other two were concentrating upon "ultimate reality," traditionally, "metaphysics." Tillich's "system building" and his basic Christian commitment are manifest contrasts. He *seems* much more affirmative about the traditions than does Heidegger and less pessimistic than Jung about the continuing power of symbols mediated by the traditions. He was, evidently, less fearful of objectifying language, though he built warnings into his system.

In spite of such differences (the examination of which could occupy a volume), the agreements strike me as deeper and more important. All three affirmed the holiness, the mysteriousness, and the graciousness of that which is ultimate. One might question this in view of Jung's discussions of "the dark side of God," which was mentioned above. However, if, as I believe, he was describing human experience and not violating his own criticisms of attempts to speak directly and objectively of the divine, something very similar may be found even in Tillich's writings such as his sermon on the 139th Psalm.[47]

This common affirmation regarding holy being is accompanied by agreement that humans can experience this mysterious presence, that this possibility is the result of divine rather than human initiative, and that the mystery is not removed in such experience. It is hardly surprising that all three have been called "mystics." The appropriateness of the term depends, of course, on how it is used, but the agreement stated here surely justifies the general applicability of this designation.

It is this general agreement which underlies the dialectical attitude toward tradition in all three. Tradition is affirmed, indeed, insisted upon, by all three. We are profoundly dependent upon it. It has brought us to where we are, and yet it contains reminders of that which we have forgotten, lost touch with. At the same time, it is not the specific formulations of the traditions which are the truth for us. In the event of the coming to presence of Being/Truth, there is re-concealing as well as revealing (Heidegger); it is the evocation of the archetypes which enables our encounter with the holy, while the archetypes are never subject to our grasp and definition (Jung); the event of revelation is in the correlation of miracle and ecstasy, not in a subject-object relating (Tillich).

For those who share such a perspective, it follows that the traditions as specifically formulated cannot be the truth for us and that to grant them, even those which some of us affirm as "Holy Scriptures," an absolute authority is to place an idolatrous barrier between ourselves and the Truth as it gives itself to us.

Our efforts, then, to interpret the traditions in such a way as to facilitate openness to the coming to presence of holy being now will require much struggle with the "texts," the vehicles which transmit the traditions. Theologians will recognize that the language of academic theology is not the primary language of faith nor a direct expression of Truth, and they will continue to explore strategies of expressive language, symbolic and narrative theologies, and mythopoesis.

But the struggle will not be just with the "texts." It will also be with ourselves. Humility, patience, and prayer will prove to be more important than erudition and cleverness. As Father Tavard wrote, " . . . only through purity of heart will wisdom emerge from the documents explaining the gospel, from the scriptures, from the monuments and texts of the past. At the present juncture, both history and theory call us to conversion."[48]

There is much in the writings of Father Tavard which makes it clear that he shares in a significant portion of the "common ground" sketched above. For example, in his *The Vision of the Trinity* he wrote,

> Faith leads us on into the mystery, not as a clear, distinct, particular expression of what God is or does, but as a structured insight, a focussed contemplation, an ordered experience which speaks to the imagination more powerfully, more deeply, than to the intellect. In the darkness of unknowing we know God. In profound obscurity the vision of the Three shines like a timid imitation of dawn, like the promise of a morning knowledge beyond all imagination and description.[49]

It would, however, be very misleading to suggest that Father Tavard fully agrees with the perspective which I have described, for while he has insisted upon the recognition of historical and cultural relativity and upon the transcendence and mystery of God, he has also made it clear that these recognitions do not warrant a departure from the authority of the great ecumenical conciliar decisions. This is clear in his judgment that Tillich's Christology is heretical. "It is unbiblical. It is not in keeping with the traditional formulations of the early Councils. It is incompatible with the theology of the Fathers and that of the medieval Doctors. It is irreconcilable with the faith of the Protestant Reformers in the sixteenth century."[50] This broad appeal is narrowed in the same context. "Orthodox Christology was formulated at Chalcedon. Every alteration of the Chalcedonian understanding of the Gospel is heterodox."[51] Father Tavard explicitly reaffirmed these judgments twenty years later in his *Images of the Christ*,[52] where he also rejected several other modern approaches to Christology because they differ from the patristic tradition.[53]

This apparent granting of authority to patristic formulations should, however, be seen in the larger context of Father Tavard's discussions of tradition. He has insisted that " . . . one must simply renounce the hope that we may have at our disposal absolute criteria that may serve as touchstones of orthodoxy."[54] He gives several reasons for the judgment that there cannot be a clear fixed standard for determining and interpreting tradition, the most basic being that "The only elements that appear to be constant are the presence of Christ and the guidance of the Spirit, this presence and this guidance being manifested in an experience which is always unique and incommunicable."[55] Hence, Christian tradition, which is made up of many traditions, is living, evolving, always in the making. "The past comes to life as tradition through the action of a contemporary living reflection which cannot avoid being contextual and conditioned by its time. Tradition exists only as a contemporary interpretation of the past in the light of the expected future."[56]

This rejection of any sort of fundamentalism is not, however, an affirmation of relativism. The past does come to life as tradition in Father Tavard's judgment, and tradition does exist as a contemporary interpretation which has authority. His rejection of such modern Christologies as Tillich's as heretical is an expression of the theologians' responsibility to discern the appropriate contemporary interpretation. It is part of the evolving of a living tradition. So also is Tillich's Christological argument with its contrasting judgments as to what is the "substance" of the biblical or the patristic witness and what is the historically and culturally relative form of expression. Both contribute to the living *sensus ecclesiae*.

Even so, it is evident that Father Tavard has significant disagreements with the perspective I have sketched above. He has made it clear (in conversation) that he rejects Carl Jung's teachings of the collective unconscious, and he certainly does not affirm the relativizing of Christianity which that entailed for Jung. Indeed, Father Tavard is convinced that there is a precomprehension of Christianity in every human culture.[57] This affirmation also reflects a rejection of Heidegger's radical reinterpretation of truth with its entailed focus upon what remained unsaid in past human responses to the self-revealing/reconcealing of holy and mysterious Being. Some of the contrast with Tillich's theology we have already noted.

This is as it should be. Open and serious dialogue is essential for the theological task. Father Tavard's teaching has been a major contribution to and an encouragement of such dialogue. Like Tillich, he has been "on the boundary," and here again, in relation to the challenges posed by the works of Heidegger, Jung, and Tillich, Father Tavard's learned and perceptive treatments of the authority of tradition provide a bridge between apparently incompatible orientations.

Notes

[1]Otto Pöggeler, *Der Denkweg Martin Heideggers* (Pfullingen: Verlag Günter Neske, 1963) 36–41.

[2]Martin Heidegger, *What Is Called Thinking?*, trans. Fred D. Wieck and J. Glenn Gray (New York: Harper and Row, 1968) 234. *Being and Time*, trans. John Macquarrie and Edward Robinson (London: SCM Press Ltd., 1962) 248–49.

[3]Heidegger, *Being and Time*, 67–273. "Letter on Humanism," *Basic Writings*, ed. David Farrell Krell (New York: Harper and Row, 1977) 228f.

[4]Martin Heidegger, "Aletheia," *Vorträge und Aufsätze*, Teil III (Pfullingen: Verlag Günter Neske, 1954) 53–78 (and many other places).

[5]Heidegger, "Letter on Humanism," *Basic Writings*, 211. Cf. William Richardson, S.J., *Heidegger: Through Phenomenology to Thought* (The Hague: Martinus Nijhoff, 1963) 6, 8.

[6]Martin Heidegger, *Holzwege* (Frankfurt am Main: Vittorio Klostermann, 1950, 1963[4]).

[7]Martin Heidegger, *Erläuterungen zu Hölderlins Dichtung* (Frankfurt am Main: Vittorio Klostermann, 1963[3]) 58ff.

[8]Ibid., 58. Also, Heidegger, "Letter on Humanism," *Basic Writings*, 218, 230.

[9]Heidegger, *Erläuterungen zu Hölderlins Dichtung*, 61–62.

[10]Ibid., 62, 66, 70.

[11]Ibid., 71.

[12]Ibid., 54, 69, et passim.

[13]Heidegger, ". . . Dichterisch Wohnet der Mensch . . .," *Vorträge und Aufsätze*, Teil II, 78. "Letter on Humanism," *Basic Writings*, 238.

[14]Martin Heidegger, "On the Essence of Truth," *Basic Writings*, 132–33.

[15]Ibid., 132.

[16]Heidegger, *Being and Time*, 41ff.

[17]Heidegger, "Aletheia," *Vorträge und Aufsätze*, 56–57.

[18]Richardson, *Heidegger: Through Phenomenology to Thought*, 89, 704.

[19]Heidegger, "Der Spruch des Anaximander," *Holzwege*, 321. Cf. "Letter on Humanism," *Basic Writings*, 221.

[20]Heidegger, *Erläuterungen zu Hölderlins Dichtung*, 84. ". . . Dichterisch Wohnet der Mensch . . .," *Vorträge und Aufsätze*, 61–78.

[21]Heidegger, *Erläuterungen zu Hölderlins Dichtung*, 23.

[22]C. G. Jung, *The Collected Works of C. G. Jung*, ed. Sir Herbert Read, Michael Fordham, Gerhard Adler, and William McGuire (Princeton: Princeton University Press, Bollingen Series XX, 1968[2]) 9i ¶¶104–10. "Approaching the Unconscious," *Man and His Symbols*, C. G. Jung, M.-L. von Franz, J. L. Henderson, J. Jacobi, and Aniela Jaffe (Garden City, N.Y.: Doubleday and Co., A Laurel Edition) 58–60.

[23]Jung, *The Collected Works of C. G. Jung*, 9ii ¶142 (and many other places).

[24]Ibid., 18 ¶1589.

[25]Ibid., 9i ¶10.

[26]Ibid., ¶11.

[27]Ibid., 11 ¶75.

[28]Ibid., ¶¶222–25.

[29]Ibid., ¶205.

[30]Ibid., ¶206.

[31]Ibid., 9i ¶283.

[32]Ibid., 11 ¶¶752–53.

[33]Ibid., 9ii ¶74.

[34]Ibid., 11 ¶¶62f.

³⁵Paul Tillich, *Systematic Theology* (Chicago: The University of Chicago Press, 1963) 3:183–84.

³⁶Ibid., 183.

³⁷Ibid., 184.

³⁸Ibid., 301–02.

³⁹Paul Tillich, *Systematic Theology* (Chicago: The University of Chicago Press, 1951) 1:60.

⁴⁰Tillich, *Systematic Theology,* 3:122.

⁴¹Tillich, *Systematic Theology,* 1:235.

⁴²Tillich, *Systematic Theology,* 3:131.

⁴³Tillich, *Systematic Theology,* 1:112.

⁴⁴Ibid., 113.

⁴⁵Ibid., 109.

⁴⁶Paul Tillich, "Theology and Symbolism," *Religious Symbolism,* ed. F. Ernest Johnson (pub. by The Institute for Religious and Social Studies; dist. by Harper and Brothers, New York, 1955) 107–16.

⁴⁷Paul Tillich, *The Shaking of the Foundations* (New York: Charles Scribner's Sons, 1953) 38–51.

⁴⁸George H. Tavard, "Tradition and Theology: A Methodological Approach," *Perspectives on Scripture and Tradition,* ed. Joseph F. Kelly (Notre Dame, Ind.: Fides Publishers, Inc., 1976) 124.

⁴⁹George H. Tavard, *The Vision of the Trinity* (Washington: University Press of America, 1981) 54.

⁵⁰George H. Tavard, *Paul Tillich and the Christian Message* (New York: Charles Scribner's Sons, 1962) 137.

⁵¹Ibid., 132.

⁵²George H. Tavard, *Images of the Christ: An Enquiry into Christology* (Washington: University Press of America, Inc., 1982) 116.

⁵³Ibid., 86–90.

⁵⁴George H. Tavard, "Tradition and Theology: A Problematic Approach," 102.

⁵⁵Ibid., 101.

⁵⁶Ibid., 92.

⁵⁷George H. Tavard, *La théologie parmi les sciences humaines: de la méthode en théologie. Le point théologique,* 15 (Paris: Éditions Beauchesne, 1975) 143.

21

Art and the Tradition: Theology, Art, and Meaning

Mary Charles Murray

In recent years a critical problem for theology has become increasingly recognised, namely, that theology is too verbal and has lost any hold of or is unable to give any account of the visual. The problem is in essence to understand what the correct relationship between the two should be, and there is a growing literature on the subject. However, despite these attempts, understanding of the problem does not seem to have advanced much at all. So in this paper I should like to argue that the reason for this is because the terms of the discussion are mistaken. The problem is always seen to be either as one of symbolism or one of aesthetics. I should like to suggest (1) that we shall not be on the way to resolving the issue until we have a new theology of the image and (2) that this theology is in itself a development of the Christian tradition. But crucial to this development is the cooperation of artists. This study is particularly appropriate in a volume offered to George Tavard, whose work on the tradition has done so much to aid the Church in its self-understanding; and it is offered to him in gratitude for all that I have learned from his work. I should like to begin my discussion by being thoroughly modern and evolutionary in approach and by asking first how did the problem arise. The origin of the problem is historical.

I. Theology and the Verbal

That theology is intrinsically verbal is not in doubt. In the Christian tradition theology is concerned with the Gospel, and whether we speak of it in English or in its original Greek form, *euaggelion,* we see that its essential nature is good news. This means from the outset that theology is bound to be verbal in expression, whether in the oral form in which most New Testament scholars think it originally existed or in the subsequent written text of the New Testament. Thus Christianity was responsible for coining a new word to describe itself and for creating a new and unique literary form. This was reinforced by the decision to retain the books of the Old Testament as scripture when Christianity left its Jewish matrix. Christianity also accepted a Greek tradition of philosophy which, in its Platonic form, had a particular theory of language. This theory included a view of the metaphysical and anthropological function of language which is generally ignored as scholars fasten on the relation Plato saw between thought and language. That language is essentially therapeutic was the view expressed by Plato in the *Republic,* and it lay behind the dialectical method adopted by Socrates; by constantly refining the language used, one would arrive at true knowledge and the healthful condition which is its result. In modern conceptions the therapeutic understanding of language is continued by the discipline of psychoanalysis, where "bad" concepts are replaced by "good" ones as a result of verbal exchanges between the therapist and the patient.[1] This account has been accepted into Christian pastoral concerns in the current fashion for counselling. Though it is impossible to discuss the matter here, our familiarity with Augustine should make us aware of the connection between this view of Plato's and the essentially therapeutic understanding of Christian doctrine.[2] In this connection the further idea that goodness can be conveyed by preaching resulted in the creation of another new literary form, the sermon. Thus the point I am making here is that Christianity has always been linguistically able to create whatever verbal form it needed to express what it considers normative about life.

Therefore because both roots of Christian theology, Hebrew scripture and Greek philosophy, favored the verbal, it is possibly for this reason that the visual form of communication was relatively neglected save as a pastoral and didactic tool. One of the abiding problems in the study of Christian art is its relatively late appearance, about 200 A.D. A possible answer may be that creative Christian energy was being devoted to the creation of literature. This may well be why Christianity did not originally create a specific corresponding theory of art or a unique art form in order to express its content in the same way.[3]

However an increasing theological reflection on its own content, which caused the rise to conscious formulation of the doctrine of the incarnation,

coupled with the constant teaching derived from Genesis that human beings are themselves formed in the image and likeness of God, made reflection on the nature of the material and the visual become an essential part
of Christian theology. Thus by the ninth century, with the Declaration of
Orthodoxy in 843 at the end of the bitterest dispute the Church has ever
witnessed, the iconoclastic controversy, the essentially Christian nature of
the visual and of art, as demanded not only by the doctrine of creation but
also by the incarnation, was clearly established. But because it came late
and was a post-New Testament development the visual has always remained
relatively undeveloped, and the tension between the verbal and the visual
within Christianity rather than their complementarity and integration has
always marked its history particularly in the West. This has been reinforced
because there is a whole history, which is particularly characteristic of the
twentieth century, of the study of theological language. It is one of the
great discoveries of our day that the balance must be restored and that to
view Christianity only as a verbal religion will no longer do. Art is part of
the subtle complexity involved in believing and of belief's expression.

If then my account of the origin of the problem is accurate, it explains
why we have always had in Western Christian theology a lopsided account
of the nature and function of the visual. This still goes on even in the area
of the discussion of symbolism, which has been a great preoccupation of
twentieth-century theologians. Theology it seems to me has been responsible for much confusion in its discussion of symbols. It has also, as is often
the case, hailed this topic as a possible means of its salvation and as an answer to its problems just when other theoretical disciplines are questioning
the whole idea. Thus I shall turn to my second point and make some observations about theology and symbolism.

II. Theology and Symbolism

"Symbol" is a word which has immense popularity in everyday speech
and in philosophical enquiry alike. Its ubiquity is frequently commented
on in discussions and the variety of its referents likewise. This variety has
been shown to range from physical, material objects, to linguistic constructions, historical events, in fact anything. It is very confused both in meaning and also in use.[4] There have also been repeated attempts to make a
definition which would cover all cases and all have failed. What is more
or less of general agreement is that symbols come from our experience of
the physical world and are the result in part of our existence as biological.

They exercise therefore a governing control on our thought, feelings, and desires and are mediated through our imagination. Their ultimate origin as metaphysical, psychological, etc., is much disputed. We simply know that they are related to the movement of our consciousness, that they are somehow explanatory, and that they provide a basis for conscious reflection. Because of their fundamental importance, they have therefore become major expressions of religious meaning.[5]

In theology however there is particular confusion due first of all to the lack of definition. But it is also due to the fact that modern discussions of symbolism began with debates about language in the nineteenth century, as exemplified by Coleridge, and also to the fact that they were of fundamental importance to the modern psychological theories of Freud and Jung, who nevertheless differed substantially in their views of its meaning. Further, the Western Platonist tradition, inherited by theology, is capable of various interpretations and so there are further differences in the Western concept of the symbol as representing something or as participating in something. One of the main differences between Catholics and Protestants at the Reformation, for example, over the Eucharist was as to whether it represents the body of Christ or actually is the body of Christ. It is not surprising therefore that the confusions in the discussion of symbolism do not help our problem.

Furthermore, discussions of the matter in theological contexts have almost always been seen as matters of language. The issue turns on the question in what way language is symbolic, particularly the language of the Scripture and the great dogmatic statements of the Creed. Despite the unresolved nature of many of the questions concerning symbols, many leading and influential modern theologians have made them one of the central categories of their enquiry.[6] It is not surprising therefore that growing contemporary suspicion about the functions of symbols and their place within human activity does not come from within theology but from within discussions of culture and philosophy. Four main objections have been analyzed.[7] They are philosophical, psychological, linguistic, and social. The first originates in philosophical discussions from Kant to Nietzsche concerning the essential qualities of human cognition and of the power of knowing how to contact any reality outside that of language. This is really the vexed question of artistic truth. The second is influenced by Freud's critique of human identity and whether, if symbols are human psychological products, they display anything more than the expression of our own interior states. Modern critical theory generates the third objection, beginning with

Nietzsche and continued by Derrida. These critics take their stand on the metaphoricity of all language and the inability to go behind it to understand reality. Finally history, especially as a result of Nazi and Soviet propaganda, has raised the question of the meaning behind the symbols of social and political life. This is the cultural critique—how are symbols which are good to be distinguished from those which are evil? In other words if it is true that symbols are socially constructive, how are they to be prevented from causing society's destruction?

The nineteenth century had argued for the role of the symbol in human affairs by stressing that symbols could bring into prominence particular aspects of the religious dimension through aesthetic experience. In other words for the nineteenth century the link of symbolism was with aesthetics—it was not a doctrinal link. Thus because of its background preoccupation with symbolism, when theology discusses artistic questions it regards them as matters of aesthetics. So when contemporary Christian thinking interprets the notion of artistic symbolism in an ontological way, as it does, it locates it within the metaphysical realm of beauty. That the aesthetic dimension of reality is the way in which the invisible God becomes visible is the central contention of the work of Hans Urs von Balthasar and of similar thinkers.[8] Although the visual arts are referred to in the analysis, the theology of von Balthasar is not really a theology of the visual in that sense and is largely a return to the idealist nineteenth-century tradition of philosophical aesthetics.[9] Further, the aesthetic argument stands or falls on whether there is such a thing as a theological category of the beautiful. This seems to be hardly the case, since beauty is not a theme of the Old Testament and is certainly not a preoccupation at all in the New. The Scriptures contain no reflection on the nature of the beautiful in itself. Thus von Balthasar's work, and also that of Paul Tillich, is still a philosophical and therefore a verbal approach to the question. Theology still remains verbal despite the topic of the discussion. Two final points also show, I think, that theology and the visual cannot be primarily a matter of aesthetic. One is the highly successful iconography of the Orthodox Church where the fundamental idea supporting it is not that of beauty but of holiness, which is basically an ethical as much as an ontological idea.[10] The second is the fact that theology would have to have an aesthetic which embraced above all suffering as well as resurrection as its component. Suffering is not usually regarded as the normal category of the beautiful, but this is what the central doctrine of the Cross would demand.

III. Theology and Image

How then would it be possible to bring together word and image to create a new and meaningful understanding? I think we shall be able to do this by establishing a new theology not of the symbol but of the image. This theology in itself is already within the tradition and represents a development of it, in that tradition itself is usually understood as verbal. But in order to learn how to "do" the visual theologically, so to speak, the Church will need to consult artists, since they alone have the skill to develop the image, which is also a medium as well as a mental construct. The Church will never need to depend on writers in the same way, since as indicated above, it has its own form of literary expression, created by itself.

It is Irenaeus who directs us to a perception of art which is based not on aesthetics but on doctrine, for it was Irenaeus in the second century who first developed the set of theoretical principles for the image as not merely verbal.[11] The context of his discussion is important because he was arguing against the Gnostics. These groups were paradoxically the most extreme in understanding theology as verbal. For although they had an iconography, and the "Gnosis" itself was mystical in nature, the organization of the Gnostics as a group meant that this Gnosis was communicated and so made a matter of verbal proposition. In this way the knowledge was of words, a knowledge that, e.g., there were various aeons and emanations and that knowledge of God could only be obtained by knowing the right formulae. Indeed the notion of a secret tradition must have made Gnosticism include a propositional view of revelation.

Irenaeus countered by arguing that meaning cannot be reduced to mere words as they thought. He recognised that words do not function in isolation but form parts of a language. In particular he appreciated that the most characteristic form of religious language is liturgy. Above all for him, the only way to attain to truth was through the image, for God's image is known in Christ and in the human being. It is the material which conveys meaning primarily, not the verbal. Meaning is revealed in the incarnation of the divine word.[12] This led him to establish what became eventually the canon of the New Testament. For him the coherence and meaning of doctrine rested primarily on a tradition of faithful instruction.[13] So Irenaeus is rejecting an argument from philosophy and relying on tradition, because the argument from philosophy would have kept him in the essentialist mistake that the essence of Christianity is in words. This had been seen in Gnosticism's assumption that Christianity had a particular essence which could be encapsulated in the essential meaning of words. Thus Irenaeus can now work without Plato and return to a more Semitic account—this despite the aniconic idea normally associated with Judaism. In his paradoxical use of that account, Irenaeus represents an advance in thinking and in offering the image as a category for considering meaning, in effect he argues backwards from the incarnation as the *imago Dei* and as the paradigm. There is one further respect in which Irenaeus' argument shows a sophisticated understanding of language in that it uses the image of the Word to illustrate the bodily nature of language. If the image of God is the incarnation, it is not a kind of verbalism but the whole of bodily life. In other words what is true is the content not the form of expression. Irenaeus identifies the content not as the ascent from the material to the spiritual but the material itself is its highest expression.

Tradition in that kind of use is more like Wittgenstein's conception of language as use and as something creative. His contention is that meaning is more amorphous than mere verbal expression; and he argued that we should look at the function of language rather than at the notion that there is a meaning behind particular words. So when he enjoined us to ask for the "use not the meaning" he was pointing out that meaning is seen in how a language works and not in some ghostly thing behind particular words. The development of Wittgenstein's view of language is not an issue I can discuss here; but it is well known that Wittgenstein came to interpret language as a form of life, or at least to use the latter concept as a means of elucidating what and how language means. Thus meaning in its wider sense is broader than a linguistic notion—a gesture would also be part of language in his view. One of the most important things that he had to say about religious belief was that it functions like a picture by which we live. Thus in *Lectures and Conversations on Aesthetics, Psychology and Religious Belief*[14] he sees religious language as a picture that regulates one's life, so that, e.g., to consider talk of the Last Judgment as simply talk of some future event, however strange, is to make a fundamental mistake. Thus it is wrong theologically to set up a disjunction between image and word; there is no disjunction possible. There is bound to be an interrelation. Fergus Kerr recently asked what happens to theology after Wittgenstein.[15] One answer is it must study art.

IV. Theology and Art

I should now like to turn therefore to actual examples of how theology has been taught and developed by artists through their own medium. They show how the task of faith in seeking understanding is sometimes more easily carried out by the visual medium. Within the Roman Catholic theological tradition, of course, it is worth noting that Mariology is in a very large measure the creation of art. I do not wish to develop this example further here, first because it is the general problem of art which is under discussion, and second because the way in which art has created this doctrine is too complicated to use as an illustration at this point. Instead I would like to select three artists, two old masters and one new, who have specifically contributed to theology. The first is Paolo Veronese, the second is Caravaggio, and the third Paula Rego.

A. VERONESE CA. 1528–1588

In 1573 the tribunal of the Inquisition summoned before its judges the painter Paolo Caliari of Verona (Veronese) for having unsuitably in the view of the theologians painted "buffoons, drunkens, Germans (i e , Protestant heretics), dwarfs and similar vulgarities" in a painting of the Last Supper commissioned for the refectory of Ss. Giovanni e Paolo in Venice. The painting now hangs in the Accademia in Venice, and we know of the whole affair because the transcripts of the examination survive in the Venetian archives.[16] The artist excused himself on the grounds that he had painted what he saw fit and what imagination had led him to consider appropriate to fill up the spaces of so large a canvas. The judges gave him three months to change the painting or suffer penalties which are not specified in the text. Veronese did not change the painting but changed the title instead to *The Feast in the House of Levi,* the title it bears today, and the judges were satisfied.[17] It was not so much the free roaming of the imagination which frightened the inquisitors as the fact that, in their view, a painting was meant to instruct and therefore should be scrupulously true and faithful to the scriptural account. But beyond that even, it was an era of controversy in which disputes over the Eucharist were central, and Catholic belief had to be asserted against Protestant doctrine. Germans, associated with Luther's 1520 *Address* as well as the religious geography of the time, could not be envisaged as admissible to the Eucharist. That Veronese's theology had risen beyond controversy to a more ecumenical and inclusive view of the Eucharist, as having its origin in Christ's concern for all "sorts and conditions of men," is clear from his representation; and that Veronese and his accusers understood this is clear from the re-labelling. There could be no offence in depicting undesirables in the house of a Jew on sixteenth-century principles. Nowadays of course Veronese's account is theologically justified and the limited views of his sixteenth-century judges are long outdated. In other words the artist was nearer to the real theological meaning of the Scripture account and proved to be a better and more faithful channel of tradition.

B. CARAVAGGIO 1573–1610

Caravaggio's pictures were regarded by the Church as unacceptable on the grounds that they were vulgar and low. The late seventeenth-century critic Gian Pietro Bellori also describes him as an artist who "often degenerates into low and vulgar forms." An example he quotes to justify this view are the versions of the Supper at Emmaus, one in the Brera Gallery in Milan and the other hanging in the National Gallery, London.[18] His especial invective is reserved for this latter version, the earlier of the two, painted about 1599–1600. The objection appears to rest on the depiction of the two apostles as rustic characters, on the Lord shown as young and, unsuitably, without a beard, on the innkeeper serving while wearing a cap, and on a plate of fruit on the table which is out of season. Modern studies illustrate that the supposed errors are simply part of an artistic tradition. But, as Scribner shows, the criticism of Christ depicted as a beardless youth is substantial and has puzzled critics to the present day. One early copyist corrected Caravaggio by substituting an older, bearded Christ; and finally Caravaggio himself, when he returned to the subject, went back to the traditional bearded image again. Thus that the beardless Christ has significance and that the apparent aberration is a visual formula deliberately chosen to convey the essential meaning of the painting seems clear.[19] The physiognomy and gesture express a leading theological point of Catholic doctrine.

The story of the journey to Emmaus is told by Luke (24:13-35), but there is also a brief mention in Mark (16:12). Scribner, who has studied this aspect, shows that this detail is the key to Caravaggio's theological interpretation of the incident.[20] Caravaggio focuses on the moment, as is the habit of the artistic tradition before him, of Christ's unexpected revelation of himself and his disciples' surprised recognition. But the artist raises the subject matter in a new way by throwing emphasis on the gesture as the cause and effect of the revelation. Further because he has given Christ a new face, so to speak, while Christ reveals himself to his disciples in the gesture, he presents a problem of recognition to the viewer. Christ does not look like himself. In other words Caravaggio gives a reason visually why the disciples do not recognise him. In explaining visually the problem of recognition by substituting a novel image for the one in the artistic canon, Caravaggio presents a more biblical account, by basing it on more than the text of Luke. He synthesises the two gospel texts. Luke never explains why the disciples did not recognize Christ, but Mark states that Christ appeared to the disciples in another likeness. Scribner argues that Caravaggio did not merely deal successfully with the central problem of recognition, but that his intention was ultimately to show that the miracle of recognition was sacramental.[21] Traditionally theology interpreted the supper not only as a confirmation of the resurrection but as the confirmation of Christ's real presence in the Eucharist. The doctrinal controversies of the period had led to intensified Catholic emphasis on the sacramentality of the Eucharist, and Caravaggio sought to convey the same idea. In the picture the disciples' recognition is dependent wholly on the meal—all clues to Christ's identity, such as his wounds, have been removed, and his face is not that of the crucified. The recognition is that of the gesture, like that of the priest in the Mass. Thus the gesture is the sine qua non for the disciples. Only in the Eucharist does Christ reveal himself to his faithful. The doctrine itself is orthodox and traditional, but by the formal and iconographic originality of his conception Caravaggio offers an interpretation of the biblical texts in a new and very persuasive form.

C. PAULA REGO 1935–

My third example is the work of Paula Rego in her recent series of pictures which she calls *Tales from the National Gallery*.[22] Her brief had been to display the continuing relationship between the old and the new in the collections, to show the association of the past with the present. Her response to that brief is an imaginative and visual account of the nature of tradition, and she thus provides theology with an eyewitness account of how tradition works. She represents a visual commentary on the ideas of Irenaeus. The painting which most clearly demonstrates this is her *Joseph's Dream*, which is a version of the seventeenth-century French artist Philippe de Champaigne's *Vision of St. Joseph*. In the seventeenth-century version the angel appears to the sleeping Joseph to reassure him concerning the divine origin of Mary's pregnancy. Paula Rego is first of all innovative in technique. The standard way to paint a theme is to re-do it in one way or another, as we have seen in the cases of the two artists just discussed. Any references to earlier treatments, if they are made, are only by allusion. Thus Caravaggio's youthful Christ looks like those on early Christian sarcophagi. But Paula

Rego deliberately brings the past into the present by referring to a definite picture and shows it as a work in progress, being painted this time by a woman. The preceding biblical event, the annunciation, omitted by de Champaigne, is alluded to in one of the artist's working drawings which lies on the floor. The conception is masterly in the way in which it elides what is theological, what is real, and what is painted. It is also a variation on the theme of the artist and model. In addition the role of the woman as artist is significant and central in the late twentieth century. The whole painting is conceptually exceptional.

The artist says of herself with regard to Mantegna, "I steal things . . . the look of this, the look of that . . . "[23] but to a theologian this is not stealing; it represents a profound insight into and expression of the nature of tradition. Paula Rego also has another painting *Time—Past and Present* where this time three paintings are incorporated into the picture, and the little girl in this picture grows up to be the woman artist of *Joseph's Dream*. Colin Wiggins in his essay written to accompany the recent exhibition says that "in *Joseph's Dream* we see a National Gallery painting 'unpainted' so to speak, and then repainted by a new artist. But who is really painting the picture? Is it Paula Rego or the artist she has invented? Whatever the answer, Paula's work from the National Gallery paintings has extended their meaning still further."[24] If one recasts this into theological terms and asks what concept of meaning is being exemplified here, since it is clearly not that of a verbal statement, the artist is showing that she, like Veronese and Caravaggio, not only presupposes a theology but is involved in a creative process which will articulate a theology. In Paula Rego's case she articulates a theology of tradition and shows very clearly the possibility of a divine communication in the modern world. She is a very clear example of theological meaning. All three artists understand tradition, and understand it in a way which presents it as a perennial vision, and can thus reinterpret it as a theme. If we wish to understand the opening of the Gospels of Matthew and Luke in the light of today's world, we need to consult Paula Rego's paintings as well as the commentaries of scripture scholars. I would like to end by quoting her words with regard to the National Gallery. It is "a treasure house . . . it's all treasure of the greatest kind, the richest treasure in the world."[25] No theologian can read those words without thinking of the New Testament view that the kingdom of God is like a householder who brings out of his treasure new things and old.

Notes

[1]See the discussion of M. R. Miles, *Image as Insight* (Boston: 1985) 139f.

[2]As in *De Doctrina Christiana*. This seems to me to be a neglected aspect in the study of Augustine's Platonism, and should set against simple assertions of the baneful effects of Platonism on doctrine, as found e.g. in C. Gunton, "Augustine, the Trinity and the Theological Crisis of the West," *Scottish Journal of Theology* 43 (1990) 33–58.

[3]See Sister Charles Murray, *Rebirth and Afterlife*, B.A.R. International Series 100 (Oxford: 1981) Introduction p. 1f. The earliest specifically Christian art object is the fourth-century frieze sarcophagus, which had no direct precedent. See E. Kitzinger, *Byzantine Art in the Making* (London: 1977) 23.

[4]See M. J. Swiatecka, *The Idea of the Symbol* (Cambridge: 1980).

[5]See for example M. Eliade, *Symbolism, the Sacred and the Arts,* ed. D. Apostolos-Cappadona (New York: 1992).

[6]Within the Protestant tradition the work of P. Tillich is of outstanding significance, who made the discussion of symbolism, and particularly of artistic symbolism, part of his theology of culture. See his *Systematic Theology* vols. 2 and 3 (London: 1978). For a Catholic analysis see K. Rahner "The Theology of the Symbol," *Theological Investigations* (London: 1966) 4:221f.

[7]By S. Happel in his article "Symbol," *The New Dictionary of Theology*, ed. J. A. Komonchak, M. Collins, D. A. Lane (Dublin: 1987) 1001, to which I am here indebted.

[8]See H. U. von Balthasar, *The Glory of the Lord: A Theological Aesthetics* (San Francisco:1982). P. Sherry, *Spirit and Beauty. An Introduction to Theological Aesthetics* (Oxford:1992) explores the connection between the Holy Spirit and beauty.

[9]See J. Dillenberger, *A Theology of Artistic Sensibilities* (London: 1987) 225. The same is also true, I think, of Tillich. His studies on artistic questions are most conveniently to be consulted in *Paul Tillich on Art and Architecture*, ed. J. and J. Dillenberger (New York: 1989).

[10]See e.g., C. Kalokyris, "The Content of Eastern Iconography," *Concilium. Symbol and Art in Worship* 132 (1980) 9–18.

[11]In his two works *The Demonstration of the Apostolic Preaching* and *Adversus Haereses*. For the *Epideixis* see the translation of J. Armitage Robinson (London: 1920). For the *Adversus Haereses* see the edition of A. Rousseau and others, *Irénée de Lyon Contre les Hérésies. Sources Chrétiennes* vols. 263 and 264 (bk. I), 293 and 294 (bk. II), 210 and 211 (bk. III), 100.i and ii (bk. IV), 152 and 153 (bk. V) (Paris: 1965 f.).

[12]See in particular his discussion in *Adv. Haer. III* on the Incarnation, esp. 16.1f. *Sources Chrétiennes,* 286f. For his invention of his own "fruit language" as a reductio ad absurdum of Gnosticism see bk. I 11 4 *SC,* 174; and for his analysis of the various hypotheses with regard to letters, syllables, and sounds see bk. I 14 4, *SC,* 206, with his ironic remark that truth seems to have had no existence till the Greeks invented the letters of the alphabet, I 15 *SC,* 246. That God is not to be sought by means of letters, syllables, and numbers but that love produces knowledge of God is the argument of bk. II 25, 26.

[13]*Adv. Haer. III.* For a general study which makes some discussion of the image question see G. Wingren, *Man and the Incarnation. A Study in the Biblical Theology of Irenaeus,* trans. R. Mackenzie (Edinburgh and London: 1959).

[14]C. Barrett, ed., *Lectures and Conversations on Aesthetics, Psychology and Religious Belief* (Oxford: Blackwell, 1966).

[15]F. Kerr, *Theology After Wittgenstein* (Oxford: Blackwell, 1986).

[16]Gallerie dell' Accademia, Venice. This huge oil on canvas, 12.80 x 5.50 m., is one of a series of so-called Last Suppers painted by Veronese. The catalogue raisonné of the paintings is by T. Pignatti, *Veronese. L'Opera Completa* (Venice: 1976).

[17]See G. Fogolari, "Il Processo dell' Inquisizione a Paolo Veronese," *Archivio Veneto* 17 (1935) 352–86. For the translation see E. Gilmore Holt, *A Documentary History of Art* (New York: 1958) 2:69. The incident is much discussed from the historical and technical point of view, see e.g., T. Pignatti, *The Golden Century of Venetian Painting* (Los Angeles: 1979) 26–27; G. Nepi-Scire, "Convito in Casa di Levi," *Paolo Veronese Restauri,* Quaderni della Soprintendenza ai Beni Artistici e Storici di Venezia 15 (Venice: 1988) 77f.; R. Cocke, "Venice, Decorum and Veronese," ed. M. Gemin, *Nuovi Studi su Paolo Veronese* (Venice: 1990) 251.

[18]G. P. Bellori, *Le Vite di pittori, scultori et archittetti moderni* (Rome: 1672) quoted and discussed in C. Scribner III, "In Alia Effigie: Caravaggio's London Supper Emmaus," ed. D. Apostolos-Cappadona, *Art, Creativity and the Sacred* (New York: 1988) 64–79.

[19]Scribner, 65f.

[20]Scribner, 66f.

[21]Scribner, 69f.

[22]*Paula Rego, Tales from the National Gallery* (National Gallery Publications, 1991). For the picture of Philippe de Champaigne, see the reproduction p. 6. For *Joseph's Dream,* see those on pp. 8 and 9.

[23]Quoted p. 21.

[24]*Time—Past and Present,* illustrated p. 25 and p. 26. Colin Wiggins, 27.

[25]Ibid., 27.

22

Prophetic Tradition and Canonization

Simon J. De Vries

During recent years, one of the most fruitful endeavors for biblical theologians has been to study the ways in which tradition develops primitive motifs towards images of high complexity. This method applies equally to the Old and the New Testament and to materials of all periods and from a great variety of genres. In this dynamic process, meanings and intentionalities shift and themes migrate from one bearing or focus to something unimagined by the original speakers or writers. Rather than thinking of a few scriptural writers as authors, we come to see the contributions of numerous unnamed sources and of a complex web of redactors and disciples, all of which have led to the expansion of the sacred Word.

The invitation to contribute to a congratulatory volume in honor of my esteemed colleague George Tavard offers me an opportunity to share some results of my current research on the tradition history of prophetic redaction, to appear soon in book form under the title "From Old Revelation to New."[1] This study follows somewhat the same method as Michael Fishbane's influential book *Biblical Interpretation in Ancient Israel,*[2] but concentrates just on biblical prophecy and specifically on redactional expansions introduced by stereotyped temporal formulas, such as "in that day."

I. Levels of Redaction

In recent years, much has been made of the technique or discipline of "redaction criticism," which is generally distinguished from the study of literary composition as such known as "source criticism."[3] Taken in the broadest sense, redaction criticism is an analysis of the entire compositional and editorial process—oral and literary—that transforms elemental units into larger complexes through combination, restructuring, and amplification.

In theory, any or all of the following levels of redaction may have been involved in the development of any given text: (1) initial shaping and recording, (2) preliminary collocation and reshaping, (3) the establishment of major tradition complexes, (4) preeditorial supplementation, (5) definitive editing, and (6) posteditorial supplementation. Beyond the scope of redactional expansion and alteration lie two nonredactional stages of alteration: (7) scribal glossation, and (8) canonical ordering. A careful analysis of each of these levels is essential if we are to keep tradition development and the process of canonization sharply distinct from each other.

Level 1. The first redactional level, that of initial shaping and recording, involves either the author himself or an amanuensis—more probably a close disciple than a professional scribe. The fore-given material may be a block of oral tradition familiar to the author, or it may be his own fresh creation in a more appropriate form as he now seeks, from one motive or another, to preserve it in writing.[4] To use a convenient example: it seems probable that Micah himself was recording one or more of his previous utterances as he joined them with the use of the initial word in 3:1, *wā'ōmar*, "and I said." Another example might be the major call-vision complexes found in Isaiah 6:1-11, Jeremiah 1:1-14, and Ezekiel 1:1-3:15, each of which has undergone nonauthentic expansion, which, once removed, reveals a more schematic original spoken by and/or recorded by the prophet in question. These are random examples, but they illustrate the general situation that pertains to this redactional level. The purpose of Level 1 redaction in these and numerous other passages is to preserve revelatory words for those not present at their initial promulgation, perhaps reshaping them in a more effective and authoritative form.

Level 2. The second level of redaction is that of preliminary collocation and reshaping; i.e., the bringing together, with alterations and appropriate transitions, of related or similar materials, almost always from the original author. In many instances, this has proceeded by stages.

As an example of a primitive stage of collocation at this level, we may cite the drawing together of Amos' early ("call") visions in 7:1-3, 4-6, 7-9, and 8:1-3, done more likely by a disciple than by the prophet himself. Many other examples might be cited; one from Ezekiel might be the "twinning" of special oracles against the prophets in 13:1-16 and of oracles concerning the "prophetesses" in 13:17-23.

As an example of a more sophisticated type of redaction at this level, we may mention the process that lies at an early compositional level in the book of Ezekiel, a collection of oracles that are either dated or prefaced by circumstantial descriptions, or by both, in 1:1ff., 8:1ff., 14:1ff., 20:1ff., 26:1ff., 29:1ff., 31:1ff., 32:1ff., 33:21-22. Here dating and historical situationing are the prime organizing principles. Elsewhere in the prophetic corpus, thematic similarities and catchwords or phrases have been as important as chronological sequencing in ordering the particular collocations. The intent in each redactional procedure at this level is to offer a more complete and balanced presentation of the prophet's message than what might be provided by a random and atomistic recording of individual proclamations.

Level 3. The third level of redaction is that of establishing major tradition complexes, in which a variety of more primitive collocations, transmitted together, are now placed into a normative association with one another. Claus Rietzschl has done this for Jeremiah. He has identified six major tradition complexes in Jeremiah 1–24, as follows: chapters 1–6, chapters 7–10, chapters 11–13, chapters 14–17, chapters 18–20, and chapters 21–24.[5] Examples from Ezekiel might be the collection of oracles against Judah's near neighbors in chapter 25, the collection of oracles against Tyre-Sidon in chapters 26–28, and the collection of oracles against Egypt in chapters 29–32.

It need hardly be said that in this process secondary material has been integrated into the received text. These might be authentic words of the prophet or they might be redactional, but both become authoritative through combination; together they shape the major tradition complexes that together preserve what is now accepted as a given prophet's message.

Level 4. A fourth level of redaction, which may in special passages actually have occurred prior to that of Level 3, is that of ideological expansion and/or alteration prior to definitive editing (Level 5). Here we would place all new oracular materials within the prophetic books that were recorded expressly for the purpose of supplementing pre-existent units and complexes. The new units as such may have been drawn from primary materials or from earlier redactional units, as the case may be.

One random example may suggest the redactional activity that is widespread at this level throughout the prophetic collection. The account of divine judgment on Jaazaniah and Pelatiah in Ezekiel 11:1-3 expands the description of Yahweh's glory departing from the temple in the original verses of Ezekiel 8-11. This occurred prior to the formation of the collection of oracles against Israel in chapters 1–24 and certainly before the definitive editing of the book as a whole.

The essential aim of redaction at this level is apologetic. The new materials may have been drawn from published or unpublished sources, authentic or inauthentic. In the latter case, they are the free composition of a disciple/redactor endeavoring to contemporize the prophetic message for a new generation. In some instances, the underlying text is nullified or even contradicted in the light of its apparent nonfulfillment; otherwise, the purpose may simply be to make room for supplemental or superseding revelatory insights.

Level 5. The fifth level of redaction is that of definitive editing, consisting primarily of topical arrangement and appropriate prefacing. We clearly see the results in the superscriptions to the prophetic books[6] and in the gathering of three special types of oracular material; viz., judgment oracles against Israel, judgment oracles against the nations, and salvation oracles for Israel, to establish the main contours of the books Jeremiah (LXX), Ezekiel, and Zephaniah.

In some instances this type of editing occurred in stages. For example, Isaiah 1–35 must have received normative editorial shaping prior to the second editing that was designed to include the new blocks of material found in chapters 36–39 and chapters 40–66.[7] In the case of Jeremiah, some editorial reshaping occurred late enough to allow Jeremiah's collection of foreign oracles to be moved from the normative intermediate location, as seen in the LXX arrangement, to a final position in the proto-Masoretic text.

The intent of redaction at this level is to present a complete and ordered corpus of materials ascribable to a given prophet.

Level 6. A sixth level of redactional activity is similar in technique to that of Level 4, following rather than preceding definitive editing, which in most instances did not preclude the possible addition of still more new material. There can be little expectation of discovering authentic material at this late level. Examples of this very late type of redactional expansion may readily be identified in the considerable number of non-Septuagintal expansions within the prophetic collection, particularly in Jeremiah and Ezekiel. The intent of this very late supplementation would have been to reinterpret still further the divine nature and purpose in the light of altered conditions in late postexilic Judaism.

II. The Canonization Process

The complex redactional activity that proceeded at one of the six levels described was the motor by which the tradition development of the prophetic literature was driven. This activity was regularly motivated by internal forces, i.e., from within the spiritual fellowship (a prophetic school, a historically determined political-social group, or an ideological movement) that had accepted the responsibility of preserving and interpreting units of cherished material passed down from a particular prophet or from the prophets as a group. This was a dynamic—if not to say, irrepressible—process of incremental expansion.

From the first level of redaction to the last, the eschatological hope of Israel was constantly being broadened. This did not end when the individual books received their final expansion, but only when the concept of canonization had put a stop to the possibility of further internal growth. After this the *traditum* of biblical revelation became subject to one or another *traditio* of exegetical interpretation.

It is understandable that there could be no further occurrence of redactional expansion, once canonization had occurred. We need to be very self-conscious in defining what canonization actually was, carefully avoiding several recent attempts to blur the distinction between "inner-scriptural" and "extra-scriptural" interpretation. On the one hand, we are not to think of a formal declaration or determination, such as those made by the Pharisees at Jamnia or the creedal formulations of the early Church. These were actually no more than the ratification and clarification of something long before essentially determined, though now with a strongly apologetic aim. On the other hand, we are not willing to speak of redactionally expanding tradition as a process contiguous with the process of canonization or to blur the essential discontinuity between precanonical refocusing and postcanonical exegesis.

Among contemporary scholars, Brevard S. Childs has been the most active champion of the view that the ultimate "canonical" message of a particular biblical book might possess greater importance than the ideas coming to expression at individual stages in the growth of the book.[8] Childs has offered, to be sure, an admirable and necessary corrective to the once-dominant scholarly ideology that saw value and authority only in the "authentic" words of the biblical writers. As a skilled practitioner of historical and literary criticism, Childs is able to identify and appreciate the biblical word at every stage and for every circumstance. Yet he does refer to "canonization" as implicit throughout the entire process of tradition development; i.e., as a goal or ideal toward which all preliminary literary development was progressing, up to the final stage when nothing more was—or could be—added.

We must insist, on our part, that nothing was implicit or in any way predetermined in the way Scripture developed toward its final, canonical form—historical or theological. We need to take the adventitiousness of the historical process far more radically than Childs seems to do. There is in fact no historical necessity whatever in what the redactors of the prophetic tradition have created. The new images of the future that inspired them were nothing else than intuitive responses to the pressures and opportunities produced by the specific circumstances of their special times. If history had been otherwise, they would have written otherwise than they did.

We may discern three specific factors governing redactional expansion of the prophetic message: (1) their own ideology and spiritual preparation; (2) the naive belief that they were authentically saying what the original prophets might have said, or would have said, under altered conditions; and (3) the new situation or situations in which they and their people found themselves. The redactors of the prophetic collection were themselves mentally and spiritually conditioned by the very traditions they were expanding. They were anything but ingenuous in their attempt to write as they believed the original prophet in whose name they wrote would have written, given their circumstances and responsibilities. But it was above all the historical particularities of their special times and situations that were forcing—and enabling—them to write as they wrote.

To be sure, what we know as canonization might have been inevitable in the sense that what is dynamically expanding will, in the end, need to be closed off, once the forces empowering it have faded away. Many scholars are of the opinion that the drying up of prophetic inspiration is what brought prophetic tradition-development to its end, but this is to state the obvious. The question remains, "What made prophetic inspiration dry up?" There must have been historical forces at work, known or unknown. The point is that prophecy did not have to end where it ended, except only through the exigencies of particular historical forces. Our surmise is that prophecy ceased in Israel when it had become more a threat than a help to the increasingly institutionalized, i.e., nomistic, community.

A group of contemporary scholars that includes James A. Sanders occupies different ground than Childs in their virtual equation of precanonical tradition-development with canonization, and it is this that we object

to even more than against Childs's minimalizing of historical adventitiousness. To equate inner-scriptural and extra-scriptural development confuses
a process of unrestrained creativity with a subsequent process of institution-
ally bound rationalizing.

Sanders has developed what he calls a method of "comparative midrash," in which he places inner-scriptural and extra-scriptural tradition development on essentially the same basis.[9] Certain other scholars, such as
Isaac Seeligmann, have compounded this confusion by identifying inner-
scriptural expansion as "midrash," refusing to distinguish it from the rabbinical method usually referred to by the name "midrash."[10] It is to be
noted that in *Biblical Interpretation in Ancient Israel,* Michael Fishbane shows
commendable caution over against this blurring of distinctions by speaking
of distinct types or tendencies of inner-biblical "exegesis" ("legal," "ag-
gadic," and "mantic"), expressly rejecting the term "midrash" as a term
to be applied to inner-biblical expansion.

There is little opportunity within the compass of this essay to enter more
fully into the debate about canon and midrash, but one should pay attention to Magne Saebø's helpful analysis of canonization in his recent study
"Vom «Zusammen-Denken» zum Kanon."[11] Saebø explains canonization
as the endstage of a process in which the late postexilic Jewish community's
consensus ("Zusammen-Denken"), based on essential heuristic principles
that were then dominant in that community, came to be superimposed upon
the individual books that had been drawn together as sacrosanct and
authoritative Scripture. At this stage no further free expansion was allowed;
on the contrary, the application of this type of interpretive pressure began
to narrow and refine the stock of acceptable Jewish viewpoints. Elements
that were now disparate with the community's most essential beliefs were
not directly censored or removed from Scripture; they were simply brought
into a condition of relative innocuousness through rearrangement and occasional corrective comment.

Though further examples could have been cited, Saebø offers two that
are especially illuminating: (1) the "second epilogue" to *Qoheleth* (Eccl
12:12-14), which places all the rather alarming statements of the book (especially 11:9's espousal of a belief that is actually forbidden in Num 15:39)
under its concluding nomistic ban; and (2) the prepositioning of the nomistic
first Psalm as a guide to understanding the already completed Psalter. He
emphasizes that normalizing expansions and tendentious rearrangements
of this type did not develop naturally in the traditioning process, but were
superimposed from without.

As Saebø explains, Scripture was now being compared with Scripture. Viewpoints that had become offensive, or at least suspect, to the community were deprived of their appeal by the assertion of the viewpoint that had now become normative and essential. As has been said, this occurred at a juncture beyond all the redactional levels that we have described. It assumes not only that each book had now reached its "final" form and had been subjected to definitive editing, but that certain books, groups of books, or sections within books were relativized by the superior authority that had been given to certain other books, in particular the Torah.[12]

Saebø is certainly justified in his insistence that canonization did not come about mysteriously or arbitrarily, as some scholars have suggested, but entirely as a result of community consensus. This is precisely what made canonization so radically different from free tradition-development through the dynamic process of redactional expansion. No longer were individuals or groups allowed the liberty to add to what had already been laid down. It was now a matter of closing off the tradition, of subjecting the deposit of a dynamic inspirational process to the final verdict of community opinion.

There were three distinct elements within this canonization process: (1) restricting the content of Scripture and establishing the arrangement of the individual books, (2) establishing a standard text by weeding out variant readings, and (3) superimposing a normalizing viewpoint by the techniques that Saebø has described.

These three factors effectively brought the dynamic expansion of Scripture to an end. Interpretation and reinterpretation could henceforth come about only through one or another form of exegesis, including the midrashic method of the rabbis and the apologetic methodologies of the early Church.[13]

III. Conclusion

We understand, then, why there could have been no redactional level beyond the six that we have described. This is clearly seen in a comparison of the intentionalities of the six redactional levels that we have defined with that of canonization:

Level 1: to record the authoritative "words" of an individual prophet for a wider audience, as well as for posterity (cf. Isa 8:16, Jer 36:32);

Level 2: to offer a more complete and balanced presentation of the prophet's message;

Level 3:   to provide interpretive perspectives for extended blocks of material ascribed to the prophet;

Level 4:   to contemporize individual prophetic messages for a new generation by the introduction of additional revelatory insights, thereby extending, reinterpreting or superseding traditional images;

Level 5:   to present a relatively complete and ordered corpus of materials ascribable to a given prophet;

Level 6:   to reinterpret the prophetic message still further for a new age.

At all these levels there was an irrepressible dynamic development toward more pertinent appropriations of revelation; the tendency was to include as much as possible. On the contrary, the intent of canonization was to neutralize troublesome variants by stabilizing the form and content of a completed and sacrosanct Holy Scripture.

We should not lose sight of the scribal emendation that was applied to the actual text of Scripture. Some of this occurred along with the redactional process, but most of it was applied to an already canonized Scripture. This was not merely a matter of erudition applied to a close study of the scriptural text, for it too had an apologetic purpose. This is especially clear with regard to such elements as the *tiqune sopherim,* the pre-Masoretic emendations of the scribes, whose general aim is to remove scandalous readings like the statement that Job's wife urged him to "curse" God (Job 2:9). The scribes also made casual, nontendential emendations in order to rectify real and imaginary mistakes in the text out of a misguided impulse to correct one text through comparison with another, often compounding errors in the process. This too was an essentially apologetic procedure because these scribes were not merely acting in their capacity as learned scholars, but were self-consciously engaged in a pious enterprise to preserve what they thought to be a more "perfect" form of Scripture.

Especially between Protestants and Catholics, there has been debate and conflict over the question of Scripture *versus* tradition. George Tavard has perhaps done more than any other contemporary scholar to examine this polarity with insight, judiciousness, and creativity. It is this writer's fond hope that all those who desire to see further progress toward clarification on this issue may be willing, now more than ever, to examine Scripture historically and critically, examining it afresh for what it conceals to the impatient eye concerning the true relationship between tradition and canon.

The sum of this discussion is that an incremental redaction was the potent vehicle for tradition development up to the point at which the canonizing process brought it to an end. Prophetic redaction expands the prophetic consciousness; it stands for undiminished creativity in a community of charismatic individuals reinterpreting and reapplying the messages of the original prophets. Canonization is just the opposite; it represents the end of redactional activity, and at the same time the end of tradition development within Scripture. This is the sign that an institutionalized religious community has developed an orthodox ideology accompanied by magisterial control, discouraging further outbursts of enthusiasm that might seem to threaten the institution and challenge the ideology.

Notes

[1]Complete title: "From Old Revelation to New. A Tradition-historical and Redaction-critical Study of Temporal Transitions in Prophetic Tradition."

[2]Oxford: Oxford University Press, 1985.

[3]Cf. N. Perrin, *What is Redaction Criticism?* (Philadelphia: Fortress Press, 1969). The term is especially applicable to the Gospels because the so-called "Evangelists" were essentially redactors who engaged in collecting, reshaping, and amplifying blocks of source material, adding their own programmatic comments at strategic positions. Though the prophets of Israel were directly productive at the primitive levels, their original words have regularly been expanded and in some cases altered by redactors responsible for perpetuating their tradition.

[4]On the special motives that led to the recording to prophetic material, see the illuminating discussion in R. E. Clements, "Prophecy as Literature: a Reappraisal," *The Hermeneutical Quest.* Essays in Honor of James Luther Mays on His Sixty-fifth Birthday, ed. D. G. Miller (Allison Park: Pickwick, 1986) 59–76; R. E. Clements, "Patterns in the Prophetic Canon," ed. G. W. Coats and B. O. Long, *Canon and Authority* (Philadelphia: Fortress Press, 1977) 42–55.

[5]Claus Rietzschl, *Das Problem der Urrolle. Ein Beitrag zur Redaktionsgeschichte des Jeremiabuches* (Gütersloh: Mohn, 1966).

[6]Cf. G. W. Tucker, "Prophetic Superscriptions and the Growth of the Canon," *Canon and Authority,* 56–70.

[7]Cf. Marvin A. Sweeney, *Isaiah 1–4 and the Post-Exilic Understanding of the Isaianic Tradition,* Beihefte zur Zeitschrift für die alttestamentliche Wissenschaft 171 (Berlin-New York: de Gruyter, 1988) 11–25.

[8]*Biblical Theology in Crisis* (Philadelphia: Westminster, 1970) 97–122; "The Old Testament as Scripture in the Church," *Concordia Theological Monthly* 43 (1972) 709–22; "The Exegetical Significance of Canon for the Study of the Old Testament," *Congress Volume: Göttingen, 1977,* Supplements to Vetus Testamentum 29 (Leiden: Brill, 1978) 66–80; *Introduction to the Old Testament as Scripture* (Philadelphia: Fortress Press, 1979); *Old Testament Theology in a Canonical Context* (Philadelphia: Fortress Press, 1985).

[9]*Torah and Canon* (Philadelphia: Fortress Press, 1972); *Canon and Community. A Guide to Canonical Criticism* (Philadelphia: Fortress Press, 1984); "Text and Canon. Concepts and Method," *Journal of Biblical Literature* 88 (1979) 5–29. "Comparative midrash" places all tradition development, inner-scriptural as well as extra-scriptural, on essentially the same basis.

[10]Cf. Seeligmann, "Voraussetzungen der Midraschexegese," *Congress Volume. Copenhagen, 1953,* Supplements to Vetus Testamentum 1 (Leiden: Brill, 1953) 150–81. Properly speak-

ing, midrash is a "literature about a literature" (A. G. Wright, *The Literary Genre Midrash* [Staten Island, N.Y.: Alba House, 1967] 74). Although there are pre-rabbinical examples of midrash, there are none within the Old Testament apart from the two examples of what I call "proto-midrash" in 1 Chronicles 5:1-2 and 17:23-24 (De Vries, *1 and 2 Chronicles,* Forms of the Old Testament Literature 11 [Grand Rapids: Eerdmans, 1989] 54–56, 212–15).

[11]"Zum Problem des biblischen Kanons," *Jahrbuch für Biblische Theologie* 3 (Neukirchen: Neukirchener Verlag, 1988) 115–33.

[12]The fact that the Pentateuch, which contains approximately as much narrative as law, came now to be referred to as the Torah (i.e., "ritual instruction") reveals that the law as interpreted and applied within the late postexilic community had become the authoritative point of reference from which the entire biblical story was to be judged.

[13]On the development of the concept of a scriptural canon, see further P. R. Ackroyd, "The Open Canon," *Studies in the Religious Tradition of the Old Testament* (London: SCM, 1987) 208–24. Particularly useful is Ackroyd's distinction between (1) the historic canon, (2) the canon within the canon—sections chosen in various traditions of especially authoritative value, and (3) the "open canon"—the influence of various sections of Scripture upon the interpretation of others.

Georges H. Tavard Bibliography

Compiled by Marc R. Alexander

BOOKS

L'Angoisse de l'unité. Paris: Bonne Presse, 1952.

A la rencontre du Protestantisme. Paris: Le Centurion, 1954.

> English: *The Catholic Approach to Protestantism.* New York: Harper, 1955.

Transiency and Permanence: The Nature of Theology According to St. Bonaventure. Theology Series, 4. St. Bonaventure, N.Y.: Franciscan Institute Publications, 1954.

Le Protestantisme. Je sais—Je crois, 137. Paris: Librairie Arthème Fayard, 1958.

> English: *Protestantism.* Translated by Rachel Attwater. Faith and Facts, 137. London: Burns & Oates, 1959; New York: Hawthorn Books, 1959; Toronto: McClelland and Stewart, 1959.
>
> Italian: *Il Protestantesimo.* Translated by Maria Teresa Garutti. Enciclopedia Cattolica dell'Uomo d'Oggi, 137. Catania: Edizioni Paoline, 1959.
>
> English version has an additional chapter on Anglicanism.

Holy Writ or Holy Church: The Crisis of the Protestant Reformation. New York: Harper & Row, 1959.

> Reprint: Westport, Conn.: Greenwood Press, 1978.
>
> French: *Écriture ou Église? La crise de la Réforme.* Translated by C. Tunmer. Unam Sanctam, 42. Paris: Les Éditions du Cerf, 1963.

The Church, the Layman, and the Modern World. New York: Macmillan, 1959.

Petite histoire du mouvement oecuménique. Paris: Éditions Fleurus, 1960.

> English: *Two Centuries of Ecumenism: The Search for Unity.* Translated by Royce W. Hughes. New York: New American Library of World Literature, 1962; Notre Dame, Ind.: Fides Publishers Association, 1960.
>
> Portuguese: *Ecumenismo: História e Perspectivas Actuais.* Cucujães: Editorial Missões, 1962.
>
> German: *Geschichte der ökumenischen Bewegung.* Translated by Ludwig Bläser. Mainz: Matthias-Grünewald-Verlag, 1964.

Protestant Hopes and the Catholic Responsibility. Notre Dame, Ind.: Fides Publishers, 1960. 2nd edition, enlarged, 1964.

Paul Tillich and the Christian Message. New York: Charles Scribner's Sons, 1962.
> French: *Initiation à Paul Tillich: une théologie moderne.* Paris: Le Centurion, 1968.

The Quest for Catholicity: A Study in Anglicanism. New York: Herder and Herder, 1964.
> French: *La poursuite de la Catholicité: Étude sur la pensée anglicane.* Unam Sanctam, 53. Paris: Les Éditions du Cerf, 1965.

The Church Tomorrow. New York: Herder and Herder, 1965.

Dogmatic Constitution on Divine Revelation of Vatican II· Commentary and Translation. London: Darton, Longman and Todd, 1966.
> Also: Glen Rock, N.J.: Paulist Fathers, 1966.
> Commentary only also published as "Commentary on *De Revelatione.*" *Journal of Ecumenical Studies* 3 (1966) 1–35.

Les Catholiques américains. Paris: Éditions du Centurion, 1966.
> English: *Catholicism U.S.A.* Translated by Theodore DuBois. New York: Newman Press, 1969.

The Pilgrim Church. New York: Herder and Herder, 1967.

With André Caquot and Johann Michl. *Die Engel.* Handbuch der Dogmengeschichte, II/2b. Freiburg: Herder, 1968.
> French: *Les Anges.* Translated by Maurice Lefèvre. Histoire des dogmes, II/2b. Paris: Les Éditions du Cerf, 1971.
> Spanish: *Los ángeles.* Translated by Manuel Pozo. Historia de los dogmas, II/2b. Madrid: Editorial Católica, 1973.

Meditation on the Word: Perspectives for a Renewed Theology. New York: Paulist Press, 1968.

La tradition au XVIIe siècle en France et en Angleterre. Paris: Les Éditions du Cerf, 1969.
> Second part in English, *The Seventeenth-Century Tradition: A Study in Recusant Thought* (1978).

La religion à l'épreuve des idées modernes. Paris: Le Centurion, 1970.
> The English original, *The Survival of Religion,* was given at the University of Nottingham as The Firth Lectures for 1967.

Woman in Christian Tradition. Notre Dame, Ind.: University of Notre Dame Press, 1973.

La théologie parmi les sciences humaines: de la méthode en théologie. Le point théologique, 15. Paris: Éditions Beauchesne, 1975.

Wasser, Henri. *La septième vague: Poèmes.* Paris: St. Germain-des-Prés, 1976. Under penname.

The Inner Life: Foundations of Christian Mysticism. New York: Paulist Press, 1976.

A Way of Love. New York: Orbis, 1977.

L'expérience de Jean-Martin Moye: Mystique et mission. Bibliothèque de Spiritualité, 12. Paris: Éditions Beauchesne, 1978.

The Seventeenth-Century Tradition: A Study in Recusant Thought. Studies in the History of Christian Thought, 16. Leiden: E. J. Brill, 1978.

> This is the English version of the second part of *La tradition au XVIIe siècle en France et en Angleterre* (1969). The last chapter is entirely new.

Wasser, Henri. *Song for Avalokita.* Ardmore, Pa.: Dorrance, 1979. Under penname.

_____. *Le silence d'une demi-heure.* Paris: St. Germain-des-Prés, 1980. Under penname.

With Joseph A. Burgess. *Studies for Lutheran/Catholic Dialogue.* Minneapolis: Augsburg Publishing House, 1980.

The Weight of God: The Spiritual Doctrine of Emmanuel d'Alzon. Rome: Maison générali ce, 1980.

> Enlarged French edition: *Le Poids de Dieu. La Spiritualité Trinitaire d'Emmanuel d'Alzon.* Paris: Quantics, 1982.

The Vision of the Trinity. Washington: University Press of America, 1981.

> French: *La Vision de la Trinité.* Paris: Les Éditions du Cerf; Montréal: Les Éditions Bellarmin, 1989.

> Italian edition in process of translation.

Images of the Christ: An Enquiry into Christology. Washington: University Press of America, 1982.

A Theology for Ministry. Theology and Life Series, 6. Wilmington: Michael Glazier, 1983.

Justification: An Ecumenical Study. New York: Paulist Press, 1983.

With Mark Edwards. *Luther: A Reformer for the Churches. An Ecumenical Study Guide.* Philadelphia: Fortress Press and New York: Paulist Press, 1983.

Lorsque Dieu fait tout: La doctrine spirituelle du bienheureux Jean-Martin Moye. Paris: Les Éditions du Cerf, 1984.

Wasser, Henri. *Sentiers de la demeure.* Paris: St. Germain-des-Prés, 1984. Under penname.

Jean de la Croix, poète mystique. Paris: Les Éditions du Cerf, 1987.

> English: *Poetry and Contemplation in St. John of the Cross.* Athens, Ohio: Ohio University Press, 1988.

Les jardins de Saint Augustin: Lecture des "Confessions." Montréal: Les Éditions Bellarmin, 1988.

Satan. L'horizon du croyant, 5. Paris: Desclée and Ottawa, Ontario: Novalis, 1988.

> Italian: *Satana.* Translated by Francesco Caponi. Milano: Edizioni Paoline, 1990.

The Forthbringer of God: St. Bonaventure on the Virgin Mary. Chicago: Franciscan Herald Press, 1989.

A Review of Anglican Orders: The Problem and the Solution. Theology and Life Series, 31. Collegeville: A Michael Glazier Book by The Liturgical Press, 1990.

Juana Inés de la Cruz and the Theology of Beauty: The First Mexican Theology. Notre Dame, Ind.: University of Notre Dame Press, 1991.

La Trinité. Collection Bref, 40. Paris: Les Éditions du Cerf, 1991.

Le Père D'Alzon et la Croix de Jésus: Les Lettres aux Adoratrices. Rome: Pères Assomptionnistes, Maison généralice, January 1992.

The Church, Community of Salvation: An Ecumenical Ecclesiology. New Theology Series, 1. Collegeville: A Michael Glazier Book by The Liturgical Press, 1992.

ARTICLES IN BOOKS, DICTIONARIES, ENCYCLOPEDIAS, AND JOURNALS

"La théologie d'après le Bréviloque de saint Bonaventure." *L'Année théologique* 10 (1949) 201–14.

"The Assumptionists and the Work for Christian Unity." *The Eastern Churches Quarterly* 8 (1949–1950) 482–94.

"The Light of God in the Theology of St. Bonaventure." *The Eastern Churches Quarterly* 8 (1949–1950) 407–17.

"St. Bonaventure's Disputed Questions *De Theologia.*" *Recherches de théologie ancienne et médiévale* 17 (1950) 187–236.

"The Mystery of the Holy Spirit." *The Downside Review* 68 (1950) 255–70.

"Riflessioni sull'attitudine dei cattolici che avvicinano i cristiani separati." *Unitas* 5 (July–September 1950) 218–23. According to Tavard, only the Italian version is correct. The other editions have numerous unauthorized changes, including the title of the French version.

> French: "Les oeuvres d'union en Angleterre: état actuel projets." *Unitas* (October–December 1950) 195–98.

> English: "Reflections on the Catholic Approach to Separated Christians." *Unitas* (January–March 1951) 9–12.

"A Great Expectation." *Westminster Cathedral Chronicle* 45, 4 (1951) 74–75.

"On a Misreading of St. Bonaventure's Doctrine on Creation." *The Downside Review* 69 (1951) 276–88.

"Où va l'Ecclésiologie anglicane?" *L'Année théologique* 12 (1951) 63–70.

"Théologie et présence de Dieu: d'après saint Bonaventure." *L'Année théologique* 12 (1951) 321–34.

"Théologie et présence de Dieu: les voies de l'union mystique d'après un opuscule de saint Bonaventure." *L'Année théologique* 12 (1951) 233–38.

Unsigned. "Actualités Oecuméniques." *La Documentation Catholique* 49 (1952) 1253–72.

"Catholiques et protestants en Amérique latine." *La Documentation Catholique* 49 (1952) 1645–51.

"Contrats et conflits collectifs du travail. V.-La grève devant la morale." *La Documentation Catholique* 49 (1952) 365–69.

"Épiscopat et Églises libres." *La Documentation Catholique* 49 (1952) 883–88.

"La structure de l'expérience fruitive. Analyse de quelques textes de S. Bonaventure." *Études franciscaines* 3 (1952) 205–11.

"Note sur le «Groupe de Hilversum»." *La Documentation Catholique* 49 (1952) 1251–52.

"Prions pour l'unité de l'Église. La part des théologiens et la part des fidèles." *Prêtre et Apôtre* 398 (January 15, 1952) 1–2.

"Un sermon du Dr Fisher, archevêque du Cantorbéry." *La Documentation Catholique* 49 (1952) 689–92.

"The Unconditional Concern: The Theology of Paul Tillich." *Thought* 28 (1953) 234–46.

> Utilized in chapter 2 of *Paul Tillich and the Christian Message* (1962).

"Peace Among Christians." *Integrity* 7, 10 (July 1953) 33–37.

"The Pentecostal Life." *Integrity* 8, 2 (November 1953) 7–11.

"L'esprit oecuménique dans l'Evangile." *Unitas* 6, 12 (November–December 1953) 125–26.

"Some Remarks on the Liturgy as Tradition." *Worship* 28 (1953–1954) 466–71.

"Holy Church or Holy Writ: A Dilemma of the Fourteenth Century." *Church History* 23 (1954) 195–206.

> Utilized in chapter 3 of *Holy Writ or Holy Church* (1959).

"Mercy for Sinners." *Integrity* 8, 9 (June 1954) 11–17.

"Scripture, Tradition and History." *The Downside Review* 72 (1954) 232–44.

"The Form of the Servant." *The Third Hour* (1954) 60–62.

"Conversion of the Nations." *Integrity* 9, 3 (December 1954) 15–22.

"Damascus and the Present Situation." *Integrity* 8, 11 (August 1954) 20–25.

> Also in *The Church, the Layman and the Modern World* (1959) as chapter 6.

Unsigned. "A Roman Catholic Looks at Evanston." *The Living Church* (September 19, 1954) 10, 13.

————. "Ethical Issues at Evanston." *The Christian Century* (October 1954) 1265–67. Written by Tavard for a German reporter.

"Christianity and Israel: Is the Church Schismatic?" *The Downside Review* 73 (1954–1955) 347–58.

"De Oosterse kerken in de Verenigde Staten." *Het Christelijk Oosten en Hereniging* 7 (1954–1955) 57–72.

"Het Kerkbegrip te Evanston." *Het Christelijk Oosten en Hereniging* 7 (1954–1955) 109–28.

"A Forgotten Theology of Inspiration: Nikolaus Ellenbog's Refutation of *Scriptura Sola.*" *Franciscan Studies* 15 (1955) 106–22.

"L'Assemblée d'Evanston." *Lumière et vie* 19 (1955) 110–16.

"Le statut prospectif de la théologie bonaventurienne." *Revue des études augustiniennes* 1 (1955) 251–63.

"Theology in a Technological Age." *Integrity* 10, 2 (November 1955) 7–15.

> Also in *The Church, the Layman and the Modern World* (1959) as chapter 3.

"Conversion from Catholicism." *Integrity* 9, 12 (September 1955) 24–32.

"Un point de vue catholique sur l'ecclésiologie d'Evanston." *Foi et vie* 53 (January–February 1955) 54–64.

"Oecumenische Kroniek." *Het Christelijk Oosten en Hereniging* 8 (1955–1956) 265–71.

Signed Émile Gabel. "Évasion des prisonniers." *Catholicisme.* Paris: Letouzey et Ané, 1956. 4:773–75. Written by Tavard for Gabel.

————. "Franc-tireurs." *Catholicisme.* Paris: Letouzey et Ané, 1956. 4:1510–12. Written by Tavard for Gabel.

"Protestantism: Spirit vs. System." *Commonweal* 65 (1956) 281–83.

"The Transfiguration of Thought: Simone Weil's Dialectic." *The Third Hour* (1956) 52–56.

"Sacrament of the Sick." *Integrity* 10, 6 (March 1956) 25–33.

"From Free Choice to Freedom." *Integrity* 10, 5 (February 1956) 9–17.

    Also in *The Church, the Layman and the Modern World* (1959) as chapter 4.

"The Liturgical Event." *Worship* 31 (1956–1957) 319–27.

"Christianity and Israel: How Did Christ Fulfill the Law?" *The Downside Review* 75 (1957) 55–68.

"Christianity and the Philosophies of Existence." *Theological Studies* 18 (1957) 1–16.

"El Catolicismo en los Estados Unidos." *Arbor* 36 (1957) 59–76.

"The Catholic Reform in the Sixteenth Century." *Church History* 26 (1957) 275–88.

"Kroniek van de Verenigde Staten." *Het Christelijk Oosten en Hereniging* 10 (1957–1958) 211–14.

"Le Protestantisme." *Panorama* (January 1958) 20–24.

"The Coming Council." *Jubilee* 6, 12 (April 1958–1959) 8–15.

"Catholicity and Non-Catholic Christians." *The Downside Review* 77 (1959) 205–16.

"La thème de la Cité de Dieu dans le protestantisme américain." *Revue des études augustiniennes* 5 (1959) 207–21.

"Opening the Windows." *Apostolic Perspectives* 4 (1959) 17–18.

"The Intellect and the Spiritual Life." *Spiritual Life* 5 (1959) 179–92.

"The Need for Roots." *Sponsa Regis* 31 (1959) 99–106.

"Your Job in Christian Unity." *Ave Maria* (August 1959) 5–8.

"Catholic Views on Karl Barth." *The Christian Century* 76 (February 1959) 132–33.

"The Riddle of Roman Catholicism: Review Article." *Journal of Religion* 40 (1960) 43–46.

"Le Monde Luthérien." *Eaux-Vives* 205 (February 1960) 45–47.

"The Laity in the Ecumenical Movement." *The Monitor* (November 1960).

"Liturgical Themes in Recent Protestant Books." *Worship* 35 (1960–1961) 617–21.

"The Eucharist in Protestantism." *Worship* 35 (1960–1961) 184–90.

"Tradition and Scripture." *Worship* 35 (1960–1961) 375–81.

"The Eucharist." *Jubilee* 8, 2 (June 1960–1961) 8–11.

"Is *Tradition* a Problem for Catholics?" *Union Seminary Quarterly Review* 16 (1961) 375–84.

"The Recovery of an Organic Notion of Tradition." *The Liturgy and Unity in Christ.* North American Liturgical Week Proceedings 1960, 21 (1961) 122–29.

"The Role of the Laity in the Ecumenical Movement." *Crosslight* (Summer 1961) 44–52.

"Anglican Piety." *Worship* 36 (1961–1962) 496–500.

"Ecumenism Today." *Jubilee* 9, 9 (January 1961–1962) 21–25.

"Le principe protestant et le système théologique de Paul Tillich." *Revue des sciences philosophiques et théologiques* 46 (1962) 242–53.

"New Delhi and Unity." *Perspectives* 7 (1962) 96–98, 103.

"The Authority of Scripture and Tradition." *Problems of Authority: An Anglo-French Symposium.* Edited by J. M. Todd. London: Darton, Longman, and Todd, 1962. 27–42.

> French: "'L'Autorité de l'Écriture et la Tradition." *Problèmes de l'autorité. Un colloque Anglo-Français.* Unam Sanctam, 38. Paris: Les Éditions du Cerf, 1962. 39–58.

> Italian: "L'autorità della Scrittura e della Tradizione." *Problemi dell'autorità.* Biblioteca di cultura religiosi, 2a ser, 77. Roma: Edizioni Paoline, 1964. 49–74.

> German: *Probleme der Autorität.* Düsseldorf: Patmos-Verlag, 1967.

"The Face We Give the Church; Sermon Excerpts." *Catholic Messenger* 80 (1962) 10.

"The Holy Tradition." *Dialogue for Reunion: The Catholic Premises.* Edited by Leonard Swidler. New York: Herder and Herder, 1962. 54–88.

"Tradition in Early Post-Tridentine Theology." *Theological Studies* 23 (1962) 377–405.

"Vatican II: The End of the Counter Reformation." *Catholic Messenger* 80 (1962) 5–6.

"The Ecumenical Movement in Contemporary Catholicism." *The Ecumenical Dialogue at Cornell University.* Ithaca: Cornell United Religious Work, December 1962. 95–108.

"The Scope of Christian Culture." *The Christian Scholar* (Summer 1962) 118–29.

"*Dienstbaarheid* in New Delhi." *Het Christelijk Oosten en Hereniging* 15 (1962–1963) 52–72.

"Other Horizons: Reformed Piety." *Worship* 37 (1962–1963) 406–11.

"Reunion and Liturgy." *Worship* 37 (1962–1963) 69–74.

"Tillich's Christology." *Jubilee* 10, 2 (June 1962–1963) 16–19.

"Spirit and the Church." *Dialog* 1 (Summer 1962) 27–33.

And Paul Tillich. *Ecumenical Perspectives: Catholic & Ecumenical Perspectives: Protestant.* Ecumenical Exchange, 1. Kansas City: Kansas City Newman Foundation, 1963.

> Reprinted as "An Ecumenical Dialogue." *Dublin Review* 239 (1965) 162–82.

Theology of the Word. Doctrinal Pamphlet Series. Glen Rock, N.J.: Paulist Press, 1963. Also included in *Meditation on the Word,* 15–38.

"Christianity in Encounter: A Lesson in Ecumenism." *The Current* 4, 2 (1963) 91–97.

"Christopher Davenport and the Problem of Tradition." *Theological Studies* 24 (1963) 278–90.

> Utilized in *La tradition au XVIIe siècle en France et en Angleterre* (1969) and *The Seventeenth Century Tradition. A Study in Recusant Thought* (1978).

"Irenic Dimensions of the Liturgical Movement." *The American Benedictine Review* 14 (1963) 175–77.

"Scripture and Tradition in Pastoral Perspective." *The Catholic World* 198 (1963) 14–20.

"The Council and the Reform of the Church." *Continuum* 1 (1963) 295–303.

"The Laity and Ecumenism." *Perspectives* 8 (1963) 4–8.

"The Problem of Tradition Today." *Ecumenist* 1 (1963) 33–36.

> Reprinted in *Ecumenical Theology Today.* Edited by Gregory Baum. Glen Rock, N.J.: Paulist Press, 1964, 18–27

"Theology in the Catholic College." *Commonweal* 78 (1963) 273–75.

> Replies and rejoinder in 78:455–57.

"The Liturgy of the Word." *Worship* 38 (1963–1964) 620–25.

"Desmitologización del NT." *Enciclopedie de la Biblia.* 6 volumes. Barcelona: Ediciones Garriga, 1963–1965. 2:874–77.

> Italian: "Smitizzazione del NT." *Enciclopedia della Bibbia.* 6 volumes. Torino-Leumann: Elle Di Ci, 1969–1971. 6:555–60.

"Exégesis protestante, Principios de la." *Enciclopedie de la Biblia.* 6 volumes. Barcelona: Ediciones Garriga, 1963–1969. 3:338–45.

> Italian: "Esegesi Protestane, Principi della." *Enciclopedia della Bibbia.* 6 volumes. Torino-Leumann: Elle Di Ci, 1969–1971. 3:71–78.

"The Unity We Need." *Thoughts for Meditation.* With other contributions by Emil Brunner and Jay Kaufman. Series No. 4. Charlotte: Marman Productions, 1963. 1–5.

"Ecumenical Perspectives: Catholic." *Journal of Ecumenical Studies* 1 (1964) 99–105.

"Paul Tillich's System." *Commonweal* 79 (1964) 566–68.

"Scripture and Tradition—Source or Sources." *Journal of Ecumenical Studies* 1 (1964) 445–59.

"Scripture and Tradition Among Seventeenth-Century Recusants." *Theological Studies* 25 (1964) 343–85.

> Utilized in *La tradition au XVIIe siècle en France et en Angleterre* (1969) and *The Seventeenth Century Tradition. A Study in Recusant Thought* (1978).

"The Council, the Press and Theology." *The Catholic World* 199 (1964) 337–44.

"Vocacion al Ecumenismo." *Dialogos de la Cristiandad.* Edited by Luis Romeu. Salamanca: Sigueme, 1964. 285–96.

"What Anglicans Mean by Catholicity . . . Is a New Approach Possible?" *The Lamp* (June 1964) 9, 26, 28.

"Het Probleem van de Traditie te Montreal." *Het Christelijk Oosten en Hereniging* 17 (1964–1965) 19–43.

"Christ as the Answer to Existential Anguish." *Paul Tillich in Catholic Thought.* Edited by T. A. O'Meara and C. D. Weisser. Dubuque: Priory Press, 1964. 224–36.

> Also: London: Darton, Longman & Todd, 1965.

> Reprinted in *The Christian Human Situation.* Winona: St. Mary's College Press, 1967. 22–35.

"Christology as Symbol." *Paul Tillich in Catholic Thought.* Edited by T. A. O'Meara and C. D. Weisser. Dubuque: Priory Press, 1964. 207–23.

> Also: London: Darton, Longman & Todd, 1965.

"The Protestant Principle and the Theological System of Paul Tillich." *Paul Tillich in Catholic Thought.* Edited by T. A. O'Meara and C. D. Weisser. Dubuque: Priory Press, 1964. 85–96.

> Also: London: Darton, Longman & Todd, 1965.

The People of God. Doctrinal Pamphlet Series. Glen Rock, N.J.: Paulist Press, 1965.

The Presence of God. Doctrinal Pamphlet Series. Glen Rock, N.J.: Paulist Press, 1965.

"Conditional Re-Baptism." *Journal of Ecumenical Studies* 2 (1965) 480–84.

"Freedom and Responsibility in the Religious Life." *Continuum* 2 (1965) 575–86.

"Monotheism." *Catholic Encyclopedia for School and Home.* New York: McGraw-Hill, 1965. 7:315–18.

"Polytheism." *Catholic Encyclopedia for School and Home.* New York: McGraw-Hill, 1965. 8:557–58.

"The Meaning of Scripture." *Scripture and Ecumenism: Protestant, Catholic, Orthodox and Jewish.* Edited by Leonard J. Swidler. Duquesne Studies Theological Series, 3. Pittsburgh: Duquesne University Press, 1965. 59–73.

"The Mystery of the Church in the Liturgical Constitution." *Worship* 39 (1965) 11–16.

> Also in *The Pilgrim Church* (1967) as chapter 7.

"Tradition." *Catholic Encyclopedia for School and Home.* New York: McGraw-Hill, 1965. 11:37–40.

"Women in the Church: A Theological Problem?" *Ecumenist* 4 (1965) 7–10.

> Reprinted in *Ecumenical Theology II.* Edited by Gregory Baum. New York: Paulist Press, 1967. 32–40.

"Doctrinal Development." *The Catholic World* 202 (1965–1966) 336–40. Part II of a three-article series.

> Also in the pamphlet *The Changing Church* (1966) as Part II.

"The Changing Church." *The Catholic World* 202 (1965–1966) 267–70. Part I of a three-article series.

> Also in the pamphlet *The Changing Church* (1966) as Part I.

The Changing Church. Doctrinal Pamphlet Series. Glen Rock, N.J.: Paulist Press, 1966.

"Commentary on *De Revelatione.*" *Journal of Ecumenical Studies* 3 (1966) 1–35.
    Also published with a translation of *De Revelatione* as *Dogmatic Constitution on Divine Revelation of Vatican II: Commentary and Translation* (1966).

"Evolution in Moral Theology." *The Catholic World* 203 (1966) 29–32. Part III of a three-article series.
    Also in the pamphlet *The Changing Church* (1966) as Part III.

"Tentative Approaches to a Mystique of Unity." *Journal of Ecumenical Studies* 3 (1966) 503–18.

"The Council's *Declaration* on Non-Christians." *Journal of Ecumenical Studies* 3 (1966) 160–66.

"Ecumenism of the Future." *Columbia* 46 (August 1966) 19–23.

"Pacifism and America." *The Sign* (August 1966) 16. Comments with other prominent people of the time.

"Alzon, Emmanuel D'." *New Catholic Encyclopedia*. Edited by The Catholic University of America. New York: McGraw-Hill, 1967. 1.362–63.

"Assumptionists." *New Catholic Encyclopedia*. Edited by The Catholic University of America. New York: McGraw-Hill, 1967. 1:975–76.

"Decree on Ecumenism: Commentary." *American Participation in the II Vatican Council*. Edited by Vincent A. Yzermans. New York: Sheed and Ward, 1967. 321–34.

"Protestantism." *New Catholic Encyclopedia*. Edited by The Catholic University of America. New York: McGraw-Hill, 1967. 11:891–99.

"The Function of the Minister in the Eucharistic Celebration. An Ecumenical Approach." *Journal of Ecumenical Studies* 4 (1967) 629–49.
    Utilized in chapter 5 of *A Theology for Ministry* (1983).

"The New Triumphalism." *Continuum* 5 (1967) 356–60.

"Putting First Principles First." *Theology Today* 24 (1967–1968) 232–33.

"Does the Protestant Ministry have Sacramental Significance?" *Continuum* 6 (1968) 260–69.

"Ecumenism and Religious Indifference." *Chicago Studies* 7 (1968) 201–12.

"Hans Küng's Church." *Continuum* 6 (1968) 106–11.
    German: "Option für das Ursprüngliche?" *Diskussion um Hans Küng "Die Kirche"*. Edited by Hermann Häring and Josef Nolte. Article translated by Karlhermann Bergner. Freiburg: Herder, 1971. 84–91.

"Scripture and Tradition." *Journal of Ecumenical Studies* 5 (1968) 308–25.

"Theses on Future Forms of Ministry." *Journal of Ecumenical Studies* 5 (1968) 726–29.
    Also in *Pro Veritate* (Johannesburg) 7 (1968) 9–10.
    Utilized in the conclusion of *A Theology for Ministry* (1983).

"The Non-encyclical on Birth Control." *Challenge* (September–October 1968) 18–24.
    Also published in *The National Catholic Reporter* 4 (1968) 7.

"Roman Catholic Theology and Recognition of Ministry." *Journal of Ecumenical Studies* 6 (1969) 623–28.
>Also in *Eucharist and Ministry*. Edited by P. C. Empie and T. A. Murphy. Lutherans and Catholics in Dialogue, IV. Washington and New York: U.S.A. National Committee of the Lutheran World Federation and the Bishops' Committee for Ecumenical and Interreligious Affairs, 1970. 301–05. Reprinted, Minneapolis: Augsburg Publishing House, 1979.

"The Depths of the Tradition." *Continuum* 7 (1969) 427–37.

"The Present Ecumenical Movement: A Personal View." *One in Christ* 5 (1969) 248–62.

"A Catholic Perspective." *Consultation on Church Union: A Catholic Perspective.* Washington: USCC Publications Office, 1970. 28–45.

"Ecumenical Dimensions: a New Hope and Vision of Unity." *The Pilgrim People: A Vision with Hope.* Edited by Joseph Papin. Villanova University Series, 4. Villanova: The Villanova University Press, 1970. 143–67.

"Ministri Vagantes." *Journal of Ecumenical Studies* 7 (1970) 777–79.

"Pluralism or Ecumenism." *One in Christ* 6 (1970) 123–34.

"Problems of a Wider Ecumenism." *Journal of Ecumenical Studies* 7 (1970) 522–25.

"The Exit of American Catholic Theologians." *Journal of Ecumenical Studies* 7 (1970) 310–13.

"Anglican Orders—Again!" *One in Christ* 7 (1971) 46–53.

"Aspects iconographiques du problème de la tradition." *Église et Théologie* 2 (1971) 309–20.
>Dutch: "Ikonografische aspecten van het traditieprobleem." *Het Christelijk Oosten en Hereniging* 23 (1971) 23–34.

" 'Hierarchia veritatum': A Preliminary Investigation." *Theological Studies* 32 (1971) 278–89.

"On Christians and Jews . . . and Moslems." *Journal of Ecumenical Studies* 8 (1971) 341–44.

"On Method and Ministry." *Journal of Ecumenical Studies* 8 (1971) 620–22.

"A Theological Approach to Ministerial Authority." *The Jurist* 32 (1972) 311–29.
>Utilized in chapter 6 of *A Theology for Ministry* (1983).

"Can the Ministry be Re-constructed?" *Transcendence and Immanence: Reconstruction in the Light of Process Thinking. Festschrift in Honour of Joseph Papin.* Edited by Joseph Armenti. St. Meinrad, Ind.: Abbey Press, 1972. Volume 1, 85–98.
>Corrected version utilized in chapter 4 of *A Theology for Ministry* (1983).

"The *Confrontation* Correspondence." *Journal of Ecumenical Studies* 9 (1972) 101–03.

"The Mythical Structure of the Church." *Journal of Ecumenical Studies* 9 (1972) 352–55.

"La Tradición y su problemática actual." *Criterio* (August 10, 1972) 424–27.

"Ecumenism in Ethics." *Journal of Ecumenical Studies* 10 (1973) 575–76.

"Episcopacy and Apostolic Succession according to Hincmar of Reims." *Theological Studies* 34 (1973) 594–623.

"On Israel: Reflections with Sadness." *Journal of Ecumenical Studies* 10 (1973) 367–69.

"St. Bonaventure as Mystic and Theologian." *The Heritage of the Early Church: Essays in Honor of The Very Reverend Georges Vasilievich Florovsky*. Edited by David Neiman and Margaret Schatkin. Orientalia Christiana Analecta, 195. Rome: Pontificium Institutum Studiorum Orientalium, 1973. 289–306.

"Un langage oecuménique est-il possible?" *Culture et Croyance* (1973) 46–55.

"Ethical Ghettos in the Ecumenical Age." *Worldview* 17 (1974) 10–12.

"Is There a Catholic Ecclesiology?" *Catholic Theological Society of America Proceedings* 29 (1974) 367–80. Responses to this presentation on pp. 381–95.

"Succession et ordre dans la structure de l'Église." *Sanctus Bonaventura 1274–1974*. Edited by J. G. Bougerol and others. 5 volumes, 1972–1974. Rome: Collegio S. Bonaventura Grottaferrata, 1974. 4:421–46.

"The Bull *Unam Sanctam* of Boniface VIII." *Papal Primacy and the Universal Church*. Edited by P. C. Empie and T. A. Murphy. Lutherans and Catholics in Dialogue, V. Minneapolis: Augsburg Publishing House, 1974. 105–19.

"The Papacy in the Middle Ages." *Papal Primacy and the Universal Church*. Edited by P. C. Empie and T. A. Murphy, Lutherans and Catholics in Dialogue, V. Minneapolis: Augsburg Publishing House, 1974. 98–105.

"The Recognition of Ministry." *Journal of Ecumenical Studies* 11 (1974) 65–84.

"What is the Petrine Function?" *Papal Primacy and the Universal Church*. Edited by P. C. Empie and T. A. Murphy. Lutherans and Catholics in Dialogue, V. Minneapolis: Augsburg Publishing House, 1974. 208–12.

"Sexist Language in Theology?" *Theological Studies* 36 (1975) 700–24.
> Reprinted in *Women New Dimensions*. Edited by Walter J. Burghardt. New York: Paulist Press, 1977. 124–48.

"The Roman Catholic Church." *The Ordination of Women: Pro and Con*. Edited by Michael P. Hamilton and Nancy S. Montgomery. New York: Morehouse-Barlow, 1975. 112–25.

"Locating the Divine." *Worldview* (June 1975) 45–46.

"A Theologian Challenges Margaret Farley's Position." *Women and Catholic Priesthood: An Expanded Vision*. Edited by Anne Marie Gardiner, S.S.N.D. New York: Paulist Press, 1976. 52–57.

"The Papacy and Christian Symbolism." *Journal of Ecumenical Studies* 13 (1976) 345–58.
> Utilized in chapter 7 of *A Theology for Ministry* (1983).
> Spanish: "Papado y simbolism cristiano," *Selecciones de teologia* (1978) 230–35.

"Tradition in Theology: A Methodological Approach." *Perspectives on Scripture and Tradition*. Edited by Joseph F. Kelly. Notre Dame, Ind.: Fides Publishers, 1976. 105–25.

"Tradition in Theology: A Problematic Approach." *Perspectives on Scripture and Tradition*. Edited by Joseph F. Kelly. Notre Dame, Ind.: Fides Publishers, 1976. 84–104.

"Antiphon: a Review." *The Story* (November 1976) 7.

"Beyond Male and Female." *Catholic Charismatic* 1 (1977) 39–43.

"Is the Papacy an Object of Faith." *One in Christ* 13 (1977) 220–28.

"Paul and the Status of Women." *Crosstalk* 6 (1977). Two parts.

"The Scholastic Doctrine." *Women Priests: A Catholic Commentary on the Vatican Declaration*. Edited by Leonard Swidler and Arlene Swidler. New York: Paulist Press, 1977. 99–106.

"Methodist Dialogue." *The Tablet* 232 (1978) 197–98, 230–32.

"Infallibility: A Structural Analysis." *Teaching Authority and Infallibility in the Church*. Edited by P. C. Empie, T. A. Austin, and J. A. Burgess. Lutherans and Catholics in Dialogue, VI. Minneapolis: Augsburg Publishing House, 1978, 1980. 169–85.

"For a Theology of Dialogue." *One in Christ* 15 (1979) 11–20.

And Richard P. McBrien, John T. Finnegan, George W. MacRae, and Richard A. McCormick. "The Bilateral Consultations between the Roman Catholic Church in the United States and other Christian Communions." *Catholic Theological Society of America Proceedings* 34 (1979) 253–85.

"The Christological Tradition of the Latin Fathers." *Dialog* 18 (1979) 265–70.

"The Church as Eucharistic Communion in Medieval Theology." *Continuity and Discontinuity in Church History: Essays Presented to George Huntston Williams on the Occasion of His 65th Birthday*. Edited by F. Forrester Church and Timothy George. Studies in the History of Christian Thought, 19. Leiden: E. J. Brill, 1979. 92–103.

> Utilized in chapter 2 of *A Theology for Ministry* (1983).
>
> Another version published as "Eucharistic Communion as Horizon for Ministry." *Emmanuel* 89, 7 (September 1983) 370–77.

"Jean-Martin Moye." *Dizionario degli Instituti di Perfezione*. Roma: Edizioni Paoline, 1980. 6:180–83.

"The Anglican-Roman Catholic Agreed Statements and Their Reception." *Theological Studies* 41 (1980) 74–97.

"The Bi-lateral Dialogues: Searching for Language." *One in Christ* 16 (1980) 19–30.

"The Bi-lateral Dialogues: Speaking Together." *One in Christ* 16 (1980) 30–42.

"The Coincidence of Opposites: A Recent Interpretation of Bonaventure." *Theological Studies* 41 (1980) 576–84.

"Lutherans and Roman Catholics in Dialogue. 1980—A Year of Ecumenical Celebration." *Ecumenical Trends* 9, 1 (January 1980) 8–10.

> Reprinted as "The Augustana and the Ecumenical Fathers." *Lutheran Forum* (Pentecost 1980) 9–10.

"Dämonen. V: Kirchengeschichtlich." *Theologische Realenzyklopädie.* Edited by Gerhard Krause and Gerhard M. Müller. Berlin and New York: Walter de Gruyter, 1981. 8:286–300.

"The Christology of the Mystics." *Theological Studies* 42 (1981) 561–79.

"The Reconciliation of Ministries." *Journal of Ecumenical Studies* 18 (1981) 267–80.

"Engel. V: Kirchengeschichtlich." *Theologische Realenzyklopädie.* Edited by Gerhard Krause and Gerhard Müller. Berlin and New York: Walter de Gruyter, 1982. 9:599–609.

"Discussion Comments." *Ecclesiam suam: Première Lettre Encyclique de Paul VI.* Colloque International, Rome, October 24–26, 1980. Brescia: Istituto Paolo VI, 1982. 170–71.

"French Catholic Ecumenism." *Ecumenist* 21 (1982–1983) 41–44.

"Pourquoi Jean-Martin Moye rentra-t-il de Chine?" *Nouvelle revue de science missionaire* 39 (1983) 161–77.

"Reassessing the Reformation." *One in Christ* 19 (1983) 355–67.

"What Elements Determine the Ecumenicity of a Council?" *The Ecumenical Council: Its Significance in the Constitution of the Church.* Edited by P. Huizing and K. Walf. *Concilium* 167 (1983) 45–49.

  Also in French, Italian, Spanish, German, and Dutch.

"Review Article of Richard McBrien's *Catholicism.*" *Religious Studies Review* 9, 2 (April 1983) 116–18.

"The Future of the Church in the US. Response to a Question." *Social Justice Review* (January–February 1983) 13.

"Eucharistic Communion as Horizon for Ministry." *Emmanuel* 89, 7 (September 1983) 370–77.

"Ecclesiology." *Dictionary of the Middle Ages.* Edited by Joseph R. Strayer. New York: Charles Scribner's Sons, 1984. 4:372–78.

"Are Bi-Lateral Dialogues Obsolete?" *Ecumenical Trends* 14 (1985) 105–07.

"Reflections on the 'Unrestricted Desire to Know'." *The Josephinum Journal of Theology* 4 (1985) 3–18.

"Response to William Lazareth." *Eucharist and Ecumenical Life.* Edited by Ronald P. Byars. Lexington, Ky.: Kentucky Council of Churches, 1985. 20–23.

  Lazareth's presentation was entitled "Unity and Communion in the Body of Christ" (pp. 10–20).

"Roman Catholic Reflections on Melanchthon's *De Potestate et Primatu Papae.*" *Concordia Theological Quarterly* 49 (1985) 253–66.

"The Contemporary Relevance of Justification by Faith." *One in Christ* 21 (1985) 131–38.

"Engel." *Lexikon des Mittelalters.* München und Zürich: Artemis Verlag, 1986. 3:1906–09.

"Infallibility: a Survey and a Proposal." *One in Christ* 22 (1986) 24–43.

"Praying Together: *Communicatio in sacris* in the Decree on Ecumenism." *Vatican II: By Those Who Were There.* Edited by Alberic Stacpoole. London: Geoffrey Chapman, 1986. 202–19.

> Also: *Vatican II Revisited: By Those Who Were There.* Minneapolis: Winston Press, 1986.

"St. Augustine between Mani and Christ." *The Patristic and Byzantine Review* 5 (1986) 196–206.

"Justification: The Dilemma of the Sixteenth Century." *Philosophy and Theology* 1 (1986–1987) 267–81.

"Justification: The Problem of the Twentieth Century." *Philosophy and Theology* 1 (1986–1987) 347–60.

"Apostolic Life and Church Reform." *Christian Spirituality II: High Middle Ages and Reformation.* Edited by J. Raitt, in collaboration with B. McGinn and J. Meyendorff. World Spirituality, 17. New York: Crossroad, 1987. 1–11.

"Response to Interpretation, History and the Ecumenical Movement." *Ecumenical Trends* 16 (1987) 128–30. Response to article by Jeffrey Gros, F.S.C., 117–21.

"The Meaning of Melchizedek for Contemporary Ministry." *The Pastor as Priest.* Edited by Earl E. Shelp and Ronald H. Sunderland. Pastoral Ministry Series. New York: Pilgrim Press, 1987. 64–85.

"The Ordination of Women." *One in Christ* 23 (1987) 200–211.

"The Recognition of Ministry: What is the Priority?" *One in Christ* 23 (1987) 21–35.

"Theology and Sexuality." *Women in the World's Religions, Past and Present.* Edited by Ursula King. God: The Contemporary Discussion Series. New York: Paragon House, 1987. 68–80.

"Tradition." *The New Dictionary of Theology.* Edited by Joseph A. Komonchak, Mary Collins, and Dermot A. Lane. Wilmington: Michael Glazier, 1987. 1037–41.

"L'oecuménisme aujourd'hui." *L'Assomption et ses Oeuvres* (Spring 1987) 24–25.

"Luther's Teaching on Prayer." *Lutheran Theological Seminary Bulletin* 67 (Winter 1987) 3–22.

> Reprinted in *Encounters with Luther,* volume 4. Gettysburg: Lutheran Theological Seminary, 1990. 41–60.

"Possession." *Catholicisme.* Paris: Letouzey et Ané, 1988. 11:661–67.

"The Ordained Ministry in Historical Ambiguity." *Doctrine and Life* 38 (1988) 466–77.

"The Ordained Ministry: Where Does It Fit?" *Doctrine and Life* 38 (1988) 518–29.

"The Problem of Space and Time in the *Confessions* of St. Augustine." *Dialogue & Alliance* 2 (1988) 49–55.

> Utilized in *Les jardins de Saint Augustin: Lecture des "Confessions"* (1988).

"Tradition as Koinonia in Historical Perspective." *One in Christ* 24 (1988) 97–111.

"Ecumenical Theology and the Catholic Church." *One in Christ* 25 (1989) 103–13.

"Het probleem van de geünieerde kerken." *Het Christelijk Oosten en Hereniging* 41 (1989) 252–61.

"Justification in Dialogue." *One in Christ* 25 (1989) 299–310.

"Justification." *New Catholic Encyclopedia*. Edited by The Catholic University of America. Supplement, 1978–1988. Palatine, Ill.: Jack Heraty & Associates, 1989. 18:233–34.

And Gerald Moede and William Norgren. "Observations by Other Lutheran Dialogue Partners." *The Leuenberg Agreement and Lutheran-Reformed Relationships*. Edited by William G. Rusch and Daniel F. Martensen. Minneapolis: Augsburg, 1989. 115–22.

And R. William Franklin. "Commentary on ARC/USA Statement on Anglican Orders." *Journal of Ecumenical Studies* 27 (1990) 261–87.

"Ordination of Women." *The New Dictionary of Sacramental Worship*. Edited by Peter E. Fink, S.J. Dublin: Gill and Macmillan, 1990. 910–15.

"Puritanisme." *Catholicisme*. Paris: Letouzey et Ané, 1990. 12:316–20.

"Quakers (Société des Amis)." *Catholicisme*. Paris: Letouzey et Ané, 1990. 12:335–38.

"Réveils." *Catholicisme*. Paris: Letouzey et Ané, 1990. 12:1041–46.

"Satan dans la catéchèse." *Lumen Vitae* 45 (1990) 395–404.

"The Contemporary Role of Women in the Catholic Church." *Forty-third Annual Conference of the American Theological Library Association: Summary of Proceedings for 1989* 43 (1990) 95–103.

"The Doctrine of Justification in Ecumenical Discussions." *Ecumenical Trends* 19 (1990) 17–19.

"The Veneration of Saints as an Ecumenical Question." *One in Christ* 26 (1990) 40–50.

> Also published as "The Veneration of Saints as Ecumenical Question." *Walking Together. Roman Catholics and Ecumenism Twenty-five Years after Vatican II*. Edited by Thaddeus D. Horgan. Grand Rapids: William B. Eerdmans Publishing Company, 1990. 118–33.

> Abbreviated version: "The Veneration of Saints: an Ecumenical Question." *The Catholic World* 233 (September–October 1990) 233–39.

"The View from the Gallery." *The Catholic World* 233 (September–October 1990) 215.

"Ecumenical Relations." *Modern Catholicism: Vatican II and After*. Edited by Adrian Hastings. New York: Oxford University Press and London: SPCK, 1991. 398–421.

"Personal Reflections on d'Alzon and Ecumenism." *Vocet* 13, 1 (1991) 3.

"Vatican II, Understood and Misunderstood." *One in Christ* 27 (1991) 209–21.

"Lessons of Ecumenism for Catholic Theology." *One in Christ* 27 (1991) 346–51.

"John of the Cross and the Eucharist." *Spiritual Life* 37 (1991) 225–31.

"John Duns Scotus and the Immaculate Conception." *The One Mediator, The Saints, and Mary*. Edited by H. George Anderson, J. Francis Stafford, and Joseph A. Burgess. Lutherans and Catholics in Dialogue, VIII. Minneapolis: Augsburg Fortress, 1992. 209–17.

List of Contributors to the Tavard Festschrift

Rev. Marc R. Alexander
Diocesan Theologian
Diocese of Honolulu, Hawaii

Dr. Robert W. Bertram
Seminex Professor (emeritus) of
  Historical and Systematic
  Theology
Lutheran School of Theology at
  Chicago
St. Louis, Missouri

Dr. Joseph A. Burgess
Regent, North Dakota

Rev. David A. R. Butler
Senior Methodist Tutor and Tutor
  in Church History
The Queen's College
Birmingham

Dr. Patrick W. Carey
Associate Professor of Theology
Department of Theology
Marquette University
Milwaukee, Wisconsin

Dr. Mary Charles Murray
Reader in Historical Theology
Department of Theology
University of Nottingham
Nottingham

Professor Simon J. De Vries
Professor of Old Testament
  Emeritus
Methodist Theological School in
  Ohio
Delaware, Ohio

Rev. John Patrick Donnelly, S.J.
Professor of History
Department of History
Marquette University
Milwaukee, Wisconsin

Rev. Avery Dulles, S.J.
Laurence J. McGinley Professor of
  Religion and Society
Fordham University
Bronx, New York

Rev. Robert B. Eno, S.S.
Professor of Church History
The Catholic University of America
Washington, D.C.

Dr. R. William Franklin
Society for the Promotion of
  Religion and Learning
Professor of History and World
  Mission
General Theological Seminary
New York, New York

Dr. Eric W. Gritsch
Maryland Synod Professor of
  Church History
Director, Institute for Luther
  Studies
Gettysburg, Pennsylvania

Dr. Jeffery Hopper
Hazen G. Werner Professor of
  Theology
Methodist Theological School in
  Ohio
Delaware, Ohio

Rev. Frederick M. Jelly, O.P.
Professor of Systematics
Mount St. Mary's Seminary
Emmitsburg, Maryland

Rev. Walter H. Principe, C.S.B.
Fellow Emeritus
Pontifical Institute of Mediaeval
  Studies
Toronto, Ontario

Rev. Herbert J. Ryan, S.J.
Professor of Theology
Loyola Marymount University
Los Angeles, California

Rev. J.-M. R. Tillard, O.P.
Professor of Dogmatic Theology
Faculté Dominicaine de Théologie
Ottawa, Ontario

The Rt. Rev. Arthur A. Vogel
Bishop of West Missouri, Retired
Kansas City, Missouri

Rev. Dr. Geoffrey Wainwright
Robert E. Cushman Professor of
  Christian Theology
The Divinity School
Duke University
Durham, North Carolina

Rev. Dr. J. Robert Wright
St. Mark's Professor of Ecclesiastical
  History
General Theological Seminary
New York, New York

Rev. E. J. Yarnold, S.J.
Research Lecturer
Oxford University
Oxford

Rev. Dr. Norman Young
Professor of Systematic Theology
Queen's College
University of Melbourne
Parkville, Victoria

Index of Names

Index of Scripture References

Index of Subjects